MBA ESSENTIALS
ACCOUNTING · FINANCE · ECONOMICS

Contains select material from

Fundamental Accounting Principles, Seventeenth Edition

Kermit D. Larson
University of Texas at Austin

John J. Wild
University of Wisconsin at Madison

Barbara Chiappetta
Nassau Community College

Essentials of Corporate Finance, Fourth Edition

Stephen A. Ross
Massachusetts Institute of Technology

Randolph W. Westerfield
University of Southern California

Bradford D. Jordan
University of Kentucky

Essentials of Economics, Fifth Edition

Bradley R. Schiller
American University, Washington, D.C.

ASHFORD
UNIVERSITY
FOUNDED 1918

McGraw Hill **Learning Solutions**

Boston   Burr Ridge, IL   Dubuque, IA   New York   San Francisco   St. Louis
Bangkok   Bogotá   Caracas   Lisbon   London   Madrid
Mexico City   Milan   New Delhi   Seoul   Singapore   Sydney   Taipei   Toronto

MBA ESSENTIALS
ACCOUNTING • FINANCE • ECONOMICS
Ashford University

This book is a McGraw-Hill Learning Solutions textbook and contains select material from:
Fundamental Accounting Principles, Seventeenth Edition by Kermit D. Larson, John J. Wild, and Barbara Chiappetta. Copyright © 2005, 2002, 1999, 1996, 1993, 1990, 1987, 1984, 1981, 1978, 1975, 1972, 1969, 1966, 1963, 1959, 1955 by The McGraw-Hill Companies, Inc. All rights reserved.
Essentials of Corporate Finance, Fourth Edition by Stephen A. Ross, Randolph W. Westerfield, and Bradford D. Jordan. Copyright © 2004, 2001, 1999, 1996, by The McGraw-Hill Companies, Inc. All rights reserved.
Essentials of Economics, Fifth Edition by Bradley R. Schiller. Copyright © 2005, 2002, 1999, 1996, 1993 by The McGraw-Hill Companies, Inc. All rights reserved.
Reprinted with permission of the publisher. Many custom published texts are modified versions or adaptations of our best-selling textbooks. Some adaptations are printed in black and white to keep prices at a minimum, while others are in color.

2 3 4 5 6 7 8 9 0 OPM OPM 0 9 8

ISBN-13: 978-0-697-77527-6
ISBN-10: 0-697-77527-5

Custom Publishing Specialist: Judith Wetherington
Production Editor: Carrie Braun
Cover Design: Fairfax Hutter
Printer/Binder: OPM Digital Services

Contents

Part I: Accounting   **1**

  1. Accounting in Business   2
  2. Analyzing and Recording Transactions   46
  3. Adjusting Accounts and Preparing Financial Statements   92
  4. Completing the Accounting Cycle   134

Part II: Finance   **181**

  5. Introduction to Financial Management   183
  6. Financial Statements, Taxes, and Cash Flow   203
  7. Working with Financial Statements   230
  8. Introduction to Valuation: The Time Value of Money   269
  9. Discounted Cash Flow Valuation   294

Part III: Economics   **335**

10. The Challenge of Economics   336
11. Supply and Demand   366
12. The U.S. Economy   398
13. Money and Banks   422

Part I
Accounting

"I love chocolate, and so I'm having fun making money"—Elise Macmillan (Evan Macmillan on right)

Accounting in Business

A Look at This Chapter

Accounting plays a crucial role in the information age. In this chapter, we discuss the importance of accounting to different types of organizations and describe its many users and uses. We explain that ethics are crucial to accounting. We also describe business transactions and how they are reflected in financial statements.

A Look Ahead

Chapter 2 further describes and analyzes business transactions. We explain the analysis and recording of transactions, the ledger and trial balance, and the double-entry system. More generally, Chapters 2 through 4 focus on accounting and analysis, and they illustrate (via the accounting cycle) how financial statements reflect business activities.

CAP

Learning Objectives are organized by conceptual, analytical, and procedural.

Conceptual

C1 Explain the purpose and importance of accounting in the information age. *(p. 4)*

C2 Identify users and uses of accounting. *(p. 5)*

C3 Identify opportunities in accounting and related fields. *(p. 6)*

C4 Explain why ethics are crucial to accounting. *(p. 8)*

C5 Explain the meaning of generally accepted accounting principles, and define and apply several key principles of accounting. *(p. 9)*

Analytical

A1 Define and interpret the accounting equation and each of its components. *(p. 12)*

A2 Analyze business transactions using the accounting equation. *(p. 13)*

A3 Compute and interpret return on assets. *(p. 20)*

Procedural

P1 Identify and prepare basic financial statements and explain how they interrelate. *(p. 17)*

Decision Feature

Sweet Taste of Success

DENVER—Elise and Evan Macmillan—sister and brother entrepreneurs—aim to satisfy. "Our whole business is about customers," says Elise. These teenagers head **The Chocolate Farm (TheChocolateFarm.com),** which specializes in making chocolates and in helping their customers make them.

"We thought our business was going to be a one-day thing," says Elise, "but it turned into a real business." This meant Elise and Evan had to deal with issues such as organization form, accounting and in-formation systems, transaction analysis, and financial reports. Adds Elise, "I'm kept busy with the company's future plans and new prod-uct ideas and everything else that there is to a company."

Special attention is directed at accounting information; because without income, The Chocolate Farm would be knee-deep in cocoa. Elise and Evan were able to set up a transaction-based accounting system to profitably handle customer sales and orders. They also used accounting information to make good business decisions. Relying on sales and expense information, Elise and Evan focused efforts on their best-sellers such as *Brown Cows, Mint Sheep Munch, Pecan Turtles,* and *Pigs in Mud.* Moreover, after an analysis of the accounting information, they decided to expand and now employ more than a dozen people.

Evan admits that even with the best accounting information, one must accept some risk. We "accept the fact that it's a risk," says Evan, but that's the reality of money making. Elise concurs, "I love chocolate, and so I'm having fun making money." The Farm now produces more than $1 million per year in revenues. We could all become chocolate-lovers with results like that!

[Sources: *Ernst & Young Website,* January 2004; *The Chocolate Farm Website,* January 2004; *Entrepreneur Magazine,* May 2002; *Denver Business Journal,* January 2002; *The Wall Street Journal,* March 2003.]

*A **Decision Feature** launches each chapter showing the relevance of accounting for a real entrepreneur. An **Entrepreneurial Decision** problem at the end of the assignments returns to this feature with a mini-case.*

↖ A **Preview** opens each chapter with a summary of topics covered.

Today's world is one of information—its preparation, communication, analysis, and use. Accounting is at the heart of this information age. Knowledge of accounting gives us career opportunities and the insight to take advantage of them. By studying this book, you will learn about concepts, procedures, and analyses that will help you make better decisions throughout your life. In this chapter we describe accounting, the users and uses of accounting information, the forms and activities of organizations, and several accounting principles. We also introduce transaction analysis and financial statements.

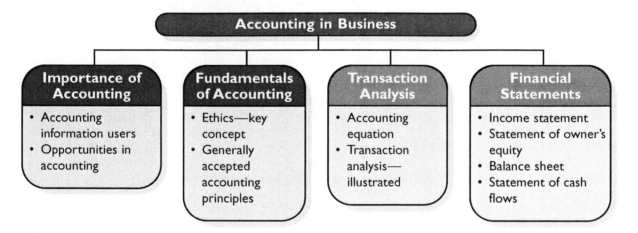

Accounting in Business

Importance of Accounting	Fundamentals of Accounting	Transaction Analysis	Financial Statements
• Accounting information users • Opportunities in accounting	• Ethics—key concept • Generally accepted accounting principles	• Accounting equation • Transaction analysis— illustrated	• Income statement • Statement of owner's equity • Balance sheet • Statement of cash flows

Importance of Accounting

C1 Explain the purpose and importance of accounting in the information age.

We live in an information age—a time of communication and immediate access to data, news, facts, and commentary. Information affects how we live, whom we associate with, and the opportunities we have. To fully benefit from the available information, we need knowledge of the information system. An information system involves the collecting, processing, and reporting of information to decision makers.

Providing information about what businesses own, what they owe, and how they perform is an important aim of accounting. **Accounting** is an information and measurement system that identifies, records, and communicates relevant, reliable, and comparable information about an organization's business activities. *Identifying* business activities requires selecting transactions and events relevant to an organization. Examples are the sale of vehicles by **Ford** and the receipt of ticket money by **TicketMaster**. *Recording* business activities requires keeping a chronological log of transactions and events measured in dollars and classified and summarized in a useful format. *Communicating* business activities requires preparing accounting reports such as financial statements. It also requires analyzing and interpreting such reports. (The financial statements and notes of **Krispy Kreme** are shown in Appendix A of this book. This appendix also shows the financial statements of **Tastykake** and **Harley-Davidson**.) Exhibit 1.1 summarizes accounting activities.

We must guard against a narrow view of accounting. The most common contact with accounting is through credit approvals, checking accounts, tax forms, and payroll. These

Exhibit 1.1

Accounting Activities

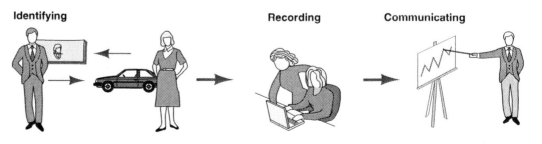

Identifying	Recording	Communicating
Select transactions and events	Log, measure and classify	Prepare, analyze and interpret

experiences are limited and tend to focus on the recordkeeping parts of accounting. **Recordkeeping, or bookkeeping,** is the recording of transactions and events, either manually or electronically. This is just one part of accounting. Accounting also identifies and communicates information on transactions and events, and it includes the crucial processes of analysis and interpretation.

Technology is a key part of modern business and plays a major role in accounting. Technology reduces the time, effort, and cost of recordkeeping while improving clerical accuracy. Some small organizations continue to perform various accounting tasks manually, but even they are impacted by information technology. As technology has changed the way we store, process, and summarize masses of data, accounting has been freed to expand. Consulting, planning, and other financial services are now closely linked to accounting. These services require sorting through data, interpreting their meaning, identifying key factors, and analyzing their implications.

Margin notes further enhance the textual material.

Point: Technology is only as useful as the accounting data available, and users' decisions are only as good as their understanding of accounting. The best software and recordkeeping cannot make up for lack of accounting knowledge.

Users of Accounting Information

Accounting is often called the *language of business* because all organizations set up an accounting information system to communicate data to help people make better decisions. Exhibit 1.2 shows that the accounting information system serves many kinds of users who can be divided into two groups: external users and internal users.

External users

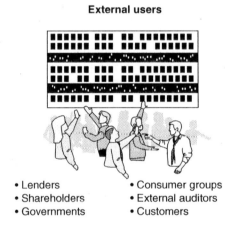

- Lenders   • Consumer groups
- Shareholders   • External auditors
- Governments   • Customers

Internal users

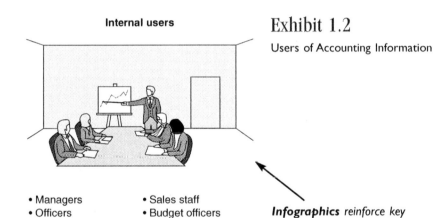

- Managers   • Sales staff
- Officers   • Budget officers
- Internal auditors   • Controllers

Exhibit 1.2

Users of Accounting Information

Infographics reinforce key concepts through visual learning.

External Information Users **External users** of accounting information are *not* directly involved in running the organization. They include shareholders (investors), lenders, directors, customers, suppliers, regulators, lawyers, brokers, and the press. External users have limited access to an organization's information. Yet many of their important decisions depend on information that is reliable, relevant, and comparable.

Financial accounting is the area of accounting aimed at serving external users by providing them with financial statements. These statements are known as *general-purpose financial statements.* The term *general-purpose* refers to the broad range of purposes for which external users rely on these statements.

Each external user has special information needs depending on the types of decisions to be made. *Lenders* (creditors) loan money or other resources to an organization. Banks, savings and loans, co-ops, and mortgage and finance companies often are lenders. Lenders look for information to help them assess whether an organization is likely to repay its loans with interest. *Shareholders* (investors) are the owners of a corporation. They use accounting reports in deciding whether to buy, hold, or sell stock. Shareholders typically elect a *board of directors* to oversee their interests in an organization. Since directors are responsible to shareholders, their information needs are similar. *External* (independent) *auditors* examine financial statements to verify that they are prepared according to generally accepted accounting principles. *Employees* and *labor unions* use financial statements to judge the fairness of

C2 Identify users and uses of accounting.

Point: World Wrestling Entertainment has more than 70 mil. shares of stock outstanding.

wages, assess future job prospects, and bargain for better wages. *Regulators* often have legal authority over certain activities of organizations. For example, the Internal Revenue Service (IRS) and other tax authorities require organizations to file accounting reports in computing taxes. Other regulators include utility boards that use accounting information to set utility rates and securities regulators that require reports for companies that sell their stock to the public.

Point: Microsoft's high income levels encouraged antitrust actions against it.

Accounting serves the needs of many other external users. *Voters, legislators,* and *government officials* use accounting information to monitor and evaluate a government's receipts and expenses. *Contributors* to nonprofit organizations use accounting information to evaluate the use and impact of their donations. *Suppliers* use accounting information to judge the soundness of a customer before making sales on credit, and *customers* use financial reports to assess the staying power of potential suppliers.

Internal Information Users   **Internal users** of accounting information are those directly involved in managing and operating an organization. They use the information to help improve the efficiency and effectiveness of an organization. **Managerial accounting** is the area of accounting that serves the decision-making needs of internal users. Internal reports are not subject to the same rules as external reports and are designed with the special needs of internal users in mind.

Decision Insight boxes highlight relevant items from practice.

↘

There are several types of internal users, and many are managers of key operating activities. *Research and development managers* need information about projected costs and revenues of proposed changes in products and services. *Purchasing managers* need to know what, when, and how much to purchase. *Human resource managers* need information about employees' payroll, benefits, performance, and compensation. *Production managers* depend on information to monitor costs and ensure quality. *Distribution managers* need reports for timely, accurate, and efficient delivery of products and services. *Marketing managers* use reports about sales and costs to target consumers, set prices, and monitor consumer needs, tastes, and price concerns. *Service managers* require information on both the costs and benefits of looking after products and services.

Decision Insight

Know-Nothing CEO   The know-nothing defense of CEOs such as **Global Crossing's** Gary Winnick and **Enron's** Jeffrey Skilling and Kenneth Lay could soon be shattered. Through novel legal moves, prosecutors are achieving convictions provided they prove that the CEO knew the company's internal picture was different than the picture shown to outsiders.

Both internal and external users rely on internal controls to monitor and control company activities. *Internal controls* are procedures set up to protect company property and equipment, ensure reliable accounting reports, promote efficiency, and encourage adherence to company policies. Examples are good records, physical controls (locks, passwords, guards), and independent reviews.

Opportunities in Accounting

C3   Identify opportunities in accounting and related fields.

Accounting information affects many aspects of our lives. When we earn money, pay taxes, invest savings, budget earnings, and plan for the future, we are influenced by accounting. Accounting has four broad areas of opportunities: financial, managerial, taxation, and accounting-related. Exhibit 1.3 lists selected opportunities in each area.

The majority of accounting opportunities are in *private accounting,* as shown in Exhibit 1.4. *Public accounting* offers the next largest number of opportunities. Still other opportunities exist in government (and not-for-profit) agencies, including business regulation and investigation of law violations.

Point: The "top 5" greatest investors of the 20th century, as compiled in a recent survey:
1. Warren Buffett, Berkshire Hathaway
2. Peter Lynch, Fidelity Funds
3. John Templeton, Templeton Group
4. Benjamin Graham & David Dodd, professors
5. George Soros, Soros Fund

Accounting specialists are highly regarded. Their professional standing often is denoted by a certificate. Certified public accountants (CPAs) must meet education and experience requirements, pass an examination, and exhibit ethical character. Many accounting specialists hold certificates in addition to or instead of the CPA. Two of the most common are the

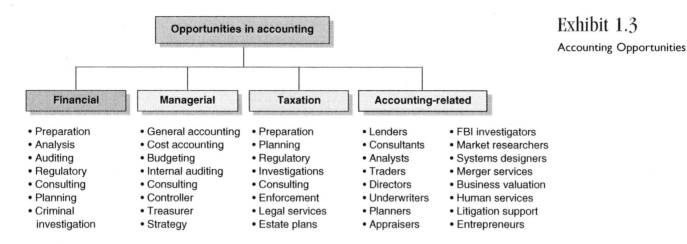

Exhibit 1.3

Accounting Opportunities

certificate in management accounting (CMA) and the certified internal auditor (CIA). Employers also look for specialists with designations such as certified bookkeeper (CB), certified payroll professional (CPP), and personal financial specialist (PFS).

Individuals with accounting knowledge are always in demand as they can help with financial analysis, strategic planning, e-commerce, product feasibility analysis, information technology, and financial management. Benefit packages can include flexible work schedules, telecommuting options, career path alternatives, casual work environments, extended vacation time, and child and elder care.

Demand for accounting specialists is boosting salaries. Exhibit 1.5 reports average annual salaries for several accounting positions. Salary variation depends on location, company size, professional designation, experience, and other factors. For example, salaries for chief financial officers (CFO) range from under $75,000 to more than $1 million per year. Likewise, salaries for bookkeepers range from under $30,000 to more than $80,000.

Exhibit 1.4

Accounting Jobs by Area

Point: The firm of Ernst & Young gave its interns a vacation at Disney World.

Point: The CFOs of Cisco Systems and Qualcom received an annual salary of more than $20 mil.

Field	Title (experience)	2003 Salary	2008 Estimate*
Public Accounting:	Partner	$181,000	$231,000
	Manager (6–8 years)	89,500	114,000
	Senior (3–5 years)	68,500	87,500
	Junior (0–2 years)	49,000	62,500
Private Accounting:	CFO	221,000	282,000
	Controller/Treasurer	140,000	179,000
	Manager (6–8 years)	83,000	106,000
	Senior (3–5 years)	69,000	88,000
	Junior (0–2 years)	47,000	60,000
Recordkeeping:	Full-charge bookkeeper	55,000	70,000
	Accounts manager	48,500	62,000
	Payroll manager	52,000	66,000
	Accounting clerk (0–1 years)	30,500	39,000

* Estimates assume a 5% compounded annual increase over current levels.

Exhibit 1.5

Accounting Salaries for Selected Fields

Point: For updated salary information:
www.AICPA.org
Abbott-Langer.com
Kforce.com

Quick Check is a chance to stop and reflect on key points.

Quick Check

1. What is the purpose of accounting?
2. What is the relation between accounting and recordkeeping?
3. Identify some advantages of technology for accounting.
4. Who are the internal and external users of accounting information?
5. Identify at least five types of managers who are internal users of accounting information.
6. What are internal controls and why are they important?

Answers—p. 26

Fundamentals of Accounting

Accounting is guided by principles, standards, concepts, and assumptions. This section describes several of these key fundamentals of accounting.

Ethics—A Key Concept

C4   Explain why ethics are crucial to accounting.

The goal of accounting is to provide useful information for decisions. For information to be useful, it must be trusted. This demands ethics in accounting. **Ethics** are beliefs that distinguish right from wrong. They are accepted standards of good and bad behavior.

Identifying the ethical path is sometimes difficult. The preferred path is a course of action that avoids casting doubt on one's decisions. For example, accounting users are less likely to trust an auditor's report if the auditor's pay depends on the success of the client. To avoid such concerns, ethics rules are often set. For example, auditors are banned from direct investment in their client and cannot accept pay that depends on figures in the client's reports. Exhibit 1.6 gives guidelines for making ethical decisions.

Point: Sarbanes-Oxley Act requires each issuer of securities to disclose whether it has adopted a code of ethics for its senior financial officers and the contents of that code.

Exhibit 1.6

Guidelines for Ethical Decision Making

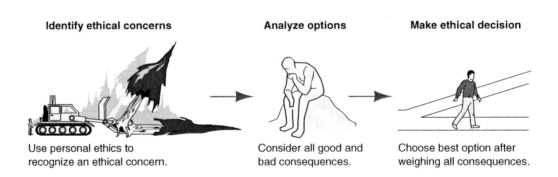

Identify ethical concerns

Use personal ethics to recognize an ethical concern.

Analyze options

Consider all good and bad consequences.

Make ethical decision

Choose best option after weighing all consequences.

Global: Business ethics differ across countries. This is due to cultural, political, legal, economic, and other important factors.

Point: A survey of executives, educators, and legislators showed that 9 of 10 participants believe organizations are troubled by ethical problems.

Point: The American Institute of Certified Public Accountants' *Code of Professional Conduct* is available at **www.AICPA.org**.

Providers of accounting information often face ethical choices as they prepare financial reports. These choices can affect the price a buyer pays and the wages paid to workers. They can even affect the success of products and services. Misleading information can lead to a wrongful closing of a division that harms workers, customers, and suppliers. There is an old saying worth remembering: *Good ethics are good business.*

Some extend ethics to *social responsibility,* which refers to a concern for the impact of actions on society. An organization's social responsibility can include donations to hospitals, colleges, community programs, and law enforcement. It also can include programs to reduce pollution, increase product safety, improve worker conditions, and support continuing education. These programs are not limited to large companies. For example, many independently owned theaters and small businesses offer discounts to students and senior citizens. Still others help sponsor events such as the Special Olympics and summer reading programs.

Graphical displays are often used to illustrate key points.

Generally Accepted Accounting Principles

Financial accounting practice is governed by concepts and rules known as **generally accepted accounting principles (GAAP)**. To use and interpret financial statements effectively, we need to understand these principles. A main purpose of GAAP is to make information in financial statements relevant, reliable, and comparable. *Relevant information* affects the decisions of its users. *Reliable information* is trusted by users. *Comparable information* is helpful in contrasting organizations.

Decision Insight

Virtuous Returns Virtue is not always its own reward. Compare the S&P 500 with the Domini Social Index (DSI), which covers 400 companies that have especially good records of social responsibility. Notice that returns for companies with socially responsible behavior are at least as high as those of the S&P 500.

Setting Accounting Principles Two main groups establish generally accepted accounting principles in the United States. The **Financial Accounting Standards Board (FASB)** is the private group that sets both broad and specific principles. The **Securities and Exchange Commission (SEC)** is the government group that establishes reporting requirements for companies that issue stock to the public.

In today's global economy, there is increased demand by external users for comparability in accounting reports. This often arises when companies wish to raise money from lenders and investors in different countries. To that end, the **International Accounting Standards Board (IASB)** issues *International Financial Reporting Standards* (*IFRS*) that identify preferred accounting practices. The IASB hopes to create more harmony among accounting practices of different countries. If standards are harmonized, one company can use a single set of financial statements in all financial markets. Many countries' standard setters support the IASB, and interest in moving U.S. GAAP toward the IASB's practices is growing, yet the IASB does not have the authority to impose its standards on companies.

Principles of Accounting Accounting principles are of two types. *General principles* are the basic assumptions, concepts, and guidelines for preparing financial statements. *Specific principles* are detailed rules used in reporting business transactions and events. General principles stem from long-used accounting practices. Specific principles arise more often from the rulings of authoritative groups.

We need to understand both general and specific principles to effectively use accounting information. Several general principles are described in this section and several others are described in later chapters. General principles are portrayed as building blocks of GAAP in Exhibit 1.7. The specific principles are described as we encounter them.

The **objectivity principle** means that accounting information is supported by independent, unbiased evidence. It demands more than a person's opinion. Information is not reliable if it is based only on what a preparer thinks might be true. A preparer can be too optimistic or pessimistic. The objectivity principle is intended to make financial statements useful by ensuring they report reliable and verifiable information.

The **cost principle** means that accounting information is based on actual cost. Cost is measured on a cash or equal-to-cash basis. This means if cash is given for a service, its cost is measured as the amount of cash paid. If something besides cash is exchanged (such as

C5 Explain the meaning of generally accepted accounting principles, and define and apply several key principles of accounting.

Point: State ethics codes require CPAs who audit financial statements to disclose areas where those statements fail to comply with GAAP. If CPAs fail to report noncompliance, they can lose their licenses and be subject to criminal action and fines.

Point: An audit examines whether financial statements are prepared using GAAP. It does *not* attest to the absolute accuracy of the statements.

Point: The largest accounting firms are Deloitte & Touche, Ernst & Young, PricewaterhouseCoopers, and KPMG.

Exhibit 1.7

Building Blocks for GAAP

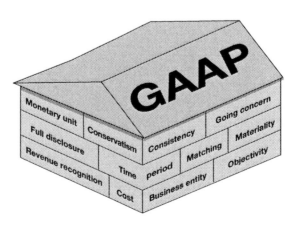

Name that Value   Abuse of the objectivity and cost principles brought down executives at **Itex Corp** who bartered assets of little or no value and then reported them at grossly inflated values—recognizing fictitious gains and assets. The deals involved difficult-to-value assets such as artwork and stamps.

Point: The cost principle is also called the *historical cost principle.*

Point: For currency conversion: **cnnfn.com/markets/currencies**

Example: Cadbury Schweppes, a leading beverage and confectionery producer, recently reported sales of £5,500 million. What is the U.S.$ equivalent of these sales if the exchange rate is £1 = $1.50? *Answer:* $8,250 million (£5,500 × $1.50).

Example: When a bookstore sells a textbook on credit is its earnings process complete? *Answer:* The bookstore can record sales for these books minus an amount expected for returns.

Point: Abuse of the entity principle was a main culprit in the collapse of Enron.

a car traded for a truck), cost is measured as the cash value of what is given up or received. The cost principle emphasizes reliability, and information based on cost is considered objective. To illustrate, suppose a company pays $5,000 for equipment. The cost principle requires that this purchase be recorded at a cost of $5,000. It makes no difference if the owner thinks this equipment is worth $7,000.

The **going-concern principle** means that accounting information reflects an assumption that the business will continue operating instead of being closed or sold. This implies, for example, that property is reported at cost instead of, say, liquidation values that assume closure.

The **monetary unit principle** means that we can express transactions and events in monetary, or money, units. Money is the common denominator in business. Examples of monetary units are the dollar in the United States, Canada, Australia, and Singapore; the pound sterling in the United Kingdom; and the peso in Mexico, the Philippines, and Chile. The monetary unit a company uses in its accounting reports usually depends on the country where it operates, but many companies today are expressing reports in more than one monetary unit.

Revenue (sales) is the amount received from selling products and services. The **revenue recognition principle** provides guidance on when a company must recognize revenue. To *recognize* means to record it. If revenue is recognized too early, a company would look more profitable than it is. If revenue is recognized too late, a company would look less profitable than it is. The following three concepts are important to revenue recognition. (1) *Revenue is recognized when earned.* The earnings process is normally complete when services are rendered or a seller transfers ownership of products to the buyer. (2) *Proceeds from selling products and services need not be in cash.* A common noncash proceed received by a seller is a customer's promise to pay at a future date, called *credit sales.* (3) *Revenue is measured by the cash received plus the cash value of any other items received.*

The **business entity principle** means that a business is accounted for separately from other business entities, including its owner. The reason for this principle is that separate information about each business is necessary for good decisions. A business entity can take one of three legal forms: *sole proprietorship, partnership,* or *corporation.*

1. A **sole proprietorship,** or simply **proprietorship,** is a business owned by one person. No special legal requirements must be met to start a proprietorship. It is a separate entity for accounting purposes, but it is *not* a separate legal entity from its owner. This means, for example, that a court can order an owner to sell personal belongings to pay a proprietorship's debt. This *unlimited liability* of a proprietorship is a disadvantage. However, an advantage is that a proprietorship's income is not subject to a business income tax but is instead reported and taxed on the owner's personal income tax return. Proprietorship characteristics are summarized in Exhibit 1.8.

2. A **partnership** is a business owned by two or more people, called *partners.* Like a proprietorship, no special legal requirements must be met in starting a partnership. The only requirement is an agreement between partners to run a business together. The agreement can be either oral or

Revenues for the New York Yankees baseball team include ticket sales, television and cable broadcasts, radio rights, concessions, and advertising. Revenues from ticket sales are earned when the Yankees play each game. Advance ticket sales are not revenues; instead, they represent a liability until the Yankees play the game for which the ticket was sold.

Characteristic	Proprietorship	Partnership	Corporation
Business entity	yes	yes	yes
Legal entity	no	no	yes
Limited liability	no*	no*	yes
Unlimited life	no	no	yes
Business taxed	no	no	yes
One owner allowed	yes	no	yes

Exhibit 1.8

Characteristics of Businesses

* Proprietorships and partnerships that are set up as LLCs provide limited liability.

written and usually indicates how income and losses are to be shared. A partnership, like a proprietorship, is *not* legally separate from its owners. This means that each partner's share of profits is reported and taxed on that partner's tax return. It also means *unlimited liability* for its partners. However, at least three types of partnerships limit liability. A *limited partnership* (*LP*) includes a general partner(s) with unlimited liability and a limited partner(s) with liability restricted to the amount invested. A *limited liability partnership* (*LLP*) restricts partners' liabilities to their own acts and the acts of individuals under their control. This protects an innocent partner from the negligence of another partner, yet all partners remain responsible for partnership debts. A *limited liability company* (*LLC*), offers the limited liability of a corporation and the tax treatment of a partnership (or proprietorship). Most proprietorships and partnerships are now organized as an LLC.

3. A **corporation** is a business legally separate from its owners, meaning it is responsible for its own acts and its own debts. Separate legal status means that a corporation can conduct business with the rights, duties, and responsibilities of a person. A corporation acts through its managers, who are its legal agents. Separate legal status also means that its owners, who are called **shareholders** (or **stockholders**), are not personally liable for corporate acts and debts. This limited liability is its main advantage. A main disadvantage is what's called *double taxation*—meaning that (1) the corporation income is taxed and (2) any distribution of income to its owners through dividends is taxed as part of the owners' personal income (usually at the 15% rate). An exception to this is an *S corporation*, a corporation with certain characteristics that give it a tax status that removes its corporate income tax. Owners of S corporations report their share of corporate income with their personal income. (*Note:* For lower income taxpayers, the dividend tax is less than 15%, and in some cases zero.) Ownership of corporations is divided into units called **shares** or **stock.** When a corporation issues only one class of stock, we call it **common stock** (or *capital stock*).

Decision Insight

Web Info Most organizations maintain Websites that include accounting information— see **Krispy Kreme's** (**KrispyKreme.com**) Website as one example. The SEC keeps an online database called EDGAR (**www.sec.gov/edgar.shtml**), which has accounting information for thousands of companies that sell their stock to the public.

Decision Insight

New Age Entrepreneurship will be the defining trend of business in this century, according to a survey of business leaders. Respondents see the biggest opportunities for entrepreneurship in technology, medicine, food services, hospitality, and information services.

Lightbulb icon highlights entrepreneurial-related info.

Decision Ethics boxes are role-playing exercises that stress ethics in accounting and business.

Decision Ethics

Entrepreneur You and a friend develop a new design for in-line skates that improves speed and performance by 25% to 40%. You plan to form a business to manufacture and market these skates. You and your friend want to minimize taxes, but your prime concern is potential lawsuits from individuals who might be injured on these skates. What form of organization do you set up?

Answer—p. 26

Point: Sole proprietorships and partnerships are usually managed on a regular basis by their owners. In a corporation, the owners (shareholders) elect a board of directors who appoint managers to run the business.

Quick Check

7. What three-step guidelines can help people make ethical decisions?
8. Why are ethics and social responsibility valuable to organizations?
9. Why are ethics crucial in accounting?
10. Who sets U.S. accounting rules?
11. How are U.S. companies affected by international accounting standards?
12. How are the objectivity and cost principles related?
13. Why is the business entity principle important?
14. Why is the revenue recognition principle important?
15. What are the three basic forms of business organization?
16. Identify the owners of corporations and the terminology for ownership units.

Answers—p. 26

Transaction Analysis and the Accounting Equation

A1 Define and interpret the accounting equation and each of its components.

To understand accounting information, we need to know how an accounting system captures relevant data about transactions, and classifies, records, and reports data.

Accounting Equation

The accounting system reflects two basic aspects of a company: what it owns and what it owes. **Assets** are resources with future benefits that are owned or controlled by a company. Examples are cash, supplies, equipment, and land. The claims on a company's assets—what it owes—are separated into owner and nonowner claims. **Liabilities** are what a company owes its nonowners (creditors) in future products or services. **Equity** (also called owner's equity or capital) refers to the claims of its owner(s). Together, liabilities and equity are the source of funds to acquire assets. The relation of assets, liabilities, and equity is reflected in the following **accounting equation:**

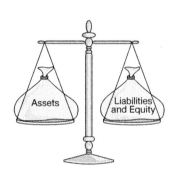

$$\textbf{Assets} = \textbf{Liabilities} + \textbf{Equity}$$

Liabilities are usually shown before equity in this equation because creditors' claims must be paid before the claims of owners. (The terms in this equation can be rearranged; for example, Assets − Liabilities = Equity.) The accounting equation applies to all transactions and events, to all companies and forms of organization, and to all points in time. To illustrate, **Krispy Kreme**'s assets equal $410,487, its liabilities equal $137,135, and its equity equals $273,352 ($ in thousands). Let's now look at the accounting equation in more detail.

Real company names are printed in bold magenta.

Point: The phrase "on credit" implies that the cash payment will occur at a future date.

Assets Assets are resources owned or controlled by a company. These resources are expected to yield future benefits. Examples are Web servers for an online services company, musical instruments for a rock band, and land for a vegetable grower. The term *receivable* is used to refer to an asset that promises a future inflow of resources. A company that provides a service or product on credit is said to have an account receivable from that customer.

Liabilities Liabilities are creditors' claims on assets. These claims reflect obligations to provide assets, products, or services to others. The term *payable* refers to a liability that promises a future outflow of resources. Examples are wages payable to employees, accounts payable to suppliers, notes payable to banks, and taxes payable to the government.

Equity Equity is the owner's claim on assets. Equity is equal to assets minus liabilities. This is the reason equity is also called *net assets* or *residual equity (interest).*

For a proprietorship, owner investments and revenues increase equity, and owner withdrawals and expenses decrease it. **Owner investments** are the assets an owner puts into the company—included under the title **Owner, Capital. Revenues** are the gross increase in equity from a company's earnings activities. Examples are consulting services provided, sales of products, facilities rented to others, and commissions from services. **Owner withdrawals** are the assets an owner takes from the company for personal use. **Expenses** decrease equity and are the cost of assets or services used to earn revenues. Examples are costs of employee time, use of supplies, and the advertising, utilities, and insurance services from others. This breakdown of equity yields the following **expanded accounting equation:**

$$\text{Assets} = \text{Liabilities} + \overbrace{\underset{\text{Capital}}{\text{Owner}} - \underset{\text{Withdrawals}}{\text{Owner}} + \text{Revenues} - \text{Expenses}}^{\textbf{Equity}}$$

Net income occurs when revenues exceed expenses. Net income increases equity. A **net loss** occurs when expenses exceed revenues, which decreases equity. The accounting equation can be used to track changes in a company's assets, liabilities, and equity, which is the focus of the next section.

Transaction Analysis

Business activities can be described in terms of transactions and events. **External transactions** are exchanges of value between two entities, which yield changes in the accounting equation. **Internal transactions** are exchanges within an entity; they can also affect the accounting equation. An example is a company's use of its supplies, which are reported as expenses when used. **Events** refer to those happenings that affect an entity's accounting equation *and* can be reliably measured. They include business events such as changes in the market value of certain assets and liabilities, and natural events such as floods and fires that destroy assets and create losses. They do not include, for example, the signing of service or product contracts, which by themselves do not impact the accounting equation.

This section uses the accounting equation to analyze 11 selected transactions and events of FastForward, a start-up consulting business, in its first month of operations. Remember that each transaction and event leaves the equation in balance and that assets *always* equal the sum of liabilities and equity.

Transaction 1: Investment by Owner On December 1, Chuck Taylor forms an athletic shoe consulting business, which he names FastForward. He sets it up as a proprietorship. Taylor owns and manages the business. The marketing plan for the business is to focus primarily on consulting with sports clubs, amateur athletes, and others who place orders for athletic shoes with manufacturers. Taylor personally invests $30,000 cash in the new company and deposits the cash in a bank account opened under the name of FastForward. After this transaction, the cash (an asset) and the owner's equity each equal $30,000. The source of increase in equity is the owner's investment, which is included in the column titled C. Taylor, Capital. (*Note:* Owner investments are always included under the title *"Owner name," Capital.*) The effect of this transaction on FastForward is reflected in the accounting equation as follows:

	Assets	=	Liabilities	+	Equity
	Cash	=			**C. Taylor, Capital**
(1)	+$30,000	=			+$30,000

Transaction 2: Purchase Supplies for Cash FastForward uses $2,500 of its cash to buy supplies of brand name athletic shoes for testing over the next few months. This transaction is an exchange of cash, an asset, for another kind of asset, supplies. It merely changes

the form of assets from cash to supplies. The decrease in cash is exactly equal to the increase in supplies. The supplies of athletic shoes are assets because of the expected future benefits from the test results of their performance. This transaction is reflected in the accounting equation as follows:

	Assets			=	Liabilities	+	Equity
	Cash	+	Supplies	=			C. Taylor, Capital
Old Bal.	$30,000			=			$30,000
(2)	−2,500	+	$2,500				
New Bal.	$27,500	+	$ 2,500	=			$30,000
		$30,000				$30,000	

Transaction 3: Purchase Equipment for Cash

FastForward spends $26,000 to acquire equipment for testing athletic shoes. Like transaction 2, transaction 3 is an exchange of one asset, cash, for another asset, equipment. The equipment is an asset because of its expected future benefits from testing athletic shoes. This purchase changes the makeup of assets but does not change the asset total. The accounting equation remains in balance.

	Assets					=	Liabilities	+	Equity
	Cash	+	Supplies	+	Equipment	=			C. Taylor, Capital
Old Bal.	$27,500	+	$2,500			=			$30,000
(3)	−26,000			+	$26,000				
New Bal.	$1,500	+	$2,500	+	$ 26,000	=			$30,000
		$30,000						$30,000	

Transaction 4: Purchase Supplies on Credit

Example: If FastForward pays $500 cash in transaction 4, how does this partial payment affect the liability to CalTech? What would be FastForward's cash balance? *Answers:* The liability to CalTech would be reduced to $6,600 and the cash balance would be reduced to $1,000.

Taylor decides he needs more supplies of athletic shoes. These additional supplies total $7,100, but as we see from the accounting equation in transaction 3, FastForward has only $1,500 in cash. Taylor arranges to purchase them on credit from CalTech Supply Company. Thus, FastForward acquires supplies in exchange for a promise to pay for them later. This purchase increases assets by $7,100 in supplies, and liabilities (called *accounts payable* to CalTech Supply) increase by the same amount. The effects of this purchase on the accounting equation follow:

	Assets					=	Liabilities	+	Equity
	Cash	+	Supplies	+	Equipment	=	Accounts Payable	+	C. Taylor, Capital
Old Bal.	$1,500	+	$2,500	+	$26,000	=			$30,000
(4)		+	7,100				+$7,100		
New Bal.	$1,500	+	$9,600	+	$26,000	=	$ 7,100	+	$30,000
		$37,100						$37,100	

Transaction 5: Provide Services for Cash

FastForward earns revenues by consulting with clients about test results on athletic shoes. It earns net income only if its revenues are greater than its expenses incurred in earning them. In one of its first jobs, FastForward provides consulting services to an athletic club and immediately collects $4,200 cash. The accounting equation reflects this increase in cash of $4,200 and in equity of $4,200. This increase in equity is identified in the far right column under Revenues because the cash is earned by providing consulting services.

	Assets					=	Liabilities	+			Equity	
	Cash	+	Supplies	+	Equipment	=	Accounts Payable	+	C. Taylor, Capital	+		Revenues
Old Bal.	$1,500	+	$9,600	+	$26,000	=	$7,100	+	$30,000			
(5)	+4,200									+		$4,200
New Bal.	$5,700	+	$9,600	+	$26,000	=	$7,100	+	$30,000	+		$ 4,200
	$41,300								$41,300			

Transactions 6 and 7: Payment of Expenses in Cash FastForward pays $1,000 rent to the landlord of the building where its store is located. Paying this amount allows FastForward to occupy the space for the month of December. The rental payment is reflected in the following accounting equation as transaction 6. FastForward also pays the biweekly $700 salary of the company's only employee. This is reflected in the accounting equation as transaction 7. Both transactions 6 and 7 are December expenses for FastForward. The costs of both rent and salary are expenses, as opposed to assets, because their benefits are used in December (they have no future benefits after December). These transactions also use up an asset (cash) in carrying out FastForward's operations. The accounting equation shows that both transactions reduce cash and equity. The far right column identifies these decreases as Expenses.

	Assets					=	Liabilities	+			Equity			
	Cash	+	Supplies	+	Equipment	=	Accounts Payable	+	C. Taylor, Capital	+	Revenues	−	Expenses
Old Bal.	$5,700	+	$9,600	+	$26,000	=	$7,100	+	$30,000	+	$4,200		
(6)	− 1,000											−	$1,000
Bal.	4,700	+	9,600	+	26,000	=	7,100	+	30,000	+	4,200	−	1,000
(7)	− 700											−	700
New Bal.	$4,000	+	$9,600	+	$26,000	=	$7,100	+	$30,000	+	$4,200	−	$ 1,700
	$39,600								$39,600				

Transaction 8: Provide Services and Facilities for Credit FastForward provides consulting services of $1,600 and rents its test facilities for $300 to an amateur sports club. The rental involves allowing club members to try recommended shoes at FastForward's testing grounds. The sports club is billed for the $1,900 total. This transaction results in a new asset, called *accounts receivable,* from this client. It also yields an increase in equity from the two revenue components reflected in the Revenues column of the accounting equation:

	Assets							=	Liabilities	+			Equity			
	Cash	+	Accounts Receivable	+	Supplies	+	Equipment	=	Accounts Payable	+	C. Taylor, Capital	+	Revenues	−	Expenses
Old Bal.	$4,000	+		+	$9,600	+	$26,000	=	$7,100	+	$30,000	+	$4,200	−	$1,700
(8)		+	$1,900									+	1,600		
												+	300		
New Bal.	$4,000	+	$ 1,900	+	$9,600	+	$26,000	=	$7,100	+	$30,000	+	$6,100	−	$1,700
	$41,500									$41,500					

Transaction 9: Receipt of Cash from Accounts Receivable The client in transaction 8 (the amateur sports club) pays $1,900 to FastForward 10 days after it is billed for consulting services. This transaction 9 does not change the total amount of assets and

does not affect liabilities or equity. It converts the receivable (an asset) to cash (another asset). It does not create new revenue. Revenue was recognized when FastForward rendered the services in transaction 8, not when the cash is now collected. This emphasis on the earnings process instead of cash flows is a goal of the revenue recognition principle and yields useful information to users. The new balances follow:

		Assets							=	Liabilities	+			Equity				
	Cash	+	Accounts Receivable	+	Supplies	+	Equipment	=	Accounts Payable	+	C. Taylor, Capital	+	Revenues	−	Expenses
Old Bal.	$4,000	+	$1,900	+	$9,600	+	$26,000	=	$7,100	+	$30,000	+	$6,100	−	$1,700
(9)	+1,900	−	1,900												
New Bal.	$5,900	+	$ 0	+	$9,600	+	$26,000	=	$7,100	+	$30,000	+	$6,100	−	$1,700
				$41,500								$41,500			

Transaction 10: Payment of Accounts Payable FastForward pays CalTech Supply $900 cash as partial payment for its earlier $7,100 purchase of supplies (transaction 4), leaving $6,200 unpaid. The accounting equation shows that this transaction decreases FastForward's cash by $900 and decreases its liability to CalTech Supply by $900. Equity does not change. This event does not create an expense even though cash flows out of FastForward (instead the expense is recorded when FastForward derives the benefits from these supplies).

		Assets							=	Liabilities	+			Equity				
	Cash	+	Accounts Receivable	+	Supplies	+	Equipment	=	Accounts Payable	+	C. Taylor, Capital	+	Revenues	−	Expenses
Old Bal.	$5,900	+	$ 0	+	$9,600	+	$26,000	=	$7,100	+	$30,000	+	$6,100	−	$1,700
(10)	− 900								− 900						
New Bal.	$5,000	+	$ 0	+	$9,600	+	$26,000	=	$6,200	+	$30,000	+	$6,100	−	$1,700
				$40,600								$40,600			

Transaction 11: Withdrawal of Cash by Owner The owner of FastForward withdraws $600 cash for personal use. Withdrawals (decreases in equity) are not reported as expenses because they are not part of the company's earnings process. Since withdrawals are not company expenses, they are not used in computing net income.

		Assets							=	Liabilities	+			Equity					
	Cash	+	Accounts Receivable	+	Supplies	+	Equipment	=	Accounts Payable	+	C. Taylor, Capital	−	C. Taylor, Withdrawals	+	Revenues	−	Expenses
Old Bal.	$5,000	+	$ 0	+	$9,600	+	$26,000	=	$6,200	+	$30,000			+	$6,100	−	$1,700
(11)	− 600												− $600				
New Bal.	$4,400	+	$ 0	+	$9,600	+	$26,000	=	$6,200	+	$30,000	−	$600	+	$6,100	−	$1,700
				$40,000									$40,000			

Summary of Transactions

We summarize in Exhibit 1.9 the effects of these 11 transactions of FastForward using the accounting equation. Two points should be noted. First, the accounting equation remains in balance after each transaction. Second, transactions can be analyzed by their effects on components of the accounting equation. For example, in transactions 2, 3, and 9, one asset increased while another decreased by equal amounts.

Exhibit 1.9

Summary of Transactions Using the Accounting Equation

	Cash	+	Accounts Receivable	+	Supplies	+	Equipment	=	Accounts Payable	+	C. Taylor, Capital	−	C. Taylor, Withdrawals	+	Revenues	−	Expenses
											Equity						
(1)	$30,000							=			$30,000						
(2)	− 2,500			+	$2,500												
Bal.	27,500			+	2,500			=			30,000						
(3)	−26,000					+	$26,000										
Bal.	1,500			+	2,500	+	26,000	=			30,000						
(4)				+	7,100				+$7,100								
Bal.	1,500			+	9,600	+	26,000	=	7,100	+	30,000						
(5)	+ 4,200													+	$4,200		
Bal.	5,700			+	9,600	+	26,000	=	7,100	+	30,000			+	4,200		
(6)	− 1,000															−	$1,000
Bal.	4,700			+	9,600	+	26,000	=	7,100	+	30,000			+	4,200	−	1,000
(7)	− 700															−	700
Bal.	4,000			+	9,600	+	26,000	=	7,100	+	30,000			+	4,200	−	1,700
(8)		+	$1,900											+	1,600		
														+	300		
Bal.	4,000	+	1,900	+	9,600	+	26,000	=	7,100	+	30,000			+	6,100	−	1,700
(9)	+ 1,900	−	1,900														
Bal.	5,900	+	0	+	9,600	+	26,000	=	7,100	+	30,000			+	6,100	−	1,700
(10)	− 900								− 900								
Bal.	5,000	+	0	+	9,600	+	26,000	=	6,200	+	30,000			+	6,100	−	1,700
(11)	− 600											−	$600				
Bal.	$ 4,400	+	$ 0	+	$ 9,600	+	$ 26,000	=	$ 6,200	+	$ 30,000	−	$ 600	+	$6,100	−	$1,700

Quick Check

17. When is the accounting equation in balance, and what does that mean?
18. How can a transaction not affect any liability and equity accounts?
19. Describe a transaction increasing equity and one decreasing it.
20. Identify a transaction that decreases both assets and liabilities.

Answers—p. 26

Financial Statements

This section shows how financial statements are prepared from the analysis of business transactions. The four financial statements and their purposes are:

P1 Identify and prepare basic financial statements and explain how they interrelate.

1. *Income statement*—describes a company's revenues and expenses along with the resulting net income or loss over a period of time due to earnings activities.
2. *Statement of owner's equity*—explains changes in equity from net income (or loss) and from the owner investments and withdrawals over a period of time.
3. *Balance sheet*—describes a company's financial position (types and amounts of assets, liabilities, and equity) at a point in time.
4. *Statement of cash flows*—identifies cash inflows (receipts) and cash outflows (payments) over a period of time.

We prepare these financial statements using the 11 selected transactions of FastForward. (These statements are technically called *unadjusted*—we explain this in Chapters 2 and 3.)

Topic Tackler 1-2

Income Statement

Point: Net income is sometimes called earnings or profit.

FastForward's income statement for December is shown at the top of Exhibit 1.10. Information about revenues and expenses is conveniently taken from the Equity columns of Exhibit 1.9. Revenues are reported first on the income statement. They include consulting revenues of $5,800 from transactions 5 and 8 and rental revenue of $300 from transaction 8. Expenses are reported after revenues. (For convenience in this chapter, we list larger amounts first, but we can sort expenses in different ways.) Rent and salary expenses are from transactions 6 and 7. Expenses reflect the costs to generate the revenues reported. Net income (or loss) is reported at the bottom of the statement and is the amount earned in December. Owner's investments and withdrawals are *not* part of income.

Point: Decision makers often compare income to the operating cash flows from the statement of cash flows to help assess how much income is in the form of cash.

Statement of Owner's Equity

The statement of owner's equity reports information about how equity changes over the reporting period. This statement shows beginning capital, events that increase it (owner investments and net income), and events that decrease it (withdrawals and net loss). Ending capital is computed in this statement and is carried over and reported on the balance sheet. FastForward's statement of owner's equity is the second report in Exhibit 1.10. The beginning capital balance is measured as of the start of business on December 1. It is zero because FastForward did not exist before then. An existing business reports the beginning balance as of the end of the prior reporting period (such as from November 30). FastForward's statement shows that Taylor's initial investment created $30,000 of equity. It also shows the $4,400 of net income earned during the period. This links the income statement to the statement of owner's equity (see line ①). The statement also reports Taylor's $600 withdrawal and FastForward's $33,800 end-of-period capital balance.

Point: The statement of owner's equity is also called the *statement of changes in owner's equity*. Note: Beg. Capital + Owner Investments + Net Income − Withdrawals = End. Capital

Balance Sheet

FastForward's balance sheet is the third report in Exhibit 1.10. This statement refers to FastForward's financial condition at the close of business on December 31. The left side of the balance sheet lists FastForward's assets: cash, supplies, and equipment. The upper right side of the balance sheet shows that FastForward owes $6,200 to creditors. Any other liabilities (such as a bank loan) would be listed here. The equity (capital) balance is $33,800. Note the link between the ending balance of the statement of owner's equity and the equity balance here—see line ②. (This presentation of the balance sheet is called the *account form:* assets on the left and liabilities and equity on the right. Another presentation is the *report form:* assets on top, followed by liabilities and then equity at the bottom. Either presentation is acceptable.)

Decision Maker boxes are role-playing exercises that stress the relevance of accounting.

Decision Maker

Retailer You open a wholesale business selling entertainment equipment to retail outlets. You find that most of your customers demand to buy on credit. How can you use the balance sheets of these customers to help you decide which ones to extend credit to?

Answer—p. 26

Statement of Cash Flows

FastForward's statement of cash flows is the final report in Exhibit 1.10. The first section reports cash flows from *operating activities.* It shows the $6,100 cash received from clients and the cash paid for supplies, rent, and employee salaries. Outflows are in parentheses to denote subtraction. Net cash provided by operating activities for December is $1,000. If cash paid exceeded cash received, we would call it "cash used by operating activities." The second section reports *investing activities,* which involve buying and selling assets such as land and equipment that are held for *long-term use* (typically more than one-year). The only investing activity is the $26,000 purchase of equipment. The third section shows cash flows from *financing activities,* which include the *long-term* borrowing and repaying of cash from lenders and the owner's cash investments and withdrawals. FastForward reports $30,000

Point: Statement of cash flows has three main sections: operating, investing, and financing.

Point: Payment for supplies is an operating activity because supplies are expected to be used up in short-term operations (typically less than one year).

FASTFORWARD
Income Statement ✓
For Month Ended December 31, 2004

Revenues:
Consulting revenue ($4,200 + $1,600)	$ 5,800	
Rental revenue	300	
Total revenues		$ 6,100

Expenses:
Rent expense	1,000	
Salaries expense	700	
Total expenses		1,700
Net income		$ 4,400

FASTFORWARD
Statement of Owner's Equity ✓
For Month Ended December 31, 2004

C. Taylor, Capital, December 1, 2004	$ 0	
Plus: Investments by owner	30,000	
Net income	4,400	34,400
		34,400
Less: Withdrawals by owner		600
C. Taylor, Capital, December 31, 2004		$33,800

FASTFORWARD
Balance Sheet ✓
December 31, 2004

Assets		Liabilities	
Cash	$ 4,400	Accounts payable	$ 6,200
Supplies	9,600	Total liabilities	6,200
Equipment	26,000		
		Equity	
		C. Taylor, Capital	33,800
Total assets	$40,000	Total liabilities and equity	$ 40,000

FASTFORWARD
Statement of Cash Flows ✓
For Month Ended December 31, 2004

Cash flows from operating activities:
Cash received from clients ($4,200 + $1,900)	$ 6,100	
Cash paid for supplies ($2,500 + $900)	(3,400)	
Cash paid for rent	(1,000)	
Cash paid to employee	(700)	
Net cash provided by operating activities		$ 1,000

Cash flows from investing activities:
Purchase of equipment	(26,000)	
Net cash used by investing activities		(26,000)

Cash flows from financing activities:
Investments by owner	30,000	
Withdrawals by owner	(600)	
Net cash provided by financing activities		29,400
Net increase in cash		$ 4,400
Cash balance, December 1, 2004		0
Cash balance, December 31, 2004		$ 4,400

Exhibit 1.10

Financial Statements and Their Links

Point: A statement's heading identifies the company, the statement title, and the date or time period.

Point: Arrow lines show how the statements are linked. ① Net income is used to compute equity. ② Equity is used to prepare the balance sheet. ③ Cash from the balance sheet is used to reconcile the statement of cash flows.

Point: The income statement, the statement of owner's equity, and the statement of cash flows are prepared for a *period* of time. The balance sheet is prepared as of a *point* in time.

Point: A single ruled line denotes an addition or subtraction. Final totals are double underlined. Negative amounts are often in parentheses.

Point: Investing activities refer to long-term asset investments by the company, *not* to owner investments.

from the owner's initial investment and the $600 owner withdrawal. The net cash effect of all transactions is a $29,400 cash inflow. The final part of the statement shows FastForward increased its cash balance by $4,400 in December. Since it started with no cash, the ending balance is also $4,400—see line ③.

Quick Check

21. Explain the link between the income statement and the statement of owner's equity.
22. Describe the link between the balance sheet and the statement of owner's equity.
23. Discuss the three major sections of the statement of cash flows.

Answers—p. 27

Decision Analysis (a section at the end of each chapter) introduces and explains ratios helpful in decision making using real company data.

Decision Analysis   Return on Assets

A *Decision Analysis* section at the end of each chapter is devoted to financial statement analysis. We organize financial statement analysis into four areas: (1) liquidity and efficiency, (2) solvency, (3) profitability, and (4) market prospects—the back inside cover has a ratio listing with definitions and grouping by area. When analyzing ratios, we need benchmarks to identify good, bad, or average levels. Common benchmarks include the company's prior levels and those of its competitors.

A3   Compute and interpret return on assets.

This chapter presents a profitability measure, that of return on assets. Return on assets is useful in evaluating management, analyzing and forecasting profits, and planning activities. **Dell Computer** has its marketing department compute return on assets for *every* mailing. *Return on assets (ROA)*, also called *return on investment (ROI)*, is defined in Exhibit 1.11.

Exhibit 1.11
Return on Assets

$$\text{Return on assets} = \frac{\text{Net income}}{\text{Average total assets}}$$

Net income is from the annual income statement, and average total assets is computed by adding the beginning and ending amounts for that same period and dividing by 2. To illustrate, **Nike** reports net income of $663.3 million in 2002. At the beginning of fiscal 2002, its total assets are $5,819.6 million and at the end of fiscal 2002, they total $6,443.0 million. Nike's return on assets for 2002 is:

$$\text{Return on assets} = \frac{\$663.3 \text{ mil.}}{(\$5,819.6 \text{ mil.} + \$6,443.0 \text{ mil.})/2} = 10.8\%$$

Is a 10.8% return on assets good or bad for Nike? To help answer this question, we compare (benchmark) Nike's return with its prior performance, the returns of competitors (such as **Reebok**, **Converse**, **Skechers**, and **Vans**), and the returns from alternative investments. Nike's return for each of the prior five years is in the second column of Exhibit 1.12, which ranges from 7.4% to 10.8%. These returns show an increase in its productive use of assets in recent years. We also compute Reebok's returns in the third column of Exhibit 1.12. In four of the five years, Nike's return exceeds Reebok's, and its average return is higher for this period. We also compare Nike's return to the normal return for manufacturers of athletic footwear and apparel (fourth column). Industry averages are available from services such as **Dun & Bradstreet**'s *Industry Norms and Key Ratios* and **Robert Morris Associates**' *Annual Statement Studies*. When compared to the industry, Nike performs well.

*Each **Decision Analysis** section ends with a role-playing scenario to show the usefulness of ratios.*

Decision Maker

Business Owner   You own a small winter ski resort that earns a 21% return on its assets. An opportunity to purchase a winter ski equipment manufacturer is offered to you. This manufacturer earns a 19% return on its assets. The industry return for this manufacturer is 14%. Do you purchase this manufacturer?

Answer—p. 26

Nike Fiscal Year	Return on Assets		
	Nike	Reebok	Industry
2002	10.8%	6.8%	3.6%
2001	10.1	5.3	6.4
2000	10.4	0.7	5.1
1999	8.5	1.4	6.4
1998	7.4	7.7	6.1

Exhibit 1.12

Nike, Reebok, and Industry Returns

*The **Demonstration Problem** is a review of key chapter content. The Planning the Solution offers strategies in solving the problem.*

Demonstration Problem

After several months of planning, Sylvia Workman started a haircutting business called Expressions. The following events occurred during its first month:

a. On August 1, Workman invested $3,000 cash and $15,000 of equipment in Expressions.

b. On August 2, Expressions paid $600 cash for furniture for the shop.

c. On August 3, Expressions paid $500 cash to rent space in a strip mall for August.

d. On August 4, it purchased $1,200 of equipment on credit for the shop (using a long-term note payable).

e. On August 5, Expressions opened for business. Cash received from services provided in the first week and a half of business (ended August 15) is $825.

f. On August 15, it provided $100 of haircutting services on account.

g. On August 17, it received a $100 check for services previously rendered on account.

h. On August 17, it paid $125 cash to an assistant for working during the grand opening.

i. Cash received from services provided during the second half of August is $930.

j. On August 31, it paid a $400 installment toward principal on the note payable entered into on August 4.

k. On August 31, Workman made a $900 cash withdrawal for personal use.

Required

1. Arrange the following asset, liability, and equity titles in a table similar to the one in Exhibit 1.9: Cash; Accounts Receivable; Furniture; Store Equipment; Note Payable; S. Workman, Capital; S. Workman, Withdrawals; Revenues; and Expenses. Show the effects of each transaction using the accounting equation.
2. Prepare an income statement for August.
3. Prepare a statement of owner's equity for August.
4. Prepare a balance sheet as of August 31.
5. Prepare a statement of cash flows for August.
6. Determine the return on assets ratio for August.

Planning the Solution

- Set up a table like Exhibit 1.9 with the appropriate columns for accounts.
- Analyze each transaction and show its effects as increases or decreases in the appropriate columns. Be sure the accounting equation remains in balance after each transaction.
- Prepare the income statement, and identify revenues and expenses. List those items on the statement, compute the difference, and label the result as *net income* or *net loss*.
- Use information in the Equity columns to prepare the statement of owner's equity.
- Use information in the last row of the transactions table to prepare the balance sheet.
- Prepare the statement of cash flows; include all events listed in the Cash column of the transactions table. Classify each cash flow as operating, investing, or financing.
- Calculate return on assets by dividing net income by average assets.

Solution to Demonstration Problem

1.

	Assets				=	Liabilities +		Equity			
	Cash	+ Accounts Receivable	+ Furniture	+ Store Equipment	=	Note Payable	+ S. Workman, Capital	− S. Workman Withdrawals	+ Revenues	− Expenses
a.	$3,000			$15,000			$18,000			
b.	− 600		+ $600							
Bal.	2,400 +		+ 600 +	15,000 =			18,000			
c.	− 500									− $500
Bal.	1,900 +		+ 600 +	15,000 =			18,000			− 500
d.				+ 1,200		+$1,200				
Bal.	1,900 +		+ 600 +	16,200 =		1,200 +	18,000			− 500
e.	+ 825								+ $825	
Bal.	2,725 +		+ 600 +	16,200 =		1,200 +	18,000		+ 825 −	500
f.		+ $100							+ 100	
Bal.	2,725 +	100	+ 600 +	16,200 =		1,200 +	18,000		+ 925 −	500
g.	+ 100	− 100								
Bal.	2,825 +	0	+ 600 +	16,200 =		1,200 +	18,000		+ 925 −	500
h.	− 125									125
Bal.	2,700 +	0	+ 600 +	16,200 =		1,200 +	18,000		+ 925 −	625
i.	+ 930								+ 930	
Bal.	3,630 +	0	+ 600 +	16,200 =		1,200 +	18,000		+ 1,855 −	625
j.	− 400					− 400				
Bal.	3,230 +	0	+ 600 +	16,200 =		800 +	18,000		+ 1,855 −	625
k.	− 900							− $900		
Bal.	$2,330 +	0	+ $600 +	$16,200 =		$ 800 +	$18,000 −	$900	+ $1,855 −	$625

2.

EXPRESSIONS
Income Statement
For Month Ended August 31

Revenues:		
Haircutting services revenue		$1,855
Expenses:		
Rent expense	$500	
Wages expense	125	
Total expenses		625
Net Income		$1,230

3.

EXPRESSIONS
Statement of Owner's Equity
For Month Ended August 31

S. Workman, Capital, August 1*		$ 0
Plus: Investments by owner	$18,000	
Net income	1,230	19,230
		19,230
Less: Withdrawals by owner		900
S. Workman, Capital, August 31		$18,330

* If Expressions had been an existing business from a prior period, the beginning capital balance would equal the Capital account balance from the end of the prior period.

4.

EXPRESSIONS			
Balance Sheet			
August 31			
Assets		**Liabilities**	
Cash	$ 2,330	Note payable	$ 800
Furniture	600	**Equity**	
Store equipment	16,200	S. Workman, Capital	18,330
Total assets	$19,130	Total liabilities and equity	$19,130

5.

EXPRESSIONS	
Statement of Cash Flows	
For Month Ended August 31	
Cash flows from operating activities:	
Cash received from customers	$1,855
Cash paid for rent	(500)
Cash paid for wages	(125)
Net cash provided by operating activities	$1,230
Cash flows from investing activities:	
Cash paid for furniture	(600)
Cash flows from financing activities:	
Cash received from owner	3,000
Cash paid for owner withdrawal	(900)
Partial repayment of (long-term) note payable	(400)
Net cash provided by financing activities	1,700
Net increase in cash	$2,330
Cash balance, August 1	0
Cash balance, August 31	$2,330

6. Return on assets $= \dfrac{\text{Net income}}{\text{Average assets}} = \dfrac{\$1,230}{(\$18,000^* + \$19,130)/2} = \dfrac{\$1,230}{\$18,565} = \underline{\underline{6.63\%}}$

* Uses the initial $18,000 investment as the begining balance for the startup period only.

Return and Risk Analysis

This appendix explains return and risk analysis and its role in business and accounting.

   Net income is often linked to **return.** Return on assets (ROA) is stated in ratio form as income divided by assets invested. For example, banks report return from a savings account in the form of an interest return such as 4%. If we invest in a savings account or in U.S. Treasury bills, we expect a return of around 2% to 7%. We could also invest in a company's stock, or even start our own business. How do we decide among these investment options? The answer depends on our trade-off between return and risk.

A4 Explain the relation between return and risk.

Celebrity Investing How do fame and fortune translate into return and risk? A poll asked people which celebrity is the best investment. Similar to business investments, many people named performers with years of earning power ahead—see results to the right.

Oprah Winfrey	27%
Steven Spielberg	19
Tiger Woods	15
Michael Jordan	14
Tom Cruise	8
Jerry Seinfeld	4
Madonna	2

Risk is the uncertainty about the return we will earn. All business investments involve risk, but some investments involve more risk than others. The lower the risk of an investment, the lower is our expected return. The reason that savings accounts pay such a low return is the low risk of not being repaid with interest (the government guarantees most savings accounts from default). If we buy a share of Nike or any other company, we might obtain a large return. However, we have no guarantee of any return; there is even the risk of loss.

The bar graph in Exhibit 1A.1 shows recent returns for bonds with different risks. *Bonds* are written promises by organizations to repay amounts loaned with interest. U.S. Treasury bonds provide a low expected return, but they also offer low risk since they are backed by the U.S. government. High-risk corporate bonds offer a much larger potential return but with much higher risk.

The trade-off between return and risk is a normal part of business. Higher risk implies higher, but riskier, expected returns. To help us make better decisions, we use accounting information to assess both return and risk.

Exhibit 1A.1
Average Returns for Bonds with Different Risks

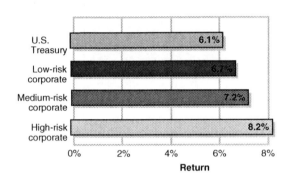

APPENDIX

1B Business Activities and the Accounting Equation

C6 Identify and describe the three major activities in organizations.

This appendix explains how the accounting equation is derived from business activities.

There are three major types of business activities: financing, investing, and operating. Each of these requires planning. *Planning* involves defining an organization's ideas, goals, and actions. Most public corporations use the *Management Discussion and Analysis* section in their annual reports to communicate plans. However, planning is not cast in stone. This adds *risk* to both setting plans and analyzing them.

Point: Management must understand accounting data to set financial goals, make financing and investing decisions, and evaluate operating performance.

Point: Investing (assets) and financing (liabilities plus equity) totals are *always* equal.

Financing *Financing activities* provide the means organizations use to pay for resources such as land, buildings, and equipment to carry out plans. Organizations are careful in acquiring and managing financing activities because they can determine success or failure. The two sources of financing are owner and nonowner. *Owner financing* refers to resources contributed by the owner along with any income the owner leaves in the organization. *Nonowner* (or *creditor*) *financing* refers to resources contributed by creditors (lenders). *Financial management* is the task of planning how to obtain these resources and to set the right mix between owner and creditor financing.

Investing *Investing activities* are the acquiring and disposing of resources (assets) that an organization uses to acquire and sell its products or services. Assets are funded by an organization's financing. Organizations differ on the amount and makeup of assets. Some require land and factories to operate. Others need only an office. Determining the amount and type of assets for operations is called *asset management*.

Invested amounts are referred to as *assets.* Financing is made up of creditor and owner financing, which hold claims on assets. Creditors' claims are called *liabilities,* and the owner's claim is called *equity.* This basic equality is called the *accounting equation* and can be written as: Assets = Liabilities + Equity.

Operating *Operating activities* involve using resources to research, develop, purchase, produce, distribute, and market products and services. Sales and revenues are the inflow of assets from selling products and services. Costs and expenses are the outflow of assets to support operating activities. *Strategic management* is the process of determining the right mix of operating activities for the type of organization, its plans, and its market.

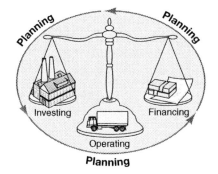

Exhibit 1B.1

Activities in Organizations

Exhibit 1B.1 summarizes business activities. Planning is part of each activity and gives them meaning and focus. Investing (assets) and financing (liabilities and equity) are set opposite each other to stress their balance. Operating activities are below investing and financing activities to show that operating activities are the result of investing and financing.

*A **Summary** organized by learning objectives concludes each chapter.*

Summary

C1 Explain the purpose and importance of accounting in the information age. Accounting is an information and measurement system that aims to identify, record, and communicate relevant, reliable, and comparable information about business activities. It helps assess opportunities, products, investments, and social and community responsibilities.

C2 Identify users and uses of accounting. Users of accounting are both internal and external. Some users and uses of accounting include (a) managers in controlling, monitoring, and planning; (b) lenders for measuring the risk and return of loans; (c) shareholders for assessing the return and risk of stock; (d) directors for overseeing management; and (e) employees for judging employment opportunities.

C3 Identify opportunities in accounting and related fields. Opportunities in accounting include financial, managerial, and tax accounting. They also include accounting-related fields such as lending, consulting, managing, and planning.

C4 Explain why ethics are crucial to accounting. The goal of accounting is to provide useful information for decision making. For information to be useful, it must be trusted. This demands ethical behavior in accounting.

C5 Explain the meaning of generally accepted accounting principles, and define and apply several key principles of accounting. Generally accepted accounting principles are a common set of standards applied by accountants. Accounting principles aid in producing relevant, reliable, and comparable information. The business entity principle means that a business is accounted for separately from its owner(s). The objectivity principle means independent, objective evidence supports the information. The cost principle means financial statements are based on actual costs incurred. The monetary unit principle assumes transactions can be reflected in money terms. The going-concern principle means financial statements assume the business will continue. The revenue recognition principle means revenue is recognized when earned.

C6^B **Identify and describe the three major activities in organizations.** Organizations carry out three major activities: financing, investing, and operating. Financing is the means used to pay for resources such as land, buildings, and machines. Investing refers to the buying and selling of resources used in acquiring and selling products and services. Operating activities are those necessary for carrying out the organization's plans.

A1 Define and interpret the accounting equation and each of its components. The accounting equation is: Assets = Liabilities + Equity. Assets are resources owned by a company. Liabilities are creditors' claims on assets. Equity is the owner's claim on assets (*the residual*). The expanded accounting equation is: Assets = Liabilities + [Owner Capital − Owner Withdrawals + Revenues − Expenses].

A2 Analyze business transactions using the accounting equation. A *transaction* is an exchange of economic consideration between two parties. Examples include exchanges of products, services, money, and rights to collect money. Transactions always have at least two effects on one or more components of the accounting equation. This equation is always in balance.

A3 Compute and interpret return on assets. Return on assets is computed as net income divided by average assets. For example, if we have an average balance of $100 in a savings account and it earns $5 interest for the year, the return on assets is $5/$100, or 5%.

A4^A **Explain the relation between return and risk.** *Return* refers to income, and *risk* is the uncertainty about the return we hope to make. All investments involve risk. The lower the risk of an investment, the lower is its expected return. Higher risk implies higher, but riskier, expected return.

P1 Identify and prepare basic financial statements and explain how they interrelate. Four financial statements report on an organization's activities: balance sheet, income statement, statement of owner's equity, and statement of cash flows.

Guidance Answers to **Decision Maker** and **Decision Ethics**

Entrepreneur (p. 11) You should probably form the business as a corporation if potential lawsuits are of prime concern. The corporate form of organization protects your personal property from lawsuits directed at the business and places only the corporation's resources at risk. A downside of the corporate form is double taxation: The corporation must pay taxes on its income, and you normally must pay taxes on any money distributed to you from the business (even though the corporation already paid taxes on this money). You should also examine the ethical and socially responsible aspects of starting a business in which you anticipate injuries to others. Formation as an LLC or S corp. should also be explored.

Retailer (p. 18) You can use the accounting equation (Assets = Liabilities + Equity) to help identify risky customers to whom you would likely not want to extend credit. A balance sheet provides amounts for each of these key components. The lower a customer's equity is relative to liabilities, the less likely you would extend credit. A low equity means the business has little value that does not already have creditor claims to it.

Business Owner (p. 20) The 19% return on assets for the manufacturer exceeds the 14% industry return (and many others). This is a positive factor for a potential purchase. Also, the purchase of this manufacturer is an opportunity to spread your risk over two businesses as opposed to one. Still, you should hesitate to purchase a business whose return of 19% is lower than your current resort's return of 21%. You are probably better off directing efforts to increase investment in your resort, assuming you can continue to earn a 21% return.

Guidance Answers to **Quick Checks**

1. Accounting is an information and measurement system that identifies, records, and communicates relevant information to help people make better decisions.

2. Recordkeeping, also called *bookkeeping*, is the recording of financial transactions and events, either manually or electronically. Recordkeeping is essential to data reliability; but accounting is this and much more. Accounting includes identifying, measuring, recording, reporting, and analyzing business events and transactions.

3. Technology offers increased accuracy, speed, efficiency, and convenience in accounting.

4. External users of accounting include lenders, shareholders, directors, customers, suppliers, regulators, lawyers, brokers, and the press. Internal users of accounting include managers, officers, and other internal decision makers involved with strategic and operating decisions.

5. Internal users (managers) include those from research and development, purchasing, human resources, production, distribution, marketing, and servicing.

6. Internal controls are procedures set up to protect assets, ensure reliable accounting reports, promote efficiency, and encourage adherence to company policies. Internal controls are crucial for relevant and reliable information.

7. Ethical guidelines are threefold: (1) identify ethical concerns using personal ethics, (2) analyze options considering all good and bad consequences, and (3) make ethical decisions after weighing all consequences.

8. Ethics and social responsibility yield good behavior, and they often result in higher income and a better working environment.

9. For accounting to provide useful information for decisions, it must be trusted. Trust requires ethics in accounting.

10. Two major participants in setting rules include the SEC and the FASB. (*Note:* Accounting rules reflect society's needs, not those of accountants or any other single constituency).

11. Most U.S. companies are not directly affected by international accounting standards. International standards are put forth as preferred accounting practices. However, stock exchanges and other parties are increasing the pressure to narrow differences in worldwide accounting practices. International accounting standards are playing an important role in that process.

12. The objectivity and cost principles are related in that most users consider information based on cost as objective. Information prepared using both principles is considered highly reliable and often relevant.

13. Users desire information about the performance of a specific entity. If information is mixed between two or more entities, its usefulness decreases.

14. The revenue recognition principle gives preparers guidelines on when to recognize (record) revenue. This is important; for example, if revenue is recognized too early, the statements report revenue sooner than it should and the business looks more profitable than it is. The reverse is also true.

15. The three basic forms of business organization are sole proprietorships, partnerships, and corporations.

16. Owners of corporations are called *shareholders* (or *stockholders*). Corporate ownership is divided into units called *shares* (or *stock*). The most basic of corporate shares is common stock (or capital stock).

17. The accounting equation is: Assets = Liabilities + Equity. This equation is always in balance, both before and after each transaction.

18. A transaction that changes the makeup of assets would not affect liability and equity accounts. FastForward's transactions 2 and 3 are examples. Each exchanges one asset for another.

19. Earning revenue by performing services, as in FastForward's transaction 5, increases equity (and assets). Incurring expenses while servicing clients, such as in transactions 6 and 7, decreases equity (and assets). Other examples include owner investments that increase equity and withdrawals that decrease equity.

20. Paying a liability with an asset reduces both asset and liability totals. One example is FastForward's transaction 10 that reduces a payable by paying cash.

21. An income statement reports a company's revenues and expenses along with the resulting net income or loss. A statement of owner's equity shows changes in equity, including that from net income or loss. Both statements report transactions occurring over a period of time.

22. The balance sheet describes a company's financial position (assets, liabilities, and equity) at a point in time. The equity account in the balance sheet is obtained from the statement of owner's equity.

23. Cash flows from operating activities report cash receipts and payments from the primary business the company engages in. Cash flows from investing activities involve cash transactions from buying and selling long-term assets. Cash flows from financing activities include long-term cash borrowings and repayments to lenders and the cash investments and withdrawals of the owner.

A list of key terms with page references concludes each chapter.

Key Terms

Key Terms are available at the book's Website for learning and testing in an online Flashcard Format.

Accounting (p. 4)
Accounting equation (p. 12)
Assets (p. 12)
Audit (p. 9)
Balance sheet (p. 17)
Bookkeeping (p. 5)
Business entity principle (p. 10)
Common stock (p. 11)
Corporation (p. 11)
Cost principle (p. 9)
Equity (p. 12)
Ethics (p. 8)
Events (p. 13)
Expanded accounting equation (p. 13)
Expenses (p. 13)
External transactions (p. 13)
External users (p. 5)
Financial accounting (p. 5)
Financial Accounting Standards Board (FASB) (p. 9)

Generally Accepted Accounting Principles (GAAP) (p. 9)
Going-concern principle (p. 10)
Income statement (p. 17)
Internal transactions (p. 13)
Internal users (p. 6)
International Accounting Standards Board (IASB) (p. 9)
Liabilities (p. 12)
Managerial accounting (p. 6)
Monetary unit principle (p. 10)
Net assets (p. 12)
Net income (p. 13)
Net loss (p. 13)
Objectivity principle (p. 9)
Owner investment (p. 13)
Owner withdrawals (p. 13)
Partnership (p. 10)

Proprietorship (p. 10)
Recordkeeping (p. 5)
Return (p. 23)
Return on assets (p. 20)
Revenues (p. 13)
Revenue recognition principle (p. 10)
Risk (p. 24)
Securities and Exchange Commission (SEC) (p. 9)
Shareholders (p. 11)
Shares (p. 11)
Sole proprietorship (p. 10)
Statement of cash flows (p. 17)
Statement of owner's equity (p. 17)
Stock (p. 11)
Stockholders (p. 11)
Withdrawals (p. 13)

Personal Interactive Quiz

Personal Interactive Quizzes A and B are available at the book's Website to reinforce and assess your learning.

Superscript letter ^{A} (^{B}) denotes assignments based on Appendix 1A (1B).

Discussion Questions

1. What is the purpose of accounting in society?

2. Identify three actual businesses that offer services and three actual businesses that offer products.

3. Why do organizations license and monitor accounting and accounting-related professionals?

4. Technology is increasingly used to process accounting data. Why then must we study and understand accounting?

5. Identify four kinds of external users and describe their uses of accounting information.

6. What are at least three questions business owners might be able to answer by looking at accounting information?

7. Describe the internal role of accounting for organizations.

8. What type of accounting information might be useful to those who carry out the marketing activities of a business?

9. Identify three types of services typically offered by accounting professionals.

10. Why is accounting described as a service activity?

11. Identify at least three tasks you would expect to be performed by government accounting professionals.

12. What work do tax accounting professionals perform in addition to preparing tax returns?

13. What ethical issues might accounting professionals face in dealing with confidential information?

14. Identify the two main categories of accounting principles.

15. What does the objectivity principle prescribe for information reported in financial statements? Why?

16. A business reports its own office stationery on the balance sheet at its $430 cost, although it cannot be sold for more than $10 as scrap paper. Which accounting principle(s) justifies this treatment?

17. Why is the revenue recognition principle needed? What does it prescribe?

18. Describe the three basic forms of business organization and their key characteristics.

19. Identify three types of organizations that can be formed as either profit-oriented entities or government (or non-profit) entities.

20. Define (a) *assets*, (b) *liabilities*, (c) *equity*, and (d) *net assets*.

21. What events or transactions change equity?

22. What do accountants mean by the term *revenue?*

23. Define *net income* and explain its computation.

24. Identify the four basic financial statements of a business.

25. What information is reported in an income statement?

26. Give two examples of expenses a business might incur.

27. What information is reported in a balance sheet?

28. The statement of cash flows reports on what major activities?

29. Define and explain return on assets.

30. [A]Explain return and risk. Discuss the trade-off between them.

31. [B]Describe the three major activities in organizations.

32. [B]Explain why investing (assets) and financing (liabilities and equity) totals are always equal.

33. Refer to the financial statements of **Krispy Kreme** in Appendix A. To what level of significance are dollar amounts rounded? What time period does its income statement cover?

34. Identify the dollar amounts of **Tastykake**'s 2002 assets, liabilities, and equity shown in its statements in Appendix A near the end of the book.

35. Access the SEC EDGAR database (**www.sec.gov**) and retrieve **Harley-Davidson**'s 2002 10-K (filed 2003-03-28). Identify its auditor. What responsibility does its independent auditor claim regarding its financial statements? **Harley-Davidson**

Red numbers denote Discussion Questions that involve decision-making.

Homework Manager 📝 *repeats all numerical Quick Study assignments on the book's Website with new numbers each time it is worked. It can be used in practice, homework, or exam mode.*

Quick Study exercises give readers a brief test of key elements.

QUICK STUDY

QS I-1
Identifying accounting users
C2

Identify the following users as either external users (E) or internal users (I).

a. Managers   **d.** FBI and CIA   **g.** Consumer group   **j.** Shareholders
b. Controllers   **e.** Sales staff   **h.** Customers   **k.** Congress
c. Business press   **f.** Brokers   **i.** Lenders   **l.** District attorney

QS I-2
Identifying accounting terms
C1

(a) Identify the meaning of these accounting-related acronyms: GAAP, SEC, and FASB, and then briefly explain the importance of each to accounting. (b) Identify the international accounting standards setting organization, and then briefly explain its purpose.

QS I-3
Accounting opportunities
C3

Identify at least three main areas of opportunities for accounting professionals. For each area, identify at least three job possibilities linked to accounting.

QS I-4
Identifying ethical concerns
C4

Accounting professionals must sometimes choose between two or more acceptable methods of accounting for business transactions and events. Explain why these situations can involve difficult matters of ethical concern.

Thinker icon highlights assignments that use decision-making skills.

Accounting provides information about an organization's business transactions and events that both affect the accounting equation and can be reliably measured. Identify at least two examples of both (*a*) business transactions and (*b*) business events that meet these requirements.

QS 1-5
Identifying transactions and events

A2

An important responsibility of many accounting professionals is to design and implement internal control procedures for organizations. Explain the purpose of internal control procedures.

QS 1-6
Explaining internal control

C1

Identify which general accounting principle best describes each of the following practices:

a. Marilyn Choi owns both Sailing Passions and Dockside Supplies. In preparing financial statements for Dockside Supplies, Choi makes sure that the expense transactions of Sailing Passions are kept separate from Dockside's statements.

b. In December 2004, A-Plus Floors received a customer's order and cash prepayment to install carpet in a new house that would not be ready for installation until March 2005. A-Plus Floors should record the revenue from the customer order in March 2005, not in December 2004.

c. If $30,000 cash is paid to buy land, the land is reported on the buyer's balance sheet at $30,000.

QS 1-7
Identifying accounting principles

C5

---

a. Total assets of HLC Financial Co. equal $40,000 and its equity is $10,000. What is the amount of its liabilities?

b. Total assets of Deep Valley Co. equal $55,000 and its liabilities and equity amounts are equal. What is the amount of its liabilities? What is the amount of its equity?

QS 1-8
Applying the accounting equation

A1

Use the accounting equation to compute the missing financial statement amounts (*a*), (*b*), and (*c*).

Company	Assets	=	Liabilities	+	Equity
1	$30,000		$ (*a*)		$20,000
2	$ (*b*)		$50,000		$30,000
3	$90,000		$10,000		$ (*c*)

QS 1-9
Applying the accounting equation

A1

Use **Harley-Davidson**'s December 31, 2002, financial statements, in Appendix A near the end of the book, to answer the following:

a. Identify the dollar amounts of Harley's 2002 (1) assets, (2) liabilities, and (3) equity.

b. Using Harley's amounts from part *a*, verify that Assets = Liabilities + Equity.

QS 1-10
Identifying and computing assets, liabilities, and equity

A2 **Harley-Davidson**

Indicate in which financial statement each item would most likely appear: income statement (I), balance sheet (B), statement of owner's equity (E), or statement of cash flows (CF).

a. Assets   **d.** Equipment   **g.** Total liabilities and equity

b. Revenues   **e.** Withdrawals   **h.** Cash from operating activities

c. Liabilities   **f.** Expenses   **i.** Net decrease (or increase) in cash

QS 1-11
Classifying items by financial statements

P1

In a recent year's financial statements, **Boeing Company**, which is the largest aerospace company in the United States, reported the following. Compute and interpret Boeing's return on assets (assume competitors average a 6% return on assets).

Sales	$21,924 million
Net income	856 million
Average total assets	21,463 million

QS 1-12
Computing and interpreting return on assets

A3

Homework Manager *repeats all numerical Exercises on the book's Website with new numbers each time they are worked. It can be used in practice, homework, or exam mode.*

EXERCISES

Exercise I-I

Distinguishing business organizations

C5

The following describe several different business organizations. Determine whether the description refers to a sole proprietorship, partnership, or corporation.

a. Ownership of Spirit Company is divided into 1,000 shares of stock.

b. Delta is owned by Sarah Gomez, who is personally liable for the debts of the business.

c. Jo Chen and Al Fitch own Financial Services, a financial services provider. Neither Chen nor Fitch has personal responsibility for the debts of Financial Services.

d. Sung Kwon and Frank Heflin own Get-It-There, a courier service. Both are personally liable for the debts of the business.

e. XLT Services does not have separate legal existence apart from the one person who owns it.

f. BioProducts does not pay income taxes and has one owner.

g. Tampa Biz pays its own income taxes and has two owners.

Exercise I-2

Identifying accounting principles

C5

Match each of the numbered descriptions with the principle it best reflects. Indicate your answer by writing the letter for the appropriate principle in the blank space next to each description.

A. General accounting principle   **E.** Specific accounting principle

B. Cost principle   **F.** Objectivity principle

C. Business entity principle   **G.** Going-concern principle

D. Revenue recognition principle

_____ **I.** Usually created by a pronouncement from an authoritative body.

_____ **2.** Financial statements reflect the assumption that the business continues operating.

_____ **3.** Derived from long-used and generally accepted accounting practices.

_____ **4.** Financial statement information is supported by evidence other than someone's opinion or belief.

_____ **5.** Every business is accounted for separately from its owner or owners.

_____ **6.** Revenue is recorded only when the earnings process is complete.

_____ **7.** Information is based on actual costs incurred in transactions.

Exercise I-3

Describing accounting responsibilities

C2   C3

Many accounting professionals work in one of the following three areas:

A. Financial accounting   **B.** Managerial accounting   **C.** Tax accounting

Identify the area of accounting that is most involved in each of the following responsibilities:

_____ **I.** External auditing.   _____ **5.** Planning transactions to minimize taxes.

_____ **2.** Cost accounting.   _____ **6.** Preparing external financial statements.

_____ **3.** Budgeting.   _____ **7.** Reviewing reports for SEC compliance.

_____ **4.** Internal auditing.   _____ **8.** Investigating violations of tax laws.

Exercise I-4

Identifying accounting users and uses

C2

Much of accounting is directed at servicing the information needs of those users that are external to an organization. Identify at least three external users of accounting information and indicate two questions they might seek to answer through their use of accounting information.

Exercise I-5

Identifying ethical concerns

C4

Assume the following role and describe a situation in which ethical considerations play an important part in guiding your decisions and actions:

a. You are a student in an introductory accounting course.

b. You are a manager with responsibility for several employees.

c. You are an accounting professional preparing tax returns for clients.

d. You are an accounting professional with audit clients that are competitors in business.

Match each of the numbered descriptions with the term or phrase it best reflects. Indicate your answer by writing the letter for the term or phrase in the blank provided.

A. Audit   **C.** Ethics   **E.** SEC   **G.** Net income
B. GAAP   **D.** Tax accounting   **F.** Public accountants   **H.** IASB

_____ **1.** Amount a business earns after paying all expenses and costs associated with its sales and revenues.

_____ **2.** An examination of an organization's accounting system and records that adds credibility to financial statements.

_____ **3.** Principles that determine whether an action is right or wrong.

_____ **4.** Accounting professionals who provide services to many clients.

_____ **5.** An accounting area that includes planning future transactions to minimize taxes paid.

Exercise 1-6
Learning the language
of business

C1–C4

Answer the following questions. (*Hint:* Use the accounting equation.)

a. Fong's Medical Supplies has assets equal to $123,000 and liabilities equal to $53,000 at year-end. What is the total equity for Fong's business at year-end?

b. At the beginning of the year, Beyonce Company's assets are $200,000 and its equity is $150,000. During the year, assets increase $70,000 and liabilities increase $30,000. What is the equity at the end of the year?

c. At the beginning of the year, New Wave Company's liabilities equal $60,000. During the year, assets increase by $80,000, and at year-end assets equal $180,000. Liabilities decrease $10,000 during the year. What are the beginning and ending amounts of equity?

Exercise 1-7
Using the accounting
equation

A1   A2

Check   (c) Beg. equity, $40,000

Determine the missing amount from each of the separate situations a, b, and c below.

	Assets	=	Liabilities	+	Equity
a.	?	=	$30,000	+	$65,000
b.	$ 89,000	=	$22,000	+	?
c.	$132,000	=	?	+	$20,000

Exercise 1-8
Using the accounting
equation

A1

Provide an example of a transaction that creates the described effects for the separate cases *a* through *g*.

a. Decreases an asset and decreases equity.

b. Increases an asset and increases a liability.

c. Decreases a liability and increases a liability.

d. Decreases an asset and decreases a liability.

e. Increases an asset and decreases an asset.

f. Increases a liability and decreases equity.

g. Increases an asset and increases equity.

Exercise 1-9
Identifying effects of
transactions on the
accounting equation

A1   A2

Mulan began a new consulting firm on January 5. The accounting equation showed the following balances after each of the company's first five transactions. Analyze the accounting equation for each transaction and describe each of the five transactions with their amounts.

Exercise 1-10
Analysis using the
accounting equation

A1   A2

		Assets							=	Liabilities	+		Equity		
Trans-action	Cash	+	Accounts Receivable	+	Office Supplies	+	Office Furniture	=	Accounts Payable	+	Mulan, Capital	+	Revenues
a.	$20,000	+	$ 0	+	$ 0	+	$ 0	=	$ 0	+	$20,000	+	$ 0
b.	19,000	+	0	+	1,500	+	0	=	500	+	20,000	+	0
c.	11,000	+	0	+	1,500	+	8,000	=	500	+	20,000	+	0
d.	11,000	+	3,000	+	1,500	+	8,000	=	500	+	20,000	+	3,000
e.	11,500	+	3,000	+	1,500	+	8,000	=	500	+	20,000	+	3,500

Exercise 1-11
Identifying effects of transactions on accounting equation

A1 A2

The following table shows the effects of five transactions (*a* through *e*) on the assets, liabilities, and equity of Bonita Boutique. Write short descriptions of the probable nature of each transaction.

	Cash	+	Accounts Receivable	+	Office Supplies	+	Land	=	Accounts Payable	+	Bonita, Capital	+	Revenues
	$ 10,500	+	$ 0	+	$1,500	+	$ 9,500	=	$ 0	+	$21,500	+	$ 0
a.	– 2,000					+	2,000						
b.				+	500				+500				
c.		+	950									+	950
d.	– 500								–500				
e.	+ 950	–	950										
	$ 8,950	+	$ 0	+	$2,000	+	$ 11,500	=	$ 0	+	$21,500	+	$950

Exercise 1-12
Identifying effects of transactions on the accounting equation and computing return on assets

A1 A2

Pamela Maben began a professional practice on June 1 and plans to prepare financial statements at the end of each month. During June, Maben (the owner) completed these transactions:

a. Owner invested $50,000 cash along with equipment that had a $10,000 market value.
b. Paid $1,600 cash for rent of office space for the month.
c. Purchased $12,000 of additional equipment on credit (due within 30 days).
d. Completed work for a client and immediately collected the $2,000 cash earned.
e. Completed work for a client and sent a bill for $7,000 to be paid within 30 days.
f. Purchased additional equipment for $8,000 cash.
g. Paid an assistant $2,400 cash as wages for the month.
h. Collected $5,000 cash on the amount owed by the client described in transaction *e.*
i. Paid $12,000 cash to settle the liability created in transaction *c.*
j. Owner withdrew $500 cash for personal use.

Required

Check Net income, $5,000

Create a table like the one in Exhibit 1.9, using the following headings for columns: Cash; Accounts Receivable; Equipment; Accounts Payable; Maben, Capital; Maben, Withdrawals; Revenues; and Expenses. Then use additions and subtractions to show the effects of the transactions on individual items of the accounting equation. Show new balances after each transaction.

Exercise 1-13
Preparing an income statement

P1

On October 1, Sasha Shandi organized Best Answers a new consulting firm. On October 31, the company's records show the following items and amounts. Use this information to prepare an October income statement for the business.

Cash	$ 2,000	Cash withdrawals by owner	$ 3,360
Accounts receivable	13,000	Consulting fees earned	15,000
Office supplies	4,250	Rent expense	2,550
Land	36,000	Salaries expense	6,000
Office equipment	28,000	Telephone expense	660
Accounts payable	7,500	Miscellaneous expenses	680

Check Net income, $5,110   Owner investments 74,000

Exercise 1-14
Preparing a statement of owner's equity P1

Use the information in Exercise 1-13 to prepare an October statement of owner's equity for Best Answers.

Use the information in Exercise 1-13 (if completed, you can also use your solution to Exercise 1-14) to prepare an October 31 balance sheet for Best Answers.

Exercise 1-15
Preparing a balance sheet P1

Use the information in Exercise 1-13 to prepare an October 31 statement of cash flows for Best Answers. Also assume the following:

a. The owner's initial investment consists of $38,000 cash and $36,000 in land.

b. The $28,000 equipment purchase is paid in cash.

c. The accounts payable balance of $7,500 consists of the $4,250 office supplies purchase and $3,250 in employee salaries yet to be paid.

d. The rent, telephone, and miscellaneous expenses are paid in cash.

e. Only $2,000 cash has been collected for the $15,000 consulting services provided.

Exercise 1-16
Preparing a statement of cash flows

P1

Check Net increase in cash, $2,000

Indicate the section where each of the following would appear on the statement of cash flows.

A. Cash flows from operating activity
B. Cash flows from investing activity
C. Cash flows from financing activity

_____ **1.** Cash paid for wages
_____ **2.** Cash withdrawal by owner
_____ **3.** Cash purchase of equipment
_____ **4.** Cash paid for advertising
_____ **5.** Cash paid on an account payable
_____ **6.** Cash invested by owner
_____ **7.** Cash received from clients
_____ **8.** Cash paid for rent

Exercise 1-17
Identifying sections of the statement of cash flows

P1

Geneva Group reports net income of $20,000 for 2005. At the beginning of 2005, Geneva Group had $100,000 in assets. By the end of 2005, assets had grown to $150,000. What is Geneva Group's 2005 return on assets? How would you assess its performance if competitors average a 10% return on assets?

Exercise 1-18
Analysis of return on assets

A3

Match each transaction or event to one of the following activities of an organization: financing activities (F), investing activities (I), or operating activities (O).

a. _____ An owner contributes resources to the business.
b. _____ An organization purchases equipment.
c. _____ An organization advertises a new product.
d. _____ The organization borrows money from a bank.
e. _____ An organization sells some of its land.

Exercise 1-19^B
Identifying business activities

C6

Problem Set B *located at the end of* **Problem Set A** *is provided for* <u>each</u> *problem to reinforce the learning process.* **Problem Set C** *(with solutions for instructors) is provided on this book's Website.*

The following financial statement information is from five separate companies:

PROBLEM SET A

	Company A	Company B	Company C	Company D	Company E
December 31, 2004:					
Assets	$45,000	$35,000	$29,000	$80,000	$123,000
Liabilities	23,500	22,500	14,000	38,000	?
December 31, 2005:					
Assets	48,000	41,000	?	125,000	112,500
Liabilities	?	27,500	19,000	64,000	75,000
During year 2005:					
Owner investments	5,000	1,500	7,750	?	4,500
Net income	7,500	?	9,000	12,000	18,000
Owner cash withdrawals	2,500	3,000	3,875	0	9,000

Problem 1-1A
Computing missing information using accounting knowledge

A1 A2

Required

1. Answer the following questions about Company A:
    a. What is the equity amount on December 31, 2004?
    b. What is the equity amount on December 31, 2005?
    c. What is the amount of liabilities on December 31, 2005?

2. Answer the following questions about Company B:
    a. What is the equity amount on December 31, 2004?
    b. What is the equity amount on December 31, 2005?

   c. What is net income for year 2005?

3. Calculate the amount of assets for Company C on December 31, 2005.

4. Calculate the amount of owner investments for Company D during year 2005.

5. Calculate the amount of liabilities for Company E on December 31, 2004.

Problem 1-2A
Identifying effects of transactions on financial statements

A1 A2

Identify how each of the following separate transactions affects financial statements. For the balance sheet, identify how each transaction affects total assets, total liabilities, and total equity. For the income statement, identify how each transaction affects net income. For the statement of cash flows, identify how each transaction affects cash flows from operating activities, cash flows from financing activities, and cash flows from investing activities. For increases, place a "+" in the column or columns. For decreases, place a "−" in the column or columns. If both an increase and a decrease occur, place a "+/−" in the column or columns. The first transaction is completed as an example.

| | | \multicolumn{3}{c}{Balance Sheet} | Income Statement | \multicolumn{3}{c}{Statement of Cash Flows} |
	Transaction	Total Assets	Total Liab.	Total Equity	Net Income	Operating Activities	Financing Activities	Investing Activities
1	Owner invests cash in business	+		+			+	
2	Receives cash for services provided							
3	Pays cash for employee wages							
4	Incurs legal costs on credit							
5	Borrows cash by signing long-term note payable							
6	Owner withdraws cash							
7	Buys land by signing note payable							
8	Provides services on credit							
9	Buys office equipment for cash							
10	Collects cash on receivable from (8)							

Problem 1-3A
Preparing an income statement

P1

The following is selected financial information for Valdez Energy Company for the year ended December 31, 2005: revenues, $65,000; expenses, $50,000; net income, $15,000.

Required

Prepare the 2005 calendar-year income statement for Valdez Energy Company.

Problem 1-4A
Preparing a balance sheet

P1

The following is selected financial information for Amico as of December 31, 2005: liabilities, $34,000; equity, $56,000; assets, $90,000.

Required

Prepare the balance sheet for Amico as of December 31, 2005.

The following is selected financial information of Trimark for the year ended December 31, 2005:

Problem 1-5A
Preparing a statement of cash flows

P1

Cash used by investing activities	$(3,000)
Net increase in cash	200
Cash used by financing activities	(3,800)
Cash from operating activities	7,000
Cash, December 31, 2004	3,300

Required

Prepare the 2005 calendar-year statement of cash flows for Trimark.

The following is selected financial information for Boardwalk for the year ended December 31, 2005:

Problem 1-6A
Preparing a statement of owner's equity

P1

B. Walk, Capital, Dec. 31, 2005	$15,000	B. Walk, Withdrawals	$2,000
Net income	9,000	B. Walk, Capital, Dec. 31, 2004	8,000

Required

Prepare the 2005 calendar-year statement of owner's equity for Boardwalk.

J. D. Simpson started The Simpson Co., a new business that began operations on May 1. Simpson Co. completed the following transactions during that first month:

Problem 1-7A
Analyzing transactions and preparing financial statements

C5 A2 P1

mhhe.com/larson

May 1   J. D. Simpson, the owner, invested $60,000 cash in the business.
    1   Rented a furnished office and paid $3,200 cash for May's rent.
    3   Purchased $1,680 of office equipment on credit.
    5   Paid $800 cash for this month's cleaning services.
    8   Provided consulting services for a client and immediately collected $4,600 cash.
  12   Provided $3,000 of consulting services for a client on credit.
  15   Paid $850 cash for an assistant's salary for the first half of this month.
  20   Received $3,000 cash payment for the services provided on May 12.
  22   Provided $2,800 of consulting services on credit.
  25   Received $2,800 cash payment for the services provided on May 22.
  26   Paid $1,680 cash for the office equipment purchased on May 3.
  27   Purchased $60 of advertising in this month's (May) local paper on credit; cash payment is due June 1.
  28   Paid $850 cash for an assistant's salary for the second half of this month.
  30   Paid $200 cash for this month's telephone bill.
  30   Paid $480 cash for this month's utilities.
  31   J. D. Simpson withdrew $1,200 cash for personal use.

Required

1. Arrange the following asset, liability, and equity titles in a table like Exhibit 1.9: Cash; Accounts Receivable; Office Equipment; Accounts Payable; J. D. Simpson, Capital; J. D. Simpson, Withdrawals; Revenues; and Expenses.
2. Show effects of the transactions on the accounts of the accounting equation by recording increases and decreases in the appropriate columns. Do not determine new account balances after each transaction. Determine the final total for each account and verify that the equation is in balance.
3. Prepare an income statement for May, a statement of owner's equity for May, a May 31 balance sheet, and a statement of cash flows for May.

Check (2) Ending balances: Cash, $61,140; Expenses, $6,440

(3) Net income, $3,960; Total assets, $62,820

Curtis Hamilton started a new business and completed these transactions during December:

Dec. 1 Curtis Hamilton transferred $56,000 cash from a personal savings account to a checking
account in the name of Hamilton Electric as its initial capital.
2 Rented office space and paid $800 cash for the December rent.
3 Purchased $14,000 of electrical equipment by paying $3,200 cash and agreeing to pay the
$10,800 balance in 30 days.
5 Purchased office supplies by paying $900 cash.
6 Completed electrical work and immediately collected $1,000 cash for the work.
8 Purchased $3,800 of office equipment on credit.
15 Completed electrical work on credit in the amount of $4,000.
18 Purchased $500 of office supplies on credit.
20 Paid $3,800 cash for the office equipment purchased on December 8.
24 Billed a client $600 for electrical work completed; the balance is due in 30 days.
28 Received $4,000 cash for the work completed on December 15.
29 Paid the assistant's salary of $1,200 cash for this month.
30 Paid $440 cash for this month's utility bill.
31 C. Hamilton withdrew $700 cash for personal use.

Required

1. Arrange the following asset, liability, and equity titles in a table like Exhibit 1.9: Cash; Accounts
Receivable; Office Supplies; Office Equipment; Electrical Equipment; Accounts Payable;
C. Hamilton, Capital; C. Hamilton, Withdrawals; Revenues; and Expenses.

Check (2) Ending balances: Cash,
$49,960, Accounts Payable, $11,300

(3) Net income, $3,160:
Total assets, $69,760

2. Use additions and subtractions to show the effects of each transaction on the accounts in the accounting equation. Show new balances after each transaction.

3. Use the increases and decreases in the columns of the table from part 2 to prepare an income
statement, a statement of owner's equity, and a statement of cash flows for the month. Also prepare a balance sheet as of the end of the month.

Analysis Component

4. Assume that the owner investment transaction on December 1 was $40,000 cash instead of $56,000
and that Hamilton Electric obtained the $16,000 difference by borrowing it from a bank. Explain
the effect of this change on total assets, total liabilities, and total equity.

Problem I-9A

Analyzing effects of transactions

C5 PI AI A2

Miranda Right started Right Consulting, a new business, and completed the following transactions
during its first year of operations:

a. M. Right invests $60,000 cash and office equipment valued at $30,000 in the business.
b. Purchased a $300,000 building to use as an office. Right paid $50,000 in cash and signed a note
payable promising to pay the $250,000 balance over the next ten years.
c. Purchased office equipment for $6,000 cash.
d. Purchased $4,000 of office supplies and $1,000 of office equipment on credit.
e. Paid a local newspaper $1,000 cash for printing an announcement of the office's opening.
f. Completed a financial plan for a client and billed that client $4,000 for the service.
g. Designed a financial plan for another client and immediately collected an $8,000 cash fee.
h. M. Right withdrew $1,800 cash from the company bank account for personal use.
i. Received a $3,000 partial cash payment from the client described in transaction *f*.
j. Made a $500 cash payment on the equipment purchased in transaction *d*.
k. Paid $2,500 cash for the office secretary's wages.

Required

1. Create a table like the one in Exhibit 1.9, using the following headings for the columns: Cash;
Accounts Receivable; Office Supplies; Office Equipment; Building; Accounts Payable; Notes
Payable; M. Right, Capital; M. Right, Withdrawals; Revenues; and Expenses.

Check (2) Ending balances:
Cash, $9,200; Expenses, $3,500

(3) Net income, $8,500

2. Use additions and subtractions to show the effects of these transactions on individual items of the
accounting equation. Show new balances after each transaction.

3. Once you have completed the table, determine the company's net income.

Coca-Cola and PepsiCo both produce and market beverages that are direct competitors. Key financial figures (in $ millions) for these businesses over the past year follow:

Key Figures	Coca-Cola	PepsiCo
Sales	$400	$250.0
Net income	50	37.5
Average invested (assets)	625	312.5

Problem 1-10A
Computing and interpreting return on assets

A3

Required

1. Compute return on assets for (a) Coca-Cola and (b) PepsiCo.

Check (1a) 8%; (1b) 12%

2. Which company is more successful in its total amount of sales to consumers?

3. Which company is more successful in returning net income from its amount invested?

Analysis Component

4. Write a one-paragraph memorandum explaining which company you would invest your money in and why. (Limit your explanation to the information provided.)

Zia manufactures, markets, and sells cellular telephones. The average total assets for Zia is $250,000. In its most recent year, Zia reported net income of $55,000 on revenues of $455,000.

Problem 1-11A
Determining expenses, liabilities, equity and return on assets

A1 A3

Required

1. What is Zia's return on assets?

2. Does return on assets seem satisfactory for Zia given that its competitors average a 12% return on assets?

3. What are total expenses for Zia in its most recent year?

Check (3) $400,000

4. What is the average total amount of liabilities plus equity for Zia?

(4) $250,000

All business decisions involve aspects of risk and return.

Problem 1-12A^A

Problem 1-12A[A]
Identifying risk and return

A4

Required

Identify both the risk and the return in each of the following activities:

1. Investing $1,000 in a 4% savings account.

2. Placing a $1,000 bet on your favorite sports team.

3. Investing $10,000 in Yahoo! stock.

4. Taking out a $10,000 college loan to earn an accounting degree.

A startup company often engages in the following transactions in its first year of operations. Classify these transactions in one of the three major categories of an organization's business activities.

Problem 1-13A[B]
Describing organizational activities

C6

A. Financing   **B.** Investing   **C.** Operating

_____ **1.** Owner investing land in business.

_____ **2.** Purchasing a building.

_____ **3.** Purchasing land.

_____ **4.** Borrowing cash from a bank.

_____ **5.** Purchasing equipment.

_____ **6.** Selling and distributing products.

_____ **7.** Paying for advertising.

_____ **8.** Paying employee wages.

An organization undertakes various activities in pursuit of business success. Identify an organization's three major business activities, and describe each activity.

Problem 1-14A[B]
Describing organizational activities C6

PROBLEM SET B

Problem 1-1B

Computing missing information using accounting knowledge

A1 A2

The following financial statement information is from five separate companies:

	Company V	Company W	Company X	Company Y	Company Z
December 31, 2004:					
Assets	$45,000	$70,000	$121,500	$82,500	$124,000
Liabilities	30,000	50,000	58,500	61,500	?
December 31, 2005:					
Assets	49,000	90,000	136,500	?	160,000
Liabilities	26,000	?	55,500	72,000	52,000
During year 2005:					
Owner investments	6,000	10,000	?	38,100	40,000
Net income	?	30,000	16,500	24,000	32,000
Owner cash withdrawals ...	4,500	2,000	0	18,000	6,000

Required

1. Answer the following questions about Company V:
   a. What is the amount of equity on December 31, 2004?
   b. What is the amount of equity on December 31, 2005?
   c. What is net income for year 2005?

2. Answer the following questions about Company W:
   a. What is the amount of equity on December 31, 2004?
   b. What is the amount of equity on December 31, 2005?
   c. What is the amount of liabilities on December 31, 2005?

3. Calculate the amount of owner investments for Company X during 2005.

4. Calculate the amount of assets for Company Y on December 31, 2005.

5. Calculate the amount of liabilities for Company Z on December 31, 2004.

Check (1b) $23,000

(2c) $32,000

(4) $137,100

Problem 1-2B

Identifying effects of transactions on financial statements

A1 A2

Identify how each of the following separate transactions affects financial statements. For the balance sheet, identify how each transaction affects total assets, total liabilities, and total equity. For the income statement, identify how each transaction affects net income. For the statement of cash flows, identify how each transaction affects cash flows from operating activities, cash flows from financing activities, and cash flows from investing activities. For increases, place a "+" in the column or columns. For decreases, place a "−" in the column or columns. If both an increase and a decrease occur, place "+/−" in the column or columns. The first transaction is completed as an example.

	Transaction	Balance Sheet			Income Statement	Statement of Cash Flows		
		Total Assets	Total Liab.	Total Equity	Net Income	Operating Activities	Financing Activities	Investing Activities
1	Owner invests cash in business	+		+			+	
2	Buys building by signing note payable							
3	Pays cash for salaries incurred							
4	Provides services for cash							
5	Pays cash for rent incurred							
6	Incurs utilities costs on credit							
7	Buys store equipment for cash							
8	Owner withdraws cash							
9	Provides services on credit							
10	Collects cash on receivable from (9)							

Selected financial information for Online Co. for the year ended December 31, 2005, follows:

Problem 1-3B
Preparing an income statement
P1

| Revenues ...... | $58,000 | Expenses .... | $30,000 | Net income ...... | $28,000 |

Required

Use the information provided to prepare the 2005 calendar-year income statement for Online Co.

The following is selected financial information for RWB Company as of December 31, 2005:

Problem 1-4B
Preparing a balance sheet
P1

| Liabilities .... | $74,000 | Equity .... | $40,000 | Assets .... | $114,000 |

Required

Use the information provided to prepare the balance sheet for RWB as of December 31, 2005.

Selected financial information of BuyRight Co. for the year ended December 31, 2005, follows:

Problem 1-5B
Preparing a statement of cash flows
P1

Cash from investing activities	$2,600
Net increase in cash	1,400
Cash from financing activities	2,800
Cash used by operating activities	(4,000)
Cash, December 31, 2004	1,300

Required

Use this information to prepare the 2005 calendar-year statement of cash flows for BuyRight.

The following is selected financial information of ComEx for the year ended December 31, 2005:

Problem 1-6B
Preparing a statement of owner's equity
P1

| C. Tex, Capital, Dec. 31, 2005 .... | $47,000 | C. Tex, Withdrawals .... | $ 8,000 |
| Net income .... | 6,000 | C. Tex, Capital, Dec. 31, 2004 .... | 49,000 |

Required

Prepare the 2005 calendar-year statement of owner's equity for ComEx.

Ken Stone launched a new business, Ken's Maintenance Co., that began operations on June 1. The following transactions were completed by the company during that first month:

Problem 1-7B
Analyzing transactions and preparing financial statements
C5 A2 P1

June 1 K. Stone invested $120,000 cash in the business.
2 Rented a furnished office and paid $4,500 cash for June's rent.
4 Purchased $2,400 of equipment on credit.
6 Paid $1,125 cash for the next week's advertising of the opening of the business.
8 Completed maintenance services for a customer and immediately collected $750 cash.
14 Completed $6,300 of maintenance services for First Union Center on credit.
16 Paid $900 cash for an assistant's salary for the first half of the month.
20 Received $6,300 cash payment for services completed for First Union Center on June 14.
21 Completed $3,500 of maintenance services for Skyway Co. on credit.
24 Completed $825 of maintenance services for Comfort Motel on credit.
25 Received $3,500 cash payment from Skyway Co. for the work completed on June 21.
26 Made payment of $2,400 cash for the equipment purchased on June 4.
28 Paid $900 cash for an assistant's salary for the second half of this month.
29 K. Stone withdrew $2,000 cash for personal use.
30 Paid $120 cash for this month's telephone bill.
30 Paid $525 cash for this month's utilities.

Required

1. Arrange the following asset, liability, and equity titles in a table like Exhibit 1.9: Cash; Accounts Receivable; Equipment; Accounts Payable; K. Stone, Capital; K. Stone, Withdrawals; Revenues; and Expenses.

Check (2) Ending balances: Cash, $118,080; Expenses, $8,070

(3) Net income, $3,305; Total assets, $121,305

2. Show the effects of the transactions on the accounts of the accounting equation by recording increases and decreases in the appropriate columns. Do not determine new account balances after each transaction. Determine the final total for each account and verify that the equation is in balance.

3. Prepare a June income statement, a June statement of owner's equity, a June 30 balance sheet, and a June statement of cash flows.

Problem 1-8B

Analyzing transactions and preparing financial statements

C5 A2 P1

Swender Excavating Co., owned by Patrick Swender, began operations in July and completed these transactions during that first month:

July 1   P. Swender invested $60,000 cash in the business as its initial capital.
     2   Rented office space and paid $500 cash for the July rent.
     3   Purchased excavating equipment for $4,000 by paying $800 cash and agreeing to pay the $3,200 balance in 30 days.
     6   Purchased office supplies for $500 cash.
     8   Completed work for a customer and immediately collected $2,200 cash for the work.
   10   Purchased $3,800 of office equipment on credit.
   15   Completed work for a customer on credit in the amount of $2,400.
   17   Purchased $1,920 of office supplies on credit.
   23   Paid $3,800 cash for the office equipment purchased on July 10.
   25   Billed a customer $5,000 for work completed; the balance is due in 30 days.
   28   Received $2,400 cash for the work completed on July 15.
   30   Paid an assistant's salary of $1,260 cash for this month.
   31   Paid $260 cash for this month's utility bill.
   31   P. Swender withdrew $1,200 cash for personal use.

Required

1. Arrange the following asset, liability, and equity titles in a table like Exhibit 1.9: Cash; Accounts Receivable; Office Supplies; Office Equipment; Excavating Equipment; Accounts Payable; P. Swender, Capital; P. Swender, Withdrawals; Revenues; and Expenses.

Check (2) Ending balances: Cash, $56,280; Accounts Payable, $5,120

(3) Net income, $7,580; Total assets, $71,500

2. Use additions and subtractions to show the effects of each transaction on the accounts in the accounting equation. Show new balances after each transaction.

3. Use the increases and decreases in the columns of the table from part 2 to prepare an income statement, a statement of owner's equity, and a statement of cash flows for the month. Also prepare a balance sheet as of the end of the month.

Analysis Component

4. Assume that Swender's $4,000 purchase of excavating equipment on July 3 was financed from an additional personal investment of another $4,000 cash in the business (instead of the purchase conditions described in the transaction). Explain the effect of this change on total assets, total liabilities, and equity.

Problem 1-9B

Analyzing effects of transactions

C5 P1 A1 A2

Tiana Moore started a new business, Tiana's Solutions, that completed the following transactions during its first year of operations:

a. T. Moore invests $95,000 cash and office equipment valued at $20,000 in the business.

b. Purchased a $120,000 building to use as an office. Moore paid $20,000 in cash and signed a note payable promising to pay the $100,000 balance over the next ten years.

c. Purchased office equipment for $20,000 cash.

d. Purchased $1,400 of office supplies and $3,000 of office equipment on credit.

e. Paid a local newspaper $400 cash for printing an announcement of the office's opening.

f. Completed a financial plan for a client and billed that client $1,800 for the service.

g. Designed a financial plan for another client and immediately collected a $2,000 cash fee.

h. T. Moore withdrew $5,000 cash from the company bank account for personal use.

i. Received $1,800 cash from the client described in transaction *f*.

j. Made a $2,000 cash payment on the equipment purchased in transaction *d*.

k. Paid $2,000 cash for the office secretary's wages.

Required

1. Create a table like the one in Exhibit 1.9, using the following headings for the columns: Cash; Accounts Receivable; Office Supplies; Office Equipment; Building; Accounts Payable; Notes Payable; T. Moore, Capital; T. Moore, Withdrawals; Revenues; and Expenses.

2. Use additions and subtractions to show the effects of these transactions on individual items of the accounting equation. Show new balances after each transaction.

Check (2) Ending balances: Cash, $49,400; Expenses, $2,400

3. Once you have completed the table, determine the company's net income.

(3) Net income, $1,400

AT&T and GTE produce and market telecommunications products and are competitors. Key financial figures (in $ millions) for these businesses over the past year follow:

Problem 1-10B
Computing and interpreting return on assets

A3

Key Figures	AT&T	GTE
Sales	$79,609	$19,957
Net income	139	2,538
Average invested (assets) . . .	87,261	37,019

Required

1. Compute return on assets for (a) AT&T and (b) GTE.

Check (1a) 0.16%, (1b) 6.9%

2. Which company is more successful in the total amount of sales to consumers?

3. Which company is more successful in returning net income from its amount invested?

Analysis Component

4. Write a one-paragraph memorandum explaining which company you would invest your money in and why. (Limit your explanation to the information provided.)

Aspen Company manufactures, markets, and sells snowmobile equipment. The average total assets for Aspen Company is $2,000,000. In its most recent year, Aspen reported net income of $100,000 on revenues of $1,200,000.

Problem 1-11B
Determining expenses, liabilities, equity, and return on assets

A1 A3

Required

1. What is Aspen Company's return on assets?

2. Does return on assets seem satisfactory for Aspen given that its competitors average a 9.5% return on assets?

3. What are the total expenses for Aspen Company in its most recent year?

Check (3) $1,100,000
(4) $2,000,000

4. What is the average total amount of liabilities plus equity for Aspen Company?

All business decisions involve aspects of risk and return.

Problem 1-12B^A
Identifying risk and return

A4

Required

Identify both the risk and the return in each of the following activities:

1. Stashing $1,000 under your mattress.

2. Placing a $500 bet on a horse running in the Kentucky Derby.

3. Investing $10,000 in Nike stock.

4. Investing $10,000 in U.S. Savings Bonds.

A startup company often engages in the following activities during its first year of operations. Classify each of the following activities into one of the three major activities of an organization:

Problem 1-13B^B
Describing organizational activities

C6

A. Financing   **B.** Investing   **C.** Operating

_____ **1.** Providing client services.   _____ **5.** Supervising workers.

_____ **2.** Obtaining a bank loan.   _____ **6.** Owner investing money in business.

_____ **3.** Purchasing machinery.   _____ **7.** Renting office space.

_____ **4.** Researching products.   _____ **8.** Paying utilities expenses.

Problem 1-14B[B]
Describing organizational
activities C6

Identify in outline format the three major business activities of an organization. For each of these activities, identify at least two specific transactions or events normally undertaken by the business's owners or managers.

PROBLEM SET C

Problem Set C is available at the book's Website to further reinforce and assess your learning.

This serial problem starts in this chapter and continues throughout most chapters of the book. It is most readily solved if you use the Working Papers that accompany this book.

SERIAL PROBLEM

Success Systems

On October 1, 2004, Kay Breeze launched a computer services company, **Success Systems,** that is organized as a sole proprietorship and provides consulting services, computer system installations, and custom program development. Breeze adopts the calendar year for reporting purposes and expects to prepare the company's first set of financial statements on December 31, 2004.

Required

Create a table like the one in Exhibit 1.9 using the following headings for columns: Cash; Accounts Receivable; Computer Supplies; Office Equipment; Accounts Payable; K. Breeze, Capital; K. Breeze, Withdrawals; Revenues; and Expenses. Then use additions and subtractions to show the effects of the October transactions for Success Systems on the individual items of the accounting equation. Show new balances after each transaction.

Oct. 1 Kay Breeze invested $55,000 cash, a $20,000 computer system, and $8,000 of office equipment in the business.
      3 Purchased $1,420 of computer supplies on credit from Cain Office Products.
      6 Billed Easy Leasing $4,800 for services performed in installing a new Web server.
      8 Paid $1,420 cash for the computer supplies purchased from Cain Office Products on October 3.
     10 Hired Sherry Adams as a part-time assistant for $125 per day, as needed.
     12 Billed Easy Leasing another $1,400 for services performed.
     15 Received $4,800 cash from Easy Leasing on its account.
     17 Paid $805 cash to repair computer equipment damaged when moving it.
     20 Paid $1,940 cash for an advertisement in the local newspaper.
     22 Received $1,400 cash from Easy Leasing on its account.
     28 Billed Clark Company $5,208 for services performed.
     31 Paid $875 cash for Sherry Adams's wages for seven days of work.
     31 Breeze withdrew $3,600 cash for personal use.

Check   Ending balances: Cash, $52,560; Revenues, $11,408; Expenses, $3,620

Beyond the Numbers (BTN) is a special problem section aimed to refine communication, conceptual, analysis, and research skills. It includes many activities helpful in developing an active learning environment.

BEYOND THE NUMBERS

REPORTING IN ACTION

A1 A3 A4

BTN 1-1   Key financial figures for **Krispy Kreme**'s fiscal year ended February 2, 2003, follow:

Key Figure	In Thousands
Liabilities + Equity	$410,487
Net income	33,478
Revenues	491,549

Required

1. What is the total amount of assets invested in Krispy Kreme?

2. What is Krispy Kreme's return on assets? Its assets at February 3, 2002, equal $255,376 (in thousands).   **Check**   (2) 10.1%

3. How much are total expenses for Krispy Kreme?

4. Does Krispy Kreme's return on assets seem satisfactory if competitors average a 3% return?

Roll On

5. Access Krispy Kreme's financial statements (Form 10-K) for fiscal years ending after February 2, 2003, from its Website (**KrispyKreme.com**) or from the SEC Website (**www.sec.gov**). Compute its return on assets for those fiscal years. Compare the February 2, 2003, fiscal year-end return on assets to any subsequent years' returns you are able to compute, and interpret the results.

BTN 1-2   Key comparative figures ($ thousands) for both **Krispy Kreme** and **Tastykake** follow:

**COMPARATIVE
ANALYSIS**

A1   A3   A4

Key Figure	Krispy Kreme	Tastykake
Liabilities + Equity	$410,487	$116,560
Net income	33,478	2,000*
Revenues (sales)	491,549	162,263

* Restructuring charges are removed from income.

Required

1. What is the total amount of assets invested in (*a*) Krispy Kreme and (*b*) Tastykake?

2. What is the return on assets for (*a*) Krispy Kreme and (*b*) Tastykake? Krispy Kreme's beginning-year assets equal $255,376 (in thousands) and Tastykake's beginning-year assets equal $116,137 (in thousands).   **Check**   (2b) 1.7%

3. How much are expenses for (*a*) Krispy Kreme and (*b*) Tastykake?

4. Is return on assets satisfactory for (*a*) Krispy Kreme and (*b*) Tastykake? (Assume competitors average a 3% return.)

5. What can you conclude about Krispy Kreme and Tastykake from these computations?

BTN 1-3   Juanita Cruz works in a public accounting firm and hopes to eventually be a partner. The management of Allnet Company invites Cruz to prepare a bid to audit Allnet's financial statements. In discussing the audit fee, Allnet's management suggests a fee range in which the amount depends on the reported profit of Allnet. The higher its profit, the higher will be the audit fee paid to Cruz's firm.

**ETHICS
CHALLENGE**

C4   C5

Required

1. Identify the parties potentially affected by this audit and the fee plan proposed.

2. What are the ethical factors in this situation? Explain.

3. Would you recommend that Cruz accept this audit fee arrangement? Why or why not?

4. Describe some ethical considerations guiding your recommendation.

BTN 1-4   Refer to this chapter's opening feature about **The Chocolate Farm**. Assume that the Macmillans wish to expand The Chocolate Farm to include a store devoted to selling food decorations related to the main business. They meet with a loan officer of a Denver bank to discuss a loan.

**COMMUNICATING
IN PRACTICE**

A1   C2

Required

1. Prepare a half-page report outlining the information you would request from the Macmillans if you were the loan officer.

2. Indicate whether the information you request and your loan decision are affected by the form of business organization for the proposed Chocolate Farm store.

TAKING IT TO THE NET

A3

mhhe.com/larson

BTN 1-5 Visit the EDGAR database at (www.sec.gov). Access the Form 10-K report of World Wrestling Entertainment (ticker WWE) filed on July 26, 2002.

Required

1. On page 16 of the 10-K report you will find comparative income statements of WWE for the years 1998–2002. How would you describe the revenue trend for WWE over this five-year period?
2. Has the WWE been profitable (see net income) over this five-year period?

TEAMWORK IN ACTION

C1

BTN 1-6 Teamwork is important in today's business world. Successful teams schedule convenient meetings, maintain regular communications, and cooperate with and support their members. This assignment aims to establish support/learning teams, initiate discussions, and set meeting times.

Required

1. Form teams and open a team discussion to determine a regular time and place for your team to meet between each scheduled class meeting. Notify your instructor via a memorandum or e-mail message as to when and where your team will hold regularly scheduled meetings.
2. Develop a list of telephone numbers and/or e-mail addresses of your teammates.

— Book's Website provides free and easy access to all articles for every Business Week Activity.

BUSINESS WEEK ACTIVITY   C1

mhhe.com/larson

BTN 1-7 *Business Week* publishes a ranking of the top 1,000 companies based on several performance measures. This issue is called the *Business Week Global 1000*. Obtain the July 14, 2003, publication of this issue—this book's Website maintains free access to this article.

Required

1. What are the top 10 companies on the basis of market value?
2. Are any of the top 10 companies in the same industry?
3. How many of the top 10 based on market capitalization are not U.S. companies?

ENTREPRENEURIAL DECISION

A1   A2

Check (2) 25%

BTN 1-8 Refer to this chapter's opening feature about **The Chocolate Farm**. Assume the Macmillans decide to open a small retail store to supplement their chocolate operations.

Required

1. The Macmillans obtain a $50,000 bank loan and contribute $30,000 of their own assets to support the opening of the new store.
   a. What is the new store's total amount of liabilities plus equity?
   b. What is the new store's total amount of assets?
2. If the Macmillans earn $20,000 of income in the first year the retail store operates, compute the store's return on assets (assume average assets equal $80,000). Assess its performance if competitors average a 10% return.

HITTING THE ROAD

C2

BTN 1-9 You are to interview a local business owner. (This can be a friend or relative.) Opening lines of communication with members of the business community can provide personal benefits of business networking. If you do not know the owner, you should call ahead to introduce yourself and explain your position as a student and your assignment requirements. You should request a thirty minute appointment for a face-to-face or phone interview to discuss the form of organization and operations of the business. Be prepared to make a good impression.

Required

1. Identify and describe the main operating activities and the form of organization for this business.
2. Determine and explain why the owner(s) chose this particular form of organization.
3. Identify any special advantages and/or disadvantages the owner(s) experiences in operating with this form of business organization.

BTN 1-10   **Grupo Bimbo (GrupoBimbo.com)** is a leader in the baking industry and also competes with both **Krispy Kreme** and **Tastykake**. Key financial figures for Grupo Bimbo follow:

Key Figure*	Pesos in Millions
Average assets	27,750
Net income	1,003
Revenues	41,373
Return on assets	3.6%

* Figures prepared in accordance with Generally Accepted
Accounting Principles in Mexico.

Required

1. Identify any concerns you have in comparing Grupo Bimbo's income, revenue, liabilities, and equity figures to those of Krispy Kreme and Tastykake (in BTN 1-2) for purposes of making business decisions.

2. Identify any concerns you have in comparing Grupo Bimbo's return on assets ratio to those of Krispy Kreme and Tastykake (in BTN 1-2) for purposes of making business decisions.

"I want everything done . . . like, yesterday"—Tanya York

Analyzing and Recording Transactions

A Look Back

Chapter 1 considered the role of accounting in the information age and introduced financial statements. We described different forms of organizations and identified users and uses of accounting. We explained the accounting equation and applied it to transaction analysis.

A Look at This Chapter

This chapter focuses on the accounting process. We describe transactions and source documents as inputs for analysis. We explain the analysis and recording of transactions. The accounting equation, T-account, general ledger, trial balance, and debits and credits are shown as useful tools in the accounting process.

A Look Ahead

Chapter 3 extends our focus on processing information. We explain the importance of adjusting accounts and the procedures in preparing financial statements.

CAP

Conceptual

C1 Explain the steps in processing transactions. *(p. 48)*

C2 Describe source documents and their purpose. *(p. 49)*

C3 Describe an account and its use in recording transactions. *(p. 49)*

C4 Describe a ledger and a chart of accounts. *(p. 52)*

C5 Define *debits* and *credits* and explain their role in double-entry accounting. *(p. 53)*

Analytical

A1 Analyze the impact of transactions on accounts and financial statements. *(p. 57)*

A2 Compute the debt ratio and describe its use in analyzing company performance. *(p. 67)*

Procedural

P1 Record transactions in a journal and post entries to a ledger. *(p. 55)*

P2 Prepare and explain the use of a trial balance. *(p. 64)*

P3 Prepare financial statements from business transactions. *(p. 65)*

Against Long Odds

LOS ANGELES—Tanya York produced her first film at 19. Since then she has produced hundreds of films with her company **York Entertainment (YorkEntertainment.com).** York's company has become an urban powerhouse and distributes its titles under the York Urban, York Latino, and York En Espanol labels. Says York, "I'm Jamaican myself, so I can kind of relate to being a minority in a world where so much is aimed at the majority, so, in that way I'm happy to be able to offer films with an urban appeal."

York insists that the business and accounting side of production is as important as the artistic side. "With producing you're involved in all aspects of the entertainment industry," she says, "the creative side as well as the business side." York knows that attention to financial statements and know-how of the accounting system of debits and credits is crucial to success. An understanding of the accounting details enabled York to assess and enhance her company's profitability and financial position.

York relies on the financial numbers in devising strategies to enhance income. At the same time, she does not lose sight of giving the public what they want. Adds York, "I don't see my job as changing the public [demands]." Instead she fulfills them. This includes filling her movies with stars like Ice T, Kurupt, Destiny's Child, Kool Mo Dee, and Mac 10.

York continues to grow her company. With revenues near $20 million, she shows a keen understanding of accounting information in making good business decisions. Still, she insists anyone can use such information in a business to achieve similar success. "I came to America and through hard work built a company."

Without a doubt, Tanya York has not only tasted success but is living it. Adds York, "I like to always have new challenges in front of me."

[Sources: *York Entertainment Website,* January 2004; *Cinescape,* 2002; *Rolling Out Urban Style,* January 2002; *Entrepreneur,* November 2002; *Los Angeles Daily News,* February 2003.]

Financial statements report on the financial performance and condition of an organization. Knowledge of their preparation, organization, and analysis is important. A main goal of this chapter is to illustrate how transactions are recorded, how they are reflected in financial statements, and how they impact analysis of financial statements. Debits and credits are introduced and identified as a tool in helping understand and process transactions.

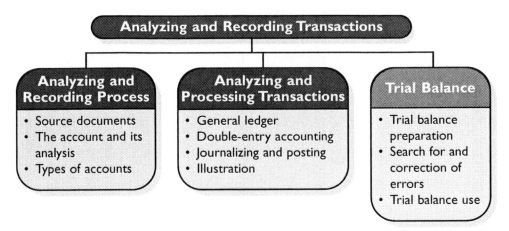

Analyzing and Recording Transactions

Analyzing and Recording Process	Analyzing and Processing Transactions	Trial Balance
• Source documents • The account and its analysis • Types of accounts	• General ledger • Double-entry accounting • Journalizing and posting • Illustration	• Trial balance preparation • Search for and correction of errors • Trial balance use

Analyzing and Recording Process

The accounting process identifies business transactions and events, analyzes and records their effects, and summarizes and presents information in reports and financial statements. These reports and statements are used for making investing, lending, and other business decisions. The steps in the accounting process that focus on *analyzing and recording* transactions and events are shown in Exhibit 2.1.

Exhibit 2.1

The Analyzing and Recording Process

Analyze each transaction and event from source documents

Record relevant transactions and events in a journal

Post journal information to ledger accounts

Prepare and analyze the trial balance

C1   Explain the steps in processing transactions.

Business transactions and events are the starting points. Relying on source documents, transactions and events are analyzed using the accounting equation to understand how they affect company performance and financial position. These effects are recorded in accounting records, informally referred to as the *accounting books,* or simply the *books.* Additional steps such as posting and then preparing a trial balance help summarize and classify the effects of transactions and events. Ultimately, the accounting process provides information in useful reports or financial statements to decision makers.

Source Documents

Source documents identify and describe transactions and events entering the accounting process. They are the sources of accounting information and can be in either hard copy or electronic form. Examples are sales tickets, checks, purchase orders, bills from suppliers, employee earnings records, and bank statements. To illustrate, when an item is purchased on credit, the seller usually prepares at least two copies of a sales invoice. One copy is given to the buyer. Another copy, often sent electronically, results in an entry in the seller's information system to record the sale. Sellers use invoices for recording sales and for control; buyers use them for recording purchases and for monitoring purchasing activity. Note that many cash registers record information for each sale on a tape or electronic file locked inside the register. This record can be used as a source document for recording sales in the accounting records. Source documents, especially if obtained from outside the organization, provide objective and reliable evidence about transactions and events and their amounts.

C2 Describe source documents and their purpose.

Point: To ensure that all sales are rung up on the register, most sellers require customers to have their receipts to exchange or return purchased items.

> ### Decision Ethics
>
> **Cashier** Your manager requires that you, as cashier, immediately enter each sale. Recently, lunch hour traffic has increased and the assistant manager asks you to avoid delays by taking customers' cash and making change without entering sales. The assistant manager says she will add up cash and enter sales after lunch. She says that, in this way, the register will always match the cash amount when the manager arrives at three o'clock. What do you do?
>
> Answer p. 72

The Account and Its Analysis

An **account** is a record of increases and decreases in a specific asset, liability, equity, revenue, or expense item. Information from an account is analyzed, summarized, and presented in reports and financial statements. The **general ledger,** or simply **ledger,** is a record containing all accounts used by a company. The ledger is often in electronic form. While most companies' ledgers contain similar accounts, a company may use one or more unique accounts because of its type of operations. Accounts are arranged into three general categories (based on the accounting equation), as shown in Exhibit 2.2.

C3 Describe an account and its use in recording transactions.

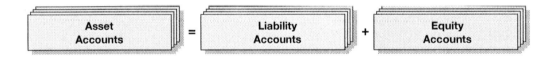

Exhibit 2.2

Accounts Organized by the Accounting Equation

Asset Accounts Assets are resources owned or controlled by a company and that have expected future benefits. Most accounting systems include (at a minimum) separate accounts for the assets described here.

A *Cash* account reflects a company's cash balance. All increases and decreases in cash are recorded in the Cash account. It includes money and any medium of exchange that a bank accepts for deposit (coins, checks, money orders, and checking account balances).

Accounts receivable are held by a seller and refer to promises of payment from customers to sellers. These transactions are often called *credit sales* or *sales on account* (or *on credit*). Accounts receivable are increased by credit sales and are decreased by customer payments. A company needs a separate record for each customer, but for now, we use the simpler practice of recording all increases and decreases in receivables in a single account called Accounts Receivable.

A *note receivable,* or promissory note, is a written promise of another entity to pay a definite sum of money on a specified future date to the holder of the note. A company holding a promissory note signed by another entity has an asset that is recorded in a Note (or Notes) Receivable account.

Prepaid accounts (also called *prepaid expenses*) are assets that represent prepayments of future expenses (*not* current expenses). When the expenses are later incurred, the amounts in prepaid accounts are transferred to expense accounts. Common examples of prepaid

Point: Customers and others who owe a company are called its **debtors.**

Point: A college parking fee is a prepaid account from the student's standpoint. At the beginning of the term, it represents an asset that entitles a student to park on or near campus. The benefits of the parking fee expire as the term progresses. At term-end, prepaid parking (asset) equals zero as it has been entirely recorded as parking expense.

Point: Prepaid accounts that apply to current *and* future periods are assets. These assets are adjusted at the end of each period to reflect only those amounts that have not yet expired and to record as expenses those amounts that have expired.

accounts include prepaid insurance, prepaid rent, and prepaid services (such as club memberships). Prepaid accounts expire with the passage of time (such as with rent) or through use (such as with prepaid meal tickets). When financial statements are prepared, prepaid accounts are adjusted so that (1) all expired and used prepaid accounts are recorded as regular expenses and (2) all unexpired and unused prepaid accounts are recorded as assets (reflecting future use in future periods). To illustrate, when an insurance fee, called a *premium,* is paid in advance, the cost is typically recorded in the asset account Prepaid Insurance. Over time, the expiring portion of the insurance cost is removed from this asset account and reported in expenses on the income statement. Any unexpired portion remains in Prepaid Insurance and is reported on the balance sheet as an asset. (An exception exists for prepaid accounts that will expire or be used before the end of the current accounting period when financial statements are prepared. In this case, the prepayments *can* be recorded immediately as expenses.)

Supplies are assets until they are used. When they are used up, their costs are reported as expenses. The costs of unused supplies are recorded in a Supplies asset account. Supplies are often grouped by purpose—for example office supplies and store supplies. *Office supplies* include stationery, paper, toner, and pens. *Store supplies* include packaging materials, plastic and paper bags, gift boxes and cartons, and cleaning materials. The costs of these unused supplies can be recorded in an Office Supplies or a Store Supplies asset account. When supplies are used, their costs are transferred from the asset accounts to expense accounts.

Point: Some assets are described as *intangible* because they do not have physical existence or their benefits are highly uncertain. A recent balance sheet for Coca-Cola Company shows nearly $3.5 billion in intangible assets.

Equipment is an asset. When equipment is used and gets worn down its cost is gradually reported as an expense (called depreciation). Equipment is often grouped by its purpose—for example, office equipment and store equipment. *Office equipment* includes computers, printers, desks, chairs, shelves, and other office equipment. Costs incurred for these items are recorded in an Office Equipment asset account. The Store Equipment account includes the costs of assets used in a store such as counters, showcases, ladders, hoists, and cash registers.

Buildings such as stores, offices, warehouses, and factories are assets because they provide expected future benefits to those who control or own them. Their costs are recorded in a Buildings asset account. When several buildings are owned, separate accounts are sometimes kept for each of them.

The cost of *land* owned by a business is recorded in a Land account. The cost of buildings located on the land is separately recorded in one or more building accounts.

Decision Insight

Boss-Aid   Entrepreneurs were asked whom they would want—if they could have anyone—to help run their businesses for a week. Bill Gates led, with 24%, followed by Donald Trump and Warren Buffet—see selected survey results.

Bill Gates	24%
Donald Trump	6.8
Warren Buffet	5.8
Lee Iacocca	5.2
Ross Perot	3.1
Hillary Clinton	1.4

Liability Accounts   Liabilities are claims (by creditors) against assets, which means they are obligations to transfer assets or provide products or services to other entities. **Creditors** are individuals and organizations that own the right to receive payments from a company. If a company fails to pay its obligations, the law gives creditors a right to force the sale of that company's assets to obtain the money to meet creditors' claims. When assets are sold under these conditions, creditors are paid first, but only up to the amount of their claims. Any remaining money, the residual, goes to the owners of the company. Creditors often use a balance sheet to help decide whether to loan money to a company. A loan is less risky if the borrower's liabilities are small in comparison to assets because there are more resources than claims on resources. The more common liability accounts are described here.

Point: Accounts Payable are also called *Trade Payables.*

Accounts payable refer to oral or implied promises to pay later, which commonly arise from purchases of merchandise. Payables can also arise from purchases of supplies, equipment, and services. Accounting systems keep separate records about each creditor. We describe these individual records in Chapter 4.

A *note payable* refers to a formal promise, usually denoted by the signing of a promissory note, to pay a future amount. It is recorded in either a Short-Term Note Payable account or a Long-Term Note Payable account, depending on when it must be repaid. We explain details of short- and long-term classification in Chapter 4.

Unearned Revenue refers to a liability that is settled in the future when a company delivers its products or services. When customers pay in advance for products or services (before revenue is earned), the revenue recognition principle requires that the seller consider this payment as unearned revenue. Examples of unearned revenue include magazine subscriptions collected in advance by a publisher, sales of gift certificates by stores, and season ticket sales by sports teams. The seller would record these in liability accounts such as Unearned Subscriptions, Unearned Store Sales, and Unearned Ticket Revenue. When products and services are later delivered, the earned portion of the unearned revenue is transferred to revenue accounts such as Subscription Fees, Store Sales, and Ticket Sales.[1]

> **Decision Insight**
>
> **Cash Spread** The **Green Bay Packers** have *Unearned Revenues* of nearly $40 million in advance ticket sales. When the team plays its regular season home games, it settles this liability to its ticket holders and transfers the amount earned to *Ticket Revenues*.
>
>

Point: If a subscription is cancelled the publisher should refund the unused portion to the subscriber.

Accrued liabilities are amounts owed that are not yet paid. Examples are wages payable, taxes payable, and interest payable. These are often recorded in separate liability accounts by the same title. If they are not large in amount, one or more ledger accounts can be added and reported as a single amount on the balance sheet. (Financial statements often have amounts reported that are a summation of several ledger accounts.)

Equity Accounts The owner's claim on a company's assets is called *equity* or *owner's equity*. Equity is the owners' *residual interest* in the assets of a business after deducting liabilities. There are four subcategories of equity: owner's capital, owner's withdrawals, revenues, and expenses. We show this visually in Exhibit 2.3 by expanding the accounting equation.

Point: Equity is also called *net assets*.

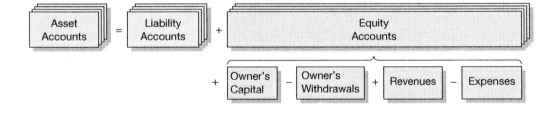

Exhibit 2.3

Expanded Accounting Equation

When an owner invests in a company, the invested amount is recorded in an account titled **Owner, Capital** (where the owner's name is inserted in place of "owner"). An account called *C. Taylor, Capital* is used for FastForward. Any further investments are recorded in this account. When the owner withdraws assets for personal use the withdrawal decreases both the company's assets and its total equity. (Owners of proprietorships cannot receive salaries because they are not legally separate from their companies and cannot enter into salary, or any other, contracts with themselves.) Withdrawals are

Point: The Owner's Withdrawals account (also called *Drawing* or *Personal* account) is sometimes referred to as a *contra equity* account because it reduces the normal balance of equity.

---

[1] In practice, account titles vary. As one example, Subscription Fees is sometimes called Subscription Fees Revenue, Subscription Fees Earned, or Earned Subscription Fees. As another example, Rent Earned is sometimes called Rent Revenue, Rental Revenue, or Earned Rent Revenue. We must use good judgment when reading financial statements because titles can differ even within the same industry. For example, product sales are called *revenues* at **Krispy Kreme,** but *net sales* at **Tastykake.** Generally, the term *revenues* or *fees* is more commonly used with service businesses, and *net sales* or *sales* with product businesses.

Point: The withdrawal of assets by the owners of a corporation is called a *dividend*.

not expenses of the business. They are simply the opposite of owner investments. An Owner, Withdrawals account is used in recording withdrawals by the owner. An account called *C. Taylor, Withdrawals,* is used to record Taylor's withdrawals from FastForward.

Revenues and expenses are the final two categories of equity. Examples of revenue accounts are Sales, Commissions Earned, Professional Fees Earned, Rent Earned, and Interest Revenue. *Revenues increase equity* and result from products or services provided to customers. Examples of expense accounts are Advertising Expense, Store Supplies Expense, Office Salaries Expense, Office Supplies Expense, Rent Expense, Utilities Expense, and Insurance Expense. *Expenses decrease equity* and result from assets or services used in a company's operations. The variety of revenues and expenses can be seen by looking at the *chart of accounts* that follows the index at the back of this book. (Different companies sometimes use different account titles than those in this book's chart of accounts. For example, some might use Interest Revenue instead of Interest Earned, or Rental Expense instead of Rent Expense. It is important only that an account title describe the item it represents.)

Decision Insight

Sports Accounts The **Boston Celtics** report the following major revenue and expense accounts:

Revenues	Expenses
Basketball ticket sales	Team salaries
TV & radio broadcast fees	Game costs
Advertising revenues	NBA franchise costs
Basketball playoff receipts	Promotional costs

Analyzing and Processing Transactions

This section explains several crucial tools and processes that comprise an accounting system. These include a ledger, T-accounts, debits and credits, double-entry accounting, journalizing, and posting.

Ledger and Chart of Accounts

C4 Describe a ledger and a chart of accounts.

The collection of all accounts for an information system is called a *ledger* (or *general ledger*). If accounts are in files on a hard drive, the sum of those files is the ledger. If the accounts are pages in a file, that file is the ledger. A company's size and diversity of operations affect the number of accounts needed. A small company can get by with as few as 20 or 30 accounts; a large company can require several thousand. The **chart of accounts** is a list of all accounts a company uses and includes an identification number assigned to each account. A small business might use the following numbering system for its accounts:

Decision Insight

Accoun-tech Using technology, **Sears** shrank its annual financial plan from 100 flowcharts with more than 300 steps to just *one* sheet of paper with 25 steps! Technology also allows Sears execs to analyze budgets and financial plans on their PCs. Sears says it slashed $100 million in recordkeeping costs.

101–199	Asset accounts
201–299	Liability accounts
301–399	Equity accounts
401–499	Revenue accounts
501–699	Expense accounts

These numbers provide a three-digit code that is useful in recordkeeping. In this case, the first digit assigned to asset accounts is a 1, the first digit assigned to liability accounts is a 2, and so on. The second and third digits relate to the accounts' subcategories. Exhibit 2.4 shows a partial chart of accounts for FastForward.

Account Number	Account Name		Account Number	Account Name
101	Cash		301	C. Taylor, Capital
106	Accounts receivable		302	C. Taylor, Withdrawals
126	Supplies		403	Consulting revenue
128	Prepaid insurance		406	Rental revenue
167	Equipment		622	Salaries expense
201	Accounts payable		637	Insurance expense
236	Unearned consulting revenue		640	Rent expense
			652	Supplies expense
			690	Utilities expense

Exhibit 2.4

Partial Chart of Accounts for FastForward

Debits and Credits

A **T-account** represents a ledger account and is a tool used to understand the effects of one or more transactions. Its name comes from its shape like the letter *T*. The layout of a T-account (shown in Exhibit 2.5) is (1) the account title on top, (2) a left, or debit side, and (3) a right, or credit, side.

The left side of an account is called the **debit** side, often abbreviated *Dr*. The right side is called the **credit** side, abbreviated *Cr*.[2] To enter amounts on the left side of an account is to *debit* the account. To enter amounts on the right side is to *credit* the account. Do not make the error of thinking that the terms *debit* and *credit* mean increase or decrease. Whether a debit or a credit is an increase or decrease depends on the account. In an account where a debit is an increase, the credit is a decrease; in an account where a debit is a decrease, the credit is an increase. The difference between total debits and total credits for an account, including any beginning balance, is the **account balance.** When the sum of debits exceeds the sum of credits, the account has a *debit balance*. It has a *credit balance* when the sum of credits exceeds the sum of debits. When the sum of debits equals the sum of credits, the account has a *zero balance*.

C5 Define *debits* and *credits* and explain their role in double-entry accounting.

Point: Think of debit and credit as accounting directions for left and right.

Account Title	
(Left side)	(Right side)
Debit	**Credit**

Exhibit 2.5

The T-Account

Double-Entry Accounting

Double-entry accounting requires that each transaction affect, and be recorded in, at least two accounts. It also means the *total amount debited must equal the total amount credited* for each transaction. Thus, the sum of the debits for all entries must equal the sum of the credits for all entries, and the sum of debit account balances in the ledger must equal the sum of credit account balances.

The system for recording debits and credits follows from the usual accounting equation—see Exhibit 2.6. Two points are important here. First, like any simple mathematical relation, net increases or decreases on one side have equal net effects on the other side. For example, a net increase in assets must be accompanied by an identical net increase on the liabilities

"Total debits equal total credits for each entry."

Assets		=	Liabilities		+	Equity	
Debit for increases	Credit for decreases		Debit for decreases	Credit for increases		Debit for decreases	Credit for increases
+	−		−	+		−	+

Exhibit 2.6

Debits and Credits in the Accounting Equation

---

[2] These abbreviations are remnants of 18th-century English recordkeeping practices where the terms *debitor* and *creditor* were used instead of *debit* and *credit*. The abbreviations use the first and last letters of these terms, just as we still do for Saint (St.) and Doctor (Dr.).

Point: Debits and credits do not mean favorable or unfavorable. A debit to an asset increases it, as does a debit to an expense. A credit to a liability increases it, as does a credit to a revenue.

and equity side. Recall that some transactions affect only one side of the equation, meaning that two or more accounts on one side are affected, but their net effect on this one side is zero. Second, the left side is the *normal balance* side for assets, and the right side is the *normal balance* side for liabilities and equity. This matches their layout in the accounting equation where assets are on the left side of this equation, and liabilities and equity are on the right.

Equity increases from revenues and owner investments and it decreases from expenses and owner withdrawals. These important equity relations are conveyed by expanding the accounting equation to include debits and credits in double-entry form as shown in Exhibit 2.7.

Exhibit 2.7

Debit and Credit Effects for Component Accounts

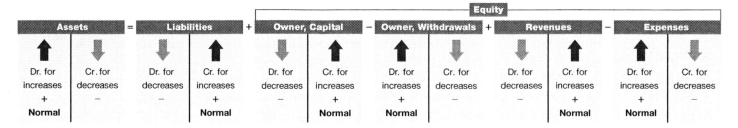

Increases (credits) to capital and revenues *increase* equity; increases (debits) to withdrawals and expenses *decrease* equity. The normal balance of each account (asset, liability, capital, withdrawals, revenue, or expense) refers to the left or right (debit or credit) side where *increases* are recorded. Understanding these diagrams and rules is required to prepare, analyze, and interpret financial statements.

The T-account for FastForward's Cash account, reflecting its first 11 transactions (from Exhibit 1.9), is shown in Exhibit 2.8. The total increases in its Cash account are $36,100, the total decreases are $31,700, and the account's debit balance is $4,400.

Exhibit 2.8

Computing the Balance for a T-Account

Cash			
Investment by owner	30,000	Purchase of supplies	2,500
Consulting services revenue earned	4,200	Purchase of equipment	26,000
Collection of account receivable	1,900	Payment of rent	1,000
		Payment of salary	700
		Payment of account payable	900
		Withdrawal by owner	600
Balance	4,400		

Point: The ending balance is on the side with the largest dollar amount.

Quick Check

1. Identify examples of accounting source documents.
2. Explain the importance of source documents.
3. Identify each of the following as either an asset, a liability, or equity: (*a*) Prepaid Rent, (*b*) Unearned Fees, (*c*) Building, (*d*) Wages Payable, and (*e*) Office Supplies.
4. What is an account? What is a ledger?
5. What determines the number and types of accounts a company uses?
6. Does *debit* always mean increase and *credit* always mean decrease?
7. Describe a chart of accounts.

Answers—pp. 72–73

Journalizing and Posting Transactions

Processing transactions is a crucial part of accounting. The four usual steps of this process are depicted in Exhibit 2.9. Steps 1 and 2—involving transaction analysis and double-entry accounting—were introduced in prior sections. This section extends that discussion and focuses on steps 3 and 4 of the accounting process. Step 3 is to record each transaction in a journal. A **journal** gives a complete record of each transaction in one place. It also shows debits and credits for each transaction. The process of recording transactions in a journal is called **journalizing.** Step 4 is to transfer (or *post*) entries from the journal to the ledger. The process of transferring journal entry information to the ledger is called **posting.**

P1   Record transactions in a journal and post entries to a ledger.

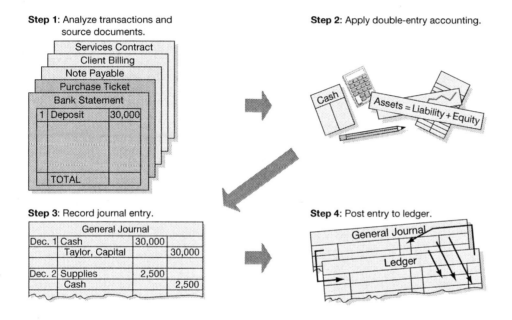

Exhibit 2.9

Steps in Processing Transactions

Journalizing Transactions   The process of journalizing transactions requires an understanding of a journal. While companies can use various journals, every company uses a **general journal.** It can be used to record any transaction and includes the following information about each transaction: (1) date of transaction, (2) titles of affected accounts, (3) dollar amount of each debit and credit, and (4) explanation of the transaction. Exhibit 2.10 shows how the first two transactions of FastForward are recorded in a general journal. This process is similar for manual and computerized systems. Computerized journals are often designed to look like a manual journal page, and also include error-checking routines that ensure debits equal credits for each entry. Shortcuts allow recordkeepers to select account names and numbers from pull-down menus.

To record entries in a general journal, apply these steps; refer to the entries in Exhibit 2.10 when reviewing these steps. ① Date the transaction: Enter the year at the top of the first column and the month and day on the first line of each journal entry. ② Enter titles

GENERAL JOURNAL

Date	Account Titles and Explanation	PR	Debit	Credit
				Page 1
2004 Dec. 1	Cash		30,000	
	C. Taylor, Capital			30,000
	Investment by owner.			
Dec. 2	Supplies		2,500	
	Cash			2,500
	Purchased supplies for cash.			

Exhibit 2.10

Partial General Journal for FastForward

of accounts debited and then enter amounts in the Debit column on the same line. Account titles are taken from the chart of accounts and are aligned with the left margin of the Account Titles and Explanation column. ③ Enter titles of accounts credited and then enter amounts in the Credit column on the same line. Account titles are from the chart of accounts and are indented from the left margin of the Account Titles and Explanation column to distinguish them from debited accounts. ④ Enter a brief explanation of the transaction on the line below the entry (it often references a source document). This explanation is indented about half as far as the credited account titles to avoid confusing it with accounts, and it is italicized.

A blank line is left between each journal entry for clarity. When a transaction is first recorded, the **posting reference (PR) column** blank is left blank (in a manual system). Later, when posting entries to the ledger, the identification numbers of the individual ledger accounts are entered in the PR column.

Balance Column Account   T-accounts are simple and direct means to show how the accounting process works. However, actual accounting systems need more structure and therefore use **balance column accounts,** as in Exhibit 2.11.

Exhibit 2.11

Cash Account in Balance Column Format

Date	Explanation	PR	Debit	Credit	Balance
Cash				Account No. 101	
2004 Dec. 1		G1	30,000		30,000
Dec. 2		G1		2,500	27,500
Dec. 3		G1		26,000	1,500
Dec. 10		G1	4,200		5,700

The balance column account format is similar to a T-account in having columns for debits and credits. It is different in including transaction date and explanation columns. It also has a column with the balance of the account after each entry is recorded. To illustrate, FastForward's Cash account in Exhibit 2.11 is debited on December 1 for the $30,000 owner investment, yielding a $30,000 debit balance. The account is credited on December 2 for $2,500, yielding a $27,500 debit balance. On December 3, it is credited again, this time for $26,000, and its debit balance is reduced to $1,500. The Cash account is debited for $4,200 on December 10, and its debit balance increases to $5,700; and so on.

The heading of the Balance column does not show whether it is a debit or credit balance. Instead, an account is assumed to have a *normal balance*. Unusual events can sometimes temporarily give an account an abnormal balance. An *abnormal balance* refers to a balance on the side where decreases are recorded. For example, a customer might mistakenly overpay a bill. This gives that customer's account receivable an abnormal (credit) balance. An abnormal balance is often identified by circling it or by entering it in red or some other unusual color. A zero balance for an account is usually shown by writing zeros or a dash in the Balance column to avoid confusion between a zero balance and one omitted in error.

Posting Journal Entries   Step 4 of processing transactions is to post journal entries to ledger accounts (see Exhibit 2.9). To ensure that the ledger is up-to-date, entries are posted as soon as possible. This might be daily, weekly, or when time permits. All entries must be posted to the ledger before financial statements are prepared to ensure that account balances are up-to-date. When entries are posted to the ledger, the debits in journal entries are transferred into ledger accounts as debits, and credits are transferred into ledger accounts as credits. Exhibit 2.12 shows the four steps to post a journal entry. First, identify the ledger account that is debited in the entry; then, in the ledger, enter the entry date, the journal and page in its PR column, the debit amount, and the new balance of the ledger account. (The letter *G* shows it came from the General Journal. Second, enter the ledger account number in the PR column of the journal. Steps three and four repeat the first two steps for credit entries and amounts. The posting process creates a link between the ledger and the jour-

Point: There are no exact rules for writing journal entry explanations. An explanation should be short yet describe why an entry is made.

Point: Computerized systems often provide a code beside a balance such as *dr.* or *cr.* to identify its balance.

Point: A journal is often referred to as the *book of original entry.* The ledger is referred to as the *book of final entry* because financial statements are prepared from it.

Point: Posting is automatic and immediate with accounting software.

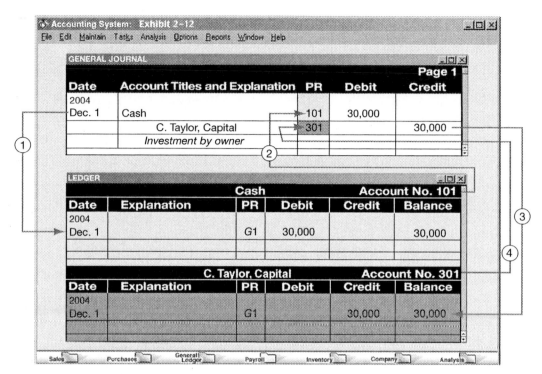

Exhibit 2.12

Posting an Entry to the Ledger

Key:
1. Identify debit account in Ledger: enter date, journal page, amount, and balance.
2. Enter the debit account number from the Ledger in the PR column of the journal.
3. Identify credit account in Ledger: enter date, journal page, amount, and balance.
4. Enter the credit account number from the Ledger in the PR column of the journal.

Point: The fundamental concepts of a manual (pencil-and-paper) system are identical to those of a computerized information system.

nal entry. This link is a useful cross-reference for tracing an amount from one record to another.

Point: Explanations are typically included in ledger accounts only for unusual transactions or events.

Analyzing Transactions—An Illustration

We return to the activities of FastForward to show how double-entry accounting is useful in analyzing and processing transactions. Analysis of each transaction follows the four steps of Exhibit 2.9. First, we review the transaction and any source documents. Second, we analyze the transaction using the accounting equation. Third, we use double-entry accounting to record the transaction in journal entry form. Fourth, the entry is posted (for simplicity, we use T-accounts to represent ledger accounts). We also identify the financial statements affected by each transaction. Study each transaction thoroughly before proceeding to the next transaction. The first 11 transactions are from Chapter 1, and we analyze five additional December transactions of FastForward (numbered 12 through 16) that were omitted earlier.

A1 Analyze the impact of transactions on accounts and financial statements.

Topic Tackler 2-1

1. Investment by Owner

Cash		101
(1)	30,000	

C. Taylor, Capital		301
	(1)	30,000

Transaction: Chuck Taylor invests $30,000 cash in FastForward.

Analysis:

Assets	=	Liabilities	+	Equity
Cash				**Capital**
+30,000	=	0	+	30,000

Double entry:

(1)	Cash	101	30,000	
	C. Taylor, Capital	301		30,000

Statements affected:[3] BLS and SCF

*FAST**Forward***

---

[3] We use abbreviations for the statements: income statement (IS), balance sheet (BLS), statement of cash flows (SCF), and statement of owner's equity (SOE).

2. Purchase Supplies for Cash

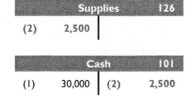

Transaction: FastForward pays $2,500 cash for supplies.

Analysis:

	Assets		=	Liabilities	+	Equity
	Cash	**Supplies**				
	−2,500	+2,500	=	0	+	0

Changes the composition of assets but not the total.

Double entry:

(2)	Supplies	126	2,500	
	Cash	101		2,500

Statements affected: BLS and SCF

3. Purchase Equipment for Cash

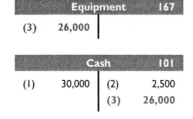

Transaction: FastForward pays $26,000 cash for equipment.

Analysis:

	Assets		=	Liabilities	+	Equity
	Cash	**Equipment**				
	−26,000	+26,000	=	0	+	0

Changes the composition of assets but not the total.

Double entry:

(3)	Equipment	167	26,000	
	Cash	101		26,000

Statements affected: BLS and SCF

4. Purchase Supplies on Credit

	Supplies		126
(2)	2,500		
(4)	7,100		

	Accounts Payable		201
		(4)	7,100

Transaction: FastForward purchases $7,100 of supplies on credit from a supplier.

Analysis:

	Assets	=	Liabilities	+	Equity
	Supplies		**Accounts Payable**		
	+7,100	=	+7,100	+	0

Double entry:

(4)	Supplies	126	7,100	
	Accounts Payable	201		7,100

Statements affected: BLS

5. Provide Services for Cash

	Cash		101	
(1)	30,000	(2)	2,500	
(5)	4,200	(3)	26,000	

	Consulting Revenue		403
		(5)	4,200

Transaction: FastForward provides consulting services and immediately collects $4,200 cash.

Analysis:

	Assets	=	Liabilities	+	Equity
	Cash				**Consulting Revenue**
	+4,200	=	0	+	+4,200

Double entry:

(5)	Cash	101	4,200	
	Consulting Revenue	403		4,200

Statements affected: BLS, IS, SCF, and SOE

6. Payment of Expense in Cash

Rent Expense	640
(6) 1,000	

Cash	101
(1) 30,000	(2) 2,500
(5) 4,200	(3) 26,000
	(6) 1,000

Transaction: FastForward pays $1,000 cash for December rent.

Analysis:

Assets	=	Liabilities	+	Equity
Cash				**Rent Expense**
−1,000	=	0		−1,000

Double entry:

(6)	Rent Expense	640	1,000	
	Cash	101		1,000

Statements affected: BLS, IS, SCF, and SOE

7. Payment of Expense in Cash

Salaries Expense	622
(7) 700	

Cash	101
(1) 30,000	(2) 2,500
(5) 4,200	(3) 26,000
	(6) 1,000
	(7) 700

Transaction: FastForward pays $700 cash for employee salary.

Analysis:

Assets	=	Liabilities	+	Equity
Cash				**Salaries Expense**
−700	=	0		−700

Double entry:

(7)	Salaries Expense	622	700	
	Cash	101		700

Statements affected: BLS, IS, SCF, and SOE

Point: *Salary* usually refers to compensation for an employee who receives a fixed amount for a given time period, whereas *wages* usually refers to compensation based on time worked.

8. Provide Consulting and Rental Services on Credit

Accounts Receivable	106
(8) 1,900	

Consulting Revenue	403
	(5) 4,200
	(8) 1,600

Rental Revenue	406
	(8) 300

Transaction: FastForward provides consulting services of $1,600 and rents its test facilities for $300. The customer is billed $1,900 for these services.

Analysis:

Assets	=	Liabilities	+	Equity	
Accounts Receivable				**Consulting Revenue**	**Rental Revenue**
+1,900	=	0		+1,600	+300

Double entry:

(8)	Accounts Receivable	106	1,900	
	Consulting Revenue	403		1,600
	Rental Revenue	406		300

Statements affected: BLS, IS, and SOE

Point: Transaction 8 is a **compound journal entry,** which affects three or more accounts.

9. Receipt of Cash on Account

Cash	101
(1) 30,000	(2) 2,500
(5) 4,200	(3) 26,000
(9) 1,900	(6) 1,000
	(7) 700

Accounts Receivable	106
(8) 1,900	(9) 1,900

Transaction: FastForward receives $1,900 cash from the client billed in transaction 8.

Analysis:

Assets		=	Liabilities	+	Equity
Cash	**Accounts Receivable**				
+1,900	−1,900	=	0	+	0

Double entry:

(9)	Cash	101	1,900	
	Accounts Receivable	106		1,900

Statements affected: BLS and SCF

Point: The *revenue recognition principle* requires revenue to be recognized when earned, which is when the company provides products or services to a customer. This is not necessarily the same time that the customer pays. A customer can pay before or after products or services are provided.

10. Partial Payment of Accounts Payable

Accounts Payable			201
(10)	900	(4)	7,100

Cash			101
(1)	30,000	(2)	2,500
(5)	4,200	(3)	26,000
(9)	1,900	(6)	1,000
		(7)	700
		(10)	900

Transaction: FastForward pays CalTech Supply $900 cash toward the payable of transaction 4.

Analysis:

Assets	=	Liabilities	+	Equity
Cash		**Accounts Payable**		
−900	=	−900	+	0

Double entry:

(10)	Accounts Payable	201	900	
	Cash	101		900

Statements affected: BLS and SCF

11. Withdrawal of Cash by Owner

C. Taylor, Withdrawals			302
(11)	600		

Cash			101
(1)	30,000	(2)	2,500
(5)	4,200	(3)	26,000
(9)	1,900	(6)	1,000
		(7)	700
		(10)	900
		(11)	600

Transaction: Chuck Taylor withdraws $600 cash from FastForward for personal use.

Analysis:

Assets	=	Liabilities	+	Equity
Cash				**Withdrawals**
−600	=	0		−600

Double entry:

(11)	C. Taylor, Withdrawals	302	600	
	Cash	101		600

Statements affected: BLS, SCF, and SOE

12. Receipt of Cash for Future Services

Cash			101
(1)	30,000	(2)	2,500
(5)	4,200	(3)	26,000
(9)	1,900	(6)	1,000
(12)	3,000	(7)	700
		(10)	900
		(11)	600

Unearned Consulting Revenue			236
		(12)	3,000

Transaction: FastForward receives $3,000 cash in advance of providing consulting services to a customer.

Analysis:

Assets	=	Liabilities	+	Equity
		Unearned		
Cash		**Consulting Revenue**		
+3,000	=	+3,000	+	0

Accepting $3,000 cash obligates FastForward to perform future services and is a liability. No revenue is earned until services are provided.

Double entry:

(12)	Cash	101	3,000	
	Unearned Consulting Revenue	236		3,000

Statements affected: BLS and SCF

Point: Luca Pacioli is considered a pioneer in accounting and the first to devise double-entry accounting.

13. Pay Cash for Future Insurance Coverage

Prepaid Insurance			128
(13)	2,400		

Cash			101
(1)	30,000	(2)	2,500
(5)	4,200	(3)	26,000
(9)	1,900	(6)	1,000
(12)	3,000	(7)	700
		(10)	900
		(11)	600
		(13)	2,400

Transaction: FastForward pays $2,400 cash (insurance premium) for a 24-month insurance policy. Coverage begins on December 1.

Analysis:

Assets		=	Liabilities	+	Equity
	Prepaid				
Cash	**Insurance**				
−2,400	+2,400	=	0	+	0

Changes the composition of assets from cash to prepaid insurance. Expense is incurred as insurance coverage expires.

Double entry:

(13)	Prepaid Insurance	128	2,400	
	Cash	101		2,400

Statements affected: BLS and SCF

14. Purchase Supplies for Cash

Supplies		126
(2)	2,500	
(4)	7,100	
(14)	120	

Cash		101
(1)	30,000	(2)	2,500
(5)	4,200	(3)	26,000
(9)	1,900	(6)	1,000
(12)	3,000	(7)	700
		(10)	900
		(11)	600
		(13)	2,400
		(14)	120

Transaction: FastForward pays $120 cash for supplies.

Analysis:

	Assets		=	Liabilities	+	Equity
	Cash	**Supplies**				
	−120	+120	=	0	+	0

Double entry:

(14)	Supplies	126	120	
	Cash	101		120

Statements affected: BLS and SCF

15. Payment of Expense in Cash

Utilities Expense		690
(15)	230	

Cash		101
(1)	30,000	(2)	2,500
(5)	4,200	(3)	26,000
(9)	1,900	(6)	1,000
(12)	3,000	(7)	700
		(10)	900
		(11)	600
		(13)	2,400
		(14)	120
		(15)	230

Transaction: FastForward pays $230 cash for December utilities expense.

Analysis:

	Assets	=	Liabilities	+	Equity
	Cash				**Utilities Expense**
	−230	=	0		−230

Double entry:

(15)	Utilities Expense	690	230	
	Cash	101		230

Statements affected: BLS, IS, SCF, and SOE

16. Payment of Expense in Cash

Salaries Expense		622
(7)	700	
(16)	700	

Cash		101
(1)	30,000	(2)	2,500
(5)	4,200	(3)	26,000
(9)	1,900	(6)	1,000
(12)	3,000	(7)	700
		(10)	900
		(11)	600
		(13)	2,400
		(14)	120
		(15)	230
		(16)	700

Transaction: FastForward pays $700 cash in employee salary for work performed in the latter part of December.

Analysis:

	Assets	=	Liabilities	+	Equity
	Cash				**Salaries Expense**
	−700	=	0		−700

Double entry:

(16)	Salaries Expense	622	700	
	Cash	101		700

Statements affected: BLS, IS, SCF, and SOE

Point: We could merge transactions 15 and 16 into one *compound entry*.

Accounting Equation Analysis

Point: Technology does not provide the judgment required to analyze most business transactions. Analysis requires the expertise of skilled and ethical professionals.

Exhibit 2.13 shows the accounts (in T-account form) of FastForward after all 16 transactions are recorded, posted and the balances computed. The accounts are grouped into three major columns corresponding to the accounting equation: assets, liabilities, and equity. Note several important points. First, as with each transaction, the totals for the three columns must obey the accounting equation. Specifically, assets equal $42,070 ($3,950 + $0 + $9,720 + $2,400 + $26,000); liabilities equal $9,200 ($6,200 + $3,000); and equity equals $32,870 ($30,000 − $600 + $5,800 + $300 − $1,400 − $1,000 − $230). These numbers prove the accounting equation: Assets of $42,070 = Liabilities of $9,200 + Equity of $32,870. Second, the capital, withdrawals, revenue, and expense accounts reflect the transactions that change equity. Their balances underlie the statement of owner's equity. Third, the revenue and expense account balances will be summarized and reported in the income statement. Fourth, increases and decreases in the cash account make up the elements reported in the statement of cash flows.

Exhibit 2.13

Ledger for FastForward (in T-Account Form)

Assets = Liabilities + Equity

Cash   101

(1)	30,000	(2)	2,500
(5)	4,200	(3)	26,000
(9)	1,900	(6)	1,000
(12)	3,000	(7)	700
		(10)	900
		(11)	600
		(13)	2,400
		(14)	120
		(15)	230
		(16)	700
Balance	3,950		

Accounts Receivable   106

(8)	1,900	(9)	1,900
Balance	0		

Supplies   126

(2)	2,500
(4)	7,100
(14)	120
Balance	9,720

Prepaid Insurance   128

(13)	2,400

Equipment   167

(3)	26,000

Accounts Payable   201

(10)	900	(4)	7,100
		Balance	6,200

Unearned Consulting Revenue 236

		(12)	3,000

C. Taylor, Capital   301

		(1)	30,000

C. Taylor, Withdrawals   302

(11)	600

Consulting Revenue   403

		(5)	4,200
		(8)	1,600
		Balance	5,800

Rental Revenue   406

		(8)	300

Salaries Expense   622

(7)	700
(16)	700
Balance	1,400

Rent Expense   640

(6)	1,000

Utilities Expense   690

(15)	230

Accounts in this white area reflect those reported on the income statement.

$42,070	=	$9,200	+	$32,870

Quick Check

8. What types of transactions increase equity? What types decrease equity?

9. Why are accounting systems called *double entry*?

10. For each transaction, double-entry accounting requires which of the following: (*a*) Debits to asset accounts must create credits to liability or equity accounts, (*b*) a debit to a liability account must create a credit to an asset account, or (*c*) total debits must equal total credits.

11. An owner invests $15,000 cash along with equipment having a market value of $23,000 in a proprietorship. Prepare the necessary journal entry.

12. Explain what a compound journal entry is.

13. Why are posting reference numbers entered in the journal when entries are posted to ledger accounts?

Answers—p. 73

Trial Balance

Double-entry accounting requires the sum of debit account balances to equal the sum of credit account balances. A trial balance is used to verify this. A **trial balance** is a list of accounts and their balances at a point in time. Account balances are reported in the appropriate debit or credit column of a trial balance. Exhibit 2.14 shows the trial balance for FastForward after its 16 entries have been posted to the ledger. (This is an *unadjusted* trial balance—Chapter 3 will explain the necessary adjustments.)

Point: Knowing how financial statements are prepared improves our analysis of them.

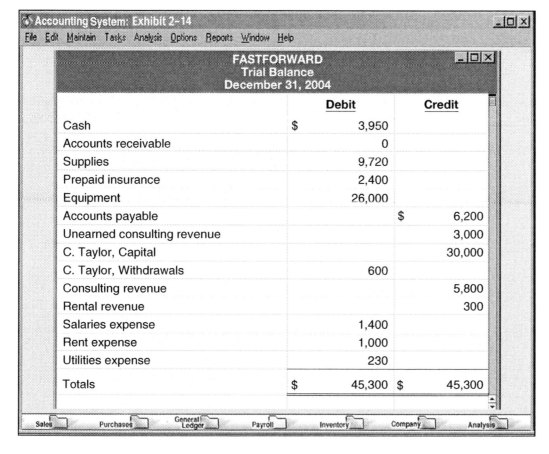

Exhibit 2.14

Trial Balance (unadjusted)

FASTFORWARD
Trial Balance
December 31, 2004

	Debit	Credit
Cash	$ 3,950	
Accounts receivable	0	
Supplies	9,720	
Prepaid insurance	2,400	
Equipment	26,000	
Accounts payable		$ 6,200
Unearned consulting revenue		3,000
C. Taylor, Capital		30,000
C. Taylor, Withdrawals	600	
Consulting revenue		5,800
Rental revenue		300
Salaries expense	1,400	
Rent expense	1,000	
Utilities expense	230	
Totals	$ 45,300	$ 45,300

Preparing a Trial Balance

Preparing a trial balance involves three steps:

1. List each account title and its amount (from ledger) in the trial balance. If an account has a zero balance, list it with a zero in its normal balance column (or omit it entirely).
2. Compute the total of debit balances and the total of credit balances.
3. Verify (*prove*) total debit balances equal total credit balances.

The total of debit balances equals the total of credit balances for the trial balance in Exhibit 2.14. Note that equality of these two totals does not guarantee that no errors were made. For example, the column totals still will be equal when a debit or credit of a correct amount is made to a wrong account. Another error that does not cause unequal column totals is when equal debits and credits of an incorrect amount are entered.

Point: The ordering of accounts in a trial balance typically follows their identification number from the chart of accounts.

Point: A trial balance is *not* a financial statement but a mechanism for checking equality of debits and credits in the ledger. Financial statements do not have debit and credit columns.

Searching for and Correcting Errors If the trial balance does not balance (when its columns are not equal), the error (or errors) must be found and corrected. An efficient way to search for an error is to check the journalizing, posting, and trial balance preparation in *reverse order.* Step 1 is to verify that the trial balance columns are correctly added. If step 1 fails to find the error, step 2 is to verify that account balances are accurately entered from the ledger. Step 3 is to see whether a debit (or credit) balance is mistakenly listed in the trial balance as a credit (or debit). A clue to this error is when the difference between total debits and total credits equals twice the amount of the incorrect account balance. If the error is still undiscovered, Step 4 is to recompute each account balance in the ledger. Step 5 is to verify that each journal entry is properly posted. Step 6 is to verify that the original journal entry has equal debits and credits. At this point, any errors should be uncovered.[4]

Example: If a credit to Unearned Revenue were incorrectly posted from the journal as a credit to the Revenue ledger account, would the ledger still balance? Would the financial statements be correct? *Answers:* The ledger would balance, but liabilities would be understated, equity would be overstated, and income would be overstated (all because of overstated revenues).

If an error in a journal entry is discovered before the error is posted, it can be corrected in a manual system by drawing a line through the incorrect information. The correct information is written above it to create a record of change for the auditor. Many computerized systems allow the operator to replace the incorrect information directly.

If an error in a journal entry is not discovered until after it is posted, do not strike through both erroneous entries in the journal and ledger. Instead, correct this error by creating a *correcting entry* that removes the amount from the wrong account and records it to the correct account. As an example, suppose a $100 purchase of supplies is journalized with an incorrect debit to Equipment, and then this incorrect entry is posted to the ledger. The Supplies ledger account balance is understated by $100, and the Equipment ledger account balance is overstated by $100. The correcting entry is: debit Supplies and credit Equipment (both for $100).

Point: The IRS requires companies to keep records that can be audited.

---

[4] *Transposition* occurs when two digits are switched, or transposed, within a number. If transposition is the only error, it yields a difference between the two trial balance totals that is evenly divisible by 9. For example, assume that a $691 debit in an entry is incorrectly posted to the ledger as $619. Total credits in the trial balance are then larger than total debits by $72 ($691 − $619). The $72 error is *evenly* divisible by 9 (72/9 = 8). The first digit of the quotient (in our example it is 8) equals the difference between the digits of the two transposed numbers (the 9 and the 1). The number of digits in the quotient also tells the location of the transposition, starting from the right. The quotient in our example had only one digit (8), so it tells us the transposition is in the first digit. Consider another example where a transposition error involves posting $961 instead of the correct $691. The difference in these numbers is $270, and its quotient is 30 (270/9). The quotient has two digits, so it tells us to check the second digit from the right for a transposition of two numbers that have a difference of 3.

Using a Trial Balance to Prepare Financial Statements

This section shows how to prepare *financial statements* from the trial balance in Exhibit 2.14 and information on the December transactions of FastForward. The statements differ from those in Chapter 1 because of several additional transactions. These statements are also more precisely called *unadjusted statements* because we need to make some further accounting adjustments (described in Chapter 3).

How financial statements are linked in time is illustrated in Exhibit 2.15. A balance sheet reports on an organization's financial position at a *point in time*. The income statement, statement of owner's equity, and statement of cash flows report on financial performance over a *period of time*. The three statements in the middle column of Exhibit 2.15 link balance sheets from the beginning to the end of a reporting period. They explain how financial position changes from one point to another.

Preparers and users (including regulatory agencies) determine the length of the reporting period. A one-year, or annual, reporting period is common, as are semiannual, quarterly, and monthly periods. The one-year reporting period is known as the *accounting,* or *fiscal, year*. Businesses whose accounting year begins on January 1 and ends on December 31 are known as *calendar-year* companies. Many companies choose a fiscal year ending on a date other than December 31. **Krispy Kreme** is a *noncalendar-year* company as reflected in the headings of its February 2 year-end financial statements in Appendix A near the end of the book.

P3 Prepare financial statements from business transactions.

Exhibit 2.15

Links between Financial Statements Across Time

Topic Tackler 2-2

Point: A statement's heading lists the 3 W's: **W**ho—name of organization, **W**hat—name of statement, **W**hen—statement's point in time or period of time.

Income Statement   An income statement reports the revenues earned less the expenses incurred by a business over a period of time. FastForward's income statement for December is shown at the top of Exhibit 2.16. Information about revenues and expenses is conveniently taken from the trial balance in Exhibit 2.14. Net income of $3,470 is reported at the bottom of the statement. Owner investments and withdrawals are *not* part of income.

Statement of Owner's Equity   The statement of owner's equity reports information about how equity changes over the reporting period. FastForward's statement of owner's equity is the second report in Exhibit 2.16. It shows the $30,000 owner investment plus the $3,470 of net income earned during the month. It also reports the $600 withdrawal and the $32,870 end-of-month equity (capital) balance. (The beginning capital balance in the statement of owner's equity is rarely zero. An exception is for the first period of a company's operations. The beginning capital balance in January 2005 is $32,870, which is December's ending balance.)

"I'LL TELL YOU, HARRIS, THEY DON'T MAKE ACCOUNTANTS LIKE THEY USED TO. THOSE I HAD IN THE '90's, NEVER BROUGHT ME FIGURES LIKE THESE."

Balance Sheet   The balance sheet reports the financial position of a company at a point in time, usually at the end of a month, quarter, or year. FastForward's balance sheet is the third report in Exhibit 2.16. This statement refers to FastForward's financial condition at the close of business on December 31. The left side of the balance sheet lists its assets: cash, supplies, prepaid insurance, and equipment. The upper right side of the balance sheet shows that it owes $6,200 to creditors and $3,000 in services to customers who paid in advance.

Point: An income statement is also called an *earnings statement, a statement of operations,* or a *P&L (profit and loss) statement.* A balance sheet is also called a *statement of financial position.*

Entrepreneur You open a wholesale business selling entertainment equipment to retail outlets. You find that most of your customers demand to buy on credit. How can you use the balance sheets of these customers to decide which ones to extend credit to?

Answer—p. 72

Point: While revenues increase equity and expenses decrease equity, the amounts are not reported in detail in the statement of owner's equity. Instead, their effects are reflected through net income.

The equity section shows an ending capital balance of $32,870. Note the link between the ending balance of the statement of owner's equity and the capital balance here. (Recall that this presentation of the balance sheet is called the *account form:* assets on the left and liabilities and equity on the right. Another presentation is the *report form:* assets on top, followed by liabilities and then equity. Either presentation is acceptable.)

Presentation Issues   Dollar signs are not used in journals and ledgers. They do appear in financial statements and other reports such as trial balances. The usual practice is to put dollar signs beside only the first and last numbers in a column. **Krispy Kreme**'s

Exhibit 2.16

Financial Statements and Their Links

Point: Arrow lines show how the statements are linked.

Point: To *foot* a column of numbers is to add them.

FASTFORWARD
Income Statement
For Month Ended December 31, 2004

Revenues		
Consulting revenue ($4,200 + $1,600)	$ 5,800	
Rental revenue	300	
Total revenues		$ 6,100
Expenses		
Rent expense	1,000	
Salaries expense	1,400	
Utilities expense	230	
Total expenses		2,630
Net income		$ 3,470

FASTFORWARD
Statement of Owner's Equity
For Month Ended December 31, 2004

C. Taylor, Capital, December 1, 2004		$ 0
Plus: Investments by owner	$30,000	
Net income	3,470	33,470
		33,470
Less: Withdrawals by owner		600
C. Taylor, Capital, December 31, 2004		$32,870

FASTFORWARD
Balance Sheet
December 31, 2004

Assets		Liabilities	
Cash	$ 3,950	Accounts payable	$ 6,200
Supplies	9,720	Unearned revenue	3,000
Prepaid insurance . .	2,400	Total liabilities	9,200
Equipment	26,000		
		Equity	
		C. Taylor, Capital	32,870
Total assets	$42,070	Total liabilities and equity .	$ 42,070

financial statements in Appendix A show this. When amounts are entered in a journal, ledger, or trial balance, commas are optional to indicate thousands, millions, and so forth. However, commas are always used in financial statements. Companies also commonly round amounts in reports to the nearest dollar, or even to a higher level. Krispy Kreme is typical of many companies in that it rounds its financial statement amounts to the nearest thousand. This decision is based on the perceived impact of rounding for users' business decisions.

Example: How would the balance sheet in Exhibit 2.16 change if FastForward pays $2,000 of its payable on December 31 using its Cash account? What would be the new amount of total assets? Would the balance sheet still balance? *Answers:* Cash would be $1,950, accounts payable would be $4,200, total assets (and liabilities plus equity) would be $40,070, and the balance sheet would still balance.

Quick Check

14. Where are dollar signs typically entered in financial statements?
15. If a $4,000 debit to Equipment in a journal entry is incorrectly posted to the ledger as a $4,000 credit, and the ledger account has a resulting debit balance of $20,000, what is the effect of this error on the Trial Balance column totals?
16. Describe the link between the income statement and the statement of owner's equity.
17. Explain the link between the balance sheet and the statement of owner's equity.
18. Define and describe revenues and expenses.
19. Define and describe assets, liabilities, and equity.

Answers—p. 73

Debt Ratio

Decision Analysis

An important business objective is gathering information to help assess a company's risk of failing to pay its debts. Companies finance their assets with either liabilities or equity. A company that finances a relatively large portion of its assets with liabilities is said to have a high degree of *financial leverage*. Higher financial leverage involves greater risk because liabilities must be repaid and often require regular interest payments (equity financing does not). The risk that a company might not be able to meet such required payments is higher if it has more liabilities (is more highly leveraged). One way to assess the risk associated with a company's use of liabilities is to compute the **debt ratio** as in Exhibit 2.17.

A2 Compute the debt ratio and describe its use in analyzing company performance.

$$\text{Debt ratio} = \frac{\text{Total liabilities}}{\text{Total assets}}$$

Exhibit 2.17

Debt Ratio

To see how to apply the debt ratio, let's look at **Stride Rite**'s liabilities and assets. Stride Rite makes Keds, Pro-Keds, and other footwear. Exhibit 2.18 computes and reports its debt ratio at the end of each year from 1998 to 2002.

Stride Rite's debt ratio ranges from a low of 0.24 to a high of 0.31. Its ratio is low compared with the industry ratio. Stride Rite reports that it carries no long-term debt, which is unusual. This analysis implies a low risk from its financial leverage. Is this good or bad? To answer that question we

Point: Compare the equity amount to the liability amount to assess the extent of owner versus nonowner financing.

Exhibit 2.18

Computation and Analysis of Debt Ratio

	2002	2001	2000	1999	1998
Total liabilities (in mil.)	$ 82	$100	$110	$101	$102
Total assets (in mil.)	$335	$362	$359	$351	$347
Debt ratio	0.24	0.28	0.31	0.29	0.29
Industry debt ratio	0.45	0.49	0.48	0.46	0.52

Investor You consider buying stock in **Converse**. As part of your analysis, you compute its debt ratio for 2001, 2002, and 2003 as: 0.35, 0.74, and 0.94, respectively. Based on the debt ratio, is Converse a low-risk investment? Has the risk of buying Converse stock changed over this period? (*Note:* The industry ratio averages 0.40.)

Answer—p. 72

need to compare the company's return on the borrowed money to the rate it is paying creditors. If the company's return is higher, it is successfully borrowing money to make more money. Be aware that a company's success with making money from borrowed money can quickly turn unprofitable if its own return drops below the rate it is paying creditors.

Demonstration Problem

(*Note:* This problem extends the demonstration problem of Chapter 1.) After several months of planning, Sylvia Workman started a haircutting business called Expressions. The following events occurred during its first month:

a. On August 1, Workman invested $3,000 cash and $15,000 of equipment in Expressions.

b. On August 2, Expressions paid $600 cash for furniture for the shop.

c. On August 3, Expressions paid $500 cash to rent space in a strip mall for August.

d. On August 4, it purchased $1,200 of equipment on credit for the shop (using a long-term note payable).

e. On August 5, Expressions opened for business. Cash received from services provided in the first week and a half of business (ended August 15) is $825.

f. On August 15, it provided $100 of haircutting services on account.

g. On August 17, it received a $100 check for services previously rendered on account.

h. On August 17, it paid $125 to an assistant for working during the grand opening.

i. Cash received from services provided during the second half of August is $930.

j. On August 31, it paid a $400 installment toward principal on the note payable entered into on August 4.

k. On August 31, Workman made a $900 cash withdrawal for personal use.

Required

1. Open the following ledger accounts in balance column format (account numbers are in parentheses): Cash (101); Accounts Receivable (102); Furniture (161); Store Equipment (165); Note Payable (240); S. Workman, Capital (301); S. Workman, Withdrawals (302); Haircutting Services Revenue (403); Wages Expense (623); and Rent Expense (640). Prepare general journal entries for the transactions.

2. Post the journal entries from (1) to the ledger accounts.

3. Prepare a trial balance as of August 31.

4. Prepare an income statement for August.

5. Prepare a statement of owner's equity for August.

6. Prepare a balance sheet as of August 31.

7. Determine the debt ratio as of August 31.

Extended Analysis

8. In the coming months, Expressions will experience a greater variety of business transactions. Identify which accounts are debited and which are credited for the following transactions. (*Hint:* You need to use some accounts not opened in part 1.)

a. Purchase supplies with cash.

b. Pay cash for future insurance coverage.

c. Receive cash for services to be provided in the future.

d. Purchase supplies on account.

Planning the Solution

- Analyze each transaction and use the debit and credit rules to prepare a journal entry for each.
- Post each debit and each credit from journal entries to their ledger accounts and cross-reference each amount in the posting reference (PR) columns of the journal and ledger.
- Calculate each account balance and list the accounts with their balances on a trial balance.
- Verify that total debits in the trial balance equal total credits.
- To prepare the income statement, identify revenues and expenses. List those items on the statement, compute the difference, and label the result as *net income* or *net loss*.
- Use information in the ledger to prepare the statement of owner's equity.
- Use information in the ledger to prepare the balance sheet.
- Calculate the debt ratio by dividing total liabilities by total assets.
- Analyze the future transactions to identify the accounts affected and apply debit and credit rules.

Solution to Demonstration Problem

1. General journal entries:

GENERAL JOURNAL   Page 1

Date	Account Titles and Explanation	PR	Debit	Credit
Aug. 1	Cash	101	3,000	
	Store Equipment	165	15,000	
	S. Workman, Capital	301		18,000
	Owner's investment.			
2	Furniture	161	600	
	Cash	101		600
	Purchased furniture for cash.			
3	Rent Expense	640	500	
	Cash	101		500
	Paid rent for August.			
4	Store Equipment	165	1,200	
	Note Payable	240		1,200
	Purchased additional equipment on credit.			
15	Cash	101	825	
	Haircutting Services Revenue	403		825
	Cash receipts from 10 days of operations.			
15	Accounts Receivable	102	100	
	Haircutting Services Revenue	403		100
	To record revenue for services provided on account.			
17	Cash	101	100	
	Accounts Receivable	102		100
	To record cash received as payment on account.			
17	Wages Expense	623	125	
	Cash	101		125
	Paid wages to assistant.			
31	Cash	101	930	
	Haircutting Services Revenue	403		930
	Cash receipts from second half of August.			
31	Note Payable	240	400	
	Cash	101		400
	Paid an installment on the note payable.			
31	S. Workman, Withdrawals	302	900	
	Cash	101		900
	Cash withdrawal by owner.			

2. Post journal entries from (part 1) to the ledger accounts:

General Ledger

Cash   **Account No. 101**

Date	PR	Debit	Credit	Balance
Aug. 1	G1	3,000		3,000
2	G1		600	2,400
3	G1		500	1,900
15	G1	825		2,725
17	G1	100		2,825
17	G1		125	2,700
31	G1	930		3,630
31	G1		400	3,230
31	G1		900	2,330

Accounts Receivable   **Account No. 102**

Date	PR	Debit	Credit	Balance
Aug. 15	G1	100		100
17	G1		100	0

Furniture   **Account No. 161**

Date	PR	Debit	Credit	Balance
Aug. 2	G1	600		600

Store Equipment   **Account No. 165**

Date	PR	Debit	Credit	Balance
Aug. 1	G1	15,000		15,000
4	G1	1,200		16,200

Note Payable   **Account No. 240**

Date	PR	Debit	Credit	Balance
Aug. 4	G1		1,200	1,200
31	G1	400		800

S. Workman, Capital   **Account No. 301**

Date	PR	Debit	Credit	Balance
Aug. 1	G1		18,000	18,000

S. Workman, Withdrawals   **Account No. 302**

Date	PR	Debit	Credit	Balance
Aug. 31	G1	900		900

Haircutting Services Revenue   **Account No. 403**

Date	PR	Debit	Credit	Balance
Aug. 15	G1		825	825
15	G1		100	925
31	G1		930	1,855

Wages Expense   **Account No. 623**

Date	PR	Debit	Credit	Balance
Aug. 17	G1	125		125

Rent Expense   **Account No. 640**

Date	PR	Debit	Credit	Balance
Aug. 3	G1	500		500

3. Prepare a trial balance from the ledger:

EXPRESSIONS
Trial Balance
August 31

	Debit	Credit
Cash	$ 2,330	
Accounts receivable	0	
Furniture	600	
Store equipment	16,200	
Note payable		$ 800
S. Workman, Capital		18,000
S. Workman, Withdrawals	900	
Haircutting services revenue		1,855
Wages expense	125	
Rent expense	500	
Totals	$20,655	$20,655

4.

EXPRESSIONS Income Statement For Month Ended August 31		
Revenues		
Haircutting services revenue		$1,855
Operating expenses		
Rent expense	$500	
Wages expense	125	
Total operating expenses		625
Net Income		$1,230

5.

EXPRESSIONS Statement of Owner's Equity For Month Ended August 31		
S. Workman, Capital, August 1		$ 0
Plus: Investments by owner	$18,000	
Net income	1,230	19,230
		19,230
Less: Withdrawals by owner		900
S. Workman, Capital, August 31		$18,330

6.

EXPRESSIONS Balance Sheet August 31			
Assets		**Liabilities**	
Cash	$ 2,330	Note payable	$ 800
Furniture	600	**Equity**	
Store equipment	16,200	S. Workman, Capital	18,330
Total assets	$19,130	Total liabilities and equity	$19,130

7. Debt ratio $= \dfrac{\text{Total liabilities}}{\text{Total assets}} = \dfrac{\$800}{\$19,130} = \mathbf{4.18\%}$

8a. Supplies *debited*   **8c.** Cash *debited*
        Cash *credited*   Unearned Services Revenue *credited*
8b. Prepaid Insurance *debited*   **8d.** Supplies *debited*
        Cash *credited*   Accounts Payable *credited*

Summary

C1 **Explain the steps in processing transactions.** The accounting process identifies business transactions and events, analyzes and records their effects, and summarizes and prepares information useful in making decisions. Transactions and events are the starting points in the accounting process. Source documents help in their analysis. The effects of transactions and events are recorded in journals. Posting along with a trial balance helps summarize and classify these effects.

C2 **Describe source documents and their purpose.** Source documents identify and describe transactions and events. Examples are sales tickets, checks, purchase orders, bills, and bank statements. Source documents provide objective and reliable evidence, making information more useful.

C3 **Describe an account and its use in recording transactions.** An account is a detailed record of increases and decreases in a specific asset, liability, equity, revenue, or expense. Information from accounts is analyzed, summarized, and presented in reports and financial statements for decision makers.

C4 **Describe a ledger and a chart of accounts.** The ledger (or general ledger) is a record containing all accounts used by a company and their balances. It is referred to as the *books*. The chart of accounts is a list of all accounts and usually includes an identification number assigned to each account.

C5 **Define *debits* and *credits* and explain their role in double-entry accounting.** *Debit* refers to left, and *credit* refers to right. Debits increase assets, expenses, and withdrawals while credits decrease them. Credits increase liabilities, owner capital, and revenues; debits decrease them. Double-entry accounting means each transaction affects at least two accounts and has at least one debit and one credit. The system for recording debits and credits follows from the accounting equation. The left side of an account is the normal balance for assets, withdrawals, and expenses, and the right side is the normal balance for liabilities, capital, and revenues.

A1 **Analyze the impact of transactions on accounts and financial statements.** We analyze transactions using concepts of double-entry accounting. This analysis is performed by determining a transaction's effects on accounts. These effects are recorded in journals and posted to ledgers.

A2 **Compute the debt ratio and describe its use in analyzing company performance.** A company's debt ratio is computed as total liabilities divided by total assets. It reveals how much of the assets are financed by creditor (nonowner) financing. The higher this ratio, the more risk a company faces because liabilities must be repaid at specific dates.

P1 **Record transactions in a journal and post entries to a ledger.** Transactions are recorded in a journal. Each entry in a journal is posted to the accounts in the ledger. This provides information that is used to produce financial statements. Balance column accounts are widely used and include columns for debits, credits, and the account balance.

P2 **Prepare and explain the use of a trial balance.** A trial balance is a list of accounts from the ledger showing their debit or credit balances in separate columns. The trial balance is a summary of the ledger's contents and is useful in preparing financial statements and in revealing recordkeeping errors.

P3 **Prepare financial statements from business transactions.** The balance sheet, the statement of owner's equity, the income statement, and the statement of cash flows use data from the trial balance (and other financial statements) for their preparation.

Guidance Answers to **Decision Maker** and **Decision Ethics**

Cashier The advantages to the process proposed by the assistant manager include improved customer service, fewer delays, and less work for you. However, you should have serious concerns about internal control and the potential for fraud. In particular, the assistant manager could steal cash and simply enter fewer sales to match the remaining cash. You should reject her suggestion without the manager's approval. Moreover, you should have an ethical concern about the assistant manager's suggestion to ignore store policy.

Entrepreneur We can use the accounting equation (Assets = Liabilities + Equity) to help us identify risky customers to whom we would likely not want to extend credit. A balance sheet provides amounts for each of these key components. The lower a customer's equity is relative to liabilities, the less likely you would extend credit. A low equity means the business has little value that does not already have creditor claims to it.

Investor The debt ratio suggests the stock of Converse is of higher risk than normal and that this risk is rising. The average industry ratio of 0.40 further supports this conclusion. The 2003 debt ratio for Converse is twice the industry norm. Also, a debt ratio approaching 1.0 indicates little to no equity.

Guidance Answers to **Quick Checks**

1. Examples of source documents are sales tickets, checks, purchase orders, charges to customers, bills from suppliers, employee earnings records, and bank statements.

2. Source documents serve many purposes, including recordkeeping and internal control. Source documents, especially if obtained from outside the organization, provide objective and reliable evidence about transactions and their amounts.

3.

Assets	Liabilities	Equity
a,c,e	b,d	—

4. An account is a record in an accounting system that records and stores the increases and decreases in a specific asset, liability, equity, revenue, or expense. The ledger is a collection of all the accounts of a company.

5. A company's size and diversity affect the number of accounts in its accounting system. The types of accounts depend on information the company needs to both effectively operate and report its activities in financial statements.

6. No. Debit and credit both can mean increase or decrease. The particular meaning in a circumstance depends on the *type of account*. For example, a debit increases the balance of asset, withdrawals, and expense accounts, but it decreases the balance of liability, capital, and revenue accounts.

7. A chart of accounts is a list of all of a company's accounts and their identification numbers.

8. Equity is increased by revenues and by owner investments. Equity is decreased by expenses and owner withdrawals.

9. The name *double entry* is used because all transactions affect at least two accounts. There must be at least one debit in one account and at least one credit in another account.

10. Answer is (c).

11.

Cash	15,000	
Equipment	23,000	
Owner, Capital		38,000
Investment by owner of cash and equipment.		

12. A compound journal entry affects three or more accounts.

13. Posting reference numbers are entered in the journal when posting to the ledger as a cross-reference that allows the record-keeper or auditor to trace debits and credits from one record to another.

14. At a minimum, dollar signs are placed beside the first and last numbers in a column. It is also common to place dollar signs beside any amount that appears after a ruled line to indicate that an addition or subtraction has occurred.

15. The Equipment account balance is incorrectly reported at $20,000—it should be $28,000. The effect of this error understates the trial balance's Debit column total by $8,000. This results in an $8,000 difference between the column totals.

16. An income statement reports a company's revenues and expenses along with the resulting net income or loss. A statement of owner's equity reports changes in equity, including that from net income or loss. Both statements report transactions occurring over a period of time.

17. The balance sheet describes a company's financial position (assets, liabilities, and equity) at a point in time. The capital account in the balance sheet is obtained from the statement of owner's equity.

18. Revenues are inflows of assets in exchange for products or services provided to customers as part of the main operations of a business. Expenses are outflows or the using up of assets that result from providing products or services to customers.

19. Assets are the resources a business owns or controls that carry expected future benefits. Liabilities are the obligations of a business, representing the claims of others against the assets of a business. Equity reflects the owner's claims on the assets of the business after deducting liabilities.

Key Terms

Key Terms are available at the book's Website for learning and testing in an online Flashcard Format.

Account (p. 49)	**Debit** (p. 53)	**Owner, capital** (p. 51)
Account balance (p. 53)	**Debt ratio** (p. 67)	**Posting** (p. 55)
Balance column account (p. 56)	**Double-entry accounting** (p. 53)	**Posting reference (PR) column** (p. 56)
Chart of accounts (p. 52)	**General journal** (p. 55)	**Source documents** (p. 49)
Compound journal entry (p. 59)	**Journal** (p. 55)	**T-account** (p. 53)
Credit (p. 53)	**Journalizing** (p. 55)	**Trial balance** (p. 63)
Creditors (p. 50)	**Ledger** (p. 49)	**Unearned revenue** (p. 51)

Personal Interactive Quiz

Personal Interactive Quizzes A and B are available at the book's Website to reinforce and assess your learning.

Discussion Questions

1. Provide the names of two (a) asset accounts, (b) liability accounts, and (c) equity accounts.

2. What is the difference between a note payable and an account payable?

3. Discuss the steps in processing business transactions.

4. What kinds of transactions can be recorded in a general journal?

5. Are debits or credits typically listed first in general journal entries? Are the debits or the credits indented?

6. If assets are valuable resources and asset accounts have debit balances, why do expense accounts have debit balances?

7. Should a transaction be recorded first in a journal or the ledger? Why?

8. Why does the recordkeeper prepare a trial balance?

9. If a wrong amount is journalized and posted to the accounts, how should the error be corrected?

10. Identify the four financial statements of a business.

11. What information is reported in an income statement?

12. Why does the user of an income statement need to know the time period that it covers?

13. What information is reported in a balance sheet?

14. Define (*a*) *assets*, (*b*) *liabilities*, (*c*) *equity*, and (*d*) *net assets*.

15. Which financial statement is sometimes called the *statement of financial position?*

16. Review the **Krispy Kreme** balance sheet in Appendix A. Identify three accounts on its balance sheet that carry debit balances and three accounts on its balance sheet that carry credit balances.

17. Review the **Tastykake** balance sheet in Appendix A. Identify two different liability accounts that include the word *payable* in the account title.

18. Locate **Harley-Davidson**'s income statement in Appendix A. What is the title of its revenue account?   **Harley-Davidson**

 Red numbers denote Discussion Questions that involve decision-making.

Homework Manager repeats all Quick Study assignments on the book's Website with new numbers each time they are worked. It can be used in practice, homework, or exam mode.

QUICK STUDY

QS 2-1

Identifying source documents

C2

Identify the items from the following list that are likely to serve as source documents:

a. Bank statement	**d.** Trial balance	**g.** Company revenue account
b. Sales ticket	**e.** Telephone bill	**h.** Balance sheet
c. Income statement	**f.** Invoice from supplier	**i.** Prepaid insurance

---

QS 2-2

Identifying financial statement items

C3 P3

Identify the financial statement(s) where each of the following items appears. Use I for income statement, E for statement of owner's equity, and B for balance sheet:

a. Service fees earned	**d.** Accounts payable	**g.** Office supplies
b. Owner cash withdrawal	**e.** Cash	**h.** Prepaid rent
c. Office equipment	**f.** Utilities expenses	**i.** Unearned fees

---

QS 2-3

Linking debit or credit with normal balance

C5

Indicate whether a debit or credit *decreases* the normal balance of each of the following accounts:

a. Office Supplies	**e.** Salaries Expense	**i.** Interest Revenue
b. Repair Services Revenue	**f.** Owner Capital	**j.** Owner Withdrawals
c. Interest Payable	**g.** Prepaid Insurance	**k.** Unearned Revenue
d. Accounts Receivable	**h.** Buildings	**l.** Accounts Payable

---

QS 2-4

Analyzing debit or credit by account

C5 A1

Identify whether a debit or credit yields the indicated change for each of the following accounts:

a. To increase Store Equipment	**f.** To decrease Unearned Revenue
b. To increase Owner Withdrawals	**g.** To decrease Prepaid Insurance
c. To decrease Cash	**h.** To increase Notes Payable
d. To increase Utilities Expense	**i.** To decrease Accounts Receivable
e. To increase Fees Earned	**j.** To increase Owner Capital

QS 2-5

Identifying normal balance

C5

Identify whether the normal balances (in parentheses) assigned to the following accounts are correct or incorrect.

a. Office supplies (Debit)	**d.** Wages Expense (Credit)	**g.** Wages Payable (Credit)
b. Owner Withdrawals (Credit)	**e.** Cash (Debit)	**h.** Building (Debit)
c. Fees Earned (Debit)	**f.** Prepaid Insurance (Credit)	

Prepare journal entries for each of the following selected transactions:

a. On January 13, Chico Chavez opens a landscaping business called Showcase Yards by investing $70,000 cash along with equipment having a $30,000 value.

b. On January 21, Showcase Yards purchases office supplies on credit for $280.

c. On January 29, Showcase Yards receives $7,800 cash for performing landscaping services.

d. On January 30, Showcase Yards receives $1,000 cash in advance of providing landscaping services to a customer.

QS 2-6
Preparing journal entries
P1

A trial balance has total debits of $20,000 and total credits of $24,500. Which one of the following errors would create this imbalance? Explain.

a. A $2,250 debit to Rent Expense in a journal entry is incorrectly posted to the ledger as a $2,250 credit, leaving the Rent Expense account with a $3,000 debit balance.

b. A $4,500 debit to Salaries Expense in a journal entry is incorrectly posted to the ledger as a $4,500 credit, leaving the Salaries Expense account with a $750 debit balance.

c. A $2,250 credit to Consulting Fees Earned in a journal entry is incorrectly posted to the ledger as a $2,250 debit, leaving the Consulting Fees Earned account with a $6,300 credit balance.

QS 2-7
Identifying a posting error
P2

Indicate the financial statement on which each of the following items appears. Use I for income statement, E for statement of owner's equity, and B for balance sheet:

a. Office Supplies   **e.** Salaries Expense   **h.** Buildings

b. Services Revenue   **f.** Equipment   **i.** Interest Revenue

c. Interest Payable   **g.** Prepaid Insurance   **j.** Withdrawals

d. Accounts Receivable

QS 2-8
Classifying accounts in financial statements
P3

 Homework Manager repeats all Exercises on the book's Website with new numbers each time they are worked. It can be used in practice, homework, or exam mode.

For each of the following (1) identify the type of account as an asset, liability, equity, revenue, or expense, (2) enter *debit* (*Dr.*) or *credit* (*Cr.*) to identify the kind of entry that would increase the account balance, and (3) identify the normal balance of the account.

a. Unearned Revenue   **e.** Land   **i.** Cash

b. Accounts Payable   **f.** Owner Capital   **j.** Equipment

c. Postage Expense   **g.** Accounts Receivable   **k.** Fees Earned

d. Prepaid Insurance   **h.** Owner Withdrawals   **l.** Wages Expense

EXERCISES

Exercise 2-1
Identifying type and normal balances of accounts
C3 C5

Tavon Co. recently notified a client that it must pay a $48,000 fee for services provided. Tavon agreed to accept the following three items in full payment: (1) $7,500 cash, (2) computer equipment worth $75,000, and (3) assume responsibility for a $34,500 note payable related to the computer equipment. The entry Tavon makes to record this transaction includes which one or more of the following?

a. $34,500 increase in a liability account   **d.** $48,000 increase in an asset account

b. $7,500 increase in the Cash account   **e.** $48,000 increase in a revenue account

c. $7,500 increase in a revenue account

Exercise 2-2
Analyzing effects of transactions on accounts
A1

Exercise 2-3
Analyzing account entries and balances

A1

Use the information in each of the following separate cases to calculate the unknown amount:

a. During October, Shandra Company had $97,500 of cash receipts and $101,250 of cash disbursements. The October 31 Cash balance was $16,800. Determine how much cash the company had at the close of business on September 30.

b. On September 30, Li Ming Co. had a $97,500 balance in Accounts Receivable. During October, the company collected $88,950 from its credit customers. The October 31 balance in Accounts Receivable was $100,500. Determine the amount of sales on account that occurred in October.

c. Nasser Co. had $147,000 of accounts payable on September 30 and $136,500 on October 31. Total purchases on account during October were $270,000. Determine how much cash was paid on accounts payable during October.

Exercise 2-4
Preparing general journal entries

A1 P1

Prepare general journal entries for the following transactions of a new business called Pose for Pics.

Aug.   1   Hashim Paris, the owner, invested $7,500 cash and $32,500 of photography equipment in the business.
       1   Paid $3,000 cash for an insurance policy covering the next 24 months.
       5   Purchased office supplies for $1,400 cash.
      20   Received $2,650 cash in photography fees earned.
      31   Paid $875 cash for August utilities.

Exercise 2-5
Preparing T-accounts and a trial balance

C3 P2

Use the information in Exercise 2-4 to prepare an August 31 trial balance for Pose-for-Pics. Open these T-accounts: Cash; Office Supplies; Prepaid Insurance; Photography Equipment; H. Paris, Capital; Photography Fees Earned; and Utilities Expense. Post the general journal entries to these T-accounts (which will serve as the ledger), and prepare a trial balance.

Exercise 2-6
Recording effects of transactions in T-accounts

C5 A1

Record the transactions below for Dejonge Company by recording the debit and credit entries directly in the following T-accounts: Cash; Accounts Receivable; Office Supplies; Office Equipment; Accounts Payable; Dejonge, Capital; Dejonge, Withdrawals; Fees Earned; and Rent Expense. Use the letters beside each transaction to identify entries. Determine the ending balance of each T-account.

a. Robert Dejonge invested $12,750 cash in the business.

b. Purchased office supplies for $375 cash.

c. Purchased $7,050 of office equipment on credit.

d. Received $1,500 cash as fees for services provided to a customer.

e. Paid $7,050 cash to settle the payable for the office equipment purchased in transaction c.

f. Billed a customer $2,700 as fees for services provided.

g. Paid the monthly rent with $525 cash.

Check   Cash ending balance, $6,425

h. Collected $1,125 cash toward the account receivable created in transaction f.

i. Dejonge withdrew $1,000 cash for personal use.

Exercise 2-7
Preparing a trial balance   P2

After recording the transactions of Exercise 2-6 in T-accounts and calculating the balance of each account, prepare a trial balance. Use May 31, 2005, as its report date.

Examine the following transactions and identify those that create revenues for Jade Services, a company owned by Mia Jade. Prepare general journal entries to record those transactions and explain why the other transactions did not create revenues.

a. Mia Jade invests $38,250 cash in the business.

b. Provided $1,350 of services on credit.

c. Provided services to a client and received $1,575 cash.

d. Received $9,150 cash from a client in payment for services to be provided next year.

e. Received $4,500 cash from a client in partial payment of an account receivable.

f. Borrowed $150,000 cash from the bank by signing a promissory note.

Exercise 2-8
Analyzing and journalizing
revenue transactions

A1 P1

Examine the following transactions and identify those that create expenses for Jade Services. Prepare general journal entries to record those transactions and explain why the other transactions did not create expenses.

a. Paid $14,100 cash for office supplies that were purchased more than 1 year ago.

b. Paid $1,125 cash for the two-week salary of the receptionist.

c. Paid $45,000 cash for equipment.

d. Paid $930 cash for monthly utilities.

e. Owner withdrew $5,000 cash for personal use.

Exercise 2-9
Analyzing and journalizing
expense transactions

A1 P1

On October 1, Ming Lue organized a new consulting firm called Tech Today. On October 31, the company's records show the following items and amounts. Use this information to prepare an October income statement for the business.

Exercise 2-10
Preparing an income
statement

C4 P3

Cash	$ 8,360	M. Lue, Withdrawals	$ 3,000
Accounts receivable	17,000	Consulting fees earned	17,000
Office supplies	3,250	Rent expense	4,550
Patents	46,000	Salaries expense	8,000
Office equipment	18,000	Telephone expense	560
Accounts payable	8,000	Miscellaneous expenses	280
M. Lue, Capital	84,000		

Check   Net income, $3,610

Use the information in Exercise 2-10 to prepare an October statement of owner's equity for Tech Today.

Exercise 2-11
Preparing a statement
of owner's equity   P3

Use the information in Exercise 2-10 (if completed, you can also use your solution to Exercise 2-11) to prepare an October 31 balance sheet for Tech Today.

Exercise 2-12
Preparing a balance sheet   P3

A sole proprietorship had the following assets and liabilities at the beginning and end of a recent year:

Exercise 2-13
Computing net income

A1 P3

	Assets	Liabilities
Beginning of the year	$ 70,000	$30,000
End of the year	115,000	46,000

Determine the net income earned or net loss incurred by the business during the year for each of the following *separate* cases:

a. Owner made no investments in the business and withdrew no assets during the year.

b. Owner made no investments in the business but withdrew $1,250 per month for personal use.

c. Owner withdrew no assets during the year but invested an additional $45,000 cash.

d. Owner withdrew $1,250 per month for personal use and invested an additional $25,000 cash.

Exercise 2-14

Analyzing changes in a company's equity

C5   P3

Compute the missing amount in each of the following separate companies *a* through *d*:

File Edit View Insert Format Tools Data Window Help

A	(a)	(b)	(c)	(d)
Equity, December 31, 2004	$ 0	$ 0	$ 0	$ 0
Owner investments during the year	120,000	?	87,000	210,000
Owner withdrawals during the year	?	54,000	10,000	55,000
Net income (loss) for the year	31,500	81,000	(4,000)	?
Equity, December 31, 2005	102,000	99,000	?	110,000

Exercise 2-15

Interpreting and describing transactions from T-accounts

C1   A1

Assume the following T-accounts reflect Joy Co.'s general ledger and that seven transactions *a* through *g* are posted to them. Provide a short description of each transaction. Include the amounts in your descriptions.

Cash

(a)	7,000	(b)	3,600
(e)	2,500	(c)	600
		(f)	2,400
		(g)	700

Office Supplies

(c)	600	
(d)	200	

Prepaid Insurance

(b)	3,600	

Equipment

(a)	5,600	
(d)	9,400	

Automobiles

(a)	11,000	

Accounts Payable

	(f)	2,400	(d)	9,600

D. Joy, Capital

	(a)	23,600

Delivery Services Revenue

	(e)	2,500

Gas and Oil Expense

(g)	700	

Exercise 2-16

Preparing general journal entries   A1   P1

Use information from the T-accounts in Exercise 2-15 to prepare general journal entries for each of the seven transaction *a* through *g*.

Exercise 2-17

Identifying effects of posting errors on the trial balance   A1   P2

Posting errors are identified in the following table. In column (1), enter the amount of the difference between the two (debit and credit) trial balance columns due to the error. In column (2), identify the trial balance column (debit or credit) with the larger amount if they are not equal. In column (3), identify the account(s) affected by the error. In column (4), indicate the amount by which the account(s) in column (3) is (are) under- or overstated. Answers for the first error are given.

	Description of Posting Error	(1) Difference between Debit and Credit Columns	(2) Column with the Larger Total	(3) Identify Account(s) Incorrectly Stated	(4) Amount that Account(s) is Over- or Understated
a.	$2,400 debit to Rent Expense is posted as a $1,590 debit.	$810	Credit	Rent Expense	Rent Expense understated $810
b.	$4,050 credit to Cash is posted twice as two credits to Cash.				
c.	$9,900 debit to the owner's withdrawals account is debited to owner's capital.				
d.	$2,250 debit to Prepaid Insurance is posted as a debit to Insurance Expense.				
e.	$42,000 debit to Machinery is posted as a debit to Accounts Payable.				
f.	$4,950 credit to Services Revenue is posted as a $495 credit.				
g.	$1,440 debit to Store Supplies is not posted.				

You are told the column totals in a trial balance are not equal. After careful analysis, you discover only one error. Specifically, a correctly journalized credit purchase of a computer for $16,950 is posted from the journal to the ledger with a $16,950 debit to Office Equipment and another $16,950 debit to Accounts Payable. The balance of the Office Equipment account has a debit balance of $40,100 on the trial balance. Answer each of the following questions and compute the dollar amount of any misstatement:

Exercise 2-18
Analyzing a trial balance error

A1   P2

a. Is the debit column total of the trial balance overstated, understated, or correctly stated?

b. Is the credit column total of the trial balance overstated, understated, or correctly stated?

c. Is the balance of the Office Equipment account overstated, understated, or correctly stated in the trial balance?

d. Is the balance of the Accounts Payable account overstated, understated, or correctly stated in the trial balance?

e. If the debit column total of the trial balance is $360,000 before correcting the error, what is the total of the credit column before correction?

a. Calculate the debt ratio and the return on assets using the year-end information for each of the following six separate companies ($ in thousands):

Exercise 2-19
Interpreting the debt ratio and return on assets

A2

	Case	Assets		Liabilities		Average Assets		Net Income
1	**Case**	**Assets**		**Liabilities**		**Average Assets**		**Net Income**
2	Company 1	$	90,500	$	12,000	$	100,000	$ 20,000
3	Company 2		64,000		47,000		40,000	3,800
4	Company 3		32,500		26,500		50,000	660
5	Company 4		147,000		56,000		200,000	21,000
6	Company 5		92,000		31,000		40,000	7,500
7	Company 6		104,500		51,500		70,000	12,000

b. Of the six companies, which business relies most heavily on creditor financing?

c. Of the six companies, which business relies most heavily on equity financing?

d. Which two companies indicate the greatest risk?

e. Which two companies earn the highest return on assets?

f. Which one company would investors likely prefer based on the risk-return relation?

PROBLEM SET A

Problem 2-1A
Preparing and posting general journal entries; preparing a trial balance

C4 C5 A1 P1 P2

Check (2) Ending balances: Cash, $73,900; Accounts Receivable, $4,240; Accounts Payable, $800

(3) Total debits, $137,440

Roberto Ricci opens a computer consulting business called Viva Consultants and completes the following transactions in its first month of operations:

April	1	Ricci invests $100,000 cash along with office equipment valued at $24,000 in the business.
	2	Prepaid $7,200 cash for twelve months' rent for office space. (*Hint:* Debit Prepaid Rent for $7,200.)
	3	Made credit purchases for $12,000 in office equipment and $2,400 in office supplies. Payment is due within 10 days.
	6	Completed services for a client and immediately received $2,000 cash.
	9	Completed an $8,000 project for a client, who must pay within 30 days.
	13	Paid $14,400 cash to settle the account payable created on April 3.
	19	Paid $6,000 cash for the premium on a 12-month insurance policy. (*Hint:* Debit Prepaid Insurance for $6,000.)
	22	Received $6,400 cash as partial payment for the work completed on April 9.
	25	Completed work for another client for $2,640 on credit.
	28	Ricci withdrew $6,200 cash for personal use.
	29	Purchased $800 of additional office supplies on credit.
	30	Paid $700 cash for this month's utility bill.

Required

1. Prepare general journal entries to record these transactions (use account titles listed in part 2).

2. Open the following ledger accounts—their account numbers are in parentheses (use the balance column format): Cash (101); Accounts Receivable (106); Office Supplies (124); Prepaid Insurance (128); Prepaid Rent (131); Office Equipment (163); Accounts Payable (201); R. Ricci, Capital (301); R. Ricci, Withdrawals (302); Services Revenue (403); and Utilities Expense (690). Post journal entries from part 1 to the ledger accounts and enter the balance after each posting.

3. Prepare a trial balance as of the end of this month's operations.

Problem 2-2A
Preparing and posting journal entries; preparing a trial balance

C4 C5 A1 P1 P2

Shelton Engineering completed the following transactions in the month of June.

a. Shania Shelton, the owner, invested $105,000 cash, office equipment with a value of $6,000, and $45,000 of drafting equipment to launch the business.

b. Purchased land worth $54,000 for an office by paying $5,400 cash and signing a long-term note payable for $48,600.

c. Purchased a portable building with $75,000 cash and moved it onto the land acquired in *b*.

d. Paid $6,000 cash for the premium on an 18-month insurance policy.

e. Completed and delivered a set of plans for a client and collected $5,700 cash.

f. Purchased $22,500 of additional drafting equipment by paying $10,500 cash and signing a long-term note payable for $12,000.

g. Completed $12,000 of engineering services for a client. This amount is to be received in 30 days.

h. Purchased $2,250 of additional office equipment on credit.

i. Completed engineering services for $18,000 on credit.

j. Received a bill for rent of equipment that was used on a recently completed job. The $1,200 rent must be paid within 30 days.

k. Collected $7,200 cash in partial payment from the client described in transaction *g*.

l. Paid $1,500 cash for wages to a drafting assistant.

m. Paid $2,250 cash to settle the account payable created in transaction *h*.

n. Paid $675 cash for minor repairs to the drafting equipment.

o. Shelton withdrew $9,360 cash for personal use.

p. Paid $1,500 cash for wages to a drafting assistant.

q. Paid $3,000 cash for advertisements in the local newspaper during June.

Required

1. Prepare general journal entries to record these transactions (use the account titles listed in part 2).

2. Open the following accounts—their account numbers are in parentheses (use the balance column format): Cash (101); Accounts Receivable (106); Prepaid Insurance (108); Office Equipment (163); Drafting Equipment (164); Building (170); Land (172); Accounts Payable (201); Notes Payable (250); S. Shelton, Capital (301); S. Shelton, Withdrawals (302); Engineering Fees Earned (402); Wages Expense (601); Equipment Rental Expense (602); Advertising Expense (603); and Repairs Expense (604). Post the journal entries from part 1 to the accounts and enter the balance after each posting.

3. Prepare a trial balance as of the end of this month's operations.

Check (2) Ending balances: Cash, $2,715; Accounts Receivable, $22,800; Accounts Payable, $1,200

(3) Trial balance totals, $253,500

Santo Birch opens a Web consulting business called Show-Me-the-Money Consultants and completes the following transactions in March:

March	1	Birch invested $150,000 cash along with $22,000 of office equipment in the business.
	2	Prepaid $6,000 cash for six months' rent for an office. (*Hint:* Debit Prepaid Rent for $6,000.)
	3	Made credit purchases of office equipment for $3,000 and office supplies for $1,200. Payment is due within 10 days.
	6	Completed services for a client and immediately received $4,000 cash.
	9	Completed a $7,500 project for a client, who must pay within 30 days.
	10	Paid $4,200 cash to settle the account payable created on March 3.
	19	Paid $5,000 cash for the premium on a 12-month insurance policy.
	22	Received $3,500 cash as partial payment for the work completed on March 9.
	25	Completed work for another client for $3,820 on credit.
	29	Birch withdrew $5,100 cash for personal use.
	30	Purchased $600 of additional office supplies on credit.
	31	Paid $200 cash for this month's utility bill.

Problem 2-3A
Preparing and posting general journal entries; preparing a trial balance

C4 C5 A1 P1 P2

mhhe.com/larson

Required

1. Prepare general journal entries to record these transactions (use the account titles listed in part 2).

2. Open the following accounts—their account numbers are in parentheses (use the balance column format): Cash (101); Accounts Receivable (106); Office Supplies (124); Prepaid Insurance (128); Prepaid Rent (131); Office Equipment (163); Accounts Payable (201); S. Birch, Capital (301); S. Birch, Withdrawals (302); Services Revenue (403); and Utilities Expense (690). Post the journal entries from part 1 to the accounts and enter the balance after each posting.

3. Prepare a trial balance as of the end of this month's operations.

Check (2) Ending balances: Cash, $137,000; Accounts Receivable, $7,820; Accounts Payable, $600

(3) Total debits, $187,920

The accounting records of Crist Crate Services show the following assets and liabilities as of December 31, 2004, and 2005:

Problem 2-4A
Computing net income from equity analysis, preparing a balance sheet, and calculating the debt ratio

C3 A1 A2 P3

mhhe.com/larson

	December 31	
	2004	**2005**
Cash	$ 52,500	$ 18,750
Accounts receivable	28,500	22,350
Office supplies	4,500	3,300
Office equipment	138,000	147,000
Trucks	54,000	54,000
Building	0	180,000
Land	0	45,000
Accounts payable	7,500	37,500
Note payable	0	105,000

Late in December 2005, the business purchased a small office building and land for $225,000. The business paid $120,000 cash toward the purchase and a $105,000 note payable was signed for the balance. Crist had to invest $35,000 cash in the business to enable it to pay the $120,000 cash. Crist also withdraws $3,000 cash per month from the business for personal use.

Required

Check (2) Net income, $58,900

1. Prepare balance sheets for the business as of December 31, 2004, and 2005. (Remember that total equity equals the difference between assets and liabilities.)

2. By comparing equity amounts from the balance sheets and using the additional information presented in this problem, prepare a calculation to show how much net income was earned by the business during 2005.

(3) Debt ratio, 30.29%

3. Compute the 2005 year-end debt ratio for the business.

Problem 2-5A
Analyzing account balances and reconstructing transactions

C1 C4 A1 P2

Carlos Beltran started an engineering firm called Beltran Engineering. He began operations and completed seven transactions in May, which included his initial investment of $17,000 cash. After these transactions, the ledger included the following accounts with normal balances:

Cash	$26,660
Office supplies	660
Prepaid insurance	3,200
Office equipment	16,500
Accounts payable	16,500
C. Beltran, Capital	17,000
C. Beltran, Withdrawals	3,740
Engineering fees earned	24,000
Rent expense	6,740

Required

Check (1) Trial balance totals, $57,500

1. Prepare a trial balance for this business at the end of May.

Analysis Components

2. Analyze the accounts and their balances and prepare a list that describes each of the seven most likely transactions and their amounts.

(3) Cash paid, $14,340

3. Prepare a report of cash received and cash paid showing how the seven transactions in part 2 yield the $26,660 ending Cash balance.

Problem 2-6A
Recording transactions; posting to ledger; preparing a trial balance

C4 A1 P1 P2

Business transactions completed by Eric Piburn during the month of September are as follows:

a. Piburn invested $23,000 cash along with office equipment valued at $12,000 in a new sole proprietorship named EP Consulting.

b. Purchased land valued at $8,000 and a building valued at $33,000. The purchase is paid with $15,000 cash and a long-term note payable for $26,000.

c. Purchased $600 of office supplies on credit.

d. Piburn invested his personal automobile in the business. The automobile has a value of $7,000 and is to be used exclusively in the business.

e. Purchased $1,100 of additional office equipment on credit.

f. Paid $800 cash salary to an assistant.

g. Provided services to a client and collected $2,700 cash.

h. Paid $430 cash for this month's utilities.

i. Paid $600 cash to settle the account payable created in transaction *c*.

j. Purchased $4,000 of new office equipment by paying $2,400 cash and trading in old equipment with a recorded net cost and value of $1,600. (*Hint:* Credit Office Equipment (old) for $1,600.)

k. Completed $2,400 of services for a client, who must pay within 30 days.

l. Paid $800 cash salary to an assistant.

m. Received $1,000 cash on the receivable created in transaction *k*.

n. Piburn withdrew $1,050 cash from the business for personal use.

Required

1. Prepare general journal entries to record these transactions (use the account titles listed in part 2).

2. Open the following accounts—their account numbers are in parentheses (use the balance column format): Cash (101); Accounts Receivable (106); Office Supplies (108); Office Equipment (163); Automobiles (164); Building (170); Land (172); Accounts Payable (201); Notes Payable (250); E. Piburn, Capital (301); E. Piburn, Withdrawals (302); Fees Earned (402); Salaries Expense (601); and Utilities Expense (602). Post the journal entries from part 1 to the accounts and enter the balance after each posting.

3. Prepare a trial balance as of the end of this month's operations.

Check (2) Ending balances: Cash, $5,620; Office Equipment, $15,500

(3) Trial balance totals, $74,200

Lummus Management Services opens for business and completes these transactions in September:

Sept.   1   Rhonda Lummus, the owner, invests $28,000 cash along with office equipment valued at $25,000 in the business.

2   Prepaid $10,500 cash for twelve months' rent for office space. (*Hint:* Debit Prepaid Rent for $10,500.)

4   Made credit purchases for $9,000 in office equipment and $1,200 in office supplies. Payment is due within 10 days.

8   Completed work for a client and immediately received $2,600 cash.

12   Completed a $13,400 project for a client, who must pay within 20 days.

13   Paid $10,200 cash to settle the account payable created on September 4.

19   Paid $5,200 cash for the premium on an 18-month insurance policy. (*Hint:* Debit Prepaid Insurance for $5,200.)

22   Received $7,800 cash as partial payment for the work completed on September 12.

24   Completed work for another client for $1,900 on credit.

28   Lummus withdrew $5,300 cash for personal use.

29   Purchased $1,700 of additional office supplies on credit.

30   Paid $460 cash for this month's utility bill.

Required

1. Prepare general journal entries to record these transactions (use account titles listed in part 2).

2. Open the following ledger accounts—their account numbers are in parentheses (use the balance column format): Cash (101); Accounts Receivable (106); Office Supplies (124); Prepaid Insurance (128); Prepaid Rent (131); Office Equipment (163); Accounts Payable (201); R. Lummus, Capital (301); R. Lummus, Withdrawals (302); Service Fees Earned (401); and Utilities Expense (690). Post journal entries from part 1 to the ledger accounts and enter the balance after each posting.

3. Prepare a trial balance as of the end of this month's operations.

PROBLEM SET B

Problem 2-1B
Preparing and posting general journal entries; preparing a trial balance

C4 C5 A1 P1 P2

Check (2) Ending balances: Cash, $6,740; Accounts Receivable, $7,500; Accounts Payable, $1,700

(3) Total debits, $72,600

At the beginning of April, Brooke Grechus launched a custom computer programming company called Softways. The company had the following transactions during April:

a. Brooke Grechus invested $45,000 cash, office equipment with a value of $4,500, and $28,000 of computer equipment in the company.

b. Purchased land worth $24,000 for an office by paying $4,800 cash and signing a long-term note payable for $19,200.

c. Purchased a portable building with $21,000 cash and moved it onto the land acquired in *b*.

Problem 2-2B
Preparing and posting journal entries; preparing a trial balance

C4 C5 A1 P1 P2

d. Paid $6,600 cash for the premium on a two-year insurance policy.

e. Provided services to a client and collected $3,200 cash.

f. Purchased $3,500 of additional computer equipment by paying $700 cash and signing a long-term note payable for $2,800.

g. Completed $3,750 of services for a client. This amount is to be received within 30 days.

h. Purchased $750 of additional office equipment on credit.

i. Completed client services for $9,200 on credit.

j. Received a bill for rent of a computer testing device that was used on a recently completed job. The $320 rent must be paid within 30 days.

k. Collected $4,600 cash from the client described in transaction *i*.

l. Paid $1,600 cash for wages to an assistant.

m. Paid $750 cash to settle the account payable created in transaction *h*.

n. Paid $425 cash for minor repairs to the computer equipment.

o. Grechus withdrew $3,875 cash for personal use.

p. Paid $1,600 cash for wages to an assistant.

q. Paid $800 cash for advertisements in the local newspaper during April.

Required

1. Prepare general journal entries to record these transactions (use the account titles listed in part 2).

Check (2) Ending balances: Cash, $10,650; Accounts Receivable, $8,350; Accounts Payable, $320

2. Open the following accounts—their account numbers are in parentheses (use the balance column format): Cash (101); Accounts Receivable (106); Prepaid Insurance (108); Office Equipment (163); Computer Equipment (164); Building (170); Land (172); Accounts Payable (201); Notes Payable (250); B. Grechus, Capital (301); B. Grechus, Withdrawals (302); Fees Earned (402); Wages Expense (601); Computer Rental Expense (602); Advertising Expense (603); and Repairs Expense (604). Post the journal entries from part 1 to the accounts and enter the balance after each posting.

(3) Trial balance totals, $115,970

3. Prepare a trial balance as of the end of this month's operations.

Problem 2-3B
Preparing and posting general journal entries; preparing a trial balance

C4 C5 A1 P1 P2

Shaw Management Services opens for business and completes these transactions in November:

Nov. 1 Kita Shaw, the owner, invested $30,000 cash along with $15,000 of office equipment in the business.

2 Prepaid $4,500 cash for six months' rent for an office. (*Hint:* Debit Prepaid Rent for $4,500.)

4 Made credit purchases of office equipment for $2,500 and of office supplies for $600. Payment is due within 10 days.

8 Completed work for a client and immediately received $3,400 cash.

12 Completed a $10,200 project for a client, who must pay within 30 days.

13 Paid $3,100 cash to settle the account payable created on November 4.

19 Paid $1,800 cash for the premium on a 24-month insurance policy.

22 Received $5,200 cash as partial payment for the work completed on November 12.

24 Completed work for another client for $1,750 on credit.

28 Shaw withdrew $5,300 cash for personal use.

29 Purchased $249 of additional office supplies on credit.

30 Paid $531 cash for this month's utility bill.

Required

1. Prepare general journal entries to record these transactions (use account titles listed in part 2).

Check (2) Ending balances: Cash, $23,369; Accounts Receivable, $6,750; Accounts Payable, $249

2. Open the following accounts—their account numbers are in parentheses (use the balance column format): Cash (101); Accounts Receivable (106); Office Supplies (124); Prepaid Insurance (128); Prepaid Rent (131); Office Equipment (163); Accounts Payable (201); K. Shaw, Capital (301); K. Shaw, Withdrawals (302); Services Revenue (403); and Utilities Expense (690). Post the journal entries from part 1 to the accounts and enter the balance after each posting.

(3) Total debits, $60,599

3. Prepare a trial balance as of the end of this month's operations.

The accounting records of Schmit Co. show the following assets and liabilities as of December 31, 2004, and 2005:

Problem 2-4B
Computing net income from equity analysis, preparing a balance sheet, and computing the debt ratio

C3   A1   A2   P3

	December 31	
	2004	**2005**
Cash	$14,000	$ 10,000
Accounts receivable	25,000	30,000
Office supplies	10,000	12,500
Office equipment	60,000	60,000
Machinery	30,500	30,500
Building	0	260,000
Land	0	65,000
Accounts payable	5,000	15,000
Note payable	0	260,000

Late in December 2005, the business purchased a small office building and land for $325,000. The business paid $65,000 cash toward the purchase and a $260,000 note payable was signed for the balance. Schmit had to invest an additional $25,000 cash to enable it to pay the $65,000 cash. Schmit also withdraws $1,000 cash per month from the business for personal use.

Required

1. Prepare balance sheets for the business as of December 31, 2004, and 2005. (Remember that total equity equals the difference between assets and liabilities.)

2. By comparing equity amounts from the balance sheets and using the additional information presented in the problem, prepare a calculation to show how much net income was earned by the business during 2005.

3. Calculate the December 31, 2005, debt ratio for the business.

Check   (2) Net income, $45,500

(3) Debt ratio, 58.76%

Miguel Gould started a Web consulting firm called Gould Solutions. He began operations and completed seven transactions in April that resulted in the following accounts, which all have normal balances:

Problem 2-5B
Analyzing account balances and reconstructing transactions

C1   C4   A1   P2

Cash	$12,485
Office supplies	560
Prepaid rent	1,500
Office equipment	11,450
Accounts payable	11,450
M. Gould, Capital	10,000
M. Gould, Withdrawals	6,200
Consulting fees earned	16,400
Operating expenses	5,655

Required

1. Prepare a trial balance for this business at the end of April.

Check   (1) Trial balance total, $37,850

Analysis Component

2. Analyze the accounts and their balances and prepare a list that describes each of the seven most likely transactions and their amounts.

3. Present a report that shows how the seven transactions in part 2 yield the $12,485 Cash balance.

(3) Cash paid, $13,915

Czekai Consulting completed the following transactions during June:

a. Chris Czekai, the sole proprietor, invested $80,000 cash along with office equipment valued at $30,000 in the new business.

b. Purchased land valued at $30,000 and a building valued at $170,000. The purchase is paid with $40,000 cash and a long-term note payable for $160,000.

Problem 2-6B
Recording transactions; posting to ledger; preparing a trial balance

C4   A1   P1   P2

c. Purchased $2,400 of office supplies on credit.

d. Czekai invested her personal automobile in the business. The automobile has a value of $18,000 and is to be used exclusively in the business.

e. Purchased $6,000 of additional office equipment on credit.

f. Paid $1,500 cash salary to an assistant.

g. Provided services to a client and collected $6,000 cash.

h. Paid $800 cash for this month's utilities.

i. Paid $2,400 cash to settle the account payable created in transaction *c*.

j. Purchased $20,000 of new office equipment by paying $18,600 cash and trading in old equipment with a recorded net cost and value of $1,400. (*Hint:* Credit Office Equipment (old) for $1,400.)

k. Completed $5,200 of services for a client, who must pay within 30 days.

l. Paid $1,500 cash salary to an assistant.

m. Received $3,800 cash on the receivable created in transaction *k*.

n. Czekai withdrew $6,400 cash from the business for personal use.

Required

1. Prepare general journal entries to record these transactions (use the account titles listed in part 2).

Check (2) Ending balances: Cash, $18,600; Office Equipment, $54,600

2. Open the following accounts—their account numbers are in parentheses (use the balance column format): Cash (101); Accounts Receivable (106); Office Supplies (108); Office Equipment (163); Automobiles (164); Building (170); Land (172); Accounts Payable (201); Notes Payable (250); C. Czekai, Capital (301); C. Czekai, Withdrawals (302); Fees Earned (402); Salaries Expense (601); and Utilities Expense (602). Post the journal entries from part 1 to the accounts and enter the balance after each posting.

(3) Trial balance totals, $305,200

3. Prepare a trial balance as of the end of this month's operations.

PROBLEM SET C

Problem Set C is available at the book's Website to further reinforce and assess your learning.

SERIAL PROBLEM

Success Systems

(This serial problem started in Chapter 1 and continues through most of the book. If the Chapter 1 segment was not completed, the problem can begin at this point. It is helpful, but not necessary, to use the Working Papers that accompany this book.)

On October 1, 2004, Kay Breeze launched a computer services company called Success Systems, which is organized as a sole proprietorship and provides consulting services, computer system installations, and custom program development. Breeze adopts the calendar year for reporting purposes and expects to prepare the company's first set of financial statements on December 31, 2004. The company's initial chart of accounts follows:

Account	No.	Account	No.
Cash	101	K. Breeze, Capital	301
Accounts Receivable	106	K. Breeze, Withdrawals	302
Computer Supplies	126	Computer Services Revenue	403
Prepaid Insurance	128	Wages Expense	623
Prepaid Rent	131	Advertising Expense	655
Office Equipment	163	Mileage Expense	676
Computer Equipment	167	Miscellaneous Expenses	677
Accounts Payable	201	Repairs Expense—Computer	684

Required

1. Prepare journal entries to record each of the following transactions for Success Systems.

Oct. 1   Breeze invested $55,000 cash, a $20,000 computer system, and $8,000 of office equipment in the business.
2   Paid $3,300 cash for four months' rent. (*Hint:* Debit Prepaid Rent for $3,300.)
3   Purchased $1,420 of computer supplies on credit from Cain Office Products.
5   Paid $2,220 cash for one year's premium on a property and liability insurance policy. (*Hint:* Debit Prepaid Insurance for $2,220.)
6   Billed Easy Leasing $4,800 for services performed in installing a new Web server.
8   Paid $1,420 cash for the computer supplies purchased from Cain Office Products on October 3.
10   Hired Sherry Adams as a part-time assistant for $125 per day, as needed.
12   Billed Easy Leasing another $1,400 for services performed.
15   Received $4,800 cash from Easy Leasing on its account.
17   Paid $805 cash to repair computer equipment damaged when moving it.
20   Paid $1,940 cash for an advertisement in the local newspaper.
22   Received $1,400 cash from Easy Leasing on its account.
28   Billed Clark Company $5,208 for services performed.
31   Paid $875 cash for Sherry Adams's wages for seven days' work.
31   Breeze withdrew $3,600 cash for personal use.
Nov. 1   Reimbursed Breeze in cash for business automobile mileage allowance (Breeze logged 1,000 miles at $0.32 per mile).
2   Received $4,633 cash from Chang Corporation for computer services performed.
5   Purchased computer supplies for $1,125 cash from Cain Office Products.
8   Billed Gomez Co. $5,668 for services performed.
13   Received notification from Alex's Engineering Co. that Success Systems' bid of $3,950 for an upcoming project is accepted.
18   Received $2,208 cash from Clark Company as partial payment of the October 28 bill.
22   Donated $250 cash to the United Way in the company's name.
24   Completed work for Alex's Engineering Co. and sent it a bill for $3,950.
25   Sent another bill to Clark Company for the past-due amount of $3,000.
28   Reimbursed Breeze in cash for business automobile mileage (1,200 miles at $0.32 per mile).
30   Paid $1,750 cash for Sherry Adams's wages for 14 days' work.
30   Breeze withdrew $2,000 cash for personal use.

2. Open ledger accounts (in balance column format) and post the journal entries from part 1 to them.

3. Prepare a trial balance as of the end of November.

BEYOND THE NUMBERS

BTN 2-1   Refer to **Krispy Kreme**'s financial statements in Appendix A for the following questions.

REPORTING IN ACTION

A1 A2

Required

1. What amount of total liabilities does it report for each of the fiscal years ended 2002 and 2003?
2. What amount of total assets does it report for each of the fiscal years ended 2002 and 2003?
3. Calculate its debt ratio for each of the fiscal years ended 2002 and 2003.
4. In which fiscal year did it employ more financial leverage (2002 or 2003)? Explain.

Roll On

5. Access its financial statements (10-K report) for a fiscal year ending after February 2, 2003, from its Website (**KrispyKreme.com**) or the SEC's EDGAR database (**www.sec.gov**). Recompute its debt ratio for any subsequent year's data and compare it with the February 2, 2003, debt ratio.

**COMPARATIVE
ANALYSIS**

A1   A2

BTN 2-2 Key comparative figures ($ thousands) for both **Krispy Kreme** and **Tastykake** follow:

Key Figures	Krispy Kreme		Tastykake	
	Current Year	Prior Year	Current Year	Prior Year
Total liabilities	$131,942	$ 65,218	$ 69,035	$ 61,072
Total assets	410,487	255,376	116,560	116,137

1. What is the debt ratio for Krispy Kreme in the current year and the prior year?

2. What is the debt ratio for Tastykake in the current year and the prior year?

3. Which of the two companies has a higher degree of financial leverage? What does this imply?

**ETHICS
CHALLENGE**

C1   C2

BTN 2-3 Review the *Decision Ethics* case from the first part of this chapter involving the cashier. The guidance answer suggests that you should not comply with the assistant manager's request.

Required

Propose and evaluate two other courses of action you might consider, and explain why.

**COMMUNICATING
IN PRACTICE**

C1   C3   A1   P3

BTN 2-4 Amy Renkmeyer is an aspiring entrepreneur and your friend. She is having difficulty understanding the purposes of financial statements and how they fit together across time.

Required

Write a one-page memorandum to Renkmeyer explaining the purposes of the four financial statements and how they are linked across time.

**TAKING IT TO
THE NET**

A1

mhhe.com/larson

BTN 2-5 Access EDGAR online (**www.sec.gov**) and locate the 10-K report of **Amazon.com** (ticker AMZN) filed on January 24, 2002. Review its financial statements reported for fiscal years ended 1999, 2000, and 2001 to answer the following questions:

Required

1. What are the amounts of its net losses reported for each of these three years?

2. Does Amazon's operations provide cash or use cash for each of these three years?

3. If Amazon has a 2000 net loss and a net use of cash in operations in 2000, how is it possible that its cash balance at December 31, 2000, shows an increase relative to its balance at January 1, 2000?

**TEAMWORK IN
ACTION**

C1   C3   C5   A1

BTN 2-6 The expanded accounting equation consists of assets, liabilities, capital, withdrawals, revenues, and expenses. It can be used to reveal insights into changes in a company's financial position.

Required

1. Form *learning teams* of six (or more) members. Each team member must select one of the six components and each team must have at least one expert on each component: (*a*) assets, (*b*) liabilities, (*c*) capital, (*d*) withdrawals, (*e*) revenues, and (*f*) expenses.

2. Form *expert teams* of individuals who selected the same component in part 1. Expert teams are to draft a report that each expert will present to his or her learning team addressing the following:

    a. Identify for its component the (i) increase and decrease side of the account and (ii) normal balance side of the account.

    b. Describe a transaction, with amounts, that increases its component.

c. Using the transaction and amounts in (*b*), verify the equality of the accounting equation and then explain any effects on the income statement and statement of cash flows.

d. Describe a transaction, with amounts, that decreases its component.

e. Using the transaction and amounts in (*d*), verify the equality of the accounting equation and then explain any effects on the income statement and statement of cash flows.

3. Each expert should return to his/her learning team. In rotation, each member presents his/her expert team's report to the learning team. Team discussion is encouraged.

BTN 2-7 Read the article "Leveraged for Success" in the April 18, 2002, issue of *Business Week*.

Required

1. Explain why debt financing can be a less expensive alternative than equity financing.

2. What can happen if a company takes on too much debt?

3. Name five companies cited by the article that are using a high degree of leverage but still maintaining top credit ratings.

BUSINESS WEEK ACTIVITY

A2

mhhe.com/larson

BTN 2-8 Liang Lu is a young entrepreneur who operates Lu Music Services, offering singing lessons and instruction on musical instruments. Lu wishes to expand but needs a loan. The bank requests Lu to prepare a balance sheet and key financial ratios. Lu has not kept formal records but is able to provide the following accounts and their amounts as of December 31, 2005:

ENTREPRENEURIAL DECISION

A1 A2 P3

Cash	$ 1,800	Accounts Receivable	$4,800	Prepaid Insurance . .	$ 750
Prepaid Rent	4,700	Store Supplies	3,300	Equipment	25,000
Accounts Payable . . .	1,100	Unearned Lesson Fees	7,800	Total Equity*	31,450
Annual net income . .	20,000				

* The total equity amount reflects all owner investments, owner withdrawals, revenues, and expenses as of December 31, 2005.

Required

1. Prepare a balance sheet as of December 31, 2005, for Lu Music Services.

2. Compute Lu's debt ratio and its return on assets (from Chapter 1). Assume average assets equal its ending balance.

3. Do you think the prospects of a $15,000 bank loan are good? Why or why not?

BTN 2-9 Assume that Tanya York of **York Entertainment** wants to grow company revenues by 10% each year for the next five years. York has determined that achieving that revenue growth will require additional financing. Accordingly, the company has sought and been offered a $5 million line of credit by a Los Angeles bank to help fund current operations and new movie projects. York is not required to use the line of credit, but it does have preapproval to use the line of credit as needed. If the line of credit is used, an annual interest rate of 8% will be charged on the money borrowed.

A1 A2 P3

Required

1. What will York's annual revenues be in five years if the revenue growth target rate is achieved?

2. If York decides to borrow against the line of credit, what must it do to successfully employ financial leverage?

BTN 2-10 Obtain a recent copy of the most prominent newspaper distributed in your area. Research the classified section and prepare a report answering the following questions (attach relevant classified clippings to your report). Alternatively, you may want to search the Web for the required information. One suitable Website is **America's Job Bank (www.AJB.org)**. For documentation, you should print copies of Websites accessed.

HITTING THE ROAD

C1

1. Identify the number of listings for accounting positions and the various accounting job titles.

2. Identify the number of listings for other job titles, with examples, that require or prefer accounting knowledge/experience but are not specifically accounting positions.

3. Specify the salary range for the accounting and accounting-related positions if provided.

4. Indicate the job that appeals to you, the reason for its appeal, and its requirements.

GLOBAL DECISION

A2

BTN 2-11 Grupo Bimbo (GrupoBimbo.com) competes with several companies, including **Krispy Kreme** and **Tastykake**. Key financial ratios for the current fiscal year follow:

Key Figure	Grupo Bimbo	Krispy Kreme	Tastykake
Return on assets	3.6%	10.1%	1.7%
Debt ratio	56.0%	32.1%	59.2%

Required

1. Which company is most profitable according to return on assets?

2. Which company is most risky according to the debt ratio?

3. Which company deserves increased investment based on a joint analysis of return on assets and the debt ratio?

"Stay focused and keep doing what you believe in"—Melody Kulp (second from left; David Reinstein is on the far left)

Adjusting Accounts and Preparing Financial Statements

A Look Back

Chapter 2 explained the analysis and recording of transactions. We showed how to apply and interpret company accounts, T-accounts, double-entry accounting, ledgers, postings, and trial balances.

A Look at This Chapter

This chapter explains the timing of reports and the need to adjust accounts. Adjusting accounts is important for recognizing revenues and expenses in the proper period. We describe the adjusted trial balance and how it is used to prepare financial statements.

A Look Ahead

Chapter 4 highlights the completion of the accounting cycle. We explain the important final steps in the accounting process. These include closing procedures, the post-closing trial balance, and reversing entries.

CAP

Conceptual

C1 Explain the importance of periodic reporting and the time period principle. *(p. 94)*

C2 Explain accrual accounting and how it makes financial statements more useful. *(p. 95)*

C3 Identify the types of adjustments and their purpose. *(p. 97)*

Analytical

A1 Explain how accounting adjustments link to financial statements. *(p. 104)*

A2 Compute profit margin and describe its use in analyzing company performance. *(p. 108)*

Procedural

P1 Prepare and explain adjusting entries. *(p. 97)*

P2 Explain and prepare an adjusted trial balance. *(p. 105)*

P3 Prepare financial statements from an adjusted trial balance. *(p. 106)*

Sparkling Financials

EL SEGUNDO, CA—One afternoon 23-year-old Melody Kulp was playing outside with the young cousin of a friend when she placed yard-picked flowers in the girl's hair and thought how much prettier they looked than headbands or hair clips. The next day, with some silk flowers and Velcro she purchased, Kulp made similar hair accessories, called them *Sparkles,* and began wearing them.

When a friend wore one to work at Fred Segal's, the shop's buyer asked to meet with Kulp about putting together a product line. Kulp quickly organized a business—dubbed **Mellies** (**Mellies.com**)—and then converted a 10′ × 10′ room in her house into a minifactory. The rest is the stuff of Hollywood movies.

After only three years, Mellies is a $40 million accessories company. With her 25-year-old partner David Reinstein, Melody Kulp now manages 15 employees and plans to launch a cosmetics line.

The young entrepreneurs learned a lot in a hurry. She had to meet creditors and bankers, set up a reliable accounting system, draw up financial statements, and analyze and interpret financial data. It was at times overwhelming, says Kulp, but "the key is to stay focused and keep doing what you believe in."

Kulp knows how important a timely and reliable accounting system is for Mellies' continued success. Historical and projected financial statements have enabled her company to obtain the necessary financing to propel it to new heights.

This chapter focuses on the accounting system underlying financial statements. Says Kulp, "We've got the system set up where we can look ahead, rather than live day to day." That look ahead reveals sparkling financials.

[Sources: Mellies Website, January 2004; *Success Publishing,* 2000; *Entrepreneur,* November 2000.]

Financial statements reflect revenues when earned and expenses when incurred. This is known as *accrual accounting*. Accrual accounting requires several steps. We described many of these steps in Chapter 2. We showed how companies use accounting systems to collect information about *external* transactions and events. We also explained how journals, ledgers, and other tools are useful in preparing financial statements. This chapter describes the accounting process for producing useful information involving *internal* transactions and events. An important part of this process is adjusting the account balances so that financial statements at the end of a reporting period reflect the effects of all transactions. We then explain the important steps in preparing financial statements.

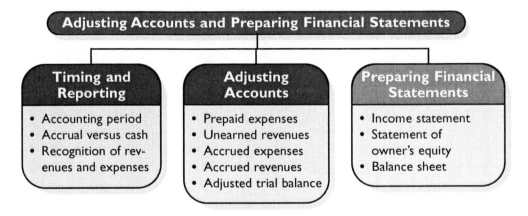

Adjusting Accounts and Preparing Financial Statements

Timing and Reporting	**Adjusting Accounts**	**Preparing Financial Statements**
• Accounting period • Accrual versus cash • Recognition of revenues and expenses	• Prepaid expenses • Unearned revenues • Accrued expenses • Accrued revenues • Adjusted trial balance	• Income statement • Statement of owner's equity • Balance sheet

Timing and Reporting

Regular, or periodic, reporting is an important part of the accounting process. This section describes the impact on the accounting process of the point in time or the period of time that a report refers to.

The Accounting Period

C1   Explain the importance of periodic reporting and the time period principle.

"Krispy Kreme announces earnings per share of . . ."

The value of information is often linked to its timeliness. Useful information must reach decision makers frequently and promptly. To provide timely information, accounting systems prepare reports at regular intervals. This results in an accounting process impacted by the time period (or periodicity) principle. The **time period principle** assumes that an organization's activities can be divided into specific time periods such as a month, a three-month quarter, a six-month interval, or a year. Exhibit 3.1 shows various **accounting,** or *reporting,*

Exhibit 3.1

Accounting Periods

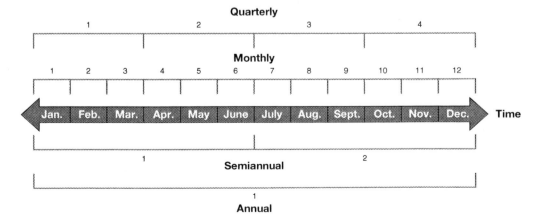

periods. Most organizations use a year as their primary accounting period. Reports covering a one-year period are known as **annual financial statements.** Many organizations also prepare **interim financial statements** covering one, three, or six months of activity.

The annual reporting period is not always a calendar year ending on December 31. An organization can adopt a **fiscal year** consisting of any 12 consecutive months. It is also acceptable to adopt an annual reporting period of 52 weeks. For example, **Gap**'s fiscal year consistently ends the final week of January or the first week of February each year.

Companies with little seasonal variation in sales often choose the calendar year as their fiscal year. For example, the financial statements of **Marvel Enterprises** reflect a fiscal year that ends on December 31. Companies experiencing seasonal variations in sales often choose a **natural business year** end, which is when sales activities are at their lowest level for the year. The natural business year for retailers such as **Wal-Mart**, **Dell**, and **FUBU** usually ends around January 31, after the holiday season.

Accrual Basis versus Cash Basis

After external transactions and events are recorded for an accounting period, several accounts still need adjustments before their balances appear in financial statements. This need arises because internal transactions and events remain unrecorded. **Accrual basis accounting** uses the adjusting process to recognize revenues when earned and to match expenses with revenues.

Cash basis accounting recognizes revenues when cash is received and records expenses when cash is paid. This means that cash basis net income for a period is the difference between cash receipts and cash payments. Cash basis accounting is not consistent with generally accepted accounting principles.

It is commonly held that accrual accounting better reflects business performance than information about cash receipts and payments. Accrual accounting also increases the *comparability* of financial statements from one period to another. Yet cash basis accounting is useful for several business decisions—which is the reason companies must report a statement of cash flows.

To see the difference between these two accounting systems, let's consider FastForward's Prepaid Insurance account. FastForward paid $2,400 for 24 months of insurance coverage beginning on December 1, 2004. Accrual accounting requires that $100 of insurance expense be reported on December's income statement. Another $1,200 of expense is reported in year 2005, and the remaining $1,100 is reported as expense in the first 11 months of 2006. Exhibit 3.2 illustrates this allocation of insurance cost across these three years. The accrual basis balance sheet reports any unexpired premium as a Prepaid Insurance asset.

A cash basis income statement for December 2004 reports insurance expense of $2,400, as shown in Exhibit 3.3. The cash basis income statements for years 2005 and 2006 report

C2   Explain accrual accounting and how it makes financial statements more useful.

Topic Tackler 3-1

Point: IBM's revenues from services to customers are recorded when services are performed. Its revenues from product sales are recorded when products are shipped.

Exhibit 3.2

Accrual Basis Accounting for Allocating Prepaid Insurance to Expense

Transaction: Purchase 24 months' insurance beginning December 2004	**Insurance Expense 2004**				**Insurance Expense 2005**				**Insurance Expense 2006**			
	Jan $0	Feb $0	Mar $0	Apr $0	Jan $100	Feb $100	Mar $100	Apr $100	Jan $100	Feb $100	Mar $100	Apr $100
	May $0	June $0	July $0	Aug $0	May $100	June $100	July $100	Aug $100	May $100	June $100	July $100	Aug $100
	Sept $0	Oct $0	Nov $0	Dec $100	Sept $100	Oct $100	Nov $100	Dec $100	Sept $100	Oct $100	Nov $100	Dec $0

Exhibit 3.3

Cash Basis Accounting for Allocating Prepaid Insurance to Expense

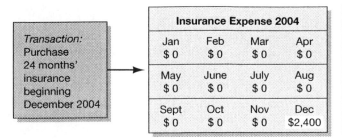

Transaction: Purchase 24 months' insurance beginning December 2004	**Insurance Expense 2004**				**Insurance Expense 2005**				**Insurance Expense 2006**			
	Jan $0	Feb $0	Mar $0	Apr $0	Jan $0	Feb $0	Mar $0	Apr $0	Jan $0	Feb $0	Mar $0	Apr $0
	May $0	June $0	July $0	Aug $0	May $0	June $0	July $0	Aug $0	May $0	June $0	July $0	Aug $0
	Sept $0	Oct $0	Nov $0	Dec $2,400	Sept $0	Oct $0	Nov $0	Dec $0	Sept $0	Oct $0	Nov $0	Dec $0

Point: Recording revenue early overstates current-period revenue and income; recording it late understates current-period revenue and income.

no insurance expense. The cash basis balance sheet never reports an insurance asset because it is immediately expensed. Note that reported income for 2004–2006 fails to match the cost of insurance with the insurance benefits received for those years and months.

Recognizing Revenues and Expenses

We use the time period principle to divide a company's activities into specific time periods, but not all activities are complete when financial statements are prepared. Thus, adjustments often are required to get correct account balances.

We rely on two principles in the adjusting process: revenue recognition and matching. Chapter 1 explained that the *revenue recognition principle* requires that revenue be recorded when earned, not before and not after. Most companies earn revenue when they provide services and products to customers. A major goal of the adjusting process is to have revenue recognized (reported) in the time period when it is earned.

The **matching principle** aims to record expenses in the same accounting period as the revenues that are earned as a result of these expenses. This matching of expenses with the revenue benefits is a major part of the adjusting process.

Matching expenses with revenues often requires us to predict certain events. When we use financial statements, we must understand that they require estimates and therefore include measures that are not precise. **Walt Disney**'s annual report explains that its production costs from movies are matched to revenues based on a ratio of current revenues from the movie divided by its predicted total revenues.

Point: Recording expense early overstates current-period expense and understates current-period income; recording it late understates current-period expense and overstates current-period income.

Adjusting Accounts

The process of adjusting accounts involves analyzing each account balance and the transactions and events that affect it to determine any needed adjustments. An **adjusting entry** is recorded to bring an asset or liability account balance to its proper amount. This entry also updates a related expense or revenue account.

C3 Identify the types of adjustments and their purpose.

Framework for Adjustments

Adjustments are necessary for transactions and events that extend over more than one period. It is helpful to group adjustments by the timing of cash receipt or cash payment in relation to the recognition of the related revenues or expenses. Exhibit 3.4 identifies four types of adjustments.

Topic Tackler 3-2

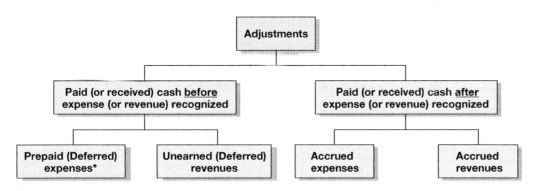

Exhibit 3.4

Types of Adjustments

*Includes depreciation.

The left side of this exhibit shows prepaid expenses (including depreciation) and unearned revenues, which reflect transactions when cash is paid or received *before* a related expense or revenue is recognized. They are also called *deferrals* because the recognition of an expense (or revenue) is *deferred* until after the related cash is paid (or received). The right side of this exhibit shows accrued expenses and accrued revenues, which reflect transactions when cash is paid or received *after* a related expense or revenue is recognized. Adjusting entries are necessary for each of these so that revenues, expenses, assets, and liabilities are correctly reported. It is helpful to remember that each adjusting entry affects one or more income statement accounts *and* one or more balance sheet accounts (but not the Cash account).

Point: Adjusting is a 3-step process: (1) Compute current account balance, (2) Compute what current account balance should be, and (3) Record entry to get from step 1 to step 2.

Prepaid (Deferred) Expenses

Prepaid expenses refer to items *paid for* in advance of receiving their benefits. Prepaid expenses are assets. When these assets are used, their costs become expenses. Adjusting entries for prepaids increase expenses and decrease assets as shown in the T-accounts of Exhibit 3.5. Such adjustments reflect transactions and events that use up prepaid expenses (including passage of time). To illustrate the accounting for prepaid expenses, this section focuses on prepaid insurance, supplies, and depreciation.

P1 Prepare and explain adjusting entries.

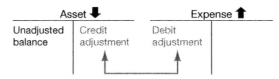

Exhibit 3.5

Adjusting for Prepaid Expenses

Prepaid Insurance We illustrate prepaid insurance using FastForward's payment of $2,400 for 24 months of insurance benefits beginning on December 1, 2004. With the passage of time, the benefits of the insurance gradually expire and a portion of the Prepaid

Insurance asset becomes expense. For instance, one month's insurance coverage expires by December 31, 2004. This expense is $100, or 1/24 of $2,400. The adjusting entry to record this expense and reduce the asset, along with T-account postings, follows:

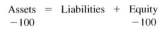

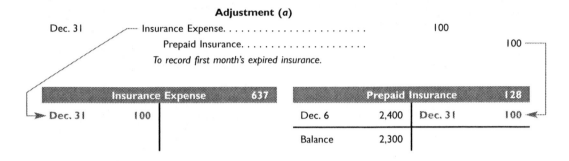

Adjustment (a)

Assets = Liabilities + Equity
−100   −100

After adjusting and posting, the $100 balance in Insurance Expense and the $2,300 balance in Prepaid Insurance are ready for reporting in financial statements. *Not* making the adjustment on or before December 31 would (1) understate expenses by $100 and overstate net income by $100 for the December income statement and (2) overstate both prepaid insurance (assets) and equity (because of net income) by $100 in the December 31 balance sheet. It is also evident from Exhibit 3.2 that 2005's adjustments must transfer a total of $1,200 from Prepaid Insurance to Insurance Expense, and 2006's adjustments must transfer the remaining $1,100 to Insurance Expense.

Supplies   Supplies are a prepaid expense often requiring adjustment. To illustrate, FastForward purchased $9,720 of supplies in December and used some of them. When financial statements are prepared at December 31, the cost of supplies used during December must be recognized. When FastForward computes (takes inventory of) its remaining unused supplies at December 31, it finds $8,670 of supplies remaining of the $9,720 total supplies. The $1,050 difference between these two amounts is December's supplies expense. The adjusting entry to record this expense and reduce the Supplies asset account, along with T-account postings, follows:

Adjustment (b)

Assets = Liabilities + Equity
−1,050   −1,050

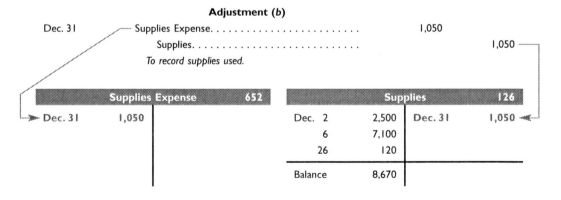

The balance of the Supplies account is $8,670 after posting—equaling the cost of the remaining supplies. *Not* making the adjustment on or before December 31 would (1) understate expenses by $1,050 and overstate net income by $1,050 for the December income statement and (2) overstate both supplies and equity (because of net income) by $1,050 in the December 31 balance sheet.

Other Prepaid Expenses   Other prepaid expenses, such as Prepaid Rent, are accounted for exactly as Insurance and Supplies are. We should also note that some prepaid expenses are both paid for and fully used up within a single accounting period. One example is when a company pays monthly rent on the first day of each month. This payment creates a prepaid expense on the first day of each month that fully expires by the end of the month. In these special cases, we can record the cash paid with a debit to an expense account instead of an asset account. This practice is described more completely later in the chapter.

Depreciation A special category of prepaid expenses is **plant assets,** which refers to long-term tangible assets used to produce and sell products and services. Plant assets are expected to provide benefits for more than one

---

Decision Maker

Investor A small publishing company signs a well-known athlete to write a book. The company pays the athlete $500,000 to sign plus future book royalties. A note to the company's financial statements says that "prepaid expenses include $500,000 in author signing fees to be matched against future expected sales." Is this accounting for the signing bonus acceptable? How does it affect your analysis?

Answer—p. 114

---

period. Examples of plant assets are buildings, machines, vehicles, and fixtures. All plant assets, with a general exception for land, eventually wear out or decline in usefulness. The costs of these assets are deferred but are gradually reported as expenses in the income statement over the assets' useful lives (benefit periods). **Depreciation** is the process of allocating the costs of these assets over their expected useful lives. Depreciation expense is recorded with an adjusting entry similar to that for other prepaid expenses.

Point: Depreciation does not necessarily measure the decline in market value.

To illustrate, recall that FastForward purchased equipment for $26,000 in early December to use in earning revenue. This equipment's cost must be depreciated. The equipment is expected to have a useful life (benefit period) of four years and to be worth about $8,000 at the end of four years. This means the *net* cost of this equipment over its useful life is $18,000 ($26,000 − $8,000). We can use any of several methods to allocate this $18,000 net cost to expense. FastForward uses a method called **straight-line depreciation,** which allocates equal amounts of an asset's net cost to depreciation during its useful life. Dividing the $18,000 net cost by the 48 months in the asset's useful life gives a monthly cost of $375 ($18,000/48). The adjusting entry to record monthly depreciation expense, along with T-account postings, follows:

Point: An asset's expected value at the end of its useful life is called *salvage value.*

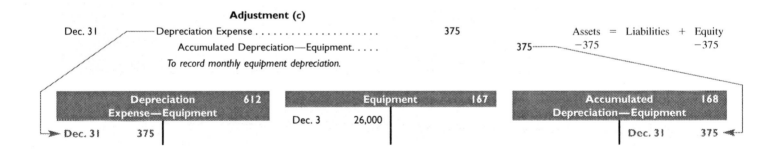

After posting the adjustment, the Equipment account ($26,000) less its Accumulated Depreciation ($375) account equals the $25,625 net cost of the 47 remaining months in the benefit period. The $375 balance in the Depreciation Expense account is reported in the December income statement. *Not* making the adjustment at December 31 would (1) understate expenses by $375 and overstate net income by $375 for the December income statement and (2) overstate both assets and equity (because of income) by $375 in the December 31 balance sheet.

The accumulated depreciation is kept in a separate contra account. A **contra account** is an account linked with another account, it has an opposite normal balance, and it is reported as a subtraction from that other account's balance. For instance, FastForward's contra account of Accumulated Depreciation—Equipment is subtracted from the Equipment account in the balance sheet (see Exhibit 3.7).

Point: The cost principle requires an asset to be initially recorded at acquisition cost. Depreciation causes the asset's book value (cost less accumulated depreciation) to decline over time.

Decision Maker

Entrepreneur   You are preparing an offer to purchase a family-run restaurant. The depreciation schedule for the restaurant's building and equipment shows costs of $175,000 and accumulated depreciation of $155,000. This leaves a net for building and equipment of $20,000. Is this information useful in helping you decide on a purchase offer?

Answer—p. 115

A contra account allows balance sheet readers to know both the full costs of assets and the total amount of depreciation. By knowing both these amounts, decision makers can better assess a company's capacity and its need to replace assets. For example, FastForward's balance sheet shows both the $26,000 original cost of equipment and the $375 balance in the accumulated depreciation contra account. This information reveals that the equipment is close to new. If FastForward reports equipment only at its net amount of $25,625, users cannot assess the equipment's age or its need for replacement. The title of the contra account, *Accumulated Depreciation,* indicates that this account includes total depreciation expense for all prior periods for which the asset was used. To illustrate, the Equipment and the Accumulated Depreciation accounts appear as in Exhibit 3.6 on February 28, 2005, after three months of adjusting entries.

Exhibit 3.6

Accounts after Three Months of Depreciation Adjustments

Equipment		167
Dec. 3	26,000	

Accumulated Depreciation—Equipment		168
	Dec. 31	375
	Jan. 31	375
	Feb. 28	375
	Balance	1,125

Point: The net cost of equipment is also called the *depreciable basis.*

The $1,125 balance in the accumulated depreciation account is subtracted from its related $26,000 asset cost. The difference ($24,875) between these two balances is the cost of the asset that has not yet been depreciated. This difference is called the **book value,** or *net amount,* which equals the asset's costs less its accumulated depreciation. These account balances are reported in the assets section of the February 28 balance sheet in Exhibit 3.7.

Exhibit 3.7

Equipment and Accumulated Depreciation on February 28 Balance Sheet

Assets		
Cash		$ _____
⋮		
Equipment	$26,000	
Less accumulated depreciation	1,125	24,875
Total Assets		$ _____

Commonly titled *Equipment, net*

Unearned (Deferred) Revenues

The term **unearned revenues** refers to cash received in advance of providing products and services. Unearned revenues, also called *deferred revenues,* are liabilities. When cash is accepted, an obligation to provide products or services is accepted. As products or services are provided, the unearned revenues become *earned* revenues. Adjusting entries for unearned revenues involve increasing revenues and decreasing unearned revenues, as shown in Exhibit 3.8.

Exhibit 3.8

Adjusting for Unearned Revenues

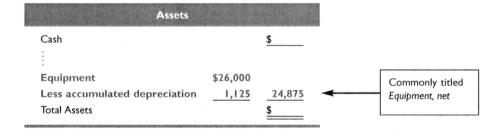

Liability ↓		Revenue ↑
Debit adjustment	Unadjusted balance	Credit adjustment

Point: To *defer* is to postpone. We postpone reporting amounts received as revenues until they are earned.

An example of unearned revenues is from **The New York Times Company**, which reports unexpired (unearned) subscriptions of more than $60 million: "Proceeds from . . . subscriptions are deferred at the time of sale and are recognized in earnings on a pro rata basis over the terms of the subscriptions."

Unearned revenues are more than 10% of the current liabilities for the Times. Another example comes from the **Boston Celtics**. When the Celtics receive cash from advance ticket sales and broadcast fees, they record it in an unearned revenue account called *Deferred Game Revenues*. The Celtics recognize this unearned revenue with adjusting entries on a game-by-game basis. Since the NBA regular season begins in October and ends in April, revenue recognition is mainly limited to this period. For a recent season, the Celtics' quarterly revenues were $0 million for July–September; $34 million for October–December; $48 million for January–March; and $17 million for April–June.

FastForward has unearned revenues. It agreed on December 26 to provide consulting services to a client for a fixed fee of $3,000 for 60 days. On that same day, this client paid the 60-day fee in advance, covering the period December 27 to February 24. The entry to record the cash received in advance is

Dec. 26	Cash	3,000	
	Unearned Consulting Revenue		3,000
	Received advance payment for services over the		
	next 60 days.		

Assets = Liabilities + Equity
+3,000   +3,000

This advance payment increases cash and creates an obligation to do consulting work over the next 60 days. As time passes, FastForward will earn this payment through consulting. By December 31, it has provided five days' service and earned 5/60 of the $3,000 unearned revenue. This amounts to $250 ($3,000 × 5/60). The *revenue recognition principle* implies that $250 of unearned revenue must be reported as revenue on the December income statement. The adjusting entry to reduce the liability account and recognize earned revenue, along with T-account postings, follows:

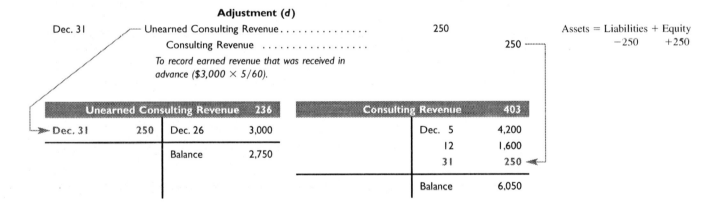

Adjustment (d)

Dec. 31	Unearned Consulting Revenue.	250	
	Consulting Revenue		250
	To record earned revenue that was received in		
	advance ($3,000 × 5/60).		

Assets = Liabilities + Equity
−250   +250

Unearned Consulting Revenue 236		
Dec. 31	250	Dec. 26	3,000
		Balance	2,750

Consulting Revenue 403	
Dec. 5	4,200
12	1,600
31	250
Balance	6,050

The adjusting entry transfers $250 from unearned revenue (a liability account) to a revenue account. *Not* making the adjustment (1) understates revenue and net income by $250 in the December income statement and (2) overstates unearned revenue and understates equity by $250 on the December 31 balance sheet.

Accrued Expenses

Accrued expenses refer to costs that are incurred in a period but are both unpaid and unrecorded. Accrued expenses must be reported on the income statement of the period when incurred. Adjusting entries for recording accrued expenses involves increasing expenses and increasing liabilities as shown in Exhibit 3.9. This adjustment

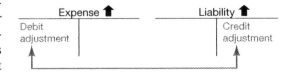

Exhibit 3.9

Adjusting for Accrued Expenses

recognizes expenses incurred in a period but not yet paid. Common examples of accrued expenses are salaries, interest, rent, and taxes. We use salaries and interest to show how to adjust accounts for accrued expenses.

Accrued Salaries Expense   FastForward's employee earns $70 per day, or $350 for a five-day workweek beginning on Monday and ending on Friday. This employee is paid every two weeks on Friday. On December 12 and 26, the wages are paid, recorded in the journal, and posted to the ledger. The calendar in Exhibit 3.10 shows three working days after the December 26 payday (29, 30, and 31). This means the employee has earned three days' salary by the close of business on Wednesday, December 31, yet this salary cost is not paid or recorded.

Exhibit 3.10

Salary Accrual and Paydays

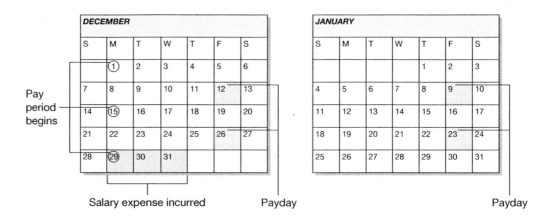

The financial statements would be incomplete if FastForward fails to report the added expense and liability to the employee for unpaid salary from December 29–31. The adjusting entry to account for accrued salaries, along with T-account postings, follows:

Assets = Liabilities + Equity
+210   −210

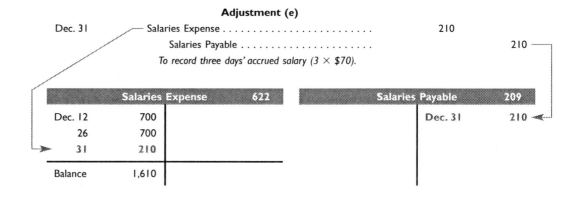

Salaries expense of $1,610 is reported on the December income statement and $210 of salaries payable (liability) is reported in the balance sheet. *Not* making the adjustment (1) understates salaries expense and overstates net income by $210 in the December income statement and (2) understates salaries payable (liabilities) and overstates equity by $210 on the December 31 balance sheet.

Accrued Interest Expense   Companies commonly have accrued interest expense on notes payable and other long-term liabilities at the end of a period. Interest expense is incurred with the passage of time. Unless interest is paid on the last day of an accounting period, we need to adjust for interest expense incurred but not yet paid. This means we must accrue interest cost from the most recent payment date up to the end of the period. The formula for computing accrued interest is:

Principal amount owed × Annual interest rate × Fraction of year since last payment date.

To illustrate, if a company has a $6,000 loan from a bank at 6% annual interest, then 30 days' accrued interest expense is $30—computed as $6,000 × 0.06 × 30/360. The adjusting entry would be to debit Interest Expense for $30 and credit Interest Payable for $30.

Point: Interest computations assume a 360-day year.

Future Payment of Accrued Expenses Adjusting entries for accrued expenses foretell cash transactions in future periods. Specifically, accrued expenses at the end of one accounting period result in *cash payments* in a *future* period(s). To illustrate, recall that FastForward recorded accrued salaries of $210. On January 9, the first payday of the next period, the following entry settles the accrued liability (salaries payable) and records salaries expense for seven days of work in January:

Jan. 9			
	Salaries Payable (3 days at $70 per day)	210	
	Salaries Expense (7 days at $70 per day)	490	
	Cash		700
	Paid two weeks' salary including three days accrued in December.		

Assets = Liabilities + Equity
−700   −210   −490

The $210 debit reflects the payment of the liability for the three days' salary accrued on December 31. The $490 debit records the salary for January's first seven working days (including the New Year's Day holiday) as an expense of the new accounting period. The $700 credit records the total amount of cash paid to the employee.

Accrued Revenues

The term **accrued revenues** refers to revenues earned in a period that are both unrecorded and not yet received in cash (or other assets). An example is a technician who bills customers only when the job is done. If one-third of a job is complete by the end of a period, then the technician must record one-third of the expected billing as revenue in that period—even though there is no billing or collection. The adjusting entries for accrued revenues increase assets and increase revenues as shown in Exhibit 3.11. Accrued revenues commonly arise from services, products, interest, and rent. We use service fees and interest to show how to adjust for accrued revenues.

Point: Accrued revenues are also called *accrued assets.*

Exhibit 3.11

Adjusting for Accrued Revenues

Accrued Services Revenue Accrued revenues are not recorded until adjusting entries are made at the end of the accounting period. These accrued revenues are earned but unrecorded because either the buyer has not yet paid for them or the seller has not yet billed the buyer. FastForward provides an example. In the second week of December, it agreed to provide 30 days of consulting services to a local sports club for a fixed fee of $2,700. The terms of the initial agreement call for FastForward to provide services from December 12, 2004, through January 10, 2005, or 30 days of service. The club agrees to pay FastForward $2,700 on January 10, 2005, when the service period is complete. At December 31, 2004, 20 days of services have already been provided. Since the contracted services are not yet entirely provided, FastForward has neither billed the club nor recorded the services already provided. Still, FastForward has earned two-thirds of the 30-day fee, or $1,800 ($2,700 × 20/30). The *revenue recognition principle* implies that it must report the $1,800 on the December income statement. The balance sheet also must report that the club owes FastForward $1,800.

The year-end adjusting entry to account for accrued services revenue is

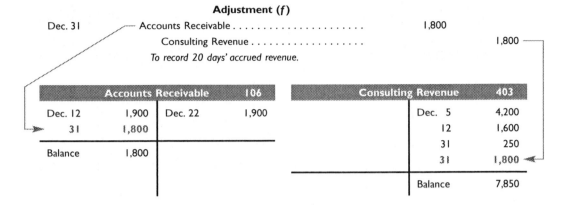

Adjustment (f)

Assets = Liabilities + Equity
+1,800   +1,800

Dec. 31	Accounts Receivable........................	1,800	
	Consulting Revenue...................		1,800
	To record 20 days' accrued revenue.		

Accounts Receivable			106
Dec. 12	1,900	Dec. 22	1,900
31	1,800		
Balance	1,800		

Consulting Revenue		403
	Dec. 5	4,200
	12	1,600
	31	250
	31	1,800
	Balance	7,850

Example: What is the adjusting entry if the 30-day consulting period began on December 22? *Answer:* One-third of the fee is earned:
Accounts Receivable... 900
   Consulting Revenue... 900

Accounts receivable are reported on the balance sheet at $1,800, and the $7,850 of consulting revenue is reported on the income statement. *Not* making the adjustment would understate (1) both consulting revenue and net income by $1,800 in the December income statement and (2) both accounts receivable (assets) and equity by $1,800 on the December 31 balance sheet.

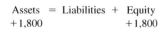

Decision Maker

Loan Officer The owner of an electronics store applies for a business loan. The store's financial statements reveal large increases in current-year revenues and income. Analysis shows that these increases are due to a promotion that let consumers buy now and pay nothing until January 1 of next year. The store recorded these sales as accrued revenue. Does your analysis raise any concerns?

Answer—p. 115

Accrued Interest Revenue In addition to the accrued interest expense we described earlier, interest can yield an accrued revenue when a debtor owes money (or other assets) to a company. If a company is holding notes or accounts receivable that produce interest revenue, we must adjust the accounts to record any earned and yet uncollected interest revenue. The adjusting entry is similar to the one for accruing services revenue. Specifically, we debit Interest Receivable (asset) and credit Interest Revenue.

Future Receipt of Accrued Revenues Accrued revenues at the end of one accounting period result in *cash receipts* in a *future* period(s). To illustrate, recall that FastForward made an adjusting entry for $1,800 to record 20 days' accrued revenue earned from its consulting contract. When FastForward receives $2,700 cash on January 10 for the entire contract amount, it makes the following entry to remove the accrued asset (accounts receivable) and recognize the revenue earned in January. The $2,700 debit reflects the cash received. The $1,800 credit reflects the removal of the receivable, and the $900 credit records the revenue earned in January.

Assets = Liabilities + Equity
+2,700   +900
−1,800

Jan. 10	Cash.................................	2,700	
	Accounts Receivable (20 days at $90 per day)		1,800
	Consulting Revenue (10 days at $90 per day)		900
	Received cash for the accrued asset and recorded earned consulting revenue.		

Links to Financial Statements

A1 Explain how accounting adjustments link to financial statements.

The process of adjusting accounts is intended to bring an asset or liability account balance to its correct amount. It also updates a related expense or revenue account. These adjustments are necessary for transactions and events that extend over more than one period. (Adjusting entries are posted like any other entry.)

Exhibit 3.12 summarizes the four types of transactions requiring adjustment. Understanding this exhibit is important to understanding the adjusting process and its

Exhibit 3.12

	Before Adjusting		
Category	Balance Sheet	Income Statement	Adjusting Entry
Prepaid expenses†	Asset overstated	Expense understated	Dr. Expense
	Equity overstated		Cr. Asset*
Unearned revenues†	Liability overstated	Revenue understated	Dr. Liability
	Equity understated		Cr. Revenue
Accrued expenses	Liability understated	Expense understated	Dr. Expense
	Equity overstated		Cr. Liability
Accrued revenues	Asset understated	Revenue understated	Dr. Asset
	Equity understated		Cr. Revenue

Summary of Adjustments and Financial Statement Links

* For depreciation, the credit is to Accumulated Depreciation (contra asset).

† Exhibit assumes that Prepaid Expenses are initially recorded as assets and that Unearned Revenues are initially recorded as liabilities.

importance to financial statements. Remember that each adjusting entry affects one or more income statement accounts *and* one or more balance sheet accounts (but not cash).

Information about some adjustments is not always available until several days or even weeks after the period-end. This means that some adjusting and closing entries are recorded later than, but dated as of, the last day of the period. One example is a company that receives a utility bill on January 10 for costs incurred for the month of December. When it receives the bill, the company records the expense and the payable as of December 31. Other examples include long-distance phone usage and costs of many Web billings. The December income statement reflects these additional expenses incurred, and the December 31 balance sheet includes these payables, although the amounts were not actually known on December 31.

Decision Ethics

Financial Officer At year-end, the president instructs you, the financial officer, not to record accrued expenses until next year because they will not be paid until then. The president also directs you to record in current-year sales a recent purchase order from a customer that requires merchandise to be delivered two weeks after the year-end. Your company would report a net income instead of a net loss if you carry out these instructions. What do you do?

Answer—p. 115

Quick Check

6. If an adjusting entry for accrued revenues of $200 at year-end is omitted, what is this error's effect on the year-end income statement and balance sheet?

7. What is a contra account? Explain its purpose.

8. What is an accrued expense? Give an example.

9. Describe how an unearned revenue arises. Give an example.

Answers—p. 115

Adjusted Trial Balance

An **unadjusted trial balance** is a list of accounts and balances prepared *before* adjustments are recorded. An **adjusted trial balance** is a list of accounts and balances prepared *after* adjusting entries have been recorded and posted to the ledger.

Exhibit 3.13 shows both the unadjusted and the adjusted trial balances for FastForward at December 31, 2004. The order of accounts in the trial balance is usually set up to match the order in the chart of accounts. Notice that several new accounts arise from the adjusting entries. Each adjustment is identified by a letter in parentheses that links it to an adjusting entry explained earlier. Each amount in the Adjusted Trial Balance columns is computed by taking that account's amount from the Unadjusted Trial Balance columns and adding or subtracting any adjustment(s). To illustrate, Supplies has a $9,720 Dr. balance in the unadjusted columns. Subtracting the $1,050 Cr. amount shown in the adjustments

P2 Explain and prepare an adjusted trial balance.

Exhibit 3.13

Unadjusted and Adjusted Trial Balances

Acct. No.	Account Title	Unadjusted Trial Balance Dr.	Unadjusted Trial Balance Cr.	Adjustments Dr.	Adjustments Cr.	Adjusted Trial Balance Dr.	Adjusted Trial Balance Cr.
		FASTFORWARD Trial Balances December 31, 2004					
101	Cash	$ 3,950				$ 3,950	
106	Accounts receivable	0		(f) $1,800		1,800	
126	Supplies	9,720			(b) $1,050	8,670	
128	Prepaid insurance	2,400			(a) 100	2,300	
167	Equipment	26,000				26,000	
168	Accumulated depreciation—Equip.		$ 0		(c) 375		$ 375
201	Accounts payable		6,200				6,200
209	Salaries payable		0		(e) 210		210
236	Unearned consulting revenue		3,000	(d) 250			2,750
301	C. Taylor, Capital		30,000				30,000
302	C. Taylor, Withdrawals	600				600	
403	Consulting revenue		5,800		(d) 250		7,850
					(f) 1,800		
406	Rental revenue		300				300
612	Depreciation expense—Equip.	0		(c) 375		375	
622	Salaries expense	1,400		(e) 210		1,610	
637	Insurance expense	0		(a) 100		100	
640	Rent expense	1,000				1,000	
652	Supplies expense	0		(b) 1,050		1,050	
690	Utilities expense	230				230	
	Totals	$45,300	$45,300	$3,785	$3,785	$47,685	$47,685

columns yields an adjusted $8,670 Dr. balance for Supplies. An account can have more than one adjustment, such as for Consulting Revenue. Also, some accounts might not require adjustment for this period, such as Accounts Payable.

Preparing Financial Statements

P3 Prepare financial statements from an adjusted trial balance.

We can prepare financial statements directly from information in the *adjusted* trial balance. An adjusted trial balance (see the right-most columns in Exhibit 3.13) includes all accounts and balances appearing in financial statements, and is easier to work from than the entire ledger when preparing financial statements.

Exhibit 3.14 shows how revenue and expense balances are transferred from the adjusted trial balance to the income statement (red lines). The net income and the withdrawals amount is then used to prepare the statement of owner's equity (black lines). Asset and liability balances on the adjusted trial balance are then transferred to the balance sheet (blue lines). The ending capital is determined on the statement of owner's equity and transferred to the balance sheet (green lines).

Point: Sarbanes-Oxley Act requires that financial statements filed with the SEC be certified by the CEO and CFO, including a declaration that the statements fairly present the issuer's operations and financial condition. Violators can receive a $5,000,000 fine and/or 20 years imprisonment.

We usually prepare financial statements in the following order: income statement, statement of owner's equity, and balance sheet. This order makes sense since the balance sheet uses information from the statement of owner's equity, which in turn uses information from the income statement. The statement of cash flows is usually the final statement prepared.

Exhibit 3.14

Preparing the Financial Statements (Adjusted Trial Balance from Exhibit 3.13)

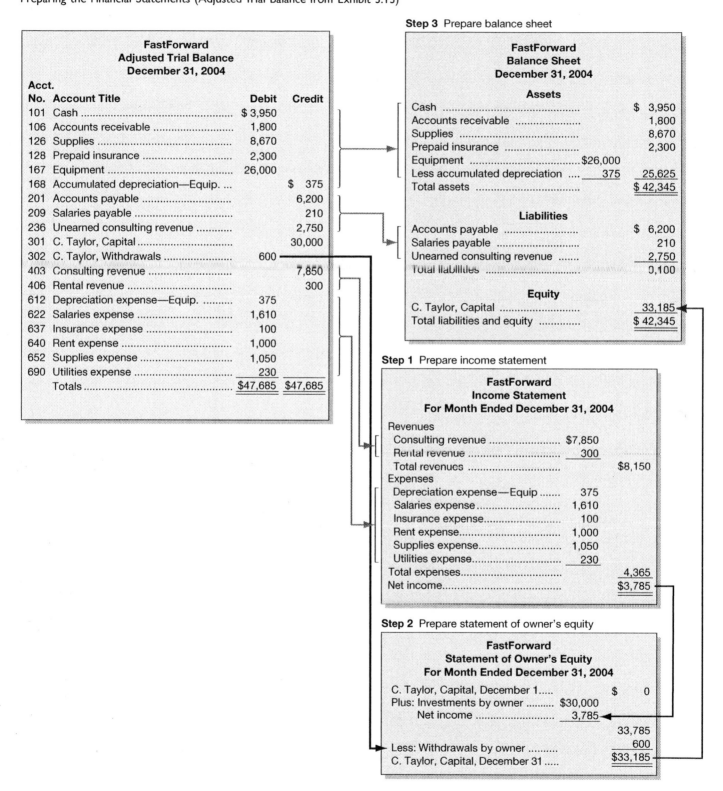

Step 3 Prepare balance sheet

FastForward
Adjusted Trial Balance
December 31, 2004

Acct. No.	Account Title	Debit	Credit
101	Cash	$ 3,950	
106	Accounts receivable	1,800	
126	Supplies	8,670	
128	Prepaid insurance	2,300	
167	Equipment	26,000	
168	Accumulated depreciation—Equip.		$ 375
201	Accounts payable		6,200
209	Salaries payable		210
236	Unearned consulting revenue		2,750
301	C. Taylor, Capital		30,000
302	C. Taylor, Withdrawals	600	
403	Consulting revenue		7,850
406	Rental revenue		300
612	Depreciation expense—Equip.	375	
622	Salaries expense	1,610	
637	Insurance expense	100	
640	Rent expense	1,000	
652	Supplies expense	1,050	
690	Utilities expense	230	
	Totals	$47,685	$47,685

FastForward
Balance Sheet
December 31, 2004

Assets

Cash		$ 3,950
Accounts receivable		1,800
Supplies		8,670
Prepaid insurance		2,300
Equipment	$26,000	
Less accumulated depreciation	375	25,625
Total assets		$ 42,345

Liabilities

Accounts payable	$ 6,200
Salaries payable	210
Unearned consulting revenue	2,750
Total liabilities	9,160

Equity

C. Taylor, Capital	33,185
Total liabilities and equity	$ 42,345

Step 1 Prepare income statement

FastForward
Income Statement
For Month Ended December 31, 2004

Revenues
Consulting revenue	$7,850	
Rental revenue	300	
Total revenues		$8,150

Expenses
Depreciation expense—Equip	375	
Salaries expense	1,610	
Insurance expense	100	
Rent expense	1,000	
Supplies expense	1,050	
Utilities expense	230	
Total expenses		4,365
Net income		$3,785

Step 2 Prepare statement of owner's equity

FastForward
Statement of Owner's Equity
For Month Ended December 31, 2004

C. Taylor, Capital, December 1		$ 0
Plus: Investments by owner	$30,000	
Net income	3,785	
		33,785
Less: Withdrawals by owner		600
C. Taylor, Capital, December 31		$33,185

Quick Check

10. Music-Mart records $1,000 of accrued salaries on December 31. Five days later, on January 5 (the next payday), salaries of $7,000 are paid. What is the January 5 entry?

11. Jordan Air has the following information in its unadjusted and adjusted trial balances:

	Unadjusted		Adjusted	
	Debit	Credit	Debit	Credit
Prepaid insurance	$6,200		$5,900	
Salaries payable		$ 0		$1,400

What are the adjusting entries that Jordan Air likely recorded?

12. What accounts are taken from the adjusted trial balance to prepare an income statement?

13. In preparing financial statements from an adjusted trial balance, what statement is usually prepared second?

Answers—p. 115

Decision Analysis   Profit Margin

A2   Compute profit margin and describe its use in analyzing company performance.

A useful measure of a company's operating results is the ratio of its net income to net sales. This ratio is called **profit margin,** or *return on sales,* and is computed as in Exhibit 3.15.

Exhibit 3.15
Profit Margin

$$\text{Profit margin} = \frac{\text{Net income}}{\text{Net sales}}$$

This ratio is interpreted as reflecting the percent of profit in each dollar of sales. To illustrate how we compute and use profit margin, let's look at the results of **Limited Brands, Inc.,** in Exhibit 3.16 for the period 2000–2003.

Exhibit 3.16
Limited Brands's Profit Margin

	2003	2002	2001	2000
Net income (in mil.)	$ 502	$ 519	$ 428	$ 461
Net sales (in mil.)	$8,445	$8,423	$9,080	$8,765
Profit margin	5.9%	6.2%	4.7%	5.3%
Industry profit margin	1.8%	1.5%	2.5%	2.9%

The Limited's average profit margin is 5.5% during this period. This favorably compares to the average industry profit margin of 2.2%. Moreover, Limited's most recent two years' profit margins are markedly better than earlier years.

Thus, while 2001 was a difficult year for Limited in generating profits on its sales, Limited's performance has slightly improved in 2002–2003. Future success, of course, depends on Limited maintaining and preferably increasing its profit margin.

Demonstration Problem 1

The following information relates to Fanning's Electronics on December 31, 2005. The company, which uses the calendar year as its annual reporting period, initially records prepaid and unearned items in balance sheet accounts (assets and liabilities, respectively).

a. The company's weekly payroll is $8,750, paid each Friday for a five-day workweek. December 31, 2005, falls on a Monday, but the employees will not be paid their wages until Friday, January 4, 2006.

b. Eighteen months earlier, on July 1, 2004, the company purchased equipment that cost $20,000. Its useful life is predicted to be five years, at which time the equipment is expected to be worthless (zero salvage value).

c. On October 1, 2005, the company agreed to work on a new housing development. The company is paid $120,000 on October 1 in advance of future installation of similar alarm systems in 24 new homes. That amount was credited to the Unearned Services Revenue account. Between October 1 and December 31, work on 20 homes was completed.

d. On September 1, 2005, the company purchased a 12-month insurance policy for $1,800. The transaction was recorded with an $1,800 debit to Prepaid Insurance.

e. On December 29, 2005, the company performed a $7,000 service that has not been billed and not recorded as of December 31, 2005.

Required

1. Prepare any necessary adjusting entries on December 31, 2005, in relation to transactions and events *a* through *e*.

2. Prepare T-accounts for the accounts affected by adjusting entries, and post the adjusting entries. Determine the adjusted balances for the Unearned Revenue and the Prepaid Insurance accounts.

3. Complete the following table and determine the amounts and effects of your adjusting entries on the year 2005 income statement and the December 31, 2005, balance sheet. Use up (down) arrows to indicate an increase (decrease) in the Effect columns.

Entry	Amount in the Entry	Effect on Net Income	Effect on Total Assets	Effect on Total Liabilities	Effect on Total Equity

Planning the Solution

- Analyze each situation to determine which accounts need to be updated with an adjustment.
- Calculate the amount of each adjustment and prepare the necessary journal entries.
- Show the amount of each adjustment in the designated accounts, determine the adjusted balance, and identify the balance sheet classification of the account.
- Determine each entry's effect on net income for the year and on total assets, total liabilities, and total equity at the end of the year.

Solution to Demonstration Problem 1

1. Adjusting journal entries.

(a) Dec. 31	Wages Expense.........................	1,750	
	Wages Payable.....................		1,750
	To accrue wages for the last day of the year		
	($8,750 × 1/5).		
(b) Dec. 31	Depreciation Expense—Equipment	4,000	
	Accumulated Depreciation—Equipment.....		4,000
	To record depreciation expense for the year		
	($20,000/5 years = $4,000 per year).		
(c) Dec. 31	Unearned Services Revenue................	100,000	
	Services Revenue.....................		100,000
	To recognize services revenue earned		
	($120,000 × 20/24).		

[continued on next page]

[continued from previous page]

(d) Dec. 31	Insurance Expense.	600	
	Prepaid Insurance.		600
	To adjust for expired portion of insurance *($1,800 × 4/12).*		
(e) Dec. 31	Accounts Receivable	7,000	
	Services Revenue.		7,000
	To record services revenue earned.		

2. T-accounts for adjusting journal entries *a* through *e*.

Wages Expense			Wages Payable	
(a)	1,750		(a)	1,750

Depreciation Expense—Equipment			Accumulated Depreciation—Equipment	
(b)	4,000		(b)	4,000

Unearned Revenue			Services Revenue	
	Unadj. Bal.	120,000	(c)	100,000
(c) 100,000			(e)	7,000
	Adj. Bal.	20,000	Adj. Bal.	107,000

Insurance Expense			Prepaid Insurance	
(d)	600		Unadj. Bal.	1,800
			(d)	600

Accounts Receivable				
(e)	7,000		Adj. Bal. 1,200	

3. Financial statement effects of adjusting journal entries.

Entry	Amount in the Entry	Effect on Net Income	Effect on Total Assets	Effect on Total Liabilities	Effect on Total Equity
a	$ 1,750	$ 1,750 ↓	No effect	$ 1,750 ↑	$ 1,750 ↓
b	4,000	4,000 ↓	$4,000 ↓	No effect	4,000 ↓
c	100,000	100,000 ↑	No effect	$100,000 ↓	100,000 ↑
d	600	600 ↓	$ 600 ↓	No effect	600 ↓
e	7,000	7,000 ↑	$7,000 ↑	No effect	7,000 ↑

Demonstration Problem 2

Use the following adjusted trial balance to answer questions 1–3.

CHOI COMPANY
Adjusted Trial Balance
December 31

	Debit	Credit
Cash	$ 3,050	
Accounts receivable	400	
Prepaid insurance	830	
Supplies	80	
Equipment	217,200	

[continued on next page]

[continued from previous page]

Accumulated depreciation—Equipment		$ 29,100
Wages payable		880
Interest payable		3,600
Unearned rent		460
Long-term notes payable		150,000
M. Choi, Capital		40,340
M. Choi, Withdrawals	21,000	
Rent earned		57,500
Wages expense	25,000	
Utilities expense	1,900	
Insurance expense	3,200	
Supplies expense	250	
Depreciation expense—Equipment	5,970	
Interest expense	3,000	
Totals	$281,880	$281,880

1. Prepare the annual income statement from the adjusted trial balance of Choi Company.

Answer:

CHOI COMPANY Income Statement For Year Ended December 31		
Revenues		
Rent earned		$57,500
Expenses		
Wages expense	$25,000	
Utilities expense	1,900	
Insurance expense	3,200	
Supplies expense	250	
Depreciation expense—Equipment	5,970	
Interest expense	3,000	
Total expenses		39,320
Net income		$18,180

2. Prepare a statement of owner's equity from the adjusted trial balance of Choi Company. Choi's capital account balance of $40,340 consists of a $30,340 beginning-year balance, plus a $10,000 owner investment during the current year.

Answer:

CHOI COMPANY Statement of Owner's Equity For Year Ended December 31		
M. Choi, Beginning-year Capital, December 31		$30,340
Plus: Owner investments	$10,000	
Net income	18,180	28,180
		58,520
Less: Withdrawals by owner		21,000
M. Choi, Year-end Capital, December 31		$37,520

3. Prepare a balance sheet from the adjusted trial balance of Choi Company.

Answer:

CHOI COMPANY
Balance Sheet
December 31

Assets

Cash		$ 3,050
Accounts receivable		400
Prepaid insurance		830
Supplies		80
Equipment	$217,200	
Less accumulated depreciation	29,100	188,100
Total assets		$192,460

Liabilities

Wages payable		$ 880
Interest payable		3,600
Unearned rent		460
Long-term note payable		150,000
Total liabilities		154,940

Equity

M. Choi, Capital		37,520
Total liabilities and equity		$192,460

Alternative Accounting for Prepayments

This appendix explains an alternative in accounting for prepaid expenses and unearned revenues.

Recording the Prepayment of Expenses in Expense Accounts

P4 Identify and explain alternatives in accounting for prepaids.

An alternative method is to record *all* prepaid expenses with debits to expense accounts. If any prepaids remain unused or unexpired at the end of an accounting period, then adjusting entries must transfer the cost of the unused portions from expense accounts to prepaid expense (asset) accounts. This alternative method is acceptable. The financial statements are identical under either method, but the adjusting entries are different. To illustrate the differences between these two methods, let's look at FastForward's cash payment of December 6 for 24 months of insurance coverage beginning on December 1. FastForward recorded that payment with a debit to an asset account, but it could have recorded a debit to an expense account. These alternatives are shown in Exhibit 3A.1.

Exhibit 3A.1

Alternative Initial Entries for Prepaid Expenses

		Payment Recorded as Asset	Payment Recorded as Expense
Dec. 6	Prepaid Insurance	2,400	
	Cash	2,400	
Dec. 6	Insurance Expense		2,400
	Cash		2,400

At the end of its accounting period on December 31, insurance protection for one month has expired. This means $100 ($2,400/24) of insurance coverage expired and is an expense for December. The adjusting entry depends on how the original payment was recorded. This is shown in Exhibit 3A.2.

		Payment Recorded as Asset	Payment Recorded as Expense
Dec. 31	Insurance Expense	100	
	Prepaid Insurance	100	
Dec. 31	Prepaid Insurance		2,300
	Insurance Expense		2,300

Exhibit 3A.2

Adjusting Entry for Prepaid Expenses for the Two Alternatives

When these entries are posted to the accounts in the ledger, we can see that these two methods give identical results. The December 31 adjusted account balances in Exhibit 3A.3 show Prepaid Insurance of $2,300 and Insurance Expense of $100 for both methods.

Exhibit 3A.3

Account Balances under Two Alternatives for Recording Prepaid Expenses

Payment Recorded as Asset				Payment Recorded as Expense		
Prepaid Insurance		**128**		**Prepaid Insurance**		**128**
Dec. 6	2,400	Dec. 31	100	Dec. 31	2,300	
Balance	2,300					

Insurance Expense		**637**		**Insurance Expense**		**637**
Dec. 31	100			Dec. 6	2,400	Dec. 31	2,300
				Balance	100	

Recording the Prepayment of Revenues in Revenue Accounts

As with prepaid expenses, an alternative method is to record *all* unearned revenues with credits to revenue accounts. If any revenues are unearned at the end of an accounting period, then adjusting entries must transfer the unearned portions from revenue accounts to unearned revenue (liability) accounts. This alternative method is acceptable. The adjusting entries are different for these two alternatives, but the financial statements are identical. To illustrate the accounting differences between these two methods, let's look at FastForward's December 26 receipt of $3,000 for consulting services covering the period December 27 to February 24. FastForward recorded this transaction with a credit to a liability account. The alternative is to record it with a credit to a revenue account, as shown in Exhibit 3A.4.

		Receipt Recorded as Liability	Receipt Recorded as Revenue
Dec. 26	Cash	3,000	
	Unearned Consulting Revenue	3,000	
Dec. 26	Cash		3,000
	Consulting Revenue		3,000

Exhibit 3A.4

Alternative Initial Entries for Unearned Revenues

By the end of its accounting period on December 31, FastForward has earned $250 of this revenue. This means $250 of the liability has been satisfied. Depending on how the initial receipt is recorded, the adjusting entry is as shown in Exhibit 3A.5.

		Receipt Recorded as Liability	Receipt Recorded as Revenue
Dec. 31	Unearned Consulting Revenue	250	
	Consulting Revenue	250	
Dec. 31	Consulting Revenue		2,750
	Unearned Consulting Revenue		2,750

Exhibit 3A.5

Adjusting Entry for Unearned Revenues for the Two Alternatives

After adjusting entries are posted, the two alternatives give identical results. The December 31 adjusted account balances in Exhibit 3A.6 show unearned consulting revenue of $2,750 and consulting revenue of $250 for both methods.

Exhibit 3A.6

Account Balances under Two Alternatives for Recording Unearned Revenues

Receipt Recorded as Liability			Receipt Recorded as Revenue		
Unearned Consulting Revenue		**236**	**Unearned Consulting Revenue**		**236**
Dec. 31	250	Dec. 26	3,000		Dec. 31	2,750
		Balance	2,750		
Consulting Revenue		**403**	**Consulting Revenue**		**403**
	Dec. 31	250	Dec. 31	2,750	Dec. 26	3,000
				Balance	250

Summary

C1 Explain the importance of periodic reporting and the time period principle. The value of information is often linked to its timeliness. To provide timely information, accounting systems prepare periodic reports at regular intervals. The time period principle assumes that an organization's activities can be divided into specific time periods for periodic reporting.

C2 Explain accrual accounting and how it makes financial statements more useful. Accrual accounting recognizes revenue when earned and expenses when incurred—not necessarily when cash inflows and outflows occur. This information is valuable in assessing a company's financial position and performance.

C3 Identify the types of adjustments and their purpose. Adjustments can be grouped according to the timing of cash receipts and cash payments relative to when they are recognized as revenues or expenses as follows: prepaid expenses, unearned revenues, accrued expenses, and accrued revenues. Adjusting entries are necessary so that revenues, expenses, assets, and liabilities are correctly reported.

A1 Explain how accounting adjustments link to financial statements. Accounting adjustments bring an asset or liability account balance to its correct amount. They also update related expense or revenue accounts. Every adjusting entry affects one or more income statement accounts *and* one or more balance sheet accounts. An adjusting entry never affects cash.

A2 Compute profit margin and describe its use in analyzing company performance. *Profit margin* is defined as the reporting period's net income divided by its net sales. Profit margin reflects on a company's earnings activities by showing how much income is in each dollar of sales.

P1 Prepare and explain adjusting entries. *Prepaid expenses* refer to items paid for in advance of receiving their

benefits. Prepaid expenses are assets. Adjusting entries for prepaids involve increasing (debiting) expenses and decreasing (crediting) assets. *Unearned* (or *prepaid*) *revenues* refer to cash received in advance of providing products and services. Unearned revenues are liabilities. Adjusting entries for unearned revenues involves increasing (crediting) revenues and decreasing (debiting) unearned revenues. *Accrued expenses* refer to costs incurred in a period that are both unpaid and unrecorded. Adjusting entries for recording accrued expenses involve increasing (debiting) expenses and increasing (crediting) liabilities. *Accrued revenues* refer to revenues earned in a period that are both unrecorded and not yet received in cash. Adjusting entries for recording accrued revenues involve increasing (debiting) assets and increasing (crediting) revenues.

P2 Explain and prepare an adjusted trial balance. An adjusted trial balance is a list of accounts and balances prepared after recording and posting adjusting entries. Financial statements are often prepared from the adjusted trial balance.

P3 Prepare financial statements from an adjusted trial balance. Revenue and expense balances are reported on the income statement. Asset, liability, and equity balances are reported on the balance sheet. We usually prepare statements in the following order: income statement, statement of owner's equity, balance sheet, and statement of cash flows.

P4ᴬ Identify and explain alternatives in accounting for prepaids. Charging all prepaid expenses to expense accounts when they are purchased is acceptable. When this is done, adjusting entries must transfer any unexpired amounts from expense accounts to asset accounts. Crediting all unearned revenues to revenue accounts when cash is received is also acceptable. In this case, the adjusting entries must transfer any unearned amounts from revenue accounts to unearned revenue accounts.

Guidance Answers to **Decision Maker** and **Decision Ethics**

Investor Prepaid expenses are items paid for in advance of receiving their benefits. They are assets and are expensed as they are used up. The publishing company's treatment of the signing bonus

is acceptable provided future book sales can at least match the $500,000 expense. As an investor, you are concerned about the risk of future book sales. The riskier the likelihood of future book sales is, the more likely your analysis is to treat the $500,000, or a portion of it, as an expense, not a prepaid expense (asset).

Entrepreneur Depreciation is a process of cost allocation, not asset valuation. Knowing the depreciation schedule is not especially useful in your estimation of what the building and equipment are currently worth. Your own assessment of the age, quality, and usefulness of the building and equipment is more important.

Loan Officer Your concern in lending to this store arises from analysis of current-year sales. While increased revenues and income are fine, your concern is with collectibility of these promotional sales. If the owner sold products to customers with poor records of paying bills, then collectibility of these sales is low. Your analysis must assess this possibility and recognize any expected losses.

Financial Officer Omitting accrued expenses and recognizing revenue early can mislead financial statement users. One action is to request a second meeting with the president so you can explain that accruing expenses when incurred and recognizing revenue when earned are required practices. If the president persists, you might discuss the situation with legal counsel and any auditors involved. Your ethical action might cost you this job, but the potential pitfalls for falsification of statements, reputation loss, personal integrity, and other costs are too great.

Guidance Answers to Quick Checks

1. An annual reporting (or accounting) period covers one year and refers to the preparation of annual financial statements. The annual reporting period is not always a calendar year that ends on December 31. An organization can adopt a fiscal year consisting of any consecutive 12 months or 52 weeks.

2. Interim financial statements (covering less than one year) are prepared to provide timely information to decision makers.

3. The revenue recognition principle and the matching principle lead most directly to the adjusting process.

4. No. Cash basis accounting is not consistent with the matching principle because it reports expenses when paid, not in the period when revenue is earned as a result of those expenses.

5. No expense is reported in 2005. Under cash basis accounting, the entire $4,800 is reported as an expense in April 2004 when the premium is paid.

6. If the accrued revenues adjustment of $200 is not made, then both revenues and net income are understated by $200 on the current year's income statement, and both assets and equity are understated by $200 on the balance sheet.

7. A contra account is an account that is subtracted from the balance of a related account. Use of a contra account provides more information than simply reporting a net amount.

8. An accrued expense is a cost incurred in a period that is both unpaid and unrecorded prior to adjusting entries. One example is salaries earned but not yet paid at period-end.

9. An unearned revenue arises when a firm receives cash (or other assets) from a customer before providing the services or products to the customer. A magazine subscription paid in advance is one example; season ticket sales is another.

10.
Salaries Payable	1,000	
Salaries Expense	6,000	
Cash		7,000

Paid salary including accrual from December.

11. The probable adjusting entries of Jordan Air are:

| Insurance Expense | 300 | |
| Prepaid Insurance | | 300 |

To record insurance expired.

| Salaries Expense | 1,400 | |
| Salaries Payable | | 1,400 |

To record accrued salaries.

12. Revenue accounts and expense accounts.

13. Statement of owner's equity.

Key Terms

Key Terms are available at the book's Website for learning and testing in an online Flashcard Format.

Accounting period (p. 94)	**Cash basis accounting** (p. 95)	**Prepaid expenses** (p. 97)
Accrual basis accounting (p. 95)	**Contra account** (p. 99)	**Profit margin** (p. 108)
Accrued expenses (p. 101)	**Depreciation** (p. 99)	**Straight-line depreciation method** (p. 99)
Accrued revenues (p. 103)	**Fiscal year** (p. 95)	**Time period principle** (p. 94)
Adjusted trial balance (p. 105)	**Interim financial statements** (p. 95)	**Unadjusted trial balance** (p. 105)
Adjusting entry (p. 97)	**Matching principle** (p. 96)	**Unearned revenues** (p. 100)
Annual financial statements (p. 95)	**Natural business year** (p. 95)	
Book value (p. 100)	**Plant assets** (p. 99)	

Personal Interactive Quiz

Personal Interactive Quizzes A and B are available at the book's Website to reinforce and assess your learning.

Superscript letter [A] *denotes assignments based on Appendix 3A.*

Discussion Questions

1. What is the difference between the cash basis and the accrual basis of accounting?

2. Why is the accrual basis of accounting generally preferred over the cash basis?

3. What type of business is most likely to select a fiscal year that corresponds to its natural business year instead of the calendar year?

4. Where is a prepaid expense reported in the financial statements?

5. What type of asset(s) requires adjusting entries to record depreciation?

6. What contra account is used when recording and reporting the effects of depreciation? Why is it used?

7. Where is unearned revenue reported in financial statements?

8. What is an accrued revenue? Give an example.

9. [A]If a company initially records prepaid expenses with debits to expense accounts, what type of account is debited in the adjusting entries for those prepaid expenses?

10. Review the balance sheet of **Krispy Kreme** in Appendix A. Identify two asset accounts that require adjustment before annual financial statements can be prepared. What would be the effect on the income statement if these two asset accounts were not adjusted?

11. Review the balance sheet of **Tastykake** in Appendix A. In addition to Prepayments, identify two accounts (either assets or liabilities) requiring adjusting entries.

12. Refer to **Harley-Davidson**'s balance sheet in Appendix A. If it made an adjustment for unpaid wages at year-end, where would the Accrued Wages Expense be reported on its balance sheet? **Harley-Davidson**

Red numbers denote Discussion Questions that involve decision-making.

Homework Manager 🖱 *repeats all numerical Quick Study assignments on the book's Website with new numbers each time they are worked. It can be used in practice, homework, or exam mode.* ↘

QUICK STUDY

QS 3-1

Identifying accounting adjustments

C3

Classify the following adjusting entries as involving prepaid expenses (PE), unearned revenues (UR), accrued expenses (AE), or accrued revenues (AR).

a. _____ To record revenue earned that was previously received as cash in advance.

b. _____ To record annual depreciation expense.

c. _____ To record wages expense incurred but not yet paid (nor recorded).

d. _____ To record revenue earned but not yet billed (nor recorded).

e. _____ To record expiration of prepaid insurance.

QS 3-2

Adjusting prepaid expenses

P1

a. On July 1, 2005, Beyonce Company paid $1,800 for six months of insurance coverage. No adjustments have been made to the Prepaid Insurance account, and it is now December 31, 2005. Prepare the journal entry to reflect expiration of the insurance as of December 31, 2005.

b. Tyrell Company has a Supplies account balance of $1,000 on January 1, 2005. During 2005, it purchased $3,000 of supplies. As of December 31, 2005, a supplies inventory shows $1,300 of supplies available. Prepare the adjusting journal entry to correctly report the balance of the Supplies account and the Supplies Expense account as of December 31, 2005.

QS 3-3

Adjusting for depreciation

P1

a. Carlos Company purchases $30,000 of equipment on January 1, 2005. The equipment is expected to last five years and be worth $5,000 at the end of that time. Prepare the entry to record one year's depreciation expense for the equipment as of December 31, 2005.

b. Chavez Company purchases $40,000 of land on January 1, 2005. The land is expected to last indefinitely. What depreciation adjustment, if any, should be made with respect to the Land account as of December 31, 2005?

a. Eager receives $20,000 cash in advance for 4 months of legal services on October 1, 2005, and records it by debiting Cash and crediting Unearned Revenue both for $20,000. It is now December 31, 2005, and Eager has provided legal services as planned. What adjusting entry should Eager make to account for the work performed from October 1 through December 31, 2005?

b. S. Morford started a new publication called *Contest News*. Her subscribers pay $48 to receive 12 issues. With every new subscriber, Morford debits Cash and credits Unearned Subscription Revenue for the amounts received. Morford has 100 new subscribers as of July 1, 2005. She sends *Contest News* to each of these subscribers every month from July through December. Assuming no changes in subscribers, prepare the journal entry that Morford must make as of December 31, 2005, to adjust the Subscription Revenue account and the Unearned Subscription Revenue account.

QS 3-4
Adjusting for unearned revenues

A1 P1

Matia Mouder employs one college student every summer in her coffee shop. The student works the five weekdays and is paid on the following Monday. (For example, a student who works Monday through Friday, June 1 through June 5, is paid for that work on Monday, June 8.) Mouder adjusts her books monthly, if needed, to show salaries earned but unpaid at month-end. The student works the last week of July—Friday is August 1. If the student earns $100 per day, what adjusting entry must Mouder make on July 31 to correctly record accrued salaries expense for July?

QS 3-5
Accruing salaries

A1 P1

Adjusting entries affect at least one balance sheet account and at least one income statement account. For the following entries, identify the account to be debited and the account to be credited. Indicate which of the accounts is the income statement account and which is the balance sheet account.

a. Entry to record revenue earned that was previously received as cash in advance.

b. Entry to record annual depreciation expense.

c. Entry to record wage expenses incurred but not yet paid (nor recorded).

d. Entry to record revenue earned but not yet billed (nor recorded).

e. Entry to record expiration of prepaid insurance.

QS 3-6
Recording and analyzing adjusting entries

A1

During the year, Lola Co. recorded prepayments of expenses in asset accounts, and cash receipts of unearned revenues in liability accounts. At the end of its annual accounting period, the company must make three adjusting entries: (1) accrue salaries expense, (2) adjust the Unearned Services Revenue account to recognize earned revenue, and (3) record services revenue earned for which cash will be received the following period. For each of these adjusting entries (1), (2), and (3), indicate the account from *a* through *g* to be debited and the account to be credited.

a. Accounts Receivable   **e.** Unearned Services Revenue

b. Prepaid Salaries   **f.** Salaries Expense

c. Cash   **g.** Services Revenue

d. Salaries Payable

QS 3-7
Preparing adjusting entries

C3 P1

The following information is taken from Cruz Company's unadjusted and adjusted trial balances:

	Unadjusted		Adjusted	
	Debit	Credit	Debit	Credit
Prepaid insurance	$4,100		$3,700	
Interest payable		$ 0		$800

Given this information, which of the following is likely included among its adjusting entries?

a. A $400 credit to Prepaid Insurance and an $800 debit to Interest Payable.

b. A $400 debit to Insurance Expense and an $800 debit to Interest Payable.

c. A $400 debit to Insurance Expense and an $800 debit to Interest Expense.

QS 3-8
Interpreting adjusting entries

C2 P2

In its first year of operations, Harden Co. earned $39,000 in revenues and received $33,000 cash from these customers. The company incurred expenses of $22,500 but had not paid $2,250 of them at year-end. Harden also prepaid $3,750 cash for expenses that would be incurred the next year. Calculate the first year's net income under both the cash basis and the accrual basis of accounting.

QS 3-9
Computing accrual and cash income

C1 C2

QS 3-10
Determining effects of
adjusting entries

C3 A1

In making adjusting entries at the end of its accounting period, Gomez Consulting failed to record $1,600 of insurance coverage that had expired. This $1,600 cost had been initially debited to the Prepaid Insurance account. The company also failed to record accrued salaries expense of $1,000. As a result of these two oversights, the financial statements for the reporting period will [choose one] (1) understate assets by $1,600; (2) understate expenses by $2,600; (3) understate net income by $1,000; or (4) overstate liabilities by $1,000.

QS 3-11
Analyzing profit margin

A2

Yang Company reported net income of $37,925 and net sales of $390,000 for the current year. Calculate Yang's profit margin and interpret the result. Assume that Yang's competitors' average profit margin is 15%.

QS 3-12^A
Preparing adjusting entries

C3 P4

Diego Consulting initially records prepaid and unearned items in income statement accounts. Given Diego Consulting's accounting practices, which of the following applies to the preparation of adjusting entries at the end of its first accounting period?

a. Earned but unbilled (and unrecorded) consulting fees are recorded with a debit to Unearned Consulting Fees and a credit to Consulting Fees Earned.

b. Unpaid salaries are recorded with a debit to Prepaid Salaries and a credit to Salaries Expense.

c. The cost of unused office supplies is recorded with a debit to Supplies Expense and a credit to Office Supplies.

d. Unearned fees (on which cash was received in advance earlier in the period) are recorded with a debit to Consulting Fees Earned and a credit to Unearned Consulting Fees.

Homework Manager repeats all numerical Exercises on the book's Website with new numbers each time they are worked. It can be used in practice, homework, or exam mode.

EXERCISES

Exercise 3-1
Classifying adjusting entries

C3

In the blank space beside each adjusting entry, enter the letter of the explanation A through F that most closely describes the entry:

A. To record this period's depreciation expense.

B. To record accrued salaries expense.

C. To record this period's use of a prepaid expense.

D. To record accrued interest revenue.

E. To record accrued interest expense.

F. To record the earning of previously un-earned income.

_____	1.	Salaries Expense	13,280	
		Salaries Payable		13,280
_____	2.	Interest Expense	2,208	
		Interest Payable		2,208
_____	3.	Insurance Expense	3,180	
		Prepaid Insurance		3,180
_____	4.	Unearned Professional Fees	19,250	
		Professional Fees Earned		19,250
_____	5.	Interest Receivable	3,300	
		Interest Revenue		3,300
_____	6.	Depreciation Expense	38,217	
		Accumulated Depreciation		38,217

Exercise 3-2
Preparing adjusting entries

P1

For each of the following separate cases, prepare adjusting entries required for financial statements for the year ended (or date of) December 31, 2005. (Assume that prepaid expenses are initially recorded in asset accounts and that fees collected in advance of work are initially recorded as liabilities.)

a. One-third of the work related to $30,000 cash received in advance is performed this period.

b. Wages of $9,000 are earned by workers but not paid as of December 31, 2005.

c. Depreciation on the company's equipment for 2005 is $19,127.

d. The Office Supplies account had a $480 debit balance on December 31, 2004. During 2005, $5,349 of office supplies is purchased. A physical count of supplies at December 31, 2005, shows $587 of supplies available.

e. The Prepaid Insurance account had a $5,000 balance on December 31, 2004. An analysis of insurance policies shows that $2,200 of unexpired insurance benefits remain at December 31, 2005.

Check (e) Dr. Insurance Expense, $2,800; (f) Cr. Interest Revenue, $750

f. The company has earned (but not recorded) $750 of interest from investments in CDs for the year ended December 31, 2005. The interest revenue will be received on January 10, 2006.

g. The company has a bank loan and has incurred (but not recorded) interest expenses of $3,500 for the year ended December 31, 2005. The company must pay the interest on January 2, 2006.

Prepare adjusting journal entries for the year ended (or date of) December 31, 2005, for each of these separate situations. Assume that prepaid expenses are initially recorded in asset accounts. Also assume that fees collected in advance of work are initially recorded as liabilities.

Exercise 3-3
Preparing adjusting entries

P1

a. Depreciation on the company's equipment for 2005 is computed to be $16,000.

b. The Prepaid Insurance account had a $7,000 debit balance at December 31, 2005, before adjusting for the costs of any expired coverage. An analysis of the company's insurance policies showed that $1,040 of unexpired insurance coverage remains.

c. The Office Supplies account had a $300 debit balance on December 31, 2004; and $2,680 of office supplies was purchased during the year. The December 31, 2005, physical count showed $354 of supplies available.

Check (c) Dr. Office Supplies Expense, $2,626; (e) Dr. Insurance Expense, $4,600

d. One-half of the work related to $10,000 cash received in advance was performed this period.

e. The Prepaid Insurance account had a $5,600 debit balance at December 31, 2005, before adjusting for the costs of any expired coverage. An analysis of insurance policies showed that $4,600 of coverage had expired.

f. Wage expenses of $4,000 have been incurred but are not paid as of December 31, 2005.

Pablo Management has five part-time employees, each of whom earns $100 per day. They are normally paid on Fridays for work completed Monday through Friday of the same week. They were paid in full on Friday, December 28, 2005. The next week, the five employees worked only four days because New Year's Day was an unpaid holiday. Show (a) the adjusting entry that would be recorded on Monday, December 31, 2005, and (b) the journal entry that would be made to record payment of the employees' wages on Friday, January 4, 2006.

Exercise 3-4
Adjusting and paying accrued wages

C1 P1

Determine the missing amounts in each of these four separate situations a through d:

Exercise 3-5
Determining cost flows through accounts

C1 A1 P1

	a	b	c	d
Supplies available—prior year-end	$ 300	$1,600	$1,360	?
Supplies purchased during the current year	2,100	5,400	?	$6,000
Supplies available—current year-end	750	?	1,840	800
Supplies expense for the current year	?	1,300	9,600	6,575

The following three separate situations require adjusting journal entries to prepare financial statements as of April 30. For each situation, present both the April 30 adjusting entry and the subsequent entry during May to record the payment of the accrued expenses.

Exercise 3-6
Adjusting and paying accrued expenses

A1 P1

a. On April 1, the company retained an attorney at a flat monthly fee of $2,500. This amount is payable on the 12th of the following month.

b. A $780,000 note payable requires 9.6% annual interest, or $6,240 to be paid at the end of each 30 days. The interest was last paid on April 20 and the next payment is due on May 20. As of April 30, $2,080 of interest has accrued.

Check (b) May 20 Dr. Interest Expense, $4,160

c. Total weekly salaries expense for all employees is $9,000. This amount is paid at the end of the day on Friday of each five-day workweek. April 30 falls on Tuesday of this year, which means that the employees had worked two days since the last payday. The next payday is May 3.

Exercise 3-7
Determining assets and expenses for accrual and cash accounting

C2

On March 1, 2003, a company paid a $16,200 premium on a 36-month insurance policy for coverage beginning on that date. Refer to that policy and fill in the blanks in the following table:

	Balance Sheet Insurance Asset Using		Insurance Expense Using	
	Accrual Basis	Cash Basis		Accrual Basis	Cash Basis
Dec. 31, 2003	$_____	$_____	2003	$_____	$_____
Dec. 31, 2004	_____	_____	2004	_____	_____
Dec. 31, 2005	_____	_____	2005	_____	_____
Dec. 31, 2006	_____	_____	2006	_____	_____
			Total	$_____	$_____

Check 2005 insurance expense: Accrual, $5,400; Cash, $0. Dec. 31, 2005, asset: Accrual, $900; Cash, $0.

Exercise 3-8
Analyzing and preparing adjusting entries

A1 P1 P3

Following are two income statements for Kendis Co. for the year ended December 31. The left column is prepared before any adjusting entries are recorded, and the right column includes the effects of adjusting entries. The company records cash receipts and payments related to unearned and prepaid items in balance sheet accounts. Analyze the statements and prepare the eight adjusting entries that likely were recorded. (*Note:* 30% of the $6,000 adjustment for Fees Earned has been earned but not billed, and the other 70% has been earned by performing services that were paid for in advance.)

KENDIS CO. Income Statements For Year Ended December 31		
	Unadjusted	Adjusted
Revenues		
Fees earned	$24,000	$30,000
Commissions earned	42,500	42,500
Total revenues	66,500	72,500
Expenses		
Depreciation expense—Computers	0	1,500
Depreciation expense—Office furniture	0	1,750
Salaries expense	12,500	14,950
Insurance expense	0	1,300
Rent expense	4,500	4,500
Office supplies expense	0	480
Advertising expense	3,000	3,000
Utilities expense	1,250	1,320
Total expenses	21,250	28,800
Net income	$45,250	$43,700

Exercise 3-9
Computing and interpreting profit margin

A2

Use the following information to compute profit margin for each separate company *a* through *e*:

	Net Income	**Net Sales**		**Net Income**	**Net Sales**
a.	$ 5,390	$ 44,830	**d.**	$55,234	$1,458,999
b.	87,644	398,954	**e.**	70,158	435,925
c.	93,385	257,082			

Which of the five companies is the most profitable according to the profit margin ratio? Interpret that company's profit margin ratio.

Exercise 3-10[A]
Adjusting for prepaids recorded as expenses and unearned revenues recorded as revenues

P4

On-The-Mark Construction began operations on December 1. In setting up its accounting procedures, the company decided to debit expense accounts when it prepays its expenses and to credit revenue accounts when customers pay for services in advance. Prepare journal entries for items *a* through *d* and the adjusting entries as of its December 31 period-end for items *e* through *g*.

a. Supplies are purchased on December 1 for $3,000 cash.

b. The company prepaid its insurance premiums for $1,440 cash on December 2.

c. On December 15, the company receives an advance payment of $12,000 cash from a customer for remodeling work.

d. On December 28, the company receives $3,600 cash from another customer for remodeling work to be performed in January.

e. A physical count on December 31 indicates that On-The-Mark has $1,920 of supplies available.

f. An analysis of the insurance policies in effect on December 31 shows that $240 of insurance coverage had expired.

g. As of December 31, only one remodeling project has been worked on and completed. The $6,300 fee for this project had been received in advance.

Check (f) Cr. Insurance Expense, $1,200; (g) Dr. Remodeling Fees Earned, $9,300

Cosmo Company experienced the following events and transactions during July:

Exercise 3-11[A]
Recording and reporting revenues received in advance

P4

July 1 Received $2,000 cash in advance of performing work for Jill Dwyer.
6 Received $8,400 cash in advance of performing work for Lisa Poe.
12 Completed the job for Dwyer.
18 Received $7,500 cash in advance of performing work for Vern Hillsman.
27 Completed the job for Poe.
31 None of the work for Hillsman has been performed.

a. Prepare journal entries (including any adjusting entries as of the end of the month) to record these events using the procedure of initially crediting the Unearned Fees account when payment is received from a customer in advance of performing services.

b. Prepare journal entries (including any adjusting entries as of the end of the month) to record these events using the procedure of initially crediting the Fees Earned account when payment is received from a customer in advance of performing services.

c. Under each method, determine the amount of earned fees reported on the income statement for July and the amount of unearned fees reported on the balance sheet as of July 31.

Check (c) Fees Earned, $10,400

For each of the following entries, enter the letter of the explanation that most closely describes it in the space beside each entry. (You can use letters more than once.)

PROBLEM SET A

Problem 3-1A
Identifying adjusting entries with explanations

C3 P1

A. To record receipt of unearned revenue.
B. To record this period's earning of prior unearned revenue.
C. To record payment of an accrued expense.
D. To record receipt of an accrued revenue.
E. To record an accrued expense.
F. To record an accrued revenue.
G. To record this period's use of a prepaid expense.
H. To record payment of a prepaid expense.
I. To record this period's depreciation expense.

___	1.	Rent Expense	2,000
		Prepaid Rent	2,000
___	2.	Interest Expense	1,000
		Interest Payable	1,000
___	3.	Depreciation Expense	4,000
		Accumulated Depreciation	4,000
___	4.	Unearned Professional Fees	3,000
		Professional Fees Earned	3,000
___	5.	Insurance Expense	4,200
		Prepaid Insurance	4,200
___	6.	Salaries Payable	1,400
		Cash	1,400
___	7.	Prepaid Rent	4,500
		Cash	4,500
___	8.	Salaries Expense	6,000
		Salaries Payable	6,000
___	9.	Interest Receivable	5,000
		Interest Revenue	5,000
___	10.	Cash	9,000
		Accounts Receivable (from consulting)	9,000
___	11.	Cash	7,500
		Unearned Professional Fees	7,500
___	12.	Cash	2,000
		Interest Receivable	2,000

Problem 3-2A
Preparing adjusting and
subsequent journal entries

C1 A1 P1

Maja Co. follows the practice of recording prepaid expenses and unearned revenues in balance sheet accounts. Maja's annual accounting period ends on December 31, 2005. The following information concerns the adjusting entries to be recorded as of that date:

a. The Office Supplies account started the year with a $3,000 balance. During 2005, the company purchased supplies for $12,400, which was added to the Office Supplies account. The inventory of supplies available at December 31, 2005, totaled $2,640.

b. An analysis of the company's insurance policies provided these facts:

Policy	Date of Purchase	Months of Coverage	Cost
A	April 1, 2004	24	$15,840
B	April 1, 2005	36	13,068
C	August 1, 2005	12	2,700

The total premium for each policy was paid in full (for all months) at the purchase date, and the Prepaid Insurance account was debited for the full cost. (Note that year-end adjusting entries for Prepaid Insurance were properly recorded in all prior years.)

c. The company has 15 employees, who earn a total of $2,100 in salaries each working day. They are paid each Monday for their work in the five-day workweek ending on the previous Friday. Assume that December 31, 2005, is a Tuesday, and all 15 employees worked the first two days of that week. Because New Year's Day is a paid holiday, they will be paid salaries for five full days on Monday, January 6, 2006.

d. The company purchased a building on January 1, 2005. It cost $855,000 and is expected to have a $45,000 salvage value at the end of its predicted 30-year life.

e. Since the company is not large enough to occupy the entire building it owns, it rented space to a tenant at $2,400 per month, starting on November 1, 2005. The rent was paid on time on November 1, and the amount received was credited to the Rent Earned account. However, the tenant has not paid the December rent. The company has worked out an agreement with the tenant, who has promised to pay both December and January rent in full on January 15. The tenant has agreed not to fall behind again.

f. On November 1, the company rented space to another tenant for $2,175 per month. The tenant paid five months' rent in advance on that date. The payment was recorded with a credit to the Unearned Rent account.

Required

Check (1*b*) Dr. Insurance Expense, $12,312 (1*d*) Dr. Depreciation Expense, $27,000

1. Use the information to prepare adjusting entries as of December 31, 2005.

2. Prepare journal entries to record the first subsequent cash transaction in 2006 for parts *c* and *e*.

Problem 3-3A
Preparing adjusting entries,
adjusted trial balance, and
financial statements

A1 P1 P2 P3

mhhe.com/larson

Watson Technical Institute (WTI), a school owned by Tom Watson, provides training to individuals who pay tuition directly to the school. WTI also offers training to groups in off-site locations. Its unadjusted trial balance as of December 31, 2005, follows. WTI initially records prepaid expenses and unearned revenues in balance sheet accounts. Descriptions of items *a* through *h* that require adjusting entries on December 31, 2005, follow.

Additional Information Items

a. An analysis of the school's insurance policies shows that $3,000 of coverage has expired.

b. An inventory count shows that teaching supplies costing $2,600 are available at year-end 2005.

c. Annual depreciation on the equipment is $12,000.

d. Annual depreciation on the professional library is $6,000.

e. On November 1, the school agreed to do a special six-month course (starting immediately) for a client. The contract calls for a monthly fee of $2,200, and the client paid the first five months' fees in advance. When the cash was received, the Unearned Training Fees account was credited. The fee for the sixth month will be recorded when it is collected in 2006.

f. On October 15, the school agreed to teach a four-month class (beginning immediately) for an individual for $3,000 tuition per month payable at the end of the class. The services are being provided as agreed, and no payment has yet been received.

g. The school's two employees are paid weekly. As of the end of the year, two days' wages have accrued at the rate of $100 per day for each employee.

h. The balance in the Prepaid Rent account represents rent for December.

WATSON TECHNICAL INSTITUTE Unadjusted Trial Balance December 31, 2005		
	Debit	**Credit**
Cash	$ 26,000	
Accounts receivable	0	
Teaching supplies	10,000	
Prepaid insurance	15,000	
Prepaid rent	2,000	
Professional library	30,000	
Accumulated depreciation—Professional library		$ 9,000
Equipment	70,000	
Accumulated depreciation—Equipment		16,000
Accounts payable		36,000
Salaries payable		0
Unearned training fees		11,000
T. Watson, Capital		63,600
T. Watson, Withdrawals	40,000	
Tuition fees earned		102,000
Training fees earned		38,000
Depreciation expense—Professional library	0	
Depreciation expense—Equipment	0	
Salaries expense	48,000	
Insurance expense	0	
Rent expense	22,000	
Teaching supplies expense	0	
Advertising expense	7,000	
Utilities expense	5,600	
Totals	$ 275,600	$ 275,600

Required

1. Prepare T-accounts (representing the ledger) with balances from the unadjusted trial balance.

2. Prepare the necessary adjusting journal entries for items *a* through *h* and post them to the T-accounts. Assume that adjusting entries are made only at year-end.

3. Update balances in the T-accounts for the adjusting entries and prepare an adjusted trial balance.

4. Prepare Watson Technical Institute's income statement and statement of owner's equity for the year 2005 and prepare its balance sheet as of December 31, 2005.

Check   (2e) Cr. Training Fees Earned, $4,400; (2f) Cr. Tuition Fees Earned, $7,500; (3) Adj. Trial balance totals, $301,500; (4) Net income, $38,500; Ending T. Watson, Capital $62,100

A six-column table for JJW Company follows. The first two columns contain the unadjusted trial balance for the company as of July 31, 2005. The last two columns contain the adjusted trial balance as of the same date.

Required

Analysis Component

1. Analyze the differences between the unadjusted and adjusted trial balances to determine the eight adjustments that likely were made. Show the results of your analysis by inserting these adjustment amounts in the table's two middle columns. Label each adjustment with a letter *a* through *h* and provide a short description of it at the bottom of the table.

Problem 3-4A
Interpreting unadjusted and adjusted trial balances, and preparing financial statements

C3 A1 P1 P2 P3

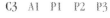

mhhe.com/larson

Preparation Component

2. Use the information in the adjusted trial balance to prepare the company's (*a*) income statement and its statement of owner's equity for the year ended July 31, 2005 (*note:* J. Winner, Capital at July 31, 2004, was $28,420, and the current-year withdrawals were $10,000), and (*b*) the balance sheet as of July 31, 2005.

	Unadjusted Trial Balance		Adjustments		Adjusted Trial Balance	
Cash	$ 27,000				$ 27,000	
Accounts receivable	12,000				22,460	
Office supplies	18,000				3,000	
Prepaid insurance	7,320				4,880	
Office equipment	92,000				92,000	
Accum. depreciation— Office equip.		$ 12,000				$ 18,000
Accounts payable		9,300				10,200
Interest payable		0				800
Salaries payable		0				6,600
Unearned consulting fees		16,000				14,300
Long-term notes payable		44,000				44,000
J. Winner, Capital		28,420				28,420
J. Winner, Withdrawals	10,000				10,000	
Consulting fees earned		156,000				168,160
Depreciation expense— Office equip.	0				6,000	
Salaries expense	71,000				77,600	
Interest expense	1,400				2,200	
Insurance expense	0				2,440	
Rent expense	13,200				13,200	
Office supplies expense	0				15,000	
Advertising expense	13,800				14,700	
Totals	$265,720	$265,720			$290,480	$290,480

Problem 3-5A

Preparing financial statements from the adjusted trial balance and calculating profit margin

P3 A1 A2

The adjusted trial balance for Callahay Company as of December 31, 2005, follows:

	Debit	Credit
Cash	$ 22,000	
Accounts receivable	44,000	
Interest receivable	10,000	
Notes receivable (due in 90 days)	160,000	
Office supplies	8,000	
Automobiles	160,000	
Accumulated depreciation—Automobiles		$ 42,000
Equipment	130,000	
Accumulated depreciation—Equipment		10,000
Land	70,000	
Accounts payable		88,000
Interest payable		12,000
Salaries payable		11,000
Unearned fees		22,000
Long-term notes payable		130,000
J. Callahay, Capital		247,800
J. Callahay, Withdrawals	38,000	

[continued on next page]

[continued from previous page]

Fees earned		420,000
Interest earned		16,000
Depreciation expense—Automobiles	18,000	
Depreciation expense—Equipment	10,000	
Salaries expense	180,000	
Wages expense	32,000	
Interest expense	24,000	
Office supplies expense	26,000	
Advertising expense	50,000	
Repairs expense—Automobiles	16,800	
Totals	$998,800	$998,800

Required

1. Use the information in the adjusted trial balance to prepare (*a*) the income statement for the year ended December 31, 2005; (*b*) the statement of owner's equity for the year ended December 31, 2005; and (*c*) the balance sheet as of December 31, 2005.

2. Calculate the profit margin for year 2005.

Check (1) Total assets, $552,000

Quisp Co. had the following transactions in the last two months of its year ended December 31:

Nov. 1 Paid $1,500 cash for future newspaper advertising.
1 Paid $2,160 cash for 12 months of insurance through October 31 of the next year.
30 Received $3,300 cash for future services to be provided to a customer.
Dec. 1 Paid $2,700 cash for a consultant's services to be received over the next three months.
15 Received $7,650 cash for future services to be provided to a customer.
31 Of the advertising paid for on November 1, $900 worth is not yet used.
31 A portion of the insurance paid for on November 1 has expired. No adjustment was made in November to Prepaid Insurance.
31 Services worth $1,200 are not yet provided to the customer who paid on November 30.
31 One-third of the consulting services paid for on December 1 have been received.
31 The company has performed $3,000 of services that the customer paid for on December 15.

Problem 3-6A[A]
Recording prepaid expenses and unearned revenues

P1 P4

Required

1. Prepare entries for these transactions under the method that records prepaid expenses as assets and records unearned revenues as liabilities. Also prepare adjusting entries at the end of the year.

2. Prepare entries for these transactions under the method that records prepaid expenses as expenses and records unearned revenues as revenues. Also prepare adjusting entries at the end of the year.

Analysis Component

3. Explain why the alternative sets of entries in requirements 1 and 2 do not result in different financial statement amounts.

For each of the following entries, enter the letter of the explanation that most closely describes it in the space beside each entry. (You can use letters more than once.)

A. To record payment of a prepaid expense.
B. To record this period's use of a prepaid expense.
C. To record this period's depreciation expense.
D. To record receipt of unearned revenue.
E. To record this period's earning of prior unearned revenue.
F. To record an accrued expense.
G. To record payment of an accrued expense.
H. To record an accrued revenue.
I. To record receipt of accrued revenue.

PROBLEM SET B

Problem 3-1B
Identifying adjusting entries with explanations

C3 P1

_____	1.	Unearned Professional Fees	6,000	
		Professional Fees Earned		6,000
_____	2.	Interest Receivable	3,500	
		Interest Revenue		3,500
_____	3.	Salaries Payable	9,000	
		Cash		9,000
_____	4.	Depreciation Expense	8,000	
		Accumulated Depreciation		8,000
_____	5.	Cash	9,000	
		Unearned Professional Fees		9,000
_____	6.	Insurance Expense	4,000	
		Prepaid Insurance		4,000
_____	7.	Interest Expense	5,000	
		Interest Payable		5,000
_____	8.	Cash	1,500	
		Accounts Receivable (from services)		1,500
_____	9.	Salaries Expense	7,000	
		Salaries Payable		7,000
_____	10.	Cash	1,000	
		Interest Receivable		1,000
_____	11.	Prepaid Rent	3,000	
		Cash		3,000
_____	12.	Rent Expense	7,500	
		Prepaid Rent		7,500

Problem 3-2B
Preparing adjusting and subsequent journal entries

C1 A1 P1

Nomo Co. follows the practice of recording prepaid expenses and unearned revenues in balance sheet accounts. Nomo's annual accounting period ends on October 31, 2005. The following information concerns the adjusting entries that need to be recorded as of that date:

a. The Office Supplies account started the fiscal year with a $500 balance. During the fiscal year, the company purchased supplies for $3,650, which was added to the Office Supplies account. The supplies available at October 31, 2005, totaled $700.

b. An analysis of the company's insurance policies provided these facts:

Policy	Date of Purchase	Months of Coverage	Cost
A	April 1, 2004	24	$3,000
B	April 1, 2005	36	3,600
C	August 1, 2005	12	660

The total premium for each policy was paid in full (for all months) at the purchase date, and the Prepaid Insurance account was debited for the full cost. (Note that year-end adjusting entries for Prepaid Insurance were properly recorded in all prior fiscal years.)

c. The company has four employees, who earn a total of $800 for each workday. They are paid each Monday for their work in the five-day workweek ending on the previous Friday. Assume that October 31, 2005, is a Monday, and all five employees worked the first day of that week. They will be paid salaries for five full days on Monday, November 7, 2005.

d. The company purchased a building on November 1, 2004, that cost $155,000 and is expected to have a $20,000 salvage value at the end of its predicted 25-year life.

e. Since the company does not occupy the entire building it owns, it rented space to a tenant at $600 per month, starting on September 1, 2005. The rent was paid on time on September 1, and the amount received was credited to the Rent Earned account. However, the October rent has not been paid. The company has worked out an agreement with the tenant, who has promised to pay both October and November rent in full on November 15. The tenant has agreed not to fall behind again.

f. On September 1, the company rented space to another tenant for $525 per month. The tenant paid five months' rent in advance on that date. The payment was recorded with a credit to the Unearned Rent account.

Required

1. Use the information to prepare adjusting entries as of October 31, 2005.

2. Prepare journal entries to record the first subsequent cash transaction in 2006 for parts *c* and *e*.

Check (1*b*) Dr. Insurance Expense, $2,365; (1*d*) Dr. Depreciation Expense, $5,400.

Following is the unadjusted trial balance for Alcorn Institute as of December 31, 2005, which initially records prepaid expenses and unearned revenues in balance sheet accounts. The Institute provides one-on-one training to individuals who pay tuition directly to the business and offers extension training to groups in off-site locations. Shown after the trial balance are items *a* through *h* that require adjusting entries as of December 31, 2005.

Problem 3-3B
Preparing adjusting entries, adjusted trial balance, and financial statements

A1 P1 P2 P3

ALCORN INSTITUTE Unadjusted Trial Balance December 31, 2005	Debit	Credit
Cash	$ 50,000	
Accounts receivable	0	
Teaching supplies	60,000	
Prepaid insurance	18,000	
Prepaid rent	2,600	
Professional library	10,000	
Accumulated depreciation—Professional library		$ 1,500
Equipment	30,000	
Accumulated depreciation—Equipment		16,000
Accounts payable		12,200
Salaries payable		0
Unearned training fees		27,600
M. Alcorn, Capital		68,500
M. Alcorn, Withdrawals	20,000	
Tuition fees earned		105,000
Training fees earned		62,000
Depreciation expense—Professional library	0	
Depreciation expense—Equipment	0	
Salaries expense	43,200	
Insurance expense	0	
Rent expense	28,600	
Teaching supplies expense	0	
Advertising expense	18,000	
Utilities expense	12,400	
Totals	$ 292,800	$292,800

Additional Information Items

a. An analysis of the Institute's insurance policies shows that $6,400 of coverage has expired.

b. An inventory count shows that teaching supplies costing $2,500 are available at year-end 2005.

c. Annual depreciation on the equipment is $4,000.

d. Annual depreciation on the professional library is $2,000.

e. On November 1, the Institute agreed to do a special four-month course (starting immediately) for a client. The contract calls for a $4,600 monthly fee, and the client paid the first two months' fees in advance. When the cash was received, the Unearned Training Fees account was credited. The last two months' fees will be recorded when collected in 2006.

f. On October 15, the Institute agreed to teach a four-month class (beginning immediately) to an individual for $2,200 tuition per month payable at the end of the class. The class started on October 15, but no payment has yet been received.

g. The Institute's only employee is paid weekly. As of the end of the year, three days' wages have accrued at the rate of $180 per day.

h. The balance in the Prepaid Rent account represents rent for December.

Required

1. Prepare T-accounts (representing the ledger) with balances from the unadjusted trial balance.

2. Prepare the necessary adjusting journal entries for items *a* through *h*, and post them to the T-accounts. Assume that adjusting entries are made only at year-end.

3. Update balances in the T-accounts for the adjusting entries and prepare an adjusted trial balance.

4. Prepare Alcorn Institute's income statement and statement of owner's equity for the year 2005, and prepare its balance sheet as of December 31, 2005.

Problem 3-4B
Interpreting unadjusted and adjusted trial balances, and preparing financial statements

C3   A1   P1   P2   P3

A six-column table for Daxu Consulting Company follows. The first two columns contain the unadjusted trial balance for the company as of December 31, 2005, and the last two columns contain the adjusted trial balance as of the same date.

	Unadjusted Trial Balance		Adjustments		Adjusted Trial Balance	
Cash	$ 48,000				$ 48,000	
Accounts receivable	70,000				76,660	
Office supplies	30,000				7,000	
Prepaid insurance	13,200				8,600	
Office equipment	150,000				150,000	
Accumulated depreciation— Office equip.		$ 30,000				$ 40,000
Accounts payable		36,000				42,000
Interest payable		0				1,600
Salaries payable		0				11,200
Unearned consulting fees		30,000				17,800
Long-term notes payable		80,000				80,000
D. Chen, Capital		70,200				70,200
D. Chen, Withdrawals	10,000				10,000	
Consulting fees earned		264,000				282,860
Depreciation expense— Office equip.	0				10,000	
Salaries expense	115,600				126,800	
Interest expense	6,400				8,000	
Insurance expense	0				4,600	
Rent expense	24,000				24,000	
Office supplies expense	0				23,000	
Advertising expense	43,000				49,000	
Totals	$510,200	$510,200			$545,660	$545,660

Required

Analysis Component

1. Analyze the differences between the unadjusted and adjusted trial balances to determine the eight adjustments that likely were made. Show the results of your analysis by inserting these adjustment amounts in the table's two middle columns. Label each adjustment with a letter *a* through *h* and provide a short description of it at the bottom of the table.

Preparation Component

2. Use the information in the adjusted trial balance to prepare this company's (*a*) income statement and its statement of owner's equity for the year ended December 31, 2005 (*note:* D. Chen, Capital at December 31, 2004, was $70,200, and the current-year withdrawals were $10,000), and (*b*) the balance sheet as of December 31, 2005.

The adjusted trial balance for Lightning Courier as of December 31, 2005, follows:

Problem 3-5B
Preparing financial statements
from the adjusted trial balance
and calculating profit margin

P3 A1 A2

	Debit	Credit
Cash	$ 48,000	
Accounts receivable	110,000	
Interest receivable	6,000	
Notes receivable (due in 90 days)	200,000	
Office supplies	12,000	
Trucks	124,000	
Accumulated depreciation—Trucks		$ 48,000
Equipment	260,000	
Accumulated depreciation—Equipment		190,000
Land	90,000	
Accounts payable		124,000
Interest payable		22,000
Salaries payable		30,000
Unearned delivery fees		110,000
Long-term notes payable		190,000
J. Hallam, Capital		115,000
J. Hallam, Withdrawals	40,000	
Delivery fees earned		580,000
Interest earned		24,000
Depreciation expense—Trucks	24,000	
Depreciation expense—Equipment	46,000	
Salaries expense	64,000	
Wages expense	290,000	
Interest expense	25,000	
Office supplies expense	33,000	
Advertising expense	26,400	
Repairs expense—Trucks	34,600	
Totals	$1,433,000	$1,433,000

Required

1. Use the information in the adjusted trial balance to prepare (a) the income statement for the year ended December 31, 2005, (b) the statement of owner's equity for the year ended December 31, 2005, and (c) the balance sheet as of December 31, 2005.

2. Calculate the profit margin for year 2005.

Check (1) Total assets, $612,000

Quake Co. had the following transactions in the last two months of its fiscal year ended May 31:

Problem 3-6B[A]
Recording prepaid expenses and
unearned revenues

P1 P4

Apr. 1 Paid $3,450 cash for future consulting services.
    1 Paid $2,700 cash for 12 months of insurance through March 31 of the next year.
    30 Received $7,500 cash for future services to be provided to a customer.
May 1 Paid $3,450 cash for future newspaper advertising.
    23 Received $9,450 cash for future services to be provided to a customer.
    31 Of the consulting services paid for on April 1, $1,500 worth has been received.
    31 A portion of the insurance paid for on April 1 has expired. No adjustment was made in April to Prepaid Insurance.
    31 Services worth $3,600 are not yet provided to the customer who paid on April 30.
    31 Of the advertising paid for on May 1, $1,050 worth is not yet used.
    31 The company has performed $4,500 of services that the customer paid for on May 23.

Required

1. Prepare entries for these transactions under the method that records prepaid expenses and unearned revenues in balance sheet accounts. Also prepare adjusting entries at the end of the year.

2. Prepare entries for these transactions under the method that records prepaid expenses and unearned revenues in income statement accounts. Also prepare adjusting entries at the end of the year.

Analysis Component

3. Explain why the alternative sets of entries in parts 1 and 2 do not result in different financial statement amounts.

PROBLEM SET C

Problem Set C is available at the book's Website to further reinforce and assess your learning.

SERIAL PROBLEM

Success Systems

This serial problem began in Chapter 1 and continues through most of the book. If previous chapter segments were not completed, the serial problem can still begin at this point. It is helpful, but not necessary, that you use the Working Papers that accompany the book.

After the success of the company's first two months, Kay Breeze continues to operate Success Systems. (Transactions for the first two months are described in the serial problem of Chapter 2.) The November 30, 2004, unadjusted trial balance of Success Systems (reflecting its transactions for October and November of 2004) follows:

No.	Account Title	Debit	Credit
101	Cash	$ 48,052	
106	Accounts receivable	12,618	
126	Computer supplies	2,545	
128	Prepaid insurance	2,220	
131	Prepaid rent	3,300	
163	Office equipment	8,000	
164	Accumulated depreciation—Office equipment		$ 0
167	Computer equipment	20,000	
168	Accumulated depreciation—Computer equipment		0
201	Accounts payable		0
210	Wages payable		0
236	Unearned computer services revenue		0
301	K. Breeze, Capital		83,000
302	K. Breeze, Withdrawals	5,600	
403	Computer services revenue		25,659
612	Depreciation expense—Office equipment	0	
613	Depreciation expense—Computer equipment	0	
623	Wages expense	2,625	
637	Insurance expense	0	
640	Rent expense	0	
652	Computer supplies expense	0	
655	Advertising expense	1,940	
676	Mileage expense	704	
677	Miscellaneous expenses	250	
684	Repairs expense—Computer	805	
	Totals	$108,659	$108,659

Success Systems had the following transactions and events in December 2004:

Dec. 2 Paid $1,025 cash to Hilldale Mall for Success Systems' share of mall advertising costs.
   3 Paid $500 cash for minor repairs to the company's computer.
   4 Received $3,950 cash from Alex's Engineering Co. for the receivable from November.
   10 Paid cash to Sherry Adams for six days of work at the rate of $125 per day.

14 Notified by Alex's Engineering Co. that Success's bid of $7,000 on a proposed project has been accepted. Alex's paid a $1,500 cash advance to Success Systems.

15 Purchased $1,100 of computer supplies on credit from Cain Office Products.

16 Sent a reminder to Gomez Co. to pay the fee for services recorded on November 8.

20 Completed a project for Chang Corporation and received $5,625 cash.

22–26 Took the week off for the holidays.

28 Received $3,000 cash from Gomez Co. on its receivable.

29 Reimbursed Breeze's business automobile mileage (600 miles at $0.32 per mile).

31 Breeze withdrew $1,500 cash for personal use.

The following additional facts are collected for use in making adjusting entries prior to preparing financial statements for the company's first three months:

a. The December 31 inventory count of computer supplies shows $580 still available.

b. Three months have expired since the 12-month insurance premium was paid in advance.

c. As of December 31, Sherry Adams has not been paid for four days of work at $125 per day.

d. The company's computer is expected to have a four-year life with no salvage value.

e. The office equipment is expected to have a five-year life with no salvage value.

f. Prepaid rent for three of the four months has expired.

Required

1. Prepare journal entries to record each of the December transactions and events for Success Systems. Post these entries to the accounts in the ledger.

2. Prepare adjusting entries to reflect *a* through *f*. Post these entries to the accounts in the ledger.

3. Prepare an adjusted trial balance as of December 31, 2004.

4. Prepare an income statement for the three months ended December 31, 2004.

5. Prepare a statement of owner's equity for the three months ended December 31, 2004.

6. Prepare a balance sheet as of December 31, 2004.

Check (3) Adjusted trial balance totals, $119,034

(6) Total assets, $93,248

BEYOND THE NUMBERS

BTN 3-1 Refer to **Krispy Kreme**'s financial statements in Appendix A to answer the following:

1. Identify and write down the revenue recognition principle as explained in the chapter.

2. Research Krispy Kreme's footnotes to discover how it applies the revenue recognition principle. Report what you discover.

3. What is Krispy Kreme's profit margin for 2003 and for 2002?

REPORTING IN ACTION

C1 C2 A1 A2

Roll On

4. Access Krispy Kreme's financial statements (10-K) for fiscal years ending after February 2, 2003, at its Website (**KrispyKreme.com**) or the SEC's EDGAR database (**www.sec.gov**). Compare the February 2, 2003, fiscal year profit margin to any subsequent year's profit margin that you are able to calculate.

BTN 3-2 Key figures for the recent two years of both **Krispy Kreme** and **Tastykake** follow:

COMPARATIVE ANALYSIS

A2

Key Figures	Krispy Kreme		Tastykake	
($ thousands)	Current Year	Prior Year	Current Year	Prior Year
Net income	$ 33,478	$ 26,378	$ 2,000*	$ 8,048*
Net sales	491,549	394,354	162,263	166,245

* Net income without restructuring charges.

Required

1. Compute profit margins for (*a*) Krispy Kreme and (*b*) Tastykake for the two years of data shown.

2. Which company is more successful on the basis of profit margin? Explain.

ETHICS CHALLENGE

C1 C2 A1

BTN 3-3   Jackie Bergez works for Sea Biscuit Co. She and Bob Welch, her manager, are preparing adjusting entries for annual financial statements. Bergez computes depreciation and records it as

Depreciation Expense—Equipment	123,000	
Accumulated Depreciation—Equipment		123,000

Welch agrees with her computation but says the credit entry should be directly to the Equipment account. He argues that while accumulated depreciation is technically correct, "it is less hassle not to use a contra account and just credit the Equipment account directly. And besides, the balance sheet shows the same amount for total assets under either method."

Required

1. How should depreciation be recorded? Do you support Bergez or Welch?

2. Evaluate the strengths and weaknesses of Welch's reasons for preferring his method.

3. Indicate whether the situation Bergez faces is an ethical problem.

COMMUNICATING IN PRACTICE

C1 A2

BTN 3-4   The class should be divided into teams. Teams are to select an industry (such as automobile manufacturing, airlines, defense contractors), and each team member is to select a different company in that industry. Each team member is to acquire the annual report of the company selected. Annual reports can be downloaded from company Websites or from the SEC's EDGAR database at (**www.SEC.gov**).

Required

1. Use the annual report to compute the return on assets, debt ratio, and profit margin.

2. Communicate with team members via a meeting, e-mail, or telephone to discuss the meaning of the ratios, how different companies compare to each other, and the industry norm. The team must prepare a single memo reporting the ratios for each company and identifying the conclusions or consensus of opinion reached during the team's discussion. The memo is to be copied and distributed to the instructor and all classmates.

TAKING IT TO THE NET

C1 A2

mhhe.com/larson

BTN 3-5   Access the **Cannondale** promotional Website (**Cannondale.com**).

1. What is the primary product that Cannondale sells?

2. Review its form 10-K. You can access this from the EDGAR system (**www.SEC.gov**). You must scroll down the form to find the financial statements.

3. What is Cannondale's fiscal year-end?

4. What are Cannondale's net sales for the annual period ended June 29, 2002?

5. What is Cannondale's net income for the annual period ended June 29, 2002?

6. Compute Cannondale's profit margin ratio for the annual period ended June 29, 2002.

7. Do you think its decision to use a year-end of late June or early July relates to its natural business year?

TEAMWORK IN ACTION

C3 A1 P1

BTN 3-6   Four types of adjustments are described in the chapter: (1) prepaid expenses, (2) unearned revenues, (3) accrued expenses, and (4) accrued revenues.

Required

1. Form *learning teams* of four (or more) members. Each team member must select one of the four adjustments as an area of expertise (each team must have at least one expert in each area).

2. Form *expert teams* from the individuals who have selected the same area of expertise. Expert teams are to discuss and write a report that each expert will present to his or her learning team addressing the following:

   a. Description of the adjustment and why it's necessary.

   b. Example of a transaction or event, with dates and amounts, that requires adjustment.

c. Adjusting entry(ies) for the example in requirement *b*.

d. Status of the affected account(s) before and after the adjustment in requirement *c*.

e. Effects on financial statements of not making the adjustment.

3. Each expert should return to his or her learning team. In rotation, each member should present his or her expert team's report to the learning team. Team discussion is encouraged.

BTN 3-7 Read the article "It's Like When Someone Robs a Bank," in the August 19, 2002, issue of *Business Week*. (Access the book's Website for a free link.)

BUSINESS WEEK ACTIVITY

C2

mhhe.com/larson

Required

1. Describe the type of overall accounting reform that FASB Chairman Herz favors.

2. What does Herz assert as being at the core of most recent scandals in corporate America?

3. What is meant by "principles-based accounting"?

4. Why is "principles-based accounting" controversial?

BTN 3-8 Melody Kulp of **Mellies** (see chapter's opening feature) is aware of Robin Drucker, who operates a collection agency. For a 50% commission, Drucker collects on accounts receivables for her clients' customers who are delinquent in their payments. For example, assume that a company turns over a $100 accounts receivable to Drucker. If she can collect the $100 from the customer, Drucker keeps $50 and remits the other $50 to her client. Kulp is negotiating with Drucker to offer her a discount from the normal 50% commission that Drucker charges. Kulp has proposed a fee of 40% on amounts collected by Drucker, and leaving 60% of the receivable for Mellies. Currently, Mellies uses a different collection agency that charges a 50% commission.

ENTREPRENEURIAL DECISION

A2

Required

1. Why would a company hire a collection agency to pursue its accounts receivable?

2. Assume that Mellies' profit margin is 8%. What is Mellies' net income on sales of $40 million?

3. Assume that Mellies currently pays 2% of its $40 million sales to collection agencies. What is the current amount of commission expense Mellies pays to collect delinquent accounts?

4. If Mellies is able to successfully negotiate with the Drucker agency for the reduced collection fee, how will its commission expense for collecting accounts change?

5. How would Mellies' profit margin change if it hires the Drucker collection agency at a 40% commission?

BTN 3-9 Visit the Website of a major company that interests you. Use the Investor Relations link at the Website to obtain the toll-free telephone number of the Investor Relations Department. Call the company, ask to speak to Investor Relations, and request a copy of the company's most recent annual report. You should receive the requested report within one to two weeks. Once you have received your report, consult it throughout the term to see the principles that you are learning in class are being applied in practice.

HITTING THE ROAD

C1

BTN 3-10 **Grupo Bimbo** is a major producer and distributor of bakery products. Access its 2002 annual financial report at the company's Website (**GrupoBimbo.com**) to answer the following questions.

GLOBAL DECISION

A2 C1 C2

Required

1. Identify and report the revenue recognition policy applied by Grupo Bimbo?

2. What are the five types of assets depreciated by Grupo Bimbo? Which two assets classified as property, plant, and equipment are not depreciated?

3. What is Grupo Bimbo's profit margin for both fiscal years ended 2002 and 2001?

"Snowskates let you live out your skateboarding fantasies on the snow"—Andy Wolf

4

Completing the Accounting Cycle

A Look Back

Chapter 3 explained the timing of reports. We described why adjusting accounts is important for recognizing revenues and expenses in the proper period. We explained how to prepare an adjusted trial balance and use it in preparing financial statements.

A Look at This Chapter

This chapter emphasizes the final steps in the accounting process and reviews the entire accounting cycle. We explain the closing process, including accounting procedures and the use of a post-closing trial balance. We show how a work sheet aids in preparing financial statements. A classified balance sheet and its use in analyzing information are explained.

CAP

Conceptual

C1 Explain why temporary accounts are closed each period. *(p. 140)*

C2 Identify steps in the accounting cycle. *(p. 143)*

C3 Explain and prepare a classified balance sheet. *(p. 146)*

Analytical

A1 Compute the current ratio and describe what it reveals about a company's financial condition. *(p. 148)*

Procedural

P1 Prepare a work sheet and explain its usefulness. *(p. 136)*

P2 Describe and prepare closing entries. *(p. 141)*

P3 Explain and prepare a post-closing trial balance. *(p. 143)*

Snowskate on Upstart

PORTLAND—Andy Wolf was a frustrated skateboarder when he moved to Portland a few years ago because of its snow-covered surroundings for much of the year. Wolf toyed with the idea of making a skateboard for snow. His answer was the "snowskate"—similar in size and shape to a skateboard but ridden without bindings to allow *shove-its* and *flip tricks* that aren't possible with snowboards. He now heads the upstart **Premier Snowskate (PremierSnowsk8.com),** the maker of snowskates.

Wolf says his early business experiences were tough as people reacted to him as if "all he knows how to do is ride a snowboard and play Nintendo." People were wrong. One of Wolf's first goals was to control costs. "I wanted to keep the price under $100 retail," says Wolf; "that's how I sourced my materials." He also monitored revenues and kept track of financial performance. Closing procedures were important in helping identify the proper costs and revenues for specific periods. He also relied on classified balance sheets so that he would know what was due and when.

Still, it was tough. "It was still a job," says Wolf. "I had to handle my business, do my own deals, set up my traveling, and work with reps." Accounting work sheets helped Wolf identify temporary and permanent accounts, make crucial adjustments, and prepare and analyze financial reports. Yet the final business decisions were his to make.

Today, his decisions look good as forward-thinking resorts are building snowskate parks. "We're finding that resorts are totally into it," says Wolf. "Either embrace it or have it run them over."

Now for Wolf: How is he dealing with success? "I kind of hate to admit it," says Wolf, "but snowskates are going mainstream." From skateboarder to entrepreneur who uses accounting data—that must hurt. However, with annual sales projected to top $3 million this year, the hurt is tolerable. Admits Wolf, "I'm pretty damn lucky."

[Sources: *Premier Snowskates Website*, January 2004; *Entrepreneur Magazine*, May 2002; *Snowskates Underground*, May 2001; *USA Today*, January 2003; *Sports Guide*, December 2002; *Transworld Snowboarding*, February 2003.]

Many of the important steps leading to financial statements were explained in earlier chapters. We described how transactions and events are analyzed, journalized, and posted. This chapter describes important adjustments that are often necessary to properly reflect revenues when earned and expenses when incurred. This chapter also describes financial statement preparation. It explains the closing process that readies revenue, expense, and withdrawal accounts for the next reporting period and updates the capital account.

A work sheet is shown to be a useful tool for these final steps and in preparing financial statements. It also explains how accounts are classified on a balance sheet to increase their usefulness to decision makers.

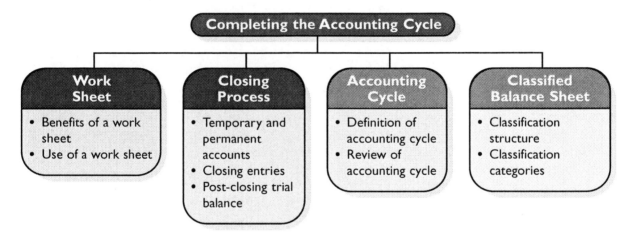

Completing the Accounting Cycle

Work Sheet	Closing Process	Accounting Cycle	Classified Balance Sheet
• Benefits of a work sheet • Use of a work sheet	• Temporary and permanent accounts • Closing entries • Post-closing trial balance	• Definition of accounting cycle • Review of accounting cycle	• Classification structure • Classification categories

Work Sheet as a Tool

Information preparers use various analyses and internal documents when organizing information for internal and external decision makers. Internal documents are often called **working papers.** One widely used working paper is the **work sheet,** which is a useful tool for preparers in working with accounting information. It is usually not available to external decision makers.

Benefits of a Work Sheet

P1 Prepare a work sheet and explain its usefulness.

A work sheet is *not* a required report, yet using a manual or electronic work sheet has several potential benefits. Specifically, a work sheet:

■ Aids the preparation of financial statements.

■ Reduces the possibility of errors when working with many accounts and adjustments.

■ Links accounts and adjustments to their impacts in financial statements.

■ Assists in planning and organizing an audit of financial statements—as it can be used to reflect any adjustments necessary.

■ Helps in preparing interim (monthly and quarterly) financial statements when the journalizing and posting of adjusting entries are postponed until the year-end.

■ Shows the effects of proposed or "what if" transactions.

Point: Since a work sheet is *not* a required report or an accounting record, its format is flexible and can be modified by its user to fit his/her preferences.

Decision Insight

Accoun-tech An electronic work sheet using spreadsheet software such as Excel allows us to easily change numbers, assess the impact of alternative strategies, and quickly prepare financial statements at less cost. It can also increase the available time for analysis and interpretation.

Use of a Work Sheet

When a work sheet is used to prepare financial statements, it is constructed at the end of a period before the adjusting process. The complete work sheet includes a list of the accounts, their balances and adjustments, and their sorting into financial statement columns. It provides two columns each for the unadjusted trial balance, the adjustments, the adjusted trial balance, the income statement, and the balance sheet (including the statement of owner's equity). To describe and interpret the work sheet, we use the information from FastForward. Preparing the work sheet has five important steps. Each step, 1 through 5, is color-coded and explained with reference to Exhibits 4.1 and 4.2.

1 Step 1. Enter Unadjusted Trial Balance

Refer to Exhibit 4.1. The first step in preparing a work sheet is to list the title of every account and its account number that is expected to appear on its financial statements. This includes all accounts in the ledger plus any new ones from adjusting entries. Most adjusting entries—including expenses from salaries, supplies, depreciation, and insurance—are predictable and recurring. The unadjusted balance for each account is then entered in the appropriate Debit or Credit column of the unadjusted trial balance columns. The totals of these two columns must be equal. Exhibit 4.1 shows FastForward's work sheet after completing this first step. Sometimes blank lines are left on the work sheet based on past experience to indicate where lines will be needed for adjustments to certain accounts. Exhibit 4.1 shows Consulting Revenue as one example. An alternative is to squeeze adjustments on one line or to combine the effects of two or more adjustments in one amount. In the unusual case when an account is not predicted, we can add a new line for such an account following the *Totals* line.

2 Step 2. Enter Adjustments

Refer to Exhibit 4.1a (turn over first transparency). The second step in preparing a work sheet is to enter adjustments in the Adjustments columns. The adjustments shown are the same ones shown in Exhibit 3.13. An identifying letter links the debit and credit of each adjusting entry. This is called *keying* the adjustments. After preparing a work sheet, adjusting entries must still be entered in the journal and posted to the ledger. The Adjustments columns provide the information for those entries.

Point: A recordkeeper often can complete the procedural task of journalizing and posting adjusting entries by using a work sheet and the guidance that *keying* provides.

3 Step 3. Prepare Adjusted Trial Balance

Refer to Exhibit 4.1b (turn over second transparency). The adjusted trial balance is prepared by combining the adjustments with the unadjusted balances for each account. As an example, the Prepaid Insurance account has a $2,400 debit balance in the Unadjusted Trial Balance columns. This $2,400 debit is combined with the $100 credit in the Adjustments columns to give Prepaid Insurance a $2,300 debit in the Adjusted Trial Balance columns. The totals of the Adjusted Trial Balance columns confirm the equality of debits and credits.

Point: To avoid omitting the transfer of an account balance, start with the first line (cash) and continue in account order.

4 Step 4. Sort Adjusted Trial Balance Amounts to Financial Statements

Refer to Exhibit 4.1c (turn over third transparency). This step involves sorting account balances from the adjusted trial balance to their proper financial statement columns. Expenses go to the Income Statement Debit column and revenues to the Income Statement Credit column. Assets and withdrawals go to the Balance Sheet & Statement of Owner's Equity Debit column. Liabilities and owner's capital go to the Balance Sheet & Statement of Owner's Equity Credit column.

5 Step 5. Total Statement Columns, Compute Income or Loss, and Balance Columns

Refer to Exhibit 4.1d (turn over fourth transparency). Each financial statement column (from Step 4) is totaled. The difference between the totals of the Income Statement columns is net income or net loss. This occurs because revenues are entered in the Credit column and expenses in the Debit column. If the Credit total exceeds the Debit total, there is net income. If the Debit total exceeds the Credit total, there is a net loss. For FastForward, the Credit total exceeds the Debit total, giving a $3,785 net income.

[continued on p. 140]

Exhibit 4.1

Work Sheet with Unadjusted Trial Balance

| File Edit View Insert Format Tools Data Window Help | | | | | | | | | | |

FastForward
Work Sheet
For Month Ended December 31, 2004

No.	Account	Unadjusted Trial Balance		Adjustments		Adjusted Trial Balance		Income Statement		Balance Sheet & Statement of Owner's Equity	
		Dr.	Cr.	Dr.	Cr.	Dr.	Cr.	Dr.	Cr.	Dr.	Cr.
101	Cash	3,950									
106	Accounts receivable	0									
126	Supplies	9,720									
128	Prepaid insurance	2,400									
167	Equipment	26,000									
168	Accumulated depreciation—Equip.		0								
201	Accounts payable		6,200								
209	Salaries payable		0								
236	Unearned consulting revenue		3,000								
301	C. Taylor, Capital		30,000								
302	C. Taylor, Withdrawals	600									
403	Consulting revenue		5,800								
406	Rental revenue		300								
612	Depreciation expense—Equip.	0									
622	Salaries expense	1,400									
637	Insurance expense	0									
640	Rent expense	1,000									
652	Supplies expense	0									
690	Utilities expense	230									
	Totals	45,300	45,300								

List all accounts from the ledger and those expected to arise from adjusting entries.

Enter all amounts available from ledger accounts. Column totals must be equal.

A work sheet collects and summarizes information used to prepare adjusting entries, financial statements, and closing entries.

Exhibit 4.1a

Enter Adjustments in the Work Sheet

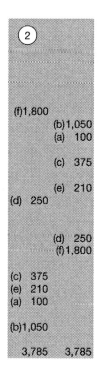

Enter adjustment amounts and use letters to cross-reference debit and credit adjustments. Column totals must be equal.

Exhibit 4.1b
Compute and Enter Amounts for the Adjusted Trial Balance

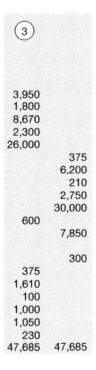

	③
3,950	
1,800	
8,670	
2,300	
26,000	
	375
	6,200
	210
	2,750
	30,000
600	
	7,850
	300
375	
1,610	
100	
1,000	
1,050	
230	
47,685	47,685

Combine unadjusted trial balance amounts with the adjustments to get the adjusted trial balance amounts. Column totals must be equal.

Exhibit 4.1c

Extend the Adjusted Trial Balance Amounts to the Financial Statement Columns

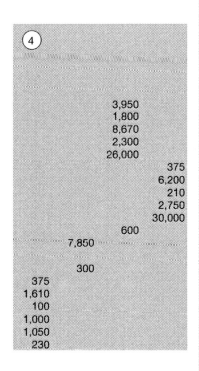

Extend all revenue and expense amounts to the income statement columns.

Extend all asset, liability, capital, and withdrawals amounts to these columns.

These column totals will differ by the amount of net income or loss.

Exhibit 4.1d
Compute and Enter the Net Income or Loss and Complete the Work Sheet

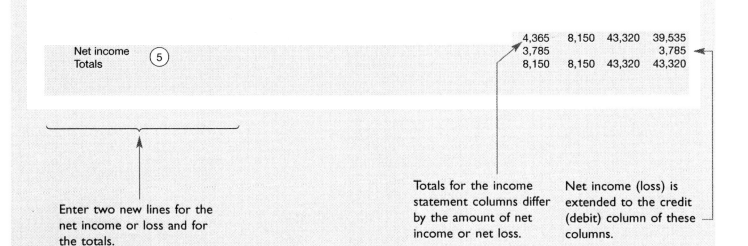

	4,365	8,150	43,320	39,535
Net income ⑤	3,785			3,785
Totals	8,150	8,150	43,320	43,320

Enter two new lines for the net income or loss and for the totals.

Totals for the income statement columns differ by the amount of net income or net loss.

Net income (loss) is extended to the credit (debit) column of these columns.

Exhibit 4.2

Financial Statements Prepared from the Work Sheet

FASTFORWARD
Income Statement
For Month Ended December 31, 2004

Revenues		
Consulting revenue	$ 7,850	
Rental revenue	300	
Total revenues		$ 8,150
Expenses		
Depreciation expense—Equipment	375	
Salaries expense	1,610	
Insurance expense	100	
Rent expense	1,000	
Supplies expense	1,050	
Utilities expense	230	
Total expenses		4,365
Net income		$ 3,785

FASTFORWARD
Statement of Owner's Equity
For Month Ended December 31, 2004

C. Taylor, Capital, December 1		$ 0
Add: Investment by owner	$30,000	
Net income	3,785	33,785
		33,785
Less: Withdrawals by owner		600
C. Taylor, Capital, December 31		$33,185

FASTFORWARD
Balance Sheet
December 31, 2004

Assets		
Cash		$ 3,950
Accounts receivable		1,800
Supplies		8,670
Prepaid insurance		2,300
Equipment	$26,000	
Accumulated depreciation—Equipment	(375)	25,625
Total assets		$42,345
Liabilities		
Accounts payable		$ 6,200
Salaries payable		210
Unearned consulting revenue		2,750
Total liabilities		9,160
Equity		
C. Taylor, Capital		33,185
Total liabilities and equity		$42,345

The net income from the Income Statement columns is then entered in the Balance Sheet & Statement of Owner's Equity Credit column. Adding net income to the last Credit column implies that it is to be added to owner's capital. If a loss occurs, it is added to the Debit column. This implies that it is to be subtracted from owner's capital. The ending balance of owner's capital does not appear in the last two columns as a single amount, but it is computed in the statement of owner's equity using these account balances. When net income or net loss is added to the proper Balance Sheet & Statement of Owner's Equity column, the totals of the last two columns must balance. If they do not, one or more errors have been made. The error can either be mathematical or involve sorting one or more amounts to incorrect columns.

Work Sheet Applications and Analysis

A work sheet does not substitute for financial statements. It is a tool we can use at the end of an accounting period to help organize data and prepare financial statements. FastForward's financial statements are shown in Exhibit 4.2. Its income statement amounts are taken from the Income Statement columns of the work sheet. Similarly, amounts for its balance sheet and its statement of owner's equity are taken from the Balance Sheet & Statement of Owner's Equity columns of the work sheet.

A work sheet is also useful to journalize adjusting entries as the information is in the Adjustments columns. It is important to remember that a work sheet is not a journal. This means that even when a work sheet is prepared, it is necessary to both journalize adjustments and post them to the ledger.

Work sheets are also useful in analyzing the effects of proposed, or what-if, transactions. This is done by entering financial statement amounts in the Unadjusted (what-if) columns. Proposed transactions are then entered in the Adjustments columns. We then compute "adjusted" amounts from these proposed transactions. The extended amounts in the financial statement columns show the effects of these proposed transactions. These financial statement columns yield **pro forma financial statements** because they show the statements *as if* the proposed transactions occurred.

Quick Check

1. Where do we get the amounts to enter in the Unadjusted Trial Balance columns of a work sheet?

2. What are the advantages of using a work sheet to help prepare adjusting entries?

3. What are the overall benefits of a work sheet?

Answers—p. 159

Closing Process

C1 Explain why temporary accounts are closed each period.

The **closing process** is an important step at the end of an accounting period *after* financial statements have been completed. It prepares accounts for recording the transactions and the events of the *next* period. In the closing process we must (1) identify accounts for closing, (2) record and post the closing entries, and (3) prepare a post-closing trial balance. The purpose of the closing process is twofold. First, it resets revenue, expense, and withdrawals account balances to zero at the end of each period. This is done so that these accounts can properly measure income and withdrawals for the next period. Second, it helps in summarizing a period's revenues and expenses. This section explains the closing process.

Temporary and Permanent Accounts

Temporary (or *nominal*) **accounts** accumulate data related to one accounting period. They include all income statement accounts, the withdrawals account, and the Income Summary account. They are temporary because the accounts are opened at the beginning of a period, used to record transactions and events for that period, and then closed at the end of the period. *The closing process applies only to temporary accounts.* **Permanent** (or *real*) **accounts** report on activities related to one or more future accounting periods. They carry their ending balances into the next period and generally consist of all balance sheet accounts. These asset, liability, and equity accounts are not closed.

Recording Closing Entries

To record and post **closing entries** is to transfer the end-of-period balances in revenue, expense, and withdrawals accounts to the permanent capital account. Closing entries are necessary at the end of each period after financial statements are prepared because

■ Revenue, expense, and withdrawals accounts must begin each period with zero balances.
■ Owner's capital must reflect revenues, expenses, and withdrawals.

An income statement aims to report revenues and expenses for a *specific accounting period.* The statement of owner's equity reports similar information, including withdrawals. Since revenue, expense, and withdrawals accounts must accumulate information separately for each period, they must start each period with zero balances. To close these accounts, we transfer their balances first to an account called *Income Summary.* **Income Summary** is a temporary account (only used for the closing process) that contains a credit for the sum of all revenues (and gains) and a debit for the sum of all expenses (and losses). Its balance equals net income or net loss and it is transferred to the capital account. Next, the withdrawals account balance is transferred to the capital account. After these closing entries are posted, the revenue, expense, withdrawals, and Income Summary accounts have zero balances. These accounts are then said to be *closed* or *cleared.*

Exhibit 4.3 uses the adjusted account balances of FastForward (from the Adjusted Trial Balance columns of Exhibit 4.1 or from the left side of Exhibit 4.4) to show the four steps necessary to close its temporary accounts. We explain each step.

Step 1: Close Credit Balances in Revenue Accounts to Income Summary
The first closing entry transfers credit balances in revenue (and gain) accounts to the Income Summary account. We bring accounts with credit balances to zero by debiting them. For FastForward, this journal entry is step 1 in Exhibit 4.4. This entry closes revenue accounts and leaves them with zero balances. The accounts are now ready to record revenues when they occur in the next period. The $8,150 credit entry to Income Summary equals total revenues for the period.

Step 2: Close Debit Balances in Expense Accounts to Income Summary
The second closing entry transfers debit balances in expense (and loss) accounts to the Income Summary account. We bring expense accounts' debit balances to zero by crediting them. With a balance of zero, these accounts are ready to accumulate a record of expenses for the next period. This second closing entry for FastForward is step 2 in Exhibit 4.4. Exhibit 4.3 shows that posting this entry gives each expense account a zero balance.

Step 3: Close Income Summary to Owner's Capital
After steps 1 and 2, the balance of Income Summary is equal to December's net income of $3,785. The third closing entry transfers the balance of the Income Summary account to the capital account. This entry closes the Income Summary account and is step 3 in Exhibit 4.4. The Income Summary account has a zero balance after posting this entry. It continues to have a zero balance until the closing process again occurs at the end of the next period. (If a net loss occurred because

---

Temporary Accounts

| Revenues |
| Expenses |
| Owner Withdrawals |
| Income Summary |

Permanent Accounts

| Assets |
| Liabilities |
| Owner Capital |

Topic Tackler 4-1

Point: To understand the closing process, focus on its *outcomes—updating* the capital account balance to its proper ending balance, and getting *temporary accounts* to show *zero balances* for purposes of accumulating data for the next period.

P2   Describe and prepare closing entries.

Point: It is possible to close revenue and expense accounts directly to owner's capital. Computerized accounting systems do this.

Point: The Income Summary is used only for closing entries.

Exhibit 4.3

Four-Step Closing Process

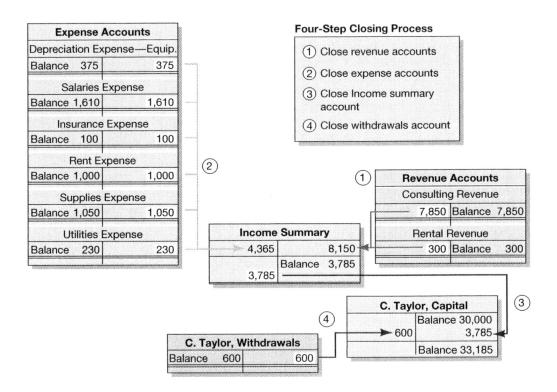

Exhibit 4.4

Preparing Closing Entries

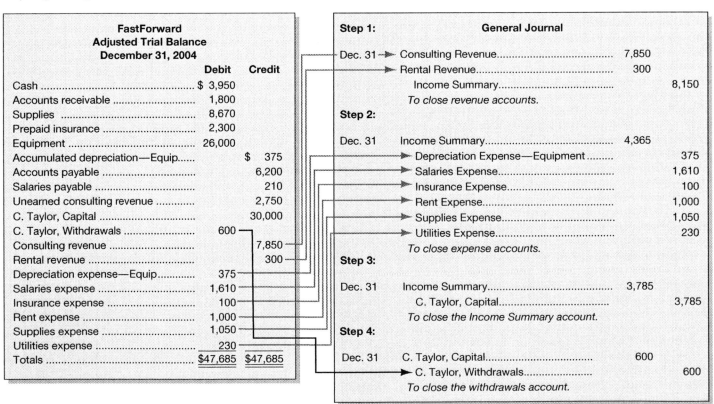

expenses exceeded revenues, the third entry is reversed: debit Owner Capital and credit Income Summary.)

Step 4: Close Withdrawals Account to Owner's Capital The fourth closing entry transfers any debit balance in the withdrawals account to the owner's capital account—see step 4 in Exhibit 4.4. This entry gives the withdrawals account a zero balance, and the account is now ready to accumulate next period's withdrawals. This entry also reduces the capital account balance to the $33,185 amount reported on the balance sheet.

Notice that we can select the accounts and amounts needing to be closed by identifying individual revenue, expense, and withdrawals accounts in the ledger. This is illustrated in Exhibit 4.4 where we prepare closing entries using the adjusted trial balance.[1] (Information for closing entries is also in the financial statement columns of the work sheet.)

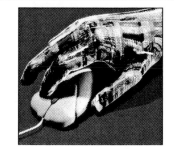

Post-Closing Trial Balance

Exhibit 4.5 shows the entire ledger of FastForward as of December 31 after adjusting and closing entries are posted. (The transaction and adjusting entries are in Chapters 2 and 3.) Note that the temporary accounts (revenues, expenses, and withdrawals) have balances equal to zero.

A **post-closing trial balance** is a list of permanent accounts and their balances from the ledger after all closing entries have been journalized and posted. It lists the balances for all accounts not closed. These accounts comprise a company's assets, liabilities, and equity, which are identical to those in the balance sheet. The aim of a post-closing trial balance is to verify that (1) total debits equal total credits for permanent accounts and (2) all temporary accounts have zero balances. FastForward's post-closing trial balance is shown in Exhibit 4.6. The post-closing trial balance usually is the last step in the accounting process.

P3 Explain and prepare a post-closing trial balance.

Accounting Cycle

The term **accounting cycle** refers to the steps in preparing financial statements. It is called a *cycle* because the steps are repeated each reporting period. Exhibit 4.7 shows the 10 steps in the cycle, beginning with analyzing transactions and ending with a post-closing trial balance or reversing entries. Steps 1 through 3 usually occur regularly as a company enters into transactions. Steps 4 through 9 are done at the end of a period. Reversing entries in step 10 are optional and are explained in Appendix 4A.

C2 Identify steps in the accounting cycle.

---

[1] The closing process has focused on proprietorships. It is identical for partnerships with the exception that each owner has separate capital and withdrawals accounts (for steps 3 and 4). The closing process for a corporation is similar with the exception that it uses a Retained Earnings account instead of a Capital account, and a Dividend account instead of a Withdrawals account.

Exhibit 4.5

General Ledger after the Closing Process for FastForward

Asset Accounts

Cash — Acct. No. 101

Date	Explan.	PR	Debit	Credit	Balance
2004					
Dec. 1		G1	30,000		30,000
2		G1		2,500	27,500
3		G1		26,000	1,500
5		G1	4,200		5,700
6		G1		2,400	3,300
12		G1		1,000	2,300
12		G1		700	1,600
22		G1	1,900		3,500
24		G1		900	2,600
24		G1		600	2,000
26		G1	3,000		5,000
26		G1		120	4,880
26		G1		230	4,650
26		G1		700	**3,950**

Accounts Receivable — Acct. No. 106

Date	Explan.	PR	Debit	Credit	Balance
2004					
Dec. 12		G1	1,900		1,900
22		G1		1,900	0
31	Adj.	G1	1,800		**1,800**

Supplies — Acct. No. 126

Date	Explan.	PR	Debit	Credit	Balance
2004					
Dec. 2		G1	2,500		2,500
6		G1	7,100		9,600
26		G1	120		9,720
31	Adj.	G1		1,050	**8,670**

Prepaid Insurance — Acct. No. 128

Date	Explan.	PR	Debit	Credit	Balance
2004					
Dec. 6		G1	2,400		2,400
31	Adj.	G1		100	**2,300**

Equipment — Acct. No. 167

Date	Explan.	PR	Debit	Credit	Balance
2004					
Dec. 3		G1	26,000		**26,000**

Accumulated Depreciation—Equipment — Acct. No. 168

Date	Explan.	PR	Debit	Credit	Balance
2004					
Dec. 31	Adj.	G1		375	**375**

Liability and Equity Accounts

Accounts Payable — Acct. No. 201

Date	Explan.	PR	Debit	Credit	Balance
2004					
Dec. 6		G1		7,100	7,100
24		G1	900		**6,200**

Salaries Payable — Acct. No. 209

Date	Explan.	PR	Debit	Credit	Balance
2004					
Dec. 31	Adj	G1		210	**210**

Unearned Consulting Revenue — Acct. No. 236

Date	Explan.	PR	Debit	Credit	Balance
2004					
Dec. 26		G1		3,000	3,000
31	Adj.	G1	250		**2,750**

C. Taylor, Capital — Acct. No. 301

Date	Explan.	PR	Debit	Credit	Balance
2004					
Dec. 1		G1		30,000	30,000
31	Closing	G1		3,785	33,785
31	Closing	G1	600		33,185

C. Taylor, Withdrawals — Acct. No. 302

Date	Explan.	PR	Debit	Credit	Balance
2004					
Dec. 24		G1	600		600
31	Closing	G1		600	0

Revenue and Expense Accounts (including Income Summary)

Consulting Revenue — Acct. No. 403

Date	Explan.	PR	Debit	Credit	Balance
2004					
Dec. 5		G1		4,200	4,200
12		G1		1,600	5,800
31	Adj.	G1		250	6,050
31	Adj.	G1		1,800	7,850
31	Closing	G1	7,850		0

Rental Revenue — Acct. No. 406

Date	Explan.	PR	Debit	Credit	Balance
2004					
Dec. 12		G1		300	300
31	Closing	G1	300		0

Depreciation Expense—Equipment — Acct. No. 612

Date	Explan.	PR	Debit	Credit	Balance
2004					
Dec. 31	Adj.	G1	375		375
31	Closing	G1		375	0

Salaries Expense — Acct. No. 622

Date	Explan.	PR	Debit	Credit	Balance
2004					
Dec. 12		G1	700		700
26		G1	700		1,400
31	Adj.	G1	210		1,610
31	Closing	G1		1,610	0

Insurance Expense — Acct. No. 637

Date	Explan.	PR	Debit	Credit	Balance
2004					
Dec. 31	Adj.	G1	100		100
31	Closing	G1		100	0

Rent Expense — Acct. No. 640

Date	Explan.	PR	Debit	Credit	Balance
2004					
Dec. 12		G1	1,000		1,000
31	Closing	G1		1,000	0

Supplies Expense — Acct. No. 652

Date	Explan.	PR	Debit	Credit	Balance
2004					
Dec. 31	Adj.	G1	1,050		1,050
31	Closing	G1		1,050	0

Utilities Expense — Acct. No. 690

Date	Explan.	PR	Debit	Credit	Balance
2004					
Dec. 26		G1	230		230
31	Closing	G1		230	0

Income Summary — Acct. No. 901

Date	Explan.	PR	Debit	Credit	Balance
2004					
Dec. 31	Closing	G1		8,150	8,150
31	Closing	G1	4,365		3,785
31	Closing	G1	3,785		0

Exhibit 4.6

Post-Closing Trial Balance

FASTFORWARD
Post-Closing Trial Balance
December 31, 2004

	Debit	Credit
Cash	$ 3,950	
Accounts receivable	1,800	
Supplies	8,670	
Prepaid insurance	2,300	
Equipment	26,000	
Accumulated depreciation—Equipment		$ 375
Accounts payable		6,200
Salaries payable		210
Unearned consulting revenue		2,750
C. Taylor, Capital		33,185
Totals	$42,720	$42,720

Exhibit 4.7

Steps in the Accounting Cycle*

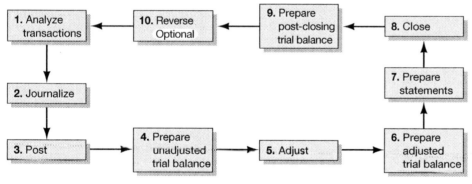

Explanations

1. Analyze transactions	Analyze transactions to prepare for journalizing.
2. Journalize	Record accounts, including debits and credits, in a journal.
3. Post	Transfer debits and credits from the journal to the ledger.
4. Prepare unadjusted trial balance	Summarize unadjusted ledger accounts and amounts.
5. Adjust	Record adjustments to bring account balances up to date; journalize and post adjusting entries.
6. Prepare adjusted trial balance	Summarize adjusted ledger accounts and amounts.
7. Prepare statements	Use adjusted trial balance to prepare financial statements.
8. Close	Journalize and post entries to close temporary accounts.
9. Prepare post-closing trial balance	Test clerical accuracy of the closing procedures.
10. Reverse (optional)	Reverse certain adjustments in the next period—optional step; see Appendix 4A.

*Steps 4, 6, and 9 can be done on a work sheet. A work sheet is useful in planning adjustments, but adjustments (step 5) must always be journalized and posted. Steps 3, 4, 6, and 9 are automatic with a computerized system.

Quick Check

4. What are the major steps in preparing closing entries?
5. Why are revenue and expense accounts called *temporary*? Can you identify and list any other temporary accounts?
6. What accounts are listed on the post-closing trial balance?

Answers—p. 159

Classified Balance Sheet

C3 Explain and prepare a classified balance sheet.

Our discussion to this point has been limited to unclassified financial statements. This section describes a classified balance sheet. An **unclassified balance sheet** is one whose items are broadly grouped into assets, liabilities, and equity. One example is FastForward's balance sheet in Exhibit 4.2. A **classified balance sheet** organizes assets and liabilities into important subgroups that provide more information to decision makers.

Topic Tackler 4-2

Classification Structure

A classified balance sheet has no required layout, but it usually contains the categories in Exhibit 4.8. One of the more important classifications is the separation between current and noncurrent items for both assets and liabilities. Current items are those expected to come due (either collected or owed) within one year or the company's operating cycle, whichever is longer. The **operating cycle** is the time span from when *cash is used* to acquire goods and services until *cash is received* from the sale of those goods and services. "Operating"

Exhibit 4.8

Typical Categories in a Classified Balance Sheet

Assets	Liabilities and Equity
Current assets	Current liabilities
Noncurrent assets	Noncurrent liabilities
Long-term investments	Equity
Plant assets	
Intangible assets	

refers to company operations and "cycle" refers to the circular flow of cash used for company inputs and then cash received from its outputs. The length of a company's operating cycle depends on its activities. For a service company, the operating cycle is the time span between (1) paying employees who perform the services and (2) receiving cash from customers. For a merchandiser selling products, the operating cycle is the time span between (1) paying suppliers for merchandise and (2) receiving cash from customers.

Point: Current is also called *short term*, and noncurrent is also called *long term*.

Most operating cycles are less than one year. This means most companies use a one-year period in deciding which assets and liabilities are current. A few companies have an operating cycle longer than one year. For instance, producers of certain beverages (wine) and products (ginseng) that require aging for several years have operating cycles longer than one year. A balance sheet lists current assets before noncurrent assets and current liabilities before noncurrent liabilities. This consistency in presentation allows users to quickly identify current assets that are most easily converted to cash and current liabilities that are shortly coming due. Items in current assets and current liabilities are listed in the order of how quickly they will be converted to, or paid in, cash.

Classification Categories

This section describes the most common categories in a classified balance sheet. The balance sheet for Snowboarding Components in Exhibit 4.9 shows these typical categories. Its assets are classified as either current or noncurrent. Its noncurrent assets include three main categories: long-term investments, plant assets, and intangible assets. Its liabilities are classified as either current or long term. Not all companies use the same categories of assets and liabilities for their balance sheets. K2's balance sheet lists only three asset classes: current assets; property, plant and equipment; and other assets.

Point: Short-term investments maturing within three months are combined with cash on both the balance sheet and cash flow statement. This combination is called *cash and cash equivalents*.

Current Assets **Current assets** are cash and other resources that are expected to be sold, collected, or used within one year or the company's operating cycle, whichever is longer. Examples are cash, short-term investments, accounts receivable, short-term notes receivable, goods for sale (called *merchandise* or *inventory*), and prepaid expenses. The individual prepaid expenses of a company are usually small in amount compared to many other assets and are often combined and shown as a single item. The prepaid expenses in Exhibit 4.9 likely include items such as prepaid insurance, prepaid rent, office supplies,

Exhibit 4.9

Example of a Classified Balance Sheet

SNOWBOARDING COMPONENTS Balance Sheet January 31, 2005			
Assets			
Current assets			
Cash		$ 6,500	
Short-term investments		2,100	
Accounts receivable		4,400	
Merchandise inventory		27,500	
Prepaid expenses		2,400	
Total current assets			$ 42,900
Long-term investments			
Notes receivable		1,500	
Investments in stocks and bonds		18,000	
Land held for future expansion		48,000	
Total long-term investments			67,500
Plant assets			
Store equipment	$ 33,200		
Less accumulated depreciation	8,000	25,200	
Buildings	170,000		
Less accumulated depreciation	45,000	125,000	
Land		73,200	
Total plant assets			223,400
Intangible assets			10,000
Total assets			$343,800
Liabilities			
Current liabilities			
Accounts payable		$15,300	
Wages payable		3,200	
Notes payable		3,000	
Current portion of long-term liabilities		7,500	
Total current liabilities			$ 29,000
Long-term liabilities (net of current portion)			150,000
Total liabilities			179,000
Equity			
I. Hawk, Capital			164,800
Total liabilities and equity			$343,800

and store supplies. Prepaid expenses are usually listed last because they will not be converted to cash (instead, they are used).

Long-Term Investments A second major balance sheet classification is **long-term** (or *noncurrent*) **investments.** Notes receivable and investments in stocks and bonds are long-term assets when they are expected to be held for more than the longer of one year or the operating cycle. Land held for future expansion is a long-term investment because it is *not* used in operations.

Plant Assets Plant assets are tangible assets that are both *long lived* and *used to produce or sell products and services.* Examples are equipment, machinery, buildings, and land that are used to produce or sell products and services. The order listing for plant assets is usually from most liquid to least liquid such as equipment and machinery to buildings and land.

Global: In the U.K. and many countries influenced by U.K. reporting, noncurrent assets are listed first and current assets are listed second.

Point: Plant assets are also called **fixed assets; property, plant and equipment;** or **long-lived assets.**

Intangible Assets   **Intangible assets** are long-term resources that benefit business operations. They usually lack physical form and have uncertain benefits. Examples are patents, trademarks, copyrights, franchises, and goodwill. Their value comes from the privileges or rights granted to or held by the owner. **Huffy Corporation** reports intangible assets of $48.1 million, which is more than 15 percent of its total assets. Its intangibles include trademarks, patents, and licensing agreements.

Current Liabilities   **Current liabilities** are obligations due to be paid or settled within one year or the operating cycle, whichever is longer. They are usually settled by paying out current assets such as cash. Current liabilities often include accounts payable, notes payable, wages payable, taxes payable, interest payable, and unearned revenues. Also, any portion of a long-term liability due to be paid within one year or the operating cycle, whichever is longer, is a current liability. Unearned revenues are current liabilities when they will be settled by delivering products or services within one year or the operating cycle, whichever is longer. Current liabilities are reported in the order of those to be settled first.

Point: Many financial ratios are distorted if accounts are not classified correctly. We must be especially careful when analyzing accounts whose balances are separated into short and long term.

Long-Term Liabilities   **Long-term liabilities** are obligations *not* due within one year or the operating cycle, whichever is longer. Notes payable, mortgages payable, bonds payable, and lease obligations are common long-term liabilities. If a company has both short- and long-term items in each of these categories, they are commonly separated into two accounts in the ledger.

Point: Many companies report two or more subgroups for long-term liabilities. See the balance sheets in Appendix A for examples.

Equity   Equity is the owner's claim on assets. For a proprietorship, this claim is reported in the equity section with an owner's capital account. (For a partnership, the equity section reports a capital account for each partner. For a corporation, the equity section is divided into two main subsections, common stock and retained earnings.)

Quick Check

7. Identify which of the following assets are classified as (1) current assets or (2) plant assets: (a) land used in operations, (b) office supplies, (c) receivables from customers due in 10 months, (d) insurance protection for the next nine months, (e) trucks used to provide services to customers, (f) trademarks.
8. Cite two examples of assets classified as investments on the balance sheet.
9. Explain the operating cycle for a service company.

Answers—p. 155

Decision Analysis   Current Ratio

A1   Compute the current ratio and describe what it reveals about a company's financial condition.

An important use of financial statements is to help assess a company's ability to pay its debts in the near future. Such analysis affects decisions by suppliers when allowing a company to buy on credit. It also affects decisions by creditors when lending money to a company, including loan terms such as interest rate, due date, and collateral requirements. It can also affect a manager's decisions about using cash to pay existing debts when they come due. The **current ratio** is an important measure of a company's ability to pay its short-term obligations. It is defined in Exhibit 4.10 as current assets divided by current liabilities:

Exhibit 4.10

Current Ratio

$$\text{Current ratio} = \frac{\text{Current assets}}{\text{Current liabilities}}$$

Using financial information from **Limited Brands, Inc.,** we compute its current ratio for the recent four-year period. The results are in Exhibit 4.11.

Fiscal Year ($ Millions)	2003	2002	2001	2000
Current assets	$3,606	$2,784	$2,068	$2,285
Current liabilities	$1,259	$1,454	$1,000	$1,236
Current ratio	2.9	1.9	2.1	1.8
Industry current ratio	2.8	2.9	3.3	3.4

Exhibit 4.11

Limited Brands's Current Ratio

Limited Brands's current ratio rose to 2.9 in 2003 compared to lower ratios for prior years. Still, the current ratio for each of these years suggests that the company's short-term obligations can be covered with its short-term assets. However, if its ratio would approach 1.0, Limited would expect to face challenges in covering liabilities. If the ratio were *less* than 1.0, current liabilities would exceed current assets, and the company's ability to pay short-term obligations would be in doubt.

Decision Maker

Analyst   You are analyzing the financial condition of a fitness club to assess its ability to meet upcoming loan payments. You compute its current ratio as 1.2. You also find that a major portion of accounts receivable is due from one client who has not made any payments in the past 12 months. Removing this receivable from current assets drops the current ratio to 0.7. What do you conclude?

Answer—p. 158

Demonstration Problem

The partial work sheet of Midtown Repair Company at December 31, 2005, follows:

	Adjusted Trial Balance		Income Statement		Balance Sheet and Statement of Owner's Equity	
	Debit	**Credit**	**Debit**	**Credit**	**Debit**	**Credit**
Cash	95,600					
Notes receivable (current)	50,000					
Prepaid insurance	16,000					
Prepaid rent	4,000					
Equipment	170,000					
Accumulated depreciation—Equipment		57,000				
Accounts payable		52,000				
Long-term notes payable		63,000				
C. Trout, Capital		178,500				
C. Trout, Withdrawals	30,000					
Repair services revenue		180,800				
Interest revenue		7,500				
Depreciation expense—Equipment	28,500					
Wages expense	85,000					
Rent expense	48,000					
Insurance expense	6,000					
Interest expense	5,700					
Totals	538,800	538,800				

Required

1. Complete the work sheet by extending the adjusted trial balance totals to the appropriate financial statement columns.
2. Prepare closing entries for Midtown Repair Company.

3. Set up the Income Summary and the C. Trout, Capital account in the general ledger (in balance column format) and post the closing entries to these accounts.

4. Determine the balance of the C. Trout, Capital account to be reported on the December 31, 2005, balance sheet.

5. Prepare an income statement, statement of owner's equity, and classified balance sheet (in report form) as of December 31, 2005.

Planning the Solution

- Extend the adjusted trial balance account balances to the appropriate financial statement columns.
- Prepare entries to close the revenue accounts to Income Summary, to close the expense accounts to Income Summary, to close Income Summary to the capital account, and to close the withdrawals account to the capital account.
- Post the first and second closing entries to the Income Summary account. Examine the balance of income summary and verify that it agrees with the net income shown on the work sheet.
- Post the third and fourth closing entries to the capital account.
- Use the work sheet's two right-most columns and your answer in part 4 to prepare the classified balance sheet.

Solution to Demonstration Problem

1. Completing the work sheet:

	Adjusted Trial Balance		Income Statement		Balance Sheet and Statement of Owner's Equity	
	Debit	**Credit**	**Debit**	**Credit**	**Debit**	**Credit**
Cash	95,600				95,600	
Notes receivable (current)	50,000				50,000	
Prepaid insurance	16,000				16,000	
Prepaid rent	4,000				4,000	
Equipment	170,000				170,000	
Accumulated depreciation—Equipment		57,000				57,000
Accounts payable		52,000				52,000
Long-term notes payable		63,000				63,000
C. Trout, Capital		178,500				178,500
C. Trout, Withdrawals	30,000				30,000	
Repair services revenue		180,800		180,800		
Interest revenue		7,500		7,500		
Depreciation expense—Equipment	28,500		28,500			
Wages expense	85,000		85,000			
Rent expense	48,000		48,000			
Insurance expense	6,000		6,000			
Interest expense	5,700		5,700			
Totals	538,800	538,800	173,200	188,300	365,600	350,500
Net Income			15,100			15,100
Totals			188,300	188,300	365,600	365,600

2. Closing entries:

Dec. 31	Repair Services Revenue	180,800	
	Interest Revenue........................	7,500	
	Income Summary.....................		188,300
	To close revenue accounts.		

[continued on next page]

[continued from previous page]

Dec. 31	Income Summary	173,200	
	Depreciation Expense—Equipment		28,500
	Wages Expense		85,000
	Rent Expense		48,000
	Insurance Expense		6,000
	Interest Expense		5,700
	To close expense accounts.		
Dec. 31	Income Summary	15,100	
	C. Trout, Capital.		15,100
	To close the Income Summary account.		
Dec. 31	C. Trout, Capital	30,000	
	C. Trout, Withdrawals.		30,000
	To close the withdrawals account.		

3. Set up the Income Summary and the capital ledger accounts and post the closing entries.

	Income Summary				Account No. 901
Date	**Explanation**	**PR**	**Debit**	**Credit**	**Balance**
2005					
Jan. 1	Beginning balance				0
Dec. 31	Close revenue accounts			188,300	188,300
31	Close expense accounts		173,200		15,100
31	Close income summary		15,100		0

	C. Trout, Capital				Account No. 301
Date	**Explanation**	**PR**	**Debit**	**Credit**	**Balance**
2005					
Jan. 1	Beginning balance				178,500
Dec. 31	Close Income Summary			15,100	193,600
31	Close C. Trout, Withdrawals		30,000		163,600

4. The final capital balance of $163,600 (from part 3) will be reported on the December 31, 2005 balance sheet. The final capital balance reflects the increase due to the net income earned during the year and the decrease for the owner's withdrawals during the year.

5.

MIDTOWN REPAIR COMPANY		
Income Statement		
For Year Ended December 31, 2005		
Revenues		
Repair services revenue	$180,800	
Interest revenue	7,500	
Total revenues		$188,300
Expenses		
Depreciation expense—Equipment	28,500	
Wages expense	85,000	
Rent expense	48,000	
Insurance expense	6,000	
Interest expense	5,700	
Total expenses		173,200
Net income		$ 15,100

MIDTOWN REPAIR COMPANY Statement of Owner's Equity For Year Ended December 31, 2005		
C. Trout, Capital, December 31, 2004		$178,500
Add: Investment by owner	$ 0	
Net income	15,100	15,100
		193,600
Less: Withdrawals by owner		30,000
C. Trout, Capital, December 31, 2005		$163,600

MIDTOWN REPAIR COMPANY Balance Sheet December 31, 2005		
Assets		
Current assets		
Cash		$ 95,600
Notes receivable		50,000
Prepaid insurance		16,000
Prepaid rent		4,000
Total current assets		165,600
Plant assets		
Equipment	$170,000	
Less: Accumulated depreciation—Equipment	(57,000)	
Total plant assets		113,000
Total assets		$278,600
Liabilities		
Current liabilities		
Accounts payable		$ 52,000
Long-term liabilities		
Long-term notes payable		63,000
Total liabilities		115,000
Equity		
C. Trout, Capital		163,600
Total liabilities and equity		$278,600

APPENDIX

Reversing Entries

Point: As a general rule, adjusting entries that create new asset or liability accounts are likely candidates for reversing.

Reversing entries are optional. They are recorded in response to accrued assets and accrued liabilities that were created by adjusting entries at the end of a reporting period. The purpose of reversing entries is to simplify a company's recordkeeping. Exhibit 4A.1 shows an example of FastForward's reversing entries. The top of the exhibit shows the adjusting entry FastForward recorded on December 31 for its employee's earned but unpaid salary. The entry recorded three days' salary of $210, which increased December's total salary expense to $1,610. The entry also recognized a liability of $210. The expense is reported on December's income statement. The expense account is then closed. The

Accrue salaries expense on December 31, 2004

Salaries Expense 210
    Salaries Payable 210

Salaries Expense

Date	Expl.	Debit	Credit	Balance
2004				
Dec. 12	(7)	700		700
26	(16)	700		1,400
31	(e)	210		1,610

Salaries Payable

Date	Expl.	Debit	Credit	Balance
2004				
Dec. 31	(e)		210	210

Exhibit 4A.1

Reversing Entries for an Accrued Expense

— OR —

No reversing entry recorded on January 1, 2005

NO ENTRY

Salaries Expense

Date	Expl.	Debit	Credit	Balance
2005				

Salaries Payable

Date	Expl.	Debit	Credit	Balance
2004				
Dec. 31	(e)		210	210
2005				

Reversing entry recorded on January 1, 2005

Salaries Payable 210
    Salaries Expense 210

Salaries Expense*

Date	Expl.	Debit	Credit	Balance
2005				
Jan. 1			210	(210)

Salaries Payable

Date	Expl.	Debit	Credit	Balance
2004				
Dec. 31	(e)		210	210
2004				
Jan. 1		210		0

Pay the accrued and current salaries on January 9, the first payday in 2005

Salaries Expense 490
Salaries Payable 210
    Cash 700

Salaries Expense

Date	Expl.	Debit	Credit	Balance
2005				
Jan. 9		490		**490**

Salaries Payable

Date	Expl.	Debit	Credit	Balance
2004				
Dec. 31	(e)		210	210
2005				
Jan. 9		210		0

Salaries Expense 700
    Cash 700

Salaries Expense*

Date	Expl.	Debit	Credit	Balance
2005				
Jan. 1			210	(210)
Jan. 9		700		**490**

Salaries Payable

Date	Expl.	Debit	Credit	Balance
2004				
Dec. 31	(e)		210	210
2005				
Jan. 1		210		0

Under both approaches, the expense and liability accounts have identical balances after the cash payment on January 9.

Salaries Expense $490
Salaries Payable .... $ 0

*Circled numbers in the *Balance* column indicate abnormal balances.

ledger on January 1, 2005, shows a $210 liability and a zero balance in the Salaries Expense account. At this point, the choice is made between using or not using reversing entries.

Accounting *without* Reversing Entries

The path down the left side of Exhibit 4A.1 is described in the chapter. To summarize here, when the next payday occurs on January 9, we record payment with a compound entry that debits both the expense and liability accounts and credits Cash. Posting that entry creates a $490 balance in the expense account and reduces the liability account balance to zero because the debt has been settled. The disadvantage of this approach is the slightly more complex entry required on January 9. Paying the accrued liability means that this entry differs from the routine entries made on all other paydays. To construct the proper entry on January 9, we must recall the effect of the December 31 adjusting entry. Reversing entries overcome this disadvantage.

Accounting *with* Reversing Entries

P4 Prepare reversing entries and explain their purpose.

The right side of Exhibit 4A.1 shows how a reversing entry on January 1 overcomes the disadvantage of the January 9 entry when not using reversing entries. A reversing entry is the exact opposite of an adjusting entry. For FastForward, the Salaries Payable liability account is debited for $210, meaning that this account now has a zero balance after the entry is posted. The Salaries Payable account temporarily understates the liability, but this is not a problem since financial statements are not prepared before the liability is settled on January 9. The credit to the Salaries Expense account is unusual because it gives the account an *abnormal credit balance*. We highlight an abnormal balance by circling it. Because of the reversing entry, the January 9 entry to record payment is straightforward. This entry debits the Salaries Expense account and credits Cash for the full $700 paid. It is the same as all other entries made to record 10 days' salary for the employee. Notice that after the payment entry is posted, the Salaries Expense account has a $490 balance that reflects seven days' salary of $70 per day (see the lower right side of Exhibit 4A.1). The zero balance in the Salaries Payable account is now correct. The lower section of Exhibit 4A.1 shows that the expense and liability accounts have exactly the same balances whether reversing entries are used or not. This means that both approaches yield identical results.

Summary

C1   Explain why temporary accounts are closed each period. Temporary accounts are closed at the end of each accounting period for two main reasons. First, the closing process updates the capital account to include the effects of all transactions and events recorded for the period. Second, it prepares revenue, expense, and withdrawals accounts for the next reporting period by giving them zero balances.

C2   Identify steps in the accounting cycle. The accounting cycle consists of 10 steps: (1) analyze transactions, (2) journalize, (3) post, (4) prepare an unadjusted trial balance, (5) adjust accounts, (6) prepare an adjusted trial balance, (7) prepare statements, (8) close, (9) prepare a post-closing trial balance, and (10) prepare (optional) reversing entries.

C3   Explain and prepare a classified balance sheet. Classified balance sheets report assets and liabilities in two categories: current and noncurrent. Noncurrent assets often include long-term investments, plant assets, and intangible assets. Owner's equity for proprietorships (and partnerships) report the capital account balance. A corporation separates equity into common stock and retained earnings.

A1   Compute the current ratio and describe what it reveals about a company's financial condition. A company's current ratio is defined as current assets divided by current liabilities. We use it to evaluate a company's ability to pay its current liabilities out of current assets.

P1   Prepare a work sheet and explain its usefulness. A work sheet can be a useful tool in preparing and analyzing financial statements. It is helpful at the end of a period in preparing adjusting entries, an adjusted trial balance, and financial statements. A work sheet usually contains five pairs of columns: Unadjusted Trial Balance, Adjustments, Adjusted Trial Balance, Income Statement, and Balance Sheet & Statement of Owner's Equity.

P2   Describe and prepare closing entries. Closing entries involve four steps: (1) close credit balances in revenue (and gain) accounts to Income Summary, (2) close debit balances in expense (and loss) accounts to Income Summary, (3) close Income Summary to the capital account, and (4) close withdrawals account to owner's capital.

P3   Explain and prepare a post-closing trial balance. A post-closing trial balance is a list of permanent accounts and their balances after all closing entries have been journalized and posted. Its purpose is to verify that (1) total debits equal total credits for permanent accounts and (2) all temporary accounts have zero balances.

P4^A   Prepare reversing entries and explain their purpose. Reversing entries are an optional step. They are applied to accrued expenses and revenues. The purpose of reversing entries is to simplify subsequent journal entries. Financial statements are unaffected by the choice to use or not use reversing entries.

Guidance Answers to **Decision Maker** and **Decision Ethics**

Entrepreneur   Yes, you are concerned about the absence of a depreciation adjustment. Equipment does depreciate, and financial statements must recognize this occurrence. Its absence suggests an error or a misrepresentation.

Analyst   A current ratio of 1.2 suggests that current assets are sufficient to cover current liabilities, but it implies a minimal buffer in case of errors in measuring current assets or current liabilities. Removing tardy receivables reduces the current ratio to 0.7. Your assessment is that the club will have some difficulty meeting its loan payments.

Guidance Answers to **Quick Checks**

1. Amounts in the Unadjusted Trial Balance columns are taken from current account balances in the ledger. The balances for new accounts expected to arise from adjusted entries can be left blank or set at zero.

2. A work sheet offers the advantage of listing on one page all necessary information to make adjusting entries.

3. A work sheet can help in (a) accounting efficiency and avoiding errors, (b) linking transactions and events to their effects in financial statements, (c) showing adjustments for audit purposes, (d) preparing interim financial statements, and (e) showing effects from proposed, or what-if, transactions.

4. The major steps in preparing closing entries are to close (1) credit balances in revenue accounts to Income Summary, (2) debit balances in expense accounts to Income Summary, (3) Income Summary to owner's capital, and (4) any withdrawals account to owner's capital.

5. Revenue (and gain) and expense (and loss) accounts are called *temporary* because they are opened and closed each period. The Income Summary and owner's withdrawals accounts are also temporary.

6. Permanent accounts make up the post-closing trial balance. These accounts are asset, liability, and equity accounts.

7. Current assets: (*b*), (*c*), (*d*). Plant assets: (*a*), (*e*). Item (*f*) is an intangible asset.

8. Investment in common stock, investment in bonds, and land held for future expansion.

9. For a service company, the operating cycle is the usual time between (1) paying employees who do the services and (2) receiving cash from customers for services provided.

Key Terms

Key Terms are available at the book's Website for learning and testing in an online Flashcard Format.

Accounting cycle (p. 147)
Classified balance sheet (p. 150)
Closing entries (p. 145)
Closing process (p. 140)
Current assets (p. 150)
Current liabilities (p. 152)
Current ratio (p. 152)

Income Summary (p. 145)
Intangible assets (p. 152)
Long-term investments (p. 151)
Long-term liabilities (p. 152)
Operating cycle (p. 150)
Permanent accounts (p. 145)
Post-closing trial balance (p. 147)

Pro forma financial statements (p. 144)
Reversing entries (p. 156)
Temporary accounts (p. 145)
Unclassified balance sheet (p. 150)
Working papers (p. 136)
Work sheet (p. 136)

Personal Interactive Quiz

Personal Interactive Quizzes A and B are available at the book's Website to reinforce and assess your learning.

Superscript letter ^{A} *denotes assignments based on Appendix 4A.*

Discussion Questions

1. What accounts are affected by closing entries? What accounts are not affected?

2. What two purposes are accomplished by recording closing entries?

3. What are the steps in recording closing entries?

4. What is the purpose of the Income Summary account?

5. Explain whether an error has occurred if a post-closing trial balance includes a Depreciation Expense account.

6. What tasks are aided by a work sheet?

7. Why are the debit and credit entries in the Adjustments columns of the work sheet identified with letters?

8. What is a company's operating cycle?

9. What classes of assets and liabilities are shown on a typical classified balance sheet?

10. How is unearned revenue classified on the balance sheet?

11. What are the characteristics of plant assets?

12.^{A}How do reversing entries simplify recordkeeping?

13.^{A}If a company recorded accrued salaries expense of $500 at the end of its fiscal year, what reversing entry could be made? When would it be made?

14. Refer to the balance sheet for **Krispy Kreme** in Appendix A. What five noncurrent asset categories are used on its classified balance sheet?

15. Refer to **Tastykake**'s balance sheet in Appendix A. Identify the accounts listed as current liabilities.

16. Refer to **Harley-Davidson**'s financial statements **Harley-Davidson** in Appendix A. What journal entry was likely recorded as of December 31, 2002, to close its Income Summary account?

 Red numbers denote Discussion Questions that involve decision-making.

Homework Manager *repeats all numerical Quick Study assignments on the book's Website with new numbers.*

QUICK STUDY

QS 4-1
Determining effects of closing entries

C1 P2

Argosy Company began the current period with a $14,000 credit balance in the D. Argosy, Capital account. At the end of the period, the company's adjusted account balances include the following temporary accounts with normal balances:

Service fees earned	$35,000		Interest revenue	$3,500
Salaries expense	19,000		D. Argosy, Withdrawals	6,000
Depreciation expense	4,000		Utilities expense	2,300

After closing the revenue and expense accounts, what will be the balance of the Income Summary account? After all closing entries are journalized and posted, what will be the balance of the D. Argosy, Capital account?

QS 4-2
Identifying the accounting cycle

C2

List the following steps of the accounting cycle in their proper order:
a. Preparing the post-closing trial balance.
b. Posting the journal entries.
c. Journalizing and posting adjusting entries.
d. Preparing the adjusted trial balance.
e. Journalizing and posting closing entries.
f. Analyzing transactions and events.
g. Preparing the financial statements.
h. Preparing the unadjusted trial balance.
i. Journalizing transactions and events.

QS 4-3
Classifying balance sheet items

C3

The following are common categories on a classified balance sheet:
A. Current assets
B. Long-term investments
C. Plant assets
D. Intangible assets
E. Current liabilities
F. Long-term liabilities

For each of the following items, select the letter that identifies the balance sheet category where the item typically would appear.
_____ **1.** Trademarks
_____ **2.** Accounts receivable
_____ **3.** Land not currently used in operations
_____ **4.** Notes payable (due in three years)
_____ **5.** Cash
_____ **6.** Wages payable
_____ **7.** Store equipment
_____ **8.** Accounts payable

QS 4-4
Identifying current accounts and computing the current ratio

C3 A1

Compute Jamar Company's current ratio using the following information:

Accounts receivable	$15,000		Long-term notes payable	$20,000
Accounts payable	10,000		Office supplies	1,800
Buildings	42,000		Prepaid insurance	2,500
Cash	6,000		Unearned services revenue	4,000

QS 4-5
Interpreting a work sheet

P1

The following information is taken from the work sheet for Wayman Company as of December 31, 2005. Using this information, determine the amount for K. Wayman, Capital, that should be reported on its December 31, 2005, balance sheet.

	Income Statement		Balance Sheet and Statement of Owner's Equity	
	Dr.	**Cr.**	**Dr.**	**Cr.**
K.Wayman, Capital				65,000
K.Wayman, Withdrawals			32,000	
Totals	115,000	174,000		

In preparing a work sheet, indicate the financial statement Debit column to which a normal balance in the following accounts should be extended. Use IS for the Income Statement Debit column and BS for the Balance Sheet and Statement of Owner's Equity Debit column.

_____ **a.** Insurance expense   _____ **d.** Depreciation expense—Equipment

_____ **b.** Equipment   _____ **e.** Prepaid rent

_____ **c.** Owner, Withdrawals   _____ **f.** Accounts receivable

QS 4-6
Applying a work sheet
P1

List the following steps in preparing a work sheet in their proper order by writing numbers 1–5 in the blank spaces provided.

a. _____ Prepare an adjusted trial balance on the work sheet.

b. _____ Prepare an unadjusted trial balance on the work sheet.

c. _____ Enter adjustments data on the work sheet.

d. _____ Extend adjusted balances to appropriate financial statement columns.

e. _____ Total the statement columns, compute net income (loss), and complete work sheet.

QS 4-7
Ordering work sheet steps
P1

The ledger of Terrel Company includes the following unadjusted normal balances: Prepaid Rent $800, Services Revenue $11,600, and Wages Expense $5,000. Adjusting entries are required for **(a)** accrued rent expense $240; **(b)** accrued services revenue $180; and **(c)** accrued wages expense $160. Enter these unadjusted balances and the necessary adjustments on a work sheet and complete the work sheet for these accounts. *Note:* You must include the following accounts: Accounts Receivable, Wages Payable, and Rent Expense.

QS 4-8
Preparing a partial work sheet
P1

The ledger of Avril Company includes the following accounts with normal balances: L. Avril, Capital $6,000; L. Avril, Withdrawals $400; Services Revenue $10,000; Wages Expense $5,200; and Rent Expense $800. Prepare the necessary closing entries at December 31.

QS 4-9
Prepare closing entries from the ledger   P2

Identify the accounts listed in QS 4-9 that would be included in a post-closing trial balance.

QS 4-10
Identify post-closing accounts   P3

On December 31, 2004, Yates Co. prepared an adjusting entry for $6,700 of earned but unrecorded management fees. On January 16, 2005, Yates received $15,500 cash in management fees, which included the accrued fees earned in 2004. Assuming the company uses reversing entries, prepare the January 1, 2005, reversing entry and the January 16, 2005, cash receipt entry.

QS 4-11[A]
Reversing entries
P4

Homework Manager repeats all numerical Exercises on the book's Website with new numbers.

Use the March 31 fiscal year-end information from the following ledger accounts (assume that all accounts have normal balances) to prepare closing journal entries and then post those entries to the appropriate ledger accounts.

EXERCISES

Exercise 4-1
Preparing and posting closing entries
P2

General Ledger										

M. Mallon, Capital   Acct. No. 301

Date	PR	Debit	Credit	Balance
Mar. 31	G2			42,000

Salaries Expense   Acct. No. 622

Date	PR	Debit	Credit	Balance
Mar. 31	G2			21,000

[continued on next page]

[continued from previous page]

M. Mallon, Withdrawals				Acct. No. 302
Date	PR	Debit	Credit	Balance
Mar. 31	G2			25,000

Insurance Expense				Acct. No. 637
Date	PR	Debit	Credit	Balance
Mar. 31	G2			4,500

Check M. Mallon, Capital (ending balance), $38,900

Services Revenue				Acct. No. 401
Date	PR	Debit	Credit	Balance
Mar. 31	G2			74,000

Rent Expense				Acct. No. 640
Date	PR	Debit	Credit	Balance
Mar. 31	G2			9,600

Depreciation Expense				Acct. No. 603
Date	PR	Debit	Credit	Balance
Mar. 31	G2			17,000

Income Summary				Acct. No. 901
Date	PR	Debit	Credit	Balance

Exercise 4-2

Preparing closing entries and a post-closing trial balance

P2 P3

The adjusted trial balance for Schwepker Marketing Co. follows. Complete the four right-most columns of the table by first entering information for the four closing entries (keyed *1* through *4*) and second by completing the post-closing trial balance.

No.	Account Title	Adjusted Trial Balance		Closing Entry Information		Post-Closing Trial Balance	
		Dr.	Cr.	Dr.	Cr.	Dr.	Cr.
101	Cash	$ 8,200					
106	Accounts receivable	24,000					
153	Equipment	41,000					
154	Accumulated depreciation—Equipment		$ 16,500				
193	Franchise	30,000					
201	Accounts payable		14,000				
209	Salaries payable		3,200				
233	Unearned fees		2,600				
301	C. Schwepker, Capital		64,500				
302	C. Schwepker, Withdrawals	14,400					
401	Marketing fees earned		79,000				
611	Depreciation expense—Equipment	11,000					
622	Salaries expense	31,500					
640	Rent expense	12,000					
677	Miscellaneous expenses	7,700					
901	Income summary						
	Totals	$179,800	$179,800				

Exercise 4-3

Preparing closing entries and a post-closing trial balance

C1 P2 P3

The following adjusted trial balance contains the accounts and balances of Showers Company as of December 31, 2005, the end of its fiscal year. (1) Prepare the December 31, 2005, closing entries for Showers Company. (2) Prepare the December 31, 2005, post-closing trial balance for Showers Company.

No.	Account Title	Debit	Credit
101	Cash	$18,000	
126	Supplies	12,000	
128	Prepaid insurance	2,000	
167	Equipment	23,000	
168	Accumulated depreciation—Equipment		$ 6,500
301	R. Showers, Capital		46,600

[continued on next page]

[continued from previous page]

		Debit	Credit
302	R. Showers, Withdrawals	6,000	
404	Services revenue		36,000
612	Depreciation expense—Equipment	2,000	
622	Salaries expense	21,000	
637	Insurance expense	1,500	
640	Rent expense	2,400	
652	Supplies expense	1,200	
	Totals	$89,100	$89,100

Check (2) R. Showers, Capital (ending), $48,500; Total debits, $55,000

Use the following adjusted trial balance of Webb Trucking Company to prepare a classified balance sheet as of December 31, 2005.

Exercise 4-4
Preparing a classified balance sheet

C3

Account Title	Debit	Credit
Cash	$ 7,000	
Accounts receivable	16,500	
Office supplies	2,000	
Trucks	170,000	
Accumulated depreciation—Trucks		$ 35,000
Land	75,000	
Accounts payable		11,000
Interest payable		3,000
Long-term notes payable		52,000
K. Webb, Capital		161,000
K. Webb, Withdrawals	19,000	
Trucking fees earned		128,000
Depreciation expense—Trucks	22,500	
Salaries expense	60,000	
Office supplies expense	7,000	
Repairs expense—Trucks	11,000	
Totals	$390,000	$390,000

Check Total assets, $235,500; K. Webb, Capital, $169,500

Use the information in the adjusted trial balance reported in Exercise 4-4 to prepare Webb Trucking Company's (1) income statement, and (2) statement of owner's equity. The K. Webb, Capital account balance is $161,000 at December 31, 2004.

Exercise 4-5
Preparing the financial statements

C2

Use the information in the adjusted trial balance reported in Exercise 4-4 to compute the current ratio as of the balance sheet date. Interpret the current ratio for this company. (Assume that the industry norm for the current ratio is 1.5.)

Exercise 4-6
Computing the current ratio

A1

Calculate the current ratio in each of the following separate cases. Identify the company case with the strongest liquidity position. (These cases represent competing companies in the same industry.)

Exercise 4-7
Computing and analyzing the current ratio

A1

	Current Assets	Current Liabilities
Case 1	$ 78,000	$31,000
Case 2	104,000	75,000
Case 3	44,000	48,000
Case 4	84,500	80,600
Case 5	60,000	99,000

Exercise 4-8
Preparing adjusting entries from a work sheet

P1

Use the following information from the Adjustments columns of a 10-column work sheet to prepare the necessary adjusting journal entries (*a*) through (*e*):

No.	Account Title	Debit	Credit
109	Interest receivable	(d) $ 580	
124	Office supplies		(b) $1,650
128	Prepaid insurance		(a) 900
164	Accumulated depreciation—Office equipment		(c) 3,300
209	Salaries payable		(e) 660
409	Interest revenue		(d) 580
612	Depreciation expense—Office equipment	(c) 3,300	
620	Office salaries expense	(e) 660	
636	Insurance expense—Office equipment	(a) 432	
637	Insurance expense—Store equipment	(a) 468	
650	Office supplies expense	(b) 1,650	
	Totals	$7,090	$7,090

Exercise 4-9
Extending adjusted account balances on a work sheet

P1

These 16 accounts are from the Adjusted Trial Balance columns of a company's 10-column work sheet. In the blank space beside each account, write the letter of the appropriate financial statement column (A, B, C, or D) to which a normal account balance is extended.

A. Debit column for the Income Statement columns.
B. Credit column for the Income Statement columns.
C. Debit column for the Balance Sheet and Statement of Owner's Equity columns.
D. Credit column for the Balance Sheet and Statement of Owner's Equity columns.

_____ **1.** Office Supplies   _____ **9.** Service Fees Revenue
_____ **2.** Accounts Payable   _____ **10.** Insurance Expense
_____ **3.** Owner, Capital   _____ **11.** Accumulated Depreciation
_____ **4.** Wages Payable   _____ **12.** Interest Revenue
_____ **5.** Machinery   _____ **13.** Accounts Receivable
_____ **6.** Interest Receivable   _____ **14.** Rent Expense
_____ **7.** Interest Expense   _____ **15.** Depreciation Expense
_____ **8.** Owner, Withdrawals   _____ **16.** Cash

Exercise 4-10
Extending accounts in a work sheet

P1

The Adjusted Trial Balance columns of a 10-column work sheet for Poppe Company follow. Complete the work sheet by extending the account balances into the appropriate financial statement columns and by entering the amount of net income for the reporting period.

No.	Account Title	Debit	Credit
101	Cash	$ 6,000	
106	Accounts receivable	26,200	
153	Trucks	41,000	
154	Accumulated depreciation—Trucks		$ 16,500
183	Land	30,000	
201	Accounts payable		14,000
209	Salaries payable		3,200
233	Unearned fees		2,600
301	J. Poppe, Capital		64,500
302	J. Poppe, Withdrawals	14,400	
401	Plumbing fees earned		79,000
611	Depreciation expense—Trucks	5,500	
622	Salaries expense	37,000	
640	Rent expense	12,000	
677	Miscellaneous expenses	7,700	
	Totals	$179,800	$179,800

Check   Net income, $16,800

These partially completed Income Statement columns from a 10-column work sheet are for Red Sail Rental Co. (1) Use the information to determine the amount that should be entered on the net income line of the work sheet. (2) Prepare Red Sail's closing entries. The owner, L. Welch, did not make any withdrawals this period.

Account Title	Debit	Credit
Rent earned		102,000
Salaries expense	45,300	
Insurance expense	6,400	
Dock rental expense	15,000	
Boat supplies expense	3,200	
Depreciation expense—Boats	19,500	
Totals		
Net income		
Totals		

The following unadjusted trial balance contains the accounts and balances of Dalton Delivery Company as of December 31, 2005, its first year of operations. (1) Use the following information about the company's adjustments to complete a 10-column work sheet for Dalton.

a. Unrecorded depreciation on the trucks at the end of the year is $35,000.

b. The total amount of accrued interest expense at year-end is $8,000.

c. The cost of unused office supplies still available at year-end is $1,000.

(2) Prepare the year-end closing entries for Dalton, and determine the capital amount to be reported on the year-end balance sheet.

Account Title	Debit	Credit
Cash	$ 14,000	
Accounts receivable	33,000	
Office supplies	4,000	
Trucks	340,000	
Accumulated depreciation—Trucks		$ 70,000
Land	150,000	
Accounts payable		22,000
Interest payable		6,000
Long-term notes payable		104,000
V. Dalton, Capital		322,000
V. Dalton, Withdrawals	38,000	
Delivery fees earned		256,000
Depreciation expense—Truck	45,000	
Salaries expense	120,000	
Office supplies expense	14,000	
Interest expense	6,000	
Repairs expense—trucks	16,000	
Totals	$780,000	$780,000

The following two events occurred for Totten Co. on October 31, 2005, the end of its fiscal year:

a. Totten rents a building from its owner for $3,200 per month. By a prearrangement, the company delayed paying October's rent until November 5. On this date, the company paid the rent for both October and November.

b. Totten rents space in a building it owns to a tenant for $750 per month. By prearrangement, the tenant delayed paying the October rent until November 8. On this date, the tenant paid the rent for both October and November.

Required

1. Prepare adjusting entries that Totten must record for these events as of October 31.

2. Assuming Totten does *not* use reversing entries, prepare journal entries to record Totten's payment of rent on November 5 and the collection of rent on November 8 from Totten's tenant.

3. Assuming that Totten uses reversing entries, prepare reversing entries on November 1 and the journal entries to record Totten's payment of rent on November 5 and the collection of rent on November 8 from Totten's tenant.

Exercise 4-14^A
Preparing reversing entries

P4

Hinson Company records prepaid assets and unearned revenues in balance sheet accounts. The following information was used to prepare adjusting entries for Hinson Company as of August 31, the end of the company's fiscal year:

a. The company has earned $5,000 in unrecorded service fees.

b. The expired portion of prepaid insurance is $2,700.

c. The company has earned $1,900 of its Unearned Service Fees account balance.

d. Depreciation expense for office equipment is $2,300.

e. Employees have earned but have not been paid salaries of $2,400.

Prepare any necessary reversing entries for the accounting adjustments *a* through *e* assuming that Hinson uses reversing entries in its accounting system.

PROBLEM SET A

Problem 4-1A
Determining balance sheet classifications

C3

In the blank space beside each numbered balance sheet item, enter the letter of its balance sheet classification. If the item should not appear on the balance sheet, enter a Z in the blank.

A. Current assets   **D.** Intangible assets   **F.** Long-term liabilities
B. Long-term investments   **E.** Current liabilities   **G.** Equity
C. Plant assets

_____ **1.** Accumulated depreciation—Trucks
_____ **2.** Cash
_____ **3.** Buildings
_____ **4.** Store supplies
_____ **5.** Office equipment
_____ **6.** Land (used in operations)
_____ **7.** Repairs expense
_____ **8.** Office supplies
_____ **9.** Current portion of long-term note payable

_____ **10.** Long-term investment in stock
_____ **11.** Depreciation expense—Building
_____ **12.** Prepaid rent
_____ **13.** Interest receivable
_____ **14.** Taxes payable
_____ **15.** Automobiles
_____ **16.** Notes payable (due in 3 years)
_____ **17.** Accounts payable
_____ **18.** Prepaid insurance
_____ **19.** Owner, Capital
_____ **20.** Unearned services revenue

Problem 4-2A
Applying the accounting cycle

C1 C2 P2 P3

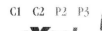
mhhe.com/larson

On April 1, 2005, Jennifer Stafford created a new travel agency, See-It-Now Travel. The following transactions occurred during the company's first month:

April 1 Stafford invested $20,000 cash and computer equipment worth $40,000 in the business.
    2 Rented furnished office space by paying $1,700 cash for the first month's (April) rent.
    3 Purchased $1,100 of office supplies for cash.
    10 Paid $3,600 cash for the premium on a 12-month insurance policy. Coverage begins on April 11.
    14 Paid $1,800 cash for two weeks' salaries earned by employees.
    24 Collected $7,900 cash on commissions from airlines on tickets obtained for customers.
    28 Paid another $1,800 cash for two weeks' salaries earned by employees.
    29 Paid $250 cash for minor repairs to the company's computer.
    30 Paid $650 cash for this month's telephone bill.
    30 Stafford withdrew $1,500 cash for personal use.

The company's chart of accounts follows:

101	Cash	405	Commissions Earned
106	Accounts Receivable	612	Depreciation Expense—Computer Equip.
124	Office Supplies	622	Salaries Expense
128	Prepaid Insurance	637	Insurance Expense
167	Computer Equipment	640	Rent Expense
168	Accumulated Depreciation—Computer Equip.	650	Office Supplies Expense
209	Salaries Payable	684	Repairs Expense
301	J. Stafford, Capital	688	Telephone Expense
302	J. Stafford, Withdrawals	901	Income Summary

Required

1. Use the balance column format to set up each ledger account listed in its chart of accounts.

2. Prepare journal entries to record the transactions for April and post them to the ledger accounts. The company records prepaid and unearned items in balance sheet accounts.

3. Prepare an unadjusted trial balance as of April 30.

4. Use the following information to journalize and post adjusting entries for the month:

    a. Two-thirds of one month's insurance coverage has expired.

    b. At the end of the month, $700 of office supplies are still available.

    c. This month's depreciation on the computer equipment is $600.

    d. Employees earned $320 of unpaid and unrecorded salaries as of month-end.

    e. The company earned $1,650 of commissions that are not yet billed at month-end.

5. Prepare the income statement and the statement of owner's equity for the month of April and the balance sheet at April 30, 2005.

6. Prepare journal entries to close the temporary accounts and post these entries to the ledger.

7. Prepare a post-closing trial balance.

Check (3) Unadj. trial balance totals, $67,900

(4a) Dr. Insurance Expense, $200

(5) Net income, $1,830; Capital (4/30/2005), $60,330; Total assets, $60,650

(7) P-C trial balance totals, $61,250

The adjusted trial balance of Kobe Repairs on December 31, 2005, follows:

Problem 4-3A
Preparing trial balances, closing entries, and financial statements

C3 P2 P3

mhhe.com/larson

No.	Account Title	Debit	Credit
	KOBE REPAIRS Adjusted Trial Balance December 31, 2005		
101	Cash	$ 13,000	
124	Office supplies	1,200	
128	Prepaid insurance	1,950	
167	Equipment	48,000	
168	Accumulated depreciation—Equipment		$ 4,000
201	Accounts payable		12,000
210	Wages payable		500
301	S. Kobe, Capital		40,000
302	S. Kobe, Withdrawals	15,000	
401	Repair fees earned		77,750
612	Depreciation expense—Equipment	4,000	
623	Wages expense	36,500	
637	Insurance expense	700	
640	Rent expense	9,600	
650	Office supplies expense	2,600	
690	Utilities expense	1,700	
	Totals	$134,250	$134,250

Required

Check (1) Ending capital balance, $47,650

(2) P-C trial balance totals, $64,150

1. Prepare an income statement and a statement of owner's equity for the year 2005, and a classified balance sheet at December 31, 2005. There are no owner investments in 2005.

2. Enter the adjusted trial balance in the first two columns of a six-column table. Use columns three and four for closing entry information and the last two columns for a post-closing trial balance. Insert an Income Summary account as the last item in the trial balance.

3. Enter closing entry information in the six-column table and prepare journal entries for them.

Analysis Component

4. Assume for this part only that:

    a. None of the $700 insurance expense had expired during the year. Instead, assume it is a prepayment of the next period's insurance protection.

    b. There are no earned and unpaid wages at the end of the year. (*Hint:* Reverse the $500 wages payable accrual.)

    Describe the financial statement changes that would result from these two assumptions.

Problem 4-4A

Preparing closing entries, financial statements, and ratios

C3 A1 P2

The adjusted trial balance for Sharp Construction as of December 31, 2005, follows:

	SHARP CONSTRUCTION Adjusted Trial Balance December 31, 2005		
No.	**Account Title**	**Debit**	**Credit**
101	Cash	$ 4,000	
104	Short-term investments	22,000	
126	Supplies	7,100	
128	Prepaid insurance	6,000	
167	Equipment	39,000	
168	Accumulated depreciation—Equipment		$ 20,000
173	Building	130,000	
174	Accumulated depreciation—Building		55,000
183	Land	45,000	
201	Accounts payable		15,500
203	Interest payable		1,500
208	Rent payable		2,500
210	Wages payable		1,500
213	Property taxes payable		800
233	Unearned professional fees		6,500
251	Long-term notes payable		66,000
301	J. Sharp, Capital		82,700
302	J. Sharp, Withdrawals	12,000	
401	Professional fees earned		96,000
406	Rent earned		13,000
407	Dividends earned		1,900
409	Interest earned		1,000
606	Depreciation expense—Building	10,000	
612	Depreciation expense—Equipment	5,000	
623	Wages expense	31,000	
633	Interest expense	4,100	
637	Insurance expense	9,000	
640	Rent expense	12,400	
652	Supplies expense	6,400	
682	Postage expense	3,200	
683	Property taxes expense	4,000	
684	Repairs expense	7,900	
688	Telephone expense	2,200	
690	Utilities expense	3,600	
	Totals	$363,900	$363,900

J. Sharp invested $50,000 cash in the business during year 2005 (the December 31, 2004, credit balance of the J. Sharp, Capital account was $32,700). Sharp Construction is required to make a $6,600 payment on its long-term notes payable during 2006.

Required

1. Prepare the income statement and the statement of owner's equity for the calendar-year 2005, and the classified balance sheet at December 31, 2005.

2. Prepare the necessary closing entries at December 31, 2005.

3. Use the information in the financial statements to compute these ratios: (a) return on assets (total assets at December 31, 2004, was $200,000), (b) debt ratio, (c) profit margin ratio (use total revenues as the denominator), and (d) current ratio.

Check (1) Total assets (12/31/2005), $178,100; Net income, $13,100

The following unadjusted trial balance is for Adams Construction Co. as of the end of its 2005 fiscal year. The June 30, 2004, credit balance of the owner's capital account was $52,660, and the owner invested $25,000 cash in the company during the 2005 fiscal year.

Problem 4-5A
Preparing a work sheet, adjusting and closing entries, and financial statements

File Edit View Insert Format Tools Data Window Help			
	A	**B**	**C**	**D**

ADAMS CONSTRUCTION CO.
Unadjusted Trial Balance
June 30, 2005

No.	Account Title	Debit	Credit
101	Cash	$ 17,500	
126	Supplies	8,900	
128	Prepaid insurance	6,200	
167	Equipment	131,000	
168	Accumulated depreciation—Equipment		$ 25,250
201	Accounts payable		5,800
203	Interest payable		0
208	Rent payable		0
210	Wages payable		0
213	Property taxes payable		0
251	Long-term notes payable		24,000
301	S. Adams, Capital		77,660
302	S. Adams, Withdrawals	30,000	
401	Construction fees earned		134,000
612	Depreciation expense—Equipment	0	
623	Wages expense	45,860	
633	Interest expense	2,640	
637	Insurance expense	0	
640	Rent expense	13,200	
652	Supplies expense	0	
683	Property taxes expense	4,600	
684	Repairs expense	2,810	
690	Utilities expense	4,000	
	Totals	$ 266,710	$ 266,710

Required

1. Prepare a 10-column work sheet for fiscal year 2005, starting with the unadjusted trial balance and including adjustments based on these additional facts:

a. The supplies available at the end of fiscal year 2005 had a cost of $3,200.

b. The cost of expired insurance for the fiscal year is $3,900.

c. Annual depreciation on equipment is $8,500.

d. The June utilities expense of $550 is not included in the unadjusted trial balance because the bill arrived after the trial balance was prepared. The $550 amount owed needs to be recorded.

e. The company's employees have earned $1,600 of accrued wages at fiscal year-end.

f. The rent expense incurred and not yet paid or recorded at fiscal year-end is $200.

g. Additional property taxes of $900 have been assessed for this fiscal year but have not been paid or recorded in the accounts.

h. The long-term note payable bears interest at 1% per month. The unadjusted Interest Expense account equals the amount paid for the first 11 months of the 2005 fiscal year. The $240 accrued interest for June has not yet been paid or recorded. (Note that the company is required to make a $5,000 payment toward the note payable during the 2006 fiscal year.)

2. Use the work sheet to enter the adjusting and closing entries; then journalize them.

3. Prepare the income statement and the statement of owner's equity for the year ended June 30 and the classified balance sheet at June 30, 2005.

Analysis Component

4. Analyze the following separate errors and describe how each would affect the 10-column work sheet. Explain whether the error is likely to be discovered in completing the work sheet and, if not, the effect of the error on the financial statements.

   a. Assume that the adjustment for supplies used consisted of a credit to Supplies for $3,200 and a debit for $3,200 to Supplies Expense.

   b. When the adjusted trial balance in the work sheet is completed, the $17,500 Cash balance is incorrectly entered in the Credit column.

Problem 4-6A[A]

Preparing adjusting, reversing, and next period entries

P4

The following six-column table for Bullseye Ranges includes the unadjusted trial balance as of December 31, 2005.

| | | BULLSEYE RANGES | | | | |
| | | December 31, 2005 | | | | |
Account Title	Unadjusted Trial Balance		Adjustments		Adjusted Trial Balance	
	Dr.	Cr.	Dr.	Cr.	Dr.	Cr.
Cash	$ 13,000					
Accounts receivable	0					
Supplies	5,500					
Equipment	130,000					
Accumulated depreciation—						
Equipment		$ 25,000				
Interest payable		0				
Salaries payable		0				
Unearned member fees		14,000				
Notes payable		50,000				
T. Allen, Capital		58,250				
T. Allen, Withdrawals	20,000					
Member fees earned		53,000				
Depreciation expense—						
Equipment	0					
Salaries expense	28,000					
Interest expense	3,750					
Supplies expense	0					
Totals	$200,250	$200,250				

Required

1. Complete the six-column table by entering adjustments that reflect the following information:

   a. As of December 31, 2005, employees had earned $900 of unpaid and unrecorded salaries. The next payday is January 4, at which time $1,600 of salaries will be paid.

   b. The cost of supplies still available at December 31, 2005, is $2,700.

   c. The notes payable requires an interest payment to be made every three months. The amount of unrecorded accrued interest at December 31, 2005, is $1,250. The next interest payment, at an amount of $1,500, is due on January 15, 2006.

   d. Analysis of the unearned member fees account shows $5,600 remaining unearned at December 31, 2005.

   e. In addition to the member fees included in the revenue account balance, the company has earned another $9,100 in unrecorded fees that will be collected on January 31, 2006. The company is also expected to collect $8,000 on that same day for new fees earned in January 2006.

   f. Depreciation expense for the year is $12,500.

2. Prepare journal entries for the adjustments entered in the six-column table for part 1.

3. Prepare journal entries to reverse the effects of the adjusting entries that involve accruals.

4. Prepare journal entries to record the cash payments and cash collections described for January.

In the blank space beside each numbered balance sheet item, enter the letter of its balance sheet classification. If the item should not appear on the balance sheet, enter a *Z* in the blank.

A. Current assets

B. Long-term investments

C. Plant assets

D. Intangible assets

E. Current liabilities

F. Long-term liabilities

G. Equity

_____ **1.** Machinery

_____ **2.** Prepaid insurance

_____ **3.** Current portion of long-term note payable

_____ **4.** Interest receivable

_____ **5.** Rent receivable

_____ **6.** Land (used in operations)

_____ **7.** Copyrights

_____ **8.** Rent revenue

_____ **9.** Depreciation expense—Trucks

_____ **10.** Long-term investment in stock

_____ **11.** Office supplies

_____ **12.** Interest payable

_____ **13.** Owner, Capital

_____ **14.** Notes receivable (due in 120 days)

_____ **15.** Accumulated depreciation—Trucks

_____ **16.** Salaries payable

_____ **17.** Commissions earned

_____ **18.** Interest payable

_____ **19.** Office equipment

_____ **20.** Notes payable (due in 5 years)

PROBLEM SET B

Problem 4-1B
Determining balance sheet classifications

C3

On July 1, 2005, Lucinda Fogle created a new self-storage business, KeepSafe Co. The following transactions occurred during the company's first month:

July 1 Fogle invested $20,000 cash and buildings worth $120,000 in the business.
       2 Rented equipment by paying $1,800 cash for the first month's (July) rent.
       5 Purchased $2,300 of office supplies for cash.
      10 Paid $5,400 cash for the premium on a 12-month insurance policy. Coverage begins on July 11.
      14 Paid an employee $900 cash for two weeks' salary earned.
      24 Collected $8,800 cash for storage fees from customers.
      28 Paid another $900 cash for two weeks' salary earned by an employee.
      29 Paid $850 cash for minor repairs to a leaking roof.
      30 Paid $300 cash for this month's telephone bill.
      31 Fogle withdrew $1,600 cash for personal use.

The company's chart of accounts follows:

Problem 4-2B
Applying the accounting cycle

C1 C2 P2 P3

101	Cash	401	Storage Fees Earned
106	Accounts Receivable	606	Depreciation Expense—Buildings
124	Office Supplies	622	Salaries Expense
128	Prepaid Insurance	637	Insurance Expense
173	Buildings	640	Rent Expense
174	Accumulated Depreciation—Buildings	650	Office Supplies Expense
209	Salaries Payable	684	Repairs Expense
301	L. Fogle, Capital	688	Telephone Expense
302	L. Fogle, Withdrawals	901	Income Summary

Required

1. Use the balance column format to set up each ledger account listed in its chart of accounts.

2. Prepare journal entries to record the transactions for July and post them to the ledger accounts. Record prepaid and unearned items in balance sheet accounts.

3. Prepare an unadjusted trial balance as of July 31.

4. Use the following information to journalize and post adjusting entries for the month:

   a. Two-thirds of one month's insurance coverage has expired.

   b. At the end of the month, $1,550 of office supplies are still available.

   c. This month's depreciation on the buildings is $1,200.

   d. An employee earned $180 of unpaid and unrecorded salary as of month-end.

   e. The company earned $950 of storage fees that are not yet billed at month-end.

5. Prepare the income statement and the statement of owner's equity for the month of July and the balance sheet at July 31, 2005.

6. Prepare journal entries to close the temporary accounts and post these entries to the ledger.

7. Prepare a post-closing trial balance.

Problem 4-3B

Preparing trial balances, closing entries, and financial statements

C3   P2   P3

Heel-To-Toe-Shoes' adjusted trial balance on December 31, 2005, follows:

No.	Account Title	Debit	Credit
	HEEL-TO-TOE SHOES		
	Adjusted Trial Balance		
	December 31, 2005		
101	Cash	$ 13,450	
125	Store supplies	4,140	
128	Prepaid insurance	2,200	
167	Equipment	33,000	
168	Accumulated depreciation—Equipment		$ 9,000
201	Accounts payable		1,000
210	Wages payable		3,200
301	P. Holt, Capital		31,650
302	P. Holt, Withdrawals	16,000	
401	Repair fees earned		62,000
612	Depreciation expense—Equipment	3,000	
623	Wages expense	28,400	
637	Insurance expense	1,100	
640	Rent expense	2,400	
651	Store supplies expense	1,300	
690	Utilities expense	1,860	
	Totals	$106,850	$106,850

Required

1. Prepare an income statement and a statement of owner's equity for the year 2005, and a classified balance sheet at December 31, 2005. There are no owner investments in 2005.

2. Enter the adjusted trial balance in the first two columns of a six-column table. Use the middle two columns for closing entry information and the last two columns for a post-closing trial balance. Insert an Income Summary account as the last item in the trial balance.

3. Enter closing entry information in the six-column table and prepare journal entries for them.

Analysis Component

4. Assume for this part only that:

   a. None of the $1,100 insurance expense had expired during the year. Instead, assume it is a prepayment of the next period's insurance protection.

   b. There are no earned and unpaid wages at the end of the year. (*Hint:* Reverse the $3,200 wages payable accrual.)

   Describe the financial statement changes that would result from these two assumptions.

The adjusted trial balance for Giovanni Co. as of December 31, 2005, follows:

Problem 4-4B
Preparing closing entries, financial
statements, and ratios

C3   A1   P2

GIOVANNI CO.
Adjusted Trial Balance
December 31, 2005

No.	Account Title	Debit	Credit
101	Cash	$ 6,400	
104	Short-term investments	10,200	
126	Supplies	3,600	
128	Prepaid insurance	800	
167	Equipment	18,000	
168	Accumulated depreciation—Equipment		$ 3,000
173	Building	90,000	
174	Accumulated depreciation—Building		9,000
183	Land	28,500	
201	Accounts payable		2,500
203	Interest payable		1,400
208	Rent payable		200
210	Wages payable		1,180
213	Property taxes payable		2,330
233	Unearned professional fees		650
251	Long-term notes payable		32,000
301	J. Giovanni, Capital		91,800
302	J. Giovanni, Withdrawals	6,000	
401	Professional fees earned		47,000
406	Rent earned		3,600
407	Dividends earned		500
409	Interest earned		1,120
606	Depreciation expense—Building	2,000	
612	Depreciation expense—Equipment	1,000	
623	Wages expense	17,500	
633	Interest expense	1,200	
637	Insurance expense	1,425	
640	Rent expense	1,800	
652	Supplies expense	900	
682	Postage expense	310	
683	Property taxes expense	3,825	
684	Repairs expense	579	
688	Telephone expense	421	
690	Utilities expense	1,820	
	Totals	$196,280	$196,280

J. Giovanni invested $30,000 cash in the business during year 2005 (the December 31, 2004, credit balance of the J. Giovanni, Capital account was $61,800). Giovanni Company is required to make a $6,400 payment on its long-term notes payable during 2006.

Required

1. Prepare the income statement and the statement of owner's equity for the calendar year 2005 and the classified balance sheet at December 31, 2005.

2. Prepare the necessary closing entries at December 31, 2005.

3. Use the information in the financial statements to calculate these ratios: (a) return on assets (total assets at December 31, 2004, was $150,000), (b) debt ratio, (c) profit margin ratio (use total revenues as the denominator), and (d) current ratio.

Check   (1) Total assets (12/31/2005),
$145,500; Net income, $19,440

Problem 4-5B

Preparing a work sheet, adjusting and closing entries, and financial statements

C3 P1 P2

The following unadjusted trial balance is for Crush Demolition Company as of the end of its April 30, 2005, fiscal year. The April 30, 2004, credit balance of the owner's capital account was $36,900, and the owner invested $30,000 cash in the company during the 2005 fiscal year.

No.	Account Title	Debit	Credit
	CRUSH DEMOLITION COMPANY		
	Unadjusted Trial Balance		
	April 30, 2005		
101	Cash	$ 9,000	
126	Supplies	18,000	
128	Prepaid insurance	14,600	
167	Equipment	140,000	
168	Accumulated depreciation—Equipment		$ 10,000
201	Accounts payable		16,000
203	Interest payable		0
208	Rent payable		0
210	Wages payable		0
213	Property taxes payable		0
251	Long-term notes payable		20,000
301	J. Bonair, Capital		66,900
302	J. Bonair, Withdrawals	24,000	
401	Demolition fees earned		177,000
612	Depreciation expense—Equipment	0	
623	Wages expense	51,400	
633	Interest expense	2,200	
637	Insurance expense	0	
640	Rent expense	8,800	
652	Supplies expense	0	
683	Property taxes expense	8,400	
684	Repairs expense	6,700	
690	Utilities expense	6,800	
	Totals	$ 289,900	$ 289,900

Required

1. Prepare a 10-column work sheet for fiscal year 2005, starting with the unadjusted trial balance and including adjustments based on these additional facts:

   a. The supplies available at the end of fiscal year 2005 had a cost of $8,100.

   b. The cost of expired insurance for the fiscal year is $11,500.

   c. Annual depreciation on equipment is $18,000.

   d. The April utilities expense of $700 is not included in the unadjusted trial balance because the bill arrived after the trial balance was prepared. The $700 amount owed needs to be recorded.

   e. The company's employees have earned $2,200 of accrued wages at fiscal year-end.

   f. The rent expense incurred and not yet paid or recorded at fiscal year-end is $5,360.

   g. Additional property taxes of $450 have been assessed for this fiscal year but have not been paid or recorded in the accounts.

   h. The long-term note payable bears interest at 1% per month. The unadjusted Interest Expense account equals the amount paid for the first 11 months of the 2005 fiscal year. The $200 accrued interest for April has not yet been paid or recorded. (Note that the company is required to make a $4,000 payment toward the note payable during the 2006 fiscal year.)

2. Use the work sheet to enter the adjusting and closing entries; then journalize them.

Check   (3) Total assets, $132,200; current liabilities, $28,910; Net income, $44,390

3. Prepare the income statement and the statement of owner's equity for the year ended April 30, and the classified balance sheet at April 30, 2005.

Analysis Component

4. Analyze the following separate errors and describe how each would affect the 10-column work sheet. Explain whether the error is likely to be discovered in completing the work sheet and, if not, the effect of the error on the financial statements.

a. Assume the adjustment for expiration of the insurance coverage consisted of a credit to Prepaid Insurance for $3,100 and a debit for $3,100 to Insurance Expense.

b. When the adjusted trial balance in the work sheet is completed, the $6,700 Repairs Expense account balance is extended to the Debit column of the balance sheet columns.

The following six-column table for Solutions Co. includes the unadjusted trial balance as of December 31, 2005:

Problem 4-6B^A
Preparing adjusting, reversing, and next period entries

P4

Account Title	Unadjusted Trial Balance Dr.	Unadjusted Trial Balance Cr.	Adjustments Dr.	Adjustments Cr.	Adjusted Trial Balance Dr.	Adjusted Trial Balance Cr.
SOLUTIONS CO. December 31, 2005						
Cash	$ 9,000					
Accounts receivable	0					
Supplies	6,600					
Machinery	40,100					
Accumulated depreciation—Machinery		$15,800				
Interest payable		0				
Salaries payable		0				
Unearned rental fees		5,200				
Notes payable		20,000				
G. Clay, Capital		13,200				
G. Clay, Withdrawals	10,500					
Rental fees earned		37,000				
Depreciation expense—Machinery	0					
Salaries expense	23,500					
Interest expense	1,500					
Supplies expense	0					
Totals	$91,200	$91,200				

Required

1. Complete the six-column table by entering adjustments that reflect the following information:

   a. As of December 31, 2005, employees had earned $420 of unpaid and unrecorded wages. The next payday is January 4, at which time $1,250 in wages will be paid.

   b. The cost of supplies still available at December 31, 2005, is $2,450.

   c. The notes payable requires an interest payment to be made every three months. The amount of unrecorded accrued interest at December 31, 2005, is $500. The next interest payment, at an amount of $600, is due on January 15, 2006.

   d. Analysis of the unearned rental fees shows that $3,100 remains unearned at December 31, 2005.

   e. In addition to the machinery rental fees included in the revenue account balance, the company has earned another $2,350 in unrecorded fees that will be collected on January 31, 2006. The company is also expected to collect $4,400 on that same day for new fees earned in January 2006.

   f. Depreciation expense for the year is $3,800.

Check (1) Adjusted trial balance totals, $98,270

2. Prepare journal entries for the adjustments entered in the six-column table for part 1.

3. Prepare journal entries to reverse the effects of the adjusting entries that involve accruals.

4. Prepare journal entries to record the cash payments and cash collections described for January.

PROBLEM SET C

Problem Set C is available at the book's Website to further reinforce and assess your learning.

SERIAL PROBLEM

Success Systems P2 P3

(This serial problem began in Chapter 1 and continues through most of the book. If previous chapter segments were not completed, the serial problem can begin at this point. It is helpful, but not necessary, that you use the Working Papers that accompany the book.)

The December 31, 2004, adjusted trial balance of Success Systems (reflecting its transactions from October through December of 2004) follows:

No.	Account Title	Debit	Credit
101	Cash	$ 58,160	
106	Accounts receivable	5,668	
126	Computer supplies	580	
128	Prepaid insurance	1,665	
131	Prepaid rent	825	
163	Office equipment	8,000	
164	Accumulated depreciation—Office equipment		$ 400
167	Computer equipment	20,000	
168	Accumulated depreciation—Computer equipment		1,250
201	Accounts payable		1,100
210	Wages payable		500
236	Unearned computer services revenue		1,500
301	K. Breeze, Capital		83,000
302	K. Breeze, Withdrawals	7,100	
403	Computer services revenue		31,284
612	Depreciation expense—Office equipment	400	
613	Depreciation expense—Computer equipment	1,250	
623	Wages expense	3,875	
637	Insurance expense	555	
640	Rent expense	2,475	
652	Computer supplies expense	3,065	
655	Advertising expense	2,965	
676	Mileage expense	896	
677	Miscellaneous expenses	250	
684	Repairs expense—Computer	1,305	
901	Income summary		0
	Totals	$119,034	$119,034

Required

Check Post-closing trial balance totals, $94,898

1. Record and post the necessary closing entries for Success Systems.
2. Prepare a post-closing trial balance as of December 31, 2004.

BEYOND THE NUMBERS

REPORTING IN ACTION

C1 P2

BTN 4-1   Refer to **Krispy Kreme**'s financial statements in Appendix A to answer the following:

Required

1. For the fiscal year ended February 2, 2003, what amount will be credited to Income Summary to summarize its revenues earned?
2. For the fiscal year ended February 2, 2003, what amount will be debited to Income Summary to summarize its expenses incurred?

3. For the fiscal year ended February 2, 2003, what will be the balance of its Income Summary account before it is closed?

4. In its statement of cash flows for the year ended February 2, 2003, what amount of cash is paid in dividends to common stockholders?

Roll On

5. Access Krispy Kreme's annual report for fiscal years ending after February 2, 2003, at its Website (**KrispyKreme.com**) or the SEC's EDGAR database (**www.sec.gov**). How has the amount of net income closed to Income Summary changed in the fiscal years ending after February 2, 2003? How has the amount of cash paid as dividends changed in the fiscal years ending after February 2, 2003?

BTN 4-2   Key figures ($ thousands) for the recent two years of both **Krispy Kreme** and **Tastykake** follow:

COMPARATIVE ANALYSIS

A1

Key Figures	Krispy Kreme		Tastykake	
	Current Year	Prior Year	Current Year	Prior Year
Current assets	$141,128	$101,769	$36,095	$35,169
Current liabilities	59,687	52,533	19,307	16,885

Required

1. Compute the current ratio for both years and both companies.

2. Which has the better ability to pay short-term obligations according to the current ratio?

3. Analyze and comment on each company's current ratios for the past two years.

4. How do Krispy Kreme's and Tastykake's current ratios compare to their industry average ratio of about 1.0 to 1.2?

BTN 4-3   On January 20, 2005, Jennifer Nelson, the accountant for Travon Enterprises, is feeling pressure to complete the annual financial statements. The company president has said he needs up-to-date financial statements to share with the bank on January 21 at a dinner meeting that has been called to discuss Travon's obtaining loan financing for a special building project. Jennifer knows that she will not be able to gather all the needed information in the next 24 hours to prepare the entire set of adjusting entries that must be posted before the financial statements accurately portray the company's performance and financial position for the fiscal period ended December 31, 2004. Jennifer ultimately decides to estimate several expense accruals at the last minute. When deciding on estimates for the expenses, she uses low estimates because she does not want to make the financial statements look worse than they are. Jennifer finishes the financial statements before the deadline and gives them to the president without mentioning that several accounts use estimated balances.

ETHICS CHALLENGE

C2

Required

1. Identify several courses of action that Jennifer could have taken instead of the one she took.

2. If you were in Jennifer's situation, what would you have done? Briefly justify your response.

BTN 4-4   Assume that one of your classmates states that a company's books should be ongoing and therefore not closed until that business is terminated. Write a one-half page memo to this classmate explaining the concept of the closing process by drawing analogies between (1) a scoreboard for an athletic event and the revenue and expense accounts of a business or (2) a sports team's record book and the capital account. (*Hint:* Think about what would happen if the scoreboard is not cleared before the start of a new game.)

COMMUNICATING IN PRACTICE

C1 P2

TAKING IT TO THE NET

A1

mhhe.com/larson

BTN 4-5 Access **Motley Fool**'s discussion of the current ratio at **Fool.com/School/Valuation/ CurrentAndQuickRatio.htm**. (Note that if the page changed, search the site for the *current ratio*.)

Required

1. What level for the current ratio is generally regarded as sufficient to meet near-term operating needs?

2. Once you have calculated the current ratio for a company, what should you compare it against?

3. What are the implications for a company that has a current ratio that is too high?

TEAMWORK IN ACTION

P1 P2 P3

BTN 4-6 The unadjusted trial balance and information for the accounting adjustments of Noseworthy Investigators follow. Each team member involved in this project is to assume one of the four responsibilities listed. After completing each of these responsibilities, the team should work together to prove the accounting equation utilizing information from teammates (1 and 4). If your equation does not balance, you are to work as a team to resolve the error. The team's goal is to complete the task as quickly and accurately as possible.

Unadjusted Trial Balance		
Account Title	Debit	Credit
Cash	$15,000	
Supplies	11,000	
Prepaid insurance	2,000	
Equipment	24,000	
Accumulated depreciation—Equipment		$ 6,000
Accounts payable		2,000
D. Noseworthy, Capital		31,000
D. Noseworthy, Withdrawals	5,000	
Investigation fees earned		32,000
Rent expense	14,000	
Totals	$71,000	$71,000

Additional Year-End Information

a. Insurance that expired in the current period amounts to $1,200.

b. Equipment depreciation for the period is $3,000.

c. Unused supplies total $4,000 at period-end.

d. Services in the amount of $500 have been provided but have not been billed or collected.

Responsibilities for Individual Team Members

1. Determine the accounts and adjusted balances to be extended to the balance sheet columns of the work sheet for Noseworthy. Also determine total assets and total liabilities.

2. Determine the adjusted revenue account balance and prepare the entry to close this account.

3. Determine the adjusted account balances for expenses and prepare the entry to close these accounts.

4. Prepare T-accounts for both D. Noseworthy, Capital (reflecting the unadjusted trial balance amount) and Income Summary. Prepare the third and fourth closing entries. Ask teammates assigned to parts 2 and 3 for the postings for Income Summary. Obtain amounts to complete the third closing entry and post both the third and fourth closing entries. Provide the team with the ending capital account balance.

5. The entire team should prove the accounting equation using post-closing balances.

HITTING THE ROAD

C2

BTN 4-7 Select a company that you can visit in person or interview on the telephone. Call ahead to the company to arrange a time when you can interview an employee (preferably an accountant) who helps prepare the annual financial statements. Inquire about the following aspects of its *accounting cycle:*

1. Does it prepare interim financial statements? What time period(s) is used for interim statements?

2. Does the company use the cash or accrual basis of accounting?

3. Does the company use a work sheet in preparing financial statements? Why or why not?

4. Does the company use a spreadsheet program? If so, which software program is used?

5. How long does it take after the end of its reporting period to complete annual statements?

BTN 4-8 Read the article "Weighing the Balance Sheet" in the April 1, 2002, issue of *Business Week*.

BUSINESS WEEK ACTIVITY

A1 C3

mhhe.com/larson

Required

1. This article explains how to evaluate whether a company has a financially strong balance sheet. What does the author of this article look for when evaluating the debt level carried by companies?

2. The article reports a table showing 12 companies that passed the test for strong balance sheets. Identify the range of the current ratio for these 12 companies and name the company with the highest and the company with the lowest current ratios.

3. What is the range of the return on assets ratio for the 12 companies with attractive numbers according to the article? Identify the company with the highest and the company with the lowest return on assets.

4. Some investors will not buy tobacco or asbestos-related companies even if they have a very strong balance sheet. What risk factor are these investors concerned with so that it is more important for these companies than the level of debt on their balance sheets?

BTN 4-9 Review this chapter's opening feature involving Andy Wolf and his startup company, **Premier Snowskates**.

ENTREPRENEURIAL DECISION

A1 C3 P2

Required

1. What is a conservative estimate for the units of snowskates that will be sold if annual sales are $3 million and Andy Wolf meets his targeted retail price?

2. What ratios studied in Chapters 1 through 4 do you recommend that Andy use to monitor the financial performance of his company?

3. What portions of the classified balance sheet do you believe are most relevant in assisting Andy in discovering what obligations are due and when?

4. What objectives are met when Andy applies closing procedures each fiscal year?

BTN 4-10 Grupo Bimbo (**GrupoBimbo.com**) is a leader in the baking and foods industry. Key financial information (millions of pesos) for Grupo Bimbo for its recent fiscal years follows:

GLOBAL DECISION

A1

Key Figures*	Current Year	Prior Year
Current assets	$7,155	$4,867
Current liabilities	5,409	4,026

*Key figures prepared in accordance with accounting principles generally accepted in Mexico.

Required

1. Compute the current ratio for Grupo Bimbo for both the current and prior years.

2. Comment on the level and the change in the current ratios computed in part 1.

Part II
Finance

5 Introduction to Financial Management

Apple Computer began as a two-man partnership in a garage. It grew rapidly and, by 1985, became a large publicly traded corporation with 60 million shares of stock and a total market value in excess of $1 billion. At that time, the firm's more visible cofounder, 30-year-old Steven Jobs, owned 7 million shares of Apple stock worth about $120 million.

Despite his stake in the company and his role in its founding and success, Jobs was forced to relinquish operating responsibilities in 1985 when Apple's financial performance turned sour, and he subsequently resigned altogether.

Of course, you can't keep a good entrepreneur down. Jobs formed Pixar Animation Studios, the company that is responsible for the animation in the hit movies *Toy Story, A Bug's Life,* and *Toy Story 2*. Pixar went public in 1995, and, following an enthusiastic reception by the stock market, Jobs's 80 percent stake was valued at about $1.1 billion. Finally, just to show that what goes around comes around, in 1997, Apple's future was still in doubt, and the company, struggling for relevance in a "Wintel" world, decided to go the sequel route when it hired a new interim chief executive officer (CEO): Steven Jobs! How successful was he at his new (old) job? In January 2000, Apple's board of directors granted Jobs stock options worth

TO GET THE MOST OUT OF THE CHAPTER, WHEN YOU ARE FINISHED STUDYING IT, MAKE SURE YOU HAVE A GOOD UNDERSTANDING OF:

- The basic types of financial management decisions and the role of the financial manager.

- The goal of financial management.

- The financial implications of the different forms of business organization.

- The conflicts of interest that can arise between managers and owners.

$200 million and threw in $90 million for the purchase and care of a Gulfstream V jet. Board member Edgar Woolard stated, "This guy has saved the company."

Understanding Jobs's journey from garage-based entrepreneur to corporate executive to ex-employee and, finally, to CEO takes us into issues involving the corporate form of organization, corporate goals, and corporate control, all of which we discuss in this chapter.

To begin our study of financial management, we address two central issues. First: What is corporate, or business, finance and what is the role of the financial manager? Second: What is the goal of financial management?

5.1 | FINANCE: A QUICK LOOK

Check out the companion web site for this text at **www.mhhe.com/rwj**.

Before we plunge into our study of "corp. fin.," we think a quick overview of the finance field might be a good idea. Our goal is to clue you in on some of the most important areas in finance and some of the career opportunities available in each. We also want to illustrate some of the ways finance fits in with other areas such as marketing, management, and accounting.

The Four Basic Areas

Traditionally, financial topics are grouped into four main areas:

1. Corporate finance
2. Investments
3. Financial institutions
4. International finance

We discuss each of these next.

For job descriptions in finance and other areas, visit **www.careers-in-business.com**.

Corporate Finance   The first of these four areas, corporate finance, is the main subject of this book. We begin covering this subject with our next section, so we will wait until then to get into any details. One thing we should note is that the term *corporate finance* seems to imply that what we cover is only relevant to corporations, but the truth is that almost all of the topics we consider are much broader than that. Maybe *business finance* would be a little more descriptive, but even this is too narrow because at least half of the subjects we discuss in the pages ahead are really basic financial ideas and principles applicable across all the various areas of finance and beyond.

Investments   Broadly speaking, the investments area deals with financial assets such as stocks and bonds. Some of the more important questions include

1. What determines the price of a financial asset such as a share of stock?
2. What are the potential risks and rewards associated with investing in financial assets?
3. What is the best mixture of the different types of financial assets to hold?

Students who specialize in the investments area have various career opportunities. Being a stockbroker is one of the most common. Stockbrokers often work for large companies such as Merrill Lynch, advising customers on what types of investments to consider and helping them make buy and sell decisions. Financial advisers play a similar role, but are not necessarily brokers.

Portfolio management is a second investments-related career path. Portfolio managers, as the name suggests, manage money for investors. For example, individual investors frequently buy into mutual funds. Such funds are simply a means of pooling money that is then invested by a portfolio manager. Portfolio managers also invest and manage money for pension funds, insurance companies, and many other types of institutions.

Security analysis is a third area. A security analyst researches individual investments, such as stock in a particular company, and makes a determination as to whether the price is right. To do so, an analyst delves deeply into company and industry reports, along with a variety of other information sources. Frequently, brokers and portfolio managers rely on security analysts for information and recommendations.

These investments-related areas, like many areas in finance, share an interesting feature. If they are done well, they can be very rewarding financially (translation: You can make a lot of money). The bad news, of course, is that they can be very demanding and very competitive, so they are definitely not for everybody.

Financial Institutions Financial institutions are basically businesses that deal primarily in financial matters. Banks and insurance companies would probably be the most familiar to you. Institutions such as these employ people to perform a wide variety of finance-related tasks. For example, a commercial loan officer at a bank would evaluate whether a particular business has a strong enough financial position to warrant extending a loan. At an insurance company, an analyst would decide whether a particular risk was suitable for insuring and what the premium should be.

International Finance International finance isn't so much an area as it is a specialization within one of the main areas we described above. In other words, careers in international finance generally involve international aspects of either corporate finance, investments, or financial institutions. For example, some portfolio managers and security analysts specialize in non-U.S. companies. Similarly, many U.S. businesses have extensive overseas operations and need employees familiar with such international topics as exchange rates and political risk. Banks frequently are asked to make loans across country lines, so international specialists are needed there as well.

Why Study Finance?

Who needs to know finance? In a word, you. In fact, there are many reasons you need a working knowledge of finance even if you are not planning a finance career. We explore some of these next.

Marketing and Finance If you are interested in marketing, you need to know finance because, for example, marketers constantly work with budgets, and they need to understand how to get the greatest payoff from marketing expenditures and programs. Analyzing costs and benefits of projects of all types is one of the most important aspects of finance, so the tools you learn in finance are vital in marketing research, the design of marketing and distribution channels, and product pricing, just to name a few areas.

Financial analysts rely heavily on marketing analysts, and the two frequently work together to evaluate the profitability of proposed projects and products. As we will see in a later chapter, sales projections are a key input in almost every type of new product analysis, and such projections are often developed jointly between marketing and finance.

Beyond this, the finance industry employs marketers to help sell financial products such as bank accounts, insurance policies, and mutual funds. Financial services marketing is one of the most rapidly growing types of marketing, and successful financial services marketers are very well compensated. To work in this area, you obviously need to understand financial products.

Accounting and Finance   For accountants, finance is required reading. In smaller businesses in particular, accountants are often required to make financial decisions as well as perform traditional accounting duties. Further, as the financial world continues to grow more complex, accountants have to know finance to understand the implications of many of the newer types of financial contracts and the impact they have on financial statements. Beyond this, cost accounting and business finance are particularly closely related, sharing many of the same subjects and concerns.

Financial analysts make extensive use of accounting information; they are some of the most important end users. Understanding finance helps accountants recognize what types of information are particularly valuable and, more generally, how accounting information is actually used (and abused) in practice.

Management and Finance   One of the most important areas in management is strategy. Thinking about business strategy without simultaneously thinking about financial strategy is an excellent recipe for disaster, and, as a result, management strategists must have a very clear understanding of the financial implications of business plans.

In broader terms, management employees of all types are expected to have a strong understanding of how their jobs impact profitability, and they are also expected to be able to work within their areas to improve profitability. This is precisely what studying finance teaches you: What are the characteristics of activities that create value?

You and Finance   Perhaps the most important reason to know finance is that you will have to make financial decisions that will be very important to you personally. Today, for example, when you go to work for almost any type of company, you will be asked to decide how you want to invest your retirement funds. We'll see in a later chapter that what you choose to do can make an enormous difference in your future financial well-being. On a different note, is it your dream to start your own business? Good luck if you don't understand basic finance before you start; you'll end up learning it the hard way. Want to know how big your student loan payments are going to be before you take out that next loan? Maybe not, but we'll show you how to calculate them anyway.

These are just a few of the ways that finance will affect your personal and business lives. Whether you want to or not, you are going to have to examine and understand financial issues, and you are going to have to make financial decisions. We want you to do so wisely, so keep reading.

CONCEPT QUESTIONS

5.1a   What are the major areas in finance?

5.1b   Besides wanting to pass this class, why do you need to understand finance?

5.2 | BUSINESS FINANCE AND THE FINANCIAL MANAGER

Now we proceed to define business finance and the financial manager's job.

What Is Business Finance?

Imagine you were to start your own business. No matter what type you started, you would have to answer the following three questions in some form or another:

1. What long-term investments should you take on? That is, what lines of business will you be in and what sorts of buildings, machinery, and equipment will you need?
2. Where will you get the long-term financing to pay for your investment? Will you bring in other owners or will you borrow the money?
3. How will you manage your everyday financial activities such as collecting from customers and paying suppliers?

These are not the only questions, but they are among the most important. Business finance, broadly speaking, is the study of ways to answer these three questions. We'll be looking at each of them in the chapters ahead.

The Financial Manager

For current issues facing CFOs, see **www.cfo.com**.

The financial management function is usually associated with a top officer of the firm, often called the chief financial officer (CFO) or vice president of finance. Figure 5.1 is a simplified organizational chart that highlights the finance activity in a large firm. As shown, the vice president of finance coordinates the activities of the treasurer and the

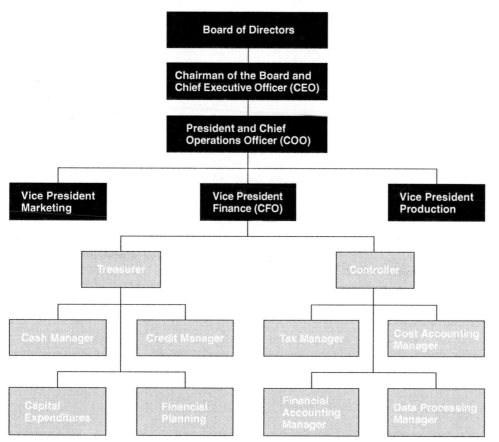

FIGURE 5.1

A simplified organizational chart. The exact titles and organization differ from company to company.

controller. The controller's office handles cost and financial accounting, tax payments, and management information systems. The treasurer's office is responsible for managing the firm's cash and credit, its financial planning, and its capital expenditures. These treasury activities are all related to the three general questions raised above, and the chapters ahead deal primarily with these issues. Our study thus bears mostly on activities usually associated with the treasurer's office. In a smaller firm, the treasurer and controller might be the same person, and there would be only one office.

Financial Management Decisions

As our discussion above suggests, the financial manager must be concerned with three basic types of questions. We consider these in greater detail next.

capital budgeting

The process of planning and managing a firm's long-term investments.

Capital Budgeting   The first question concerns the firm's long-term investments. The process of planning and managing a firm's long-term investments is called **capital budgeting**. In capital budgeting, the financial manager tries to identify investment opportunities that are worth more to the firm than they cost to acquire. Loosely speaking, this means that the value of the cash flow generated by an asset exceeds the cost of that asset.

Regardless of the specific investment under consideration, financial managers must be concerned with how much cash they expect to receive, when they expect to receive it, and how likely they are to receive it. Evaluating the *size, timing,* and *risk* of future cash flows is the essence of capital budgeting. In fact, whenever we evaluate a business decision, the size, timing, and risk of the cash flows will be, by far, the most important things we will consider.

capital structure

The mixture of debt and equity maintained by a firm.

Capital Structure   The second question for the financial manager concerns how the firm obtains the financing it needs to support its long-term investments. A firm's **capital structure** (or financial structure) refers to the specific mixture of long-term debt and equity the firm uses to finance its operations. The financial manager has two concerns in this area. First: How much should the firm borrow? Second: What are the least expensive sources of funds for the firm?

In addition to deciding on the financing mix, the financial manager has to decide exactly how and where to raise the money. The expenses associated with raising long-term financing can be considerable, so different possibilities must be carefully evaluated. Also, businesses borrow money from a variety of lenders in a number of different ways. Choosing among lenders and among loan types is another job handled by the financial manager.

working capital

A firm's short-term assets and liabilities.

Working Capital Management   The third question concerns **working capital** management. The term *working capital* refers to a firm's short-term assets, such as inventory, and its short-term liabilities, such as money owed to suppliers. Managing the firm's working capital is a day-to-day activity that ensures the firm has sufficient resources to continue its operations and avoid costly interruptions. This involves a number of activities related to the firm's receipt and disbursement of cash.

Some questions about working capital that must be answered are the following: (1) How much cash and inventory should we keep on hand? (2) Should we sell on credit to our customers? (3) How will we obtain any needed short-term financing? If we borrow in the short term, how and where should we do it? This is just a small sample of the issues that arise in managing a firm's working capital.

Conclusion   The three areas of corporate financial management we have described—capital budgeting, capital structure, and working capital management—are very broad categories. Each includes a rich variety of topics, and we have indicated only a few of the questions that arise in the different areas. The chapters ahead contain greater detail.

CONCEPT QUESTIONS

5.2a What is the capital budgeting decision?

5.2b What do you call the specific mixture of long-term debt and equity that a firm chooses to use?

5.2c Into what category of financial management does cash management fall?

FORMS OF BUSINESS ORGANIZATION | 5.3

Large firms in the United States, such as IBM and Exxon, are almost all organized as corporations. We examine the three different legal forms of business organization—sole proprietorship, partnership, and corporation—to see why this is so.

Sole Proprietorship

A **sole proprietorship** is a business owned by one person. This is the simplest type of business to start and is the least regulated form of organization. For this reason, there are more proprietorships than any other type of business, and many businesses that later become large corporations start out as small proprietorships.

The owner of a sole proprietorship keeps all the profits. That's the good news. The bad news is that the owner has *unlimited liability* for business debts. This means that creditors can look to the proprietor's personal assets for payment. Similarly, there is no distinction between personal and business income, so all business income is taxed as personal income.

The life of a sole proprietorship is limited to the owner's life span, and, importantly, the amount of equity that can be raised is limited to the proprietor's personal wealth. This limitation often means that the business is unable to exploit new opportunities because of insufficient capital. Ownership of a sole proprietorship may be difficult to transfer since this requires the sale of the entire business to a new owner.

Partnership

A **partnership** is similar to a proprietorship, except that there are two or more owners (partners). In a *general partnership,* all the partners share in gains or losses, and all have unlimited liability for *all* partnership debts, not just some particular share. The way partnership gains (and losses) are divided is described in the *partnership agreement.* This agreement can be an informal oral agreement, such as "let's start a lawn mowing business," or a lengthy, formal written document.

In a *limited partnership,* one or more *general partners* will run the business and have unlimited liability, but there will be one or more *limited partners* who do not actively participate in the business. A limited partner's liability for business debts is limited to the amount that partner contributes to the partnership. This form of organization is common in real estate ventures, for example.

The advantages and disadvantages of a partnership are basically the same as those for a proprietorship. Partnerships based on a relatively informal agreement are easy and inexpensive to form. General partners have unlimited liability for partnership debts, and the partnership terminates when a general partner wishes to sell out or dies. All income is taxed

sole proprietorship
A business owned by a single individual.

For more information on forms of business organization, see the "Small Business" section at **www.nolo.com**.

partnership
A business formed by two or more individuals or entities.

For more in-depth legal information concerning partnerships, go to **www.business-law.freeadvice.com/partnerships/**.

as personal income to the partners, and the amount of equity that can be raised is limited to the partners' combined wealth. Ownership by a general partner is not easily transferred because a new partnership must be formed. A limited partner's interest can be sold without dissolving the partnership, but finding a buyer may be difficult.

Because a partner in a general partnership can be held responsible for all partnership debts, having a written agreement is very important. Failure to spell out the rights and duties of the partners frequently leads to misunderstandings later on. Also, if you are a limited partner, you must not become deeply involved in business decisions unless you are willing to assume the obligations of a general partner. The reason is that if things go badly, you may be deemed to be a general partner even though you say you are a limited partner.

Based on our discussion, the primary disadvantages of sole proprietorships and partnerships as forms of business organization are (1) unlimited liability for business debts on the part of the owners, (2) limited life of the business, and (3) difficulty of transferring ownership. These three disadvantages add up to a single, central problem: The ability of such businesses to grow can be seriously limited by an inability to raise cash for investment.

Corporation

corporation

A business created as a distinct legal entity owned by one or more individuals or entities.

The **corporation** is the most important form (in terms of size) of business organization in the United States. A corporation is a legal "person" separate and distinct from its owners, and it has many of the rights, duties, and privileges of an actual person. Corporations can borrow money and own property, can sue and be sued, and can enter into contracts. A corporation can even be a general partner or a limited partner in a partnership, and a corporation can own stock in another corporation.

Not surprisingly, starting a corporation is somewhat more complicated than starting the other forms of business organization. Forming a corporation involves preparing *articles of incorporation* (or a charter) and a set of *bylaws*. The articles of incorporation must contain a number of things, including the corporation's name, its intended life (which can be forever), its business purpose, and the number of shares that can be issued. This information must normally be supplied to the state in which the firm will be incorporated. For most legal purposes, the corporation is a "resident" of that state.

The bylaws are rules describing how the corporation regulates its own existence. For example, the bylaws describe how directors are elected. The bylaws may be amended or extended from time to time by the stockholders.

In a large corporation, the stockholders and the managers are usually separate groups. The stockholders elect the board of directors, who then select the managers. Management is charged with running the corporation's affairs in the stockholders' interests. In principle, stockholders control the corporation because they elect the directors.

As a result of the separation of ownership and management, the corporate form has several advantages. Ownership (represented by shares of stock) can be readily transferred, and the life of the corporation is therefore not limited. The corporation borrows money in its own name. As a result, the stockholders in a corporation have limited liability for corporate debts. The most they can lose is what they have invested.

The relative ease of transferring ownership, the limited liability for business debts, and the unlimited life of the business are the reasons why the corporate form is superior when it comes to raising cash. If a corporation needs new equity, it can sell new shares of stock and attract new investors. The number of owners can be huge; larger corporations have many thousands or even millions of stockholders. For example, AT&T has about 4.8 million stockholders and Cisco has about 4 million.

The corporate form has a significant disadvantage. Since a corporation is a legal person, it must pay taxes. Moreover, money paid out to stockholders in the form of dividends

TABLE 5.1

International corporations

You can find the translation for any business type at: **www. corporateinformation. com/definitions.html**.

Company	Country of Origin	Type of Company	Translation
Bayerische Motoren Werke (BMW) AG	Germany	Aktiengesellschaft	Corporation
Dornier GmbH	Germany	Gesellschaft mit beschränkter Haftung	Company with limited liability
Rolls-Royce PLC	United Kingdom	Public limited company	Public limited company
Shell UK Ltd.	United Kingdom	Limited	Corporation
Unilever NV	Netherlands	Naamloze Vennootschap	Limited liability company
Fiat SpA	Italy	Società per Azioni	Public limited company
Saab AB	Sweden	Aktiebolag	Joint stock company
Peugeot SA	France	Société Anonyme	Joint stock company

is taxed again as income to those stockholders. This is *double taxation,* meaning that corporate profits are taxed twice: at the corporate level when they are earned and again at the personal level when they are paid out.

As of 2001, all 50 states had enacted laws allowing for the creation of a relatively new form of business organization, the limited liability company (LLC). The goal of this entity is to operate and be taxed like a partnership but retain limited liability for owners, so an LLC is essentially a hybrid of partnership and corporation. Although states have differing definitions for LLCs, the more important scorekeeper is the Internal Revenue Service (IRS). The IRS will consider an LLC a corporation, thereby subjecting it to double taxation, unless it meets certain specific criteria. In essence, an LLC cannot be too corporationlike, or it will be treated as one by the IRS. LLCs have become common. For example, Goldman, Sachs and Co., one of Wall Street's last remaining partnerships, decided to convert from a private partnership to an LLC (it later "went public," becoming a publicly held corporation). Large accounting firms and law firms by the score have converted to LLCs.

How hard is it to form an LLC? Visit **www.llc.com** to find out.

A Corporation by Another Name . . .

The corporate form has many variations around the world. Exact laws and regulations differ, of course, but the essential features of public ownership and limited liability remain. These firms are often called *joint stock companies, public limited companies,* or *limited liability companies.*

Table 5.1 gives the names of a few well-known international corporations, their country of origin, and a translation of the abbreviation that follows the company name.

CONCEPT QUESTIONS

5.3a What are the three forms of business organization?

5.3b What are the primary advantages and disadvantages of sole proprietorships and partnerships?

5.3c What is the difference between a general and a limited partnership?

5.3d Why is the corporate form superior when it comes to raising cash?

5.4 | THE GOAL OF FINANCIAL MANAGEMENT

To study financial decision making, we first need to understand the goal of financial management. Such an understanding is important because it leads to an objective basis for making and evaluating financial decisions.

Profit Maximization

Profit maximization would probably be the most commonly cited business goal, but this is not a very precise objective. Do we mean profits this year? If so, then actions such as deferring maintenance, letting inventories run down, and other short-run, cost-cutting measures will tend to increase profits now, but these activities aren't necessarily desirable.

The goal of maximizing profits may refer to some sort of "long-run" or "average" profits, but it's unclear exactly what this means. First, do we mean something like accounting net income or earnings per share? As we will see, these numbers may have little to do with what is good or bad for the firm. Second, what do we mean by the long run? As a famous economist once remarked, in the long run, we're all dead! More to the point, this goal doesn't tell us the appropriate trade-off between current and future profits.

The Goal of Financial Management in a Corporation

Find a business finance magazine site that discusses current issues facing the financial executive at **www. businessfinancemag. com**.

The financial manager in a corporation makes decisions for the stockholders of the firm. Given this, instead of listing possible goals for the financial manager, we really need to answer a more fundamental question: From the stockholders' point of view, what is a good financial management decision?

If we assume stockholders buy stock because they seek to gain financially, then the answer is obvious: Good decisions increase the value of the stock, and poor decisions decrease it.

Given our observations, it follows that the financial manager acts in the shareholders' best interests by making decisions that increase the value of the stock. The appropriate goal for the financial manager in a corporation can thus be stated quite easily:

> The goal of financial management is to maximize the current value per share of the existing stock.

The goal of maximizing the value of the stock avoids the problems associated with the different goals we discussed above. There is no ambiguity in the criterion, and there is no short-run versus long-run issue. We explicitly mean that our goal is to maximize the *current* stock value. Of course, maximizing stock value is the same thing as maximizing the market price per share.

A More General Financial Management Goal

Given our goal as stated above (maximize the value of the stock), an obvious question comes up: What is the appropriate goal when the firm has no traded stock? Corporations are certainly not the only type of business, and the stock in many corporations rarely changes hands, so it's difficult to say what the value per share is at any given time.

As long as we are dealing with for-profit businesses, only a slight modification is needed. The total value of the stock in a corporation is simply equal to the value of the owners' equity. Therefore, a more general way of stating our goal is:

The Costs of Unethical Conduct

The business world can, and does, severely punish unethical conduct. One recent example concerns Arthur Andersen LLP. Arthur Andersen was one of the "Big Five" accounting firms in the late 1990s. One of Andersen's biggest clients was Enron, the natural gas and energy giant, which was one of the 10 largest corporations in the United States.

Enron filed for bankruptcy in December 2001 amid allegations that the firm's financial statements were deliberately misleading. How could this happen? Like all major firms, Enron employed an independent, outside auditor to look over its books and certify that its financial statements were accurate. Enron's auditor was Arthur Andersen, and Andersen had approved years of Enron financial statements that ultimately overstated the company's profits by nearly $600 million and understated its debt by more than $1 billion.

Why would an accounting firm agree to misrepresent a client's financial statements? To understand, it helps to know that accounting firms such as Andersen began life as companies that performed outside audits and helped companies prepare taxes. In the 1980s, auditors began to use their financial expertise to provide other services such as valuing assets, assisting with mergers, and tax planning. With the growth of computers, the auditors even began advising on the computer systems used by client companies.

The consulting business grew rapidly. In 1976, accounting fees for the biggest firms represented 70 percent of revenue. By 1998, that number had dropped to 34 percent, and many clients were paying much more for consulting than auditing. In 2000, for example, SBC Communications reported audit fees of $3.0 million, but it paid $35.3 million more in other fees; AT&T paid $7.0 million for audit fees and $48.4 million for other services; and General Electric paid $23.9 million for audit fees and a whopping $79.7 million in nonaudit fees.

Substantial non-audit fees may create conflicts of interest that are very difficult to ethically resolve. The earliest Andersen mention of accounting problems at Enron was contained in email in February 2001. The email discussed almost all of the questionable accounting practices at Enron. But the email went on to point out that Enron generated fees of $52 million in 2000 for Andersen and was expected to be a $100-million-per-year client in the near future.

So what happened to Arthur Andersen in the wake of the Enron debacle? In an industry where reputation is everything, you would expect a massive fallout. That is exactly what happened. Andersen quickly fired most of the partners in the Houston office that were responsible for the Enron audit in an effort to save its reputation. It quickly came out that several of these partners had shredded documents after the problems with Enron became public. One of the partners claimed the shredding was at the direction of an Andersen lawyer.

By March 2002, at least 24 companies had dropped Andersen as their auditor. The list was impressive and, at the same time, devastating to Andersen. Merck, for example, dropped Andersen after a 30-year relationship, and Delta Airlines dropped Andersen after a 52-year relationship. Other clients to drop Andersen included Freddie Mac, SunTrust Bank, and FedEx.

Things got worse. In addition to civil lawsuits, Andersen was charged with obstruction of justice in criminal court for shredding documents. Large groups of international Andersen partners began leaving the company. Then, defections reached U.S. partners. Tax partners left to work for Deloitte & Touche, and more than 400 partners in the western United States left for KPMG.

In August, 2002, Andersen closed its public auditing practice. A few months later, a federal judge sentenced Andersen to five years probation and fined it $500,000 for obstruction of justice.

Maximize the market value of the existing owners' equity.

With this goal in mind, it doesn't matter whether the business is a proprietorship, a partnership, or a corporation. For each of these, good financial decisions increase the market value of the owners' equity and poor financial decisions decrease it.

Finally, our goal does not imply that the financial manager should take illegal or unethical actions in the hope of increasing the value of the equity in the firm. What we mean is that the financial manager best serves the owners of the business by identifying goods and services that add value to the firm because they are desired and valued in the free

Business ethics are considered at **www.business-ethics.com**.

marketplace. Our *Reality Bytes* on page 193 shows what can happen when companies choose to engage in unethical practices.

CONCEPT QUESTIONS

5.4a   What is the goal of financial management?

5.4b   What are some shortcomings of the goal of profit maximization?

5.5 | THE AGENCY PROBLEM AND CONTROL OF THE CORPORATION

We've seen that the financial manager in a corporation acts in the best interests of the stockholders by taking actions that increase the value of the firm's stock. However, we've also seen that in large corporations ownership can be spread over a huge number of stockholders. This dispersion of ownership arguably means that management effectively controls the firm. In this case, will management necessarily act in the best interests of the stockholders? Put another way, might not management pursue its own goals at the stockholders' expense? We briefly consider some of the arguments below.

Agency Relationships

The relationship between stockholders and management is called an *agency relationship*. Such a relationship exists whenever someone (the principal) hires another (the agent) to represent his or her interest. For example, you might hire someone (an agent) to sell a car that you own while you are away at school. In all such relationships, there is a possibility of conflict of interest between the principal and the agent. Such a conflict is called an **agency problem**.

agency problem

The possibility of conflict of interest between the owners and management of a firm.

Suppose you hire someone to sell your car and you agree to pay her a flat fee when she sells the car. The agent's incentive in this case is to make the sale, not necessarily to get you the best price. If you paid a commission of, say, 10 percent of the sales price instead of a flat fee, then this problem might not exist. This example illustrates that the way an agent is compensated is one factor that affects agency problems.

Management Goals

To see how management and stockholder interests might differ, imagine that a corporation is considering a new investment. The new investment is expected to favorably impact the stock price, but it is also a relatively risky venture. The owners of the firm will wish to take the investment (because the share value will rise), but management may not because there is the possibility that things will turn out badly and management jobs will be lost. If management does not take the investment, then the stockholders may lose a valuable opportunity. This is one example of an *agency cost*.

It is sometimes argued that, left to themselves, managers would tend to maximize the amount of resources over which they have control, or, more generally, business power or wealth. This goal could lead to an overemphasis on business size or growth. For example, cases where management is accused of overpaying to buy another company just to increase the size of the business or to demonstrate corporate power are not uncommon. Obviously, if overpayment does take place, such a purchase does not benefit the owners of the purchasing company.

Our discussion indicates that management may tend to overemphasize organizational survival to protect job security. Also, management may dislike outside interference, so independence and corporate self-sufficiency may be important goals.

Do Managers Act in the Stockholders' Interests?

Whether managers will, in fact, act in the best interests of stockholders depends on two factors. First, how closely are management goals aligned with stockholder goals? This question relates to the way managers are compensated. Second, can management be replaced if they do not pursue stockholder goals? This issue relates to control of the firm. As we will discuss, there are a number of reasons to think that, even in the largest firms, management has a significant incentive to act in the interests of stockholders.

Managerial Compensation Management will frequently have a significant economic incentive to increase share value for two reasons. First, managerial compensation, particularly at the top, is usually tied to financial performance in general and oftentimes to share value in particular. For example, managers are frequently given the option to buy stock at a fixed price. The more the stock is worth, the more valuable is this option. The second incentive managers have relates to job prospects. Better performers within the firm will tend to get promoted. More generally, those managers who are successful in pursuing stockholder goals will be in greater demand in the labor market and thus command higher salaries.

In fact, managers who are successful in pursuing stockholder goals can reap enormous rewards. For example, Michael Dell, CEO of Dell Computer, received about $236 million in 2001 alone, which is less than George Lucas ($250 million), but way more than Britney Spears ($38.5 million). For the five-year period ending in 2001, Sanford Weill of Citigroup received well over $785 million. However, these numbers pale in comparison to what some execs at Web-related companies have received. For example, including the value of stock options and other items, Margaret Whitman of on-line auctioneer eBay received a total pay package valued (as of March 2000) right at $1 billion!

Control of the Firm Control of the firm ultimately rests with stockholders. They elect the board of directors, who, in turn, hires and fires management. The mechanism by which unhappy stockholders can act to replace existing management is called a *proxy fight*. A proxy is the authority to vote someone else's stock. A proxy fight develops when a group solicits proxies in order to replace the existing board, and thereby replace existing management. As our nearby *Reality Bytes* box shows, proxy fights can occur for other reasons as well.

Another way that management can be replaced is by takeover. Those firms that are poorly managed are more attractive as acquisitions than well-managed firms because a greater profit potential exists. Thus, avoiding a takeover by another firm gives management another incentive to act in the stockholders' interests. Information on executive compensation, along with a ton of other information, can be easily found on the Web for almost any public company. Our nearby *Work the Web* box shows you how to get started.

Conclusion The available theory and evidence are consistent with the view that stockholders control the firm and that stockholder wealth maximization is the relevant goal of the corporation. Even so, there will undoubtedly be times when management goals are pursued at the expense of the stockholders, at least temporarily.

WORK THE WEB

The Web is a great place to learn about individual companies, and there are a slew of sites available to help you. Try pointing your Web browser to finance.yahoo.com. Once there, you should see something like this on the page:

YAHOO! FINANCE

Welcome | Sign In

Yahoo! Finance   Friday, April 19 2002 10pm

Enter symbol(s)   [Get] Symbol Lookup

To look up a company, you must know its "ticker symbol" (or just ticker for short), which is a unique one to four-letter identifier. You can click on the "Symbol Lookup" link and type in the company's name to find the ticker. For example, we typed in "XMSR," which is the ticker symbol for XM Satellite, the satellite radio provider, and selected the "Detailed" quote from the drop-down menu. Here is a portion of what we got:

XM SATELLITE (NasdaqNM:XMSR) - Trade: Choose Brokerage

Last Trade 3:59pm · **10.42**	Change -0.92 (-8.11%)	Prev Cls 11.34	Open 11.32	Volume 3,997,000	XMSR 1-May-2002 (C)Yahoo!
Day's Range 9.86 - 11.43	Bid 10.21	Ask 10.30	P/E N/A	Mkt Cap 924.3M	Avg Vol 1,618,636
52-wk Range 4.02 - 20.68	Bid Size 500	Ask Size 100	P/S 433.96	Div/Shr N/A	Div Date N/A
1y Target Est 18.37	EPS (ttm) -5.89	EPS Est -5.31	PEG N/A	Yield N/A	Ex-Div N/A

Chart, Financials, Historical Prices, Insider, Messages, News, Options
Profile, Reports, Research, SEC Filings, Upgrades, more...

There is a lot of information here and a lot of links for you to explore, so have at it. By the end of the term, we hope it all makes sense to you!

Agency problems are not unique to corporations; they exist whenever there is a separation of ownership and management. This separation is most pronounced in corporations, but it certainly exists in partnerships and proprietorships as well.

Stakeholders

Our discussion thus far implies that management and stockholders are the only parties with an interest in the firm's decisions. This is an oversimplification, of course. Employees, customers, suppliers, and even the government all have a financial interest in the firm.

stakeholder

Someone other than a stockholder or creditor who potentially has a claim on the cash flows of the firm.

These various groups are called **stakeholders** in the firm. In general, a stakeholder is someone other than a stockholder or creditor who potentially has a claim on the cash flows of the firm. Such groups will also attempt to exert control over the firm, perhaps to the detriment of the owners.

CONCEPT QUESTIONS

5.5a   What is an agency relationship?

5.5b   What are agency problems and how do they arise? What are agency costs?

5.5c   What incentives do managers in large corporations have to maximize share value?

Fight!

Proxy fights often occur when dissident shareholders attempt to gather proxies from other shareholders to remove directors from the company's board. They also occur for other corporate matters, most notably the vote on a merger. For example, in early 2002, the proposed merger between Hewlett-Packard (HP) and Compaq became one of the most widely followed, bitterly contested, and expensive proxy fights in history. In the end, it was estimated that well over $100 million was spent on the contest.

The two most prominent members of the proxy battle were Walter B. Hewlett, an heir to one of the cofounders of HP and also a member of the company's board of directors, and Carly Fiorina, the CEO of HP. Ms. Fiorina had been brought in to revive HP in 1999. Under her guidance, HP set aggressive growth targets. At first, the company met those targets, but it soon began to fall short. When sales declined, Ms. Fiorina laid off workers, reduced travel expenses, and closed offices, but profits continued to fall. This decline led to doubts regarding Ms. Fiorina's ability to lead HP. It was in this environment that the planned merger with Compaq was announced.

Soon after the merger was proposed, Mr. Hewlett voiced his opposition. Then the David and Lucille Packard Foundation and David Woodley Packard (heir to the other cofounder) announced their opposition, so heirs of both cofounders opposed the merger. Together they owned or controlled about 18 percent of the outstanding HP stock. Soon both sides began visiting large institutional shareholders to court their votes.

About midway between the announcement and the vote on the merger, things began to heat up. In a letter to shareholders, Ms. Fiorina called Mr. Hewlett "a musician and academic." She also criticized his lack of business experience and went on to argue that he had no real plan for the company. Mr. Hewlett later recanted his previously stated desire for Ms. Fiorina to stay on if the merger failed and stated, "This time we don't want someone learning on the job," a reference to Ms. Fiorina's lack of experience as CEO. He then attacked Ms. Fiorina for her "$25 billion mistake." Several of the members of the board of directors struck back, implying they would resign if the merger failed.

Mr. Hewlett also was upset at the pay package for Ms. Fiorina and Michael Capellas, the CEO of Compaq, which the board had discussed if the merger went through. Under the proposed deal, Ms. Fiorina and Mr. Capellas would receive a total of $115 million. The board insisted that the package was not final, therefore irrelevant. Mr. Hewlett responded by releasing the minutes of the board meeting and supporting documents, which the board considered a breach of confidentiality.

As you would expect from a race with so much acrimony, the vote was close, but in the end shareholders voted to approve the merger. But this was not the end of the story. Mr. Hewlett filed a lawsuit charging coercion in the voting process, contending that Ms. Fiorina illegally influenced Deutsche Bank into changing its proxy vote from negative to positive. Deutsche Bank held millions of proxies, and since the merger was approved by a very slim margin, those proxies were critical. Mr. Hewlett contended that Ms. Fiorina told Deutsche Bank that if it didn't vote for the merger, HP would find another investment bank, costing Deutsche Bank millions of dollars per year in revenue. This potential conflict of interest even brought in the SEC to investigate. In the end, the courts sided with HP, and the merger went through in April 2002. That same month, Mr. Hewlett ended his term on the HP board.

FINANCIAL MARKETS AND THE CORPORATION | 5.6

We've seen that the primary advantages of the corporate form of organization are that ownership can be transferred more quickly and easily than with other forms and that money can be raised more readily. Both of these advantages are significantly enhanced by the existence of financial markets, and financial markets play an extremely important role in corporate finance.

Cash Flows to and from the Firm

The interplay between the corporation and the financial markets is illustrated in Figure 5.2. The arrows in Figure 5.2 trace the passage of cash from the financial markets to the firm and from the firm back to the financial markets.

197

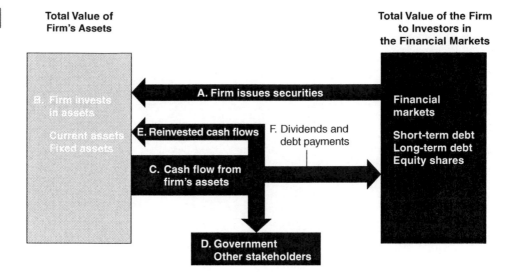

Total Value of
Firm's Assets

Total Value of the Firm
to Investors in
the Financial Markets

A. Firm issues securities

B. Firm invests in assets

Current assets
Fixed assets

E. Reinvested cash flows

F. Dividends and debt payments

C. Cash flow from firm's assets

D. Government
Other stakeholders

Financial markets

Short-term debt
Long-term debt
Equity shares

A. Firm issues securities to raise cash.
B. Firm invests in assets.
C. Firm's operations generate cash flow.
D. Cash is paid to government as taxes.
    Other stakeholders may receive cash.
E. Reinvested cash flows are plowed back
    into firm.
F. Cash is paid out to investors in the form
    of interest and dividends.

Suppose we start with the firm selling shares of stock and borrowing money to raise cash. Cash flows to the firm from the financial markets (A). The firm invests the cash in current and fixed (or long-term) assets (B). These assets generate some cash (C), some of which goes to pay corporate taxes (D). After taxes are paid, some of this cash flow is reinvested in the firm (E). The rest goes back to the financial markets as cash paid to creditors and shareholders (F).

A financial market, like any market, is just a way of bringing buyers and sellers together. In financial markets, it is debt and equity securities that are bought and sold. Financial markets differ in detail, however. The most important differences concern the types of securities that are traded, how trading is conducted, and who the buyers and sellers are. Some of these differences are discussed next.

Primary versus Secondary Markets

Financial markets function as both primary and secondary markets for debt and equity securities. The term *primary market* refers to the original sale of securities by governments and corporations. The *secondary markets* are those in which these securities are bought and sold after the original sale. Equities are, of course, issued solely by corporations. Debt securities are issued by both governments and corporations. In the discussion that follows, we focus on corporate securities only.

To learn more about the SEC, visit **www.sec.gov**.

Primary Markets   In a primary-market transaction, the corporation is the seller, and the transaction raises money for the corporation. Corporations engage in two types of primary-market transactions: public offerings and private placements. A public offering, as the name suggests, involves selling securities to the general public, whereas a private placement is a negotiated sale involving a specific buyer.

By law, public offerings of debt and equity must be registered with the Securities and Exchange Commission (SEC). Registration requires the firm to disclose a great deal of information before selling any securities. The accounting, legal, and selling costs of public offerings can be considerable.

Partly to avoid the various regulatory requirements and the expense of public offerings, debt and equity are often sold privately to large financial institutions such as life insurance companies or mutual funds. Such private placements do not have to be registered with the SEC and do not require the involvement of underwriters (investment banks that specialize in selling securities to the public).

Secondary Markets   A secondary-market transaction involves one owner or creditor selling to another. It is therefore the secondary markets that provide the means for transferring ownership of corporate securities. Although a corporation is only directly involved in a primary-market transaction (when it sells securities to raise cash), the secondary markets are still critical to large corporations. The reason is that investors are much more willing to purchase securities in a primary-market transaction when they know that those securities can later be resold if desired.

Dealer versus auction markets   There are two kinds of secondary markets: *auction* markets and *dealer* markets. Generally speaking, dealers buy and sell for themselves, at their own risk. A car dealer, for example, buys and sells automobiles. In contrast, brokers and agents match buyers and sellers, but they do not actually own the commodity that is bought or sold. A real estate agent, for example, does not normally buy and sell houses.

Dealer markets in stocks and long-term debt are called *over-the-counter* (OTC) markets. Most trading in debt securities takes place over the counter. The expression *over the counter* refers to days of old when securities were literally bought and sold at counters in offices around the country. Today, a significant fraction of the market for stocks and almost all of the market for long-term debt have no central location; the many dealers are connected electronically.

Auction markets differ from dealer markets in two ways. First, an auction market, or exchange, has a physical location (like Wall Street). Second, in a dealer market, most of the buying and selling is done by the dealer. The primary purpose of an auction market, on the other hand, is to match those who wish to sell with those who wish to buy. Dealers play a limited role.

Trading in corporate securities   The equity shares of most of the large firms in the United States trade in organized auction markets. The largest such market is the New York Stock Exchange (NYSE), which accounts for more than 85 percent of all the shares traded in auction markets. Other auction exchanges include the American Stock Exchange (AMEX) and regional exchanges such as the Pacific Stock Exchange.

In addition to the stock exchanges, there is a large OTC market for stocks. In 1971, the National Association of Securities Dealers (NASD) made available to dealers and brokers an electronic quotation system called NASDAQ (NASD Automated Quotations system, pronounced "naz-dak" and now spelled "Nasdaq"). There are roughly three times as many companies on Nasdaq as there are on NYSE, but they tend to be much smaller in size and trade less actively. There are exceptions, of course. Both Microsoft and Intel trade OTC, for example. Nonetheless, the total value of Nasdaq stocks is significantly less than the total value of NYSE stocks.

There are many large and important financial markets outside the United States, of course, and U.S. corporations are increasingly looking to these markets to raise cash. The Tokyo Stock Exchange and the London Stock Exchange (TSE and LSE, respectively) are two well-known examples. The fact that OTC markets have no physical location means that

To learn more about the exchanges, visit **www.nyse.com** and **www.nasdaq.com**.

The Tokyo Stock Exchange in English: **www.tse.or.jp/english**.

The London Stock Exchange: **www. londonstockexchange. com**.

national borders do not present a great barrier, and there is now a huge international OTC debt market. Because of globalization, financial markets have reached the point where trading in many instruments never stops; it just travels around the world.

Listing   Stocks that trade on an organized exchange are said to be *listed* on that exchange. In order to be listed, firms must meet certain minimum criteria concerning, for example, asset size and number of shareholders. These criteria differ for different exchanges.

NYSE has the most stringent requirements of the exchanges in the United States. For example, to be listed on NYSE, a company is expected to have a market value for its publicly held shares of at least $60 million and a total of at least 2,000 shareholders with at least 100 shares each. There are additional minimums on earnings, assets, and number of shares outstanding.

CONCEPT QUESTIONS

5.6a   What is a dealer market? How do dealer and auction markets differ?

5.6b   What is the largest auction market in the United States?

5.6c   What does *OTC* stand for? What is the large OTC market for stocks called?

SUMMARY AND CONCLUSIONS

This chapter has introduced you to some of the basic ideas in business finance. In it, we saw that:

1. Business finance has three main areas of concern:
    a.   Capital budgeting. What long-term investments should the firm take?
    b.   Capital structure. Where will the firm get the long-term financing to pay for its investments? In other words, what mixture of debt and equity should we use to fund our operations?
    c.   Working capital management. How should the firm manage its everyday financial activities?

2. The goal of financial management in a for-profit business is to make decisions that increase the value of the stock, or, more generally, increase the market value of the equity.

3. The corporate form of organization is superior to other forms when it comes to raising money and transferring ownership interests, but it has the significant disadvantage of double taxation.

4. There is the possibility of conflicts between stockholders and management in a large corporation. We called these conflicts agency problems and discussed how they might be controlled and reduced.

Of the topics we've discussed thus far, the most important is the goal of financial management. Throughout the text, we will be analyzing many different financial decisions, but we always ask the same question: How does the decision under consideration affect the value of the equity in the firm?

CRITICAL THINKING AND CONCEPTS REVIEW

5.1   **The Financial Management Decision Process.**   What are the three types of financial management decisions? For each type of decision, give an example of a business transaction that would be relevant.

5.2   **Sole Proprietorships and Partnerships.**   What are the four primary disadvantages to the sole proprietorship and partnership forms of business organization? What benefits are there to these types of business organization as opposed to the corporate form?

5.3   **Corporations.**   What is the primary disadvantage of the corporate form of organization? Name at least two of the advantages of corporate organization.

5.4   **Corporate Finance Organization.**   In a large corporation, what are the two distinct groups that report to the chief financial officer? Which group is the focus of corporate finance?

5.5   **Goal of Financial Management.**   What goal should always motivate the actions of the firm's financial manager?

5.6   **Agency Problems.**   Who owns a corporation? Describe the process whereby the owners control the firm's management. What is the main reason that an agency relationship exists in the corporate form of organization? In this context, what kinds of problems can arise?

5.7   **Primary versus Secondary Markets.**   You've probably noticed coverage in the financial press of an initial public offering (IPO) of a company's securities. Is an IPO a primary-market transaction or a secondary-market transaction?

5.8   **Auction versus Dealer Markets.**   What does it mean when we say the New York Stock Exchange is an auction market? How are auction markets different from dealer markets? What kind of market is Nasdaq?

5.9   **Not-for-Profit Firm Goals.**   Suppose you were the financial manager of a not-for-profit business (a not-for-profit hospital, perhaps). What kinds of goals do you think would be appropriate?

5.10   **Ethics and Firm Goals.**   Can our goal of maximizing the value of the stock conflict with other goals, such as avoiding unethical or illegal behavior? In particular, do you think subjects such as customer and employee safety, the environment, and the general good of society fit in this framework, or are they essentially ignored? Try to think of some specific scenarios to illustrate your answer.

5.11   **International Firm Goal.**   Would our goal of maximizing the value of the stock be different if we were thinking about financial management in a foreign country? Why or why not?

5.12   **Agency Problems.**   Suppose you own stock in a company. The current price per share is $25. Another company has just announced that it wants to buy your company and will pay $35 per share to acquire all the outstanding stock. Your company's management immediately begins fighting off this hostile bid. Is management acting in the shareholders' best interests? Why or why not?

5.13   **Agency Problems and Corporate Ownership.**   Corporate ownership varies around the world. Historically, individuals have owned the majority of shares in public corporations in the United States. In Germany and Japan, however, banks, other large financial institutions, and other companies own most of the stock in public corporations. Do you think agency problems are likely to be more or less severe in Germany and Japan than in the United States? Why? In recent years, large financial institutions such as mutual funds and pension funds have been becoming the dominant owners of stock in the United States, and these institutions are becoming more active in corporate affairs. What are the implications of this trend for agency problems and corporate control?

5.14   Executive Compensation.   Critics have charged that compensation to top management in the United States is simply too high and should be cut back. For example, focusing on large corporations, Michael Eisner of Disney has been one of the best-compensated CEOs in the United States, earning about $73 million in 2001 alone and $737 million over the 1997–2001 period. Are such amounts excessive? In answering, it might be helpful to recognize that superstar athletes such as Tiger Woods, top entertainers such as Jim Carrey and Julia Roberts, and many others at the top of their respective fields earn at least as much, if not a great deal more.

What's On the Web?

5.1   Listing Requirements.   This chapter discussed some of the listing requirements for the NYSE and Nasdaq. Find the complete listing requirements for the New York Stock Exchange at www.nyse.com and Nasdaq at www.nasdaq.com. Which exchange has more stringent listing requirements? Why don't the exchanges have the same listing requirements?

5.2   Business Formation.   As you may (or may not) know, many companies incorporate in Delaware for a variety of reasons. Visit Bizfilings at www.bizfilings.com to find out why. Which state has the highest fee for incorporation? For an LLC? While at the site, look at the FAQ section regarding corporations and LLCs.

5.3   Organizational Structure.   The organizational structure chart in the text is a simplified version. Go to www.conference-board.org, follow the "Organization Charts" link, and then the "Click here to see a sample chart" link. What are the differences in the two diagrams? Who reports to the chief financial officer? How many vice presidents does this company have?

6 Financial Statements, Taxes, and Cash Flow

**THERE ARE BASICALLY FOUR THINGS THAT
YOU SHOULD BE CLEAR ON WHEN YOU HAVE
FINISHED STUDYING THIS CHAPTER:**

▩ The difference between accounting
value (or "book" value) and market
value.

▩ The difference between accounting
income and cash flow.

▩ The difference between average and
marginal tax rates.

▩ How to determine a firm's cash flow
from its financial statements.

W hen exactly is revenue really revenue? It used to be easy to tell, but lately it's become downright dot-complicated! Consider, for example, priceline.com, the on-line service that lets consumers bid their own price for airline tickets, car rentals, hotel rooms, and the like. Priceline takes on-line bids from consumers and, if a bid fits the seller's requirements, fills the order by buying the good or service and immediately reselling it to the bidder. Here is where it gets interesting: Although priceline.com might own the item for no more than a nanosecond, it records the entire price paid by the customer as revenue. Of course, it also records the cost of the item sold as a cost of the sale, but in the world of Internet stocks, where revenue growth seems to matter a great deal, the practice certainly should give investors pause.

Priceline is not alone, however, in employing what some view as questionable accounting practices. WebMD, the Internet health company, provided content for "health channels" in return for a portion of the advertising revenues generated by the sites. But, by prearranged agreement, WebMD then turned right around and paid a sizable chunk of the advertising money it received back to its partner in the form of commissions. WebMD booked all of the money coming in as revenue even though part of it had been previously committed for return to the site owner. VerticalNet, another Internet-based company, routinely booked revenue from barter transactions even though the transactions were essentially swaps of goods or services and no cash actually changed hands.

These examples are troublesome because they seem to suggest that a company's financial performance depends on accounting decisions; but, as we will see, this is not true. Instead, this chapter shows that underneath all the accounting numbers lurks the financial truth. Our job is to uncover that truth by examining the all-important substance known as *cash flow*.

In this chapter, we examine financial statements, taxes, and cash flow. Our emphasis is not on preparing financial statements. Instead, we recognize that financial statements are frequently a key source of information for financial decisions, so our goal is to briefly examine such statements and point out some of their more relevant features. We pay special attention to some of the practical details of cash flow.

As you read, pay particular attention to two important differences: (1) the difference between accounting value and market value and (2) the difference between accounting income and cash flow. These distinctions will be important throughout the book.

6.1 | THE BALANCE SHEET

The **balance sheet** is a snapshot of the firm. It is a convenient means of organizing and summarizing what a firm owns (its *assets*), what a firm owes (its *liabilities*), and the difference between the two (the firm's *equity*) at a given point in time. Figure 6.1 illustrates how the balance sheet is constructed. As shown, the left-hand side lists the assets of the firm, and the right-hand side lists the liabilities and equity.

balance sheet
Financial statement showing a firm's accounting value on a particular date.

Assets: The Left-Hand Side

Assets are classified as either *current* or *fixed.* A fixed asset is one that has a relatively long life. Fixed assets can either be *tangible,* such as a truck or a computer, or *intangible,* such as a trademark or patent. A current asset has a life of less than one year. This means that the asset will normally convert to cash within 12 months. For example, inventory would

FIGURE 6.1

The balance sheet.
Left side: Total value of assets. Right side: Total value of liabilities and shareholders' equity.

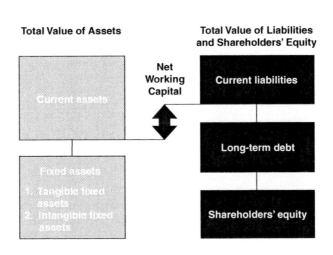

204

normally be purchased and sold within a year and is thus classified as a current asset. Obviously, cash itself is a current asset. Accounts receivable (money owed to the firm by its customers) is also a current asset.

Two excellent sites for company financial information are **finance.yahoo.com** and **money.cnn.com**.

Liabilities and Owners' Equity: The Right-Hand Side

The firm's liabilities are the first thing listed on the right-hand side of the balance sheet. These are classified as either *current* or *long-term*. Current liabilities, like current assets, have a life of less than one year (meaning they must be paid within the year), and they are listed before long-term liabilities. Accounts payable (money the firm owes to its suppliers) is one example of a current liability.

A debt that is not due in the coming year is classified as a long-term liability. A loan that the firm will pay off in five years is one such long-term debt. Firms borrow over the long term from a variety of sources. We will tend to use the terms *bonds* and *bondholders* generically to refer to long-term debt and long-term creditors, respectively.

Disney has a good investor site at **www.disney.com**.

Finally, by definition, the difference between the total value of the assets (current and fixed) and the total value of the liabilities (current and long-term) is the *shareholders' equity*, also called *common equity* or *owners' equity*. This feature of the balance sheet is intended to reflect the fact that, if the firm were to sell all of its assets and use the money to pay off its debts, then whatever residual value remained would belong to the shareholders. So, the balance sheet "balances" because the value of the left-hand side always equals the value of the right-hand side. That is, the value of the firm's assets is equal to the sum of its liabilities and shareholders' equity:[1]

$$\text{Assets} = \text{Liabilities} + \text{Shareholders' equity} \qquad [6.1]$$

This is the balance sheet identity, or equation, and it always holds because shareholders' equity is defined as the difference between assets and liabilities.

Net Working Capital

As shown in Figure 6.1, the difference between a firm's current assets and its current liabilities is called **net working capital**. Net working capital is positive when current assets exceed current liabilities. Based on the definitions of current assets and current liabilities, this means that the cash that will become available over the next 12 months exceeds the cash that must be paid over that same period. For this reason, net working capital is usually positive in a healthy firm.

net working capital
Current assets less current liabilities.

A firm has current assets of $100, net fixed assets of $500, short-term debt of $70, and long-term debt of $200. What does the balance sheet look like? What is shareholders' equity? What is net working capital?

In this case, total assets are $100 + 500 = $600 and total liabilities are $70 + 200 = $270, so shareholders' equity is the difference: $600 − 270 = $330. The balance sheet would thus look like:

---

[1]The terms *owners' equity*, *shareholders' equity*, and *stockholders' equity* are used interchangeably to refer to the equity in a corporation. The term *net worth* is also used. Variations exist in addition to these.

Assets		Liabilities and Shareholders' Equity	
Current assets	$100	Current liabilities	$ 70
Net fixed assets	500	Long-term debt	200
		Shareholders' equity	330
		Total liabilities and	
Total assets	$600	shareholders' equity	$600

Net working capital is the difference between current assets and current liabilities, or $100 − 70 = $30.

Table 6.1 shows a simplified balance sheet for the fictitious U.S. Corporation. There are three particularly important things to keep in mind when examining a balance sheet: liquidity, debt versus equity, and market value versus book value.

Liquidity

Liquidity refers to the speed and ease with which an asset can be converted to cash. Gold is a relatively liquid asset; a custom manufacturing facility is not. Liquidity really has two dimensions: ease of conversion versus loss of value. Any asset can be converted to cash quickly if we cut the price enough. A highly liquid asset is therefore one that can be quickly sold without significant loss of value. An illiquid asset is one that cannot be quickly converted to cash without a substantial price reduction.

Assets are normally listed on the balance sheet in order of decreasing liquidity, meaning that the most liquid assets are listed first. Current assets are relatively liquid and include cash and those assets that we expect to convert to cash over the next 12 months. Accounts receivable, for example, represent amounts not yet collected from customers on sales

Annual and quarterly financial statements (and lots more) for most public U.S. corporations can be found in the EDGAR database at **www.sec.gov**.

TABLE 6.1

Balance sheets for U.S. Corporation

U.S. CORPORATION
Balance Sheets as of December 31, 2002 and 2003
($ in Millions)

	2002	2003		2002	2003
Assets			**Liabilities and Owners' Equity**		
Current assets			Current liabilities		
Cash	$ 104	$ 160	Accounts payable	$ 232	$ 266
Accounts receivable	455	688	Notes payable	196	123
Inventory	553	555	Total	$ 428	$ 389
Total	$1,112	$1,403			
Fixed assets					
Net fixed assets	$1,644	$1,709	Long-term debt	$ 408	$ 454
			Owners' equity		
			Common stock and		
			paid-in surplus	600	640
			Retained earnings	1,320	1,629
			Total	$1,920	$2,269
			Total liabilities and		
Total assets	$2,756	$3,112	owners' equity	$2,756	$3,112

already made. Naturally, we hope these will convert to cash in the near future. Inventory is probably the least liquid of the current assets, at least for many businesses.

Fixed assets are, for the most part, relatively illiquid. These consist of tangible things such as buildings and equipment that don't convert to cash at all in normal business activity (they are, of course, used in the business to generate cash). Intangible assets, such as a trademark, have no physical existence but can be very valuable. Like tangible fixed assets, they won't ordinarily convert to cash and are generally considered illiquid.

Liquidity is valuable. The more liquid a business is, the less likely it is to experience financial distress (that is, difficulty in paying debts or buying needed assets). Unfortunately, liquid assets are generally less profitable to hold. For example, cash holdings are the most liquid of all investments, but they sometimes earn no return at all—they just sit there. There is therefore a trade-off between the advantages of liquidity and forgone potential profits.

Debt versus Equity

To the extent that a firm borrows money, it usually gives first claim to the firm's cash flow to creditors. Equity holders are only entitled to the residual value, the portion left after creditors are paid. The value of this residual portion is the shareholders' equity in the firm, which is just the value of the firm's assets less the value of the firm's liabilities:

$$\text{Shareholders' equity} = \text{Assets} - \text{Liabilities}$$

This is true in an accounting sense because shareholders' equity is defined as this residual portion. More importantly, it is true in an economic sense: If the firm sells its assets and pays its debts, whatever cash is left belongs to the shareholders.

The use of debt in a firm's capital structure is called *financial leverage.* The more debt a firm has (as a percentage of assets), the greater is its degree of financial leverage. As we discuss in later chapters, debt acts like a lever in the sense that using it can greatly magnify both gains and losses. So, financial leverage increases the potential reward to shareholders, but it also increases the potential for financial distress and business failure.

The home page for the Financial Accounting Standards Board (FASB) is **www.fasb.org**.

Market Value versus Book Value

The true value of any asset is its *market* value, which is simply the amount of cash we would get if we actually sold it. In contrast, the values shown on the balance sheet for the firm's assets are *book values* and generally are not what the assets are actually worth. Under **Generally Accepted Accounting Principles (GAAP)**, audited financial statements in the United States generally show assets at *historical cost.* In other words, assets are "carried on the books" at what the firm paid for them, no matter how long ago they were purchased or how much they are worth today.

For current assets, market value and book value might be somewhat similar since current assets are bought and converted into cash over a relatively short span of time. In other circumstances, they might differ quite a bit. Moreover, for fixed assets, it would be purely a coincidence if the actual market value of an asset (what the asset could be sold for) were equal to its book value. For example, a railroad might own enormous tracts of land purchased a century or more ago. What the railroad paid for that land could be hundreds or thousands of times less than what it is worth today. The balance sheet would nonetheless show the historical cost.

Managers and investors will frequently be interested in knowing the market value of the firm. This information is not on the balance sheet. The fact that balance sheet assets are listed at cost means that there is no necessary connection between the total assets shown and the market value of the firm. Indeed, many of the most valuable assets that a firm might

Generally Accepted Accounting Principles (GAAP)
The common set of standards and procedures by which audited financial statements are prepared.

have—good management, a good reputation, talented employees—don't appear on the balance sheet at all.

Similarly, the owners' equity figure on the balance sheet and the true market value of the equity need not be related. For financial managers, then, the accounting value of the equity is not an especially important concern; it is the market value that matters. Henceforth, whenever we speak of the value of an asset or the value of the firm, we will normally mean its *market value.* So, for example, when we say the goal of the financial manager is to increase the value of the stock, we mean the market value of the stock.

EXAMPLE 6.2 | **Market versus Book Values**

The Klingon Corporation has fixed assets with a book value of $700 and an appraised market value of about $1,000. Net working capital is $400 on the books, but approximately $600 would be realized if all the current accounts were liquidated. Klingon has $500 in long-term debt, both book value and market value. What is the book value of the equity? What is the market value?

We can construct two simplified balance sheets, one in accounting (book value) terms and one in economic (market value) terms:

KLINGON CORPORATION
Balance Sheets
Market Value versus Book Value

Assets	Book	Market	Liabilities and Shareholders' Equity	Book	Market
Net working capital	$ 400	$ 600	Long-term debt	$ 500	$ 500
Net fixed assets	700	1,000	Shareholders' equity	600	1,100
	$1,100	$1,600		$1,100	$1,600

In this example, shareholders' equity is actually worth almost twice as much as what is shown on the books. The distinction between book and market values is important precisely because book values can be so different from true economic value.

CONCEPT QUESTIONS

6.1a   What is the balance sheet identity?

6.1b   What is liquidity? Why is it important?

6.1c   What do we mean by financial leverage?

6.1d   Explain the difference between accounting value and market value. Which is more important to the financial manager? Why?

6.2 | THE INCOME STATEMENT

income statement
Financial statement summarizing a firm's performance over a period of time.

The **income statement** measures performance over some period of time, usually a quarter or a year. The income statement equation is:

$$\text{Revenues} - \text{Expenses} = \text{Income} \qquad [6.2]$$

If you think of the balance sheet as a snapshot, then you can think of the income statement as a video recording covering the period between a before and an after picture. Table 6.2 gives a simplified income statement for U.S. Corporation.

The first thing reported on an income statement would usually be revenue and expenses from the firm's principal operations. Subsequent parts include, among other things, financing expenses such as interest paid. Taxes paid are reported separately. The last item is *net income* (the so-called bottom line). Net income is often expressed on a per-share basis and called *earnings per share (EPS)*.

As indicated, U.S. paid cash dividends of $103. The difference between net income and cash dividends, $309, is the addition to retained earnings for the year. This amount is added to the cumulative retained earnings account on the balance sheet. If you'll look back at the two balance sheets for U.S. Corporation, you'll see that retained earnings did go up by this amount, $1,320 + 309 = $1,629.

Earnings and Dividends per Share | **EXAMPLE 6.3**

Suppose U.S. had 200 million shares outstanding at the end of 2003. Based on the income statement in Table 6.2, what was EPS? What were dividends per share?

From the income statement, U.S. had a net income of $412 million for the year. Total dividends were $103 million. Since 200 million shares were outstanding, we can calculate earnings per share and dividends per share as follows:

Earnings per share = Net income/Total shares outstanding
= $412/200 = $2.06 per share

Dividends per share = Total dividends/Total shares outstanding
= $103/200 = $.515 per share

When looking at an income statement, the financial manager needs to keep three things in mind: GAAP, cash versus noncash items, and time and costs.

GAAP and the Income Statement

An income statement prepared using GAAP will show revenue when it accrues. This is not necessarily when the cash comes in. The general rule (the realization principle) is to

U.S. CORPORATION 2003 Income Statement ($ in Millions)		
Net sales		$1,509
Cost of goods sold		750
Depreciation		65
Earnings before interest and taxes		$ 694
Interest paid		70
Taxable income		$ 624
Taxes		212
Net income		$ 412
Dividends	$103	
Addition to retained earnings	309	

TABLE 6.2

Income statement for U.S. Corporation

A Bitter Pill for McKesson's Stockholders

Want to know a quick way to eliminate $9 billion worth of the market value of your company's stock? It's easy; just write off about $42 million in sales as being of questionable quality. While no company aspires to doing such a thing, that's exactly what happened at McKesson HBOC Inc., the big health care supply management and information technology company, at the end of April 1999.

McKesson's tale of woe dates back to its acquisition three months earlier of HBO & Co., a health care information management business, for $12 billion in stock. While many investors panned the acquisition, citing the lack of available synergies between the two companies, none anticipated the bad news that was to come. A major consideration in the acquisition price was the rapid growth in sales at HBO. Sales growth had recently been very strong, with what one analyst called "a string of remarkable quarters."

All of that came crashing down in April, however. At issue were sales contracts for software HBO provided to hospitals and doctors for tracking finances, clinical outcomes, and similar items. The sales were apparently booked in full at the time they were contracted despite the fact that the contracts contained contingencies that hadn't yet been met. Although McKesson believed the contingencies would eventually be removed, it conceded that, until they were, the sales should not have been recorded as revenue. In fact, the restatement of these sales effectively cut in half the sales growth from these types of contracts for HBO for the previous year.

The ultimate disposition of these sales is instructive because it emphasizes the differences between accounting income and cash flow and what investors think of the two. The contracts were booked as sales even though the company might never receive a bit of the cash it expected from the contracts. Investors did not take the news well. When the company restated its earnings for the previous quarter and then slashed its profit projection for the coming fiscal year from $3 a share to $2.50 per share, stockholders voted with their feet, ultimately trimming the stock price by 48 percent, from $65.75 down to $34.50. That's fully 75 percent of the value of the acquisition cost of HBO in the first place. However, investors weren't done yet, as the value of the company's stock further declined to below $19 a share in early 2000. As this example makes clear, not all sales are cash inflows, and investors know the difference when confronted with the discrepancies between the two.

recognize revenue when the earnings process is virtually complete and the value of an exchange of goods or services is known or can be reliably determined. In practice, this principle usually means that revenue is recognized at the time of sale, which need not be the same as the time of collection.

Expenses shown on the income statement are based on the matching principle. The basic idea here is to first determine revenues as described above and then match those revenues with the costs associated with producing them. So, if we manufacture a product and then sell it on credit, the revenue is realized at the time of sale. The production and other costs associated with the sale of that product would likewise be recognized at that time. Once again, the actual cash outflows may have occurred at some very different times.

As a result of the way revenues and expenses are reported, the figures shown on the income statement may not be at all representative of the actual cash inflows and outflows that occurred during a particular period. The accompanying *Reality Bytes* box illustrates just how important the difference can be.

Noncash Items

noncash items
Expenses charged against revenues that do not directly affect cash flow, such as depreciation.

A primary reason that accounting income differs from cash flow is that an income statement contains **noncash items**. The most important of these is *depreciation*. Suppose a firm purchases a fixed asset for $5,000 and pays in cash. Obviously, the firm has a $5,000 cash outflow at the time of purchase. However, instead of deducting the $5,000 as an expense, an accountant might depreciate the asset over a five-year period.

210

If the depreciation is straight-line and the asset is written down to zero over that period, then $5,000/5 = $1,000 would be deducted each year as an expense.[2] The important thing to recognize is that this $1,000 deduction isn't cash—it's an accounting number. The actual cash outflow occurred when the asset was purchased.

The depreciation deduction is simply another application of the matching principle in accounting. The revenues associated with an asset would generally occur over some length of time. So the accountant seeks to match the expense of purchasing the asset with the benefits produced from owning it.

As we will see, for the financial manager, the actual timing of cash inflows and outflows is critical in coming up with a reasonable estimate of market value, so we need to learn how to separate the cash flows from the noncash accounting entries. In reality, the difference between cash flow and accounting income can be pretty dramatic. For example, media company Clear Channel Communications reported a net loss of $332 million for the first quarter of 2001. Sounds bad, but Clear Channel also reported a *positive* cash flow of $324 million! The reason the difference is so large is that Clear Channel has particularly big noncash deductions related to, among other things, the acquisition of radio stations.

Time and Costs

It is often useful to think of the future as having two distinct parts: the short run and the long run. These are not precise time periods. The distinction has to do with whether costs are fixed or variable. In the long run, all business costs are variable. Given sufficient time, assets can be sold, debts can be paid, and so on.

If our time horizon is relatively short, however, some costs are effectively fixed—they must be paid no matter what (property taxes, for example). Other costs such as wages to laborers and payments to suppliers are still variable. As a result, even in the short run, the firm can vary its output level by varying expenditures in these areas.

The distinction between fixed and variable costs is important, at times, to the financial manager, but the way costs are reported on the income statement is not a good guide as to which costs are which. The reason is that, in practice, accountants tend to classify costs as either product costs or period costs.

Product costs include such things as raw materials, direct labor expense, and manufacturing overhead. These are reported on the income statement as costs of goods sold, but they include both fixed and variable costs. Similarly, period costs are incurred during a particular time period and might be reported as selling, general, and administrative expenses. Once again, some of these period costs may be fixed and others may be variable. The company president's salary, for example, is a period cost and is probably fixed, at least in the short run.

The balance sheets and income statement we have been using thus far are hypothetical. Our nearby *Work the Web* box shows how to find actual balance sheets and income statements on-line for almost any company.

CONCEPT QUESTIONS

6.2a What is the income statement equation?

6.2b What are the three things to keep in mind when looking at an income statement?

6.2c Why is accounting income not the same as cash flow?

---

[2]By "straight-line," we mean that the depreciation deduction is the same every year. By "written down to zero," we mean that the asset is assumed to have no value at the end of five years.

WORK THE WEB

The U.S. Securities and Exchange Commission (SEC) requires that most public companies file regular reports, including annual and quarterly financial statements. The SEC has a public site named EDGAR at www.sec.gov that makes these reports available free. We went to "Search for Company Filings" and then "Quick Forms Lookup." On the search form, we entered "Microsoft" and then selected 10-K from the drop-down menu.

EDGAR Form Pick Search

Revised May 2001

This search allows you to look up filings by specifying the form type and the company name or company CIK. The search covers all EDGAR filings on the website from **1993** through **2002**.

Enter Company Name:	Microsoft
OR Enter CIK:	

Select Form Type:	Common:	10-K		Select Date Range:	Start:	1993
	OR Other:				End:	2002

Search

Here is a partial view of what we got:

Your search matched **8** of **2132491** documents.

No.	Company	Format	Form Type	Filing Date	Size
1	MICROSOFT CORP	[text] [html]	10-K	09/18/2001	262127
2	MICROSOFT CORP	[text] [html]	10-K	09/28/2000	457956
3	MICROSOFT CORP	[text] [html]	10-K	09/28/1999	289775
4	MICROSOFT CORP	[text]	10-K	09/25/1998	178170
5	MICROSOFT CORP	[text]	10-K	09/29/1997	198534
6	MICROSOFT CORP	[text]	10-K	09/27/1996	147565
7	MICROSOFT CORP	[text]	10-K	09/25/1995	189572
8	MICROSOFT CORP	[text]	10-K	09/27/1994	442763

As of the date of this search, EDGAR had eight of these reports for Microsoft available for download. The 10-K is the annual report filed with the SEC. It includes, among other things, the list of officers and their salaries, financial statements for the previous fiscal year, and an explanation by the company for the financial results. Here is an exercise for you: Go to the "Quick Forms Lookup" page and follow the "form type" link to find a description of the different forms companies must file with the SEC.

6.3 | TAXES

Taxes can be one of the largest cash outflows that a firm experiences. For example, for the fiscal year 2001, Wal-Mart's earnings before taxes were about $9.1 billion. Its tax bill,

Taxable Income		Tax Rate
$ 0–	50,000	15%
50,001–	75,000	25
75,001–	100,000	34
100,001–	335,000	39
335,001–	10,000,000	34
10,000,001–	15,000,000	35
15,000,001–	18,333,333	38
18,333,334+		35

TABLE 6.3

Corporate tax rates

including all taxes paid worldwide, was a whopping $3.5 billion, or about 38 percent of its pretax earnings. The size of the tax bill is determined through the tax code, an often-amended set of rules. In this section, we examine corporate tax rates and how taxes are calculated. Taxes for partnerships and proprietorships are computed using the personal income tax schedules; we don't discuss these here, but the general procedures are the same as for corporate taxes.

If the various rules of taxation seem a little bizarre or convoluted to you, keep in mind that the tax code is the result of political, not economic, forces. As a result, there is no reason why it has to make economic sense.

Corporate Tax Rates

Corporate tax rates in effect for 2003 are shown in Table 6.3. A peculiar feature is that corporate tax rates are not strictly increasing. As shown, corporate tax rates rise from 15 percent to 39 percent, but they drop back to 34 percent on income over $335,000. They then rise to 38 percent and subsequently fall to 35 percent.

According to the originators of the current tax rules, there are only four corporate rates: 15 percent, 25 percent, 34 percent, and 35 percent. The 38 and 39 percent brackets arise because of "surcharges" applied on top of the 34 and 35 percent rates. A tax is a tax is a tax, however, so there are really six corporate tax brackets, as we have shown.

The IRS has a great web site! (**www.irs.gov**)

Average versus Marginal Tax Rates

In making financial decisions, it is frequently important to distinguish between average and marginal tax rates. Your **average tax rate** is your tax bill divided by your taxable income, in other words, the percentage of your income that goes to pay taxes. Your **marginal tax rate** is the extra tax you would pay if you earned one more dollar. The percentage tax rates shown in Table 6.3 are all marginal rates. Put another way, the tax rates in Table 6.3 apply to the part of income in the indicated range only, not all income.

The difference between average and marginal tax rates can best be illustrated with a simple example. Suppose our corporation has a taxable income of $200,000. What is the tax bill? From Table 6.3, we can figure our tax bill as:

average tax rate
Total taxes paid divided by total taxable income.

marginal tax rate
Amount of tax payable on the next dollar earned.

$$.15(\$\ 50,000) = \$\ 7,500$$
$$.25(\$\ 75,000 - 50,000) = 6,250$$
$$.34(\$100,000 - 75,000) = 8,500$$
$$.39(\$200,000 - 100,000) = \underline{39,000}$$
$$\underline{\underline{\$61,250}}$$

Our total tax is thus $61,250.

In our example, what is the average tax rate? We had a taxable income of $200,000 and a tax bill of $61,250, so the average tax rate is $61,250/200,000 = 30.625%. What is the marginal tax rate? If we made one more dollar, the tax on that dollar would be 39 cents, so our marginal rate is 39 percent.

EXAMPLE 6.4   **Deep in the Heart of Taxes**

Algernon, Inc., has a taxable income of $85,000. What is its tax bill? What is its average tax rate? Its marginal tax rate?

From Table 6.3, the tax rate applied to the first $50,000 is 15 percent; the rate applied to the next $25,000 is 25 percent; and the rate applied after that up to $100,000 is 34 percent. So Algernon must pay .15 × $50,000 + .25 × 25,000 + .34 × (85,000 − 75,000) = $17,150. The average tax rate is thus $17,150/85,000 = 20.18%. The marginal rate is 34 percent since Algernon's taxes would rise by 34 cents if it had another dollar in taxable income.

Table 6.4 summarizes some different taxable incomes, marginal tax rates, and average tax rates for corporations. Notice how the average and marginal tax rates come together at 35 percent.

With a *flat-rate* tax, there is only one tax rate, and this rate is the same for all income levels. With such a tax, the marginal tax rate is always the same as the average tax rate. As it stands now, corporate taxation in the United States is based on a modified flat-rate tax, which becomes a true flat rate for the highest incomes.

In looking at Table 6.4, notice that the more a corporation makes, the greater is the percentage of taxable income paid in taxes. Put another way, under current tax law, the average tax rate never goes down, even though the marginal tax rate does. As illustrated, for corporations, average tax rates begin at 15 percent and rise to a maximum of 35 percent.

It will normally be the marginal tax rate that is relevant for financial decision making. The reason is that any new cash flows will be taxed at that marginal rate. Since financial decisions usually involve new cash flows or changes in existing ones, this rate will tell us the marginal effect on our tax bill.

There is one last thing to notice about the tax code as it affects corporations. It's easy to verify that the corporate tax bill is just a flat 35 percent of taxable income if our taxable income is more than $18.33 million. Also, for the many midsize corporations with taxable incomes in the $335,000 to $10,000,000 range, the tax rate is a flat 34 percent. Since we will usually be talking about large corporations, you can assume that the average and marginal tax rates are 35 percent unless we explicitly say otherwise.

TABLE 6.4

Corporate taxes and tax rates

(1) Taxable Income	(2) Marginal Tax Rate	(3) Total Tax	(3)/(1) Average Tax Rate
$ 45,000	15%	$ 6,750	15.00%
70,000	25	12,500	17.86
95,000	34	20,550	21.63
250,000	39	80,750	32.30
1,000,000	34	340,000	34.00
17,500,000	38	6,100,000	34.86
50,000,000	35	17,500,000	35.00
100,000,000	35	35,000,000	35.00

CONCEPT QUESTIONS

6.3a What is the difference between a marginal and an average tax rate?

6.3b Do the wealthiest corporations receive a tax break in terms of a lower tax rate? Explain.

CASH FLOW | 6.4

At this point, we are ready to discuss perhaps one of the most important pieces of financial information that can be gleaned from financial statements: *cash flow*. By cash flow, we simply mean the difference between the number of dollars that came in and the number that went out. For example, if you were the owner of a business, you might be very interested in how much cash you actually took out of your business in a given year. How to determine this amount is one of the things we discuss next.

There is no standard financial statement that presents this information in the way that we wish. We will therefore discuss how to calculate cash flow for U.S. Corporation and point out how the result differs from that of standard financial statement calculations. Important note: there is a standard financial accounting statement called the *statement of cash flows,* but it is concerned with a somewhat different issue that should not be confused with what is discussed in this section.

From the balance sheet identity, we know that the value of a firm's assets is equal to the value of its liabilities plus the value of its equity. Similarly, the cash flow from the firm's assets must equal the sum of the cash flow to creditors and the cash flow to stockholders (or owners, if the business is not a corporation):

$$\text{Cash flow from assets} = \text{Cash flow to creditors} \\ + \text{Cash flow to stockholders} \qquad \textbf{[6.3]}$$

This is the cash flow identity. What it reflects is the fact that a firm generates cash through its various activities, and that cash either is used to pay creditors or else is paid out to the owners of the firm. We discuss the various things that make up these cash flows next.

Cash Flow from Assets

Cash flow from assets involves three components: operating cash flow, capital spending, and change in net working capital. **Operating cash flow** refers to the cash flow that results from the firm's day-to-day activities of producing and selling. Expenses associated with the firm's financing of its assets are not included since they are not operating expenses.

In the normal course of events, some portion of the firm's cash flow is reinvested in the firm. *Capital spending* refers to the net spending on fixed assets (purchases of fixed assets less sales of fixed assets). Finally, *the change in net working capital* is the amount spent on net working capital. It is measured as the change in net working capital over the period being examined and represents the net increase in current assets over current liabilities. The three components of cash flow are examined in more detail below. In all our examples, all amounts are in millions of dollars.

Operating Cash Flow To calculate operating cash flow (OCF), we want to calculate revenues minus costs, but we don't want to include depreciation since it's not a cash outflow, and we don't want to include interest because it's a financing expense. We do want to include taxes, because taxes are, unfortunately, paid in cash.

cash flow from assets

The total of cash flow to creditors and cash flow to stockholders, consisting of the following: operating cash flow, capital spending, and changes in net working capital.

operating cash flow

Cash generated from a firm's normal business activities.

If we look at U.S. Corporation's income statement (Table 6.2), we see that earnings before interest and taxes (EBIT) are $694. This is almost what we want since it doesn't include interest paid. We need to make two adjustments. First, recall that depreciation is a noncash expense. To get cash flow, we first add back the $65 in depreciation since it wasn't a cash deduction. The other adjustment is to subtract the $212 in taxes since these were paid in cash. The result is operating cash flow:

U.S. CORPORATION	
2003 Operating Cash Flow	
Earnings before interest and taxes	$694
+ Depreciation	65
− Taxes	212
Operating cash flow	$547

U.S. Corporation thus had a 2003 operating cash flow of $547.

Operating cash flow is an important number because it tells us, on a very basic level, whether or not a firm's cash inflows from its business operations are sufficient to cover its everyday cash outflows. For this reason, a negative operating cash flow is often a sign of trouble.

There is an unpleasant possibility for confusion when we speak of operating cash flow. In accounting practice, operating cash flow is often defined as net income plus depreciation. For U.S. Corporation, this would amount to $412 + 65 = $477. The accounting definition of operating cash flow differs from ours in one important way: Interest is deducted when net income is computed. Notice that the difference between the $547 operating cash flow we calculated and this $477 is $70, the amount of interest paid for the year. This definition of cash flow thus considers interest paid to be an operating expense. Our definition treats it properly as a financing expense. If there were no interest expense, the two definitions would be the same.

To finish our calculation of cash flow from assets for U.S. Corporation, we need to consider how much of the $547 operating cash flow was reinvested in the firm. We consider spending on fixed assets first.

Capital Spending   Net capital spending is just money spent on fixed assets less money received from the sale of fixed assets. At the end of 2002, net fixed assets for U.S. Corporation (Table 6.1) were $1,644. During the year, we wrote off (depreciated) $65 worth of fixed assets on the income statement. So, if we didn't purchase any new fixed assets, net fixed assets would have been $1,644 − 65 = $1,579 at year's end. The 2003 balance sheet shows $1,709 in net fixed assets, so we must have spent a total of $1,709 − 1,579 = $130 on fixed assets during the year:

Ending net fixed assets	$1,709
− Beginning net fixed assets	1,644
+ Depreciation	65
Net investment in fixed assets	$ 130

This $130 is our net capital spending for 2003.

Could net capital spending be negative? The answer is yes. This would happen if the firm sold off more assets than it purchased. The *net* here refers to purchases of fixed assets net of any sales of fixed assets.

Change in Net Working Capital In addition to investing in fixed assets, a firm will also invest in current assets. For example, going back to the balance sheet in Table 6.1, we see that at the end of 2003, U.S. had current assets of $1,403. At the end of 2002, current assets were $1,112, so, during the year, U.S. invested $1,403 − 1,112 = $291 in current assets.

As the firm changes its investment in current assets, its current liabilities will usually change as well. To determine the change in net working capital, the easiest approach is just to take the difference between the beginning and ending net working capital (NWC) figures. Net working capital at the end of 2003 was $1,403 − 389 = $1,014. Similarly, at the end of 2002, net working capital was $1,112 − 428 = $684. So, given these figures, we have:

Ending NWC	$1,014
− Beginning NWC	684
Change in NWC	$ 330

Net working capital thus increased by $330. Put another way, U.S. Corporation had a net investment of $330 in NWC for the year.

Conclusion Given the figures we've come up with, we're ready to calculate cash flow from assets. The total cash flow from assets is given by operating cash flow less the amounts invested in fixed assets and net working capital. So, for U.S., we have:

U.S. CORPORATION	
2003 Cash Flow from Assets	
Operating cash flow	$547
− Net capital spending	130
− Change in NWC	330
Cash flow from assets	$ 87

From the cash flow identity above, this $87 cash flow from assets equals the sum of the firm's cash flow to creditors and its cash flow to stockholders. We consider these next.

It wouldn't be at all unusual for a growing corporation to have a negative cash flow. As we shall see below, a negative cash flow means that the firm raised more money by borrowing and selling stock than it paid out to creditors and stockholders that year.

A Note on "Free" Cash Flow Cash flow from assets sometimes goes by a different name, **free cash flow**. Of course, there is no such thing as "free" cash (we wish!). Instead, the name refers to cash that the firm is free to distribute to creditors and stockholders because it is not needed for working capital or fixed asset investments. We will stick with "cash flow from assets" as our label for this important concept because, in practice, there is some variation in exactly how free cash flow is computed; different users calculate it in different ways. Nonetheless, whenever you hear the phrase "free cash flow," you

free cash flow
Another name for cash flow from assets.

should understand that what is being discussed is cash flow from assets or something quite similar.

Cash Flow to Creditors and Stockholders

cash flow to creditors

A firm's interest payments to creditors less net new borrowings.

cash flow to stockholders

Dividends paid out by a firm less net new equity raised.

The cash flows to creditors and stockholders represent the net payments to creditors and owners during the year. They are calculated in a similar way. **Cash flow to creditors** is interest paid less net new borrowing; **cash flow to stockholders** is dividends paid less net new equity raised.

Cash Flow to Creditors   Looking at the income statement in Table 6.2, we see that U.S. paid $70 in interest to creditors. From the balance sheets in Table 6.1, long-term debt rose by $454 − 408 = $46. So, U.S. Corporation paid out $70 in interest, but it borrowed an additional $46. Net cash flow to creditors is thus:

U.S. CORPORATION 2003 Cash Flow to Creditors	
Interest paid	$70
− Net new borrowing	46
Cash flow to creditors	$24

Cash flow to creditors is sometimes called *cash flow to bondholders;* we will use these terms interchangeably.

Cash Flow to Stockholders   From the income statement, dividends paid to stockholders amount to $103. To get net new equity raised, we need to look at the common stock and paid-in surplus account. This account tells us how much stock the company has sold. During the year, this account rose by $40, so $40 in net new equity was raised. Given this, we have:

U.S. CORPORATION 2003 Cash Flow to Stockholders	
Dividends paid	$103
− Net new equity raised	40
Cash flow to stockholders	$ 63

The cash flow to stockholders for 2003 was thus $63.

Conclusion

The last thing that we need to do is to verify that the cash flow identity holds to be sure that we didn't make any mistakes. From above, cash flow from assets is $87. Cash flow to creditors and stockholders is $24 + 63 = $87, so everything checks out. Table 6.5 contains a summary of the various cash flow calculations for future reference.

As our discussion indicates, it is essential that a firm keep an eye on its cash flow. The following serves as an excellent reminder of why doing so is a good idea, unless the firm's owners wish to end up in the "Po' " house.

I. The cash flow identity

Cash flow from assets = Cash flow to creditors (bondholders)
   + Cash flow to stockholders (owners)

II. Cash flow from assets

Cash flow from assets = Operating cash flow
   − Net capital spending
   − Change in net working capital (NWC)

where

Operating cash flow = Earnings before interest and taxes (EBIT)
   + Depreciation − Taxes

Net capital spending = Ending net fixed assets − Beginning net fixed assets
   + Depreciation

Change in NWC = Ending NWC − Beginning NWC

III. Cash flow to creditors (bondholders)

Cash flow to creditors = Interest paid − Net new borrowing

IV. Cash flow to stockholders (owners)

Cash flow to stockholders = Dividends paid − Net new equity raised

TABLE 6.5

Cash flow summary

Quoth the Banker, "Watch Cash Flow"

Once upon a midnight dreary as I pondered weak and weary
Over many a quaint and curious volume of accounting lore,
Seeking gimmicks (without scruple) to squeeze through
   some new tax loophole,
Suddenly I heard a knock upon my door,
   Only this, and nothing more.

Then I felt a queasy tingling and I heard the cash a-jingling
As a fearsome banker entered whom I'd often seen before.
His face was money-green and in his eyes there could be seen
Dollar-signs that seemed to glitter as he reckoned up the score.
   "Cash flow," the banker said, and nothing more.

I had always thought it fine to show a jet black bottom line.
But the banker sounded a resounding, "No.
Your receivables are high, mounting upward toward the sky;
Write-offs loom. What matters is cash flow."
   He repeated, "Watch cash flow."

Then I tried to tell the story of our lovely inventory
Which, though large, is full of most delightful stuff.
But the banker saw its growth, and with a mighty oath
He waved his arms and shouted, "Stop! Enough!
   Pay the interest, and don't give me any guff!"

Next I looked for noncash items which could add ad infinitum
To replace the ever-outward flow of cash,
But to keep my statement black I'd held depreciation back,
And my banker said that I'd done something rash.
   He quivered, and his teeth began to gnash.

When I asked him for a loan, he responded, with a groan,
That the interest rate would be just prime plus eight,
And to guarantee my purity he'd insist on some security—
All my assets plus the scalp upon my pate.
   Only this, a standard rate.

Though my bottom line is black, I am flat upon my back,
My cash flows out and customers pay slow.

The growth of my receivables is almost unbelievable:
The result is certain—unremitting woe!
And I hear the banker utter an ominous low mutter,
    "Watch cash flow."

Herbert S. Bailey Jr.

Source: Reprinted from the January 13, 1975, issue of *Publishers Weekly,* published by R. R. Bowker, a Xerox company. Copyright © 1975 by the Xerox Corporation.

To which we can only add: "Amen."

An Example: Cash Flows for Dole Cola

This extended example covers the various cash flow calculations discussed in the chapter. It also illustrates a few variations that may arise.

Operating Cash Flow   During the year, Dole Cola, Inc., had sales and cost of goods sold of $600 and $300, respectively. Depreciation was $150 and interest paid was $30. Taxes were calculated at a straight 34 percent. Dividends were $30. (All figures are in millions of dollars.) What was operating cash flow for Dole? Why is this different from net income?

The easiest thing to do here is to go ahead and create an income statement. We can then pick up the numbers we need. Dole Cola's income statement is given below.

DOLE COLA **2003 Income Statement**		
Net sales		$600
Cost of goods sold		300
Depreciation		150
Earnings before interest and taxes		$150
Interest paid		30
Taxable income		$120
Taxes		41
Net income		$ 79
Dividends	$30	
Addition to retained earnings	49	

Net income for Dole was thus $79. We now have all the numbers we need. Referring back to the U.S. Corporation example and Table 6.5, we have:

DOLE COLA **2003 Operating Cash Flow**	
Earnings before interest and taxes	$150
+ Depreciation	150
− Taxes	41
Operating cash flow	$259

As this example illustrates, operating cash flow is not the same as net income, because depreciation and interest are subtracted out when net income is calculated. If you recall our earlier discussion, we don't subtract these out in computing operating cash flow because depreciation is not a cash expense and interest paid is a financing expense, not an operating expense.

Net Capital Spending Suppose beginning net fixed assets were $500 and ending net fixed assets were $750. What was the net capital spending for the year?

From the income statement for Dole, depreciation for the year was $150. Net fixed assets rose by $250. Dole thus spent $250 along with an additional $150, for a total of $400.

Change in NWC and Cash Flow from Assets Suppose Dole Cola started the year with $2,130 in current assets and $1,620 in current liabilities. The corresponding ending figures were $2,260 and $1,710. What was the change in NWC during the year? What was cash flow from assets? How does this compare to net income?

Net working capital started out as $2,130 − 1,620 = $510 and ended up at $2,260 − 1,710 = $550. The change in NWC was thus $550 − 510 = $40. Putting together all the information for Dole Cola, we have

DOLE COLA 2003 Cash Flow from Assets	
Operating cash flow	$259
− Net capital spending	400
− Change in NWC	40
Cash flow from assets	−$181

Dole had a cash flow from assets of −$181. Net income was positive at $79. Is the fact that cash flow from assets was negative a cause for alarm? Not necessarily. The cash flow here is negative primarily because of a large investment in fixed assets. If these are good investments, then the resulting negative cash flow is not a worry.

Cash Flow to Creditors and Stockholders We saw that Dole Cola had cash flow from assets of −$181. The fact that this is negative means that Dole raised more money in the form of new debt and equity than it paid out for the year. For example, suppose we know that Dole didn't sell any new equity for the year. What was cash flow to stockholders? To creditors?

Since it didn't raise any new equity, Dole's cash flow to stockholders is just equal to the cash dividend paid:

DOLE COLA 2003 Cash Flow to Stockholders	
Dividends paid	$30
− Net new equity	0
Cash flow to stockholders	$30

Now, from the cash flow identity, the total cash paid to creditors and stockholders was −$181. Cash flow to stockholders is $30, so cash flow to creditors must be equal to −$181 − 30 = −$211:

Cash flow to creditors + Cash flow to stockholders = −$181

Cash flow to creditors + $30   = −$181

Cash flow to creditors   = −$211

Since we know that cash flow to creditors is −$211 and interest paid is $30 (from the income statement), we can now determine net new borrowing. Dole must have borrowed $241 during the year to help finance the fixed asset expansion:

DOLE COLA	
2003 Cash Flow to Creditors	
Interest paid	$ 30
− Net new borrowing	241
Cash flow to creditors	−$211

CONCEPT QUESTIONS

6.4a   What is the cash flow identity? Explain what it says.

6.4b   What are the components of operating cash flow?

6.4c   Why is interest paid not a component of operating cash flow?

SUMMARY AND CONCLUSIONS

This chapter has introduced you to some of the basics of financial statements, taxes, and cash flow. In it we saw that:

1. The book values on an accounting balance sheet can be very different from market values. The goal of financial management is to maximize the market value of the stock, not its book value.
2. Net income as it is computed on the income statement is not cash flow. A primary reason is that depreciation, a noncash expense, is deducted when net income is computed.
3. Marginal and average tax rates can be different, and it is the marginal tax rate that is relevant for most financial decisions.
4. The marginal tax rate paid by the corporations with the largest incomes is 35 percent.
5. There is a cash flow identity much like the balance sheet identity. It says that cash flow from assets equals cash flow to creditors and stockholders.

The calculation of cash flow from financial statements isn't difficult. Care must be taken in handling noncash expenses, such as depreciation, and in not confusing operating costs with financing costs. Most of all, it is important not to confuse book values with market values and accounting income with cash flow.

CHAPTER REVIEW AND SELF-TEST PROBLEM

6.1 **Cash Flow for Rasputin Corporation.** This problem will give you some practice working with financial statements and figuring cash flow. Based on the following information for Rasputin Corporation, prepare an income statement for 2003 and balance sheets for 2002 and 2003. Next, following our U.S. Corporation examples in the chapter, calculate cash flow from assets for Rasputin, cash flow to creditors, and cash flow to stockholders for 2003. Use a 34 percent tax rate throughout. You can check your answers below.

	2002	2003
Sales	$3,790	$3,990
Cost of goods sold	2,043	2,137
Depreciation	975	1,018
Interest	225	267
Dividends	200	225
Current assets	2,140	2,346
Net fixed assets	6,770	7,087
Current liabilities	994	1,126
Long-term debt	2,000	2,956

■ Answer to Chapter Review and Self-Test Problem

6.1 In preparing the balance sheets, remember that shareholders' equity is the residual. With this in mind, Rasputin's balance sheets are as follows:

RASPUTIN CORPORATION
Balance Sheets as of December 31, 2002 and 2003

	2002	2003		2002	2003
Current assets	$2,140	$2,346	Current liabilities	$ 994	$1,126
Net fixed assets	6,770	7,087	Long-term debt	2,869	2,956
			Equity	5,047	5,351
			Total liabilities and		
Total assets	$8,910	$9,433	shareholders' equity	$8,910	$9,433

The income statement is straightforward:

RASPUTIN CORPORATION
2003 Income Statement

Sales		$3,990
Cost of goods sold		2,137
Depreciation		1,018
Earnings before interest and taxes		$ 835
Interest paid		267
Taxable income		$ 568
Taxes (34%)		193
Net income		$ 375
Dividends	$225	
Addition to retained earnings	150	

Notice that we've used a flat 34 percent tax rate. Also notice that the addition to retained earnings is just net income less cash dividends.

We can now pick up the figures we need to get operating cash flow:

RASPUTIN CORPORATION 2003 Operating Cash Flow	
Earnings before interest and taxes	$ 835
+ Depreciation	1,018
− Current taxes	193
Operating cash flow	$1,660

Next, we get the capital spending for the year by looking at the change in fixed assets, remembering to account for the depreciation:

Ending fixed assets	$7,087
− Beginning fixed assets	6,770
+ Depreciation	1,018
Net investment in fixed assets	$1,335

After calculating beginning and ending NWC, we take the difference to get the change in NWC:

Ending NWC	$1,220
− Beginning NWC	1,146
Change in NWC	$ 74

We now combine operating cash flow, net capital spending, and the change in net working capital to get the total cash flow from assets:

RASPUTIN CORPORATION 2003 Cash Flow from Assets	
Operating cash flow	$1,660
− Net capital spending	1,335
− Change in NWC	74
Cash flow from assets	$ 251

To get cash flow to creditors, notice that long-term borrowing increased by $87 during the year and that interest paid was $267, so:

RASPUTIN CORPORATION 2003 Cash Flow to Creditors	
Interest paid	$267
− Net new borrowing	87
Cash flow to creditors	$180

Finally, dividends paid were $225. To get net new equity, we have to do some extra calculating. Total equity was up by $5,351 − 5,047 = $304. Of this increase, $150 was from additions to retained earnings, so $154 in new equity was raised during the year. Cash flow to stockholders was thus:

RASPUTIN CORPORATION 2003 Cash Flow to Stockholders	
Dividends paid	$225
− Net new equity	154
Cash flow to stockholders	$ 71

As a check, notice that cash flow from assets ($251) does equal cash flow to creditors plus cash flow to stockholders ($180 + 71 = $251).

CRITICAL THINKING AND CONCEPTS REVIEW

6.1 **Liquidity.** What does liquidity measure? Explain the trade-off a firm faces between high-liquidity and low-liquidity levels.

6.2 **Accounting and Cash Flows.** Why is it that the revenue and cost figures shown on a standard income statement may not be representative of the actual cash inflows and outflows that occurred during a period?

6.3 **Book Values versus Market Values.** In preparing a balance sheet, why do you think standard accounting practice focuses on historical cost rather than market value?

6.4 **Operating Cash Flow.** In comparing accounting net income and operating cash flow, what two items do you find in net income that are not in operating cash flow? Explain what each is and why it is excluded in operating cash flow.

6.5 **Book Values versus Market Values.** Under standard accounting rules, it is possible for a company's liabilities to exceed its assets. When this occurs, the owners' equity is negative. Can this happen with market values? Why or why not?

6.6 **Cash Flow from Assets.** Suppose a company's cash flow from assets was negative for a particular period. Is this necessarily a good sign or a bad sign?

6.7 **Operating Cash Flow.** Suppose a company's operating cash flow was negative for several years running. Is this necessarily a good sign or a bad sign?

6.8 **Net Working Capital and Capital Spending.** Could a company's change in NWC be negative in a given year? (Hint: Yes.) Explain how this might come about. What about net capital spending?

6.9 **Cash Flow to Stockholders and Creditors.** Could a company's cash flow to stockholders be negative in a given year? (Hint: Yes.) Explain how this might come about. What about cash flow to creditors?

6.10 **Firm Values.** In December 1995, Texaco announced it would take a fourth-quarter charge of $640 million against earnings, changing its quarterly results from a profit to a loss. Texaco was not alone. Other oil companies, such as Phillips Petroleum, Mobil, and Chevron, all planned to take significant charges as well. Poor performance wasn't the issue. Instead, oil companies were forced by accounting rule changes to recalculate the value of oil fields shown on their financial statements. The new values were substantially smaller, and, as a result, the reported assets of these companies fell in value by hundreds of millions of dollars.

So, did stockholders in Texaco lose $640 million as a result of accounting rule changes? The answer: Probably not. What do you think is the basis for this conclusion?

Use the following information to answer the next two questions:

In June 2002, WorldCom, the telecommunications giant, surprised investors when it announced that it had overstated net income in the prior two years by $3.8 billion. At the center of the controversy was Scott D. Sullivan, the former CFO. WorldCom had leased telephone lines from local companies with the expectation of reselling the use of the lines at a higher price. Under GAAP, these costs should have been reported as an expense on the income statement. Reportedly, however, Mr. Sullivan ordered that the costs be treated as money spent to purchase a fixed asset, so they were to be shown on the balance sheet as an asset and subsequently depreciated.

6.11   **Corporate Ethics.**   In the wake of this scandal, Mr. Sullivan was charged with fraud. Do you think this should be considered fraud? Why? Why was this unethical?

6.12   **Net Income and Cash Flows.**   How did Mr. Sullivan's reclassifying some costs as asset purchases affect net income at the time? In the future? How did this action affect cash flows? What does this tell you about the importance of examining cash flow relative to net income?

QUESTIONS AND PROBLEMS

www.mhhe.com/rwj
Spreadsheet Templates 6, 10, 19

Basic
(Questions 1–13)

1. **Building a Balance Sheet.**   Bellaire Bat Factory, Inc., has current assets of $2,800, net fixed assets of $6,000, current liabilities of $1,600, and long-term debt of $5,200. What is the value of the shareholders' equity account for this firm? How much is net working capital?

2. **Building an Income Statement.**   Hoobstank, Inc., has sales of $425,000, costs of $210,000, depreciation expense of $63,000, interest expense of $38,000, and a tax rate of 35 percent. What is the net income for this firm?

3. **Dividends and Retained Earnings.**   Suppose the firm in Problem 2 paid out $35,000 in cash dividends. What is the addition to retained earnings?

4. **Per-Share Earnings and Dividends.**   Suppose the firm in Problem 3 had 30,000 shares of common stock outstanding. What is the earnings per share, or EPS, figure? What is the dividends per share figure?

5. **Market Values and Book Values.**   Klingon Widgets, Inc., purchased new cloaking machinery three years ago for $5 million. The machinery can be sold to the Romulans today for $4 million. Klingon's current balance sheet shows net fixed assets of $2,100,000, current liabilities of $750,000, and net working capital of $600,000. If all the current assets were liquidated today, the company would receive $1.25 million cash. What is the book value of Klingon's assets today? What is the market value?

6. **Calculating Taxes.**   The Gonas Co. had $310,000 in 2003 taxable income. Using the rates from Table 6.3 in the chapter, calculate the company's 2003 income taxes.

7. **Tax Rates.**   In Problem 6, what is the average tax rate? What is the marginal tax rate?

8. **Calculating OCF.**   Lutz, Inc., has sales of $9,620, costs of $4,840, depreciation expense of $1,300, and interest expense of $1,210. If the tax rate is 35 percent, what is the operating cash flow, or OCF?

9. **Calculating Net Capital Spending.**   Rotweiler Obedience School's December 31, 2002, balance sheet showed net fixed assets of $2.8 million, and the December 31, 2003, balance sheet showed net fixed assets of $3.1 million. The company's 2003 income statement showed a depreciation expense of $510,000. What was Rotweiler's net capital spending for 2003?

10. **Calculating Additions to NWC.**   The December 31, 2002, balance sheet of Anna's Tennis Shop, Inc., showed current assets of $800 and current liabilities of $280. The December 31, 2003, balance sheet showed current assets of $860 and current liabilities of $415. What was the company's 2003 change in net working capital, or NWC?

11. **Cash Flow to Creditors.**   The December 31, 2002, balance sheet of Rack N Pinion, Inc., showed long-term debt of $1.9 million, and the December 31, 2003, balance sheet showed long-term debt of $2.3 million. The 2003 income statement showed an interest expense of $420,000. What was the firm's cash flow to creditors during 2003?

12. **Cash Flow to Stockholders.**   The December 31, 2002, balance sheet of Rack N Pinion, Inc., showed $200,000 in the common stock account and $4.2 million in the additional paid-in surplus account. The December 31, 2003, balance sheet showed $230,000 and $4.5 million in the same two accounts, respectively. If the company paid out $120,000 in cash dividends during 2003, what was the cash flow to stockholders for the year?

13. **Calculating Total Cash Flows.**   Given the information for Rack N Pinion, Inc., in Problems 11 and 12, suppose you also know that the firm's net capital spending for 2003 was $760,000, and that the firm reduced its net working capital investment by $135,000. What was the firm's 2003 operating cash flow, or OCF?

14. **Calculating Total Cash Flows.**   Faulk Co. shows the following information on its 2003 income statement: sales = $114,000; costs = $61,200; other expenses = $3,300; depreciation expense = $9,600; interest expense = $8,400; taxes = $10,710; dividends = $3,840. In addition, you're told that the firm issued $1,700 in new equity during 2003, and redeemed $3,600 in outstanding long-term debt.

    Intermediate
    (Questions 14–22)

    a.   What is the 2003 operating cash flow?

    b.   What is the 2003 cash flow to creditors?

    c.   What is the 2003 cash flow to stockholders?

    d.   If net fixed assets increased by $11,400 during the year, what was the addition to NWC?

15. **Using Income Statements.**   Given the following information for Pierce Pizza Co., calculate the depreciation expense: sales = $30,000; costs = $19,000; addition to retained earnings = $2,100; dividends paid = $900; interest expense = $1,430; tax rate = 35 percent.

16. **Preparing a Balance Sheet.**   Prepare a balance sheet for Tim's Couch Corp. as of December 31, 2003, based on the following information: cash = $204,000; patents

and copyrights = \$798,000; accounts payable = \$605,000; accounts receivable = \$226,000; tangible net fixed assets = \$4,400,000; inventory = \$473,000; notes payable = \$193,000; accumulated retained earnings = \$3,905,000; long-term debt = \$908,000.

17. **Residual Claims.**   O'Dowd, Inc., is obligated to pay its creditors \$3,800 during the year.

    a.   What is the value of the shareholders' equity if assets equal \$4,500?

    b.   What if assets equal \$3,400?

18. **Marginal versus Average Tax Rates.**   (Refer to Table 6.3) Corporation Growth has \$82,000 in taxable income, and Corporation Income has \$8,200,000 in taxable income.

    a.   What is the tax bill for each firm?

    b.   Suppose both firms have identified a new project that will increase taxable income by \$10,000. How much in additional taxes will each firm pay? Why is this amount the same?

19. **Net Income and OCF.**   During 2003, Belyk Paving Co. had sales of \$2,400,000. Cost of goods sold, administrative and selling expenses, and depreciation expenses were \$1,440,000, \$360,000, and \$480,000, respectively. In addition, the company had an interest expense of \$180,000 and a tax rate of 35 percent. (Ignore any tax loss carryback or carryforward provisions.)

    a.   What is Belyk's net income for 2003?

    b.   What is its operating cash flow?

    c.   Explain your results in (a) and (b).

20. **Accounting Values versus Cash Flows.**   In Problem 19, suppose Belyk Paving Co. paid out \$480,000 in cash dividends. Is this possible? If no new investments were made in net fixed assets or net working capital, and if no new stock was issued during the year, what do you know about the firm's long-term debt account?

21. **Calculating Cash Flows.**   Titan Football Manufacturing had the following operating results for 2003: sales = \$10,980; cost of goods sold = \$8,100; depreciation expense = \$1,440; interest expense = \$180; dividends paid = \$270. At the beginning of the year, net fixed assets were \$7,200, current assets were \$1,800, and current liabilities were \$1,350. At the end of the year, net fixed assets were \$7,560, current assets were \$2,790, and current liabilities were \$1,620. The tax rate for 2003 was 35 percent.

    a.   What is net income for 2003?

    b.   What is the operating cash flow for 2003?

    c.   What is the cash flow from assets for 2003? Is this possible? Explain.

    d.   If no new debt was issued during the year, what is the cash flow to creditors? What is the cash flow to stockholders? Explain and interpret the positive and negative signs of your answers in (a) through (d).

22. **Calculating Cash Flows.**   Consider the following abbreviated financial statements for Cabo Wabo, Inc.:

| CABO WABO, INC. | | | | | | CABO WABO, INC. | |
| Partial Balance Sheets as of December 31, 2002 and 2003 | | | | | | 2003 Income Statement | |

	2002	2003		2002	2003	Sales	$21,300
			Liabilities and			Costs	10,680
Assets			**Owners' Equity**			Depreciation	1,800
Current assets	$1,425	$1,509	Current liabilities	$ 615	$ 903	Interest paid	324
Net fixed assets	6,600	6,900	Long-term debt	$3,600	4,200		

   a. What is owners' equity for 2002 and 2003?

   b. What is the change in net working capital for 2003?

   c. In 2003, Cabo Wabo purchased $3,000 in new fixed assets. How much in fixed assets did Cabo Wabo sell? What is the cash flow from assets for the year? (The tax rate is 35 percent.)

   d. During 2003, Cabo Wabo raised $900 in new long-term debt. How much long-term debt must Cabo Wabo have paid off during the year? What is the cash flow to creditors?

6.1   **Change in Net Working Capital.**   Find the most recent abbreviated balance sheets for General Dynamics at finance.yahoo.com. Enter the ticker symbol "GD," follow the "Research" link and the "Financials" link. Using the two most recent balance sheets, calculate the change in net working capital. What does this number mean?

6.2   **Book Values versus Market Values.**   The home page for Coca-Cola Company can be found at www.coca-cola.com. Locate the most recent annual report, which contains a balance sheet for the company. What is the book value of equity for Coca-Cola? The market value of a company is the number of shares of stock outstanding times the price per share. This information can be found at finance.yahoo.com using the ticker symbol for Coca-Cola (KO). What is the market value of equity? Which number is more relevant for shareholders?

6.3   **Net Working Capital.**   Duke Energy is one of the world's largest energy companies. Go to the company's home page at www.dukeenergy.com, follow the link to the investor's page, and locate the annual reports. What was Duke Energy's net working capital for the most recent year? Does this number seem low to you given Duke's current liabilities? Does this indicate that Duke Energy may be experiencing financial problems? Why or why not?

6.4   **Cash Flows to Stockholders and Creditors.**   Cooper Tire and Rubber Company provides financial information for investors on its web site at www.coopertires.com. Follow the "Investor Relations" link and find the most recent annual report. Using the consolidated statements of cash flows, calculate the cash flow to stockholders and the cash flow to creditors.

6.5   **Average and Marginal Tax Rates.**   Find the most recent income statement for IBM at www.ibm.com. What is the marginal tax rate for IBM? What is the average tax rate for IBM? Is the average tax rate 35 percent? Why or why not?

7 Working with Financial Statements

THE MOST IMPORTANT THING TO CARRY AWAY
FROM THIS CHAPTER IS A GOOD
UNDERSTANDING OF:

▪ How to standardize financial statements for comparison purposes.

▪ How to compute and, more importantly, interpret some common ratios.

▪ The determinants of a firm's profitability and growth.

▪ Some of the problems and pitfalls in financial statement analysis.

In the spring of 2002, shares of stock in United Parcel Service (UPS) were trading for about $60. At that price, UPS had a price-to-earnings (PE) ratio of 29, meaning that investors were willing to pay $29 for every dollar in income earned by UPS. At the same time, investors were willing to pay a stunning $554 for each dollar earned by Lone Star Steakhouse and a meager $9 and $8 for each dollar earned by Freddie Mac and Honda, respectively. And then there were stocks like (John) Deere & Co., which, despite having no earnings (a loss, actually), had a stock price of about $47 a share. Meanwhile, the average stock in the Standard and Poor's (S&P) 500 index, which contains 500 of the largest publicly traded companies in the United States, had a PE ratio of about 29, so UPS was about average in this regard.

As we look at these numbers, an obvious question arises: Why were investors willing to pay so much for a dollar of Lone Star's earnings and so much less for a dollar earned by Honda? To understand the answer, we need to delve into subjects such as relative profitability and growth potential, and we also need to know how to compare financial and operating information across companies. By a remarkable coincidence, that is precisely what this chapter is about.

The PE ratio is just one example of a financial ratio. As we will see in this chapter, there are a wide variety of such ratios, all designed to summarize specific aspects of a firm's financial position. In addition to discussing financial ratios and what they mean, we will have quite a bit to say about who uses this information and why.

Everybody needs to understand ratios. Managers will find that almost every business characteristic, from profitability to employee productivity, is summarized in some kind of ratio. Marketers examine ratios dealing with costs, markups, and margins. Production personnel focus on ratios dealing with issues such as operating efficiency. Accountants need to understand ratios because, among other things, ratios are one of the most common and important forms of financial statement information.

In fact, regardless of your field, you may very well find that your compensation is tied to some ratio or group of ratios. Perhaps that is the best reason to study up!

In Chapter 6, we discussed some of the essential concepts of financial statements and cash flows. This chapter continues where our earlier discussion left off. Our goal here is to expand your understanding of the uses (and abuses) of financial statement information.

A good working knowledge of financial statements is desirable simply because such statements, and numbers derived from those statements, are the primary means of communicating financial information both within the firm and outside the firm. In short, much of the language of business finance is rooted in the ideas we discuss in this chapter.

In the best of all worlds, the financial manager has full market value information about all of the firm's assets. This will rarely (if ever) happen. So, the reason we rely on accounting figures for much of our financial information is that we are almost always unable to obtain all (or even part) of the market information that we want. The only meaningful yardstick for evaluating business decisions is whether or not they create economic value (see Chapter 5). However, in many important situations, it will not be possible to make this judgment directly because we can't see the market value effects.

We recognize that accounting numbers are often just pale reflections of economic reality, but they frequently are the best available information. For privately held corporations, not-for-profit businesses, and smaller firms, for example, very little direct market value information exists at all. The accountant's reporting function is crucial in these circumstances.

Clearly, one important goal of the accountant is to report financial information to the user in a form useful for decision making. Ironically, the information frequently does not come to the user in such a form. In other words, financial statements don't come with a user's guide. This chapter is a first step in filling this gap.

Company financial information can be found many places on the Web, including **www.financials.com**, **www.equityweb.com**, and **www.wsrn.com**.

STANDARDIZED FINANCIAL STATEMENTS | 7.1

One obvious thing we might want to do with a company's financial statements is to compare them to those of other, similar companies. We would immediately have a problem, however. It's almost impossible to directly compare the financial statements for two companies because of differences in size.

For example, Ford and GM are obviously serious rivals in the auto market, but GM is much larger (in terms of assets), so it is difficult to compare them directly. For that matter, it's difficult to even compare financial statements from different points in time for the same company if the company's size has changed. The size problem is compounded if we try to

TABLE 7.1

PRUFROCK CORPORATION
Balance Sheets as of December 31, 2002 and 2003
($ in millions)

	2002	2003
Assets		
Current assets		
Cash *750,000 5.5%*	$ 84	$ 98
Accounts receivable *150,000 1.1%*	165	188
Inventory *450,000 3.3%*	393	422
Total *1,350,000*	$ 642	$ 708
Fixed assets		
Net plant and equipment *1,235,000 9.0%*	$2,731	$2,880
Total assets *1,358,500 2585000*	$3,373	$3,588
Liabilities and Owners' Equity		
Current liabilities		
Accounts payable	$ 312	$ 344
Notes payable	231	196
Total	$ 543	$ 540
Long-term debt	$ 531	$ 457
Owners' equity		
Common stock and paid-in surplus	$ 500	$ 550
Retained earnings	1,799	2,041
Total	$2,299	$2,591
Total liabilities and owners' equity	$3,373	$3,588

compare GM and, say, Toyota. If Toyota's financial statements are denominated in yen, then we have a size *and* a currency difference.

To start making comparisons, one obvious thing we might try to do is to somehow standardize the financial statements. One very common and useful way of doing this is to work with percentages instead of total dollars. The resulting financial statements are called **common-size statements**. We consider these next.

Common-Size Balance Sheets

For easy reference, Prufrock Corporation's 2002 and 2003 balance sheets are provided in Table 7.1. Using these, we construct common-size balance sheets by expressing each item as a percentage of total assets. Prufrock's 2002 and 2003 common-size balance sheets are shown in Table 7.2.

Notice that some of the totals don't check exactly because of rounding errors. Also notice that the total change has to be zero since the beginning and ending numbers must add up to 100 percent.

In this form, financial statements are relatively easy to read and compare. For example, just looking at the two balance sheets for Prufrock, we see that current assets were 19.7 percent of total assets in 2003, up from 19.1 percent in 2002. Current liabilities declined from 16.0 percent to 15.1 percent of total liabilities and equity over that same time. Similarly, total equity rose from 68.1 percent of total liabilities and equity to 72.2 percent.

Overall, Prufrock's liquidity, as measured by current assets compared to current liabilities, increased over the year. Simultaneously, Prufrock's indebtedness diminished as a

common-size statement

A standardized financial statement presenting all items in percentage terms. Balance sheet items are shown as a percentage of assets and income statement items as a percentage of sales.

IBM's web site has a good guide to reading financial statements. Select "Investor tools" at **www.ibm.com/ investor**.

TABLE 7.2

PRUFROCK CORPORATION
Common-Size Balance Sheets
December 31, 2002 and 2003

	2002	2003	Change
Assets			
Current assets			
Cash	2.5%	2.7%	+ .2%
Accounts receivable	4.9	5.2	+ .3
Inventory	11.7	11.8	+ .1
Total	19.1	19.7	+ .6
Fixed assets			
Net plant and equipment	80.9	80.3	− .6
Total assets	100.0%	100.0%	.0%
Liabilities and Owners' Equity			
Current liabilities			
Accounts payable	9.2%	9.6%	+ .4%
Notes payable	6.8	5.5	−1.3
Total	16.0	15.1	− .9
Long-term debt	15.7	12.7	−3.0
Owners' equity			
Common stock and paid-in surplus	14.8	15.3	+ .5
Retained earnings	53.3	56.9	+3.6
Total	68.1	72.2	+4.1
Total liabilities and owners' equity	100.0%	100.0%	.0%

TABLE 7.3

PRUFROCK CORPORATION
2003 Income Statement
($ in millions)

Sales		$2,311
Cost of goods sold		1,344
Depreciation		276
Earnings before interest and taxes		$ 691
Interest paid		141
Taxable income		$ 550
Taxes (34%)		187
Net income		$ 363
Dividends	$121	
Addition to retained earnings	242	

percentage of total assets. We might be tempted to conclude that the balance sheet has grown "stronger."

Common-Size Income Statements

A useful way of standardizing the income statement shown in Table 7.3 is to express each item as a percentage of total sales, as illustrated for Prufrock in Table 7.4.

TABLE 7.4

PRUFROCK CORPORATION Common-Size Income Statement 2003		
Sales		100.0%
Cost of goods sold		58.2
Depreciation		11.9
Earnings before interest and taxes		29.9
Interest paid		6.1
Taxable income		23.8
Taxes (34%)		8.1
Net income		15.7%
Dividends	5.2%	
Addition to retained earnings	10.5	

This income statement tells us what happens to each dollar in sales. For Prufrock, interest expense eats up $.061 out of every sales dollar, and taxes take another $.081. When all is said and done, $.157 of each dollar flows through to the bottom line (net income), and that amount is split into $.105 retained in the business and $.052 paid out in dividends.

These percentages are very useful in comparisons. For example, a very relevant figure is the cost percentage. For Prufrock, $.582 of each $1.00 in sales goes to pay for goods sold. It would be interesting to compute the same percentage for Prufrock's main competitors to see how Prufrock stacks up in terms of cost control.

CONCEPT QUESTIONS

7.1a   Why is it often necessary to standardize financial statements?

7.1b   Describe how common-size balance sheets and income statements are formed.

7.2 | RATIO ANALYSIS

financial ratios

Relationships determined from a firm's financial information and used for comparison purposes.

Another way of avoiding the problems involved in comparing companies of different sizes is to calculate and compare **financial ratios**. Such ratios are ways of comparing and investigating the relationships between different pieces of financial information. We cover some of the more common ratios next, but there are many others that we don't touch on.

One problem with ratios is that different people and different sources frequently don't compute them in exactly the same way, and this leads to much confusion. The specific definitions we use here may or may not be the same as ones you have seen or will see elsewhere. If you are ever using ratios as a tool for analysis, you should be careful to document how you calculate each one, and, if you are comparing your numbers to those of another source, be sure you know how their numbers are computed.

We will defer much of our discussion of how ratios are used and some problems that come up with using them until a bit later in the chapter. For now, for each of the ratios we discuss, several questions come to mind:

1.   How is it computed?

2.   What is it intended to measure, and why might we be interested?

3. What is the unit of measurement?

4. What might a high or low value be telling us? How might such values be misleading?

5. How could this measure be improved?

Financial ratios are traditionally grouped into the following categories:

1. Short-term solvency, or liquidity, ratios.

2. Long-term solvency, or financial leverage, ratios.

3. Asset management, or turnover, ratios.

4. Profitability ratios.

5. Market value ratios.

Go to **www.marketguide.com** and follow the "Ratio Comparison" link to examine comparative ratios for a huge number of companies.

We will consider each of these in turn. In calculating these numbers for Prufrock, we will use the ending balance sheet (2003) figures unless we explicitly say otherwise. Also notice that the various ratios are color keyed to indicate which numbers come from the **income statement** and which come from the **balance sheet**.

Short-Term Solvency, or Liquidity, Measures

As the name suggests, short-term solvency ratios as a group are intended to provide infor mation about a firm's liquidity, and these ratios are sometimes called *liquidity measures*. The primary concern is the firm's ability to pay its bills over the short run without undue stress. Consequently, these ratios focus on current assets and current liabilities.

For obvious reasons, liquidity ratios are particularly interesting to short-term creditors. Since financial managers are constantly working with banks and other short-term lenders, an understanding of these ratios is essential.

One advantage of looking at current assets and liabilities is that their book values and market values are likely to be similar. Often (though not always), these assets and liabilities just don't live long enough for the two to get seriously out of step. On the other hand, like any type of near-cash, current assets and liabilities can and do change fairly rapidly, so today's amounts may not be a reliable guide to the future.

Current Ratio   One of the best-known and most widely used ratios is the *current ratio*. As you might guess, the current ratio is defined as:

$$\text{Current ratio} = \frac{\text{Current assets}}{\text{Current liabilities}} \qquad [7.1]$$

For Prufrock, the 2003 current ratio is:

$$\text{Current ratio} = \frac{\$708}{\$540} = 1.31 \text{ times}$$

Because current assets and liabilities are, in principle, converted to cash over the following 12 months, the current ratio is a measure of short-term liquidity. The unit of measurement is either dollars or times. So, we could say Prufrock has $1.31 in current assets for every $1 in current liabilities, or we could say Prufrock has its current liabilities covered 1.31 times over.

To a creditor, particularly a short-term creditor such as a supplier, the higher the current ratio, the better. To the firm, a high current ratio indicates liquidity, but it also may indicate an inefficient use of cash and other short-term assets. Absent some extraordinary circumstances, we would expect to see a current ratio of at least 1, because a current ratio of less than 1 would mean that net working capital (current assets less current liabilities) is negative. This would be unusual in a healthy firm, at least for most types of businesses.

The current ratio, like any ratio, is affected by various types of transactions. For example, suppose the firm borrows over the long term to raise money. The short-run effect would be an increase in cash from the issue proceeds and an increase in long-term debt. Current liabilities would not be affected, so the current ratio would rise.

Finally, note that an apparently low current ratio may not be a bad sign for a company with a large reserve of untapped borrowing power.

EXAMPLE 7.1 | **Current Events**

Suppose a firm were to pay off some of its suppliers and short-term creditors. What would happen to the current ratio? Suppose a firm buys some inventory. What happens in this case? What happens if a firm sells some merchandise?

The first case is a trick question. What happens is that the current ratio moves away from 1. If it is greater than 1 (the usual case), it will get bigger, but if it is less than 1, it will get smaller. To see this, suppose the firm has $4 in current assets and $2 in current liabilities for a current ratio of 2. If we use $1 in cash to reduce current liabilities, then the new current ratio is ($4 − 1)/($2 − 1) = 3. If we reverse the original situation to $2 in current assets and $4 in current liabilities, then the change will cause the current ratio to fall to 1/3 from 1/2.

The second case is not quite as tricky. Nothing happens to the current ratio because cash goes down while inventory goes up—total current assets are unaffected.

In the third case, the current ratio would usually rise because inventory is normally shown at cost and the sale would normally be at something greater than cost (the difference is the markup). The increase in either cash or receivables is therefore greater than the decrease in inventory. This increases current assets, and the current ratio rises.

Quick (or Acid-Test) Ratio Inventory is often the least liquid current asset. It's also the one for which the book values are least reliable as measures of market value since the quality of the inventory isn't considered. Some of the inventory may later turn out to be damaged, obsolete, or lost.

More to the point, relatively large inventories are often a sign of short-term trouble. The firm may have overestimated sales and overbought or overproduced as a result. In this case, the firm may have a substantial portion of its liquidity tied up in slow-moving inventory.

To further evaluate liquidity, the *quick*, or *acid-test, ratio* is computed just like the current ratio, except inventory is omitted:

$$\text{Quick ratio} = \frac{\text{Current assets} - \text{Inventory}}{\text{Current liabilities}} \qquad [7.2]$$

Notice that using cash to buy inventory does not affect the current ratio, but it reduces the quick ratio. Again, the idea is that inventory is relatively illiquid compared to cash.

For Prufrock, this ratio in 2003 was:

$$\text{Quick ratio} = \frac{\$708 - 422}{\$540} = .53 \text{ times}$$

The quick ratio here tells a somewhat different story than the current ratio, because inventory accounts for more than half of Prufrock's current assets. To exaggerate the point, if this inventory consisted of, say, unsold nuclear power plants, then this would be a cause for concern.

Cash Ratio   A very short-term creditor might be interested in the *cash ratio:*

$$\text{Cash ratio} = \frac{\text{Cash}}{\text{Current liabilities}} \qquad \text{[7.3]}$$

You can verify that this works out to be .18 times for Prufrock.

Long-Term Solvency Measures

Long-term solvency ratios are intended to address the firm's long-run ability to meet its obligations, or, more generally, its financial leverage. These ratios are sometimes called *financial leverage ratios* or just *leverage ratios*. We consider three commonly used measures and some variations.

Total Debt Ratio   The *total debt ratio* takes into account all debts of all maturities to all creditors. It can be defined in several ways, the easiest of which is:

$$\text{Total debt ratio} = \frac{\text{Total assets} - \text{Total equity}}{\text{Total assets}}$$

$$= \frac{\$3,588 - 2,591}{\$3,588} = .28 \text{ times} \qquad \text{[7.4]}$$

In this case, an analyst might say that Prufrock uses 28 percent debt.[1] Whether this is high or low or whether it even makes any difference depends on whether or not capital structure matters, a subject we discuss in a later chapter.

Prufrock has $.28 in debt for every $1 in assets. Therefore, there is $.72 in equity ($1 − .28) for every $.28 in debt. With this in mind, we can define two useful variations on the total debt ratio, the *debt-equity ratio* and the *equity multiplier:*

$$\text{Debt-equity ratio} = \text{Total debt}/\text{Total equity}$$
$$= \$.28/\$.72 = .39 \text{ times} \qquad \text{[7.5]}$$

$$\text{Equity multiplier} = \text{Total assets}/\text{Total equity}$$
$$= \$1/\$.72 = 1.39 \text{ times} \qquad \text{[7.6]}$$

The fact that the equity multiplier is 1 plus the debt–equity ratio is not a coincidence:

$$\text{Equity multiplier} = \text{Total assets}/\text{Total equity} = \$1/\$.72 = 1.39 \text{ times}$$
$$= (\text{Total equity} + \text{Total debt})/\text{Total equity}$$
$$= 1 + \text{Debt-equity ratio} = 1.39 \text{ times}$$

The thing to notice here is that given any one of these three ratios, you can immediately calculate the other two, so they all say exactly the same thing.

The on-line Women's Business Center has more information on financial statements, ratios, and small business topics (**www.onlinewbc.gov**).

Times Interest Earned   Another common measure of long-term solvency is the *times interest earned* (TIE) *ratio.* Once again, there are several possible (and common) definitions, but we'll stick with the most traditional:

---

[1]Total equity here includes preferred stock, if there is any. An equivalent numerator in this ratio would be (Current liabilities + Long-term debt).

$$\text{Times interest earned ratio} = \frac{\text{EBIT}}{\text{Interest}}$$

$$= \frac{\$691}{\$141} = 4.9 \text{ times}$$

[7.7]

As the name suggests, this ratio measures how well a company has its interest obligations covered, and it is often called the interest coverage ratio. For Prufrock, the interest bill is covered 4.9 times over.

Cash Coverage   A problem with the TIE ratio is that it is based on EBIT, which is not really a measure of cash available to pay interest. The reason is that depreciation, a non-cash expense, has been deducted out. Since interest is most definitely a cash outflow (to creditors), one way to define the *cash coverage ratio* is

$$\text{Cash coverage ratio} = \frac{\text{EBIT} + \text{Depreciation}}{\text{Interest}}$$

$$= \frac{\$691 + 276}{\$141} = \frac{\$967}{\$141} = 6.9 \text{ times}$$

[7.8]

The numerator here, EBIT plus depreciation, is often abbreviated EBDIT (earnings before depreciation, interest, and taxes). It is a basic measure of the firm's ability to generate cash from operations, and it is frequently used as a measure of cash flow available to meet financial obligations.

Asset Management, or Turnover, Measures

We next turn our attention to the efficiency with which Prufrock uses its assets. The measures in this section are sometimes called *asset utilization ratios*. The specific ratios we discuss can all be interpreted as measures of turnover. What they are intended to describe is how efficiently, or intensively, a firm uses its assets to generate sales. We first look at two important current assets: inventory and receivables.

Inventory Turnover and Days' Sales in Inventory   During the year, Prufrock had a cost of goods sold of $1,344. Inventory at the end of the year was $422. With these numbers, *inventory turnover* can be calculated as:

$$\text{Inventory turnover} = \frac{\text{Cost of goods sold}}{\text{Inventory}}$$

$$= \frac{\$1,344}{\$422} = 3.2 \text{ times}$$

[7.9]

Ratios used to analyze technology firms can be found at **www.chalfin.com** under the "Publications" link.

In a sense, we sold off, or turned over, the entire inventory 3.2 times. As long as we are not running out of stock and thereby forgoing sales, the higher this ratio is, the more efficiently we are managing inventory.

If we know that we turned our inventory over 3.2 times during the year, then we can immediately figure out how long it took us to turn it over on average. The result is the average *days' sales in inventory:*

$$\text{Days' sales in inventory} = \frac{365 \text{ days}}{\text{Inventory turnover}}$$

$$= \frac{365}{3.2} = 114 \text{ days}$$

[7.10]

This tells us that, roughly speaking, inventory sits 114 days on average before it is sold. Alternatively, assuming we used the most recent inventory and cost figures, it will take about 114 days to work off our current inventory.

For example, we frequently hear things like "Majestic Motors has a 60 days' supply of cars." This means that, at current daily sales, it would take 60 days to deplete the available inventory. We could also say that Majestic has 60 days of sales in inventory.

Receivables Turnover and Days' Sales in Receivables Our inventory measures give some indication of how fast we can sell products. We now look at how fast we collect on those sales. The *receivables turnover* is defined in the same way as inventory turnover:

$$
\text{Receivables} = \frac{\text{Sales}}{\text{Accounts receivable}}
$$
$$
= \frac{\$2,311}{\$188} = 12.3 \text{ times}
$$

[7.11]

Loosely speaking, we collected our outstanding credit accounts and reloaned the money 12.3 times during the year.[2]

This ratio makes more sense if we convert it to days, so the *days' sales in receivables* is:

$$
\text{Days' sales in receivables} = \frac{365 \text{ days}}{\text{Receivables turnovers}}
$$
$$
= \frac{365}{12.3} = 30 \text{ days}
$$

[7.12]

Therefore, on average, we collect on our credit sales in 30 days. For obvious reasons, this ratio is very frequently called the *average collection period* (ACP).

Also note that if we are using the most recent figures, we can also say that we have 30 days' worth of sales currently uncollected. We will learn more about this subject when we study credit policy in a later chapter.

Payables Turnover | EXAMPLE 7.2

Here is a variation on the receivables collection period. How long, on average, does it take for Prufrock Corporation to *pay* its bills? To answer, we need to calculate the accounts payable turnover rate using cost of goods sold. We will assume that Prufrock purchases everything on credit.

The cost of goods sold is $1,344, and accounts payable are $344. The turnover is therefore $1,344/$344 = 3.9 times. So, payables turned over about every 365/3.9 = 94 days. On average, then, Prufrock takes 94 days to pay. As a potential creditor, we might take note of this fact.

Total Asset Turnover Moving away from specific accounts like inventory or receivables, we can consider an important "big picture" ratio, the *total asset turnover* ratio. As the name suggests, total asset turnover is:

---

[2]Here we have implicitly assumed that all sales are credit sales. If they were not, then we would simply use total credit sales in these calculations, not total sales.

$$\text{Total asset turnover} = \frac{\text{Sales}}{\text{Total assets}}$$

$$= \frac{\$2,311}{\$3,588} = .64 \text{ times}$$

[7.13]

PricewaterhouseCoopers has a useful utility for extracting EDGAR data. Try it at **edgarscan. pwcglobal.com**.

In other words, for every dollar in assets, we generated $.64 in sales.

A closely related ratio, the *capital intensity ratio,* is simply the reciprocal of (that is, 1 divided by) total asset turnover. It can be interpreted as the dollar investment in assets needed to generate $1 in sales. High values correspond to capital-intensive industries (such as public utilities). For Prufrock, total asset turnover is .64, so, if we flip this over, we get that capital intensity is $1/.64 = $1.56. That is, it takes Prufrock $1.56 in assets to create $1 in sales.

EXAMPLE 7.3   **More Turnover**

Suppose you find that a particular company generates $.40 in sales for every dollar in total assets. How often does this company turn over its total assets?

The total asset turnover here is .40 times per year. It takes 1/.40 = 2.5 years to turn assets over completely.

Profitability Measures

The three measures we discuss in this section are probably the best known and most widely used of all financial ratios. In one form or another, they are intended to measure how efficiently the firm uses its assets and how efficiently the firm manages its operations. The focus in this group is on the bottom line—net income.

Profit Margin   Companies pay a great deal of attention to their *profit margin:*

$$\text{Profit margin} = \frac{\text{Net income}}{\text{Sales}}$$

$$= \frac{\$363}{\$2,311} = 15.7\%$$

[7.14]

This tells us that Prufrock, in an accounting sense, generates a little less than 16 cents in profit for every dollar in sales.

All other things being equal, a relatively high profit margin is obviously desirable. This situation corresponds to low expense ratios relative to sales. However, we hasten to add that other things are often not equal.

For example, lowering our sales price will usually increase unit volume, but will normally cause profit margins to shrink. Total profit (or, more importantly, operating cash flow) may go up or down, so the fact that margins are smaller isn't necessarily bad. After all, isn't it possible that, as the saying goes, "Our prices are so low that we lose money on everything we sell, but we make it up in volume!"?[3]

---

[3]No, it's not; margins can be small, but they do need to be positive!

Return on Assets   *Return on assets* (ROA) is a measure of profit per dollar of assets. It can be defined several ways, but the most common is:

$$\text{Return on assets} = \frac{\text{Net income}}{\text{Total assets}}$$
$$= \frac{\$363}{\$3,588} = 10.12\%$$ **[7.15]**

Return on Equity   *Return on equity* (ROE) is a measure of how the stockholders fared during the year. Since benefiting shareholders is our goal, ROE is, in an accounting sense, the true bottom-line measure of performance. ROE is usually measured as:

$$\text{Return on equity} = \frac{\text{Net income}}{\text{Total equity}}$$
$$= \frac{\$363}{\$2,591} = 14\%$$ **[7.16]**

Therefore, for every dollar in equity, Prufrock generated 14 cents in profit, but, again, this is only correct in accounting terms.

Because ROA and ROE are such commonly cited numbers, we stress that it is important to remember they are accounting rates of return. For this reason, these measures should properly be called *return on book assets* and *return on book equity*. In addition, ROE is sometimes called *return on net worth*. Whatever it's called, it would be inappropriate to compare the result to, for example, an interest rate observed in the financial markets.

The fact that ROE exceeds ROA reflects Prufrock's use of financial leverage. We will examine the relationship between these two measures in more detail below.

Market Value Measures

Our final group of measures is based, in part, on information not necessarily contained in financial statements—the market price per share of the stock. Obviously, these measures can be calculated directly only for publicly traded companies.

We assume that Prufrock has 33 million shares outstanding and the stock sold for $88 per share at the end of the year. If we recall that Prufrock's net income was $363 million, then we can calculate that its earnings per share were:

$$\text{EPS} = \frac{\text{Net income}}{\text{Shares outstanding}} = \frac{\$363}{33} = \$11$$ **[7.17]**

Price-Earnings Ratio   The first of our market value measures, the *price-earnings,* or PE, *ratio* (or multiple), is defined as:

$$\text{PE ratio} = \frac{\text{Price per share}}{\text{Earnings per share}}$$
$$= \frac{\$88}{\$11} = 8 \text{ times}$$ **[7.18]**

In the vernacular, we would say that Prufrock shares sell for eight times earnings, or we might say that Prufrock shares have, or "carry," a PE multiple of 8.

Since the PE ratio measures how much investors are willing to pay per dollar of current earnings, higher PEs are often taken to mean that the firm has significant prospects for future growth. Of course, if a firm had no or almost no earnings, its PE would probably be quite large; so, as always, care is needed in interpreting this ratio.

Market-to-Book Ratio   A second commonly quoted measure is the *market-to-book ratio:*

$$\text{Market-to-book ratio} = \frac{\text{Market value per share}}{\text{Book value per share}}$$

$$= \frac{\$88}{2{,}591/33} = \frac{\$88}{\$78.5} = 1.12 \text{ times} \qquad \textbf{[7.19]}$$

Notice that book value per share is total equity (not just common stock) divided by the number of shares outstanding.

Since book value per share is an accounting number, it reflects historical costs. In a loose sense, the market-to-book ratio therefore compares the market value of the firm's investments to their cost. A value less than 1 could mean that the firm has not been successful overall in creating value for its stockholders.

This completes our definition of some common ratios. We could tell you about more of them, but these are enough for now. We'll leave it here and go on to discuss some ways of using these ratios instead of just how to calculate them. Table 7.5 summarizes the ratios we've discussed.

TABLE 7.5   Common financial ratios

I. Short-term solvency, or liquidity, ratios

$$\text{Current ratio} = \frac{\text{Current assets}}{\text{Current liabilities}}$$

$$\text{Quick ratio} = \frac{\text{Current assets} - \text{Inventory}}{\text{Current liabilities}}$$

$$\text{Cash ratio} = \frac{\text{Cash}}{\text{Current liabilities}}$$

II. Long-term solvency, or financial leverage, ratios

$$\text{Total debt ratio} = \frac{\text{Total assets} - \text{Total equity}}{\text{Total assets}}$$

Debt-equity ratio = Total debt/Total equity

Equity multiplier = Total assets/Total equity

$$\text{Times interest earned ratio} = \frac{\text{EBIT}}{\text{Interest}}$$

$$\text{Cash coverage ratio} = \frac{\text{EBIT} + \text{Depreciation}}{\text{Interest}}$$

III. Asset utilization, or turnover, ratios

$$\text{Inventory turnover} = \frac{\text{Cost of goods sold}}{\text{Inventory}}$$

$$\text{Days' sales in inventory} = \frac{365 \text{ days}}{\text{Inventory turnover}}$$

$$\text{Receivables turnover} = \frac{\text{Sales}}{\text{Accounts receivable}}$$

$$\text{Days' sales in receivables} = \frac{365 \text{ days}}{\text{Receivables turnover}}$$

$$\text{Total asset turnover} = \frac{\text{Sales}}{\text{Total assets}}$$

$$\text{Capital intensity} = \frac{\text{Total assets}}{\text{Sales}}$$

IV. Profitability ratios

$$\text{Profit margin} = \frac{\text{Net income}}{\text{Sales}}$$

$$\text{Return on assets (ROA)} = \frac{\text{Net income}}{\text{Total assets}}$$

$$\text{Return on equity (ROE)} = \frac{\text{Net income}}{\text{Total equity}}$$

$$\text{ROE} = \frac{\text{Net income}}{\text{Sales}} \times \frac{\text{Sales}}{\text{Assets}} \times \frac{\text{Assets}}{\text{Equity}}$$

V. Market value ratios

$$\text{Price-earnings ratio} = \frac{\text{Price per share}}{\text{Earnings per share}}$$

$$\text{Market-to-book ratio} = \frac{\text{Market value per share}}{\text{Book value per share}}$$

CONCEPT QUESTIONS

7.2a   What are the five groups of ratios? Give two or three examples of each kind.

7.2b   Turnover ratios all have one of two figures as numerators. What are these two figures? What do these ratios measure? How do you interpret the results?

7.2c   Profitability ratios all have the same figure in the numerator. What is it? What do these ratios measure? How do you interpret the results?

7.2d   Given the total debt ratio, what other two ratios can be computed? Explain how.

THE DU PONT IDENTITY | 7.3

As we mentioned in discussing ROA and ROE, the difference between these two profitability measures is a reflection of the use of debt financing, or financial leverage. We illustrate the relationship between these measures in this section by investigating a famous way of decomposing ROE into its component parts.

To begin, let's recall the definition of ROE:

$$\text{Return on equity} = \frac{\text{Net income}}{\text{Total equity}}$$

If we were so inclined, we could multiply this ratio by Assets/Assets without changing anything:

$$\text{Return on equity} = \frac{\text{Net income}}{\text{Total equity}} = \frac{\text{Net income}}{\text{Total equity}} \times \frac{\text{Assets}}{\text{Assets}}$$

$$= \frac{\text{Net income}}{\text{Assets}} \times \frac{\text{Assets}}{\text{Total equity}}$$

Notice that we have expressed the ROE as the product of two other ratios—ROA and the equity multiplier:

$$\text{ROE} = \text{ROA} \times \text{Equity multiplier} = \text{ROA} \times (1 + \text{Debt-equity ratio})$$

Looking back at Prufrock, for example, we see that the debt-equity ratio was .39 and ROA was 10.12 percent. Our work here implies that Prufrock's ROE, as we previously calculated, is:

$$\text{ROE} = 10.12\% \times 1.39 = 14\%$$

We can further decompose ROE by multiplying the top and bottom by total sales:

$$\text{ROE} = \frac{\text{Sales}}{\text{Sales}} \times \frac{\text{Net income}}{\text{Assets}} \times \frac{\text{Assets}}{\text{Total equity}}$$

If we rearrange things a bit, ROE is:

$$\text{ROE} = \underbrace{\frac{\text{Net income}}{\text{Sales}} \times \frac{\text{Sales}}{\text{Assets}}}_{\text{Return on assets}} \times \frac{\text{Assets}}{\text{Total equity}}$$

[7.20]

$$= \text{Profit margin} \times \text{Total asset turnover} \times \text{Equity multiplier}$$

Du Pont identity

Popular expression breaking ROE into three parts: operating efficiency, asset use efficiency, and financial leverage.

What we have now done is to partition ROA into its two component parts, profit margin and total asset turnover. This last expression is called the **Du Pont identity**, after the Du Pont Corporation, which popularized its use.

We can check this relationship for Prufrock by noting that the profit margin was 15.7 percent and the total asset turnover was .64. ROE should thus be:

$$\text{ROE} = \text{Profit margin} \times \text{Total asset turnover} \times \text{Equity multiplier}$$
$$= \quad 15.7\% \quad \times \quad .64 \quad \times \quad 1.39$$
$$= \quad 14\%$$

This 14 percent ROE is exactly what we had before.

The Du Pont identity tells us that ROE is affected by three things:

1. Operating efficiency (as measured by profit margin).
2. Asset use efficiency (as measured by total asset turnover).
3. Financial leverage (as measured by the equity multiplier).

Weakness in either operating or asset use efficiency (or both) will show up in a diminished return on assets, which will translate into a lower ROE.

Considering the Du Pont identity, it appears that a firm could leverage up its ROE by increasing its amount of debt. It turns out this will only happen if the firm's ROA exceeds the interest rate on the debt. More importantly, the use of debt financing has a number of other effects, and, as we discuss at some length in later chapters, the amount of leverage a firm uses is governed by its capital structure policy.

The decomposition of ROE we've discussed in this section is a convenient way of systematically approaching financial statement analysis. If ROE is unsatisfactory by some measure, then the Du Pont identity tells you where to start looking for the reasons.

CONCEPT QUESTIONS

7.3a Return on assets, or ROA, can be expressed as the product of two ratios. Which two?

7.3b Return on equity, or ROE, can be expressed as the product of three ratios. Which three?

7.4 | INTERNAL AND SUSTAINABLE GROWTH

A firm's return on assets and return on equity are frequently used to calculate two additional numbers, both of which have to do with the firm's ability to grow. We examine these next, but first we introduce two basic ratios.

Dividend Payout and Earnings Retention

You can find growth rates under the research links at **www.multexinvestor.com** and **finance.yahoo.com**.

As we have seen in various places, a firm's net income gets divided into two pieces. The first piece is cash dividends paid to stockholders. Whatever is left over is the addition to retained earnings. For example, from Table 7.3, Prufrock's net income was $363, of which $121 was paid out in dividends. If we express dividends paid as a percentage of net income, the result is the *dividend payout ratio:*

$$\text{Dividend payout ratio} = \text{Cash dividends/Net income}$$
$$= \$121/\$363 \qquad\qquad\qquad \textbf{[7.21]}$$
$$= 33\tfrac{1}{3}\%$$

What this tells us is that Prufrock pays out one-third of its net income in dividends.

Anything Prufrock does not pay out in the form of dividends must be retained in the firm, so we can define the *retention ratio* as:

$$\text{Retention ratio} = \text{Addition to retained earnings}/\text{Net income}$$
$$= \$242/\$363 \qquad\qquad\qquad \textbf{[7.22]}$$
$$= 66\frac{2}{3}\%$$

So, Prufrock retains two-thirds of its net income. The retention ratio is also known as the *plowback ratio* because it is, in effect, the portion of net income that is plowed back into the business.

Notice that net income must be either paid out or plowed back, so the dividend payout and plowback ratios have to add up to 1. Put differently, if you know one of these figures, you can figure the other one immediately.

Payout and Retention EXAMPLE 7.4

The Manson-Marilyn Corporation routinely pays out 40 percent of net income in the form of dividends. What is its plowback ratio? If net income was $800, how much did stockholders actually receive?

If the payout ratio is 40 percent, then the retention, or plowback, ratio must be 60 percent since the two have to add up to 100 percent. Dividends were 40 percent of $800, or $320.

ROA, ROE, and Growth

Investors and others are frequently interested in knowing how rapidly a firm's sales can grow. The important thing to recognize is that if sales are to grow, assets have to grow as well, at least over the long run. Further, if assets are to grow, then the firm must somehow obtain the money to pay for the needed acquisitions. In other words, growth has to be financed, and as a direct corollary, a firm's ability to grow depends on its financing policies. As the accompanying *Reality Bytes* box illustrates, properly managing growth is vital.

A firm has two broad sources of financing: *internal* and *external*. Internal financing simply refers to what the firm earns and subsequently plows back into the business. External financing refers to funds raised by either borrowing money or selling stock.

The Internal Growth Rate Suppose a firm has a policy of financing growth using only internal financing. This means that the firm won't borrow any funds and won't sell any new stock. How rapidly can the firm grow? The answer is given by the **internal growth rate**:

$$\text{Internal growth rate} = \frac{\text{ROA} \times b}{1 - \text{ROA} \times b} \qquad\qquad \textbf{[7.23]}$$

internal growth rate

The maximum possible growth rate for a firm that relies only on internal financing.

where ROA is, as usual, return on assets, and b is the retention, or plowback, ratio we just discussed.

For example, for the Prufrock Corporation, we earlier calculated ROA as 10.12 percent. We also saw that the retention ratio is $66\frac{2}{3}$ percent, or $\frac{2}{3}$, so the internal growth rate is:

$$\text{Internal growth rate} = \frac{\text{ROA} \times b}{1 - \text{ROA} \times b}$$
$$= \frac{.1012 \times \frac{2}{3}}{1 - .1012 \times \frac{2}{3}}$$
$$= 7.23\%$$

Growing Broke: A By-the-Book Case?

Suppose you start your own Web-based business, a bookstore perhaps. You might assume that after a short period of lingering in relative obscurity, a column in the *New York Times* praising your business would be just the ticket to launch you on your way. You would probably be right . . . but you might also find it's just what it would take to sink your business. That is precisely what happened to www.Positively-You.com, a Web-based bookstore operating out of Cedar Falls, Iowa.

Lyle Bowlin launched Positively-You, an on-line bookstore, in 1998 with the help of his wife. They were able to earn a small profit for four months by keeping expenses to a minimum, operating the business mostly out of their living room. Then, on February 26, 1999, a glowing review of the business appeared in an op-ed column in the *New York Times*. Virtually overnight, orders grew from an average of $2,000 a month to $50,000 a month. The Bowlins, overwhelmed by the growth, enlisted the aid of their book club group to help pack and ship the orders. Meanwhile, there were more op-ed pieces, an article in *Time* magazine, appearances on television, and even collaboration on a book designed to help others start a Web-based business. It appeared to be just the kind of favorable attention a young, growing business needs.

The brisk pace of business and the positive media attention led several of the book club members to invest a total of $50,000 in the young company. An additional $30,000 in capital was raised from another local business. The bookstore operations were moved into rented office space, and soon there was a small staff of people on the payroll. But that was just the beginning of the firm's growing pains. Positively-You's profit margins were thin, about 16 cents per dollar of merchandise sold. This compared to an estimated 20 cents per dollar profit that was being earned by Barnes&Noble.com, the fast-growing, high-volume competitor. To make matters worse, Positively-You allowed its customers to designate that 10 percent of the profit on their purchases go to the nonprofit organization of their choice. This further pared the bookstore's already thin margins. The founders hoped this would lead nonprofit organizations to steer business their way and that what the firm lacked in margins could be made up in volume. Alas, the referrals never materialized.

There were other problems as well. The company was losing money on shipping because it was matching Amazon.com's flat $2.95 shipping fee. In addition, since there wasn't enough capital for Positively-You to build its own database of books, it was forced to rent a database, which, while a cheap alternative, provided the firm little control over content or pricing. By August, sales were down to $12,000 a month, and the firm was woefully short on cash. The local business investor contributed another $10,000 to the firm, hoping to get it through the upcoming Christmas season. Meanwhile, Positively-You raised its prices even though that meant charging more than its large competitor Amazon.com in many cases.

The firm never made it to Christmas. By December 14, Positively-You was out of cash and the web site was shut down. In the end, the firm's own success was its undoing in the ultra-competitive business of being an on-line bookstore. It just didn't have the capital and cash flow to compete, and its investors eventually ended up losing everything they had put into the business. All of this might make you wonder how Amazon.com and Barnes&Noble.com can survive on such thin margins. Well, we're still waiting for them to consistently turn a profit as well, aren't we?

Thus, if Prufrock relies solely on internally generated financing, it can grow at a maximum rate of 7.23 percent per year.

The Sustainable Growth Rate   If a firm only relies on internal financing, then, through time, its total debt ratio will decline. The reason is that assets will grow, but total debt will remain the same (or even fall if some is paid off). Frequently, firms have a particular total debt ratio or equity multiplier that they view as optimal.

sustainable growth rate

The maximum possible growth rate for a firm that maintains a constant debt ratio and doesn't sell new stock.

With this in mind, we now consider how rapidly a firm can grow if (1) it wishes to maintain a particular total debt ratio and (2) it is unwilling to sell new stock. There are various reasons why a firm might wish to avoid selling stock, and equity sales by established firms are actually a relatively rare occurrence. Given these two assumptions, the maximum growth rate that can be achieved, called the **sustainable growth rate**, is:

$$\text{Sustainable growth rate} = \frac{\text{ROE} \times b}{1 - \text{ROE} \times b} \qquad \text{[7.24]}$$

Notice that this is the same as the internal growth rate, except that ROE is used instead of ROA.

Looking at Prufrock, we earlier calculated ROE as 14 percent, and we know that the retention ratio is ⅔, so we can easily calculate sustainable growth as:

$$
\begin{aligned}
\text{Sustainable growth rate} &= \frac{\text{ROE} \times b}{1 - \text{ROE} \times b} \\
&= \frac{.14 \times \frac{2}{3}}{1 - .14 \times \frac{2}{3}} \\
&= 10.29\%
\end{aligned}
$$

If you compare this sustainable growth rate of 10.29 percent to the internal growth rate of 7.23 percent, you might wonder why it is larger. The reason is that, as the firm grows, it will have to borrow additional funds if it is to maintain a constant debt ratio. This new borrowing is an extra source of financing in addition to internally generated funds, so Prufrock can expand more rapidly.

Determinants of Growth   In our previous section, we saw that the return on equity, or ROE, could be decomposed into its various components using the Du Pont identity. Since ROE appears so prominently in the determination of the sustainable growth rate, the factors important in determining ROE are also important determinants of growth.

As we saw, ROE can be written as the product of three factors:

$$\text{ROE} = \text{Profit margin} \times \text{Total asset turnover} \times \text{Equity multiplier}$$

If we examine our expression for the sustainable growth rate, we see that anything that increases ROE will increase the sustainable growth rate by making the top bigger and the bottom smaller. Increasing the plowback ratio will have the same effect.

To see how one company thinks about sustainable growth, see **www. sustainablegrowth. conoco.com**.

Putting it all together, what we have is that a firm's ability to sustain growth depends explicitly on the following four factors:

1. Profit margin. An increase in profit margin will increase the firm's ability to generate funds internally and thereby increase its sustainable growth.

2. Total asset turnover. An increase in the firm's total asset turnover increases the sales generated for each dollar in assets. This decreases the firm's need for new assets as sales grow and thereby increases the sustainable growth rate. Notice that increasing total asset turnover is the same thing as decreasing capital intensity.

3. Financial policy. An increase in the debt-equity ratio increases the firm's financial leverage. Since this makes additional debt financing available, it increases the sustainable growth rate.

4. Dividend policy. A decrease in the percentage of net income paid out as dividends will increase the retention ratio. This increases internally generated equity and thus increases internal and sustainable growth.

The sustainable growth rate is a very useful number. What it illustrates is the explicit relationship between the firm's four major areas of concern: its operating efficiency as measured by profit margin, its asset use efficiency as measured by total asset turnover, its financial policy as measured by the debt-equity ratio, and its dividend policy as measured by the retention ratio. If sales are to grow at a rate higher than the sustainable growth rate, the

TABLE 7.6

Summary of internal and sustainable growth rates

I. Internal growth rate

Internal growth rate $= \dfrac{\text{ROA} \times b}{1 - \text{ROA} \times b}$

where

> ROA = Return on assets = Net income/Total assets
>
> b = Plowback (retention) ratio
>
> = Addition to retained earnings/Net income
>
> = 1 − Dividend payout ratio

The internal growth rate is the maximum growth rate that can be achieved with no external financing of any kind.

II. Sustainable growth rate

Sustainable growth rate $= \dfrac{\text{ROE} \times b}{1 - \text{ROE} \times b}$

where

> ROE = Return on equity = Net income/Total equity
>
> b = Plowback (retention) ratio
>
> = Addition to retained earnings/Net income
>
> = 1 − Dividend payout ratio

The sustainable growth rate is the maximum growth rate that can be achieved with no external equity financing while maintaining a constant debt-equity ratio.

---

firm must increase profit margins, increase total asset turnover, increase financial leverage, increase earnings retention, or sell new shares.

The two growth rates, internal and sustainable, are summarized in Table 7.6.

CONCEPT QUESTIONS

7.4a   What does a firm's internal growth rate tell us?

7.4b   What does a firm's sustainable growth rate tell us?

7.4c   Why is the sustainable growth rate likely to be larger than the internal growth rate?

7.5 | USING FINANCIAL STATEMENT INFORMATION

Our last task in this chapter is to discuss in more detail some practical aspects of financial statement analysis. In particular, we will look at reasons for doing financial statement analysis, how to go about getting benchmark information, and some of the problems that come up in the process.

Why Evaluate Financial Statements?

As we have discussed, the primary reason for looking at accounting information is that we don't have, and can't reasonably expect to get, market value information. It is important to emphasize that, whenever we have market information, we will use it instead of accounting data. Also, if there is a conflict between accounting and market data, market data should be given precedence.

Financial statement analysis is essentially an application of "management by exception." In many cases, such analysis will boil down to comparing ratios for one business with some kind of average or representative ratios. Those ratios that seem to differ the most from the averages are tagged for further study.

Internal Uses Financial statement information has a variety of uses within a firm. Among the most important of these is performance evaluation. For example, managers are frequently evaluated and compensated on the basis of accounting measures of performance such as profit margin and return on equity. Also, firms with multiple divisions frequently compare the performance of those divisions using financial statement information.

Another important internal use of financial statement information involves planning for the future. Historical financial statement information is very useful for generating projections about the future and for checking the realism of assumptions made in those projections.

External Uses Financial statements are useful to parties outside the firm, including short-term and long-term creditors and potential investors. For example, we would find such information quite useful in deciding whether or not to grant credit to a new customer.

We would also use this information to evaluate suppliers, and suppliers would use our statements before deciding to extend credit to us. Large customers use this information to decide if we are likely to be around in the future. Credit-rating agencies rely on financial statements in assessing a firm's overall creditworthiness. The common theme here is that financial statements are a prime source of information about a firm's financial health.

We would also find such information useful in evaluating our main competitors. We might be thinking of launching a new product. A prime concern would be whether the competition would jump in shortly thereafter. In this case, we would be interested in our competitors' financial strength to see if they could afford the necessary development.

Finally, we might be thinking of acquiring another firm. Financial statement information would be essential in identifying potential targets and deciding what to offer.

Choosing a Benchmark

Given that we want to evaluate a division or a firm based on its financial statements, a basic problem immediately comes up. How do we choose a benchmark, or a standard of comparison? We describe some ways of getting started in this section.

Time-Trend Analysis One standard we could use is history. Suppose we found that the current ratio for a particular firm is 2.4 based on the most recent financial statement information. Looking back over the last 10 years, we might find that this ratio has declined fairly steadily over that period.

Based on this, we might wonder if the liquidity position of the firm has deteriorated. It could be, of course, that the firm has made changes that allow it to more efficiently use its current assets, that the nature of the firm's business has changed, or that business practices have changed. If we investigate, we might find any of these possible explanations. This is an example of what we mean by management by exception—a deteriorating time trend may not be bad, but it does merit investigation.

Peer Group Analysis The second means of establishing a benchmark is to identify firms similar in the sense that they compete in the same markets, have similar assets, and operate in similar ways. In other words, we need to identify a *peer group*. There are obvious problems with doing this since no two companies are identical. Ultimately, the choice of which companies to use as a basis for comparison is subjective.

TABLE 7.7

Selected two-digit SIC codes

Agriculture, Forestry, and Fishing	Retail Trade
01 Agriculture production—crops	54 Food stores
02 Forestry	55 Auto dealers and gas stations
Mining	58 Eating and drinking places
10 Metal mining	Finance, Insurance, and Real Estate
13 Oil and gas extraction	60 Banking
Construction	63 Insurance
15 Building construction	65 Real Estate
16 Construction other than building	Services
Manufacturing	78 Motion pictures
28 Chemicals and allied products	80 Health services
29 Petroleum refining	82 Educational services
35 Machinery, except electrical	
37 Transportation equipment	
Transportation, Communication, Electric, Gas, and Sanitary Service	
45 Transportation by air	
49 Electric, gas, and sanitary services	

Standard Industrial Classification (SIC) code

U.S. government code used to classify a firm by its type of business operations.

Learn more about NAICS at **www.naics.com**.

One common way of identifying potential peers is based on **Standard Industrial Classification (SIC) codes**. These are four-digit codes established by the U.S. government for statistical reporting purposes. Firms with the same SIC code are frequently assumed to be similar.

The first digit in an SIC code establishes the general type of business. For example, firms engaged in finance, insurance, and real estate have SIC codes beginning with 6. Each additional digit narrows down the industry. So, companies with SIC codes beginning with 60 are mostly banks and banklike businesses; those with codes beginning with 602 are mostly commercial banks; and SIC code 6025 is assigned to national banks that are members of the Federal Reserve system. Table 7.7 is a list of selected two-digit codes (the first two digits of the four-digit SIC codes) and the industries they represent.

Beginning in 1997, a new industry classification system was instituted. Specifically, the North American Industry Classification System (NAICS, pronounced "nakes") is intended to replace the older SIC codes, and it probably will eventually. Currently, however, SIC codes are widely used.

SIC codes are far from perfect. For example, suppose you were examining financial statements for Wal-Mart, the largest retailer in the United States. The relevant SIC code is 5310, Department Stores. In a quick scan of the nearest financial database, you would find about 20 large, publicly owned corporations with this same SIC code, but you might not be too comfortable with some of them. Kmart would seem to be a reasonable peer, but Neiman-Marcus also carries the same industry code. Are Wal-Mart and Neiman-Marcus really comparable?

As this example illustrates, it is probably not appropriate to blindly use SIC code–based averages. Instead, analysts often identify a set of primary competitors and then compute a set of averages based on just this group. Also, we may be more concerned with a group of the top firms in an industry, not the average firm. Such a group is called an *aspirant group,* because we aspire to be like them. In this case, a financial statement analysis reveals how far we have to go.

With these caveats about SIC codes in mind, we can now take a look at a specific industry. Suppose we are in the retail furniture business. Table 7.8 contains some condensed common-size financial statements for this industry from RMA, one of many sources of such information. Table 7.9 contains selected ratios from the same source.

TABLE 7.8   Selected financial statement information

Retail—Furniture Stores SIC# 5712 (NAICS 33711, 337121, 337122)

Comparative Historical Data				Current Data Sorted By Sales					
68	50	58	**Type of Statement** Unqualified	1	3	1	3	12	38
131	147	131	Reviewed	1	23	15	32	42	18
198	205	177	Compiled	23	67	40	25	19	3
72	72	82	Tax Returns	21	37	12	8	3	1
127	153	134	Other	9	40	13	23	20	29
					188 (4/1–9/30/99)		394 (10/1/99–3/31/00)		
4/1/97–3/31/98 ALL	4/1/98–3/31/99 ALL	4/1/99–3/31/00 ALL	**NUMBER OF STATEMENTS**	0–1 MM	1–3 MM	3–5 MM	5–10 MM	10–25 MM	25MM & OVER
596	627	582		55	170	81	91	96	89
%	%	%	**ASSETS**	%	%	%	%	%	%
6.6	8.2	8.4	Cash & Equivalents	8.4	9.8	8.1	6.4	8.7	7.5
17.4	16.6	15.8	Trade Receivables—(net)	16.3	15.2	12.3	12.6	20.0	18.4
49.8	48.4	49.0	Inventory	49.5	49.7	52.2	55.5	46.7	40.2
1.3	1.7	1.6	All Other Current	.3	.8	1.8	2.3	1.7	2.7
75.2	74.9	74.7	Total Current	74.5	75.5	74.3	76.9	77.1	68.8
16.9	16.6	17.8	Fixed Assets (net)	19.1	17.8	18.3	16.7	15.3	20.4
2.0	2.3	2.1	Intangibles (net)	2.6	1.8	1.0	.9	1.7	5.0
6.0	6.1	5.4	All Other Non-Current	3.8	4.9	6.3	5.6	5.9	5.9
100.0	100.0	100.0	Total	100.0	100.0	100.0	100.0	100.0	100.0
			LIABILITIES						
9.9	10.5	9.0	Notes Payable—Short Term	7.8	9.1	11.2	8.9	8.0	9.0
3.4	2.8	2.2	Cur. Mat.—L/T/D	3.6	2.9	1.7	1.7	1.3	1.6
18.1	18.3	18.9	Trade Payables	12.6	17.7	17.4	20.9	20.9	22.0
.3	.4	.4	Income Taxes Payable	.4	.4	.3	.8	.5	.3
14.7	17.2	18.0	All Other Current	11.5	17.7	20.3	19.1	20.4	17.0
46.4	49.2	48.5	Total Current	36.0	27.8	50.8	51.5	51.1	49.7
12.7	12.5	12.5	Long-Term Debt	18.6	13.5	9.3	15.4	8.1	11.5
.2	.2	.1	Deferred Taxes	.0	.1	.1	.1	.2	.2
3.9	5.5	5.4	All Other Non-Current	10.7	5.6	5.1	5.7	4.2	2.6
36.8	32.6	33.5	Net Worth	34.7	33.0	34.6	27.2	36.4	35.9
100.0	100.0	100.0	Total Liabilities & Net Worth	100.0	100.0	100.0	100.0	100.0	100.0
			INCOME DATA						
100.0	100.0	100.0	Net Sales	100.0	100.0	100.0	100.0	100.0	100.0
39.2	38.7	40.0	Gross Profit	43.2	39.7	40.2	40.0	38.8	39.6
36.4	36.1	37.5	Operating Expenses	41.4	37.7	37.0	37.9	36.2	36.0
2.8	2.5	2.5	Operating Profit	1.7	2.0	3.2	2.1	2.5	3.7
.5	.0	−.3	All Other Expenses (net)	−1.0	.1	.4	.6	−.7	−1.7
2.3	2.5	2.8	Profit Before Taxes	2.7	2.0	2.8	1.5	3.2	5.3

M = $ thousand; MM = $ million.

Interpretation of Statement Studies Figures: RMA cautions that the studies be regarded only as a general guideline and not as an absolute industry norm. This is due to limited samples within categories, the categorization of companies by their primary Standard Industrial Classification (SIC) number only, and different methods of operations by companies within the same industry. For these reasons, RMA recommends that the figures be used only as general guidelines in addition to other methods of financial analysis.

TABLE 7.9   Selected ratios

Retail—Furniture Stores SIC# 5712 (NAICS 33711, 337121, 337122)

Comparative Historical Data				Current Data Sorted by Sales					
			Type of Statement						
68	50	58	Unqualified	1	3	1	3	12	38
131	147	131	Reviewed	1	23	15	32	42	18
198	205	177	Compiled	23	67	40	25	19	3
72	72	82	Tax Returns	21	37	12	8	3	1
127	153	134	Other	9	40	13	23	20	29
				188 (4/1–9/30/99)		394 (10/1/99–3/31/00)			
4/1/97– 3/31/98 ALL	4/1/98– 3/31/99 ALL	4/1/99– 3/31/00 ALL		0–1MM	1–3MM	3–5MM	5–10 MM	10–25 MM	25MM & OVER
			NUMBER OF STATEMENTS						
596	627	582		55	170	81	91	96	89
			RATIOS						
2.6	2.4	2.4	Current	4.0	3.1	2.3	2.1	2.2	1.9
1.7	1.6	1.5		2.1	1.7	1.4	1.4	1.4	1.5
1.2	1.2	1.1		1.5	1.2	1.1	1.2	1.1	1.0
.9	.9	.9	Quick	1.2	1.1	.8	.6	1.0	.9
(595) .5	(622) .4	(579) .4		(54) .7	(169) .4	.3	.2	(88) .5	.5
.2	.1	.2		.2	.2	.1	.1	.2	.1
2 165.2	2 217.3	1 296.1	Sales/ Receivables	0 UND	1 373.8	1 485.5	2 194.8	2 223.7	2 230.4
11 31.9	10 35.9	9 42.2		11 33.7	8 44.9	11 34.3	7 51.8	8 45.6	9 38.9
38 9.7	32 11.5	29 12.6		49 7.5	27 13.3	21 17.4	24 15.5	34 10.7	43 8.5
72 5.1	64 5.7	70 5.2	Cost of Sales/ Inventory	75 4.9	77 4.7	69 5.3	90 4.0	59 6.2	65 5.6
118 3.1	110 3.3	108 3.4		148 2.5	106 3.4	131 2.8	124 2.9	100 3.7	91 4.0
174 2.1	156 2.3	158 2.3		227 1.6	167 2.2	171 2.1	158 2.3	122 3.0	119 3.1
20 18.0	19 19.3	17 21.8	Cost of Sales/ Payable	5 69.1	14 25.8	17 20.9	18 20.0	18 20.7	31 11.9
33 10.9	31 11.7	33 11.2		32 11.4	29 12.6	28 13.0	39 9.3	30 12.2	39 9.4
53 6.9	48 7.6	58 6.3		61 6.0	56 6.5	48 7.6	64 5.7	49 7.5	61 6.0
4.7	5.4	5.5	Sales/ Working Capital	2.4	4.6	5.4	7.3	7.0	7.3
9.9	11.4	11.9		5.6	10.2	13.5	13.1	13.8	13.9
24.5	31.7	42.3		12.4	61.4	57.7	29.7	49.6	266.1
6.4	9.4	9.8	EBIT/ Interest	5.0	8.5	9.3	5.9	20.6	17.3
(540) 2.6	(560) 3.0	(507) 3.6		(40) 2.7	(153) 3.5	(70) 2.9	(81) 3.5	(85) 6.3	(78) 5.8
1.2	1.4	1.4		1.6	1.0	1.3	1.5	2.1	2.5
3.7	5.9	6.8	Net Profit + Depr., Dep., Amort./ Cur. Mat. L/T/D		6.6	9.3	6.6	5.8	12.6
(162) 1.9	(147) 2.7	(128) 2.6			(32) 2.4	(17) 2.4	(26) 2.5	(25) 2.2	(25) 6.3
.5	1.0	1.1			.8	.8	1.1	1.4	1.5
.2	.2	.2	Fixed/ Worth	.1	.1	.2	.2	.2	.3
.4	.4	.5		.4	.4	.5	.4	.3	.6
1.1	1.3	1.4		1.6	2.5	1.3	1.1	.9	1.4
.9	.9	.9	Debt/ Worth	.7	.9	1.0	1.2	1.0	.9
1.9	2.2	2.0		1.9	1.8	2.0	2.3	2.3	1.9
4.1	5.6	5.1		8.1	8.2	6.0	3.9	4.0	5.8
30.3	39.7	40.9	% Profit Before Taxes/ Tangible Net Worth	49.1	42.4	40.4	29.1	49.3	38.1
(546) 12.7	(559) 16.9	(511) 18.5		(45) 15.6	(141) 15.6	(75) 16.2	(83) 15.5	(91) 19.2	(76) 27.9
2.4	4.7	6.5		1.3	2.9	7.2	5.8	8.1	15.8
11.1	12.5	13.2	% Profit Before Taxes/Total Assets	13.4	13.0	11.8	10.0	15.7	16.4
4.4	5.2	6.0		5.3	5.4	6.0	4.9	7.5	8.8
.5	1.3	1.7		.0	.1	1.7	1.6	2.4	4.4

(continued)

TABLE 7.9 — Selected ratios (concluded)

Retail—Furniture Stores SIC# 5712 (NAICS 33711, 337121, 337122)

Comparative Historical Data			Type of Statement	Current Data Sorted by Sales					
51.8	57.6	52.8	Sales/ Net Fixed Assets	56.3	67.3	43.7	58.1	63.1	30.8
23.0	25.3	24.5		21.7	26.8	24.2	27.9	26.3	14.2
10.5	11.9	10.5		7.8	11.8	11.3	11.8	13.6	8.3
3.6	3.9	4.0	Sales/ Total Assets	3.3	4.1	3.8	3.8	4.6	4.0
2.7	2.8	2.8		2.1	2.7	2.7	3.0	3.2	2.8
1.8	2.0	1.9		1.3	1.6	1.9	2.2	2.3	1.8
(536) .5	(557) .5	(511) .5	% Depr., Dep., Amort./Sales	(40) .5	(150) .5	(78) .5	(82) .5	(88) .4	(73) .6
.9	.8	.8		1.1	.9	.9	.8	.6	1.0
1.5	1.3	1.2		2.3	1.5	1.1	1.1	1.0	1.5
(301) 2.1	(288) 2.0	(297) 2.0	% Officers', Directors', Owners' Comp/Sales	(32) 4.9	(97) 2.9	(48) 2.3	(46) 1.6	(57) 1.5	(17) .6
3.6	3.7	3.8		7.9	4.8	3.5	2.8	2.2	1.5
6.5	6.3	6.9		11.2	7.2	5.1	6.3	4.0	6.9
8723294M	13781185M	14827349M	Net Sales ($)	33379M	319782M	313436M	666443M	1480420M	12013889M
4140881M	5596486M	6398099M	Total Assets ($)	22534M	151249M	133560M	250141M	565461M	5275154M

M = $ thousand; MM = $ million

There is a large amount of information here, most of which is self-explanatory. On the right in Table 7.8, we have current information reported for different groups based on sales. Within each sales group, common-size information is reported. For example, firms with sales in the $10 million to $25 million range have cash and equivalents equal to 8.7 percent of total assets. There are 96 companies in this group, out of 582 in all.

On the left, we have three years' worth of summary historical information for the entire group. For example, operating expenses rose from 36.4 percent of sales to 37.5 percent over that time.

Table 7.9 contains some selected ratios, again reported by sales groups on the right and time period on the left. To see how we might use this information, suppose our firm has a current ratio of 2. Based on the ratios, is this value unusual?

Looking at the current ratio for the overall group for the most recent year (third column from the left in Table 7.9), we see that three numbers are reported. The one in the middle, 1.5, is the median, meaning that half of the 582 firms had current ratios that were lower and half had bigger current ratios. The other two numbers are the upper and lower quartiles. So, 25 percent of the firms had a current ratio larger than 2.4 and 25 percent had a current ratio smaller than 1.1. Our value of 2 falls comfortably within these bounds, so it doesn't appear too unusual. This comparison illustrates how knowledge of the range of ratios is important in addition to knowledge of the average. Notice how stable the current ratio has been for the last three years.

More Ratios | EXAMPLE 7.5

Take a look at the most recent numbers reported for Sales/Receivables and EBIT/Interest in Table 7.9. What are the overall median values? What are these ratios?

If you look back at our discussion, you will see that these are the receivables turnover and the times interest earned, or TIE, ratios. The median value for receivables turnover for the entire group is

42.2 times. So, the days in receivables would be 365/42.2 = 9, which is the bold-faced number reported. The median for the TIE is 3.6 times. The number in parentheses indicates that the calculation is meaningful for, and therefore based on, only 507 of the 582 companies. In this case, the reason is probably that only 507 companies paid any significant amount of interest.

There are many sources of ratio information in addition to the one we examine here. Our nearby *Work the Web* box shows how to get this information for just about any company, along with some very useful benchmarking information. Be sure to look it over and then benchmark your favorite company.

WORK THE WEB

s we discussed in this chapter, ratios are an important tool for examining a company's performance. Gathering the necessary financial statements can be tedious and time consuming. Fortunately, many sites on the Web provide this information for free. One of the best is www.marketguide.com. We went there, entered a ticker symbol ("BUD" for Anheuser-Busch), and then selected the "Ratio Comparison" link. Here is an abbreviated look at the results:

BUD 52.490 +0.070 (0.13%)
Anheuser-Busch Companies (NYSE)
Sector: Consumer/Non-Cyclical Industry: Beverages (Alcoholic)

Financial Strength	Company	Industry	Sector	S&P 500
Quick Ratio (MRQ)	0.45	0.51	0.58	1.12
Current Ratio (MRQ)	0.90	1.10	1.13	1.65
LT Debt to Equity (MRQ)	1.47	1.26	0.96	0.67
Total Debt to Equity (MRQ)	1.47	1.29	1.26	1.04
Interest Coverage (TTM)	7.54	9.60	11.09	7.75

Most of the information is self-explanatory. Interest coverage ratio is the same as the times interest earned ratio discussed in the text. The abbreviation MRQ refers to results from the most recent quarterly financial statements, and TTM refers to results from the previous ("trailing") 12 months. Here's a question for you about Anheuser-Busch: What does it imply when the long-term debt to equity and the total debt to equity ratios are the same? The site also provides a comparison to the industry, business sector, and S&P 500 average for the ratios. Other ratios are available on the site and have five-year averages calculated. Have a look!

Problems with Financial Statement Analysis

We close out our chapter on working with financial statements by discussing some additional problems that can arise in using financial statements. In one way or another, the basic problem with financial statement analysis is that there is no underlying theory to help us identify which items or ratios to look at and to guide us in establishing benchmarks.

As we discuss in other chapters, there are many cases where financial theory and economic logic provide guidance in making judgments about value and risk. Very little such help exists with financial statements. This is why we can't say which ratios matter the most and what a high or low value might be.

What Financial Statements Don't Tell You

"Financial statements are like fine perfume: to be sniffed but not swallowed."

Abraham Brilloff

An important factor in financial markets is "transparency," which simply means that investors can see what is truly happening. To promote transparency in U.S. markets, the SEC requires audited financial statements by outside auditors who are not employees of the company being audited. These outside audits provide transparency in that they are intended to show the actual performance of the company and, when combined with GAAP-based reporting, also provide a standardized method of comparing companies.

Unfortunately, even with standardized accounting procedures, the results are often not as clear as we would like. One loophole, exploited most famously by Enron, is the use of SPEs, or special purpose entities. Before you think Enron was the only company to utilize SPEs, other companies such as Circuit City, Krispy Kreme, GE, and Dollar General have come under fire for their use of the SPE.

SPEs can be fairly complex, but the basic idea is pretty simple. In essence, a parent company creates a separate company, the SPE, to do a specific task. For example, an SPE might be formed to build a new headquarters building. The SPE borrows most of the needed funds, thereby creating a large liability; builds the building; and then rents it to the parent company. Here's the catch: Neither the building nor the debt would show up on the parent's balance sheet. By creating the SPE, the parent got the new building using "off balance sheet" financing.

There are many good reasons for using an SPE, but problems can arise from misuse. In the case of Enron, SPEs were used to hide massive amounts of debt from shareholders. Worse yet, Enron essentially guaranteed the SPEs. When the SPEs started to fail, Enron was forced to divert income to the SPEs. This was a liability that shareholders didn't know about.

Earnings management is another problem with understanding financial statements. In 2001, Waste Management, the nation's leading trash hauler, reported earnings excluding unusual, or special, expenses of 33 cents per share in the second quarter, one cent above estimates. What was really unusual were the unusual expenses. Waste Management declared a $1 million charge for painting its trucks as unusual, essentially because they were painted ahead of schedule. A $30 million consulting expense was considered unusual because it was part of a turnaround effort. If these items were included in net income, Waste Management's earnings per share would have been 30 cents per share, two cents below estimates.

Waste Management is not alone. FMC reported earnings per share of $1.58 excluding unusual expenses, but a loss of $9.62 including these expenses. Applied Micro Circuits reported a loss of $0.05 per share net of unusual expenses, but a loss of $11.18 per share including unusual expenses. Similarly, Cummins went from a $0.55 per share net income to a loss of $1.92, and Sears went from $0.96 per share to a loss of $0.60. As you can see from these examples, unusual expenses can dramatically alter the evaluation of a company's performance. When looking at an income statement, unusual expenses should be excluded, but it appears that you should examine unusual expenses with unusual skepticism.

One particularly severe problem is that many firms are conglomerates, owning more or less unrelated lines of business. The consolidated financial statements for such firms don't really fit any neat industry category. Going back to department stores, for example, Sears has an SIC code of 6710 (Holding Offices) because of its diverse financial and retailing operations. More generally, the kind of peer group analysis we have been describing is going to work best when the firms are strictly in the same line of business, the industry is competitive, and there is only one way of operating.

Another problem that is becoming increasingly common is that major competitors and natural peer group members in an industry may be scattered around the globe. The automobile industry is an obvious example. The problem here is that financial statements from outside the United States do not necessarily conform at all to GAAP (more precisely, different countries can have different GAAPs). The existence of different standards and procedures makes it very difficult to compare financial statements across national borders.

Even companies that are clearly in the same line of business may not be comparable. For example, electric utilities engaged primarily in power generation are all classified in the same group (SIC 4911). This group is often thought to be relatively homogeneous. However, utilities generally operate as regulated monopolies, so they don't compete with each other. Many have stockholders, and many are organized as cooperatives with no stockholders. There are several different ways of generating power, ranging from hydroelectric to nuclear, so the operating activities can differ quite a bit. Finally, profitability is strongly affected by regulatory environment, so utilities in different locations can be very similar but show very different profits.

Several other general problems frequently crop up. First, different firms use different accounting procedures—for inventory, for example. This makes it difficult to compare statements. Second, different firms end their fiscal years at different times. For firms in seasonal businesses (such as a retailer with a large Christmas season), this can lead to difficulties in comparing balance sheets because of fluctuations in accounts during the year. Finally, for any particular firm, unusual or transient events, such as a one-time profit from an asset sale, may affect financial performance. In comparing firms, such events can give misleading signals. Our nearby *Reality Bytes* box on page 255 examines some additional issues that have recently made headlines.

CONCEPT QUESTIONS

7.5a   What are some uses for financial statement analysis?

7.5b   What are SIC codes and how might they be useful?

7.5c   Why do we say that financial statement analysis is management by exception?

7.5d   What are some of the problems that can come up with financial statement analysis?

SUMMARY AND CONCLUSIONS

This chapter has discussed aspects of financial statement analysis, including

1. Standardized financial statements. We explained that differences in firm size make it difficult to compare financial statements, and we discussed how to form common-size statements to make comparisons easier.

2. Ratio analysis. Evaluating ratios of accounting numbers is another way of comparing financial statement information. We therefore defined and discussed a number of the most commonly reported and used financial ratios. We also discussed the famous Du Pont identity as a way of analyzing financial performance, and we examined the connection between profitability, financial policy, and growth.

3. Using financial statements. We described how to establish benchmarks for comparison purposes and discussed some of the types of information that are available. We then examined some of the potential problems that can arise.

After you have studied this chapter, we hope that you will have some perspective on the uses and abuses of financial statements. You should also find that your vocabulary of business and financial terms has grown substantially.

CHAPTER REVIEW AND SELF-TEST PROBLEMS

7.1 **Common-Size Statements.** Below are the most recent financial statements for Wildhack. Prepare a common-size income statement based on this information. How do you interpret the standardized net income? What percentage of sales goes to cost of goods sold?

WILDHACK CORPORATION
2003 Income Statement
($ in millions)

Sales	$3,756
Cost of goods sold	2,453
Depreciation	490
Earnings before interest and taxes	$ 813
Interest paid	613
Taxable income	$ 200
Taxes (34%)	68
Net income	$ 132

Dividends	$46
Addition to retained earnings	86

WILDHACK CORPORATION
Balance Sheets as of December 31, 2002 and 2003
($ in millions)

	2002	2003		2002	2003
Assets			**Liabilities and Owners' Equity**		
Current assets			Current liabilities		
Cash	$ 120	$ 88	Accounts payable	$ 124	$ 144
Accounts receivable	224	192	Notes payable	1,412	1,039
Inventory	424	368	Total	$1,536	$1,183
Total	$ 768	$ 648	Long-term debt	$1,804	$2,077
Fixed assets			Owners' equity		
Net plant			Common stock		
and equipment	$5,228	$5,354	and paid-in surplus	$ 300	$ 300
			Retained earnings	2,356	2,442
Total assets	$5,996	$6,002	Total	$2,656	$2,742
			Total liabilities		
			and owner's equity	$5,996	$6,002

7.2 **Financial Ratios.** Based on the balance sheets and income statement in the previous problem, calculate the following ratios for 2003:

Current ratio	_____
Quick ratio	_____
Cash ratio	_____
Inventory turnover	_____
Receivables turnover	_____
Days' sales in inventory	_____

Days' sales in receivables   _____

Total debt ratio   _____

Times interest earned ratio   _____

Cash coverage ratio   _____

7.3   ROE and the Du Pont Identity.   Calculate the 2003 ROE for the Wildhack Corporation and then break down your answer into its component parts using the Du Pont identity.

7.4   Sustainable Growth.   Based on the following information, what growth rate can Corwin maintain if no external financing is used? What is the sustainable growth rate?

CORWIN COMPANY
Financial Statements

Income Statement		Balance Sheet			
Sales	$2,750	Current assets	$ 600	Long-term debt	$ 200
Cost of sales	2,400	Net fixed assets	800	Equity	1,200
Tax (34%)	119	Total	$1,400	Total	$1,400
Net income	$ 231				
Dividends	$ 77				

■ Answers to Chapter Review and Self-Test Problems

7.1   We've calculated the common-size income statement below. Remember that we simply divide each item by total sales.

WILDHACK CORPORATION
2003 Common-Size Income Statement

Sales	100.0%
Cost of goods sold	65.3
Depreciation	13.0
Earnings before interest and taxes	21.6
Interest paid	16.3
Taxable income	5.3
Taxes (34%)	1.8
Net income	3.5%
Dividends	1.2%
Addition to retained earnings	2.3

Net income is 3.5 percent of sales. Since this is the percentage of each sales dollar that makes its way to the bottom line, the standardized net income is the firm's profit margin. Cost of goods sold is 65.3 percent of sales.

7.2   We've calculated the ratios below based on the ending figures. If you don't remember a definition, refer back to Table 7.5.

Current ratio	$648/$1,183	= .55 times
Quick ratio	$280/$1,183	= .24 times
Cash ratio	$88/$1,183	= .07 times

Inventory turnover	$2,453/$368	= 6.7 times
Receivables turnover	$3,756/$192	= 19.6 times
Days' sales in inventory	365/6.7	= 54.5 days
Days' sales in receivables	365/19.6	= 18.6 days
Total debt ratio	$3,260/$6,002	= 54.3%
Times interest earned ratio	$813/$613	= 1.33 times
Cash coverage ratio	$1,303/$613	= 2.13 times

7.3 The return on equity is the ratio of net income to total equity. For Wildhack, this is $132/$2,742 = 4.8%, which is not outstanding. Given the Du Pont identity, ROE can be written as:

$$
\begin{aligned}
\text{ROE} &= \text{Profit margin} \times \text{Total asset turnover} \times \text{Equity multiplier} \\
&= \$132/\$3,756 \times \quad \$3,756/\$6,002 \quad \times \quad \$6,002/\$2,742 \\
&= \quad 3.5\% \quad \times \quad\quad .626 \quad\quad \times \quad\quad 2.19 \\
&= \quad 4.8\%
\end{aligned}
$$

Notice that return on assets, ROA, is $3.5\% \times .626 = 2.2\%$.

7.4 Corwin retains $b = (1 - .33) = \frac{2}{3} \approx .67$ of net income. Return on assets is $231/$1,400 = 16.5%$. The internal growth rate is:

$$
\frac{\text{ROA} \times b}{1 - \text{ROA} \times b} = \frac{.165 \times \frac{2}{3}}{1 - .165 \times \frac{2}{3}} = 12.36\%
$$

Return on equity for Corwin is $231/$1,200 = 19.25%$, so we can calculate the sustainable growth rate as:

$$
\frac{\text{ROE} \times b}{1 - \text{ROE} \times b} = \frac{.1925 \times \frac{2}{3}}{1 - .1925 \times \frac{2}{3}} = 14.72\%
$$

CRITICAL THINKING AND CONCEPTS REVIEW

7.1 Current Ratio. What effect would the following actions have on a firm's current ratio? Assume that net working capital is positive.

a. Inventory is purchased.

b. A supplier is paid.

c. A short-term bank loan is repaid.

d. A long-term debt is paid off early.

e. A customer pays off a credit account.

f. Inventory is sold at cost.

g. Inventory is sold for a profit.

7.2 Current Ratio and Quick Ratio. In recent years, Dixie Co. has greatly increased its current ratio. At the same time, the quick ratio has fallen. What has happened? Has the liquidity of the company improved?

7.3 Current Ratio. Explain what it means for a firm to have a current ratio equal to .50. Would the firm be better off if the current ratio were 1.50? What if it were 15.0? Explain your answers.

7.4   Financial Ratios.   Fully explain the kind of information the following financial ratios provide about a firm:

a. Quick ratio

b. Cash ratio

c. Capital intensity ratio

d. Total asset turnover

e. Equity multiplier

f. Long-term debt ratio

g. Times interest earned ratio

h. Profit margin

i. Return on assets

j. Return on equity

k. Price-earnings ratio

7.5   Standardized Financial Statements.   What types of information do common-size financial statements reveal about the firm? What is the best use for these common-size statements?

7.6   Peer Group Analysis.   Explain what peer group analysis means. As a financial manager, how could you use the results of peer group analysis to evaluate the performance of your firm? How is a peer group different from an aspirant group?

7.7   Du Pont Identity.   Why is the Du Pont identity a valuable tool for analyzing the performance of a firm? Discuss the types of information it reveals as compared to ROE considered by itself.

7.8   Industry-Specific Ratios.   Specialized ratios are sometimes used in specific industries. For example, the so-called book-to-bill ratio is closely watched for semiconductor manufacturers. A ratio of .93 indicates that for every $100 worth of chips shipped over some period, only $93 worth of new orders were received. In August 1998, the North American semiconductor equipment industry's book-to-bill ratio declined to .60, the lowest level since 1995, when analysts first began following it. Three-month average shipments in August were down 5 percent from July figures, while three-month average bookings were down 14.7 percent. What is this ratio intended to measure? Why do you think it is so closely followed?

7.9   Industry-Specific Ratios.   So-called same-store sales are a very important measure for companies as diverse as McDonald's and Sears. As the name suggests, examining same-store sales means comparing revenues from the same stores or restaurants at two different points in time. Why might companies focus on same-store sales rather than total sales?

7.10   Industry-Specific Ratios.   There are many ways of using standardized financial information beyond those discussed in this chapter. The usual goal is to put firms on an equal footing for comparison purposes. For example, for auto manufacturers, it is common to express sales, costs, and profits on a per-car basis. For each of the following industries, give an example of an actual company and discuss one or more potentially useful means of standardizing financial information:

a. Public utilities

b. Large retailers

c. Airlines

d. On-line services

e. Hospitals

f. College textbook publishers

QUESTIONS AND PROBLEMS

www.mhhe.com/rwj
Spreadsheet Templates 2, 14, 15

1. **Calculating Liquidity Ratios.** SDJ, Inc., has net working capital of $900, current liabilities of $4,320, and inventory of $1,900. What is the current ratio? What is the quick ratio?

Basic
(Questions 1–25)

2. **Calculating Profitability Ratios.** Bennett's Bird Cages has sales of $41 million, total assets of $32 million, and total debt of $11 million. If the profit margin is 12 percent, what is net income? What is ROA? What is ROE?

3. **Calculating the Average Collection Period.** Pirate Lumber Yard has a current accounts receivable balance of $308,165. Credit sales for the year just ended were $2,131,516. What is the receivables turnover? The days' sales in receivables? How long did it take on average for credit customers to pay off their accounts during the past year?

4. **Calculating Inventory Turnover.** Keegan Corporation has ending inventory of $921,386, and cost of goods sold for the year just ended was $1,843,127. What is the inventory turnover? The days' sales in inventory? How long on average did a unit of inventory sit on the shelf before it was sold?

5. **Calculating Leverage Ratios.** Myrtle Golf, Inc., has a total debt ratio of .45. What is its debt-equity ratio? What is its equity multiplier?

6. **Calculating Market Value Ratios.** Sandy's Baby-sitting, Inc., had additions to retained earnings for the year just ended of $300,000. The firm paid out $220,000 in cash dividends, and it has ending total equity of $5 million. If Sandy's currently has 300,000 shares of common stock outstanding, what are earnings per share? Dividends per share? What is book value per share? If the stock currently sells for $25 per share, what is the market-to-book ratio? The price-earnings ratio?

7. **Du Pont Identity.** If Roten Rooters, Inc., has an equity multiplier of 1.60, total asset turnover of 1.05, and a profit margin of 11 percent, what is its ROE?

8. **Du Pont Identity.** Jiminy Cricket Removal has a profit margin of 12 percent, total asset turnover of 1.35, and ROE of 17.20 percent. What is this firm's debt-equity ratio?

9. **Calculating Average Payables Period.** For the past year, BDJ, Inc., had a cost of goods sold of $18,364. At the end of the year, the accounts payable balance was $3,105. How long on average did it take the company to pay off its suppliers during the year? What might a large value for this ratio imply?

10. **Equity Multiplier and Return on Equity.** Sunny Beach Chair Company has a debt-equity ratio of .80. Return on assets is 8.4 percent, and total equity is $430,000. What is the equity multiplier? Return on equity? Net income?

11. **Internal Growth.** If Highfield Hobby Shop has a 19 percent ROA and a 30 percent payout ratio, what is its internal growth rate?

12. **Sustainable Growth.** If the Rooster Driving School has a 17 percent ROE and a 40 percent payout ratio, what is its sustainable growth rate?

13. **Sustainable Growth.** Based on the following information, calculate the sustainable growth rate for Chicago Chocolate Pies:

Profit margin $= 10.2\%$

Capital intensity ratio $= .70$

Debt-equity ratio $= .50$

Net income $= \$30,000$

Dividends $= \$6,000$

What is the ROE here?

14. **Sustainable Growth.**   Assuming the following ratios are constant, what is the sustainable growth rate?

Total asset turnover $= 1.90$

Profit margin $= 6.5\%$

Equity multiplier $= 2.05$

Payout ratio $= 30\%$

Bethesda Mining Company reports the following balance sheet information for 2002 and 2003. Use this information to work Problems 15 through 17.

BETHESDA MINING COMPANY
Balance Sheets as of December 31, 2002 and 2003

	2002	2003		2002	2003
Assets			**Liabilities and Owners' Equity**		
Current assets			Current liabilities		
Cash	$ 16,150	$ 19,125	Accounts payable	$161,710	$137,830
Accounts receivable	48,734	52,816	Notes payable	74,391	96,318
Inventory	100,387	137,806			
Total	$165,271	$209,747	Total	$236,101	$234,148
Fixed Assets			Long-term debt	$150,000	$125,000
Net plant and equipment	$537,691	$535,227	Owners' equity		
			Common stock and paid-in surplus	$150,000	$150,000
			Retained earnings	166,861	235,826
			Total	$316,861	$385,826
			Total liabilities and		
Total assets	$702,962	$744,974	owners' equity	$702,962	$744,974

15. **Preparing Standardized Financial Statements.**   Prepare the 2002 and 2003 common-size balance sheets for Bethesda Mining.

16. **Calculating Financial Ratios.**   Based on the balance sheets given for Bethesda Mining, calculate the following financial ratios for each year:

    a.   Current ratio

    b.   Quick ratio

    c.   Cash ratio

    d.   Debt-equity ratio and equity multiplier

    e.   Total debt ratio

17. **Du Pont Identity.**   Suppose that the Bethesda Mining Company had sales of $1,986,382 and net income of $157,320 for the year ending December 31, 2003. Calculate the Du Pont identity.

18. **Du Pont Identity.** The Buckeye Tree Company has an ROA of 11 percent, a 9 percent profit margin, and an ROE of 24 percent. What is the company's total asset turnover? What is the equity multiplier?

19. **Return on Assets.** Tom's Toupees has a profit margin of 13 percent on sales of $22,000,000. If the firm has debt of $9,000,000 and total assets of $22,500,000, what is the firm's ROA?

20. **Calculating Internal Growth.** The most recent financial statements for Filer Manufacturing Co. are shown below:

Income Statement		Balance Sheet			
Sales	$26,205	Current assets	$17,000	Debt	$45,000
Costs	9,430	Fixed assets	51,000	Equity	23,000
Taxable income	$16,775	Total	$68,000	Total	$68,000
Tax (34%)	5,704				
Net Income	$11,071				

Assets and costs are proportional to sales. Debt and equity are not. Filer Manufacturing maintains a constant 40 percent dividend payout ratio. No external financing is possible. What is the internal growth rate?

21. **Calculating Sustainable Growth.** For Filer Manufacturing in Problem 20, what is the sustainable growth rate?

22. **Total Asset Turnover.** Kaleb's Karate Supply had a profit margin of 9 percent, sales of $15 million, and total assets of $8 million. What was total asset turnover? If management set a goal of increasing total asset turnover to 2.25 times, what would the new sales figure need to be, assuming no increase in total assets?

23. **Return on Equity.** Taylor's Cleaning Service has a total debt ratio of .70, total debt of $140,000, and net income of $14,000. What is Taylor's return on equity?

24. **Market Value Ratios.** Bill's Burgers has a current stock price of $70. For the past year the company had net income of $6,100,000, total equity of $31,000,000, and 3.4 million shares of stock outstanding. What is the earnings per share (EPS)? Price-earnings ratio? Book value per share? Market-to-book ratio?

25. **Profit Margin.** Bob's Billiards has total assets of $8,000,000 and a total asset turnover of 2.9 times. If the return on assets is 11 percent, what is Bob's profit margin?

26. **Using the Du Pont Identity.** Y3K, Inc., has sales of $3,680, total assets of $800, and a debt-equity ratio of 1.00. If its return on equity is 12 percent, what is its net income?

Intermediate
(Questions 26–43)

27. **Ratios and Fixed Assets.** The Hooya Company has a long-term debt ratio (i.e., the ratio of long-term debt to long-term debt plus equity) of 0.65 and a current ratio of 1.2. Current liabilities are $750, sales are $3,920, profit margin is 9 percent, and ROE is 18.5 percent. What is the amount of the firm's net fixed assets?

28. **Profit Margin.** In response to complaints about high prices, a grocery chain runs the following advertising campaign: "If you pay your child 50 cents to go buy $25 worth of groceries, then your child makes twice as much on the trip as we do." You've collected the following information from the grocery chain's financial statements:

(millions)	
Sales	$450.0
Net income	4.5
Total assets	105.0
Total debt	67.5

Evaluate the grocery chain's claim. What is the basis for the statement? Is this claim misleading? Why or why not?

29. **Using the Du Pont Identity.** The Celtic Company has net income of $141,200. There are currently 21.50 days' sales in receivables. Total assets are $960,000, total receivables are $138,600, and the debt-equity ratio is 1.15. What is Celtic's profit margin? Its total asset turnover? Its ROE?

30. **Calculating the Cash Coverage Ratio.** Delectable Turnip Inc.'s net income for the most recent year was $6,820. The tax rate was 34 percent. The firm paid $1,931 in total interest expense and deducted $1,380 in depreciation expense. What was Delectable Turnip's cash coverage ratio for the year?

31. **Calculating the Times Interest Earned Ratio.** For the most recent year, Nugent's Nougats, Inc., had sales of $380,000, cost of goods sold of $93,000, depreciation expense of $47,000, and additions to retained earnings of $61,420. The firm currently has 20,000 shares of common stock outstanding, and the previous year's dividends per share were $1.70. Assuming a 34 percent income tax rate, what was the times interest earned ratio?

32. **Return on Assets.** A fire has destroyed a large percentage of the financial records of the Benton Company. You have the task of piecing together information in order to release a financial report. You have found the return on equity to be 15 percent. Sales were $1,700,000, the total debt ratio was .40, and total debt was $300,000. What is the return on assets (ROA)?

33. **Ratios and Foreign Companies.** King Albert Carpet PLC had a 2003 net loss of £10,386 on sales of £161,583 (both in thousands of pounds). What was the company's profit margin? Does the fact that these figures are quoted in a foreign currency make any difference? Why? In dollars, sales were $362,814. What was the net loss in dollars?

Some recent financial statements for Smolira Golf, Inc., follow. Use this information to work Problems 34 through 37.

SMOLIRA GOLF, INC.
Balance Sheets as of December 31, 2002 and 2003

	2002	2003		2002	2003
Assets			**Liabilities and Owners' Equity**		
Current assets			Current liabilities		
Cash	$ 1,180	$ 2,122	Accounts payable	$ 1,811	$ 1,925
Accounts receivable	2,812	$ 4,116	Notes payable	1,143	907
Inventory	6,218	6,462	Other	60	218
Total	$10,210	$12,700	Total	$ 3,014	$ 3,050
Fixed Assets			Long-term debt	$ 9,815	$10,518
Net plant and equipment	$23,372	$23,816	Owners' equity Common stock and		
			paid-in surplus	$20,000	$20,000
			Retained earnings	753	2,948
			Total	$20,753	$22,948
Total assets	$33,582	$36,516	Total	$33,582	$36,516

264

SMOLIRA GOLF, INC.
2003 Income Statement

Sales	$26,800
Cost of goods sold	8,400
Depreciation	1,400
Earnings before interest and taxes	$17,000
Interest paid	1,250
Taxable income	$15,750
Taxes (34%)	5,355
Net income	$10,395

Dividends	$8,200	
Addition to retained earnings	2,195	

---

34. **Calculating Financial Ratios.**   Find the following financial ratios for Smolira Golf (use year-end figures rather than average values where appropriate):

   Short-Term Solvency Ratios

   a. Current ratio _____

   b. Quick ratio _____

   c. Cash ratio _____

   Asset Utilization Ratios

   d. Total asset turnover _____

   e. Inventory turnover _____

   f. Receivables turnover _____

   Long-Term Solvency Ratios

   g. Total debt ratio _____

   h. Debt-equity ratio _____

   i. Equity multiplier _____

   j. Times interest earned ratio _____

   k. Cash coverage ratio _____

   Profitability Ratios

   l. Profit margin _____

   m. Return on assets _____

   n. Return on equity _____

35. **Du Pont Identity.**   Construct the Du Pont identity for Smolira Golf.

36. **Market Value Ratios.**   Smolira Golf has 10,000 shares of common stock outstanding, and the market price for a share of stock at the end of 2003 was $24. What is the price-earnings ratio? What are the dividends per share? What is the market-to-book ratio at the end of 2003?

37. **Interpreting Financial Ratios.**   After calculating the ratios for Smolira Golf, you have uncovered the following industry ratios for 2003:

	Lowest Quartile	Median	Highest Quartile
Current ratio	1.2	2.2	4.5
Total asset turnover	0.8	1.2	1.5
Debt-equity ratio	.40	.52	.60
Profit margin	8.4%	11.9%	16.3%

How is Smolira Golf performing based on these ratios?

38. **Growth and Profit Margin.**   Keene Manufacturing wishes to maintain a growth rate of 8 percent a year, a debt-equity ratio of .55, and a dividend payout ratio of 40 percent. The ratio of total assets to sales is constant at 1.50. What profit margin must the firm achieve?

39. **Growth and Debt-Equity Ratio.**   A firm wishes to maintain a growth rate of 9 percent and a dividend payout ratio of 30 percent. The ratio of total assets to sales is constant at .8, and profit margin is 7 percent. If the firm also wishes to maintain a constant debt-equity ratio, what must it be?

40. **Growth and Assets.**   A firm wishes to maintain an internal growth rate of 6 percent and a dividend payout ratio of 70 percent. The current profit margin is 11 percent and the firm uses no external financing sources. What must total asset turnover be?

41. **Sustainable Growth.**   Based on the following information, calculate the sustainable growth rate for Matchbox, Inc.:

    Profit margin = 8.5%

    Total asset turnover = 1.50

    Total debt ratio = .60

    Payout ratio = 40%

    What is the ROA here?

42. **Sustainable Growth and Outside Financing.**   You've collected the following information about P.O.D., Inc.:

    Sales = $110,000

    Net income = $7,000

    Dividends = $2,100

    Total debt = $51,000

    Total equity = $24,000

    What is the sustainable growth rate for P.O.D., Inc.? If it does grow at this rate, how much new borrowing will take place in the coming year, assuming a constant debt-equity ratio? What growth rate could be supported with no outside financing at all?

43. **Constraints on Growth.**   Paglia's Pasta, Inc., wishes to maintain a growth rate of 13 percent per year and a debt-equity ratio of .30. The profit margin is 8 percent, and total asset turnover is constant at .95. Is this growth rate possible? To answer, determine what the dividend payout ratio must be. How do you interpret the result?

What's On the Web?

7.1   **Du Pont Identity.**   You can find financial statements for Walt Disney Company on the "Investor Relations" link at Disney's home page, www.disney.com. For the three most recent years, calculate the Du Pont identity for Disney. How has ROE changed over this period? How have changes in each component of the Du Pont identity affected ROE over this period?

7.2   **Ratio Analysis.**   You want to examine the financial ratios for Dell Computer Corporation. Go to www.marketguide.com and type in the ticker symbol for the company (DELL). Next, go to the comparison link. You should find financial ratios for Dell and the industry, sector, and S&P 500 averages for each ratio.

   a.   What do TTM and MRQ mean?

   b.   How do Dell's recent profitability ratios compare to their values over the past five years? To the industry averages? To the sector averages? To the S&P 500 averages? Which is the better comparison group for Dell: the industry, sector, or S&P 500 averages? Why?

c. In what areas does Dell seem to outperform its competitors based on the financial ratios? Where does Dell seem to lag behind its competitors?

d. Dell's inventory turnover ratio is much larger than that for all comparison groups. Why do you think this is?

7.3 Standardized Financial Statements. Go to the "Investors Relations" link for AT&T located at www.att.com, follow the "Annual Reports & SEC filings" link, then the most recent "Financial Report" link. You should find the income statements and balance sheets for the two most recent years at this link. Using this information, prepare the common-size income statements and balance sheets for the two years.

7.4 Sources and Uses of Cash. Find the two most recent balance sheets for 3M at the "Investor Relations" link on the web site www.mmm.com/about3m. For each account in the balance sheet, show the change during the most recent year and note whether this was a source or use of cash. Do your numbers add up and make sense? Explain your answer for total assets as compared to your answer for total liabilities and owners' equity.

7.5 Asset Utilization Ratios. Find the most recent financial statements for Wal-Mart at www.walmart.com and Boeing at www.boeing.com. Calculate the asset utilization ratio for these two companies. What does this ratio measure? Is the ratio similar for both companies? Why or why not?

8 Introduction to Valuation: The Time Value of Money

On December 2, 1982, General Motors Acceptance Corporation (GMAC), a subsidiary of General Motors, offered some securities for sale to the public. Under the terms of the deal, GMAC promised to repay the owner of one of these securities $10,000 on December 1, 2012, but investors would receive nothing until then. Investors paid GMAC $500 for each of these securities, so they gave up $500 on December 2, 1982, for the promise of a $10,000 payment 30 years later. Such a security, for which you pay some amount today in exchange for a promised lump sum to be received at a future date, is about the simplest possible type.

Is giving up $500 in exchange for $10,000 in 30 years a good deal? On the plus side, you get back $20 for every $1 you put up. That probably sounds good, but, on the downside, you have to wait 30 years to get it. What you need to know is how to analyze this trade-off; this chapter gives you the tools you need.

Specifically, our goal here is to introduce you to one of the most important principles in finance, the time value of money. What you will learn is how to determine the value today of some cash flow to be received later. This is a very basic business skill, and it underlies the analysis of many different types of investments and financing arrangements. In fact, almost all business activities, whether they originate in marketing, management, operations, or strategy, involve comparing outlays made today to benefits projected for the future. How to do this comparison is something everyone needs to understand; this chapter gets you started.

THERE ARE THREE ESSENTIAL THINGS YOU SHOULD LEARN FROM THIS CHAPTER:

- How to determine the future value of an investment made today.

- How to determine the present value of cash to be received at a future date.

- How to find the return on an investment.

One of the basic problems faced by the financial manager is how to determine the value today of cash flows expected in the future. For example, the jackpot in a PowerBall™ lottery drawing was $110 million. Does this mean the winning ticket was worth $110 million? The answer is no because the jackpot was actually going to pay out over a 20-year period at a rate of $5.5 million per year. How much was the ticket worth then? The answer depends on the time value of money, the subject of this chapter.

In the most general sense, the phrase *time value of money* refers to the fact that a dollar in hand today is worth more than a dollar promised at some time in the future. On a practical level, one reason for this is that you could earn interest while you waited; so, a dollar today would grow to more than a dollar later. The trade-off between money now and money later thus depends on, among other things, the rate you can earn by investing. Our goal in this chapter is to explicitly evaluate this trade-off between dollars today and dollars at some future time.

A thorough understanding of the material in this chapter is critical to understanding material in subsequent chapters, so you should study it with particular care. We will present a number of examples in this chapter. In many problems, your answer may differ from ours slightly. This can happen because of rounding and is not a cause for concern.

8.1 | FUTURE VALUE AND COMPOUNDING

future value (FV)

The amount an investment is worth after one or more periods.

The first thing we will study is future value. **Future value (FV)** refers to the amount of money an investment will grow to over some period of time at some given interest rate. Put another way, future value is the cash value of an investment at some time in the future. We start out by considering the simplest case, a single-period investment.

Investing for a Single Period

Suppose you were to invest $100 in a savings account that pays 10 percent interest per year. How much would you have in one year? You would have $110. This $110 is equal to your original *principal* of $100 plus $10 in interest that you earn. We say that $110 is the future value of $100 invested for one year at 10 percent, and we simply mean that $100 today is worth $110 in one year, given that 10 percent is the interest rate.

In general, if you invest for one period at an interest rate of r, your investment will grow to $(1 + r)$ per dollar invested. In our example, r is 10 percent, so your investment grows to $1 + .10 = 1.1$ dollars per dollar invested. You invested $100 in this case, so you ended up with $100 \times 1.10 = $110.

Investing for More Than One Period

Going back to our $100 investment, what will you have after two years, assuming the interest rate doesn't change? If you leave the entire $110 in the bank, you will earn $110 \times .10 = $11 in interest during the second year, so you will have a total of $110 + 11 = $121. This $121 is the future value of $100 in two years at 10 percent. Another way of looking at it is that one year from now you are effectively investing $110 at 10 percent for a year. This is a single-period problem, so you'll end up with $1.1 for every dollar invested, or $110 \times 1.1 = $121 total.

This $121 has four parts. The first part is the $100 original principal. The second part is the $10 in interest you earn in the first year, and the third part is another $10 you earn in the second year, for a total of $120. The last $1 you end up with (the fourth part) is interest you earn in the second year on the interest paid in the first year: $10 \times .10 = $1.

This process of leaving your money and any accumulated interest in an investment for more than one period, thereby reinvesting the interest, is called **compounding**. Compounding the interest means earning **interest on interest**, so we call the result **compound interest**. With **simple interest**, the interest is not reinvested, so interest is earned each period only on the original principal.

| | Interest on Interest | EXAMPLE 8.1 |

Suppose you locate a two-year investment that pays 14 percent per year. If you invest $325, how much will you have at the end of the two years? How much of this is simple interest? How much is compound interest?

At the end of the first year, you will have $325 × (1 + .14) = $370.50. If you reinvest this entire amount, and thereby compound the interest, you will have $370.50 × 1.14 = $422.37 at the end of the second year. The total interest you earn is thus $422.37 − 325 = $97.37. Your $325 original principal earns $325 × .14 = $45.50 in interest each year, for a two-year total of $91 in simple interest. The remaining $97.37 − 91 = $6.37 results from compounding. You can check this by noting that the interest earned in the first year is $45.50. The interest on interest earned in the second year thus amounts to $45.50 × .14 = $6.37, as we calculated.

compounding

The process of accumulating interest in an investment over time to earn more interest.

interest on interest

Interest earned on the reinvestment of previous interest payments.

We now take a closer look at how we calculated the $121 future value. We multiplied $110 by 1.1 to get $121. The $110, however, was $100 also multiplied by 1.1. In other words:

$$\$121 = \$110 \times 1.1$$
$$= (\$100 \times 1.1) \times 1.1$$
$$= \$100 \times (1.1 \times 1.1)$$
$$= \$100 \times 1.1^2$$
$$= \$100 \times 1.21$$

compound interest

Interest earned on both the initial principal and the interest reinvested from prior periods.

simple interest

Interest earned only on the original principal amount invested.

At the risk of belaboring the obvious, let's ask: How much would our $100 grow to after three years? Once again, in two years, we'll be investing $121 for one period at 10 percent. We'll end up with $1.1 for every dollar we invest, or $121 × 1.1 = $133.1 total. This $133.1 is thus:

$$\$133.1 = \$121 \times 1.1$$
$$= (\$110 \times 1.1) \times 1.1$$
$$= (\$100 \times 1.1) \times 1.1 \times 1.1$$
$$= \$100 \times (1.1 \times 1.1 \times 1.1)$$
$$= \$100 \times 1.1^3$$
$$= \$100 \times 1.331$$

You're probably noticing a pattern to these calculations, so we can now go ahead and state the general result. As our examples suggest, the future value of $1 invested for t periods at a rate of r per period is:

$$\text{Future value} = \$1 \times (1 + r)^t \qquad \textbf{[8.1]}$$

The expression $(1 + r)^t$ is sometimes called the *future value interest factor* (or just *future value factor*) for $1 invested at r percent for t periods and can be abbreviated as FVIF(r, t).

Compound interest

		Year	Beginning Amount	Interest Earned	Ending Amount

Future value of $100 at 10 percent

Year	Beginning Amount	Interest Earned	Ending Amount
1	$100.00	$10.00	$110.00
2	110.00	11.00	121.00
3	121.00	12.10	133.10
4	133.10	13.31	146.41
5	146.41	14.64	161.05
		Total interest $61.05	

In our example, what would your $100 be worth after five years? We can first compute the relevant future value factor as:

$$(1 + r)^t = (1 + .10)^5 = 1.1^5 = 1.6105$$

Your $100 will thus grow to:

$$\$100 \times 1.6105 = \$161.05$$

The growth of your $100 each year is illustrated in Table 8.1. As shown, the interest earned in each year is equal to the beginning amount multiplied by the interest rate of 10 percent.

In Table 8.1, notice that the total interest you earn is $61.05. Over the five-year span of this investment, the simple interest is $100 × .10 = $10 per year, so you accumulate $50 this way. The other $11.05 is from compounding.

Figure 8.1 illustrates the growth of the compound interest in Table 8.1. Notice how the simple interest is constant each year, but the compound interest you earn gets bigger every year. The size of the compound interest keeps increasing because more and more interest builds up and there is thus more to compound.

Future values depend critically on the assumed interest rate, particularly for long-lived investments. Figure 8.2 illustrates this relationship by plotting the growth of $1 for different rates and lengths of time. Notice that the future value of $1 after 10 years is about $6.20 at a 20 percent rate, but it is only about $2.60 at 10 percent. In this case, doubling the interest rate more than doubles the future value.

To solve future value problems, we need to come up with the relevant future value factors. There are several different ways of doing this. In our example, we could have multiplied 1.1 by itself five times. This would work just fine, but it would get to be very tedious for, say, a 30-year investment.

Fortunately, there are several easier ways to get future value factors. Most calculators have a key labeled "y^x." You can usually just enter 1.1, press this key, enter 5, and press the "=" key to get the answer. This is an easy way to calculate future value factors because it's quick and accurate.

Alternatively, you can use a table that contains future value factors for some common interest rates and time periods. Table 8.2 contains some of these factors. Table A.1 in Appendix A at the end of the book contains a much larger set. To use the table, find the column that corresponds to 10 percent. Then look down the rows until you come to five periods. You should find the factor that we calculated, 1.6105.

Tables such as Table 8.2 are not as common as they once were because they predate inexpensive calculators and are only available for a relatively small number of rates. Interest rates are often quoted to three or four decimal places, so the tables needed to deal with these accurately would be quite large. As a result, the "real world" has moved away from using them. We will emphasize the use of a calculator in this chapter.

A brief introduction to key financial concepts is available at **www. teachmefinance.com**.

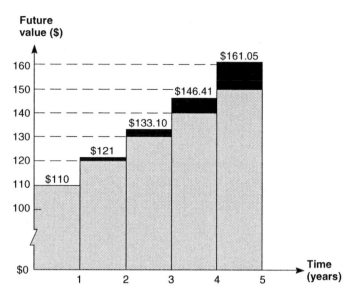

FIGURE 8.1

Future value, simple interest, and compound interest

Growth of $100 original amount at 10% per year. Blue shaded area represents the portion of the total that results from compounding of interest.

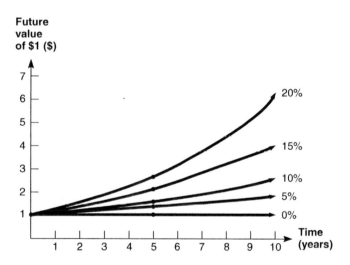

FIGURE 8.2

Future value of $1 for different periods and rates

Number of	Interest Rates				
Periods	5%	10%	15%	20%	
1	1.0500	1.1000	1.1500	1.2000	
2	1.1025	1.2100	1.3225	1.4400	
3	1.1576	1.3310	1.5209	1.7280	
4	1.2155	1.4641	1.7490	2.0736	
5	1.2763	1.6105	2.0114	2.4883	

TABLE 8.2

Future value interest factors

These tables still serve a useful purpose. To make sure you are doing the calculations correctly, pick a factor from the table and then calculate it yourself to see that you get the same answer. There are plenty of numbers to choose from.

EXAMPLE 8.2 | **Compound Interest**

You've located an investment that pays 12 percent. That rate sounds good to you, so you invest $400. How much will you have in three years? How much will you have in seven years? At the end of seven years, how much interest have you earned? How much of that interest results from compounding?

Based on our discussion, we can calculate the future value factor for 12 percent and three years as:

$$(1 + r)^t = 1.12^3 = 1.4049$$

Your $400 thus grows to:

$$\$400 \times 1.4049 = \$561.97$$

After seven years, you will have:

$$\$400 \times 1.12^7 = \$400 \times 2.2107 = \$884.27$$

Thus, you will more than double your money over seven years.

Since you invested $400, the interest in the $884.27 future value is $884.27 − 400 = $484.27. At 12 percent, your $400 investment earns $400 × .12 = $48 in simple interest every year. Over seven years, the simple interest thus totals 7 × $48 = $336. The other $484.27 − 336 = $148.27 is from compounding.

How much do you need at retirement? Check out the "Money/Retirement" link at **www.about.com**.

The effect of compounding is not great over short time periods, but it really starts to add up as the horizon grows. To take an extreme case, suppose one of your more frugal ancestors had invested $5 for you at a 6 percent interest rate 200 years ago. How much would you have today? The future value factor is a substantial $1.06^{200} = 115,125.90$ (you won't find this one in a table), so you would have $5 × 115,125.90 = $575,629.50 today. Notice that the simple interest is just $5 × .06 = $.30 per year. After 200 years, this amounts to $60. The rest is from reinvesting. Such is the power of compound interest!

EXAMPLE 8.3 | **How Much for That Island?**

To further illustrate the effect of compounding for long horizons, consider the case of Peter Minuit and the Indians. In 1626, Minuit bought all of Manhattan Island for about $24 in goods and trinkets. This sounds cheap, but the Indians may have gotten the better end of the deal. To see why, suppose the Indians had sold the goods and invested the $24 at 10 percent. How much would it be worth today?

Roughly 375 years have passed since the transaction. At 10 percent, $24 will grow by quite a bit over that time. How much? The future value factor is approximately:

$$(1 + r)^t = 1.1^{375} \approx 3,000,000,000,000,000$$

That is, 3 followed by 15 zeroes. The future value is thus on the order of $24 × 3 quadrillion, or about $72 *quadrillion* (give or take a few hundreds of trillions).

Well, $72 quadrillion is a lot of money. How much? If you had it, you could buy the United States. All of it. Cash. With money left over to buy Canada, Mexico, and the rest of the world, for that matter.

This example is something of an exaggeration, of course. In 1626, it would not have been easy to locate an investment that would pay 10 percent every year without fail for the next 375 years.

Using a Financial Calculator

Although there are the various ways of calculating future values we have described so far, many of you will decide that a financial calculator is the way to go. If you are planning on using one, you should read this extended hint; otherwise, skip it.

A financial calculator is simply an ordinary calculator with a few extra features. In particular, it knows some of the most commonly used financial formulas, so it can directly compute things like future values.

Financial calculators have the advantage that they handle a lot of the computation, but that is really all. In other words, you still have to understand the problem; the calculator just does some of the arithmetic. In fact, there is an old joke (somewhat modified) that goes like this: Anyone can make a mistake on a time value of money problem, but to really screw one up takes a financial calculator! We therefore have two goals for this section. First, we'll discuss how to compute future values. After that, we'll show you how to avoid the most common mistakes people make when they start using financial calculators.

How to Calculate Future Values with a Financial Calculator   Examining a typical financial calculator, you will find five keys of particular interest. They usually look like this:

> **N**   **I/Y**   **PMT**   **PV**   **FV**

For now, we need to focus on four of these. The keys labeled **PV** and **FV** are just what you would guess: present value and future value. The key labeled **N** refers to the *n*umber of periods, which is what we have been calling *t*. Finally, **I/Y** stands for the *i*nterest rate, which we have called *r*.[1]

If we have the financial calculator set up right (see our next section), then calculating a future value is very simple. Take a look back at our question involving the future value of $100 at 10 percent for five years. We have seen that the answer is $161.05. The exact keystrokes will differ depending on what type of calculator you use, but here is basically all you do:

1.   Enter −100. Press the **PV** key. (The negative sign is explained below.)
2.   Enter 10. Press the **I/Y** key. (Notice that we entered 10, not .10; see below.)
3.   Enter 5. Press the **N** key.

Now we have entered all of the relevant information. To solve for the future value, we need to ask the calculator what the FV is. Depending on your calculator, you either press the button labeled "CPT" (for compute) and then press **FV**, or else you just press **FV**. Either way, you should get 161.05. If you don't (and you probably won't if this is the first time you have used a financial calculator!), we will offer some help in our next section.

Before we explain the kinds of problems that you are likely to run into, we want to establish a standard format for showing you how to use a financial calculator. Using the example we just looked at, in the future, we will illustrate such problems like this:

Enter	5	10		−100	
	N	**I/Y**	**PMT**	**PV**	**FV**
Solve for					161.05

---

[1]The reason financial calculators use N and I/Y is that the most common use for these calculators is determining loan payments. In this context, N is the number of payments and I/Y is the interest rate on the loan. But, as we will see, there are many other uses of financial calculators that don't involve loan payments and interest rates.

Here is an important tip: Appendix D in the back of the book contains some more detailed instructions for the most common types of financial calculators. See if yours is included, and, if it is, follow the instructions there if you need help. Of course, if all else fails, you can read the manual that came with the calculator.

How to Get the Wrong Answer Using a Financial Calculator   There are a couple of common (and frustrating) problems that cause a lot of trouble with financial calculators. In this section, we provide some important *dos* and *don'ts*. If you just can't seem to get a problem to work out, you should refer back to this section.

There are two categories we examine: three things you need to do only once and three things you need to do every time you work a problem. The things you need to do just once deal with the following calculator settings:

1. *Make sure your calculator is set to display a large number of decimal places.* Most financial calculators only display two decimal places; this causes problems because we frequently work with numbers—like interest rates—that are very small.

2. *Make sure your calculator is set to assume only one payment per period or per year.* Most financial calculators assume monthly payments (12 per year) unless you say otherwise.

3. *Make sure your calculator is in "end" mode.* This is usually the default, but you can accidently change to "begin" mode.

If you don't know how to set these three things, see Appendix D or your calculator's operating manual. There are also three things you need to do *every time you work a problem:*

1. *Before you start, completely clear out the calculator.* This is very important. Failure to do this is the number one reason for wrong answers; you simply must get in the habit of clearing the calculator every time you start a problem. How you do this depends on the calculator (see Appendix D), but you must do more than just clear the display. For example, on a Texas Instruments BA II Plus you must press   **2nd**   then   **CLR TVM**   for *clear time value of money.* There is a similar command on your calculator. Learn it!

    Note that turning the calculator off and back on won't do it. Most financial calculators remember everything you enter, even after you turn them off. In other words, they remember all your mistakes unless you explicitly clear them out. Also, if you are in the middle of a problem and make a mistake, *clear it out and start over.* Better to be safe than sorry.

2. *Put a negative sign on cash outflows.* Most financial calculators require you to put a negative sign on cash outflows and a positive sign on cash inflows.[2] As a practical matter, this usually just means that you should enter the present value amount with a negative sign (because normally the present value represents the amount you give up today in exchange for cash inflows later). You enter a negative value on the BA II Plus by first entering a number and then pressing the   **+/−**   key. By the same token, when you solve for a present value, you shouldn't be surprised to see a negative sign.

3. *Enter the rate correctly.* Financial calculators assume that rates are quoted in percent, so if the rate is .08 (or 8 percent), you should enter 8, not .08.

If you follow these guidelines (especially the one about clearing out the calculator), you should have no problem using a financial calculator to work almost all of the problems in this and the next few chapters. We'll provide some additional examples and guidance where appropriate.

---

[2]The Texas Instruments BA-35 is an exception; it doesn't require negative signs to be entered.

CONCEPT QUESTIONS

8.1a   What do we mean by the future value of an investment?

8.1b   What does it mean to compound interest? How does compound interest differ from simple interest?

8.1c   In general, what is the future value of $1 invested at *r* per period for *t* periods?

PRESENT VALUE AND DISCOUNTING | 8.2

When we discuss future value, we are thinking of questions such as the following: What will my $2,000 investment grow to if it earns a 6.5 percent return every year for the next six years? The answer to this question is what we call the future value of $2,000 invested at 6.5 percent for six years (verify that the answer is about $2,918).

There is another type of question that comes up even more often in financial management that is obviously related to future value. Suppose you need to have $10,000 in 10 years, and you can earn 6.5 percent on your money. How much do you have to invest today to reach your goal? You can verify that the answer is $5,327.26. How do we know this? Read on.

The Single-Period Case

We've seen that the future value of $1 invested for one year at 10 percent is $1.10. We now ask a slightly different question: How much do we have to invest today at 10 percent to get $1 in one year? In other words, we know the future value here is $1, but what is the **present value (PV)**? The answer isn't too hard to figure out. Whatever we invest today will be 1.1 times bigger at the end of the year. Since we need $1 at the end of the year:

> Present value × 1.1 = $1

Or, solving for the present value:

> Present value = $1/1.1 = $.909

In this case, the present value is the answer to the following question: What amount, invested today, will grow to $1 in one year if the interest rate is 10 percent? Present value is thus just the reverse of future value. Instead of compounding the money forward into the future, we **discount** it back to the present.

present value (PV)
The current value of future cash flows discounted at the appropriate discount rate.

discount
Calculate the present value of some future amount.

Single-Period PV | EXAMPLE 8.4

Suppose you need $400 to buy textbooks next year. You can earn 7 percent on your money. How much do you have to put up today?

We need to know the PV of $400 in one year at 7 percent. Proceeding as above:

> Present value × 1.07 = $400

We can now solve for the present value:

> Present value = $400 × (1/1.07) = $373.83

Thus, $373.83 is the present value. Again, this just means that investing this amount for one year at 7 percent will result in your having a future value of $400.

From our examples, the present value of $1 to be received in one period is generally given as:

$$PV = \$1 \times [1/(1 + r)] = \$1/(1 + r)$$

We next examine how to get the present value of an amount to be paid in two or more periods into the future.

Present Values for Multiple Periods

Suppose you need to have $1,000 in two years. If you can earn 7 percent, how much do you have to invest to make sure that you have the $1,000 when you need it? In other words, what is the present value of $1,000 in two years if the relevant rate is 7 percent?

Based on your knowledge of future values, you know that the amount invested must grow to $1,000 over the two years. In other words, it must be the case that:

$$\begin{aligned}
\$1,000 &= PV \times 1.07 \times 1.07 \\
&= PV \times 1.07^2 \\
&= PV \times 1.1449
\end{aligned}$$

Given this, we can solve for the present value:

$$\text{Present value} = \$1,000/1.1449 = \$873.44$$

Therefore, $873.44 is the amount you must invest in order to achieve your goal.

EXAMPLE 8.5 | **Saving Up**

You would like to buy a new automobile. You have $50,000, but the car costs $68,500. If you can earn 9 percent, how much do you have to invest today to buy the car in two years? Do you have enough? Assume the price will stay the same.

What we need to know is the present value of $68,500 to be paid in two years, assuming a 9 percent rate. Based on our discussion, this is:

$$PV = \$68,500/1.09^2 = \$68,500/1.1881 = \$57,655.08$$

You're still about $7,655 short, even if you're willing to wait two years.

---

discount rate

The rate used to calculate the present value of future cash flows.

discounted cash flow (DCF) valuation

Valuation calculating the present value of a future cash flow to determine its value today.

As you have probably recognized by now, calculating present values is quite similar to calculating future values, and the general result looks much the same. The present value of $1 to be received t periods into the future at a discount rate of r is:

$$PV = \$1 \times [1/(1 + r)^t] = \$1/(1 + r)^t \qquad \text{[8.2]}$$

The quantity in brackets, $1/(1 + r)^t$, goes by several different names. Since it's used to discount a future cash flow, it is often called a *discount factor*. With this name, it is not surprising that the rate used in the calculation is often called the **discount rate**. We will tend to call it this in talking about present values. The quantity in brackets is also called the *present value interest factor* (or just *present value factor*) for $1 at r percent for t periods and is sometimes abbreviated as PVIF(r,t). Finally, calculating the present value of a future cash flow to determine its worth today is commonly called **discounted cash flow (DCF) valuation**.

Number of Periods	Interest Rates			
	5%	**10%**	**15%**	**20%**
1	.9524	.9091	.8696	.8333
2	.9070	.8264	.7561	.6944
3	.8638	.7513	.6575	.5787
4	.8227	.6830	.5718	.4823
5	.7835	.6209	.4972	.4019

TABLE 8.3

Present value interest factors

To illustrate, suppose you need $1,000 in three years. You can earn 15 percent on your money. How much do you have to invest today? To find out, we have to determine the present value of $1,000 in three years at 15 percent. We do this by discounting $1,000 back three periods at 15 percent. With these numbers, the discount factor is:

$$1/(1 + .15)^3 = 1/1.5209 = .6575$$

The amount you must invest is thus:

$$\$1,000 \times .6575 = \$657.50$$

We say that $657.50 is the present, or discounted, value of $1,000 to be received in three years at 15 percent.

There are tables for present value factors just as there are tables for future value factors, and you use them in the same way (if you use them at all). Table 8.3 contains a small set of these factors. A much larger set can be found in Table A.2 in Appendix A.

In Table 8.3, the discount factor we just calculated, .6575, can be found by looking down the column labeled "15%" until you come to the third row. Of course, you could use a financial calculator, as we illustrate next.

You solve present value problems on a financial calculator just like you do future value problems. For the example we just examined (the present value of $1,000 to be received in three years at 15 percent), you would do the following:

Enter	3	15			1,000
	N	**I/Y**	**PMT**	**PV**	**FV**
Solve for				−657.50	

Notice that the answer has a negative sign; as we discussed above, that's because it represents an outflow today in exchange for the $1,000 inflow later.

Deceptive Advertising | EXAMPLE 8.6

Recently, some businesses have been saying things like "Come try our product. If you do, we'll give you $100 just for coming by!" If you read the fine print, what you find out is that they will give you a savings certificate that will pay you $100 in 25 years or so. If the going interest rate on such certificates is 10 percent per year, how much are they really giving you today?

What you're actually getting is the present value of $100 to be paid in 25 years. If the discount rate is 10 percent per year, then the discount factor is:

$$1/1.1^{25} = 1/10.8347 = .0923$$

This tells you that a dollar in 25 years is worth a little more than nine cents today, assuming a 10 percent discount rate. Given this, the promotion is actually paying you about $.0923 \times \$100 = \$9.23$. Maybe this is enough to draw customers, but it's not $100.

As the length of time until payment grows, present values decline. As Example 8.6 illustrates, present values tend to become small as the time horizon grows. If you look out far enough, they will always get close to zero. Also, for a given length of time, the higher the discount rate is, the lower is the present value. Put another way, present values and discount rates are inversely related. Increasing the discount rate decreases the PV and vice versa.

The relationship between time, discount rates, and present values is illustrated in Figure 8.3. Notice that by the time we get to 10 years, the present values are all substantially smaller than the future amounts.

CONCEPT QUESTIONS

8.2a What do we mean by the present value of an investment?

8.2b The process of discounting a future amount back to the present is the opposite of doing what?

8.2c What do we mean by discounted cash flow, or DCF, valuation?

8.2d In general, what is the present value of $1 to be received in t periods, assuming a discount rate of r per period?

FIGURE 8.3

Present value of $1 for different periods and rates

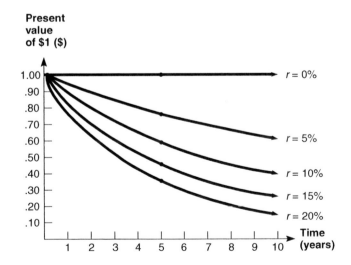

MORE ON PRESENT AND FUTURE VALUES | 8.3

If you look back at the expressions we came up with for present and future values, you will see there is a very simple relationship between the two. We explore this relationship and some related issues in this section.

Present versus Future Value

What we called the present value factor is just the reciprocal of (that is, 1 divided by) the future value factor:

Future value factor $= (1 + r)^t$

Present value factor $= 1/(1 + r)^t$

In fact, the easy way to calculate a present value factor on many calculators is to first calculate the future value factor and then press the **1/x** key to flip it over.

If we let FV_t stand for the future value after t periods, then the relationship between future value and present value can be written very simply as one of the following:

$$PV \times (1 + r)^t = FV_t$$
$$PV = FV_t/(1 + r)^t = FV_t \times [1/(1 + r)^t] \qquad \textbf{[8.3]}$$

This last result we will call the *basic present value equation*. We will use it throughout the text. There are a number of variations that come up, but this simple equation underlies many of the most important ideas in finance.

For a downloadable, Windows-based financial calculator, go to **www.calculator.org**.

Evaluating Investments | EXAMPLE 8.7

To give you an idea of how we will be using present and future values, consider the following simple investment. Your company proposes to buy an asset for $335. This investment is very safe. You will sell off the asset in three years for $400. You know you could invest the $335 elsewhere at 10 percent with very little risk. What do you think of the proposed investment?

This is not a good investment. Why not? Because you can invest the $335 elsewhere at 10 percent. If you do, after three years it will grow to:

$$\$335 \times (1 + r)^t = \$335 \times 1.1^3$$
$$= \$335 \times 1.331$$
$$= \$445.89$$

Since the proposed investment only pays out $400, it is not as good as other alternatives we have. Another way of saying the same thing is to notice that the present value of $400 in three years at 10 percent is:

$$\$400 \times [1/(1 + r)^t] = \$400/1.1^3 = \$400/1.331 = \$300.53$$

This tells us that we only have to invest about $300 to get $400 in three years, not $335. We will return to this type of analysis later on.

Determining the Discount Rate

It will turn out that we will frequently need to determine what discount rate is implicit in an investment. We can do this by looking at the basic present value equation:

$$PV = FV_t/(1 + r)^t$$

There are only four parts to this equation: the present value (PV), the future value (FV_t), the discount rate (r), and the life of the investment (t). Given any three of these, we can always find the fourth.

EXAMPLE 8.8 | **Finding r for a Single-Period Investment**

You are considering a one-year investment. If you put up $1,250, you will get back $1,350. What rate is this investment paying?

First, in this single-period case, the answer is fairly obvious. You are getting a total of $100 in addition to your $1,250. The implicit rate on this investment is thus $100/1,250 = 8 percent.

More formally, from the basic present value equation, the present value (the amount you must put up today) is $1,250. The future value (what the present value grows to) is $1,350. The time involved is one period, so we have:

$$\$1,250 = \$1,350/(1 + r)^1$$
$$1 + r = \$1,350/1,250 = 1.08$$
$$r = 8\%$$

In this simple case, of course, there was no need to go through this calculation, but, as we describe below, it gets a little harder when there is more than one period.

To illustrate what happens with multiple periods, let's say that we are offered an investment that costs us $100 and will double our money in eight years. To compare this to other investments, we would like to know what discount rate is implicit in these numbers. This discount rate is called the *rate of return*, or sometimes just *return*, on the investment. In this case, we have a present value of $100, a future value of $200 (double our money), and an eight-year life. To calculate the return, we can write the basic present value equation as:

$$PV = FV_t/(1 + r)^t$$
$$\$100 = \$200/(1 + r)^8$$

It could also be written as:

$$(1 + r)^8 = \$200/100 = 2$$

We now need to solve for r. There are three ways we could do it:

1. Use a financial calculator. (See below.)
2. Solve the equation for $1 + r$ by taking the eighth root of both sides. Since this is the same thing as raising both sides to the power of ⅛, or .125, this is actually easy to do with the **y**ˣ key on a calculator. Just enter 2, then press **y**ˣ , enter .125, and press the **=** key. The eighth root should be about 1.09, which implies that r is 9 percent.
3. Use a future value table. The future value factor for eight years is equal to 2. If you look across the row corresponding to eight periods in Table A.1, you will see that a future value factor of 2 corresponds to the 9 percent column, again implying that the return here is 9 percent.

Why does the Rule of 72 work? See **www.datachimp.com**.

Actually, in this particular example, there is a useful "back of the envelope" means of solving for r—the Rule of 72. For reasonable rates of return, the time it takes to double your money is given approximately by $72/r\%$. In our example, this means that $72/r\% = 8$ years, implying that r is 9 percent as we calculated. This rule is fairly accurate for discount rates in the 5 percent to 20 percent range.

A Quack Investment?

It used to be that trading in collectibles such as baseball cards, art, and old toys occurred mostly at auctions, swap meets, and collectible shops, all of which were limited to regional traffic. However, with the growing popularity of on-line auctions such as eBay, trading in collectibles has expanded to an international arena. The most visible form of collectible is probably the baseball card, but Furbies, Beanie Babies, and Pokémon cards have been extremely hot collectibles in the recent past. It's not just fad items that spark the collector's interest; virtually anything of sentimental value from days gone by is considered collectible, and, more and more, collectibles are being viewed as investments.

Collectibles typically provide no cash flows, except when sold, and condition and buyer sentiment are the major determinants of value. The rates of return have been staggering at times, but care is needed in interpreting them. One of the hottest collectibles in the past several years has been duck decoys. In its simplest form, a duck decoy is a carved wooden block with a weight attached that duck hunters place in the water to attract ducks. Collectible decoys are carved and painted to resemble different species of ducks. In an auction at Sotheby's, a collection of decoys sold for $11 million. What about individual decoys? The most expensive decoy ever sold was carved by a hunter in East Harwich, Maine, in 1917. The decoy was sold for $684,500 in 2001. We aren't really sure what the decoy sold for in 1917, but suppose it sold for $100. While this looks like an extraordinary return to the untrained eye, check for yourself that the actual return on the investment was about 11.09 percent per year. Plus, you had the problem of storing the decoy and keeping termites away.

Barbie dolls have historically been a hot collectible, but Barbie's tale also shows the downside of investing in collectibles. An original Barbie sold for about $3 when it was introduced in March 1959. An original in mint condition (and never removed from its package) might have been worth $7,000 in 2000, which represents a whopping return of 20.8 percent per year. However, at an auction in 2002, the top bid for a vintage 1959, in-the-box Barbie, was $4,400. If you had purchased Barbie in 2000 and sold it in 2002 you would have had a return of −20.72 percent per year (notice the negative sign). The return on your original Barbie purchased in 1959 would have dropped to 18.48 percent per year.

Stamp collecting (or philately) is a popular activity. The first postage stamp ever made in the United States was the 5-cent imperforate postage stamp. The stamp was issued in 1847 and printed in imperforate sheets, meaning no perforations, so you had to cut them apart with scissors or a razor. You could have purchased this stamp from Sothebys.com in 2002 for $600. Again, to the untrained eye it appears to be a huge gain, but the return is only 6.25 percent per year.

Looking back at these investments, the Barbie doll did the best. The problem is that to earn this return, you had to purchase the toy when it was new and store it (without opening it) for all those years. Looking ahead, the corresponding problem is predicting what the future value of the collectible will be. You can earn a positive return only if the market value of your asset rises above the purchase price at some point in the future. That, of course, is rarely assured. For example, most collectors say the Barbies that are mass-marketed at discount stores today will probably have little or no value as collectibles at any time in the future, so we don't recommend them for your retirement investing.

The nearby *Reality Bytes* box provides some examples of rates of return on collectibles. See if you can verify the numbers reported there.

Double Your Fun | EXAMPLE 8.9

You have been offered an investment that promises to double your money every 10 years. What is the approximate rate of return on the investment?

From the Rule of 72, the rate of return is given approximately by $72/r\% = 10$, so the rate is approximately $72/10 = 7.2\%$. Verify that the exact answer is 7.177 percent.

A slightly more extreme example involves money bequeathed by Benjamin Franklin, who died on April 17, 1790. In his will, he gave 1,000 pounds sterling to Massachusetts and the city of Boston. He gave a like amount to Pennsylvania and the city of Philadelphia. The money was paid to Franklin when he held political office, but he believed that politicians should not be paid for their service (it appears that this view is not widely shared by modern-day politicians).

Franklin originally specified that the money should be paid out 100 years after his death and used to train young people. Later, however, after some legal wrangling, it was agreed that the money would be paid out in 1990, 200 years after Franklin's death. By that time, the Pennsylvania bequest had grown to about $2 million; the Massachusetts bequest had grown to $4.5 million. The money was used to fund the Franklin Institutes in Boston and Philadelphia. Assuming that 1,000 pounds sterling was equivalent to 1,000 dollars, what rate of return did the two states earn (the dollar did not become the official U.S. currency until 1792)?

For Pennsylvania, the future value is $2 million and the present value is $1,000. There are 200 years involved, so we need to solve for r in the following:

$$\$1,000 = \$2 \text{ million}/(1 + r)^{200}$$
$$(1 + r)^{200} = 2,000$$

Solving for r, we see that the Pennsylvania money grew at about 3.87 percent per year. The Massachusetts money did better; verify that the rate of return in this case was 4.3 percent. Small differences can add up!

CALCULATOR HINTS

We can illustrate how to calculate unknown rates using a financial calculator using these numbers. For Pennsylvania, you would do the following:

Enter	200			-1,000	2,000,000
	N	**I/Y**	**PMT**	**PV**	**FV**
Solve for		3.87			

As in our previous examples, notice the minus sign on the present value, representing Franklin's outlay made many years ago. What do you change to work the problem for Massachusetts?

EXAMPLE 8.10 | **Saving for College**

You estimate that you will need about $80,000 to send your child to college in eight years. You have about $35,000 now. If you can earn 20 percent per year, will you make it? At what rate will you just reach your goal?

If you can earn 20 percent, the future value of your $35,000 in eight years will be:

$$FV = \$35,000 \times 1.20^8 = \$35,000 \times 4.2998 = \$150,493.59$$

So, you will make it easily. The minimum rate is the unknown r in the following:

$$FV = \$35,000 \times (1 + r)^8 = \$80,000$$
$$(1 + r)^8 = \$80,000/35,000 = 2.2857$$

Therefore, the future value factor is 2.2857. Looking at the row in Table A.1 that corresponds to eight periods, we see that our future value factor is roughly halfway between the ones shown for 10 percent

(2.1436) and 12 percent (2.4760), so you will just reach your goal if you earn approximately 11 percent. To get the exact answer, we could use a financial calculator or we could solve for r:

$$(1 + r)^8 = \$80,000/35,000 = 2.2857$$
$$1 + r = 2.2857^{(1/8)} = 2.2857^{.125} = 1.1089$$
$$r = 10.89\%$$

Only 18,262.5 Days to Retirement   **EXAMPLE 8.11**

You would like to retire in 50 years as a millionaire. If you have $10,000 today, what rate of return do you need to earn to achieve your goal?

The future value is $1,000,000. The present value is $10,000, and there are 50 years until retirement. We need to calculate the unknown discount rate in the following:

$$\$10,000 = \$1,000,000/(1 + r)^{50}$$
$$(1 + r)^{50} = 100$$

The future value factor is thus 100. You can verify that the implicit rate is about 9.65 percent.

Finding the Number of Periods

Suppose we were interested in purchasing an asset that costs $50,000. We currently have $25,000. If we can earn 12 percent on this $25,000, how long until we have the $50,000? Finding the answer involves solving for the last variable in the basic present value equation, the number of periods. You already know how to get an approximate answer to this particular problem. Notice that we need to double our money. From the Rule of 72, this will take about $72/12 = 6$ years at 12 percent.

To come up with the exact answer, we can again manipulate the basic present value equation. The present value is $25,000, and the future value is $50,000. With a 12 percent discount rate, the basic equation takes one of the following forms:

$$\$25,000 = \$50,000/1.12^t$$
$$\$50,000/25,000 = 1.12^t = 2$$

We thus have a future value factor of 2 for a 12 percent rate. We now need to solve for t. If you look down the column in Table A.1 that corresponds to 12 percent, you will see that a future value factor of 1.9738 occurs at six periods. It will thus take about six years, as we calculated. To get the exact answer, we have to explicitly solve for t (or use a financial calculator). If you do this, you will find that the answer is 6.1163 years, so our approximation was quite close in this case.

CALCULATOR HINTS

If you do use a financial calculator, here are the relevant entries:

Enter		12		−25,000	50,000
	N	**I/Y**	**PMT**	**PV**	**FV**
Solve for	6.1163				

EXAMPLE 8.12 | **Waiting for Godot**

You've been saving up to buy the Godot Company. The total cost will be $10 million. You currently have about $2.3 million. If you can earn 5 percent on your money, how long will you have to wait? At 16 percent, how long must you wait?

At 5 percent, you'll have to wait a long time. From the basic present value equation:

$2.3 = $10/1.05^t$
$1.05^t = 4.35$
$t = 30$ years

At 16 percent, things are a little better. Verify for yourself that it will take about 10 years.

This example finishes our introduction to basic time value of money concepts. Table 8.4 on page 288 summarizes present value and future value calculations for future reference. As our nearby *Work the Web* box shows, on-line calculators are widely available to handle these calculations, but it is still important to know what is going on.

SPREADSHEET STRATEGIES

Using a Spreadsheet for Time Value of Money Calculations

More and more, businesspeople from many different areas (and not just finance and accounting) rely on spreadsheets to do all the different types of calculations that come up in the real world. As a result, in this section, we will show you how to use a spreadsheet to handle the various time value of money problems we presented in this chapter. We will use Microsoft Excel™, but the commands are similar for other types of software. We assume you are already familiar with basic spreadsheet operations.

As we have seen, you can solve for any one of the following four potential unknowns: future value, present value, the discount rate, or the number of periods. With a spreadsheet, there is a separate formula for each. In Excel, these are as follows:

Learn more about using Excel for time value and other calculations at **www. studyfinance.com**.

To Find	Enter This Formula
Future value	= FV (rate,nper,pmt,pv)
Present value	= PV (rate,nper,pmt,fv)
Discount rate	= RATE (nper,pmt,pv,fv)
Number of periods	= NPER (rate,pmt,pv,fv)

In these formulas, pv and fv are present and future value, nper is the number of periods, and rate is the discount, or interest, rate.

There are two things that are a little tricky here. First, unlike a financial calculator, the spreadsheet requires that the rate be entered as a decimal. Second, as with most financial calculators, you have to put a negative sign on either the present value or the future value to solve for the rate or the number of periods. For the same reason, if you solve for a present value, the answer will have a negative sign unless you input a negative future value. The same is true when you compute a future value.

To illustrate how you might use these formulas, we will go back to an example in the chapter. If you invest $25,000 at 12 percent per year, how long until you have $50,000? You might set up a spreadsheet like this:

	A	B	C	D	E	F	G	H
1								
2	**Using a spreadsheet for time value of money calculations**							
3								
4	If we invest $25,000 at 12 percent, how long until we have $50,000? We need to solve for the							
5	unknown number of periods, so we use the formula NPER (rate, pmt, pv, fv).							
6								
7	Present value (pv):	$25,000						
8	Future value (fv):	$50,000						
9	Rate (rate):	.12						
10								
11	Periods:	**6.116255**						
12								
13	The formula entered in cell B11 is =NPER(B9,0,-B7,B8); notice that pmt is zero and that pv has a							
14	negative sign on it. Also notice that the rate is entered as a decimal, not a percentage.							

How important is the time value of money? A recent search on one Web engine returned over ?.? million hits! It is important to understand the calculations behind the time value of money, but the advent of financial calculators and spreadsheets has eliminated the need for tedious calculations. In fact, many web sites offer time value of money calculators. The following is an example from Cigna's web site, www.cigna.com. You need $40,000 in 15 years and will invest your money at 9.8 percent. How much do you need to deposit today? With the Cigna calculator, you simply enter the values and hit calculate:

Present Value / Future Value Calculator

Fill in any 3 of the 4 boxes in the form.

Present Value Amount:	$
Number of Years Invested:	15
Growth Rate:	% 9.8
Future Value Amount:	$ 40,000

CLEAR   **CALCULATE**

The results look like this:

Results

Present Value Amount	$9,841
Number of Years Invested	15 years
Growth Rate	9.8%
Future Value Amount	$40,000

Who said time value of money calculations are hard?

TABLE 8.4

Summary of time value of money calculations

I. **Symbols**
   PV = Present value, what future cash flows are worth today
   FV_t = Future value, what cash flows are worth in the future
     r = Interest rate, rate of return, or discount rate per period—typically, but not always, one year
     t = Number of periods—typically, but not always, the number of years
     C = Cash amount

II. **Future value of C invested at r percent per period for t periods**
   $FV_t = C \times (1 + r)^t$
   The term $(1 + r)^t$ is called the *future value factor.*

III. **Present value of C to be received in t periods at r percent per period**
   $PV = C/(1 + r)^t$
   The term $1/(1 + r)^t$ is called the *present value factor.*

IV. **The basic present value equation giving the relationship between present and future value is**
   $PV = FV_t/(1 + r)^t$

CONCEPT QUESTIONS

8.3a   What is the basic present value equation?

8.3b   What is the Rule of 72?

SUMMARY AND CONCLUSIONS

This chapter has introduced you to the basic principles of present value and discounted cash flow valuation. In it, we explained a number of things about the time value of money, including:

1.   For a given rate of return, the value at some point in the future of an investment made today can be determined by calculating the future value of that investment.
2.   The current worth of a future cash flow can be determined for a given rate of return by calculating the present value of the cash flow involved.
3.   The relationship between present value and future value for a given rate r and time t is given by the basic present value equation:

$$PV = FV_t/(1 + r)^t$$

As we have shown, it is possible to find any one of the four components (PV, FV_t, r, or t) given the other three.

The principles developed in this chapter will figure prominently in the chapters to come. The reason for this is that most investments, whether they involve real assets or financial assets, can be analyzed using the discounted cash flow, or DCF, approach. As a result, the DCF approach is broadly applicable and widely used in practice. Before going on, therefore, you might want to do some of the problems below.

CHAPTER REVIEW AND SELF-TEST PROBLEMS

8.1   **Calculating Future Values.** Assume you deposit $1,000 today in an account that pays 8 percent interest. How much will you have in four years?

8.2   **Calculating Present Values.** Suppose you have just celebrated your 19th birthday. A rich uncle set up a trust fund for you that will pay you $100,000 when you turn 25. If the relevant discount rate is 11 percent, how much is this fund worth today?

8.3   **Calculating Rates of Return.** You've been offered an investment that will double your money in 12 years. What rate of return are you being offered? Check your answer using the Rule of 72.

8.4   **Calculating the Number of Periods.** You've been offered an investment that will pay you 7 percent per year. If you invest $10,000, how long until you have $20,000? How long until you have $30,000?

■ Answers to Chapter Review and Self-Test Problems

8.1   We need to calculate the future value of $1,000 at 8 percent for four years. The future value factor is:

$$1.08^4 = 1.3605$$

The future value is thus $1,000 \times 1.3605 = $1,360.50.

8.2   We need the present value of $100,000 to be paid in six years at 11 percent. The discount factor is:

$$1/1.11^6 = 1/1.8704 = .5346$$

The present value is thus about $53,460.

8.3   Suppose you invest, say, $100. You will have $200 in 12 years with this investment. So, $100 is the amount you have today, the present value, and $200 is the amount you will have in 12 years, or the future value. From the basic present value equation, we have:

$$\$200 = \$100 \times (1 \times r)^{12}$$
$$2 = (1 \times r)^{12}$$

From here, we need to solve for r, the unknown rate. As shown in the chapter, there are several different ways to do this. We will take the 12th root of 2 (by raising 2 to the power of 1/12):

$$2^{(1/12)} = 1 + r$$
$$1.0595 = 1 + r$$
$$r = 5.95\%$$

Using the Rule of 72, we have $72/t = r\%$, or $72/12 = 6\%$, so our answer looks good (remember that the Rule of 72 is only an approximation).

8.4   The basic equation is:

$$\$20,000 = \$10,000 \times (1 + .07)^t$$
$$2 = (1 + .07)^t$$

If we solve for t, we get that $t = 10.24$ years. Using the Rule of 72, we get $72/7 = 10.29$ years, so, once again, our answer looks good. To get $30,000, verify for yourself that you will have to wait 16.24 years.

CRITICAL THINKING AND CONCEPTS REVIEW

8.1   Present Value.   The basic present value equation has four parts. What are they?

8.2   Compounding.   What is compounding? What is discounting?

8.3   Compounding and Periods.   As you increase the length of time involved, what happens to future values? What happens to present values?

8.4   Compounding and Interest Rates.   What happens to a future value if you increase the rate r? What happens to a present value?

8.5   Ethical Considerations.   Take a look back at Example 8.6. Is it deceptive advertising? Is it unethical to advertise a future value like this without a disclaimer?

To answer the next five questions, refer to the GMAC security we discussed to open the chapter.

8.6   Time Value of Money.   Why would GMAC be willing to accept such a small amount today ($500) in exchange for a promise to repay 20 times that amount ($10,000) in the future?

8.7   Call Provisions.   GMAC has the right to buy back the securities anytime it wishes by paying $10,000 (this is a term of this particular deal). What impact does this feature have on the desirability of this security as an investment?

8.8   Time Value of Money.   Would you be willing to pay $500 today in exchange for $10,000 in 30 years? What would be the key considerations in answering yes or no? Would your answer depend on who is making the promise to repay?

8.9   Investment Comparison.   Suppose that when GMAC offered the security for $500, the U.S. Treasury had offered an essentially identical security. Do you think it would have had a higher or lower price? Why?

8.10   Length of Investment.   The GMAC security is actively bought and sold on the New York Stock Exchange. If you looked in *The Wall Street Journal* today, do you think the price would exceed the $500 original price? Why? If you looked in the year 2006, do you think the price would be higher or lower than today's price? Why?

QUESTIONS AND PROBLEMS

www.mhhe.com/rwj
Spreadsheet Templates 3, 4, 15, 18

Basic
(Questions 1–15)

1. Simple Interest versus Compound Interest.   First Mark Bank pays 6 percent simple interest on its savings account balances, whereas First Mullineaux Bank pays 6 percent interest compounded annually. If you made a $5,000 deposit in each bank, how much more money would you earn from your First Mullineaux Bank account at the end of 10 years?

2. Calculating Future Values.   For each of the following, compute the future value:

Present Value	Years	Interest Rate	Future Value
$ 2,250	3	18%	
9,310	10	6	
81,550	17	12	
210,384	22	7	

3. Calculating Present Values. For each of the following, compute the present value:

Present Value	Years	Interest Rate	Future Value
	4	4%	$ 15,451
	9	12	51,557
	14	22	886,073
	18	20	550,164

4. Calculating Interest Rates. Solve for the unknown interest rate in each of the following:

Present Value	Years	Interest Rate	Future Value
$ 221	4		$ 307
425	8		761
25,000	16		136,771
40,200	25		255,810

5. Calculating the Number of Periods. Solve for the unknown number of years in each of the following:

Present Value	Years	Interest Rate	Future Value
$ 250		4%	$ 1,105
1,941		9	3,860
21,320		23	387,120
32,500		34	198,212

6. Calculating Interest Rates. Assume the total cost of a college education will be $300,000 when your child enters college in 18 years. You presently have $40,000 to invest. What annual rate of interest must you earn on your investment to cover the cost of your child's college education?

7. Calculating the Number of Periods. At 9 percent interest, how long does it take to double your money? To quadruple it?

8. Calculating Interest Rates. You are offered an investment that requires you to put up $10,000 today in exchange for $40,000 15 years from now. What is the annual rate of return on this investment?

9. Calculating the Number of Periods. You're trying to save to buy a new $120,000 Ferrari. You have $26,000 today that can be invested at your bank. The bank pays 3.5 percent annual interest on its accounts. How long will it be before you have enough to buy the car?

10. Calculating Present Values. Imprudential, Inc., has an unfunded pension liability of $950 million that must be paid in 20 years. To assess the value of the firm's stock, financial analysts want to discount this liability back to the present. If the relevant discount rate is 8 percent, what is the present value of this liability?

11. Calculating Present Values. You have just received notification that you have won the $2 million first prize in the Centennial Lottery. However, the prize will be awarded on your 100th birthday (assuming you're around to collect), 80 years from now. What is the present value of your windfall if the appropriate discount rate is 12 percent?

12. **Calculating Future Values.** Your coin collection contains 50 1952 silver dollars. If your grandparents purchased them for their face value when they were new, how much will your collection be worth when you retire in 2055, assuming they appreciate at a 4.25 percent annual rate?

13. **Calculating Interest Rates and Future Values.** In 1895, the first U.S. Open Golf Championship was held. The winner's prize money was $150. In 2001, the winner's check was $900,000. What was the annual percentage increase in the winner's check over this period? If the winner's prize increases at the same rate, what will it be in 2040?

14. **Calculating Present Values.** In 2001, a mechanized toy robot from the television series *Lost in Space* sold for $750. This represented a 13.86 percent annual return. For this to be true, what must the robot have sold for new in 1965?

15. **Calculating Rates of Return.** Although appealing to more refined tastes, art as a collectible has not always performed so profitably. During 1995, Christie's auctioned the William de Kooning painting *Untitled.* The highest bid of $2.2 million was rejected by the owner, who had purchased the painting at the height of the art market in 1989 for $3.52 million. Had the seller accepted the bid, what would his annual rate of return have been?

Intermediate
(Questions 16–25)

16. **Calculating Rates of Return.** Referring to the GMAC security we discussed at the very beginning of the chapter:

    a. Based upon the $500 price, what rate was GMAC paying to borrow money?

    b. Suppose that on December 1, 2002, this security's price was $6,340.81. If an investor had purchased it for $500 at the offering and sold it on this day, what annual rate of return would she have earned?

    c. If an investor had purchased the security at market on December 1, 2002, and held it until it matured, what annual rate of return would she have earned?

17. **Calculating Present Values.** Suppose you are still committed to owning a $120,000 Ferrari (see Question 9). If you believe your mutual fund can achieve an 11.5 percent annual rate of return, and you want to buy the car in 10 years on the day you turn 30, how much must you invest today?

18. **Calculating Future Values.** You have just made your first $2,000 contribution to your individual retirement account. Assuming you earn a 12 percent rate of return and make no additional contributions, what will your account be worth when you retire in 45 years? What if you wait 10 years before contributing? (Does this suggest an investment strategy?)

19. **Calculating Future Values.** You are scheduled to receive $28,000 in two years. When you receive it, you will invest it for six more years at 7 percent per year. How much will you have in eight years?

20. **Calculating the Number of Periods.** You expect to receive $40,000 at graduation in two years. You plan on investing it at 8 percent until you have $120,000. How long will you wait from now? (Better than the situation in Question 9, but still no Ferrari.)

21. **Calculating Future Values.** You have $8,000 to deposit. Roten Bank offers 12 percent per year compounded monthly (1 percent per month), while Brook Bank

offers 12 percent but will only compound annually. How much will your investment be worth in 10 years at each bank?

22. **Calculating Interest Rates.** An investment offers to quadruple your money in 36 months (don't believe it). What rate per six months are you being offered?

23. **Calculating the Number of Periods.** You can earn .3 percent per month at your bank. If you deposit $1,100, how long must you wait until your account has grown to $2,500?

24. **Calculating Present Values.** You need $50,000 in eight years. If you can earn .65 percent per month, how much will you have to deposit today?

25. **Calculating Present Values.** You have decided that you want to be a millionaire when you retire in 40 years. If you can earn a 12 percent annual return, how much do you have to invest today? What if you can earn 6 percent?

8.1 **Calculating Future Values.** Go to www.dinkytown.net and follow the "Savings Calculator" link. If you currently have $10,000 and invest this money at 9 percent, how much will you have in 30 years? Assume you will not make any additional contributions. How much will you have if you can earn 11 percent?

8.2 **Calculating the Number of Periods.** Go to www.dinkytown.net and follow the "Cool Million" link. You want to be a millionaire. You can earn 11.5 percent per year. Using your current age, at what age will you become a millionaire if you have $25,000 to invest, assuming you make no other deposits (ignore inflation)?

8.3 **Calculating the Number of Periods.** Cigna has a financial calculator available at www.cigna.com. To get to the calculator, follow the "Calculator & Tools" link, then the "Present/Future Value Calculator" link. You want to buy a Lamborghini Murciélago. The current market price of the car is $330,000 and you have $33,000. If you can earn an 11 percent return, how many years until you can buy this car (assuming the price stays the same)?

8.4 **Calculating Rates of Return.** Use the Cigna financial calculator to solve the following problem. You still want to buy the Lamborghini Murciélago, but you have $50,000 to deposit and want to buy the car in 15 years. What interest rate do you have to earn to accomplish this (assuming the price stays the same)?

8.5 **Future Values and Taxes.** Taxes can greatly affect the future value of your investment. The web site www.fincalc.com has a financial calculator that adjusts your return for taxes. Follow the "Projected Savings" link on this page to find this calculator. Suppose you have $50,000 to invest today. If you can earn a 12 percent return and no additional annual savings, how much will you have in 20 years? (Enter 0 percent as the tax rate.) Now, assume that your marginal tax rate is 27 percent. How much will you have at this tax rate?

What's On the Web?

9 Discounted Cash Flow Valuation

T he signing of big-name athletes is often accompanied by great fanfare, but the numbers are sometimes misleading. For example, in October 1998, the New York Mets signed catcher Mike Piazza to a $91 million contract, the richest deal in baseball history. Not bad, especially for someone who makes a living using the "tools of ignorance" (jock jargon for a catcher's equipment). That record didn't last long. In late 2000, the Texas Rangers offered 25-year-old Alexander Rodriguez, or "A-Rod" as his fans call him, a contract with a stated value of $250 million!

A closer look at the number shows that both Piazza and A-Rod did pretty well, but nothing like the quoted figures. Using Piazza's contract as an example, the value was reported to be $91 million, but the total was actually payable over several years. It consisted of a signing bonus of $7.5 million ($4 million payable in 1999, $3.5 million in 2002) plus a salary of $83.5 million. The salary was to be distributed as $6 million in 1999, $11 million in 2000, $12.5 million in 2001, $9.5 million in 2002, $14.5 million in 2003, and $15 million in both 2004 and 2005. A-Rod's deal was spread out over an even longer period of 10 years. So, once we consider the time value of money, neither player received the quoted amounts. How much did they really get? This chapter gives you the "tools of knowledge" to answer this question.

AFTER STUDYING THIS CHAPTER, YOU SHOULD HAVE A GOOD UNDERSTANDING OF:

- How to determine the future and present value of investments with multiple cash flows.

- How loan payments are calculated and how to find the interest rate on a loan.

- How loans are amortized or paid off.

- How interest rates are quoted (and misquoted).

In our previous chapter, we learned how to examine single, lump-sum future payments to determine their current, or present, value. This is a useful skill, but we need to go further and figure out how to handle multiple future payments because that is the much more common situation. For example, most loans (including student loans) involve receiving a lump sum today and making future payments.

More generally, most types of business decisions, including decisions concerning marketing, operations, and strategy, involve the comparison of costs incurred today with cash inflows hoped for later. Evaluating the cost-benefit trade-off requires the tools that we develop in this chapter.

Because discounted cash flow valuation is so important, students who learn this material well will find that life is much easier down the road. Getting it straight now will save you a lot of headaches later.

In our previous chapter, we covered the basics of discounted cash flow valuation. However, so far, we have only dealt with single cash flows. In reality, most investments have multiple cash flows. For example, if Sears is thinking of opening a new department store, there will be a large cash outlay in the beginning and then cash inflows for many years. In this chapter, we begin to explore how to value such investments.

When you finish this chapter, you should have some very practical skills. For example, you will know how to calculate your own car payments or student loan payments. You will also be able to determine how long it will take to pay off a credit card if you make the minimum payment each month (a practice we do not recommend). We will show you how to compare interest rates to determine which are the highest and which are the lowest, and we will also show you how interest rates can be quoted in different, and at times deceptive, ways.

FUTURE AND PRESENT VALUES OF MULTIPLE | 9.1
CASH FLOWS

Thus far, we have restricted our attention to either the future value of a lump-sum present amount or the present value of some single future cash flow. In this section, we begin to study ways to value multiple cash flows. We start with future value.

Future Value with Multiple Cash Flows

Suppose you deposit $100 today in an account paying 8 percent. In one year, you will deposit another $100. How much will you have in two years? This particular problem is relatively easy. At the end of the first year, you will have $108 plus the second $100 you deposit, for a total of $208. You leave this $208 on deposit at 8 percent for another year. At the end of this second year, the account is worth:

$208 × 1.08 = $224.64

Figure 9.1 is a *time line* that illustrates the process of calculating the future value of these two $100 deposits. Figures such as this one are very useful for solving complicated problems. Anytime you are having trouble with a present or future value problem, drawing a time line will usually help you to see what is happening.

In the first part of Figure 9.1, we show the cash flows on the time line. The most important thing is that we write them down where they actually occur. Here, the first cash

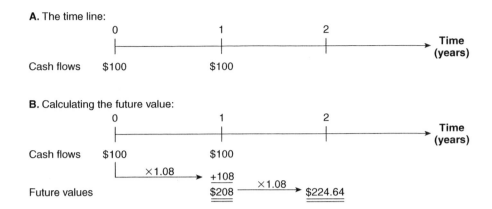

FIGURE 9.1

Drawing and using a time line

flow occurs today, which we label as Time 0. We therefore put $100 at Time 0 on the time line. The second $100 cash flow occurs one year from today, so we write it down at the point labeled as Time 1. In the second part of Figure 9.1, we calculate the future values one period at a time to come up with the final $224.64.

EXAMPLE 9.1 | Saving Up Revisited

You think you will be able to deposit $4,000 at the end of each of the next three years in a bank account paying 8 percent interest. You currently have $7,000 in the account. How much will you have in three years? In four years?

At the end of the first year, you will have:

$7,000 × 1.08 + 4,000 = $11,560

At the end of the second year, you will have:

$11,560 × 1.08 + 4,000 = $16,484.80

Repeating this for the third year gives:

$16,484.80 × 1.08 + 4,000 = $21,803.58

Therefore, you will have $21,803.58 in three years. If you leave this on deposit for one more year (and don't add to it), at the end of the fourth year you'll have:

$21,803.58 × 1.08 = $23,547.87

When we calculated the future value of the two $100 deposits, we simply calculated the balance as of the beginning of each year and then rolled that amount forward to the next year. We could have done it another, quicker way. The first $100 is on deposit for two years at 8 percent, so its future value is:

$100 × 1.08² = $100 × 1.1664 = $116.64

The second $100 is on deposit for one year at 8 percent, and its future value is thus:

$100 × 1.08 = $108.00

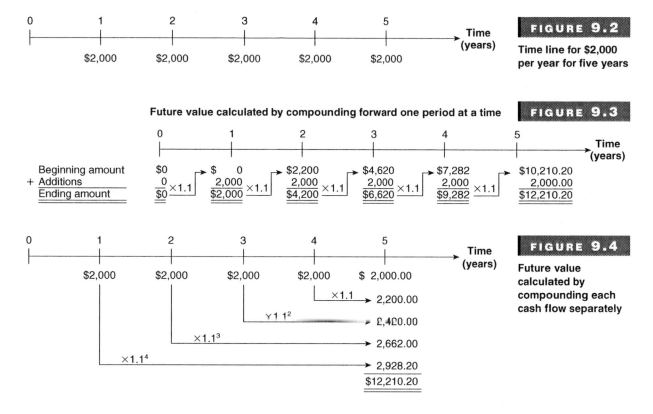

FIGURE 9.2

Time line for $2,000 per year for five years

Future value calculated by compounding forward one period at a time

FIGURE 9.3

FIGURE 9.4

Future value calculated by compounding each cash flow separately

The total future value, as we previously calculated, is equal to the sum of these two future values:

$$\$116.64 + 108 = \$224.64$$

Based on this example, there are two ways to calculate future values for multiple cash flows: (1) compound the accumulated balance forward one year at a time or (2) calculate the future value of each cash flow first and then add these up. Both give the same answer, so you can do it either way.

To illustrate the two different ways of calculating future values, consider the future value of $2,000 invested at the end of each of the next five years. The current balance is zero, and the rate is 10 percent. We first draw a time line as shown in Figure 9.2.

On the time line, notice that nothing happens until the end of the first year when we make the first $2,000 investment. This first $2,000 earns interest for the next four (not five) years. Also notice that the last $2,000 is invested at the end of the fifth year, so it earns no interest at all.

Figure 9.3 illustrates the calculations involved if we compound the investment one period at a time. As illustrated, the future value is $12,210.20.

Figure 9.4 goes through the same calculations, but it uses the second technique. Naturally, the answer is the same.

Saving Up Once Again   EXAMPLE 9.2

If you deposit $100 in one year, $200 in two years, and $300 in three years, how much will you have in three years? How much of this is interest? How much will you have in five years if you don't add additional amounts? Assume a 7 percent interest rate throughout.

We will calculate the future value of each amount in three years. Notice that the $100 earns interest for two years, and the $200 earns interest for one year. The final $300 earns no interest. The future values are thus:

$$
\begin{array}{ll}
\$100 \times 1.07^2 & = \$114.49 \\
\$200 \times 1.07 & = \ \ 214.00 \\
+\$300 & = \underline{\$300.00} \\
\text{Total future value} & = \underline{\underline{\$628.49}}
\end{array}
$$

The future value is thus $628.49. The total interest is:

$$\$628.49 - (100 + 200 + 300) = \$28.49$$

How much will you have in five years? We know that you will have $628.49 in three years. If you leave that in for two more years, it will grow to:

$$\$628.49 \times 1.07^2 = \$628.49 \times 1.1449 = \$719.56$$

Notice that we could have calculated the future value of each amount separately. Once again, be careful about the lengths of time. As we previously calculated, the first $100 earns interest for only four years, the second deposit earns three years' interest, and the last earns two years' interest:

$$
\begin{array}{lll}
\$100 \times 1.07^4 = \$100 \times 1.3108 = & \$131.08 \\
\$200 \times 1.07^3 = \$200 \times 1.2250 = & \ \ 245.01 \\
+\$300 \times 1.07^2 = \$300 \times 1.1449 = & \underline{\ \ 343.47} \\
\text{Total future value} = & \underline{\underline{\$719.56}}
\end{array}
$$

Present Value with Multiple Cash Flows

It will turn out that we will very often need to determine the present value of a series of future cash flows. As with future values, there are two ways we can do it. We can either discount back one period at a time, or we can just calculate the present values individually and add them up.

Suppose you need $1,000 in one year and $2,000 more in two years. If you can earn 9 percent on your money, how much do you have to put up today to exactly cover these amounts in the future? In other words, what is the present value of the two cash flows at 9 percent?

The present value of $2,000 in two years at 9 percent is:

$$\$2,000/1.09^2 = \$1,683.36$$

The present value of $1,000 in one year is:

$$\$1,000/1.09 = \$917.43$$

Therefore, the total present value is:

$$\$1,683.36 + 917.43 = \$2,600.79$$

To see why $2,600.79 is the right answer, we can check to see that after the $2,000 is paid out in two years, there is no money left. If we invest $2,600.79 for one year at 9 percent, we will have:

$$\$2,600.79 \times 1.09 = \$2,834.86$$

We take out $1,000, leaving $1,834.86. This amount earns 9 percent for another year, leaving us with:

$1,834.86 × 1.09 = $2,000

This is just as we planned. As this example illustrates, the present value of a series of future cash flows is simply the amount that you would need today in order to exactly duplicate those future cash flows (for a given discount rate).

An alternative way of calculating present values for multiple future cash flows is to discount back to the present one period at a time. To illustrate, suppose we had an investment that was going to pay $1,000 at the end of every year for the next five years. To find the present value, we could discount each $1,000 back to the present separately and then add the results up. Figure 9.5 illustrates this approach for a 6 percent discount rate. As shown, the answer is $4,212.37 (ignoring a small rounding error).

Alternatively, we could discount the last cash flow back one period and add it to the next-to-the-last cash flow:

$1,000/1.06 + 1,000 = $943.40 + 1,000 = $1,943.40

We could then discount this amount back one period and add it to the Year 3 cash flow:

$1,943.40/1.06 + 1,000 = $1,833.40 + 1,000 = $2,833.40

This process could be repeated as necessary. Figure 9.6 illustrates this approach and the remaining calculations.

As the accompanying *Reality Bytes* box shows, calculating present values is a vital step in comparing alternative cash flows. We will have much more to say on this subject in subsequent chapters.

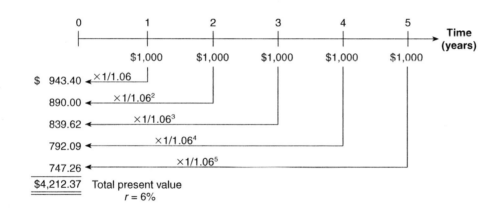

FIGURE 9.5

Present value calculated by discounting each cash flow separately

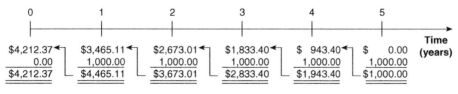

FIGURE 9.6

Present value calculated by discounting back one period at a time

Jackpot!

If you (or someone you know) is a regular lottery player, you probably already understand that you are 15–20 times more likely to get struck by lightning than you are of winning a big lottery jackpot. What are your odds of winning? Nearby, you will find a table with the odds of winning the Big Game.

However, you also know that if you are a lucky winner, you will usually have to choose to take all of your money immediately or else receive a series of payments over some number of periods.

For example, in April 2002, a 20-year-old warehouse worker from Georgia was one of three winners of the $331 million Big Game lottery. Just to show you how the odds work, it was the first lottery ticket she had ever purchased! As with most jackpots, however, the prize money was not actually all it appeared to be. To collect her full $110.3 million, the warehouse worker would have had to accept equal annual payments over 26 years, amounting to about $4,262,213 per year. As you can determine, using what you have already learned, the present value of this annuity is quite a bit less than the advertised jackpot. Assuming a discount rate of 10 percent, the present value of the payments is about $43 million, a tidy sum, but not $110 million.

Instead of taking the annuity payments, the winner chose to receive a lump-sum payment of $58,938,743 immediately. Did she make the right choice? Well, see if you don't agree that at a discount rate of about 5.96 percent she would be indifferent between the two options. (Also, remember that a lottery annuity payment is an annuity due, that is, the first annuity payment is received today.) At rates greater than that, she would be better off with the lump-sum payment.

The Virginia Lottery compares the alternatives on their web site. The table below shows your choices if you win Lotto South or the Big Game.

Big Game: Is It Worth the Gamble?	
Odds of winning Big Game jackpot:	1:76,275,360*
Odds of being killed by fireworks:	1:20,788,308
Odds of being killed by a dog bite:	1:18,016,533
Odds of being killed by lightning:	1:4,289,651
Odds of being killed in the bathtub:	1:801,923
Odds of being killed in a plane crash:	1:391,000
Odds of being killed in a car crash:	1:6,200

*Source: Big Game lottery.
All other odds from National Safety Council.

The winner of a $10 million jackpot in Lotto South can receive $5 million today or $333,333 per year for 30 years. The breakeven interest rate with these options is 5.72 percent. On the Big Game, the choice is $5 million today or $384,615 a year for 26 years, a breakeven rate of 6.68 percent. The Virginia web site will show you the alternatives, but even they don't tell you the rate of return.

Some lotteries make your decision a little tougher. The Ontario Lottery will pay you either $1,000 a week for the rest of your life or $675,000 now. (That's in Canadian dollars, by the way.) Of course, there is the chance you might die in the near future, so the lottery guarantees that your heirs will collect the $1,000 weekly payments until the 20th anniversary of the first payment or until you would have turned 91, whichever comes first. This payout scheme complicates your decision quite a bit. If you live for only the 20-year minimum, the breakeven interest rate between the two options is about 4.8 percent per year, compounded weekly. If you expect to live longer than the 20-year minimum, you might be better off accepting the $1,000 per week for life.

The Big Game and Lotto South Payout Comparison: Advertised $10 Million Jackpot—One Winner					
If There Is 1 Cash Option Winner (Lotto South or Big Game)		**If There Is 1 Annual Payout Winner for Lotto South**		**If There Is 1 Annual Payout Winner for the Big Game**	
Total payments:	1	Total payments:	30 annual	Total payments:	26 annual
One pre-tax payment:	$5,000,000	One of 30 pre-tax payments:	$ 333,333	One of 26 pre-tax payments:	$ 384,615
One after-tax* payment:	$3,450,000	One of 30 after-tax* payments:	$ 230,000	One of 26 after-tax* payments:	$ 265,385
Total pre-tax winnings:	$5,000,000	Total pre-tax winnings:	$10,000,000	Total pre-tax winnings:	$10,000,000
Total after-tax* winnings:	**$3,450,000**	Total after-tax* winnings:	**$ 6,900,000**	Total after-tax* winnings:	**$ 6,900,000**

*The assumed tax rate is 31 percent (combined state and federal).

How Much Is It Worth? | EXAMPLE 9.3

You are offered an investment that will pay you $200 in one year, $400 the next year, $600 the next year, and $800 at the end of the next year. You can earn 12 percent on very similar investments. What is the most you should pay for this one?

We need to calculate the present value of these cash flows at 12 percent. Taking them one at a time gives:

$$\begin{aligned}
\$200 \times 1/1.12^1 &= \$200/1.1200 = \$\ \ 178.57 \\
\$400 \times 1/1.12^2 &= \$400/1.2544 = \ \ \ \ 318.88 \\
\$600 \times 1/1.12^3 &= \$600/1.4049 = \ \ \ \ 427.07 \\
+\$800 \times 1/1.12^4 &= \$800/1.5735 = \ \underline{\ \ \ 508.41} \\
\text{Total present value} &= \underline{\underline{\$1,432.93}}
\end{aligned}$$

If you can earn 12 percent on your money, then you can duplicate this investment's cash flows for $1,432.93, so this is the most you should be willing to pay.

How Much Is It Worth? Part 2 | EXAMPLE 9.4

You are offered an investment that will make three $5,000 payments. The first payment will occur four years from today. The second will occur in five years, and the third will follow in six years. If you can earn 11 percent, what is the most this investment is worth today? What is the future value of the cash flows?

We will answer the questions in reverse order to illustrate a point. The future value of the cash flows in six years is:

$$\begin{aligned}
\$5,000 \times 1.11^2 + 5,000 \times 1.11 + 5,000 &= \$6,160.50 + 5,550 + 5,000 \\
&= \$16,710.50
\end{aligned}$$

The present value must be:

$$\$16,710.50/1.11^6 = \$8,934.12$$

Let's check this. Taking them one at a time, the PVs of the cash flows are:

$$\begin{aligned}
\$5,000 \times 1/1.11^6 &= \$5,000/1.8704 = \$2,673.20 \\
\$5,000 \times 1/1.11^5 &= \$5,000/1.6851 = \ \ 2,967.26 \\
+\$5,000 \times 1/1.11^4 &= \$5,000/1.5181 = \ \underline{\ \ 3,293.65} \\
\text{Total present value} &= \underline{\underline{\$8,934.12}}
\end{aligned}$$

This is as we previously calculated. The point we want to make is that we can calculate present and future values in any order and convert between them using whatever way seems most convenient. The answers will always be the same as long as we stick with the same discount rate and are careful to keep track of the right number of periods.

How to Calculate Present Values with Multiple Future Cash Flows Using a Financial Calculator

To calculate the present value of multiple cash flows with a financial calculator, we will simply discount the individual cash flows one at a time using the same technique we used in our previous chapter, so this is not really new. There is a shortcut, however, that we can show you. We will use the numbers in Example 9.3 to illustrate.

To begin, of course, we first remember to clear out the calculator! Next, from Example 9.3, the first cash flow is $200 to be received in one year and the discount rate is 12 percent, so we do the following:

Enter	1	12			200
	N	**I/Y**	**PMT**	**PV**	**FV**
Solve for				−178.57	

Now you can write down this answer to save it, but that's inefficient. All calculators have a memory where you can store numbers. Why not just save it there? Doing so cuts way down on mistakes because you don't have to write down and/or rekey numbers, and it's much faster.

Next we value the second cash flow. We need to change N to 2 and FV to 400. As long as we haven't changed anything else, we don't have to reenter I/Y or clear out the calculator, so we have:

Enter	2				400
	N	**I/Y**	**PMT**	**PV**	**FV**
Solve for				−318.88	

You save this number by adding it to the one you saved in our first calculation, and so on for the remaining two calculations.

As we will see in a later chapter, some financial calculators will let you enter all of the future cash flows at once, but we'll discuss that subject when we get to it.

A Note on Cash Flow Timing

In working present and future value problems, cash flow timing is critically important. In almost all such calculations, it is implicitly assumed that the cash flows occur at the *end* of each period. In fact, all the formulas we have discussed, all the numbers in a standard present value or future value table, and, very importantly, all the preset (or default) settings on a financial calculator or spreadsheet assume that cash flows occur at the end of each period. Unless you are very explicitly told otherwise, you should always assume that this is what is meant.

As a quick illustration of this point, suppose you are told that a three-year investment has a first-year cash flow of $100, a second-year cash flow of $200, and a third-year cash flow of $300. You are asked to draw a time line. Without further information, you should always assume that the time line looks like this:

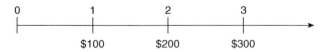

On our time line, notice how the first cash flow occurs at the end of the first period, the second at the end of the second period, and the third at the end of the third period.

How to Calculate Present Values with Multiple Future Cash Flows Using a Spreadsheet

Just as we did in our previous chapter, we can set up a basic spreadsheet to calculate the present values of the individual cash flows as follows. Notice that we have simply calculated the present values one at a time and added them up.

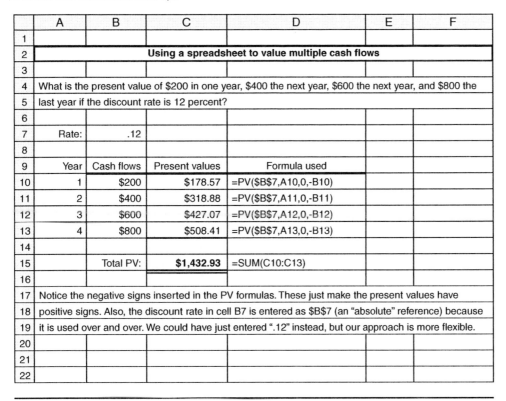

	A	B	C	D	E	F
1						
2			**Using a spreadsheet to value multiple cash flows**			
3						
4	What is the present value of $200 in one year, $400 the next year, $600 the next year, and $800 the					
5	last year if the discount rate is 12 percent?					
6						
7	Rate:	.12				
8						
9		Year	Cash flows	Present values	Formula used	
10		1	$200	$178.57	=PV($B$7,A10,0,-B10)	
11		2	$400	$318.88	=PV($B$7,A11,0,-B11)	
12		3	$600	$427.07	=PV($B$7,A12,0,-B12)	
13		4	$800	$508.41	=PV($B$7,A13,0,-B13)	
14						
15			Total PV:	$1,432.93	=SUM(C10:C13)	
16						
17	Notice the negative signs inserted in the PV formulas. These just make the present values have					
18	positive signs. Also, the discount rate in cell B7 is entered as $B$7 (an "absolute" reference) because					
19	it is used over and over. We could have just entered ".12" instead, but our approach is more flexible.					
20						
21						
22						

CONCEPT QUESTIONS

9.1a Describe how to calculate the future value of a series of cash flows.

9.1b Describe how to calculate the present value of a series of cash flows.

9.1c Unless we are explicitly told otherwise, what do we always assume about the timing of cash flows in present and future value problems?

VALUING LEVEL CASH FLOWS: | 9.2
ANNUITIES AND PERPETUITIES

We will frequently encounter situations where we have multiple cash flows that are all the same amount. For example, a very common type of loan repayment plan calls for the borrower to repay the loan by making a series of equal payments for some length of time. Almost all consumer loans (such as car loans) and home mortgages feature equal payments, usually made each month.

annuity

A level stream of cash flows for a fixed period of time.

More generally, a series of constant, or level, cash flows that occur at the end of each period for some fixed number of periods is called an ordinary **annuity**; or, more correctly, the cash flows are said to be in ordinary annuity form. Annuities appear very frequently in financial arrangements, and there are some useful shortcuts for determining their values. We consider these next.

Present Value for Annuity Cash Flows

Suppose we were examining an asset that promised to pay $500 at the end of each of the next three years. The cash flows from this asset are in the form of a three-year, $500 ordinary annuity. If we wanted to earn 10 percent on our money, how much would we offer for this annuity?

From the previous section, we know that we can discount each of these $500 payments back to the present at 10 percent to determine the total present value:

$$
\begin{aligned}
\text{Present value} &= \$500/1.1^1 + 500/1.1^2 + 500/1.1^3 \\
&= \$500/1.10 + 500/1.21 + 500/1.331 \\
&= \$454.55 + 413.22 + 375.66 \\
&= \$1{,}243.43
\end{aligned}
$$

This approach works just fine. However, we will often encounter situations where the number of cash flows is quite large. For example, a typical home mortgage calls for monthly payments over 30 years, for a total of 360 payments. If we were trying to determine the present value of those payments, it would be useful to have a shortcut.

Since the cash flows on an annuity are all the same, we can come up with a very useful variation on the basic present value equation. It turns out that the present value of an annuity of C dollars per period for t periods when the rate of return, or interest rate, is r is given by:

$$
\begin{aligned}
\text{Annuity present value} &= C \times \left(\frac{1 - \text{Present value factor}}{r} \right) \\
&= C \times \left\{ \frac{1 - [1/(1 + r)^t]}{r} \right\}
\end{aligned}
\qquad \textbf{[9.1]}
$$

The term in parentheses on the first line is sometimes called the present value interest factor for annuities and abbreviated PVIFA(r,t).

The expression for the annuity present value may look a little complicated, but it isn't difficult to use. Notice that the term in square brackets on the second line, $1/(1 + r)^t$, is the same present value factor we've been calculating. In our example just above, the interest rate is 10 percent and there are three years involved. The usual present value factor is thus:

$$
\text{Present value factor} = 1/1.1^3 = 1/1.331 = .75131
$$

To calculate the annuity present value factor, we just plug this in:

$$
\begin{aligned}
\text{Annuity present value factor} &= (1 - \text{Present value factor})/r \\
&= (1 - .75131)/.10 \\
&= .248685/.10 = 2.48685
\end{aligned}
$$

Just as we calculated before, the present value of our $500 annuity is then:

$$
\text{Annuity present value} = \$500 \times 2.48685 = \$1{,}243.43
$$

Number of Periods	Interest Rates			
	5%	10%	15%	20%
1	.9524	.9091	.8696	.8333
2	1.8594	1.7355	1.6257	1.5278
3	2.7232	2.4869	2.2832	2.1065
4	3.5460	3.1699	2.8550	2.5887
5	4.3295	3.7908	3.3522	2.9906

TABLE 9.1

Annuity present value interest factors

How Much Can You Afford?   EXAMPLE 9.5

After carefully going over your budget, you have determined you can afford to pay $632 per month towards a new sports car. You call up your local bank and find out that the going rate is 1 percent per month for 48 months. How much can you borrow?

To determine how much you can borrow, we need to calculate the present value of $632 per month for 48 months at 1 percent per month. The loan payments are in ordinary annuity form, so the annuity present value factor is:

$$\text{Annuity PV factor} = (1 - \text{Present value factor})/r$$
$$= [1 - (1/1.01^{48})]/.01$$
$$= (1 - .6203)/.01 = 37.9740$$

With this factor, we can calculate the present value of the 48 payments of $632 each as:

$$\text{Present value} = \$632 \times 37.9740 = \$24,000$$

Therefore, $24,000 is what you can afford to borrow and repay.

Annuity Tables   Just as there are tables for ordinary present value factors, there are tables for annuity factors as well. Table 9.1 contains a few such factors; Table A.3 in Appendix A contains a larger set. To find the annuity present value factor we just calculated, look for the row corresponding to three periods and then find the column for 10 percent. The number you see at that intersection should be 2.4869 (rounded to four decimal places), as we calculated. Once again, try calculating a few of these factors yourself and compare your answers to the ones in the table to make sure you know how to do it. If you are using a financial calculator, just enter $1 as the payment and calculate the present value; the result should be the annuity present value factor.

Annuity Present Values   CALCULATOR HINTS

To find annuity present values with a financial calculator, we need to use the **PMT** key (you were probably wondering what it was for). Compared to finding the present value of a single amount, there are two important differences. First, we enter the annuity cash flow using the **PMT** key, and, second, we don't enter anything for the future value, **FV**. So, for example, the problem we have been examining is a three-year, $500 annuity. If the discount rate is 10 percent, we need to do the following (after clearing out the calculator!):

Enter	3	10	500		
	N	**I/Y**	**PMT**	**PV**	**FV**
Solve for				-1,243.43	

As usual, we get a negative sign on the PV.

SPREADSHEET STRATEGIES

Annuity Present Values

Using a spreadsheet to work the same problem goes like this:

	A	B	C	D	E	F	G
1							
2	**Using a spreadsheet to find annuity present values**						
3							
4	What is the present value of $500 per year for 3 years if the discount rate is 10 percent?						
5	We need to solve for the unknown present value, so we use the formula PV(rate, nper, pmt, fv).						
6							
7	Payment amount per period:	$500					
8	Number of payments:	3					
9	Discount rate:	.1					
10							
11	Annuity present value:	$1,243.43					
12							
13	The formula entered in cell B11 is =PV(B9, B8, -B7, 0); notice that FV is zero and that pmt has a						
14	negative sign on it. Also notice that the discount rate is entered as a decimal, not a percentage.						
15							

Finding the Payment   Suppose you wish to start up a new business that specializes in the latest of health food trends, frozen yak milk. To produce and market your product, the Yakee Doodle Dandy, you need to borrow $100,000. Because it strikes you as unlikely that this particular fad will be long-lived, you propose to pay off the loan quickly by making five equal annual payments. If the interest rate is 18 percent, what will the payments be?

In this case, we know that the present value is $100,000. The interest rate is 18 percent, and there are five years. The payments are all equal, so we need to find the relevant annuity factor and solve for the unknown cash flow:

$$\text{Annuity present value} = \$100,000 = C \times (1 - \text{Present value factor})/r$$
$$\$100,000 = C \times (1 - 1/1.18^5)/.18$$
$$= C \times (1 - .4371)/.18$$
$$= C \times 3.1272$$
$$C = \$100,000/3.1272 = \$31,978$$

Therefore, you'll make five payments of just under $32,000 each.

Annuity Payments

Finding annuity payments is easy with a financial calculator. In our example just above, the PV is $100,000, the interest rate is 18 percent, and there are five years. We find the payment as follows:

Enter	5	18		100,000	
	N	**I/Y**	**PMT**	**PV**	**FV**
Solve for			−31,978		

Here we get a negative sign on the payment because the payment is an outflow for us.

Annuity Payments

Using a spreadsheet to work the same problem goes like this:

	A	B	C	D	E	F	G
1							
2		Using a spreadsheet to find annuity payments					
3							
4	What is the annuity payment if the present value is $100,000, the interest rate is 18 percent, and						
5	there are 5 periods? We need to solve for the unknown payment in an annuity, so we use the						
6	formula PMT (rate, nper, pv, fv)						
7							
8	Annuity present value:	$100,000					
9	Number of payments:	5					
10	Discount rate:	.18					
11							
12	Annuity payment:	($31,977.78)					
13							
14	The formula entered in cell B12 is =PMT(B10, B9, -B8, 0); notice that fv is zero and that the payment						
15	has a negative sign because it is an outflow to us.						

Finding the Number of Payments | EXAMPLE 9.6

You ran a little short on your spring break vacation, so you put $1,000 on your credit card. You can only afford to make the minimum payment of $20 per month. The interest rate on the credit card is 1.5 percent per month. How long will you need to pay off the $1,000?

What we have here is an annuity of $20 per month at 1.5 percent per month for some unknown length of time. The present value is $1,000 (the amount you owe today). We need to do a little algebra (or else use a financial calculator):

$$\$1{,}000 = \$20 \times (1 - \text{Present value factor})/.015$$
$$(\$1{,}000/20) \times .015 = 1 - \text{Present value factor}$$
$$\text{Present value factor} = .25 = 1/(1 + r)^t$$
$$1.015^t = 1/.25 = 4$$

At this point, the problem boils down to asking the following question: How long does it take for your money to quadruple at 1.5 percent per month? Based on our previous chapter, the answer is about 93 months:

$$1.015^{93} = 3.99 \approx 4$$

It will take you about 93/12 = 7.75 years at this rate.

Finding the Number of Payments

To solve this one on a financial calculator, do the following:

Enter	1.5		−20	1,000	
	N	**I/Y**	**PMT**	**PV**	**FV**

Solve for   93.11

Notice that we put a negative sign on the payment you must make, and we have solved for the number of months. You still have to divide by 12 to get our answer. Also, some financial calculators won't report a fractional value for N; they automatically (without telling you) round up to the next whole period (not to the nearest value). With a spreadsheet, use the function =NPER(rate,pmt,pv,fv); be sure to put in a zero for fv and to enter −20 as the payment.

Finding the Rate   The last question we might want to ask concerns the interest rate implicit in an annuity. For example, an insurance company offers to pay you $1,000 per year for 10 years if you will pay $6,710 up front. What rate is implicit in this 10-year annuity?

In this case, we know the present value ($6,710), we know the cash flows ($1,000 per year), and we know the life of the investment (10 years). What we don't know is the discount rate:

$$\$6,710 = \$1,000 \times (1 - \text{Present value factor})/r$$
$$\$6,710/1,000 = 6.71 = \{1 - [1/(1 + r)^{10}]\}/r$$

So, the annuity factor for 10 periods is equal to 6.71, and we need to solve this equation for the unknown value of r. Unfortunately, this is mathematically impossible to do directly. The only way to do it is to use a table or trial and error to find a value for r.

If you look across the row corresponding to 10 periods in Table A.3, you will see a factor of 6.7101 for 8 percent, so we see right away that the insurance company is offering just about 8 percent. Alternatively, we could just start trying different values until we got very close to the answer. Using this trial-and-error approach can be a little tedious, but, fortunately, machines are good at that sort of thing.[1]

To illustrate how to find the answer by trial and error, suppose a relative of yours wants to borrow $3,000. She offers to repay you $1,000 every year for four years. What interest rate are you being offered?

---

[1] Financial calculators rely on trial and error to find the answer. That's why they sometimes appear to be "thinking" before coming up with the answer. Actually, it is possible to directly solve for r if there are fewer than five periods, but it's usually not worth the trouble.

The cash flows here have the form of a four-year, $1,000 annuity. The present value is $3,000. We need to find the discount rate, r. Our goal in doing so is primarily to give you a feel for the relationship between annuity values and discount rates.

We need to start somewhere, and 10 percent is probably as good a place as any to begin. At 10 percent, the annuity factor is:

Annuity present value factor = $(1 - 1/1.10^4)/.10 = 3.1699$

The present value of the cash flows at 10 percent is thus:

Present value = $1,000 \times 3.1699 = $3,169.90

You can see that we're already in the right ballpark.

Is 10 percent too high or too low? Recall that present values and discount rates move in opposite directions: Increasing the discount rate lowers the PV and vice versa. Our present value here is too high, so the discount rate is too low. If we try 12 percent:

Present value = $1,000 \times (1 - 1/1.12^4)/.12 = $3,037.35

Now we're almost there. We are still a little low on the discount rate (because the PV is a little high), so we'll try 13 percent:

Present value = $1,000 \times (1 - 1/1.13^4)/.13 = $2,974.47

This is less than $3,000, so we now know that the answer is between 12 percent and 13 percent, and it looks to be about 12.5 percent. For practice, work at it for a while longer and see if you find that the answer is about 12.59 percent.

Finding the Rate

Alternatively, you could use a financial calculator to do the following:

Enter	4		1,000	-3,000	
	N	**I/Y**	**PMT**	**PV**	**FV**
Solve for		12.59			

Notice that we put a negative sign on the present value (why?). With a spreadsheet, use the function =RATE(nper,pmt,pv,fv); be sure to put in a zero for fv and to enter 1,000 as the payment and −3,000 as the pv.

Future Value for Annuities

On occasion, it's also handy to know a shortcut for calculating the future value of an annuity. As you might guess, there are future value factors for annuities as well as present value factors. In general, the future value factor for an annuity is given by:

$$\text{Annuity FV factor} = (\text{Future value factor} - 1)/r$$
$$= [(1 + r)^t - 1]/r \quad \text{[9.2]}$$

To see how we use annuity future value factors, suppose you plan to contribute $2,000 every year into a retirement account paying 8 percent. If you retire in 30 years, how much will you have?

The number of years here, t, is 30, and the interest rate, r, is 8 percent, so we can calculate the annuity future value factor as:

$$
\begin{aligned}
\text{Annuity FV factor} &= (\text{Future value factor} - 1)/r \\
&= (1.08^{30} - 1)/.08 \\
&= (10.0627 - 1)/.08 \\
&= 113.2832
\end{aligned}
$$

The future value of this 30-year, \$2,000 annuity is thus:

$$
\begin{aligned}
\text{Annuity future value} &= \$2,000 \times 113.2832 \\
&= \$226,566.4
\end{aligned}
$$

CALCULATOR HINTS

Future Values of Annuities

Of course, you could solve this problem using a financial calculator by doing the following:

Enter	30	8	−2,000		
	N	**I/Y**	**PMT**	**PV**	**FV**
Solve for					226,566.42

Notice that we put a negative sign on the payment (why?). With a spreadsheet, use the function =FV(rate,nper,pmt,pv); be sure to put in a zero for pv and to enter −2,000 as the payment.

A Note on Annuities Due

So far, we have only discussed ordinary annuities. These are the most important, but there is a variation that is fairly common. Remember that with an ordinary annuity, the cash flows occur at the end of each period. When you take out a loan with monthly payments, for example, the first loan payment normally occurs one month after you get the loan. However, when you lease an apartment, the first lease payment is usually due immediately. The second payment is due at the beginning of the second month, and so on. A lease is an example of an **annuity due**. An annuity due is an annuity for which the cash flows occur at the beginning of each period. Almost any type of arrangement in which we have to prepay the same amount each period is an annuity due.

> **annuity due**
>
> An annuity for which the cash flows occur at the beginning of the period.

There are several different ways to calculate the value of an annuity due. With a financial calculator, you simply switch it into "due" or "beginning" mode. It is very important to remember to switch it back when you are finished! Another way to calculate the present value of an annuity due can be illustrated with a time line. Suppose an annuity due has five payments of \$400 each, and the relevant discount rate is 10 percent. The time line looks like this:

Notice how the cash flows here are the same as those for a *four*-year ordinary annuity, except that there is an extra \$400 at Time 0. For practice, verify that the present value of a four-year \$400 ordinary annuity at 10 percent is \$1,267.95. If we add on the extra \$400, we get \$1,667.95, which is the present value of this annuity due.

There is an even easier way to calculate the present or future value of an annuity due. If we assume that cash flows occur at the end of each period when they really occur at the beginning, then we discount each one by one period too many. We could fix this by simply multiplying our answer by $(1 + r)$, where r is the discount rate. In fact, the relationship between the value of an annuity due and an ordinary annuity with the same number of payments is just:

Time value applications abound on the Web. See, for example, **www.collegeboard. com**, **www. 1stmortgagedirectory .com**, and **personal.fidelity.com**.

$$\text{Annuity due value} = \text{Ordinary annuity value} \times (1 + r) \qquad [9.3]$$

This works for both present and future values, so calculating the value of an annuity due involves two steps: (1) calculate the present or future value as though it were an ordinary annuity and (2) multiply your answer by $(1 + r)$.

Perpetuities

We've seen that a series of level cash flows can be valued by treating those cash flows as an annuity. An important special case of an annuity arises when the level stream of cash flows continues forever. Such an asset is called a **perpetuity** since the cash flows are perpetual. Perpetuities are also called **consols**, particularly in Canada and the United Kingdom. See Example 9.7 for an important example of a perpetuity.

perpetuity
An annuity in which the cash flows continue forever.

Since a perpetuity has an infinite number of cash flows, we obviously can't compute its value by discounting each one. Fortunately, valuing a perpetuity turns out to be the easiest possible case. The present value of a perpetuity is simply:

consol
A type of perpetuity.

$$\text{PV for a perpetuity} = C/r \qquad [9.4]$$

For example, an investment offers a perpetual cash flow of $500 every year. The return you require on such an investment is 8 percent. What is the value of this investment? The value of this perpetuity is:

$$\text{Perpetuity PV} = C/r = \$500/.08 = \$6,250$$

This concludes our discussion of valuing investments with multiple cash flows. For future reference, Table 9.2 contains a summary of the annuity and perpetuity basic calculations we described. By now, you probably think that you'll just use on-line calculators to handle annuity problems. Before you do, see our nearby *Work the Web* box.

I. Symbols
   PV = Present value, what future cash flows are worth today
   FV_t = Future value, what cash flows are worth in the future at time t
   r = Interest rate, rate of return, or discount rate per period—typically, but not always, one year
   t = Number of periods—typically, but not always, the number of years
   C = Cash amount

II. Future value of C invested per period for t periods at r percent per period
   $FV_t = C \times [(1 + r)^t - 1]/r$
   A series of identical cash flows is called an annuity, and the term $[(1 + r)^t - 1]/r$ is called the *annuity future value factor.*

III. Present value of C per period for t periods at r percent per period
   $PV = C \times \{1 - [1/(1 + r)^t]\}/r$
   The term $\{1 - [1/(1 + r)^t]\}/r$ is called the *annuity present value factor.*

IV. Present value of a perpetuity of C per period
   $PV = C/r$
   A perpetuity has the same cash flow every year forever.

TABLE 9.2

Summary of annuity and perpetuity calculations

WORK THE WEB

A s we discussed in our previous chapter, many web sites have financial calculators. One of these sites is MoneyChimp, which is located at www.datachimp.com. Suppose you are lucky enough to have $2,000,000. You think that you will be able to earn an 8 percent return. How much can you withdraw each year for the next 25 years? Here is what MoneyChimp says:

MoneyChimp Calculator - Netscape	
Mode	**Annuity Payout**
○ Future Value	
○ Present Value	Starting Principal: $ 2000000
○ Rate of Return	Return Rate: 8 %
○ Basic Investment	Years to Pay Out: 25
⦿ Annuity Payout	
○ Bond Yield	Calculate
○ Mortgage	
	Annual Payout Amount: $ 173479.22
○ More...	

According to the MoneyChimp calculator, the answer is $173,479.22. How important is it to understand what you are doing? Calculate this one for yourself, and you should get $187,357.56. Which one is right? You are, of course! What's going on is that MoneyChimp assumes (but does not tell you) that the annuity is in the form of an annuity due, not an ordinary annuity. Recall that, with an annuity due, the payments occur at the beginning of the period rather than the end of the period. The moral of the story is clear: *Caveat calculator.*

EXAMPLE 9.7 | ## Preferred Stock

Preferred stock (or preference stock) is an important example of a perpetuity. When a corporation sells preferred stock, the buyer is promised a fixed cash dividend every period (usually every quarter) forever. This dividend must be paid before any dividend can be paid to regular stockholders, hence the term *preferred*.

Suppose the Fellini Co. wants to sell preferred stock at $100 per share. A very similar issue of preferred stock already outstanding has a price of $40 per share and offers a dividend of $1 every quarter. What dividend will Fellini have to offer if the preferred stock is going to sell?

The issue that is already out has a present value of $40 and a cash flow of $1 every quarter forever. Since this is a perpetuity:

Present value = $40 = $1 × (1/$r$)
r = 2.5%

To be competitive, the new Fellini issue will also have to offer 2.5 percent *per quarter;* so, if the present value is to be $100, the dividend must be such that:

Present value = $100 = C × (1/.025)
C = $2.5 (per quarter)

9.2a   In general, what is the present value of an annuity of *C* dollars per period at a discount rate of *r* per period? The future value?

9.2b   In general, what is the present value of a perpetuity?

COMPARING RATES: THE EFFECT OF | 9.3
COMPOUNDING PERIODS

The last issue we need to discuss has to do with the way interest rates are quoted. This subject causes a fair amount of confusion because rates are quoted in many different ways. Sometimes the way a rate is quoted is the result of tradition, and sometimes it's the result of legislation. Unfortunately, at times, rates are quoted in deliberately deceptive ways to mislead borrowers and investors. We will discuss these topics in this section.

Effective Annual Rates and Compounding

If a rate is quoted as 10 percent compounded semiannually, then what this means is that the investment actually pays 5 percent every six months. A natural question then arises: Is 5 percent every six months the same thing as 10 percent per year? It's easy to see that it is not. If you invest $1 at 10 percent per year, you will have $1.10 at the end of the year. If you invest at 5 percent every six months, then you'll have the future value of $1 at 5 percent for two periods, or:

$$\$1 \times 1.05^2 = \$1.1025$$

This is $.0025 more. The reason is very simple. What has occurred is that your account was credited with $1 × .05 = 5 cents in interest after six months. In the following six months, you earned 5 percent on that nickel, for an extra 5 × .05 = .25 cent.

As our example illustrates, 10 percent compounded semiannually is actually equivalent to 10.25 percent per year. Put another way, we would be indifferent between 10 percent compounded semiannually and 10.25 percent compounded annually. Anytime we have compounding during the year, we need to be concerned about what the rate really is.

In our example, the 10 percent is called a **stated**, or **quoted**, **interest rate**. Other names are used as well. The 10.25 percent, which is actually the rate that you will earn, is called the **effective annual rate (EAR)**. To compare different investments or interest rates, we will always need to convert to effective rates. Some general procedures for doing this are discussed next.

stated interest rate
The interest rate expressed in terms of the interest payment made each period. Also, quoted interest rate.

effective annual rate (EAR)
The interest rate expressed as if it were compounded once per year.

Calculating and Comparing Effective Annual Rates

To see why it is important to work only with effective rates, suppose you've shopped around and come up with the following three rates:

    Bank A: 15 percent, compounded daily
    Bank B: 15.5 percent, compounded quarterly
    Bank C: 16 percent, compounded annually

Which of these is the best if you are thinking of opening a savings account? Which of these is best if they represent loan rates?

To begin, Bank C is offering 16 percent per year. Since there is no compounding during the year, this is the effective rate. Bank B is actually paying $.155/4 = .03875$, or 3.875 percent, per quarter. At this rate, an investment of $1 for four quarters would grow to:

$$\$1 \times 1.03875^4 = \$1.1642$$

The EAR, therefore, is 16.42 percent. For a saver, this is much better than the 16 percent rate Bank C is offering; for a borrower, it's worse.

Bank A is compounding every day. This may seem a little extreme, but it is very common to calculate interest daily. In this case, the daily interest rate is actually:

$$.15/365 = .000411$$

This is .0411 percent per day. At this rate, an investment of $1 for 365 periods would grow to:

$$\$1 \times 1.000411^{365} = \$1.1618$$

The EAR is 16.18 percent. This is not as good as Bank B's 16.42 percent for a saver, and not as good as Bank C's 16 percent for a borrower.

This example illustrates two things. First, the highest quoted rate is not necessarily the best. Second, compounding during the year can lead to a significant difference between the quoted rate and the effective rate. Remember that the effective rate is what you get or what you pay.

If you look at our examples, you see that we computed the EARs in three steps. We first divided the quoted rate by the number of times that the interest is compounded. We then added 1 to the result and raised it to the power of the number of times the interest is compounded. Finally, we subtracted the 1. If we let m be the number of times the interest is compounded during the year, these steps can be summarized simply as:

$$EAR = (1 + Quoted\ rate/m)^m - 1 \qquad \textbf{[9.5]}$$

For example, suppose you were offered 12 percent compounded monthly. In this case, the interest is compounded 12 times a year; so m is 12. You can calculate the effective rate as:

$$
\begin{aligned}
EAR &= (1 + Quoted\ rate/m)^m - 1 \\
&= (1 + .12/12)^{12} - 1 \\
&= 1.01^{12} - 1 \\
&= 1.126825 - 1 \\
&= 12.6825\%
\end{aligned}
$$

EXAMPLE 9.8 | **What's the EAR?**

A bank is offering 12 percent compounded quarterly. If you put $100 in an account, how much will you have at the end of one year? What's the EAR? How much will you have at the end of two years?

The bank is effectively offering 12%/4 = 3% every quarter. If you invest $100 for four periods at 3 percent per period, the future value is:

$$
\begin{aligned}
Future\ value &= \$100 \times 1.03^4 \\
&= \$100 \times 1.1255 \\
&= \$112.55
\end{aligned}
$$

The EAR is 12.55 percent: $100 × (1 + .1255) = $112.55.

We can determine what you would have at the end of two years in two different ways. One way is to recognize that two years is the same as eight quarters. At 3 percent per quarter, after eight quarters, you would have:

$100 \times 1.03^8 = \$100 \times 1.2668 = \$126.68$

Alternatively, we could determine the value after two years by using an EAR of 12.55 percent; so after two years you would have:

$100 \times 1.1255^2 = \$100 \times 1.2688 = \$126.68$

Thus, the two calculations produce the same answer. This illustrates an important point. Anytime we do a present or future value calculation, the rate we use must be an actual or effective rate. In this case, the actual rate is 3 percent per quarter. The effective annual rate is 12.55 percent. It doesn't matter which one we use once we know the EAR.

Quoting a Rate | **EXAMPLE 9.9**

Now that you know how to convert a quoted rate to an EAR, consider going the other way. As a lender, you know you want to actually earn 18 percent on a particular loan. You want to quote a rate that features monthly compounding. What rate do you quote?

In this case, we know that the EAR is 18 percent, and we know that this is the result of monthly compounding. Let q stand for the quoted rate. We thus have:

$$\text{EAR} = (1 + \text{Quoted rate}/m)^m - 1$$
$$.18 = (1 + q/12)^{12} - 1$$
$$1.18 = (1 + q/12)^{12}$$

We need to solve this equation for the quoted rate. This calculation is the same as the ones we did to find an unknown interest rate in Chapter 8:

$$1.18^{(1/12)} = 1 + q/12$$
$$1.18^{.08333} = 1 + q/12$$
$$1.0139 = 1 + q/12$$
$$q = .0139 \times 12$$
$$= 16.68\%$$

Therefore, the rate you would quote is 16.68 percent, compounded monthly.

EARs and APRs

Sometimes it's not altogether clear whether a rate is an effective annual rate or not. A case in point concerns what is called the **annual percentage rate (APR)** on a loan. Truth-in-lending laws in the United States require that lenders disclose an APR on virtually all consumer loans. This rate must be displayed on a loan document in a prominent and unambiguous way.

Given that an APR must be calculated and displayed, an obvious question arises: Is an APR an effective annual rate? Put another way: If a bank quotes a car loan at 12 percent APR, is the consumer actually paying 12 percent interest? Surprisingly, the answer is no. There is some confusion over this point, which we discuss next.

The confusion over APRs arises because lenders are required by law to compute the APR in a particular way. By law, the APR is simply equal to the interest rate per period multiplied by the number of periods in a year. For example, if a bank is charging 1.2 percent per month on car loans, then the APR that must be reported is $1.2\% \times 12 = 14.4\%$. So, an APR is in fact a quoted, or stated, rate in the sense we've been discussing. For

annual percentage rate (APR)

The interest rate charged per period multiplied by the number of periods per year.

example, an APR of 12 percent on a loan calling for monthly payments is really 1 percent per month. The EAR on such a loan is thus:

$$EAR = (1 + APR/12)^{12} - 1$$
$$= 1.01^{12} - 1 = 12.6825\%$$

EXAMPLE 9.10 | **What Rate Are You Paying?**

A typical credit card agreement quotes an interest rate of 18 percent APR. Monthly payments are required. What is the actual interest rate you pay on such a credit card?

Based on our discussion, an APR of 18 percent with monthly payments is really .18/12 = .015, or 1.5 percent, per month. The EAR is thus:

$$EAR = (1 + .18/12)^{12} - 1$$
$$= 1.015^{12} - 1$$
$$= 1.1956 - 1$$
$$= 19.56\%$$

This is the rate you actually pay.

The difference between an APR and an EAR probably won't be all that great, but it is somewhat ironic that truth-in-lending laws sometimes require lenders to be *un*truthful about the actual rate on a loan.

EARs, APRs, Financial Calculators, and Spreadsheets

A financial calculator will convert a quoted rate (or an APR) to an EAR and back. Unfortunately, the specific procedures are too different from calculator to calculator for us to illustrate in general terms; you'll have to consult Appendix D or your calculator's operating manual. Typically, however, what we have called EAR is labeled "EFF" (for *effective*) on a calculator. More troublesome is the fact that what we have called a quoted rate (or an APR) is labeled "NOM" (for *nominal*). Unfortunately, the term *nominal rate* has come to have a different meaning that we will see in our next chapter. So, just remember that *nominal* in this context means quoted or APR.

With a spreadsheet, we can easily do these conversions. To convert a quoted rate (or an APR) to an effective rate in Excel, for example, use the formula EFFECT(nominal_rate,npery), where nominal_rate is the quoted rate or APR and npery is the number of compounding periods per year. Similarly, to convert an EAR to a quoted rate, use NOMINAL(effect_rate,npery), where effect_rate is the EAR.

CONCEPT QUESTIONS

9.3a If an interest rate is given as 12 percent, compounded daily, what do we call this rate?

9.3b What is an APR? What is an EAR? Are they the same thing?

9.3c In general, what is the relationship between a stated interest rate and an effective interest rate? Which is more relevant for financial decisions?

LOAN TYPES AND LOAN AMORTIZATION | 9.4

Whenever a lender extends a loan, some provision will be made for repayment of the principal (the original loan amount). A loan might be repaid in equal installments, for example, or it might be repaid in a single lump sum. Because the way that the principal and interest are paid is up to the parties involved, there are actually an unlimited number of possibilities.

In this section, we describe a few forms of repayment that come up quite often; more complicated forms can usually be built up from these. The three basic types of loans are pure discount loans, interest-only loans, and amortized loans. Working with these loans is a very straightforward application of the present value principles that we have already developed.

Pure Discount Loans

The pure discount loan is the simplest form of loan. With such a loan, the borrower receives money today and repays a single lump sum at some time in the future. A one-year, 10 percent pure discount loan, for example, would require the borrower to repay $1.1 in one year for every dollar borrowed today.

Because a pure discount loan is so simple, we already know how to value one. Suppose a borrower was able to repay $25,000 in five years. If we, acting as the lender, wanted a 12 percent interest rate on the loan, how much would we be willing to lend? Put another way, what value would we assign today to that $25,000 to be repaid in five years? Based on our work in Chapter 8, we know that the answer is just the present value of $25,000 at 12 percent for five years:

$$\text{Present value} = \$25,000/1.12^5$$
$$= \$25,000/1.7623$$
$$= \$14,186$$

Pure discount loans are very common when the loan term is short, say, a year or less. In recent years, they have become increasingly common for much longer periods.

Treasury Bills | EXAMPLE 9.11

When the U.S. government borrows money on a short-term basis (a year or less), it does so by selling what are called *Treasury bills*, or *T-bills* for short. A T-bill is a promise by the government to repay a fixed amount at some time in the future, for example, 3 months or 12 months.

Treasury bills are pure discount loans. If a T-bill promises to repay $10,000 in 12 months, and the market interest rate is 7 percent, how much will the bill sell for in the market?

Since the going rate is 7 percent, the T-bill will sell for the present value of $10,000 to be paid in one year at 7 percent, or:

Present value = $10,000/1.07 = $9,345.79

Interest-Only Loans

A second type of loan has a repayment plan that calls for the borrower to pay interest each period and to repay the entire principal (the original loan amount) at some point in the future. Such loans are called *interest-only loans.* Notice that if there is just one period, a pure discount loan and an interest-only loan are the same thing.

For example, with a three-year, 10 percent, interest-only loan of $1,000, the borrower would pay $1,000 × .10 = $100 in interest at the end of the first and second years. At the end of the third year, the borrower would return the $1,000 along with another $100 in interest for that year. Similarly, a 50-year interest-only loan would call for the borrower to pay interest every year for the next 50 years and then repay the principal. In the extreme, the borrower pays the interest every period forever and never repays any principal. As we discussed earlier in the chapter, the result is a perpetuity.

Most corporate bonds have the general form of an interest-only loan. Because we will be considering bonds in some detail in the next chapter, we will defer a further discussion of them for now.

Amortized Loans

With a pure discount or interest-only loan, the principal is repaid all at once. An alternative is an *amortized loan,* with which the lender may require the borrower to repay parts of the loan amount over time. The process of paying off a loan by making regular principal reductions is called *amortizing* the loan.

A simple way of amortizing a loan is to have the borrower pay the interest each period plus some fixed amount. This approach is common with medium-term business loans. For example, suppose a business takes out a $5,000, five-year loan at 9 percent. The loan agreement calls for the borrower to pay the interest on the loan balance each year and to reduce the loan balance each year by $1,000. Since the loan amount declines by $1,000 each year, it is fully paid in five years.

In the case we are considering, notice that the total payment will decline each year. The reason is that the loan balance goes down, resulting in a lower interest charge each year, while the $1,000 principal reduction is constant. For example, the interest in the first year will be $5,000 × .09 = $450. The total payment will be $1,000 + 450 = $1,450. In the second year, the loan balance is $4,000, so the interest is $4,000 × .09 = $360, and the total payment is $1,360. We can calculate the total payment in each of the remaining years by preparing a simple *amortization schedule* as follows:

Year	Beginning Balance	Total Payment	Interest Paid	Principal Paid	Ending Balance
1	$5,000	$1,450	$ 450	$1,000	$4,000
2	4,000	1,360	360	1,000	3,000
3	3,000	1,270	270	1,000	2,000
4	2,000	1,180	180	1,000	1,000
5	1,000	1,090	90	1,000	0
Totals		$6,350	$1,350	$5,000	

Notice that, in each year, the interest paid is just given by the beginning balance multiplied by the interest rate. Also notice that the beginning balance is given by the ending balance from the previous year.

Probably the most common way of amortizing a loan is to have the borrower make a single, fixed payment every period. Almost all consumer loans (such as car loans) and mortgages work this way. For example, suppose our five-year, 9 percent, $5,000 loan was amortized this way. How would the amortization schedule look?

We first need to determine the payment. From our discussion earlier in the chapter, we know that this loan's cash flows are in the form of an ordinary annuity. In this case, we can solve for the payment as follows:

$$\$5,000 = C \times (1 - 1/1.09^5)/.09$$
$$= C \times (1 - .6499)/.09$$

This gives us:

$$C = \$5,000/3.8897$$
$$= \$1,285.46$$

The borrower will therefore make five equal payments of $1,285.46. Will this pay off the loan? We will check by filling in an amortization schedule.

In our previous example, we knew the principal reduction each year. We then calculated the interest owed to get the total payment. In this example, we know the total payment. We will thus calculate the interest and then subtract it from the total payment to get the principal portion in each payment.

In the first year, the interest is $450, as we calculated before. Since the total payment is $1,285.46, the principal paid in the first year must be:

$$\text{Principal paid} = \$1,285.46 - 450 = \$835.46$$

The ending loan balance is thus:

$$\text{Ending balance} = \$5,000 - 835.46 = \$4,164.54$$

The interest in the second year is $4,164.54 \times .09 = \$374.81$, and the loan balance declines by $1,285.46 - 374.81 = \$910.65$. We can summarize all of the relevant calculations in the following schedule:

Year	Beginning Balance	Total Payment	Interest Paid	Principal Paid	Ending Balance
1	$5,000.00	$1,285.46	$ 450.00	$ 835.46	$4,164.54
2	4,164.54	1,285.46	374.81	910.65	3,253.88
3	3,253.88	1,285.46	292.85	992.61	2,261.27
4	2,261.27	1,285.46	203.51	1,081.95	1,179.32
5	1,179.32	1,285.46	106.14	1,179.32	.00
Totals		$6,427.30	$1,427.31	$5,000.00	

Since the loan balance declines to zero, the five equal payments do pay off the loan. Notice that the interest paid declines each period. This isn't surprising since the loan balance is going down. Given that the total payment is fixed, the principal paid must be rising each period.

If you compare the two loan amortizations in this section, you will see that the total interest is greater for the equal total payment case, $1,427.31 versus $1,350. The reason for this is that the loan is repaid more slowly early on, so the interest is somewhat higher. This doesn't mean that one loan is better than the other; it simply means that one is effectively paid off faster than the other. For example, the principal reduction in the first year is $835.46 in the equal total payment case compared to $1,000 in the first case. Many web sites offer loan amortization schedules. See our nearby *Work the Web* box for an example.

SPREADSHEET
STRATEGIES

Loan Amortization Using a Spreadsheet

Loan amortization is a very common spreadsheet application. To illustrate, we will set up the problem that we have just examined, a five-year, $5,000, 9 percent loan with constant payments. Our spreadsheet looks like this:

	A	B	C	D	E	F	G	H
1								
2				**Using a spreadsheet to amortize a loan**				
3								
4			Loan amount:	$5,000				
5			Interest rate:	.09				
6			Loan term:	5				
7			Loan payment:	**$1,285.46**				
8				Note: payment is calculated using PMT(rate,nper,-pv,fv).				
9		Amortization table:						
10								
11		Year	Beginning	Total	Interest	Principal	Ending	
12			Balance	Payment	Paid	Paid	Balance	
13		1	$5,000.00	$1,285.46	$450.00	$835.46	$4,164.54	
14		2	4,164.54	1,285.46	374.81	910.65	3,253.88	
15		3	3,253.88	1,285.46	292.85	992.61	2,261.27	
16		4	2,261.27	1,285.46	203.51	1,081.95	1,179.32	
17		5	1,179.32	1,285.46	106.14	1,179.32	.00	
18		Totals		$6,427.31	$1,427.31	$5,000.00		
19								
20		Formulas in the amortization table:						
21								
22		Year	Beginning	Total	Interest	Principal	Ending	
23			Balance	Payment	Paid	Paid	Balance	
24		1	=+D4	=$D$7	=+$D$5*C13	=+D13-E13	=+C13-F13	
25		2	=+G13	=$D$7	=+$D$5*C14	=+D14-E14	=+C14-F14	
26		3	=+G14	=$D$7	=+$D$5*C15	=+D15-E15	=+C15-F15	
27		4	=+G15	=$D$7	=+$D$5*C16	=+D16-E16	=+C16-F16	
28		5	=+G16	=$D$7	=+$D$5*C17	=+D17-E17	=+C17-F17	
29								
30		Note: totals in the amortization table are calculated using the SUM formula.						
31								

Preparing an amortization table is one of the more tedious time value of money applications. Using a spreadsheet makes it relatively easy, but there are also web sites available that will prepare an amortization table very quickly and simply. One such site is LendingTree. Their web site, www.lendingtree.com, has a mortgage calculator for home loans, but the same calculations apply to most other types of loans such as car loans and student loans. To illustrate, suppose you graduate with a student loan of $20,000. You will repay the loan over the next 10 years at 7.625 percent. What are your monthly payments? Using the calculator we get:

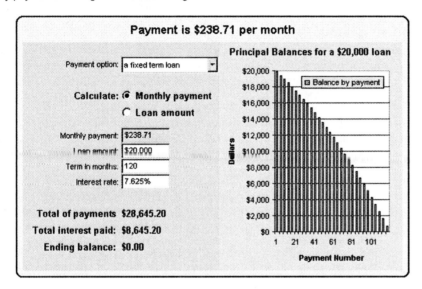

Try this example yourself and hit the "View Report" button. You will find that your first payment will consist of $111.63 in principal and $127.08 in interest. Over the life of the loan you will pay a total of $8,645.20 in interest.

We close out this discussion by noting that one type of loan may be particularly important to you. Student loans are an important source of financing for many college students, helping to cover the cost of tuition, books, new cars, condominiums, and many other things. Sometimes students do not seem to fully realize that such loans have a serious drawback: They must be repaid. See our nearby *Reality Bytes* box for a discussion.

CONCEPT QUESTIONS

9.4a   What is a pure discount loan?

9.4b   What does it mean to amortize a loan?

An Unwelcome Christmas Present

If you are reading this, we can assume that you are a college student. While you receive an education in college, and studies show that college graduates earn a higher salary on average than nongraduates, you might receive an unwelcome Christmas present if you graduate in May: student loan payments. About one-half of all college students graduate with student loans, and over 90 percent of the loans are Stafford loans. Stafford loans are available through lenders such as Sallie Mae, on-line lenders, or, in some cases, your college. Stafford loans must be paid off in 10 years, but there is a six-month grace period from the time you graduate until the first payment must be made. The good news is that the current interest rate for money borrowed since 1998 is 5.99 percent, the lowest in the 36-year history of the Stafford loan program.

If you have student loans, you went through an introductory program. Just in case you forgot, here are several of the repayment options. First, you can make equal monthly payments like most other loans. A second option is to pay only the interest on the loan for up to four years, and then begin making principal and interest payments. This means your payments at the end of the loan are higher than the equal payment option. A third option is to make payments based on a percentage of your salary. A fourth option is a graduated payment option that increases your monthly payments on a predetermined schedule. Finally, you can consolidate your loans one time. If the loan balance is high enough, you may be able to extend your payment for up to 30 years.

So how do student loans work in practice? A recent graduate from the University of Maryland with a master's degree in creative writing graduated with $40,000 in student loans. Her loan payments were $442 a month, a payment that was difficult to make on her salary as a fundraiser. She considered the percentage of salary option, which would have lowered her monthly payments to about $200 per month. However, she realized that this was just putting off the inevitable, so she took a second job to make up the difference.

A recent master's graduate from law school took a different route. His student loans totaled $109,000 and required monthly payments of $1,200 per month for 10 years. The option chosen by this lawyer was to consolidate his loans and extend his payments to 30 years. This reduced his monthly payments to about $640 per month.

A Chicago couple is using a third solution. Both the husband and wife are doctors. The wife is out of her residency and employed full time, while the husband is finishing his last year of residency. What is most unusual about this couple is the amount of student loan debt. The wife's student loan balance is $234,000, the husband's student loan balance is $310,000, and the couple has a $156,000 mortgage! The wife's student loan repayments have already started and amount to $1,750 per month. So how is the couple handling this? They are paying a total of $2,250 per month towards the wife's student loans. This will reduce the repayment period from 22 years to 13 years. The couple is also paying an additional $100 per month on their $1,500 mortgage payment. Fortunately, when the husband's residency ends, he expects his salary to triple. The couple will need it. His loan payments will be $2,349 per month. And you thought your student loan was high! Maybe MD stands for "mucho debt"!

SUMMARY AND CONCLUSIONS

This chapter rounds out your understanding of fundamental concepts related to the time value of money and discounted cash flow valuation. Several important topics were covered, including:

1. There are two ways of calculating present and future values when there are multiple cash flows. Both approaches are straightforward extensions of our earlier analysis of single cash flows.

2. A series of constant cash flows that arrive or are paid at the end of each period is called an ordinary annuity, and we described some useful shortcuts for determining the present and future values of annuities.

3. Interest rates can be quoted in a variety of ways. For financial decisions, it is important that any rates being compared be first converted to effective rates. The

relationship between a quoted rate, such as an annual percentage rate, or APR, and an effective annual rate, or EAR, is given by:

$$EAR = (1 + \text{Quoted rate}/m)^m - 1$$

where m is the number of times during the year the money is compounded, or, equivalently, the number of payments during the year.

4. Many loans are annuities. The process of paying off a loan gradually is called amortizing the loan, and we discussed how amortization schedules are prepared and interpreted.

CHAPTER REVIEW AND SELF-TEST PROBLEMS

9.1 Present Values with Multiple Cash Flows. A first-round draft choice quarterback has been signed to a three-year, $10 million contract. The details provide for an immediate cash bonus of $1 million. The player is to receive $2 million in salary at the end of the first year, $3 million the next, and $4 million at the end of the last year. Assuming a 10 percent discount rate, is this package worth $10 million? How much is it worth?

9.2 Future Value with Multiple Cash Flows. You plan to make a series of deposits in an interest-bearing account. You will deposit $1,000 today, $2,000 in two years, and $8,000 in five years. If you withdraw $3,000 in three years and $5,000 in seven years, how much will you have after eight years if the interest rate is 9 percent? What is the present value of these cash flows?

9.3 Annuity Present Value. You are looking into an investment that will pay you $12,000 per year for the next 10 years. If you require a 15 percent return, what is the most you would pay for this investment?

9.4 APR versus EAR. The going rate on student loans is quoted as 9 percent APR. The terms of the loan call for monthly payments. What is the effective annual rate, or EAR, on such a student loan?

9.5 It's the Principal That Matters. Suppose you borrow $10,000. You are going to repay the loan by making equal annual payments for five years. The interest rate on the loan is 14 percent per year. Prepare an amortization schedule for the loan. How much interest will you pay over the life of the loan?

9.6 Just a Little Bit Each Month. You've recently finished your MBA at the Darnit School. Naturally, you must purchase a new BMW immediately. The car costs about $21,000. The bank quotes an interest rate of 15 percent APR for a 72-month loan with a 10 percent down payment. What will your monthly payment be? What is the effective interest rate on the loan?

■ Answers to Chapter Review and Self-Test Problems

9.1 Obviously, the package is not worth $10 million because the payments are spread out over three years. The bonus is paid today, so it's worth $1 million. The present values for the three subsequent salary payments are:

$$\$2/1.1 + 3/1.1^2 + 4/1.1^3 \quad = \$2/1.1 + 3/1.21 + 4/1.331$$
$$= \$7.3028$$

The package is worth a total of $8.3028 million.

9.2   We will calculate the future value for each of the cash flows separately and then add the results up. Notice that we treat the withdrawals as negative cash flows:

$$
\begin{aligned}
\$1,000 \times 1.09^8 &= \quad \$1,000 \times 1.9926 = \$ \quad 1,992.60 \\
\$2,000 \times 1.09^6 &= \quad \$2,000 \times 1.6771 = \quad 3,354.20 \\
-\$3,000 \times 1.09^5 &= -\$3,000 \times 1.5386 = \quad -4,615.87 \\
\$8,000 \times 1.09^3 &= \quad \$8,000 \times 1.2950 = \quad 10,360.23 \\
-\$5,000 \times 1.09^1 &= -\$5,000 \times 1.0900 = \quad \underline{-5,450.00} \\
& \qquad\qquad \text{Total future value} = \underline{\underline{\$ \quad 5,641.12}}
\end{aligned}
$$

This value includes a small rounding error.

To calculate the present value, we could discount each cash flow back to the present or we could discount back a single year at a time. However, since we already know that the future value in eight years is $5,641.12, the easy way to get the PV is just to discount this amount back eight years:

$$
\begin{aligned}
\text{Present value} &= \$5,641.12/1.09^8 \\
&= \$5,641.12/1.9926 \\
&= \$2,831.03
\end{aligned}
$$

We again ignore a small rounding error. For practice, you can verify that this is what you get if you discount each cash flow back separately.

9.3   The most you would be willing to pay is the present value of $12,000 per year for 10 years at a 15 percent discount rate. The cash flows here are in ordinary annuity form, so the relevant present value factor is:

$$
\begin{aligned}
\text{Annuity present value factor} &= [1 - (1/1.15^{10})]/.15 \\
&= (1 - .2472)/.15 \\
&= 5.0188
\end{aligned}
$$

The present value of the 10 cash flows is thus:

$$
\begin{aligned}
\text{Present value} &= \$12,000 \times 5.0188 \\
&= \$60,225
\end{aligned}
$$

This is the most you would pay.

9.4   A rate of 9 percent with monthly payments is actually $9\%/12 = .75\%$ per month. The EAR is thus:

$$
\text{EAR} = (1 + .09/12)^{12} - 1 = 9.38\%
$$

9.5   We first need to calculate the annual payment. With a present value of $10,000, an interest rate of 14 percent, and a term of five years, the payment can be determined from:

$$
\begin{aligned}
\$10,000 &= \text{Payment} \times (1 - 1/1.14^5)/.14 \\
&= \text{Payment} \times 3.4331
\end{aligned}
$$

Therefore, the payment is $10,000/3.4331 = $2,912.84 (actually, it's $2,912.8355; this will create some small rounding errors in the schedule below). We can now prepare the amortization schedule as follows:

Year	Beginning Balance	Total Payment	Interest Paid	Principal Paid	Ending Balance
1	$10,000.00	$ 2,912.84	$1,400.00	$ 1,512.84	$8,487.16
2	8,487.16	2,912.84	1,188.20	1,724.63	6,762.53
3	6,762.53	2,912.84	946.75	1,966.08	4,796.45
4	4,796.45	2,912.84	671.50	2,241.33	2,555.12
5	2,555.12	2,912.84	357.72	2,555.12	.00
Totals		$14,564.17	$4,564.17	$10,000.00	

9.6 The cash flows on the car loan are in annuity form, so we only need to find the payment. The interest rate is $15\%/12 = 1.25\%$ per month, and there are 72 months. The first thing we need is the annuity factor for 72 periods at 1.25 percent per period:

$$
\begin{aligned}
\text{Annuity present value factor} &= (1 - \text{Present value factor})/r \\
&= [1 - (1/1.0125^{72})]/.0125 \\
&= [1 - (1/2.4459)]/.0125 \\
&= (1 - .4088)/.0125 \\
&= 47.2925
\end{aligned}
$$

The present value is the amount we finance. With a 10 percent down payment, we will be borrowing 90 percent of $21,000, or $18,900.

So, to find the payment, we need to solve for C in the following:

$$
\begin{aligned}
\$18,900 &= C \times \text{Annuity present value factor} \\
&= C \times 47.2925
\end{aligned}
$$

Rearranging things a bit, we have:

$$
\begin{aligned}
C &= \$18,900 \times (1/47.2925) \\
&= \$18,900 \times .02115 \\
&= \$399.64
\end{aligned}
$$

Your payment is just under $400 per month.

The actual interest rate on this loan is 1.25 percent per month. Based on our work in the chapter, we can calculate the effective annual rate as:

$$\text{EAR} = 1.0125^{12} - 1 = 16.08\%$$

The effective rate is about one point higher than the quoted rate.

CRITICAL THINKING AND CONCEPTS REVIEW

9.1 **Annuity Factors.**   There are four pieces to an annuity present value. What are they?

9.2 **Annuity Period.**   As you increase the length of time involved, what happens to the present value of an annuity? What happens to the future value?

9.3   **Interest Rates.**   What happens to the future value of an annuity if you increase the rate r? What happens to the present value?

9.4   **Present Value.**   The Tri-State Megabucks lottery advertises a $500,000 prize; however, the lump-sum option is $250,000. Is this deceptive advertising?

9.5   **Present Value.**   If you were an athlete negotiating a contract, would you want a big signing bonus payable immediately and smaller payments in the future, or vice versa? How about looking at it from the team's perspective?

9.6   **Present Value.**   Suppose two athletes sign 10-year contracts for $80 million. In one case, we're told that the $80 million will be paid in 10 equal installments. In the other case, we're told that the $80 million will be paid in 10 installments, but the installments will increase by 5 percent per year. Who got the better deal?

9.7   **APR and EAR.**   Should lending laws be changed to require lenders to report EARs instead of APRs? Why or why not?

9.8   **Time Value.**   On subsidized Stafford loans, a common source of financial aid for college students, interest does not begin to accrue until repayment begins. Who receives a bigger subsidy, a freshman or a senior? Explain.

9.9   **Time Value.**   In words, how would you go about valuing the subsidy on a subsidized Stafford loan?

9.10   **Time Value.**   Eligibility for a subsidized Stafford loan is based on current financial need. However, both subsidized and unsubsidized Stafford loans are repaid out of future income. Given this, do you see a possible objection to having two types?

QUESTIONS AND PROBLEMS

www.mhhe.com/rwj
Spreadsheet Templates 3, 4, 7, 31

Basic
(Questions 1–28)

1. **Present Value and Multiple Cash Flows.**   JD Shaved Ice Co. has identified an investment project with the following cash flows. If the discount rate is 10 percent, what is the present value of these cash flows? What is the present value at 18 percent? At 24 percent?

Year	Cash Flow
1	$ 700
2	300
3	1,200
4	1,600

2. **Present Value and Multiple Cash Flows.**   Investment X offers to pay you $4,000 per year for 10 years, whereas Investment Y offers to pay you $8,000 per year for 4 years. Which of these cash flow streams has the higher present value if the discount rate is 5 percent? If the discount rate is 15 percent?

3. **Future Value and Multiple Cash Flows.**   Officer, Inc., has identified an investment project with the following cash flows. If the discount rate is 8 percent,

what is the future value of these cash flows in Year 4? What is the future value at a discount rate of 11 percent? At 24 percent?

Year	Cash Flow
1	$ 500
2	900
3	1,100
4	1,300

4. **Calculating Annuity Present Value.** An investment offers $6,000 per year for 15 years, with the first payment occurring 1 year from now. If the required return is 8 percent, what is the value of the investment? What would the value be if the payments occurred for 40 years? For 75 years? Forever?

5. **Calculating Annuity Cash Flows.** If you put up $10,000 today in exchange for a 9.5 percent, 12-year annuity, what will the annual cash flow be?

6. **Calculating Annuity Values.** Your company will generate $50,000 in revenue each year for the next eight years from a new information database. The computer system needed to set up the database costs $250,000. If you can borrow the money to buy the computer system at 8.75 percent annual interest, can you afford the new system?

7. **Calculating Annuity Values.** If you deposit $2,000 at the end of each of the next 20 years into an account paying 7.5 percent interest, how much money will you have in the account in 20 years? How much will you have if you make deposits for 40 years?

8. **Calculating Annuity Values.** You want to have $50,000 in your savings account seven years from now, and you're prepared to make equal annual deposits into the account at the end of each year. If the account pays 3.75 percent interest, what amount must you deposit each year?

9. **Calculating Annuity Values.** Biktimirov's Bank offers you a $20,000, seven-year term loan at 11 percent annual interest. What will your annual loan payment be?

10. **Calculating Perpetuity Values.** Moe's Life Insurance Co. is trying to sell you an investment policy that will pay you and your heirs $10,000 per year forever. If the required return on this investment is 9 percent, how much will you pay for the policy?

11. **Calculating Perpetuity Values.** In the previous problem, suppose Moe's told you the policy costs $120,000. At what interest rate would this be a fair deal?

12. **Calculating EAR.** Find the EAR in each of the following cases:

Stated Rate (APR)	Number of Times Compounded	Effective Rate (EAR)
7%	Quarterly	
9	Monthly	
12	Daily	
16	Semiannually	

13. Calculating APR.   Find the APR, or stated rate, in each of the following cases:

Stated Rate (APR)	Number of Times Compounded	Effective Rate (EAR)
	Semiannually	9%
	Monthly	19
	Weekly	8
	Daily	15

14. Calculating EAR.   First National Bank charges 12.6 percent compounded monthly on its business loans. First United Bank charges 12.8 percent compounded semiannually. As a potential borrower, which bank would you go to for a new loan?

15. Calculating APR.   Buckeye Credit Corp. wants to earn an effective annual return on its consumer loans of 16 percent per year. The bank uses daily compounding on its loans. What interest rate is the bank required by law to report to potential borrowers? Explain why this rate is misleading to an uninformed borrower.

16. Calculating Future Values.   What is the future value of $1,420 in 12 years assuming an interest rate of 10 percent compounded semiannually?

17. Calculating Future Values.   Lowpay Credit Bank is offering 2.6 percent compounded daily on its savings accounts. If you deposit $5,000 today, how much will you have in the account in five years? In 10 years? In 20 years?

18. Calculating Present Values.   An investment will pay you $60,000 in six years. If the appropriate discount rate is 8 percent compounded daily, what is the present value?

19. EAR versus APR.   Ricky Ripov's Pawn Shop charges an interest rate of 20 percent per month on loans to its customers. Like all lenders, Ricky must report an APR to consumers. What rate should the shop report? What is the effective annual rate?

20. Calculating Loan Payments.   You want to buy a new sports coupe for $52,350, and the finance office at the dealership has quoted you an 8.6 percent APR loan for 60 months to buy the car. What will your monthly payments be? What is the effective annual rate on this loan?

21. Calculating Number of Periods.   One of your customers is delinquent on his accounts payable balance. You've mutually agreed to a repayment schedule of $400 per month. You will charge 1.4 percent per month interest on the overdue balance. If the current balance is $11,652, how long will it take for the account to be paid off?

22. Calculating EAR.   Friendly's Quick Loans, Inc., offers you "three for four, or I knock on your door." This means you get $3 today and repay $4 when you get your paycheck in one week (or else). What's the effective annual return Friendly's earns on this lending business? If you were brave enough to ask, what APR would Friendly's say you were paying?

23. Valuing Perpetuities.   Maybepay Life Insurance Co. is selling a perpetual annuity contract that pays $2,000 monthly. The contract currently sells for $130,000. What is the monthly return on this investment vehicle? What is the APR? The effective annual return?

24. Calculating Annuity Future Values.   You are to make monthly deposits of $200 into a retirement account that pays 11 percent interest compounded monthly. If your first deposit will be made one month from now, how large will your retirement account be in 30 years?

25. **Calculating Annuity Future Values.** In the previous problem, suppose you make $2,400 annual deposits into the same retirement account. How large will your account balance be in 30 years?

26. **Calculating Annuity Present Values.** Beginning three months from now, you want to be able to withdraw $1,500 each quarter from your bank account to cover college expenses over the next four years. If the account pays .50 percent interest per quarter, how much do you need to have in your bank account today to meet your expense needs over the next four years?

27. **Discounted Cash Flow Analysis.** If the appropriate discount rate for the following cash flows is 10 percent, what is the present value of the cash flows?

Year	Cash Flow
1	$600
2	800
3	400
4	900

28. **Discounted Cash Flow Analysis.** If the appropriate discount rate for the following cash flows is 11.65 percent per year, what is the present value of the cash flows?

Year	Cash Flow
1	$1,500
2	3,200
3	6,800
4	8,100

29. **Simple Interest versus Compound Interest.** First Simple Bank pays 7 percent simple interest on its investment accounts. If First Complex Bank pays interest on its accounts compounded annually, what rate should the bank set if it wants to match First Simple Bank over an investment horizon of 10 years?

Intermediate
(Questions 29–56)

30. **Calculating Annuities Due.** You want to buy a new sports car from Muscle Motors for $68,000. The contract is in the form of a 60-month annuity due at a 9.5 percent APR. What will your monthly payment be?

31. **Calculating Interest Expense.** You receive a credit card application from Shady Banks Savings and Loan offering an introductory rate of 1.80 percent per year, compounded monthly for the first six months, increasing thereafter to 21 percent compounded monthly. Assuming you transfer the $5,000 balance from your existing credit card and make no subsequent payments, how much interest will you owe at the end of the first year?

32. **Calculating the Number of Periods.** You are saving to buy a $100,000 house. There are two competing banks in your area, both offering certificates of deposit yielding 5 percent. How long will it take your initial $72,000 investment to reach the desired level at First Bank, which pays simple interest? How long at Second Bank, which compounds interest monthly?

33. **Calculating Future Values.** You have an investment that will pay you 1.12 percent per month. How much will you have per dollar invested in one year? In two years?

34. **Calculating the Number of Periods.** You have $500 today. You need $720. If you earn .75 percent per month, how many months will you wait?

35. **Comparing Cash Flow Streams.**   You've just joined the investment banking firm of Dewey, Cheatum, and Howe. They've offered you two different salary arrangements. You can have $6,100 per month for the next two years, or you can have $4,500 per month for the next two years, along with a $30,000 signing bonus today. If the interest rate is 7 percent compounded monthly, which do you prefer?

36. **Calculating Present Value of Annuities.**   Peter Lynchpin wants to sell you an investment contract that pays equal $15,000 amounts at the end of each of the next 20 years. If you require an effective annual return of 11 percent on this investment, how much will you pay for the contract today?

37. **Calculating Rates of Return.**   You're trying to choose between two different investments, both of which have up-front costs of $40,000. Investment G returns $70,000 in six years. Investment H returns $120,000 in 12 years. Which of these investments has the higher return?

38. **Present Value and Interest Rates.**   What is the relationship between the value of an annuity and the level of interest rates? Suppose you just bought a 10-year annuity of $4,000 per year at the current interest rate of 10 percent per year. What happens to the value of your investment if interest rates suddenly drop to 5 percent? What if interest rates suddenly rise to 15 percent?

39. **Calculating the Number of Payments.**   You're prepared to make monthly payments of $120, beginning at the end of this month, into an account that pays 12 percent interest compounded monthly. How many payments will you have made when your account balance reaches $40,000?

40. **Calculating Annuity Present Values.**   You want to borrow $50,000 from your local bank to buy a new sailboat. You can afford to make monthly payments of $1,300, but no more. Assuming monthly compounding, what is the highest rate you can afford on a 60-month APR loan?

41. **Calculating Present Values.**   In the 1994 NBA draft, no one was surprised when the Milwaukee Bucks took Glenn "Big Dog" Robinson with the first pick. But Robinson wanted big bucks from the Bucks: a 13-year deal worth a total of $100 million. He had to settle for about $68 million over 10 years. His contract called for $2.9 million the first year, with annual raises of $870,000. So, how big a bite did Big Dog really take? Assume a 12 percent discount rate.

42. **Calculating Present Values.**   In our previous question, we looked at the numbers for Big Dog's basketball contract. Now let's take a look at the terms for Shaquille "Shaq" O'Neal, the number one pick in 1992 who was drafted by the Orlando Magic. Shaquille signed a seven-year contract with estimated total payments of about $40 million. Although the precise terms were not disclosed, it was reported that Shaq would receive a salary of $3 million the first year, with raises of $900,000 each year thereafter. If the cash flows are discounted at the same 12 percent discount rate we used for Robinson, does the "Shaq Attack" result in the same kind of numbers? Did Robinson achieve his goal of being paid more than any other rookie in NBA history, including Shaq? Are the different contract lengths a factor? (Hint: Yes.)

43. **EAR versus APR.**   You have just purchased a new warehouse. To finance the purchase, you've arranged for a 30-year mortgage loan for 80 percent of the $1,450,000 purchase price. The monthly payment on this loan will be $9,800. What is the APR on this loan? The EAR?

44. **Present Value and Break-Even Interest.**   Consider a firm with a contract to sell an asset for $100,000 three years from now. The asset costs $67,000 to produce today.

Given a relevant discount rate on this asset of 12 percent per year, will the firm make a profit on this asset? At what rate does the firm just break even?

45. **Discount Interest Loans.** This question illustrates what is known as *discount interest.* Imagine you are discussing a loan with a somewhat unscrupulous lender. You want to borrow $12,000 for one year. The interest rate is 10 percent. You and the lender agree that the interest on the loan will be .10 × $12,000 = $1,200. So the lender deducts this interest amount from the loan up front and gives you $10,800. In this case, we say that the discount is $1,200. What's wrong here?

46. **Calculating Annuities Due.** As discussed in the text, an ordinary annuity assumes equal payments at the end of each period over the life of the annuity. An *annuity due* is the same thing except the payments occur at the beginning of each period instead. Thus, a three-year annual annuity due would have periodic payment cash flows occurring at Years 0, 1, and 2, whereas a three-year annual ordinary annuity would have periodic payment cash flows occurring at Years 1, 2, and 3.

    a. At a 10 percent annual discount rate, find the present value of a four-year ordinary annuity contract of $750 payments.

    b. Find the present value of the same contract if it is an annuity due.

47. **Present Value and Interest Rates.** You've just won the U.S. Lottery. Lottery officials offer you the choice of two alternative payouts: either $3 million today or $10 million 10 years from now. Which payout will you choose if the relevant discount rate is 0 percent? If it is 10 percent? If it is 20 percent?

48. **Calculating Present Values.** A 5-year annuity of 10 $5,000 semiannual payments will begin 9 years from now, with the first payment coming 9.5 years from now. If the discount rate is 15 percent compounded semiannually, what is the value of this annuity five years from now? What is the value three years from now? What is the current value of the annuity?

49. **Present Value and Multiple Cash Flows.** What is the present value of $920 per year, at a discount rate of 10 percent, if the first payment is received 5 years from now and the last payment is received 20 years from now?

50. **Variable Interest Rates.** A 10-year annuity pays $1,500 per month, and payments are made at the end of each month. If the interest rate is 13 percent compounded monthly for the first four years, and 9 percent compounded monthly thereafter, what is the present value of the annuity?

51. **Comparing Cash Flow Streams.** You have your choice of two investment accounts. Investment A is a 10-year annuity that features end-of-month $1,500 payments and has an interest rate of 9 percent compounded monthly. Investment B is a 7 percent annually compounded lump-sum investment, also good for 10 years. How much money would you need to invest in B today for it to be worth as much as Investment A 10 years from now?

52. **Calculating Present Value of a Perpetuity.** Given an interest rate of 7.75 percent per year, what is the value at date $t = 9$ of a perpetual stream of $510 payments that begin at date $t = 14$?

53. **Calculating EAR.** A local finance company quotes a 15 percent interest rate on one-year loans. So, if you borrow $20,000, the interest for the year will be $3,000. Because you must repay a total of $23,000 in one year, the finance company requires you to pay $23,000/12, or $1,916.67, per month over the next 12 months. Is this a 15 percent loan? What rate would legally have to be quoted? What is the effective annual rate?

54. **Calculating Future Values.**   If today is Year 0, what is the future value of the following cash flows five years from now? What is the future value 10 years from now? Assume a discount rate of 10.2 percent per year.

Year	Cash Flow
2	$30,000
3	45,000
5	75,000

55. **Amortization with Equal Payments.**   Prepare an amortization schedule for a three-year loan of $60,000. The interest rate is 11 percent per year, and the loan calls for equal annual payments. How much interest is paid in the third year? How much total interest is paid over the life of the loan?

56. **Amortization with Equal Principal Payments.**   Rework Problem 55 assuming that the loan agreement calls for a principal reduction of $20,000 every year instead of equal annual payments.

What's On the Web?

9.1   **Annuity Future Value.**   The St. Louis Federal Reserve Board has files listing historical interest rates on their web site www.stls.frb.org. Follow the link for "FRED II® (Federal Reserve Economic Data)." You will find listings for Moody's Seasoned Aaa Corporate Bond Yield and Moody's Seasoned Baa Corporate Bond Yield. (These rates are discussed in the next chapter.) If you invest $2,000 per year for the next 40 years at the most recent Aaa yield, how much will you have? What if you invest the same amount at the Baa yield?

9.2   **Loan Payments.**   Finding the time necessary until you pay off a loan is simple if you make equal payments each month. However, when paying off credit cards many individuals only make the minimum monthly payment, which is generally $10 or 2 percent to 3 percent of the balance, whichever is greater. You can find a credit card calculator at www.fincalc.com. You currently owe $10,000 on a credit card with a 17 percent interest rate and a minimum payment of $10 or 2 percent of your balance, whichever is greater. How soon will you pay off this debt if you make the minimum payment each month? How much total interest will you pay?

9.3   **Annuity Payments.**   Go to www.fcfcorp.com/onlinecalc.htm. Use the calculator to solve this problem. If you have $1,500,000 when you retire and want to withdraw an equal amount for the next 30 years, how much can you withdraw each year if you earn 7 percent? What if you earn 9 percent?

9.4   **Annuity Payments.**   The St. Louis Federal Reserve Board has files listing historical interest rates on their web site www.stls.frb.org. Follow the link for "FRED II® (Federal Reserve Economic Data)." You will find a listing for the Bank Prime Loan Rate. The file lists the monthly prime rate since January 1949 (1949.01). What is the most recent prime rate? What is the highest prime rate over this period? If you bought a house for $150,000 at the current prime rate on a 30-year mortgage with monthly payments, how much are your payments? If you had purchased the house at the same price when the prime rate was at its highest, what would your monthly payments have been?

9.5   **Loan Amortization.**   Interest.com, located at www.interest.com, has a financial calculator that will prepare a loan amortization table based on your inputs. First, follow the "Track Mortgage Rates" link and then the "View Current Mortgage Rate Averages" to find the current average interest rate for a 30-year conventional fixed rate mortgage. Now follow the "Mortgage Calculators" link, and then "Calculate the monthly payments for a particular mortgage loan" link. You want to buy a house for $200,000 on a 30-year mortgage with monthly payments at the rate quoted on the site. What percentage of your first month's payment is principal? What percentage of your last month's payment is principal? What is the total interest paid on the loan? When do you have one-half of the principal repaid? How do these numbers change if mortgage rates increase 1 percent?

Part III
Economics

The Challenge of Economics

The twentieth century was very good to the United States of America. At the beginning of that century, life was hard and short. Life expectancy was only 47 years for whites and a shockingly low 33 years for blacks and other minorities. Those people who survived infancy faced substantial risk of early death from tuberculosis, influenza, pneumonia, or gastritis. Measles, syphilis, whooping cough, malaria, typhoid, and smallpox were all life-threatening diseases at the turn of the last century.

Work was a lot harder back then, too. In 1900, one-third of all U.S. families lived on farms, where the workday began before sunrise and lasted all day. Those who lived in the cities typically worked 60 hours a week for wages of only 22 cents an hour. Hours were long, jobs were physically demanding, and workplaces were often dirty and unsafe.

People didn't have much to show for all that work. By today's standards nearly everyone was poor back then. The average income per person was less than $4,000 per year (in today's dollars). Very few people had telephones and even fewer had cars. There were no television sets, no home freezers, no microwaves, no dishwashers or central air-conditioning, and no computers. Even indoor plumbing was a luxury. Only a small elite went to college; an eighth-grade education was the norm.

All of this, of course, sounds like ancient history. Today, most of us take new cars, central air and heat, remote-control TVs, flush toilets, cell phones, and even long weekends for granted. We seldom imagine what life would be like without the abundance of goods and services we encounter daily. Nor do we often imagine how hard work might be had factories, offices, and homes not been transformed by technology.

We ought to ponder, however, how we got so affluent. Was it our high moral standards that made us rich? Was it our religious convictions? Did politics have anything to do with it? Did extending suffrage to women, ending prohibition, or repealing the military draft raise our living standards? Did the many wars fought in the twentieth century enhance our material well-being? Was the tremendous expansion of the public sector the catalyst for growth? Were we just lucky?

Some people say America has prospered because our nation was blessed with an abundance of natural resources. But other countries are larger. Many others have more oil, more arable land, more gold, more people, and more math majors. Yet few nations have prospered as much as the United States. Indeed, many countries today are no better off than the United States was a century ago.

Students of history can't ignore the role that economic *systems* might have played in these developments. In the mid-nineteenth century, Karl Marx predicted that the capitalist *system* of private ownership would eventually self-destruct. The capitalists who owned the land, the factories, and the machinery would continue exploiting the working class until it rose up and overthrew the social order. Long-term prosperity would be possible only if the state owned the means of production and managed the economy.

Things didn't work out as Marx predicted. People in the U.S. working class that Marx worried about now own their own home, a couple of cars, TVs, and DVDs, and they take expensive vacations they locate on the Internet. By contrast, the nations that adopted Marxian systems—Russia, China, North Korea, East Germany, Cuba—fell behind more market-oriented economies. The gap in living standards between communist and capitalist nations got so wide that communism effectively collapsed. People in those countries wanted a different economic system—one that would deliver the goods capitalist consumers were already enjoying. In the last decade of the twentieth century, formerly communist nations scrambled to transform their economies from centrally planned ones to more market-oriented systems. They sought the rules, the mechanisms, the engine that would propel their living standards upward.

Even in the United States the quest for greater prosperity continues. As rich as we are, we always want more. Fewer than four out of ten Americans feel that they have "most everything" they want. How will we get still *more* goods and services? Will the economic system that served us so well in the twentieth century continue to churn out more goods and services in the twenty-first century? A combination of terrorist attacks, wars in Afghanistan and Iraq, a brief recession, and a stock-market collapse in 2000–03 made many Americans anxious about the future. A 2003 public-opinion poll showed that as many as one out of three Americans expected their children to have *fewer* goods and services than they do (see Headline).

Is America's affluence an accident or the result of an effective economic system?

GROWTH PROSPECTS   HEADLINE

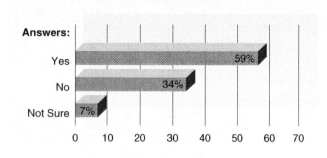

Will Your Kids Be Better Off?

Question: Do you expect your children's generation to enjoy a higher standard of living than your generation?

PERCENTAGE

Source: NBC/*Wall Street Journal* poll, January 2003.

NOTE: For living standards to keep rising, the economy must continue to grow. Will that happen? How?

And what about people in other nations? The Russian standard of living today resembles the American standard during the Great Depression of the 1930s. Even that pitiful standard is the envy of the billion or so people in Africa, Asia, and South America who subsist on incomes of less than $1 a day. How can they ever catch up with American living standards (where families are officially designated as poor if they have less than $60 a day)?

To answer these questions we need a better sense of what an economic system is and how it works. That is the foremost goal of this course. We want to know what kind of system a "market economy" really is. How does it work? Who determines the price of a textbook in a market economy? Who decides how many textbooks will be produced? Will everyone who needs a textbook get one? And why are gasoline prices so high? How about jobs? Who decides how many jobs are available or what wages they pay in a market economy? What keeps an economy growing? Or stops it in its tracks?

To understand how an economy works and what to expect from it, we'll have to ask and answer a lot of questions. Three central questions will be paramount, however. They are:

* What are the basic goals of an economic system?
* How does a market economy address these goals?
* What role should government play in shaping economic outcomes?

We won't answer all of these questions in this first chapter. But we will get a sense of what the study of economics is all about and why the answers to these central questions are both important and controversial.

The Central Problem of Scarcity

The land area of the United States stretches over 3.5 million square miles. We have a population of over 290 million, about half of whom work. We also have over $30 trillion worth of buildings and machinery. With so many resources, the United States can produce an enormous volume of output. As we've observed, however, consumers always want more, more, more. We want not only faster cars, more clothes, and larger TVs but also more roads, better schools, and more police protection. Why can't we have everything we want?

economics The study of how best to allocate scarce resources among competing uses.

The answer is fairly simple: *our* **wants** *exceed our* **resources.** As abundant as our resources might appear, they are not capable of producing everything we want. The same kind of problem makes doing homework so painful. You have only 24 hours in a day. You can spend it watching movies, shopping, hanging out with friends, sleeping, or doing your homework. With only 24 hours in a day, you've got to make choices. **Economics** offers a framework for explaining how we make such choices. The goal of economic theory is to figure out how we can best cope with scarcity. How can we use our scarce resources in the best possible way?

To answer this question, economists analyze the nature of the choices we make. Consider again your decision to read this chapter right now. Hopefully, you'll get some benefit from finishing it. You'll also incur a *cost,* however. The time you spend reading could be spent doing something else. You're probably missing a good show on TV right now. Giving up that show is the *opportunity cost* of reading this chapter. You have sacrificed the opportunity to watch TV in order to finish this homework. In general, whatever you decide to do with your time will entail an **opportunity cost,** that is, the sacrifice of a next-best alternative. The rational thing to do is to weigh the benefits of doing your homework against the implied opportunity cost, then make a choice.

opportunity cost The most desired goods and services that are forgone in order to obtain something else.

The larger society faces a similar dilemma. For the larger economy, time is also limited. So, too, are the resources needed to produce desired goods and services. To get more houses, more cars, or more movies, we need not only time but also resources to produce these things. These resources—land, labor, capital, and entrepreneurship—are the basic ingredients of production. They are called **factors of production.** The more factors of production we have, the more we can produce in a given period of time.

factors of production Resource inputs used to produce goods and services; e.g., land, labor, capital, entrepreneurship.

As we noted earlier, our available resources always fall short of our output desires. The central problem here again is **scarcity,** a situation where our desires for goods and services exceed our capacity to produce them.

scarcity Lack of enough resources to satisfy all desired uses of those resources.

Three Basic Economic Questions

The central problem of scarcity forces every society to make difficult choices. Specifically, every nation must resolve three critical questions about the use of its scarce resources:

* WHAT to produce
* HOW to produce
* FOR WHOM to produce

We will first examine the nature of each question, then review the mechanisms different countries use for answering these three basic questions.

WHAT to Produce

The WHAT question is quite simple. We've already noted that there isn't enough time in the day to do everything you want to. Nor are there enough resources in the economy to produce all the goods and services society desires. *Because wants exceed resources, we have to decide WHAT we want most, sacrificing less desired activities and goods.*

Production Possibilities   Figure 10.1 illustrates this basic dilemma. Suppose there are only two kinds of goods, "consumer goods" and "military goods." In this case, the question of WHAT to produce boils down to finding the most desirable combination of these two goods.

To make that selection, we first need to know how much of each good we *could* produce. That will depend on how many resources we have available.

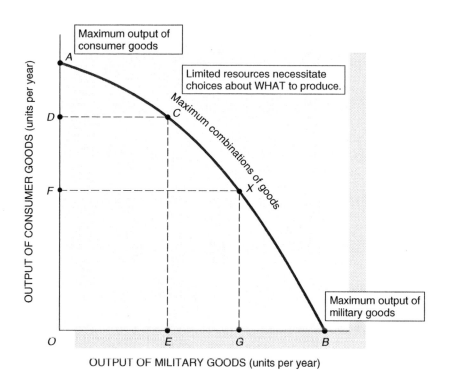

Maximum output of consumer goods

Limited resources necessitate choices about WHAT to produce.

Maximum combinations of goods

Maximum output of military goods

OUTPUT OF CONSUMER GOODS (units per year)

OUTPUT OF MILITARY GOODS (units per year)

FIGURE 10.1
A Production-Possibilities Curve

A production-possibilities curve describes the various combinations of final goods or services that could be produced in a given time period with available resources and technology. It represents a menu of output choices. Point C indicates that we could produce a *combination* of OD units of consumer goods and the quantity OE of military output. To get more military output (e.g., at point X), we have to reduce consumer output (to OF). Our objective is to select the best possible mix of output from the choices on the production-possibilities curve.

The first thing we need to do, then, is to count up our factors of production. The factors of production include:

- **Land** (including natural resources)
- **Labor** (number and skills of workers)
- **Capital** (machinery, buildings, networks)
- **Entrepreneurship** (skill in creating products, services, and processes)

The more we have of these factors, the more output we can produce. Our technological ability is also critical. The more advanced our technology—our technological and managerial abilities—the more output we will be able to produce with available factors of production. If we inventoried all our resources and technology, we could figure out what the physical *limits* to production are.

To simplify the computation, suppose we wanted to produce only consumer goods. How much *could* we produce? Surely, not an infinite amount. After assessing our stocks of land, labor, capital, and technology, we'd discover that there was a *finite* limit on such output. The *limit* is represented by point *A* in Figure 10.1. That is to say, the vertical distance from the origin (point *O*) to point *A* represents the *maximum* quantity of consumer goods that could be produced this year. To produce the quantity *A* of consumer goods, we would have to use *all* available factors of production. At point *A* no resources would be available for producing military goods. The choice of *maximum* consumer output implies *zero* military output.

We could make other choices about WHAT to produce. Point *B*, for example, illustrates another extreme. The horizontal distance from the origin (point *O*) to point *B* represents our *maximum* capacity to produce military goods. To get that much military output, we would have to devote all available resources to that single task. At point *B*, we wouldn't be producing *any* consumer goods. We would be well protected but ill-nourished and poorly clothed (wearing last year's clothes).

Our choices about WHAT to produce are not limited to the extremes of points *A* and *B*. We could instead produce a *combination* of consumer and military goods. Point *C* represents one such combination. To get to point *C*,

TABLE 10.1

Specific Production
Possibilities

The choice of WHAT to
produce eventually boils down
to specific goods and services.
Here the choices are defined in
terms of missiles or houses.
More missiles can be produced
only if some resources are
diverted from home
construction. Only one of these
output combinations can be
produced in a given time
period. Selecting that mix is a
basic economic issue.

production possibilities The
alternative combinations of goods
and services that could be
produced in a given time period
with all available resources and
technology.

| | Possible Output Combinations | | | | | |
Output	A	B	C	D	E	F
Missiles	0	50	100	150	200	250
Houses	100	90	75	55	30	0

we have to forsake maximum consumer goods output (point *A*) and use some
of our scarce resources to produce military goods. At point *C* we are producing only *OD* of consumer goods and *OE* of military goods.

Point *C* is just one of many combinations we *could* produce. We could
produce *any* combination of output represented by points along the curve in
Figure 10.1. For this reason we call it the **production-possibilities** curve; it
represents the alternative combinations of goods and services that could be
produced in a given time period with all available resources and technology.
It is, in effect, an economic menu from which some combination of goods
and services must be selected.

The production-possibilities curve puts the basic issue of WHAT to produce
in graphic terms. The same choices can be depicted in numerical terms as well.
Table 10.1, for example, illustrates specific tradeoffs between missile production
and home construction. The output mix *A* allocates all resources to home construction, leaving nothing to produce missiles. If missiles are desired, the level
of home construction must be cut back. To produce 50 missiles (mix *B*), home
construction activity must be cut back to 90. Output mixes *C* through *F* illustrate other possible choices. Only one mix of output—one choice—can be made
at any time. The question of WHAT to produce thus boils down to choosing
one specific mix of output—a single point on the production-possibilities curve.

The Choices Nations Make There is no single point on the production-
possibilities curve that is right for all nations at all times. In the United
States, the share of total output devoted to "guns" has varied greatly. During
World War II, we converted auto plants to produce military vehicles. Clothing manufacturers cut way back on consumer clothing in order to produce
more uniforms for the army, navy, and air force. The government also
forcibly drafted 12 million men and women to bear arms. By shifting
resources from the production of consumer goods to the production of military goods, we were able to move down along the production-possibilities
curve in Figure 10.1 toward point *X*. By 1944 fully 40 percent of all our output consisted of military goods. Consumer goods were so scarce that everything from butter to golf balls had to be rationed.

Figure 10.2 illustrates the rapid military buildup during World War II. The
figure also illustrates how quickly we reallocated factors of production to
consumer goods after the war ended. By 1948, less than 4 percent of U.S.
output was military goods. We had moved close to point *A* in Figure 10.1.

Peace Dividends We changed the mix of output dramatically again to fight
the Korean War. Since then, we have been slowly, if somewhat erratically,
moving along the production-possibilities curve to an ever smaller military
share. Less than 4 percent of total output now consists of military goods.

As we reduced the size of the military, we freed up more resources for the
production of civilian goods and services. In the last 20 years, the U.S. armed
forces have been reduced by nearly 600,000 personnel. As these personnel
found civilian jobs, they increased consumer output. That increase in nonmilitary output is called the *peace dividend*. Notice in Figure 10.3 how the
output of consumer goods increases from OC_1 to OC_2 as the mix of output

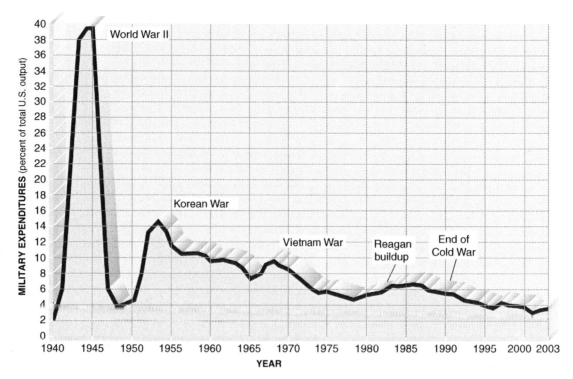

FIGURE 10.2 Military Share of Total U.S. Output

The share of total output devoted to national defense has risen sharply in wars and fallen in times of peace. The defense buildup of the 1980s increased the military share to more than 6 percent of total output. The end of the Cold War reversed that buildup, releasing resources for other uses (the peace dividend).

Source: Congressional Research Service.

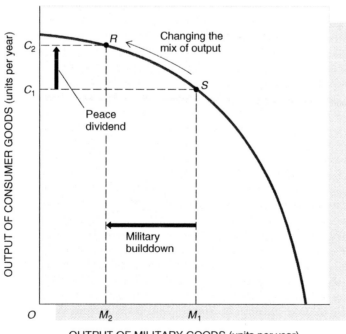

FIGURE 10.3
The Cost of War

A reduction in military output releases factors of production that can be used to produce consumer goods. The military builddown associated with the move from point S to point R enables consumption output to increase from C_1 to C_2. A military buildup reverses the process reducing output of consumer goods. The economic cost of war is measured by the implied reduction in nondefense output.

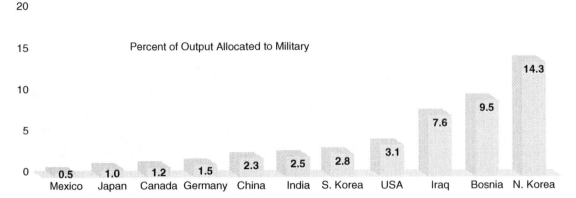

FIGURE 10.4   The Military Share of Output

The share of output allocated to the military is an indication of the opportunity cost of maintaining an army. North Korea has the highest cost, using 14 percent of its resources for military purposes. Although China and the United States have much larger armies, their military *share* of output is much smaller.

Source: World Bank (2001 data).

moves from point S to point R. That increase in consumer output is the peace dividend of a military builddown (from OM_1 to OM_2 in Figure 10.3).

The Cost of War   When a nation mobilizes for war, the process is reversed. To wage war against Iraq, for example, the government spent more than $150 billion. The *economic* cost of that effort was measured in lost consumer output. The money spent by the government on war might otherwise have been spent on schools, highways, or other nondefense projects. The National Guard personnel called up for the war would otherwise have stayed home and produced consumer goods.

In some countries the opportunity cost of military output seems far too high. North Korea, for example, has the fourth-largest army in the world. Yet North Korea is a relatively small country. Consequently, it must allocate a huge share of its resources to feed, clothe, and arm its military. As Figure 10.4 illustrates, 14 percent of North Korean output consists of military goods and services. That compares with a military share of only 3 percent in the United States.

North Korea's military has a high price tag. North Korea is a very poor country, with output per capita in the neighborhood of $1,000 per year. That is substantially less than the American standard of living was in 1900 and a tiny fraction of today's output per capita (around $38,000). Although one-third of North Korea's population lives on farms, the country cannot grow enough food to feed its population. The farm sector needs more machinery, seeds, and fertilizer; better-trained labor; and improved irrigation systems. So long as the military absorbs one-seventh of total output, however, North Korea can't afford to modernize its farm sector. The implied shortfall in food and other consumer goods is the *opportunity cost* of a large military sector (see Headline).

The Best Possible Mix   North Koreans apparently believed that a large military establishment was essential to their well-being and security. Recurrent famines and persistently low living standards compelled them to rethink that choice, however. In seeking to normalize relations with South Korea, the North Koreans are now seeking to change the mix of output in favor of more consumer goods. In September 2000, Russia pursued the same policy, cutting its military force by 30 percent (see Headline).

OPPORTUNITY COST HEADLINE

North Korea Says It Is Running Out of Food

TOKYO; March 3 (Tuesday)—North Korea issued its most dire assessment yet of its food shortages on Monday, saying that a hungry population already living on starvation rations could run out of food in as little as two weeks.

The official state news agency reported that daily rations for most people had already been cut to seven ounces a day, far below what is generally considered necessary for survival. It said that even if that ration is cut in half, "the stock will run out in mid-March."

Because of North Korea's secretive nature, it is virtually impossible to know whether its statements about the shortages are accurate. If true, millions of people could be at immediate risk of famine and starvation.

—Kevin Sullivan

Source: *Washington Post*, March 2, 1998, p. A11.

N. Korea Expanding Missile Programs

Despite international pressure to curtail its missile program, North Korea is building at least two new launch facilities for the medium-range Taepo Dong 1 and has stepped up production of short-range missiles, according to U.S. intelligence and diplomatic sources.

The projects, and a conclusion by U.S. intelligence agencies that North Korea intends to test-fire a second missile capable of striking Japan, are inflaming regional tensions, U.S. officials and Korea experts said.

—Dana Priest *and* Thomas W. Lippman

Source: *Washington Post*, November 20, 1998, p. 1.

NOTE: North Korea's inability to feed itself is due in part to its large army. Resources used for the military aren't available for producing food.

CHANGING THE OUTPUT MIX HEADLINE

Troop strength in 1998, in millions

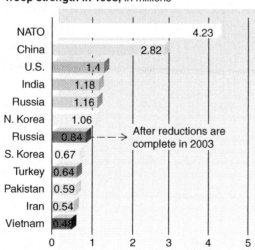

NATO	4.23
China	2.82
U.S.	1.4
India	1.18
Russia	1.16
N. Korea	1.06
Russia	0.84 → After reductions are complete in 2003
S. Korea	0.67
Turkey	0.64
Pakistan	0.59
Iran	0.54
Vietnam	0.44

Russia Tightens Its Belt

Financially strapped Russia announced cuts in its armed forces over the next three years. Here is a comparison with troop strengths of other nations:

Source: Military Balance, from *Washington Post*, September 9, 2000, p. 1.

NOTE: To raise living standards, Russia decided it had to shift more resources out of the military and into private-sector production.

What else might these women be producing?

AP/Wide World Photos

Ultimately, the designation of any particular mix of output as "best" rests on the value judgments of a society. A militaristic society would prefer a mix of output closer to point *B* in Figure 10.1. A community of pacifists would prefer a mix of output closer to point *A*. At any moment in time, ***there is one specific mix of output that is optimal for a country,*** that is, a mix that represents the best possible allocation of resources across competing uses. Locating and producing that optimal mix of output is the essence of the WHAT challenge. Of all the points along the production-possibilities curve, every nation wants to find the single point that represents the best possible mix of output.

The optimal mix of output changes when values or circumstances change. During the Cold War that persisted from 1948 to 1989, there was a general consensus that the United States needed to maintain a huge arsenal of weapons. Not everyone agreed with that conclusion, but both the Republican and Democratic political parties supported the proposition. As a result, national defense spending absorbed as much as 6.5 percent of total output in the mid-1980s. When the Soviet Union collapsed, the need for American military preparedness diminished. People felt safer and therefore placed less priority on military output. A different mix of output—one that included more nonmilitary goods—was desired. In 2001 President George W. Bush suggested that we might have moved too far in that direction. He proposed to enhance America's military readiness by producing more "guns." After the September 11, 2001 terrorist attacks on New York City and Washington, D.C. there was a broad public consensus to devote a larger share of output to national defense and homeland security.

Although society's answer to the WHAT question may change over time, ***there is only one best possible (optimal) mix of output at any given time. The first economic goal of any society is to produce that optimal mix of output.***

The same desire for an optimal mix of output drives your decisions on the use of scarce time. There is only one *best* way to use your time on any given day. If you use your time in that way, you will maximize your well-being. Other uses won't necessarily kill you, but they won't do you as much good.

Economic Growth   The selection of an optimal mix depends in part on how future-oriented one is. If you had no concern for future jobs or income, there would be little point in doing homework now. You might as well party all day if you're that present-oriented. On the other hand, if you value future jobs and income, it makes sense to allocate some present time to studying. Then you'll have more human capital (knowledge and skills) later to pursue job opportunities.

The larger society confronts the same choice between present and future consumption. We could devote all our present resources to the production of consumer goods and services. If we did, however, there wouldn't be any factors of production available to build machinery, factories, or telecommunications networks. A complete dedication to present consumption would also leave no resources for research activities. Yet these are the kinds of **investment** that enhance our capacity to produce. If we want the economy to keep growing—and our living standards to rise—we must allocate some of our scarce resources to investment rather than consumption. The resultant **economic growth** will expand our production possibilities outward, allowing us to produce more of all goods. The phenomenon of economic growth is illustrated in Figure 10.5 by the outward *shift* of the production-possibilities curve.

investment Expenditures on (production of) new plant and equipment (capital) in a given time period, plus changes in business inventories.

economic growth An increase in output (real GDP): an expansion of production possibilities.

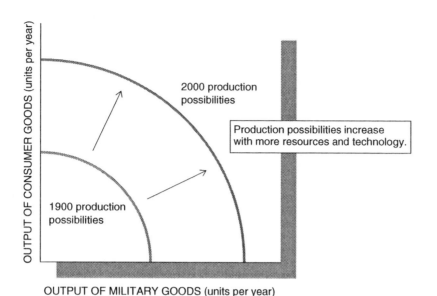

OUTPUT OF CONSUMER GOODS (units per year)

2000 production possibilities

Production possibilities increase with more resources and technology.

1900 production possibilities

OUTPUT OF MILITARY GOODS (units per year)

FIGURE 10.5
Economic Growth
Since 1900, the U.S. population has quadrupled. Investment in machinery and buildings has increased our capital stock even faster. These additional factors of production, together with advancing technology, have expanded (shifted outward) our production possibilities.

The tradeoff between consumption and investment required to attain such growth adds another level of complexity to the WHAT decision.

HOW to Produce

The second basic economic question concerns HOW we produce output. Should this class be taught in an auditorium or in small discussion sections? Should it meet twice a week or only once? Should the instructor make more use of computer aids? Should, heaven forbid, this textbook be replaced with online text files? There are numerous ways of teaching a course. Of these many possibilities, one way is presumably best, given the resources and technology available. That best way is HOW we want the course taught. Educational researchers and a good many instructors spend a lot of time trying to figure out the best way of teaching a course.

Chicken farmers do the same thing. They know they can fatten chickens up with a lot of different grains and other food. They can also vary breeding patterns, light exposure, and heat. They can use more labor in the feeder process, or more machinery. Faced with so many choices, the chicken farmers try to find the *best* way of raising chickens.

The HOW question isn't just an issue of getting more output from available inputs. It also encompasses our use of the environment. Should the waste from chicken farms be allowed to contaminate groundwater or local waterways? Or do we want to keep the water clean for other uses? Humanitarian concerns may also come into play. Should live chickens be processed without any concern for their welfare? Or should the processing be designed to minimize trauma? The HOW question encompasses all such issues. Although people may hold different views on these questions, everyone shares a common goal: ***to find an optimal method of producing goods and services.*** The best possible answer to the HOW question will entail both efficiency in the use of factors of

Should chicken farmers be free to process chickens and to dispose of waste in any way they desire? Or should the government regulate how chickens are produced?

Norm Thomas/Photo Researchers, Inc.

production and adequate safeguards for the environment and other social concerns.

FOR WHOM to Produce

The third basic economic question every society must confront is FOR WHOM? The answers to the WHAT and HOW questions determine how large an economic pie we'll bake and how we'll bake it. Then we have to slice it up. Should everyone get an equal slice of the pie? Or can some people have big pieces of the pie while others get only crumbs? In other words, *the FOR WHOM question focuses on how an economy's output is distributed across members of society.*

A pie can be divided up in many ways. Personally, I like a distribution that gives me a big slice even if that leaves less for others. Maybe you feel the same way. Whatever your feelings, however, there is likely to be a lot of disagreement about what distribution is best. Maybe we should just give everyone an equal slice. But should everyone get an equal slice even if some people helped bake the pie while others contributed nothing? The Little Red Hen of children's fables felt perfectly justified eating all the pie herself after her friends and neighbors refused to help sow the seeds, harvest the grain, or bake the pie! Should such a work-based sense of equity determine how all goods are distributed?

Karl Marx's communist vision of utopia entailed a very different FOR WHOM answer. The communist ideal is "from each according to his ability, to each according to his need." In that vision, all pitch in to bake the pie according to their abilities. Slices of the pie are distributed, however, based on need (hunger, desire) rather than on productive contributions. In a communal utopia there is no direct link between work and consumption.

Incentives   There is a risk entailed in distributing slices of the pie based on need rather than work effort. People who work hard to bake the pie may feel cheated if nonworkers get just as large a slice. Worse still, people may decide to exert less effort if they see no tangible reward to working. If that happens, the size of the pie may shrink and everyone will be worse off.

This is the kind of problem welfare programs create. Welfare programs are intended to provide a slice of the pie to people who don't have enough income to satisfy basic needs. As welfare benefits rise, however, the incentive to work diminishes. If people choose welfare checks over paychecks, total output will decline.

The same problem emerges in the tax system. If Paul is heavily taxed to provide welfare benefits to Peter, Paul may decide that hard work and entrepreneurship don't pay. To the extent that taxes discourage work, production, or investment, they shrink the size of the pie that feeds all of us.

The potential tradeoffs between taxes, welfare, and work don't compel us to dismantle all tax and welfare programs. They do emphasize, however, how difficult it is to select the right answer to the FOR WHOM question. The optimal distribution of income must satisfy our sense of fairness as well as our desire for more output.

The Mechanisms of Choice

By now, two things should be apparent. First, every society has to make difficult choices about WHAT, HOW, and FOR WHOM to produce. Second, those choices aren't easy. ***There are conflicts and tradeoffs with every*** *choice.* More of one good implies less of another. A more efficient production process may pollute the environment. Helping the poor may dull work incentives. In every case, society has to weigh the alternatives and try to find the best possible answer to each question.

How does "society" actually make such choices? What are the mechanisms we use to decide WHAT to produce, HOW, and FOR WHOM?

The Political Process

Many of these basic economic decisions are made through the political process. Consider again the decision to shrink the military share of output in the 1990s. Who made that decision? Not me. Not you. Not the mass of consumers who were streaming through real and virtual malls. No, the decisions on military buildups and builddowns were made in the political arena. The U.S. Congress made those decisions on behalf of consumers and producers. Congress also makes decisions about how many interstate highways to build, how many Head Start classes to offer, and how much space exploration to pursue.

Should *all* decisions about WHAT to produce be made in the political arena? Should Congress also decide how much ice cream will be produced, and how many DVD players? What about essentials, like food and shelter? Should decisions about the production of those goods be made in Washington, D.C., or should the mix of output be selected some other way?

The Market Mechanism

The market mechanism offers an alternative decision-making process. In a market-driven economy the process of selecting a mix of output is as familiar as grocery shopping. If you desire ice cream and have sufficient income, you simply buy ice cream. Your purchases signal to producers that ice cream is desired. By expressing the *ability and willingness to pay* for ice cream, you are telling ice cream producers that their efforts are going to be rewarded. If enough consumers feel the same way you do—and are able and willing to pay the price of ice cream—ice cream producers will churn out more ice cream.

The same kind of interaction helps determine which crops we grow. There is only so much good farmland available. Should we grow corn or beans? If consumers prefer corn, they will buy more corn and shun the beans. Farmers will quickly get the market's message and devote more of their land to corn, cutting back on bean production. In the process, the mix of output will change—moving us closer to the choice consumers have made.

The central actor in this reshuffling of resources and outputs is the **market mechanism.** *Market sales and prices send a signal to producers about what mix of output consumers want.* If you want something and have sufficient income, you buy it. If enough people do the same thing, the total sales of that product will rise, and perhaps its price will as well. Producers, seeing sales and prices rise, will be inclined to increase production. To do so, they will acquire a larger share of our available resources and use it to produce the goods we desire. No direct communication between us and the producer is required; market sales and prices convey the message and direct the market, much like an "invisible hand."

It was this ability of "the market" to select a desirable mix of output that so impressed the eighteenth-century economist Adam Smith. He argued that nations would prosper with less government interference and more reliance on the invisible hand of the marketplace. As he saw it, markets were efficient mechanisms for deciding what goods to produce, how to produce them, and

market mechanism The use of market prices and sales to signal desired outputs (or resource allocations).

even what wages to pay. Smith's writings (*The Wealth of Nations*, 1776) urged government to pursue a policy of **laissez faire**—leaving the market alone to make basic economic decisions.

laissez faire The doctrine of "leave it alone," of nonintervention by government in the market mechanism.

Central Planning

Karl Marx saw things differently. In his view, a freewheeling marketplace would cater to the whims of the rich and neglect the needs of the poor. Workers would be exploited by industrial barons and great landowners. To "leave it to the market," as Smith had proposed, would encourage exploitation. In the mid-nineteenth century, Karl Marx proposed a radical alternative: overturn the power of the elite and create a communist state in which everyone's needs would be fulfilled. Marx's writings (*Das Kapital*, 1867) encouraged communist revolutions and the development of central planning systems. The (people's) government, not the market, assumed responsibility for deciding what goods were produced, at what prices they were sold, and even who got them.

Central planning is still the principal mechanism of choice in some countries. In North Korea and Cuba, for example, the central planners decide how many cars to produce and how much bread. They then assign workers and other resources to those industries to implement their decisions. They also decide who will get the bread and the cars that are produced. Individuals cannot own factors of production nor even employ other workers for wages. The WHAT, HOW, and FOR WHOM outcomes are all directed by the central government.

Mixed Economies

Few countries still depend so fully on central planners (government) to make basic economic decisions. China, Russia, and other formerly communist nations have turned over many decisions to the market mechanism. Likewise, no nation relies exclusively on markets to fashion economic outcomes. In the United States, for example, we let the market decide how much ice cream will be produced and how many cars. We use the political process, however, to decide how many highways to construct, how many schools to build, and how much military output to produce.

mixed economy An economy that uses both market and nonmarket signals to allocate goods and resources.

Because most nations use a combination of government directives and market mechanisms to determine economic outcomes, they are called **mixed economies.** There is huge variation in that mix, however. The government-dominated economic systems in North Korea, Cuba, Laos, and Libya are starkly different from the freewheeling economies of Singapore, Bahrain, New Zealand, or the United States.

Undesirable Choices

Although differences across nations in their relative reliance on markets or government are huge, the common use of *both* market signals and government directives raises an interesting question. Why don't we let the market make *all* our output decisions? If the market does such a good job in producing the right amount of ice cream, couldn't it also decide how many highways to build or how much weaponry to produce?

Market Failure

The market does not work equally well in all situations. In fact, in some circumstances, the market mechanism might actually fail to produce the goods and services society desires. National defense is an example. Most people want to feel that their nation's borders are secure and that law and order will prevail in their communities. But few people can afford to buy an army or maintain a legal system. Even if someone were rich enough to pay for such security, he or she might decline to do so. After all, a military force and a legal system would benefit everyone in the community, not just those individuals who paid for it. Recognizing this, few people would willingly pay for national security or a system of criminal justice. They would rather spend their income on ice cream and DVD players, hoping someone else would pay for law and order. If everyone waited for a free ride, no money would be spent on national defense or a legal system. Society would end up with neither output, even though both services were widely desired.

In other situations, the market might produce *too much* of a good or service. If there were no government regulation, then anyone who had enough money could purchase and drive a car. Little kids from wealthy families could hit the highways, and so could adults with a history of drunken driving. Moreover, no one would have to spend money on emissions-control systems, lead-free gasoline, or mufflers. We could drive as fast as we wanted.

Some people would welcome unregulated roadways as a new utopia. Others, however, would be concerned about safety and pollution. They would realize that the *market's* decisions about who could drive and what kinds of cars were produced might not be so perfect. They would want the government to intervene. To assure safer and cleaner driving, people might agree to let the government regulate speed, auto emissions, and even drivers.

The Wrong Mix of Output   These and other situations suggest that the market alone might not always pick the best possible mix of output. The problem is illustrated in Figure 10.6. In principle there is a single *best* mix of output among the array of choices along the production-possibilities curve. Suppose that we could somehow divine where that mix is. In Figure 10.6 that best-possible mix is arbitrarily placed at point *X*.

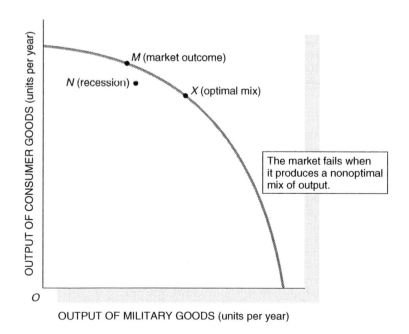

FIGURE 10.6
Market Failure

The market mechanism will allocate resources to produce a specific mix of output. In this case, however, the market-generated mix (point *M*) is not consistent with society's most desired mix (point *X*). When this happens, the market has failed.

An unregulated market might generate too much pollution. Such a market failure requires government intervention.

Gary Milburn/Tom Stack & Associates

market failure An imperfection in the market mechanism that prevents optimal outcomes.

externalities Costs (or benefits) of a market activity borne by a third party; the difference between the social and private costs (or benefits) of a market activity.

The question now is what mix of output will the *market* produce? Suppose that the market generates the mix of output represented by point *M* in Figure 10.6. Clearly, the market outcome (point *M*) is *not* the most desirable outcome (point *X*). In this case, we would conclude that the market had *failed*. **Market failure** means that the market does not produce the best possible mix of output. In Figure 10.6, the market produces too much civilian output and too little military output. When the market fails to produce the right mix of output, government intervention may be required to get to point *X*.

The market mechanism might also fail to make full use of the economy's production possibilities. If some workers cannot find jobs, the mix of output may end up *inside* the production-possibilities curve, as at point *N* in Figure 10.6. This is what happened during the Great Depression of the 1930s and in a dozen or so lesser recessions since then. When the market fails in this way, the goal of economic policy is to restore full employment by moving back onto the production-possibilities curve. To get there, government intervention may be necessary.

Too Much Pollution   The market mechanism might also select the wrong choice about HOW to produce. Consider the message that unregulated markets communicate to producers. In an unregulated market, no price would be charged for using air or waterways, since neither are owned by any individual. Producers, therefore, would regard the use of air and waterways as a "free" good. Under such circumstances it would be a lot cheaper for a factory to dump its waste into nearby waterways than to dispose of it more carefully. It would also be cheaper for power plants to let waste gases and soot go up in smoke than to install environmental safeguards. The resulting pollutants are an **externality**—a cost imposed on innocent third parties. Consumers would be worse off as the quality of the air and water deteriorated.

Profit-driven producers would seldom worry about externalities in a completely unregulated marketplace. Were profit-and-loss considerations the only determinant of HOW goods were produced, we might end up destroying the environment. To prevent such a calamity, we look to the government to regulate HOW goods are produced, thereby rectifying market failures.

Too Much Poverty   The market might also fail to distribute goods and services in the best possible way. A market system rewards people according to their value in the marketplace. Sports stars, entertainers, and corporate executives end up with huge paychecks while others toil for meager wages. Big paychecks provide access to more output; people with little paychecks get much less of what is produced.

Is this market-based system of distributing output fair? Should rich people live in mansions while poor people sleep in abandoned cars? Many observers object that the market should not be the sole arbiter of who gets shelter. If a consensus emerges that the market's way of slicing up the pie is too unfair, then taxes and income transfers (e.g., welfare benefits, Social Security) may be used to reslice the pie. Such government intervention may generate a more desirable answer to the FOR WHOM question.

Government Failure

It is relatively easy to find evidence of market failure. It is not so easy, however, to fix every failure. Karl Marx, you may recall, believed the government could always find and implement the right answers. In practice, however, central planning wasn't notably more successful than the market mechanism in answering the WHAT, HOW, and FOR WHOM questions. Indeed, the collapse of communism in the early 1990s was precipitated by recurrent failures to resolve basic economic questions. ***Just because the market fails doesn't mean that the government will necessarily offer better answers to the WHAT, HOW, and FOR WHOM questions.***

The possibility for **government failure**—intervention that fails to improve (possibly even worsens) market outcomes—is illustrated in Figure 10.7. Again, we assume the optimal mix of output is located at point X and that the market itself produces the suboptimal mix at point M. In this case, the goal of government intervention is to move the economy closer to point X. It is possible, however, that misguided intervention might move the economy to point G_1, farther away from the optimal mix. That worsening of the mix of output would represent government failure.

Government intervention might not just worsen the *mix* of output but even reduce the total *amount* of output. When the government regulates an industry, it typically employs a lot of inspectors, lawyers, and bureaucrats. It also burdens private industry with paperwork and other bureaucratic red tape. The resources used to write, enforce, and comply with government regulations produce neither consumer goods nor military goods. As a result, the final mix of output may end up at point G_2 in Figure 10.7. At G_2 the inefficiencies associated with government intervention prevent the economy from fully utilizing its productive capacity. If public opinion is any index of government failure, then the potential for failure appears alarmingly high. The accompanying Headline reveals that fewer than half of all Americans trust the federal government to do the right thing.

The government could also fail the HOW question. The centrally planned economies of Eastern Europe experienced some of the world's worst environmental problems. The huge steel mills outside Krakow, Poland, spewed

government failure Government intervention that fails to improve economic outcomes.

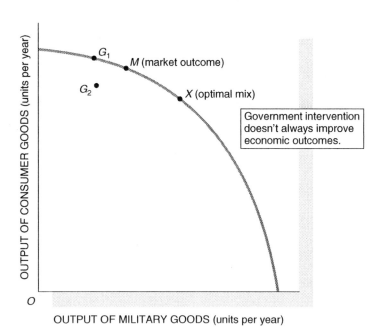

FIGURE 10.7
Government Failure

The goal of government intervention is to correct market failure. It is possible, however, that government policy might move the economy farther away from the optimal mix (to point G_1) or even inside the production-possibilities curve (point G_2).

Declining Faith in Government

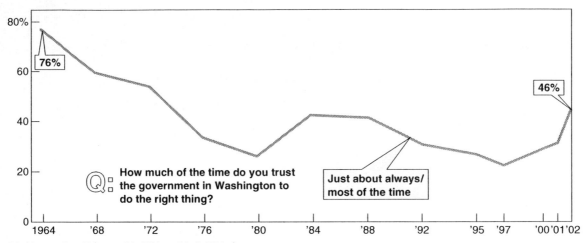

Source: *Washington Post*, February 26, 1996, p. A6. © 1996, the *Washington Post*. Reprinted with permission; ABC News poll, August 1997. CBS News Poll, January 2001. Gallup poll, September 2002.

NOTE: Government intervention is supposed to correct market failures. Most people feel, however, that the government is likely to fail as well.

more sulfur into the air than all of Western Europe's steel mills combined. The air in Budapest was so polluted that Hungarians paid for brief inhalations of compressed clean air. The factory and sewage waste from Hungary, Czechoslovakia, and Bulgaria made the Danube Europe's most polluted waterway. Worse yet, Soviet planners allowed Chernobyl to become a nuclear nightmare. Clearly, ***there is no guarantee that the visible hand of government will be any cleaner than the invisible hand of the marketplace.***

We don't have any government guarantees for the FOR WHOM question either. When the government starts reslicing the economic pie, politics may overwhelm charity. Only a small fraction of all income transfers in the United States goes to poor people. Rich people get more Social Security and Medicare benefits than poor people get in welfare benefits. And "corporate welfare" (tax breaks and subsidies) far outstrip poor people's welfare as well. As a consequence, the FOR WHOM answer generated by government intervention isn't always more equitable than that of the marketplace. Indeed, a Harvard University/*Washington Post* survey revealed that only 11 percent of all Americans believe government efforts to improve income distribution have succeeded. Forty-nine percent believe the government has made the FOR WHOM answer worse.

We have to recognize, then, that government might fail to satisfy our distributional goals.

What Economics Is All About

With so many possibilities for market and government failure, it's amazing that we ever get things right. Public policy is driven, however, by the conviction that it is better to be half right than completely wrong. That is to say, the policy challenge is to *improve* economic outcomes, even if we can't always attain perfect outcomes. To this end, **we rely on a combination of market signals and government interventions to forge better answers to the WHAT, HOW, and FOR WHOM questions.** That is the essence of a *mixed* economy.

The first goal of economic theory is to help society find better answers to the three basic questions. This requires us to first *understand* how the economy functions. How do people decide which goods to buy? How do producers decide what prices to charge? What forces determine how many job seekers will be employed? Who is helped and who is hurt by inflation?

The second goal of economic theory is to *predict* how changes in government policy or market institutions will affect economic outcomes. Will government-financed student loans affect how many students attend college? Will a drop in interest rates stimulate sales of new cars? Will a higher minimum wage reduce the number of available jobs? How will corporate mergers affect the quality or price of Internet features?

Macro vs. Micro

The study of economics is typically divided into two parts: macroeconomics and microeconomics. Macroeconomics focuses on the behavior of an entire economy—the big picture. In macroeconomics we study such national goals as full employment, control of inflation, and economic growth, without worrying about the well-being or behavior of specific individuals or groups. The essential concern of **macroeconomics** is to understand and improve the performance of the economy as a whole.

macroeconomics The study of aggregate economic behavior, of the economy as a whole.

Microeconomics is concerned with the details of this big picture. In microeconomics we focus on the individuals, firms, and government agencies that actually make up the larger economy. Our interest here is in the behavior of individual economic actors. What are their goals? How can they best achieve these goals with their limited resources? How will they respond to various incentives and opportunities?

microeconomics The study of individual behavior in the economy, of the components of the larger economy.

A primary concern of macroeconomics, for example, is to determine the impact of aggregate consumer spending on total output, employment, and prices. Very little attention is devoted to the actual content of consumer spending or its determinants. Microeconomics, on the other hand, focuses on the specific expenditure decisions of individual consumers and the forces (tastes, prices, incomes) that influence those decisions.

The distinction between macro- and microeconomics is also reflected in discussions of business investment. In macroeconomics we want to know what determines the aggregate rate of business investment and how those expenditures influence the nation's total output, employment, and prices. In microeconomics we focus on the decisions of individual businesses regarding the rate of production, the choice of factors of production, and the pricing of specific goods.

The distinction between macro- and microeconomics is a matter of convenience. In reality, macroeconomic outcomes depend on micro behavior, and micro behavior is affected by macro outcomes. Hence one cannot fully understand how an economy works until one understands how all the participants behave and why they behave as they do. But just as you can drive a car without knowing how its engine is constructed, you can observe how an economy runs without completely disassembling it. In macroeconomics we observe that the car goes faster when the accelerator is depressed and that it slows when the brake is applied. That is all we need to know in most situations. There are times, however, when the car breaks downs. When it does, we have to know something more about how the pedals work. This leads us into micro studies. How does each part work? Which ones can or should be fixed?

Theory vs. Reality

The distinction between macroeconomics and microeconomics is one of many simplifications we make in studying economic behavior. The economy is much too vast and complex to describe and explain in one course (or one lifetime). Accordingly, we focus on basic relationships, ignoring unnecessary detail. What this means is that we formulate theories, or *models*, of economic behavior, then use those theories to evaluate and design economic policy.

The economic models that economists use to explain market behavior are like maps. To get from New York to Los Angeles you don't need to know all the details of topography that lie between those two cities. Knowing where the interstate highways are is probably enough. An interstate route map therefore provides enough information to get to your destination.

The same kind of simplification is used in economic models of consumer behavior. Such models assert that when the price of a good increases, consumers will buy less of it. In reality, however, people *may* buy *more* of a good at increased prices, especially if those high prices create a certain snob appeal or if prices are expected to increase still further. In predicting consumer responses to price increases, we typically ignore such possibilities by *assuming* that the price of the good in question is the *only* thing that changes. This assumption of "other things remaining equal (unchanged)" (in Latin, ***ceteris paribus***) allows us to make straightforward predictions. If instead we described consumer responses to increased prices in any and all circumstances (allowing everything to change at once), every prediction would be accompanied by a book full of exceptions and qualifications. We would look more like lawyers than economists.

ceteris paribus The assumption of nothing else changing.

Although the assumption of *ceteris paribus* makes it easier to formulate economic theory and policy, it also increases the risk of error. Obviously, if other things do change in significant ways, our predictions (and policies) may fail. But, like weather forecasters, we continue to make predictions, knowing that occasional failure is inevitable. In so doing, we are motivated by the conviction that it is better to be approximately right than to be dead wrong.

Politics vs. Economics

Politicians cannot afford to be quite so complacent about predictions, however. Policy decisions must be made every day. And a politician's continued survival may depend on being more than approximately right. Economists can contribute to those policy decisions by offering measures of economic impact and predictions of economic behavior. But in the real world, those measures and predictions will always contain a substantial margin of error.

Even if the future were known, economic policy could not rely completely on economic theory. There are always political choices to be made. The choice of more consumer goods ("butter") or more military hardware ("guns"), for example, is not an economic decision. Rather it is a sociopolitical decision based in part on economic tradeoffs (opportunity costs). The "need" for more butter or more guns must be expressed politically—ends versus means again. Political forces are a necessary ingredient in economic policy decisions. That is not to say that all political decisions are right. It does suggest, however, that economic policies may not always conform to economic theory.

Both politics and economics are involved in the continuing debate about laissez faire and government intervention. The pendulum has swung from laissez faire (Adam Smith) to central government control (Karl Marx) and to an ill-defined middle ground where the government assumes major responsibilities for economic stability (John Maynard Keynes) and for answers to the WHAT, HOW, and FOR WHOM questions. In the 1980s the Reagan administration pushed the pendulum a bit closer to laissez faire by cutting taxes, reducing government regulation, and encouraging market incentives. The first Bush administration pushed the pendulum back a bit by expanding the government's role in education, regulation, and research. When the economy slumped in 1990–91, however, President Bush rejected advice to intervene, preferring to let the market right itself.

President Clinton thought the government should play a more active role in resolving basic economic issues. Just after he was elected, he published a "Vision for America" that spelled out a greater role for government in assuring health care, providing skills training, protecting the environment, and regulating working conditions. In this vision, well-intentioned government officials could correct market failures. The Democratic-controlled Congress of 1993–94 offered little support for Clinton's vision, however, and the Republican-controlled Congress of 1995–98 rejected it. President George W. Bush has made clear that he, too, favors less government intervention and more reliance on the market mechanism.

In part, this enduring controversy about markets versus government reflects diverse political, rather than strictly economic, views. Some people think a big public sector is undesirable, even if it improves economic performance. They see government intervention as a threat not only to economic performance but to individual liberties as well. They prefer the invisible hand of the market to the visible hand of government intervention almost every time. On the other hand, some advocates of government intervention feel that the market mechanism is inherently corrupting of human values and call on the government to limit greed, to guarantee economic security, and to protect the environment.

The debate over markets versus government also persists because of gaps in our economic understanding. For over 200 years economists have been arguing about what makes the economy tick. None of the competing theories has performed spectacularly well. Indeed, few economists have successfully predicted major economic events with any consistency. Even annual forecasts of inflation, unemployment, and output are regularly in error. Worse still, there are never-ending arguments about what caused a major economic event long after it occurred. In fact, economists are still arguing over the causes of the Great Depression of the 1930s!

Modest Expectations

In view of all these debates and uncertainties, you should not expect to learn everything there is to know about the economy in this text or course. Our goals are more modest. We want you to develop a reasonable perspective on economic behavior and an understanding of basic principles. With this foundation, you should acquire a better view of how the economy works. Daily news reports on economic events should make more sense. Congressional debates on tax and budget policies should take on more meaning. You may even develop some insights that you can apply toward running a business or planning a career.

SUMMARY

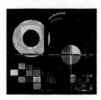

* Every nation confronts the three basic economic questions of WHAT to produce, HOW, and FOR WHOM.
* The need to select a single mix of output (WHAT) is necessitated by our limited capacity to produce. Scarcity results when our wants exceed our resources.
* The production-possibilities curve illustrates the limits to output dictated by available factors of production and technology. Points on the production-possibilities curve represent the menu of different output mixes from which we may choose.
* All production entails an opportunity cost: We can produce more of output A only if we produce less of output B. The implied reduction in output B is the opportunity cost of output A.
* The HOW question focuses on the choice of what inputs to use in production. It also encompasses choices made about environmental protection.
* The FOR WHOM question concerns the distribution of output among members of society.
* The goal of every society is to select the best possible (optimal) answers to the WHAT, HOW, and FOR WHOM questions. The optimal answers will vary with social values and production capabilities.
* The three questions can be answered by the market mechanism, by a system of central planning, or by a mixed system of market signals and government intervention.
* Price signals are the key feature of the market mechanism. Consumers signal their desires for specific goods by paying a price for these goods. Producers respond to the price signal by assembling factors of production to produce the desired output.
* Market failure occurs when the market mechanism generates the wrong mix of output, undesirable methods of production, or an inequitable distribution of income. Government intervention may fail, too, however, by not improving (or even worsening) economic outcomes.
* The study of economics focuses on the broad question of resource allocation. Macroeconomics is concerned with allocating the resources of an entire economy to achieve broad economic goals (e.g., full employment). Microeconomics focuses on the behavior and goals of individual market participants.

Terms to Remember

Define the following terms:

economics	economic growth	externalities
opportunity cost	market mechanism	government failure
factors of production	laissez faire	macroeconomics
scarcity	mixed economy	microeconomics
production possibilities	market failure	*ceteris paribus*
investment		

1. What opportunity costs did you incur in reading this chapter?
2. In Figure 10.7 government failure causes output to fall below its full potential. How might this happen? If government intervention moved the mix of output to a point between *M* and *X*, would this be government failure?
3. In 2003, President George W. Bush proposed a significant increase in military spending. What would that added spending cost us? Is this too much or too little? How can we decide?
4. Should the government build more shelters for the homeless? Where will it get the resources to do so?
5. Why might it be necessary to reduce consumer spending in order to attain faster economic growth? Would it be worth the sacrifice?
6. If auto-emissions controls weren't required, would people willingly buy and install them? Explain.
7. McDonald's recently asked its suppliers to process chickens more humanely. How much more would you be willing to pay for chicken that was humanely processed?
8. Which government income transfers do rich people receive? Who pays for them?
9. If taxes on the rich were raised to provide more housing for the poor, how would the willingness to work be affected? What would happen to total output?
10. Why is public confidence in government so low (see Headline, p. 354)? How can government failure be avoided?

1. According to Figure 10.1, what is the opportunity cost of increasing consumer output from *OF* to *OD*?
2. Draw a production-possibilities curve based on Table 10.1, labeling combinations *A–F*. What is the opportunity cost of producing 100 missiles?
3. Assume that it takes 4 hours of labor time to paint a room and 3 hours to sand a floor. If all 24 hours were spent painting, how many rooms could be painted by one worker? If a decision were made to sand two floors, how many painted rooms would have to be given up? Illustrate with a production-possibilities curve.
4. Suppose in problem 3 that a second worker became available. Illustrate the resulting change in production possibilities. Now what would be the opportunity cost of sanding two floors?
5. According to Figure 10.3, what is the cost of a war that increases military output from M_2 to M_1? What is the opportunity cost of maintaining military output at M_1?
6. On a single graph, draw production-possibilities curves for 1945 and 2000 with consumer goods and military goods as the output choices. Label points *A* and *B* to approximate the choices made in each year (see Figure 10.2 for data).
7. Assume that the schedule below describes the production possibilities confronting an economy. Using the information from the table:
   (*a*) Draw the production-possibilities curve. Be sure to label each alternative output combination (*A* through *E*).
   (*b*) Calculate and illustrate on your graph the opportunity cost of building one convenience store per week.

(c) What is the cost of producing a second convenience store? What might account for the difference?

(d) Why can't more of both outputs be produced?

(e) Which point on the curve is the most desired one? How will we find out?

Potential Weekly Output Combinations	Homeless Shelters	Convenience Stores
A	10	0
B	9	1
C	7	2
D	4	3
E	0	4

8. In 1999 the dollar value of total output was roughly $25 billion in North Korea and $400 billion in South Korea. Use the data in Figure 10.4 to compute the cost of defense spending in each country.

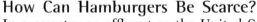

Web Activities

1. Log on to www.federalreserve.gov/releases/g17/current.

(a) Draw a production possibility curve for the U.S. measuring capital goods production on the horizontal axis and consumer goods on the vertical axis for 1982. Draw a point on this PPC map that represents the 1982 low capacity utilization. Label this point "A."

(b) Draw a second PPC map that represents current production data.

    i. Draw a point on this PPC map that represents the current capacity utilization. Label this point B. Explain your choice of location for point A.

    ii. How does the location of the current PPC compare to that of 1982?

    iii. Is point A closer to the 1982 curve than is point B to the current curve?

2. Log on to www.bea.doc.gov/bea/glance.htm and find the data for nonresidential fixed investment.

(a) How did the rate of nonresidential fixed investment change in the past two years of data available?

(b) What are the implications for the nation's production-possibilities curve?

3. Log on to www.whitehouse.gov/fsbr/employment.html and find the data for the civilian labor force.

(a) What has happened to the size of labor force over the last three years?

(b) What implications does this have for the nation's production-possibilities curve? Explain.

Living Econ

How Can Hamburgers Be Scarce?

In a country as affluent as the United States it is sometimes hard to believe that scarcity exists. In particular it is hard to believe that a product such as hamburgers is scarce. In fact, you can approach a number of fast food restaurants, anytime day or night almost, and order what seems to be an endless quantity of hamburgers. But the resources used to produce hamburgers and all other goods and services are scarce in the sense that they could be put to other uses.

More than 600,000 fast food cooks use energy and other resources to prepare our burgers. Over nine billion pounds of cattle are destined for hamburger meat every year in the United States; to make one quarter pound of beef typically requires more than one pound of feed grain and 100 gallons of water. All of these resources could be used to produce other goods or services.

On an individual level, every time you buy a hamburger you choose not to buy something else. If you work in a fast food restaurant, you will have less time for other pursuits. So, whether in your personal life or at the national level, there are finite resources and choices must be made about how to use them.

APPENDIX

Using Graphs

Economists like to draw graphs. In fact, we didn't even make it through the first chapter without a few graphs. The purpose of this appendix is to look more closely at the way graphs are drawn and used.

The basic purpose of a graph is to illustrate a relationship between two variables. Consider, for example, the relationship between grades and studying. In general, we expect that additional hours of study time will lead to higher grades. Hence we should be able to see a distinct relationship between hours of study time and grade-point average.

Suppose that we actually surveyed all the students taking this course with regard to their study time and grade-point averages. The resulting information can be compiled in a table such as Table A.1.

According to the table, students who don't study at all can expect an F in this course. To get a C, the average student apparently spends 8 hours a week studying. All those who study 16 hours a week end up with an A in the course.

These relationships between grades and studying can also be illustrated on a graph. Indeed, the whole purpose of a graph is to summarize numerical relationships.

We begin to construct a graph by drawing horizontal and vertical boundaries, as in Figure A.1. These boundaries are called the *axes* of the graph. On the vertical axis we measure one of the variables; the other variable is measured on the horizontal axis.[1]

In this case, we shall measure the grade-point average on the vertical axis. We start at the *origin* (the intersection of the two axes) and count upward, letting the distance between horizontal lines represent half (0.5) a grade point. Each horizontal line is numbered, up to the maximum grade-point average of 4.0.

The number of hours each week spent doing homework is measured on the horizontal axis. We begin at the origin again, and count to the right. The *scale* (numbering) proceeds in increments of 1 hour, up to 20 hours per week.

When both axes have been labeled and measured, we can begin to illustrate the relationship between study time and grades. Consider the typical student who does 8 hours of homework per week and has a 2.0 (C) grade-point average. We illustrate this relationship by first locating 8 hours on the horizontal axis. We then move up from that point a distance of 2.0 grade points, to point *M*. Point *M* tells us that 8 hours of study time per week is typically associated with a 2.0 grade-point average.

The rest of the information in Table A.1 is drawn (or *plotted*) on the graph in the same way. To illustrate the average grade for people who study 12

---

[1]The vertical axis is often called the *Y* axis; the horizontal axis, the *X* axis.

TABLE A.1
Hypothetical Relationship
of Grades to Study Time

Study Time (hours per week)	Grade-Point Average
16	4.0 (A)
14	3.5 (B +)
12	3.0 (B)
10	2.5 (C +)
8	2.0 (C)
6	1.5 (D +)
4	1.0 (D)
2	0.5 (F +)
0	0 (F)

hours per week, we move upward from the number 12 on the horizontal axis until we reach the height of 3.0 on the vertical axis. At that intersection, we draw another point (point *N*).

Once we have plotted the various points describing the relationship of study time to grades, we may connect them with a line or curve. This line (curve) is our summary. In this case, the line slopes upward to the right—that is, it has a *positive* slope. This slope indicates that more hours of study time are associated with *higher* grades. Were higher grades associated with *less* study time, the curve in Figure A.1 would have a *negative* slope (downward from left to right).

Slopes

The upward slope of Figure A.1 tells us that higher grades are associated with increased amounts of study time. That same curve also tells us *by how much* grades tend to rise with study time. According to point *M* in Figure A.1, the average student studies 8 hours per week and earns a C (2.0 grade-point average). In order to earn a B (3.0 grade-point average), a student apparently needs to study an average of 12 hours per week (point *N*). Hence an increase of 4 hours of study time per week is associated with a 1-point increase in grade-

FIGURE A.1
The Relationship of
Grades to Study Time

The upward (positive) slope of the curve indicates that additional studying is associated with higher grades. The average student (2.0, or C grade) studies 8 hours per week. This is indicated by point *M* on the graph.

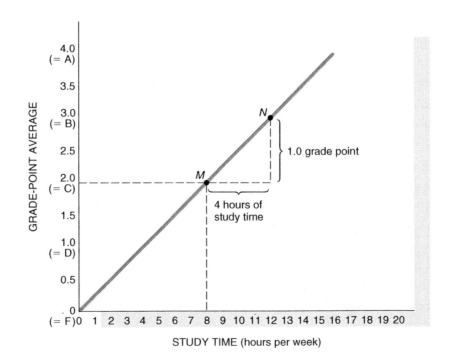

STUDY TIME (hours per week)

point average. This relationship between *changes* in study time and *changes* in grade-point average is expressed by the steepness, or *slope*, of the graph.

The slope of any graph is calculated as

$$\bullet \; \text{Slope} = \frac{\text{vertical distance between two points}}{\text{horizontal distance between two points}}$$

Some people simplify this by saying

$$\text{Slope} = \frac{\text{the rise}}{\text{the run}}$$

In our example, the vertical distance (the "rise") between points *M* and *N* represents a change in grade-point average. The horizontal distance (the "run") between these two points represents the change in study time. Hence the slope of the graph between points *M* and *N* is equal to

$$\text{Slope} = \frac{3.0 \; \text{grade} - 2.0 \; \text{grade}}{12 \; \text{hours} - 8 \; \text{hours}} = \frac{1 \; \text{grade point}}{4 \; \text{hours}}$$

In other words, a 4-hour increase in study time (from 8 to 12 hours) is associated with a 1-point increase in grade-point average (see Figure A.1).

Shifts

The relationship between grades and studying illustrated in Figure A.1 is not inevitable. It is simply a graphical illustration of student experiences, as revealed in our hypothetical survey. The relationship between study time and grades could be quite different.

Suppose that the university decided to raise grading standards, making it more difficult to achieve every grade other than an F. To achieve a C, a student now would need to study 12 hours per week, not just 8 (as in Figure A.1). Whereas students could previously expect to get a B by studying 12 hours per week, now they have to study 16 hours to get that grade.

Figure A.2 illustrates the new grading standards. Notice that the new curve lies to the right of the earlier curve. We say that the curve has *shifted* to reflect a change in the relationship between study time and grades. Point *R* indicates that 12 hours of study time now "produces" a C, not a B (point *N* on the old curve). Students who now study only 4 hours per week (point *S*) will fail. Under the old grading policy, they could have at least gotten a D. ***When a curve shifts, the underlying relationship between the two variables has changed.***

A shift may also change the slope of the curve. In Figure A.2, the new grading curve is parallel to the old one; it therefore has the same slope. Under either the new grading policy or the old one, a 4-hour increase in study time leads to a 1-point increase in grades. Therefore, the slope of both curves in Figure A.2 is

$$\text{Slope} = \frac{\text{vertical change}}{\text{horizontal change}} = \frac{1}{4}$$

This, too, may change, however, Figure A.3 illustrates such a possibility. In this case, zero study time still results in an F. But now the payoff for additional studying is reduced. Now it takes 6 hours of study time to get a D (1.0 grade point), not 4 hours as before. Likewise, another 4 hours of study time (to a total of 10) raises the grade by only two-thirds of a point.

FIGURE A.2
A Shift

When a relationship between two variables changes, the entire curve *shifts*. In this case a tougher grading policy alters the relationship between study time and grades. To get a C one must now study 12 hours per week (point *R*), not just 8 hours (point *M*).

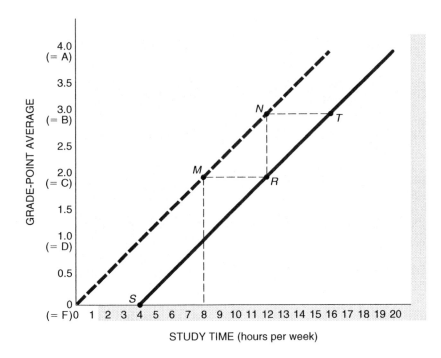

It takes 6 hours to raise the grade a full point. The slope of the new line is therefore

$$\text{Slope} = \frac{\text{vertical change}}{\text{horizontal change}} = \frac{1}{6}$$

The new curve in Figure A.3 has a smaller slope than the original curve and so lies below it. What all this means is that it now takes a greater effort to *improve* your grade.

FIGURE A.3
A Change in Slope

When a curve shifts, it may change its slope as well. In this case, a new grading policy makes each higher grade more difficult to reach. To raise a C to a B, for example, one must study 6 additional hours (compare points *J* and *K*). Earlier it took only 4 hours to move up the grade scale a full point. The slope of the line has declined from 0.25 (= 1 − 4) to 0.17 (= 1 − 6).

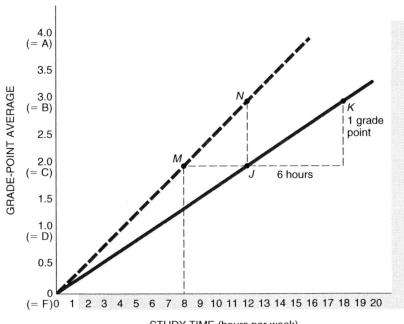

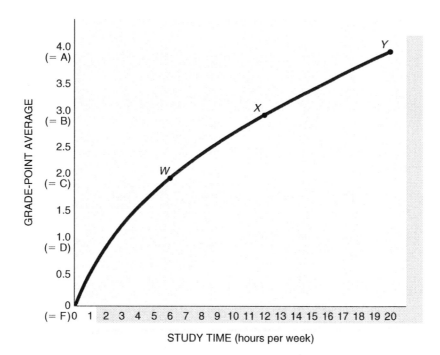

A Nonlinear Relationship
Straight lines have a constant slope, implying a constant relationship between the two variables. But the relationship (and slope) may vary. In this case. It takes 6 extra hours of study to raise a C (point *W*) to a B (point *X*) but 8 extra hours to raise a B to an A (point *Y*). The slope is decreasing as we move up the curve.

Linear vs. Nonlinear Curves

In Figures A.1–A.3, the relationship between grades and studying is represented by a straight line—that is, a *linear* curve. A distinguishing feature of linear curves is that they have the same (constant) slope throughout. In Figure A.1, it appears that *every* 4-hour increase in study time is associated with a 1-point increase in average grades. In Figure A.3, it appears that every 6-hour increase in study time leads to a 1-point increase in grades. But the relationship between studying and grades may not be linear. Higher grades may be more difficult to attain. You may be able to raise a C to a B by studying 4 hours more per week. But it may be harder to raise a B to an A. According to Figure A.4, it takes an additional 8 hours of studying to raise a B to an A. Thus the relationship between study time and grades is *nonlinear* in Figure A.4; the slope of the curve changes as study time increases. In this case, the slope decreases as study time increases. Grades continue to improve, but not so fast, as more and more time is devoted to homework. You may know the feeling.

Causation

Figure A.4 does not itself guarantee that your grade-point average will rise if you study 4 more hours per week. In fact, the graph drawn in Figure A.4 does not prove that additional study ever results in higher grades. The graph is only a summary of empirical observations. It says nothing about cause and effect. It could be that students who study a lot are smarter to begin with. If so, then less able students might not get higher grades if they studied harder. In other words, the *cause* of higher grades is debatable. At best, the empirical relationship summarized in the graph may be used to support a particular theory (e.g., that it pays to study more). Graphs, like tables, charts, and other statistical media, rarely tell their own stories; rather, they must be *interpreted* in terms of some underlying theory or expectation.

Supply and Demand

A couple of years ago a Florida man tried to sell his kidney on eBay. As his offer explained, he could supply only one kidney because he needed the other to survive. He wanted the bidding to start out at $25,000, plus expenses for the surgical removal and shipment of his kidney. He felt confident he could get at least that much money since thousands of people have potentially fatal kidney diseases.

He was right. The bids for his kidney quickly surpassed $100,000. Clearly, there were lots of people with kidney disease who were willing and able to pay high prices to get a lifesaving transplant.

The seller never got the chance to sell his kidney to the highest bidder. Although organ transplants are perfectly legal in the United States, the purchase or sale of human organs is not. When eBay learned the pending sale was illegal, they shut down the man's auction.

Despite its illegality, there is clearly a market in human kidneys. That is to say, there are people who are willing to *sell* kidneys, and others who are willing to *buy* kidneys. Those are sufficient conditions for the existence of a market. The market in kidneys happens to be illegal in the United States, but it is still a market, although illegal. The markets for drugs, prostitution, and nuclear warheads are also illegal, but still reflect the intentions of potential buyers and sellers.

Fortunately, we don't have to venture into the underworld to see how markets work. You can watch markets work by visiting eBay or other electronic auction sites. Or you can simply go to the mall and watch people shop. In either location you will observe people deciding whether to buy or sell goods at various prices. That's the essence of market activity. The goal in this chapter is to assess how markets actually function. How does the invisible hand of the market resolve the competing interests of buyers (who want low prices) and sellers (who want high prices)? Specifically,

* What determines the price of a good or service?
* How does the price of a product affect its production or consumption?
* Why do prices and production levels often change?

Market Participants

Over 290 million individual consumers, about 20 million business firms, and tens of thousands of government agencies participate directly in the U.S. economy. Millions of foreigners also participate by buying and selling goods in American markets.

Goals

All of these economic actors participate in the market in order to achieve specific goals. Consumers strive to maximize their own happiness, businesses try to maximize profits; government agencies are supposed to maximize the general welfare. Foreigners pursue these same goals, as consumers, producers, or government agencies. In every case, they strive to achieve these goals by buying the best-possible mix of goods, services, or factors of production.

Constraints

The desire of all market participants to maximize something—profits, private satisfaction, or social welfare—is not their only common trait. Another element common to all participants is their *limited resources*. You and I cannot buy everything we desire; we simply don't have enough income. As a consequence, we must make *choices* among available products. We're always hoping to get as much satisfaction as possible for the few dollars we have to spend. Likewise, business firms and government agencies must decide how *best* to use their limited resources to maximize profits or public welfare. This is the scarcity problem we examined in Chapter 10. It is central to all economic decisions.

Specialization and Exchange

market Any place where goods are bought and sold.

To maximize the returns on our limited resources, we participate in the **market,** buying and selling various goods and services. Our decision to participate in these exchanges is prompted by two considerations. First, most of us are incapable of producing everything we desire to consume. Second, even if we *could* produce all our own goods and services, it would still make sense to specialize, producing only one product and trading it for other desired goods and services.

Suppose you were capable of growing your own food, stitching your own clothes, building your own shelter, and even writing your own economics text. Even in this little utopia, it would still make sense to decide how *best* to expend your limited time and energy and to rely on others to fill in the gaps. If you were *most* proficient at growing food, you would be best off spending your time farming. You could then exchange some of your food output for the clothes, shelter, and books you desired. In the end, you'd be able to consume more goods than if you had tried to make everything yourself.

Our economic interactions with others are thus necessitated by two constraints:

* Our inability as individuals to produce all the things we desire.
* The limited amount of time, energy, and resources we possess for producing those things we could make for ourselves.

Together, these constraints lead us to specialize and interact. Most of the interactions that result take place in the market.

Market Interactions

Figure 11.1 summarizes the kinds of interactions that occur among market participants. Note, first of all, that we have identified *four separate groups of market participants:*

* *Consumers*
* *Business firms*
* *Governments*
* *Foreigners*

Domestically, the "Consumers" rectangle includes all 290 million consumers in the United States. In the "Business firms" box we have grouped all of the domestic business enterprises that buy and sell goods and services. The third participant, "Governments," includes the many separate agencies of the federal government, as well as state and local governments. Figure 11.1 also illustrates the role of foreigners.

The Two Markets

The easiest way to keep track of all this market activity is to distinguish two basic markets. Figure 11.1 does this by portraying separate circles for product markets and factor markets. In **factor markets,** factors of production are exchanged. Market participants buy or sell land, labor, or capital that can be used in the production process. When you go looking for work, for example, you are making a factor of production—your labor—available to producers. You are offering to *sell* your time and talent. The producers will hire you—*buy*

factor market Any place where factors of production (e.g., land, labor, capital, entrepreneurship) are bought and sold.

FIGURE 11.1

Market Interactions

Business firms participate in markets by supplying goods and services to product markets (point *A*) and purchasing factors of production in factor markets (*B*). Individual consumers participate in the marketplace by supplying factors of production such as their own labor (*C*) and purchasing final goods and services (*D*). Federal, state, and local governments also participate in both factor (*E*) and product markets (*F*) Foreigners participate by supplying imports, purchasing exports (*G*), and buying and selling resources (*H*).

your services in the factor market—if you are offering the skills they need at a price they are willing to pay.

Interactions within factor markets are only half the story. At the end of a hard day's work, consumers go to the grocery store (or the movies) to purchase desired goods and services—that is, to buy *products*. In this context, consumers again interact with business firms. This time, however, their roles are reversed: consumers are doing the *buying* and businesses are doing the *selling*. This exchange of goods and services occurs in **product markets.**

product market Any place where finished goods and services (products) are bought and sold.

Governments also supply goods and services to product markets. The consumer rarely buys national defense, schools, or highways directly; instead, such purchases are made indirectly through taxes and government expenditure. In Figure 11.1, the arrows running from governments through product markets to consumers serve to remind us, however, that all government output is intended "for the people." In this sense, the government acts as an intermediary, buying factors of production and providing certain goods and services consumers desire.

In Figure 11.1, the arrow connecting product markets to consumers (point D) emphasizes the fact that consumers, by definition, do not supply products. To the extent that individuals produce goods and services, they do so within the government or business sector. An individual who is a doctor, a dentist, or an economic consultant functions in two sectors. When selling services in the market, this person is regarded as a "business"; when away from the office, he or she is regarded as a "consumer." This distinction is helpful in emphasizing the role of the consumer as the final recipient of all goods and services produced.

Locating Markets Although we will refer repeatedly to two kinds of markets, it would be a little foolish to go off in search of the product and factor markets. Neither a factor market nor a product market is a single, identifiable structure. The term *market* simply refers to any place where an economic exchange occurs—where a buyer and seller interact. The exchange may take place on the street, in a taxicab, over the phone, by mail, in cyberspace, or through the classified ads of the newspaper. In some cases, the market used may in fact be quite distinguishable, as in the case of a retail store, the Chicago Commodity Exchange, or a state employment office. But whatever it looks like, *a market exists wherever and whenever an exchange takes place.*

A market exists wherever buyers and sellers interact.

© Stephen Chernin/Getty Images

Dollars and Exchange

Sometimes people exchange one good for another in the marketplace. On eBay, for example, you might convince a seller to accept some old CDs in payment for the DVD player she is selling. Or you might offer to paint someone's house in exchange for "free" rent. Such two-way exchanges are called **barter.**

barter The direct exchange of one good for another, without the use of money.

The problem with bartered exchanges is that you have to find a seller who wants whatever good you are offering in payment. This can make shopping an extremely time-consuming process. Fortunately, most market transactions are facilitated by using money as a form of payment. If you go shopping for a DVD player, you don't have to find a seller craving old CDs; all you have to do is find a seller willing to accept the dollar price you are willing to pay. Because money facilitates exchanges, ***nearly every market transaction involves an exchange of dollars for goods (in product markets) or resources (in factor markets).*** Money thus plays a critical role in facilitating market exchanges and the specialization they permit.

Supply and Demand

The two sides of each market transaction are called **supply** and **demand.** As noted earlier, we are *supplying* resources to the market when we look for a job—that is, when we offer our labor in exchange for income. But we are *demanding* goods when we shop in a supermarket—that is, when we are prepared to offer dollars in exchange for something to eat. Business firms may *supply* goods and services in product markets at the same time that they are *demanding* factors of production in factor markets.

Whether one is on the supply side or the demand side of any particular market transaction depends on the nature of the exchange, not on the people or institutions involved.

supply The ability and willingness to sell (produce) specific quantities of a good at alternative prices in a given time period, ceteris paribus.

demand The ability and willingness to buy specific quantities of a good at alternative prices in a given time period, ceteris paribus.

Demand

Although the concepts of supply and demand are useful for explaining what's happening in the marketplace, we are not yet ready to summarize the countless transactions that occur daily in both factor and product markets. Recall that ***every market transaction involves an exchange and thus some element of both supply and demand.*** Then just consider how many exchanges you alone undertake in a single week, not to mention the transactions of the other 290 million or so consumers among us. To keep track of so much action, we need to summarize the activities of many individuals.

Individual Demand

We can begin to understand how market forces work by looking more closely at the behavior of a single market participant. Let us start with Tom, a senior at Clearview College. Tom has majored in everything from art history to government in his three years at Clearview. He didn't connect to any of those fields and is on the brink of academic dismissal. To make matters worse, his parents have threatened to cut him off financially unless he gets serious about his course work. By that they mean he should enroll in courses that will lead to a job after graduation. Tom thinks he has found the perfect solution: web design. Everything associated with the Internet pays big bucks. Plus, the girls seem to think webbies are "cool." Or at least so Tom thinks. And his parents would definitely approve. So Tom has enrolled in web-design courses.

Unfortunately for Tom, he never developed computer skills. Until he got to Clearview College he thought mastering Sony's latest alien-attack video game was the pinnacle of electronic wizardry. His parents had given him a wired iMac, but he used it only for surfing hot video sites. The concept of using his computer for course work, much less developing some web content, was completely foreign to him. To compound his problems, Tom didn't have a clue about streaming, interfacing, animation, or the other concepts the web-design instructor outlined in the first lecture.

Given his circumstances, Tom was desperate to find someone who could tutor him in web design. But desperation is not enough to secure the services of a web architect. In a market-based economy, you must also be willing to *pay* for the things you want. Specifically, ***a demand exists only if someone is willing and able to pay for the good***—that is, exchange dollars for a good or service in the marketplace. Is Tom willing and able to pay for the web-design tutoring he so obviously needs?

Let us assume that Tom has some income and is willing to spend some of it to get a tutor. Under these assumptions, we can claim that Tom is a participant in the *market* for web-design services.

opportunity cost The most desired goods or services that are forgone in order to obtain something else.

But how much is Tom willing to pay? Surely, Tom is not prepared to exchange *all* his income for help in mastering web design. After all, Tom could use his income to buy more desirable goods and services. If he spent all his income on a web tutor, that help would have an extremely high **opportunity cost.** He would be giving up the opportunity to spend that income on other goods and services. He might pass his web-design class but have little else. It doesn't sound like a good idea to Tom. Even though he says he would be willing to pay *anything* to pass the web-design course, he probably has lower prices in mind. Indeed, it would be more reasonable to assume that there are *limits* to the amount Tom is willing to pay for any given quantity of web-design tutoring. These limits will be determined by how much income Tom has to spend and how many other goods and services he must forsake in order to pay for a tutor.

Tom also knows that his grade in web design will depend in part on how much tutoring service he buys. He can pass the course with only a few hours of design help. If he wants a better grade, however, the cost is going to escalate quickly.

Naturally, Tom wants it all—an A in web design and a ticket to higher-paying jobs. But here again the distinction between *desire* and *demand* is relevant. He may *desire* to master web design, but his actual proficiency will depend on how many hours of tutoring he is willing to *pay* for.

demand schedule A table showing the quantities of a good a consumer is willing and able to buy at alternative prices in a given time period, ceteris paribus.

We assume, then, that when Tom starts looking for a web-design tutor he has in mind some sort of **demand schedule,** like that described in Figure 11.2. According to row *A* of this schedule, Tom is willing and able to buy only one hour of tutoring service per semester if he must pay $50 an hour. At such an outrageous price he will learn minimal skills and pass the course. Just the bare minimum is all Tom is willing to buy at that price.

At lower prices, Tom would behave differently. According to Figure 11.2, Tom would purchase more tutoring services if the price per hour were less. At lower prices, he would not have to give up so many other goods and services for each hour of technical help. The reduced opportunity costs implied by lower service prices increase the attractiveness of professional help. Indeed, we see from row *I* of the demand schedule that Tom is willing to purchase 20 hours per semester—the whole bag of design tricks—if the price of tutoring is as low as $10 per hour.

Notice that the demand schedule doesn't tell us anything about *why* this consumer is willing to pay specific prices for various amounts of tutoring. Tom's expressed willingness to pay for web-design tutoring may reflect a desperate need to finish a web-design course, a lot of income to spend, or a relatively small desire for other goods and services. All the demand schedule tells us is what the consumer is *willing and able* to buy, for whatever reasons.

Also observe that the demand schedule doesn't tell us how many hours of design help the consumer will *actually* buy. Figure 11.2 simply states that Tom

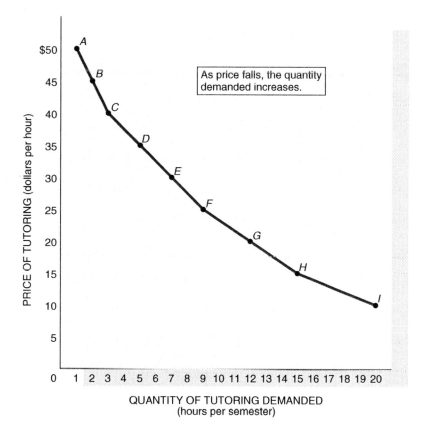

Demand Schedule

	Price of Tutoring (per hour)	Quantity of Tutoring Demanded (hours per semester)
A	$50	1
B	45	2
C	40	3
D	35	5
E	30	7
F	25	9
G	20	12
H	15	15
I	10	20

As price falls, the quantity demanded increases.

QUANTITY OF TUTORING DEMANDED
(hours per semester)

PRICE OF TUTORING (dollars per hour)

FIGURE 11.2
A Demand Schedule and Curve

A demand schedule indicates the quantities of a good a consumer is able and willing to buy at alternative prices (*ceteris paribus*). The demand schedule indicates that Tom would buy 5 hours of web-design tutoring per semester if the price were $35 per hour (row *D*). If web tutoring were less expensive (rows *E–I*). Tom would purchase a larger quantity.

A demand curve is a graphical illustration of a demand schedule. Each point on the curve refers to a specific quantity that will be demanded at a given price. If, for example, the price of web-design tutoring were $35 per hour, this curve tells us the consumer would purchase 5 hours per semester (point *D*). If web services cost $30 per hour, 7 hours per semester would be demanded (point *E*). Each point on the curve corresponds to a row in the schedule.

is *willing and able* to pay for one hour of tutoring per semester at $50 per hour, for two hours at $45 each, and so on. How much service he purchases will depend on the actual price of web services in the market. Until we know that price, we cannot tell how much service will be purchased. Hence **demand is an expression of consumer buying intentions, of a willingness to buy, not a statement of actual purchases.**

A convenient summary of buying intentions is the **demand curve,** a graphical illustration of the demand schedule. The demand curve in Figure 11.2 tells us again that this consumer is willing to pay for only one hour of web-design tutoring per semester if the price is $50 per hour (point *A*), for two if the price is $45 (point *B*), for three at $40 a hour (point *C*), and so on.

demand curve A curve describing the quantities of a good a consumer is willing and able to buy at alternative prices in a given time period, ceteris paribus.

HEADLINE　LAW OF DEMAND

Higher Alcohol Prices and Student Drinking

Raise the price of alcohol substantially and some college students will not drink or will drink less. That's the conclusion from a Harvard survey of 22,831 students at 158 colleges. Students faced with a $1 increase above the average drink price of $2.17 will be 33 percent less likely to drink at all or as much. So raising the price of alcohol in college communities could significantly lessen student drinking and its associated problems (alcohol-related deaths, property damage, unwanted sexual encounters, arrests). This could be done by raising local excise taxes, eliminating bar promotions, and forbidding all-you-can-drink events.

Source: Jenny Williams, Frank Chaloupka, and Henry Wechsler, "Are There Differential Effects of Price and Policy on College Students Drinking Intensity?" Cambridge, MA: National Bureau of Economic Research, 2002.

NOTE: The Law of Demand predicts that the quantity demanded of any good—even beer and liquor—declines as its price increases.

Once we know what the market price of web tutoring actually is, a glance at the demand curve tells us how much service this consumer will buy.

What the notion of *demand* emphasizes is that the amount we buy of a good depends on its price. We seldom if ever decide to buy only a certain quantity of a good at whatever price is charged. Instead, we enter markets with a set of desires and a limited amount of money to spend. How much we actually buy of any good will depend on its price.

A common feature of demand curves is their downward slope. As the price of a good falls, people tend to purchase more of it. In Figure 11.2 the quantity of web tutorial services demanded increases (moves rightward along the horizontal axis) as the price per hour decreases (moves down the vertical axis). This inverse relationship between price and quantity is so common we refer to it as the **law of demand.**

law of demand The quantity of a good demanded in a given time period increases as its price falls, ceteris paribus.

College administrators think the Law of Demand could be used to curb student drinking. Low retail prices and bar promotions encourage student to drink more alcohol. As the accompanying Headline explains, higher prices would reduce the quantity of alcohol demanded.

Determinants of Demand

The demand curve in Figure 11.2 has only two dimensions—quantity demanded (on the horizontal axis) and price (on the vertical axis). This seems to imply that the amount of tutorial services demanded depends only on the price of that service. This is surely not the case. A consumer's willingness and ability to buy a product at various prices depend on a variety of forces. *The determinants of market demand include*

* *Tastes* (desire for this and other goods).
* *Income* (of the consumer).
* *Other goods* (their availability and price).
* *Expectations* (for income, prices, tastes).
* *Number of buyers.*

If Tom didn't have to pass a web-design course, he would have no taste (desire) for web-page tutoring and thus no demand. If he had no income, he would not have the ability to pay and thus would still be out of the web-design market. The price and availability of other goods affect the opportunity cost of tutoring services, while expectations for income, grades, and graduation prospects would all influence his willingness to buy such services.

Ceteris Paribus

If demand is in fact such a multidimensional decision, how can we reduce it to only the two dimensions of price and quantity? This is the ***ceteris paribus*** trick we encountered earlier. To simplify their models of the world, economists focus on only one or two forces at a time and *assume* nothing else changes. We know a consumer's tastes, income, other goods, and expectations all affect the decision to buy web-design services. But **we focus on the relationship between quantity demanded and price.** That is to say, we want to know what *independent* influence price has on consumption decisions. To find out, we must isolate that one influence, price, and assume that the determinants of demand remain unchanged.

The *ceteris paribus* assumption is not as far-fetched as it may seem. People's tastes (desires) don't change very quickly. Income tends to be fairly stable from week to week. Even expectations for the future are slow to change. Accordingly, the price of a good may be the only thing that changes on any given day. In that case, a change in price may be the only thing that prompts a change in consumer behavior.

ceteris paribus The assumption of nothing else changing.

Shifts in Demand

The determinants of demand do change, of course, particularly over time. Accordingly, **the demand schedule and curve remain unchanged only so long as the underlying determinants of demand remain constant.** If the *ceteris paribus* assumption is violated—if tastes, income, other goods, or expectations change—the ability or willingness to buy will change. When this happens, the demand curve will **shift** to a new position.

Suppose, for example, that Tom won $1,000 in the state lottery. This increase in his income would greatly increase his ability to pay for tutoring services. Figure 11.3 shows the effect of this windfall on Tom's demand for tutoring services. The old demand curve, D_1, is no longer relevant. Tom's

shift in demand A change in the quantity demanded at any (every) given price.

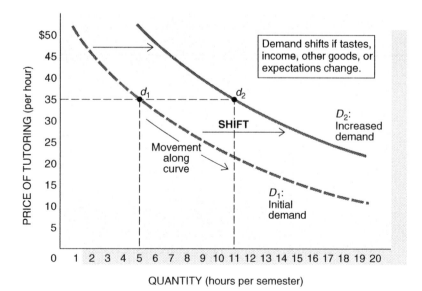

QUANTITY (hours per semester)

FIGURE 11.3
A Shift in Demand

A demand curve shows how the quantity demanded changes in response to a change in price, *if* all else remains constant. But the determinants of demand may themselves change, causing the demand curve to *shift*. In this case, an increase in income increases demand from D_1 to D_2. After this shift. Tom demands 11 hours (d_2), rather than 5 (d_1), at the price of $35. The quantity demanded at all other prices increases as well.

lottery winnings enable him to buy more tutoring services at any price. This is illustrated by the new demand curve, D_2. According to this new curve, lucky Tom is now willing and able to buy 11 hours per semester at the price of $35 per hour (point d_2). This is a large increase in demand, as previously (before winning the lottery) he demanded only 5 hours at that price (point d_1).

With his higher income, Tom can buy more tutoring services at every price. Thus *the entire demand curve shifts to the right when income goes up.* Both the old (prelottery) and the new (postlottery) demand curves are illustrated in Figure 11.3.

Income is only one of four basic determinants of demand. Changes in any of the other determinants of demand would also cause the demand curve to shift. Tom's taste for web-design tutoring might increase dramatically, for example, if his other professors made the quality of personal web pages a critical determinant of course grades. His taste (desire) for web-design services might increase even more if his parents promised to buy him a new car for passing *all* his courses. Whatever its origins, *an increase in taste (desire) or expectations also shifts the demand curve to the right.* The accompanying Headline shows how such shifts can affect the equilibrium price of a product.

Movements vs. Shifts

It is important to distinguish shifts of the demand curve from movements along the demand curve. *Movements along a demand curve are a response to price changes for that good.* Such movements assume that determinants of demand are unchanged. By contrast, *shifts of the demand curve occur when the determinants of demand change.* When tastes, income, other goods, or expectations are altered, the basic relationship between price and quantity demanded is changed (shifts).

For convenience, the distinction between movements along a demand curve and shifts of the demand curve have their own labels. Specifically, take care to distinguish

* *Changes in quantity demanded:* movements along a given demand curve, in response to price changes of that good.
* *Changes in demand:* shifts of the demand curve due to changes in tastes, income, other goods, or expectations.

The Headline on p. 374 told how higher alcohol prices could reduce college drinking. The effectiveness of higher prices depends in part, however, on *ceteris paribus.* If student incomes increased, the demand curve might shift to the right, offsetting the impact of higher prices. On the other hand, if the penalties for campus drinking were increased, altered expectations might shift the demand curve to the left, reinforcing the policy goal of lower alcohol consumption.

Tom's behavior in the web-tutoring market is subject to similar influences. A change in the *price* of tutoring will move Tom up or down his demand curve. By contrast, a change in an underlying determinant of demand will shift his entire demand curve to the left or right.

market demand The total quantities of a good or service people are willing and able to buy at alternative prices in a given time period, the sum of individual demands.

Market Demand

The same forces that change an individual's consumption behavior also move entire markets. Suppose you wanted to assess the **market demand** for web-tutoring services at Clearview College. To do that, you'd want to identify every student's demand for that service. Some students, of course, have no need

Natural Gas Prices Rise as Temps Fall

WASHINGTON—Natural gas prices are climbing quickly, shocking millions of homeowners across the country as they open their winter energy bills.

Futures prices for natural gas are up more than 130% from last year and are the highest since April 2001.

What's behind the increase:

- It's colder this winter than last winter, which was the ninth warmest in the USA since recordkeeping began in 1895, according to The Weather Channel. Last winter was the warmest on record for the Northeast. Lower temperatures this year are leading to increased demand. Forecasters anticipate lower temperatures to continue in coming weeks.
- Oil prices have been rising for months because of a general strike in Venezuela and concerns about what will happen to oil supplies if the USA goes to war

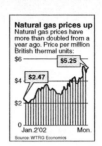

Natural gas prices up
Natural gas prices have more than doubled from a year ago. Price per million British thermal units:

against Iraq. Because natural gas can often be used in place of oil, especially in industry, a rise in oil prices usually translates into higher natural gas prices.

—Barbara Hagenbaugh

Source: *USA Today*, January 14, 2003, p. B1.

NOTE: Demand increases (shifts) when tastes increase (due, here, to colder weather), when the price of substitute goods (e.g., oil) increase, or when other determinants of demand (income, expectations) change.

or desire for professional web-design services and are not willing to pay anything for such tutoring; they do not participate in the web-design market. Other students have a desire for such services but not enough income to pay for them; they, too, are excluded from the web-design market. A large number of students, however, not only have a need (or desire) for tutoring but also are willing and able to purchase such services.

What we start with in product markets, then, is many individual demand curves. Fortunately, it is possible to combine all the individual demand curves into a single **market demand** for web-design services. Suppose you would be willing to buy one hour of tutoring services per semester at a price of $80 per hour. George, who is also desperate to learn web design, would buy two at that price; and I would buy none, since my publisher (McGraw-Hill) creates a web page for me (try mhhe.com/economics/Schiller). What would our combined (market) demand for hours of design services be at that price? Clearly, our individual inclinations indicate that we would be willing to buy a total of three hours of tutoring services per semester if the price were $80 per hour. Our combined willingness to buy—our collective market demand—is nothing more than the sum of our individual demands. The same kind of aggregation can be performed for all consumers, leading to a summary of the total market demand for web-design tutoring services at Clearview College. This *market demand is determined by the number of potential buyers and their respective tastes, incomes, other goods, and expectations.*

The Market Demand Curve

Table 11.1 provides the basic market demand schedule for a situation in which only three consumers participate in the market. Figure 11.4 illustrates the same market situation with demand curves. The three individuals who

TABLE 11.1
The Market Demand Schedule

Market demand represents the combined demands of all market participants. To determine the total quantity of tutoring demanded at any given price, we add up the separate demands of the individual consumers. Row G of this schedule indicates that a *total* quantity of 39 hours of service per semester will be demanded at a price of $20 per hour.

	Price per Hour	Quantity of Tutoring Demanded (hours per semester)			Total Demand
		Tom +	George +	Lisa =	
A	$50	1	4	0	5
B	45	2	6	0	8
C	40	3	8	0	11
D	35	5	11	0	16
E	30	7	14	1	22
F	25	9	18	3	30
G	20	12	22	5	39
H	15	15	26	6	47
I	10	20	30	7	57

participate in the market demand for web services at Clearview College obviously differ greatly, as suggested by their respective demand schedules. Tom *has* to pass his web-design classes or confront college and parental rejection. He also has a nice allowance (income), so can afford to buy a lot of tutorial help. His demand schedule is portrayed in the first column of Table 11.1 (and is identical to the one we examined in Figure 11.2). George, as we already noted, is also desperate to acquire some job skills and is willing to pay relatively high prices for web-design tutoring. His demand is summarized in the second column under "Quantity of Tutoring Demanded" in Table 11.1.

The third consumer in this market is Lisa. Lisa already knows the nuts and bolts of web design, so she doesn't have as desperate a need for tutorial services. She would like to upgrade her skills, however, especially in animation

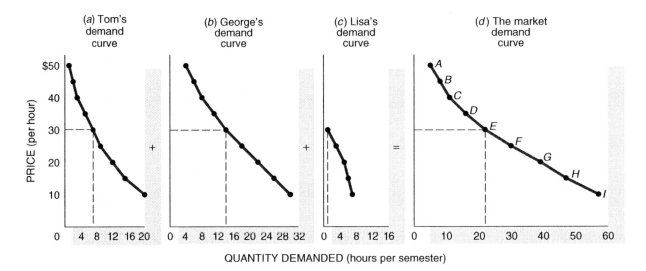

FIGURE 11.4   Construction of the Market Demand Curve

The market demand curve expresses the *combined* demands of all market participants. At a price of $30 per hour, the total quantity of web-design services demanded would be 22 hours per semester (point *E*): 7 hours demanded by Tom, 14 by George, and 1 by Lisa.

and e-commerce applications. But her limited budget precludes paying a lot for help. She will buy some technical support only if the price falls to $30 per hour. Should tutors cost less, she'd even buy quite a few hours of design services.

The differing personalities and consumption habits of Tom, George, and Lisa are expressed in their individual demand schedules and associated curves, as depicted in Table 11.1 and Figure 11.4. To determine the *market* demand for tutoring services from this information, we simply add up these three separate demands. The end result of this aggregation is, first, a *market* demand schedule (the last column in Table 11.1) and, second, the resultant *market* demand curve (the curve in Figure 11.4*d*). These market summaries describe the various quantities of tutoring services that Clearview College students are *willing and able* to purchase each semester at various prices.

The Use of Demand Curves

So why does anybody care what the demand curve for web-design tutoring looks like? What's the point of doing all this arithmetic and drawing so many graphs?

If you were a web designer at Clearview College, you'd certainly like to have the information depicted in Figure 11.4. What the market demand curve tells us is how much tutoring service could be sold at various prices to Clearview students. Suppose you hoped to sell 30 hours at a price of $30 per hour. According to Figure 11.4 (point *E*), students will buy only 22 hours at that price. Hence, you won't attain your sales goal. You could find that out by posting ads on campus and waiting for a response. It would be a lot easier, however, if you knew in advance what the demand curve looked like.

People who promote music concerts need the same kind of information. They want to fill the stadium with screaming fans. But fans have limited income and

Would this many fans show up if concert prices were higher?
AP/Wide World Photos

desires for other goods. Accordingly, the number of fans who will buy concert tickets depends on the price. If the promoter sets the price too high, there will be lots of empty seats at the concert. If the price is set too low, the promoter may lose potential sales revenue. What the promoter wants to know is what price will induce a quantity demanded that conforms to the number of available seats. If the promoter could consult a demand curve, the correct price would be evident.

Supply

Even if we knew what the demand for every good looked like, we couldn't predict what quantities would be bought. The demand curve tells us only how much consumers are willing and able to buy at specific prices. We don't know the price yet, however. To find out what price will be charged, we've got to know something about the behavior of people who *sell* goods and services. That is to say, we need to examine the *supply* side of the marketplace. The **market supply** of a good reflects the collective behavior of all firms that are willing and able to sell that good at various prices.

market supply The total quantities of a good that sellers are willing and able to sell at alternative prices in a given time period, ceteris paribus.

Determinants of Supply

Let's return to the Clearview campus for a moment. What we need to know now is how much tutorial web service people are willing and able to provide. Generally speaking, web-page design can be fun, but it can also be drudge work, especially when you're doing it for someone else. Software programs like PhotoShop, Flash, and Fireworks have made web-page design easier and more creative. But teaching someone else to design web pages is still work. So few people offer to supply web services just for the fun of it. Web designers do it for money. Specifically, they do it to earn income that they, in turn, can spend on goods and services they desire.

How much income must be offered to induce web designers to do a job depends on a variety of things. The **_determinants of market supply include_**

* **_Technology_**   * **_Taxes and subsidies_**
* **_Factor costs_**   * **_Expectations_**
* **_Other goods_**   * **_Number of sellers_**

The technology of web design, for example, is always getting easier and more creative. With a program like PageOut, for example, it's very easy to create a bread-and-butter web page. A continuous stream of new software programs (e.g., Fireworks, Dreamweaver) keeps stretching the possibilities for graphics, animation, interactivity, and content. These technological advances mean that web-design services can be supplied more quickly and cheaply. They also make _teaching_ web design easier. As a result, they induce people to supply more web-design services at every price.

How much tutoring is offered at any given price also depends on the cost of factors of production. If the software programs needed to create web pages are cheap (or, better yet, free!), web designers can afford to charge lower prices. If the required software inputs are expensive, however, they will have to charge more money per hour for their services.

Other goods can also affect the willingness to supply web-design services. If you can make more income waiting tables than you can designing web pages, why would you even boot up the computer? As the prices paid for other goods and services change, they will influence people's decisions about whether to offer web services.

In the real world, the decision to supply goods and services is also influenced by the long arm of Uncle Sam. Federal, state, and local governments impose taxes on income earned in the marketplace. When tax rates are high, people get to keep less of the income they earn. Some people may conclude that tutoring is no longer worth the hassle and withdraw from the market.

Expectations are also important on the supply side of the market. If web designers expect higher prices, lower costs, or reduced taxes, they may be more willing to learn new software programs. On the other hand, if they have poor expectations about the future, they may just sell their computers and find something else to do.

Finally, we note that the number of available web designers will affect the quantity of service offered for sale at various prices. If there are lots of willing web designers on campus, a large quantity of tutoring services will be available.

The Market Supply Curve

Figure 11.5 illustrates the market supply curve of web services at Clearview College. Like market demand, the market supply curve is the sum of all the individual supplier decisions about how much output to produce at any given price. The market supply curve slopes upward to the right, indicating that

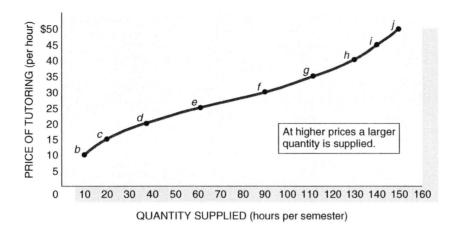

FIGURE 11.5
The Market Supply Curve

The market supply curve indicates the *combined* sales intentions of all market participants. If the price of tutoring were $25 per hour (point *e*), the *total* quantity of tutoring service supplied would be 62 hours per semester. This quantity is determined by adding together the supply decisions of all individual producers.

larger quantities will be offered at higher prices. This basic **law of supply** reflects the fact that increased output typically entails higher costs and so will be forthcoming only at higher prices. Higher prices may also increase profits and so entice producers to supply greater quantities.

Note that Figure 11.5 illustrates the *market* supply. We have not bothered to construct separate supply curves for each person who is able and willing to supply web services on the Clearview campus. We have skipped that first step and gone right to the *market* supply curve. Like the market demand curve, however, the market supply curve is based on the supply decisions of individual producers. The curve itself is computed by adding up the quantities each producer is willing and able to supply at every given price. Point *f* in Figure 11.5 tells us that those individuals are collectively willing and able to produce 90 hours of tutoring per semester at a price of $30 per hour. The rest of the points on the supply curve tell us how many hours of tutoring will be offered at other prices.

None of the points on the market supply curve (Figure 11.5) tells us how much tutoring service is actually being sold on the Clearview campus. *Market supply is an expression of sellers' intentions, of the ability and willingness to sell, not a statement of actual sales.* My next-door neighbor may be *willing* to sell his 1986 Honda Civic for $8,000, but it is most unlikely that he will ever find a buyer at that price. Nevertheless, his *willingness* to sell his car at that price is part of the *market supply* of used cars.

Shifts in Supply

As with demand, there is nothing sacred about any given set of supply intentions. Supply curves *shift* when the underlying determinants of supply change. Thus we again distinguish

* *Changes in quantity supplied:* movements along a given supply curve.
* *Changes in supply:* shifts of the supply curve.

Our Latin friend *ceteris paribus* is once again the decisive factor. If the price of tutoring services is the only thing changing, then we can **track changes in quantity supplied along the supply curve** in Figure 11.5. But if *ceteris paribus* is violated—if technology, factor costs, other goods, taxes, or expectations change—then **changes in supply are illustrated by shifts of the supply curve.** The accompanying Headline illustrates how a leftward shift in the supply of electricity worsened California's 2000–2001 energy crisis.

law of supply The quantity of a good supplied in a given time period increases as its price increases, ceteris paribus.

HEADLINE   SUPPLY SHIFT

California Forced to Turn the Lights Off

LOS ANGELES, Jan. 17—Out of power and out of options, California ordered rolling blackouts across the state today, its most desperate move yet in an energy crisis that is spinning out of control.

The widely scattered blackouts affecting some half-million customers began at midday. With only minutes of warning, sections of San Francisco, Silicon Valley, the state capital of Sacramento and a few other smaller cities went dark . . .

The immediate cause of the blackouts was a large power plant suddenly going offline in Northern California this morning. More important is that some wholesale energy suppliers refused to sell power to California's financially struggling utility companies, which are having great difficulty paying for power.

After a week of dire warnings and coast-to-coast negotiations on the state's predicament, managers of California's electrical system—or power grid—said they resorted to blackouts because demand overwhelmed dwindling supplies and a frantic effort to beg or borrow electricity from other states failed.

"This situation is not going to get any prettier unless we find some magical megawatts from somewhere," Patrick Dorinson, a spokesman for the California Independent System Operator, the agency that distributes power through most of the state, said this afternoon.

The operators of the state's power grid said that some wholesale power providers declined to sell energy to

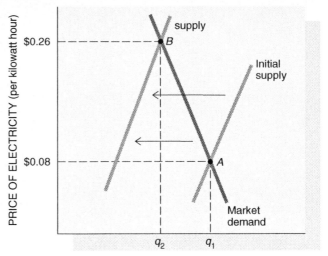

California until the operators called the suppliers today pleading for more power hour by hour and invoking Energy Secretary Bill Richardson's emergency order requiring the providers to come to California's aid. Richardson extended that order again today.

—Rene Sanchez and William Booth

Source: *Washington Post*, January 18, 2001, p. 1.

NOTE: If an underlying determinant of supply changes, the entire supply curve shifts. Mechanical breakdowns and supplier anxiety about prospects for getting paid reduced the quantity of electricity supplied at any given price in early 2001.

Equilibrium

We can now determine the price and quantity of web-tutoring services being sold at Clearview College. The market supply curve expresses the *ability and willingness* of producers to sell web services at various prices. The market demand curve illustrates the *ability and willingness* of Tom, George, and Lisa to buy web services at those same prices. When we put the two curves together, we see that **only one price and quantity are compatible with the existing intentions of both buyers and sellers.** This **equilibrium price** occurs at the intersection of the two curves in Figure 11.6. Once it is established, web tutoring services will cost $20 per hour. At that price, campus web designers will sell a total of 39 hours of tutoring service per semester—the same amount that students wish to buy at that price.

equilibrium price The price at which the quantity of a good demanded in a given time period equals the quantity supplied.

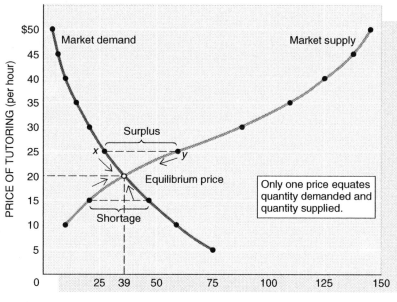

FIGURE 11.6
Market Surplus or
Shortage

Only at equilibrium is the quantity demanded equal to the quantity supplied. In this case, the equilibrium price is $20 per hour, and 39 hours is the equilibrium quantity. At higher prices, a market surplus exists—the quantity supplied exceeds the quantity demanded. At prices below equilibrium, a market shortage exists.

The intersection of the demand and supply curves in the graph represents equilibrium price and output in this market.

QUANTITY (hours per semester)

Price per Hour	Quantity Supplied (hours per semester)		Quantity Demanded (hours per semester)
$50	148		5
45	140		8
40	130	market	11
35	114	surplus	16
30	90		22
25	62		30
20	39	**equilibrium**	39
15	20	market	47
10	10	shortage	57

Market Clearing

An equilibrium doesn't imply that everyone is happy with the prevailing price or quantity. Notice in Figure 11.6, for example, that some students who want to buy web tutoring don't get any. These would-be buyers are arrayed along the demand curve *below* the equilibrium. Because the price they are *willing* to pay is less than the equilibrium price, they don't get any tutoring.

Likewise, there are would-be sellers in the market who don't sell as many web services as they might like. These people are arrayed along the supply curve *above* the equilibrium. Because they insist on being paid a price that is higher than the equilibrium price, they don't actually sell anything.

Although not everyone gets full satisfaction from the market equilibrium, that unique outcome is efficient. The equilibrium price and quantity reflect a compromise between buyers and sellers. No other compromise yields a quantity demanded that is exactly equal to the quantity supplied.

The Invisible Hand The equilibrium price is not determined by any single individual. Rather it is determined by the collective behavior of many buyers and sellers, each acting out his or her own demand or supply schedule. It is this kind of impersonal price determination that gave rise to Adam Smith's

HEADLINE   MARKET SHORTAGE

For Fans, What's 4 Nights for U2?

After an 80-hour ordeal—four nights stuffed in a car, three days breathing bus exhaust, scarfing Cokes and franks, running blocks for pit stops—the three University of Maryland seniors who camped out at RFK Stadium prevailed. They beat the scalpers to U2 concert tickets.

At 8 A.M. today they would be, if all went as planned, first in line at the RFK box office. By 9 A.M. the 52,000-seat stadium will sell out, predicted a Ticketmaster official.

"It's what you got to do to get good seats," said Crawford Conniff, 22, stretched out near the stadium among traffic island dandelions.

"We have unlimited time," said Mike Collins, 22. "If we had a job making 50 grand, we could pay $150 to scalpers."

Actually, $150 sounds cheap for the $28.50 face-value tickets. Today's ticket sale for the Aug. 15 concert, one of the summer's hottest, is likely to ignite an orgy of profiteering.

When the band played Los Angeles, scalpers scored up to $1,200 a ticket for prime seats. In Washington, as early as Tuesday, ticket brokers had stationed students, unemployed, and even homeless people at ticket outlets to snap up hundreds of choice seats.

—Laura Blumenfeld

Source: ©1992, the Washington Post. *Washington Post,* April 25, 1992, p. Al. Reprinted with permission.

NOTE: A below-equilibrium price creates a market shortage. When that happens, another method of distributing tickets—like time in line—must be used to determine who gets the available tickets.

characterization of the market mechanism as the invisible hand. In attempting to explain how the market mechanism works, the famed eighteenth-century economist noted a certain feature of market prices. The market behaves as if some unseen force (the invisible hand) were examining each individual's supply or demand schedule, then selecting a price that assured an equilibrium. In practice, the process of price determination is not so mysterious; rather, it is a simple one of trial and error.

Surplus and Shortage

Suppose for the moment that someone were to spread the word on the Clearview campus that tutors were available at only $15 per hour. Tom, George, and Lisa would be standing in line to get help with their web classes, but campus web designers would not be willing to supply the quantity desired at that price. As Figure 11.6 confirms, at $15 per page, the quantity demanded (47 hours per semester) would greatly exceed the quantity supplied (20 hours per semester). In this situation, we speak of a **market shortage,** that is, an excess of quantity demanded over quantity supplied. At a price of $15 a page, the shortage amounts to 27 hours of web service.

When a market shortage exists, not all consumer demands can be satisfied. Some people who are *willing* to buy tutoring services at the going price ($15) will not be able to do so. To assure themselves of good grades. Tom, George, Lisa, or some other consumer may offer to pay a *higher* price, thus initiating a move up the demand curve of Figure 11.6. The higher prices offered will in turn induce other enterprising students to offer more web tutoring, thus ensuring an upward movement along the market supply curve. Thus a higher price tends to call forth a greater quantity supplied, as reflected in the upward-sloping supply curve. Notice, again, that the *desire* to tutor web design has not changed: only the quantity supplied has responded to a change in price.

The accompanying Headline illustrates what happens at music concerts when tickets are priced below equilibrium. More fans were willing to pay

market shortage The amount by which the quantity demanded exceeds the quantity supplied at a given price: excess demand.

MARKET SHORTAGE   HEADLINE

Buyers Line Up for Sony's PlayStation 2

Teenage boys line up outside an electronics store as the hour approaches midnight. If that scene sounds vaguely familiar, undoubtedly you remember the last videogame system that every teenager in America (and even some adults) had to have. Now, they must have another one. And at 12:01 A.M. today, the Sony PlayStation 2 went on sale.

"I want to be the first kid on the block to have one," said James Willis, 35, in line in front of the Electronic Boutique at the Fashion Centre at Pentagon City. The store planned to open at midnight and remain open until 2:30 A.M. to meet the perceived needs of hard-core game customers, some of whom signed up for the $299 videogame console as long ago as last December.

But most major electronics retailers, including CompUSA, Best Buy, and Circuit City, said they would open at the normal hour this morning, doling out the games on a first-come, first-served basis.

Sony expects to ship 1.3 million to 1.4 million PlayStation 2s to the U.S. market this year, But the demand appears to be much higher. One analyst, Greg Durkin at Alexander Associates, estimated that demand for the game system could be as high as 4 million customers.

—Nicholas Johnston and Mike Musgrove

Source: *Washington Post*, October 26, 2000, p. EI.

NOTE: If price is below equilibrium, the quantity demanded exceeds the quantity supplied. The willingness to pay $299 didn't assure purchase of a PlayStation 2 in 2000.

$28.50 for the 1992 U2 concerts than the stadiums could accommodate. At below equilibrium prices, the market mechanism was no longer the sole arbiter of FOR WHOM the concert is produced. Admission required not just the ticket price but also the willingness to stand in line—sometimes for days. Consumers with a low opportunity cost for their time (e.g., nonworking students) are more likely to stand in line. Once they get the tickets, they may even resell them at higher prices to high-paid businesspeople who have more income and a higher opportunity cost for waiting in line. Such "scalping" would not be possible if the initial price of the tickets had been set by supply and demand.

A similar situation occurred when Sony started selling the PlayStation 2 in October 2000. At the initial price of $299, the quantity demanded greatly exceeded the quantity supplied (see Headline on this page). To get a PlayStation 2, people had to spend hours in line or pay a premium price in resale markets like eBay.

A very different sequence of events occurs when a market surplus exits. Suppose for the moment that the web designers at Clearview College believed tutoring services could be sold for $25 per hour rather than the equilibrium price of $20. From the demand and supply schedules depicted in Figure 11.6, we can foresee the consequences. At $25 per hour, campus web designers would be offering more web-tutoring services (point *y*) than Tom, George, and Lisa were willing to buy (point *x*) at that price. A **market surplus** of web services would exist, in that more tutoring was being offered for sale (supplied) than students cared to purchase at the available price.

As Figure 11.6 indicates, at a price of $25 per hour, a market surplus of 32 hours per semester exists. Under these circumstances, campus web designers would be spending many idle hours at their computers, waiting for customers to appear. Their waiting will be in vain, because the quantity of tutoring demanded will not increase until the price of tutoring falls. That is the clear message of the demand curve. The tendency of quantity demanded to increase as price falls is illustrated in Figure 11.6 by a movement along the

market surplus The amount by which the quantity supplied exceeds the quantity demanded at a given price: excess supply.

HEADLINE   MARKET SURPLUS

U2 Tour Turning Out 2 Be "Disaster" in Ticket Sales

Industry insiders tell me U2's "Pop-Mart" tour, which hits Denver tonight, is the lowest-grossing stadium tour in the history of rock 'n' roll. "It's a disaster," they're saying. The lavish production, which arrived in Denver with 500 tons of equipment in 75 trailer trucks, sold out in Las Vegas when it opened last week but attracted only 30,500 fans in second-date San Diego. Sales are soft in numerous U.S. markets on the band's projected world tour. There's a lot out there competing for our fun-ticket bucks—and U2 tickets cost $37.50 to $52.50 plus service charges.

—Bill Husted

Source: *Denver Post*, May 1, 1997, p. A2. Reprinted by permission of the *Denver Post*.

NOTE: Empty seats in a stadium, on an airplane, or in a theater imply a market surplus: a larger quantity is supplied than demanded at the existing price.

demand curve from point *x* to lower prices and greater quantity demanded. As we move down the market demand curve, the desire for tutoring does not change, but the quantity people are able and willing to buy increases. Web designers at Clearview would have to reduce price from $25 (point *y*) to $20 per hour in order to attract enough buyers.

U2 learned the difference between market shortage and surplus the hard way. The group began another tour in April 1997, with scheduled concerts in 80 cities over a period of 14 months. This time around, however, U2 was charging as much as $52.50 a ticket—nearly double the 1992 price. By the time they got to the second city, they were playing in stadiums with lots of empty seats (see Headline). The apparent market surplus led critics to label the 1997 PopMart tour a disaster. For their 2001 Elevation Tour, U2 offered festival seating for only $35. By this process of trial and error, U2 ultimately located the equilibrium price for their concerts.

What we observe, then, is that **whenever the market price is set above or below the equilibrium price, either a market surplus or a market shortage will emerge.** To overcome a surplus or shortage, buyers and sellers will change their behavior. Only at the *equilibrium* price will no further adjustments be required.

Business firms can discover equilibrium market prices by trial and error. If they find that consumer purchases are not keeping up with production, they may conclude that price is above the equilibrium. To get rid of their accumulated inventory, they will have to lower their prices (by a Grand End-of-Year Sale, perhaps). In the happy situation where consumer purchases are outpacing production, a firm might conclude that its price was a trifle too low and give it a nudge upward. In either case, the equilibrium price can be established after a few trials in the marketplace.

Changes in Equilibrium

The collective actions of buyers and sellers will quickly establish an equilibrium price for any product. No particular equilibrium price is permanent, however. The equilibrium price established in the Clearview College web-services market, for example, was the unique outcome of specific demand and supply schedules. Those schedules are valid for only a certain time and place. They will rule the market only so long as the assumption of *ceteris paribus* holds. In reality, tastes, incomes, the price and availability of other

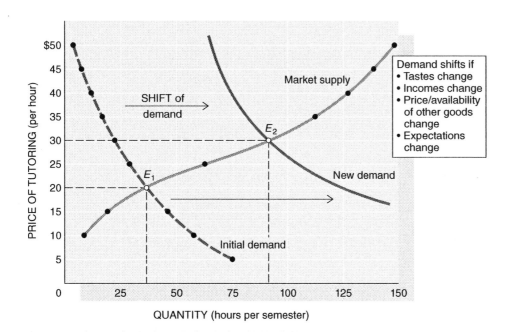

FIGURE 11.7
A New Equilibrium

A rightward shift of the demand curve indicates that consumers are willing and able to buy a larger quantity at every price. As a consequence, a new equilibrium is established (point E_2), at a higher price and greater quantity. A shift of the demand curve occurs only when the assumption of *ceteris paribus* is violated—when one of the determinants of demand changes.

The equilibrium would also be altered if the determinants of supply changed, causing a shift of the market supply curve.

goods, or expectations could change at any time. When this happens, *ceteris paribus* will be violated and the demand curve will have to be redrawn. Such a shift of the demand curve will lead to a new equilibrium price and quantity. Indeed, ***the equilibrium price will change whenever the supply or demand curve shifts.***

We can illustrate how equilibrium prices change by taking one last look at the Clearview College web-services market. Our original supply and demand curves, together with the resulting equilibrium (point E_1), are depicted in Figure 11.7. Now suppose that the professors at Clearview begin requiring more technical expertise in their web-design courses. These increased course requirements will affect market demand. Tom, George, and Lisa will suddenly be willing to buy more web services (tutors) at every price than they were before. That is to say, the *demand* for web services will increase. We can represent this increased demand by a rightward *shift* of the market demand curve, as illustrated in Figure 11.7.

Note that the new demand curve intersects the (unchanged) market supply curve at a new price (point E_2); the equilibrium price is now $30 per hour. This new equilibrium price will persist until either the demand curve or the supply curve shifts again.

Supply and Demand Shifts   The accompanying Headline illustrates what can happen to the equilibrium price when *both* demand and supply shift. Colder temperatures in the 2000–01 winter increased the demand for natural gas (heating oil). At the same time, shrinking reserves and pipeline problems reduced the supply of gas. As a result, the price of natural gas nearly tripled between January 2000 and January 2001.

The kinds of price changes described here are quite common. A few moments in a stockbroker's office or a glance through the stock pages of the daily newspaper should be testimony enough to the fluid character of market prices. If thousands of stockholders decide to sell IBM shares tomorrow, you can be sure that the market price of that stock will drop. Notice how often other prices—in the grocery store, the music store, or at the gas station—change. Then determine whether it was supply, demand, or both curves that shifted.

HEADLINE   BEEF PRICES ON THE WAY UP

Canadian Import Ban, Demand Cited

Stock up the freezer if you like steak because beef prices at the supermarket are on their way up.

And they're likely to stay there for a while.

U.S. cattle prices are at a record high, say economists with the U.S. Department of Agriculture. They've increased 34% since July, and this month, the benchmark price of Nebraska choice steers went from $90 to $116 per 100 pounds. A year ago, the price per 100 pounds was $64.

"We've seen increases in the last 10 days," said Jim Robb, director of the Livestock Marketing Information Center in Denver. "Choice T-bone steak and New York strip steak, those prices are double what they were three weeks ago."

Prices are up because of a set of circumstances that Robb calls "Completely unprecedented." First, consumer demand for beef has increased nearly 10% since 1998 after declining for 20 years.

Recent increases in consumption may be due in part [to] the increasing popularity of high protein diets, such as this summer's blockbuster South Beach diet and the venerable Atkins diet.

The rising prices
Here is the price per 100 pounds of 65–80% choice cattle, the kind that most commonly end up on retail shelves, in the five major cattle markets:

$115.20

$120

$80

$40

$0

8/17/03   10/19/03

Source: Livestock Marketing Information Center
By Julie Snider, USA TODAY

Second, as Wayne Purcell of the Research Institute on Livestock Pricing at Virginia Tech points out, the U.S. banned imports of Canadian cattle and beef five months ago. The ban was imposed because of the discovery of a case of mad cow disease there last spring and reduced cattle and meat imports to the USA by 9%.

Consumers already may be feeling the impact, whether they're eating out or at home.

—Elizabeth Weise

Source: *USA TODAY*, October 24, 2003, p. 1.

NOTE: If demand increases (shifts right) and supply decreases (shifts left), the equilibrium price can increase sharply.

Disequilibrium Pricing

The ability of the market to achieve equilibrium price and quantity is evident. Nevertheless, people are often upset with those outcomes. At Clearview College, the students buying tutoring services are likely to feel that the price of such services is too high. On the other hand, campus web designers may feel that they are getting paid too little for their tutorial services.

Price Ceilings

price ceiling Upper limit imposed on the price of a good.

Sometimes consumers are able to convince the government to intervene on their behalf by setting a limit on prices. In many cities, for example, poor people and their advocates have convinced local governments that rents are too high. High rents, they argue, make housing prohibitively expensive for the poor, leaving them homeless or living in crowded, unsafe quarters. They ask government to impose a *limit* on rents in order to make housing affordable for everyone. Two hundred local governments—including New York City, Boston, Washington, D.C., and San Francisco—have responded with rent controls. In all cases, rent controls are a **price ceiling**—an upper limit imposed on the price of a good or service.

FIGURE 11.8
Price Ceilings Create Shortages

Many cities impose rent controls to keep housing affordable. Consumers respond to the below-equilibrium price ceiling (p_c) by demanding more housing (q_d vs. q_e). But the quantity of housing supplied diminishes as landlords convert buildings to other uses (e.g., condos) or simply let rental units deteriorate. New construction also slows. The result is a housing shortage ($q_d - q_s$) and an actual reduction in available housing ($q_e - q_s$).

Rent controls have a very visible effect in making housing more afford-able. But such controls are *disequilibrium* prices and will change housing decisions in less visible and unintended ways. Figure 11.8 illustrates the prob-lem. In the absence of government intervention, the quantity of housing consumed (q_e) and the prevailing rent (p_e) would be established by the inter-section of market supply and demand curves (point E). Not everyone would be housed to their satisfaction in this equilibrium. Some of those people on the low end of the demand curve (below p_e) simply do not have enough income to pay the equilibrium rent p_e. They may be living with relatives or roommates they would rather not know. Or, in extreme cases, they may even be homeless.

To remedy this situation, the city government imposes a rent ceiling of p_c. This lower price seemingly makes housing more affordable for everyone, including the poor. At the controlled rent p_c, people are willing and able to consume a lot more housing: the quantity demanded increases from q_e to q_d at point A.

But what about the quantity of housing *supplied*? Rent controls do not increase the number of housing units available. On the contrary, price con-trols tend to have the opposite effect. Notice in Figure 11.8 how the quan-tity *supplied* falls from q_e to q_s when the rent ceiling is enacted. When the quantity supplied slides down the supply curve from point E to point B, there is less housing available than there was before. Thus *price ceilings have three predictable effects; they*

* *Increase the quantity demanded.*
* *Decrease the quantity supplied.*
* *Create a market shortage.*

You may well wonder where the "lost" housing went. The houses did not disappear. Some landlords simply decided that renting their units was no longer worth the effort. They chose, instead, to sell the units, convert them to condominiums, or even live in them themselves. Other landlords stopped maintaining their buildings, letting the units deteriorate. The rate of new construction slowed. too, as builders decided that rent control made new construction less profitable. Slowly but surely the quantity of housing declines from q_e to q_s. Hence **there will be less housing for everyone when rent controls are imposed to make housing more affordable for some.**

Figure 11.8 illustrates another problem. The rent ceiling p_c has created a housing shortage—a gap between the quantity demanded (q_d) and the quantity supplied (q_s). Who will get the increasingly scarce housing? The market would have settled this FOR WHOM question by permitting rents to rise and allocating available units to those consumers willing and able to pay the rent p_e. Now, however, rents cannot rise and we have lots of people clamoring for housing that is not available. A different method of distributing goods must be found. Vacant units will go to those who learn of them first, patiently wait on waiting lists, or offer a gratuity to the landlord or renting agent. In New York City, where rent control has been the law for 60 years, people "sell" their rent-controlled apartments when they move elsewhere.

Price Floors

price floor Lower limit imposed on the price of a good.

Artificially high (above-equilibrium) prices create similar problems in the marketplace. A **price floor** is a minimum price imposed by the government for a good or service. The objective is to raise the price of the good and create more income for the seller. Federal minimum wage laws, for example, forbid most employers from paying less than $5.15 an hour for labor.

Price floors were also common in the farm sector. To stabilize farmers' incomes, the government offers price guarantees for certain crops. In 1985, for example, the government set a price guarantee of 18 cents per pound for domestically grown cane sugar. If the market price of sugar falls below 18 cents; the government promises to buy at the guaranteed price. Hence farmers know they can sell their sugar for 18 cents per pound, regardless of market demand.

Figure 11.9 illustrates the consequences of the price floor. The price guarantee (18¢) lies above the equilibrium price p_e (otherwise it would have no effect). At that higher price, farmers supply more sugar (q_s versus q_e). However, consumers are not willing to buy that much sugar: at that price; they demand only the quantity q_d. Hence, the **price floor has three predictable effects; it**

* *Increases the quantity supplied.*
* *Reduces the quantity demanded.*
* *Creates a market surplus.*

government failure Government intervention that fails to improve economic outcomes.

In 2001 the market surplus amounted to more than a *million tons* of sugar. The federal government ended up buying this surplus for more than $350 million. As for consumers, they ended up paying more for sugar than an unregulated market would charge. They also had to pay higher taxes to finance the government's sugar purchases. Furthermore, the mix of output now included more sugar than people would want if they had to pay the true costs of sugar directly. This is a classic case of **government failure:** society ends up with the wrong mix of output (too much sugar), an increased tax burden (to pay for the surplus), and an altered distribution of income (enriched sugar growers).

Laissez Faire

The apparent inefficiencies of price ceilings and floors imply that market outcomes are best left alone. This is a conclusion reached long ago by Adam

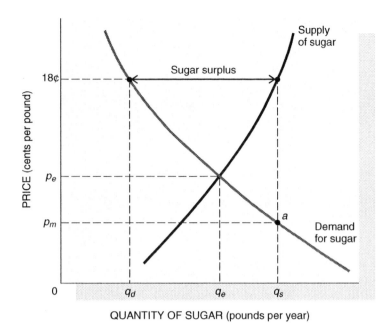

FIGURE 11.9

Price Floors Create
Surplus

The U.S. Department of
Agriculture sets a minimum
price for sugar at 18 cents. If
the market price drops below
18 cents, the government will
buy the resulting surplus.

Farmers respond by
producing the quantity q_s.
Consumers would purchase the
quantity q_s, however, only if the
market price dropped to p_m
(point a on the demand curve).
The government thus has to
purchase and store the surplus
$q_s - q_d$.

Smith, the founder of modern economic theory. In 1776 he advocated a
policy of **laissez faire**—literally, "leave it alone." As he saw it, the market
mechanism was an efficient procedure for allocating resources and distributing incomes. The government should set and enforce the rules of the marketplace, but otherwise not interfere. Interference with the market—through
price ceilings, floors, or other regulation—was likely to cause more problems
than it could hope to solve.

laissez faire The doctrine of
"leave it alone," of
nonintervention by government in
the market mechanism.

The policy of laissez faire is motivated not only by the potential pitfalls of
government intervention but also by the recognition of how well the market
mechanism can work. Recall our visit to Clearview College, where the price
and quantity of tutoring services had to be established. There was no central
agency that set the price of tutoring service or determined how much tutoring service would be done at Clearview College. Instead, both the price of web
services and its quantity were determined by the **market mechanism**—the
interactions of many independent (decentralized) buyers and sellers.

market mechanism The use of
market prices and sales to signal
desired outputs (or resource
allocations).

WHAT, HOW, FOR WHOM Notice how the market mechanism resolved the
basic economic questions of WHAT, HOW, and FOR WHOM. The WHAT
question refers to how much web tutoring to include in society's mix of output. The answer at Clearview College was 39 hours per semester. This decision was not reached in a referendum but instead in the market equilibrium
(see Figure 11.6). In the same way but on a larger scale, millions of consumers and a handful of auto producers decide to include 15 million cars
and trucks in each year's mix of output.

The market mechanism will also determine HOW these goods are produced. Profit-seeking producers will strive to produce web services and
automobiles in the most efficient way. They will use market prices to decide
not only WHAT to produce but also what resources to use in the production
process.

Finally, the invisible hand of the market will determine who gets the goods
produced. At Clearview College, who got tutorial help in web design? Only
those students who were willing and able to pay $20 per hour for that service.

FOR WHOM are all those automobiles produced each year? The answer is the same: those consumers who are willing and able to pay the market price for a new car.

Optimal, Not Perfect   Not everyone is happy with these answers, of course. Tom would like to pay only $10 an hour for web tutoring. And some of the Clearview students do not have enough income to buy any assistance. They think it is unfair that they have to master web design on their own while richer students can have someone tutor them. Students who cannot afford cars are even less happy with the market's answer to the FOR WHOM question.

Although the outcomes of the marketplace are not perfect, they are often optimal. Optimal outcomes are the best possible, given the level and distribution of incomes and scarce resources. In other words, we expect the choices made in the marketplace to be the best possible choices for each participant. Why do we draw such a conclusion? Because Tom and George and everybody in our little Clearview College drama had (and continue to have) absolute freedom to make their own purchase and consumption decisions. And also because we assume that sooner or later they will make the choices they find most satisfying. The results are thus *optimal*, in the sense that everyone has done as well as can be expected, given his or her income and talents.

The optimality of market outcomes provides a powerful argument for *laissez faire*. In essence, the laissez-faire doctrine recognizes that decentralized markets not only work, but also give individuals the opportunity to maximize their satisfaction. In this context, government interference is seen as a threat to the attainment of the "right" mix of output and other economic goals. Since its development by Adam Smith in 1776, the laissez-faire doctrine has had a profound impact on the way the economy functions and what government does (or doesn't do).

POLICY PERSPECTIVES

Free Tuition in California!

In 2000 the state of California introduced a free-tuition program for residents of that state. Beginning in 2003, any high school senior in the state with at least a B average and family income below certain thresholds is guaranteed free admission to public universities in that state. Should a student prefer to go to a private college, the state will pay $9,708 per year in tuition.

What makes the Cal Grant Program so remarkable—and expensive—is how high the qualifying income threshold is. For students in four-person families, the qualifying income threshold is $66,200. Because that threshold is so high, as many as one-third of all graduating high school seniors in California will be eligible for free tuition.

The state will also provide free tuition for high school students with a C average if their families have incomes of less than half the threshold of B students. Specifically, a C student from a family with income of less than $34,800 can get free tuition as well.

Demand Effects   California's free-tuition program will have a major impact on the *demand* for college. By reducing the effective price of tuition to zero, the state will induce a movement down the demand curve to a much greater quantity demanded. By making college so accessible, the program will also alter expectations, shifting demand to the right. The tuition subsidy for attending private schools represents additional income that will also shift the demand curve rightward. As a result, the state expects at least 100,000 more students to demand a college education.

Supply Responses   But where will all these students enroll? California's colleges were already overflowing before this new tuition program was introduced. In fact, state subsidies had long kept tuition below its equilibrium level. The resulting shortage forced thousands of qualified students to attend schools elsewhere. An increase in demand will only exacerbate the shortage problem.

To make this program work, the state will have to increase the *supply* of college educational services. This may require the state to build more classrooms, hire more professors, construct more dorms, and pave more parking lots. Or the state may expand the use of electronic classrooms rather than brick-and-mortar classrooms. In either case, the state will now have to focus on the *supply* side of the market to assure the increased demand can be accommodated. The budget pressures that hit the state in 2002–2003 precluded such a response. This imbalance between supply and demand caused a *shortage* in the college market and a lot of frustrated applicants.

SUMMARY

* Consumers, business firms, government agencies, and foreigners participate in the marketplace by offering to buy or sell goods and services, or factors of production. Participation is motivated by the desire to maximize utility (consumers), profits (business firms), or the general welfare (government agencies).
* All interactions in the marketplace involve the exchange of either factors of production or finished products. Although the actual exchanges can take place anywhere, we say that they take place in product markets or factor markets, depending on what is being exchanged.
* People who are willing and able to buy a particular good at some price are part of the market demand for that product. All those who are willing and able to sell that good at some price are part of the market supply. Total market demand or supply is the sum of individual demands or supplies.
* Supply and demand curves illustrate how the quantity demanded or supplied changes in response to a change in the price of that good. Demand curves slope downward; supply curves slope upward.
* The determinants of market demand include the number of potential buyers and their respective tastes (desires), incomes, other goods, and expectations. If any of these determinants changes, the demand curve shifts. Movements along a demand curve are induced only by a change in the price of that good.
* The determinants of market supply include technology, factor costs, other goods, taxes, expectations, and the number of sellers. Supply shifts when these underlying determinants change.
* The quantity of goods or resources actually exchanged in each market depends on the behavior of all buyers and sellers, as summarized in

market supply and demand curves. At the point where the two curves intersect, an equilibrium price—the price at which the quantity demanded equals the quantity supplied—will be established.

* A distinctive feature of the market equilibrium is that it is the only price–quantity combination that is acceptable to buyers and sellers alike. At higher prices, sellers supply more than buyers are willing to purchase (a market surplus); at lower prices, the amount demanded exceeds the quantity supplied (a market shortage). Only the equilibrium price clears the market.

* Price ceilings and floors are disequilibrium prices imposed on the marketplace. Such price controls create an imbalance between quantities demanded and supplied.

* The market mechanism is a device for establishing prices and product and resource flows. As such, it may be used to answer the basic economic questions of WHAT to produce, HOW to produce it, and FOR WHOM. Its apparent efficiency prompts the call for laissez faire—a policy of government nonintervention in the marketplace.

Terms to Remember

Define the following terms:

market	demand curve	market shortage
factor market	law of demand	market surplus
product market	*ceteris paribus*	price ceiling
barter	shift in demand	price floor
supply	market demand	government failure
demand	market supply	laissez faire
opportunity cost	law of supply	market mechanism
demand schedule	equilibrium price	

Questions for Discussion

1. What does the supply and demand for human kidneys look like? If a market in kidneys were legal, who would get them? How does a law prohibiting kidney sales affect the quantity of kidney transplants or their distribution?

2. In the web-tutoring market, what forces might cause
   (a) A rightward shift of demand?
   (b) A leftward shift of demand?
   (c) A rightward shift of supply?
   (d) A leftward shift of supply?
   (e) An increase in the equilibrium price?

3. Did the price of tuition at your school change this year? What might have caused that?

4. What was the market situation for the 1992 and 1997 U2 concerts (pp. 384 and 386)? Why didn't the concerts' promoters set equilibrium prices?

5. When concert tickets are priced below equilibrium, who gets them? Is this distribution of tickets fairer than a pure market distribution? Is it more efficient? Who gains or loses if all the tickets are resold (scalped) at the market-clearing price?

6. Is there a shortage of on-campus parking at your school? How might the shortage be resolved?

7. If departing tenants sell access to rent-controlled apartments, who is likely to end up with the apartments? How else might scarce rent-controlled apartments be distributed?

8. If rent controls are so counterproductive, why do cities impose them? How else might the housing problems of poor people be solved?

9. In 2003, Cruz Bustamante, the lieutenant governor of California, proposed a price ceiling on gasoline. Is this a good idea?

10. Why did Sony set the initial price of the PlayStation 2 below equilibrium (see Headline, p. 385). Should Sony have immediately raised the price?

Problems

1. Using Figure 11.7 as a guide, determine the approximate size of the market surplus or shortage that would exist at a price of (*a*) $40 (*b*) $20.

2. Illustrate the different market situations for the 1992 and 1997 U2 concerts, assuming constant supply and demand curves. What is the equilibrium price? (see Headlines on pp. 384 and 386).

3. Given the following data, (*a*) construct market supply and demand curves and identify the equilibrium price; and (*b*) identify the amount of shortage or surplus that would exist at a price of $4.

Participant	Quantity Demanded (per week)				
A. Price	$5	$4	$3	$2	$1
B. Demand side					
Al	1	2	3	4	5
Betsy	0	1	1	1	2
Casey	2	2	3	3	4
Daisy	1	3	4	4	6
Eddie	1	2	2	3	5
Market total	—	—	—	—	—

Participant	Quantity Supplied (per week)				
A. Price	$5	$4	$3	$2	$1
C. Supply side					
Alice	3	3	3	3	3
Butch	7	5	4	4	2
Connie	6	4	3	3	1
Dutch	6	5	4	3	0
Ellen	4	2	2	2	1
Market total	—	—	—	—	—

4. Suppose that the good described in problem 3 became so popular that every consumer demanded one additional unit at every price. Illustrate this increase in market demand and identify the new equilibrium. Which curve has shifted? Along which curve has there been a movement of price and quantity?

5. Illustrate each of the following events with supply or demand shifts in the domestic car market:
   (*a*) The U.S. economy falls into a recession.
   (*b*) U.S. auto workers go on strike.
   (*c*) Imported cars become more expensive.
   (*d*) The price of gasoline increases.

6. Graph the effects on price and quantity of California's free-tuition program (see Policy Perspectives beginning p. 392).
7. Assume the following data describe the gasoline market

Price per gallon	$1.00	1.25	1.50	1.75	2.00	2.25	2.50
Quantity demanded	26	25	24	23	22	21	20
Quantity supplied	16	20	24	28	32	36	40

   (a) What is the equilibrium price?
   (b) If supply at every price is reduced by 5 gallons, what will the new equilibrium price be?
   (c) If the government freezes the price of gasoline at its initial price, how much of a surplus or shortage will exist when supply is reduced as described above?
   (d) Illustrate your answers on a graph.
8. Graph the response of students to higher alcohol prices, as discussed in the Headline on p. 374.
9. Graph the changes in the beef market during 2003, as described in the Headline on p. 388.

Web Activities

1. Log on to www.whitehouse.gov/fsbr/income.html and find the data on real per capita income.
   (a) What has happened to the value of real per capita income?
   (b) Assuming that the size of the workforce has remained relatively constant, use supply and demand analysis to explain why real income has increased.
2. Log on to www.cnn.com or www.msnbc.com and do a search using the keywords "crude oil prices." Find an article that discusses recent changes in the price of crude oil.
   (a) Discuss the reasons stated in the article explaining why the price of crude oil has changed.
   (b) Use supply and demand graphs to illustrate what is being discussed in the article.
3. Log on to www.ebay.com and record the price bids for some item during a 30-minute period. Use supply and demand analysis to explain the initial shortage in the market and how the bidding process is correcting the imbalance.

Living Econ

How Can I Communicate with a Large Corporation?

Most of us spend a fair amount of time in the product market. On a typical morning you might stop at the coffee shop on your way to class, purchase your lunch at a fast food restaurant, gas up your vehicle at the corner gas station, and rent a DVD from the video store.

But for all the time we spend in the product market, few of us ever take the time to communicate directly with a business or producer. Or, at least that's what we think. Yet companies must know what we want to buy and what we're willing to pay because we keep going back into the product market and offering them additional dollars for more stuff. So how can a business know this information if we don't call or e-mail them?

You and I send a very strong signal to producers every time we go into the product market. When we make a purchase, we tell producers, "I like this product and I'm willing to pay this price for it." If we choose not to buy the product, we are also sending a signal. Maybe we are stating, "This price is too high," or perhaps we are announcing, "This product is ugly and totally useless." Either way, producers are listening to what we have to say through the purchasing choices we make. The next time you buy a pair of jeans at the mall, picture yourself yelling, "I love these pants and they are definitely worth $78."

The U.S. Economy

We are surrounded by the economy but never really see it. We see only fragments, never the entirety. We see boutiques at the mall, never total retail sales. We visit virtual stores in cyberspace but can't begin to describe the dimensions of e-commerce. We pump gas at the service station but have no notion of how many millions of barrels of oil are consumed each day. We know every detail on our paychecks but don't have a clue about how much income the entire workforce earns. Nor can many of us tell how our own income stacks up against that of the average U.S. household, much less that of earlier generations or other nations. Such details simply aren't a part of our daily agendas. For most people, the "economy" is just a vague reference to a mass of meaningless statistics.

The intent of this chapter is to provide a more user-friendly picture of the U.S. economy. This profile of the economy is organized around the three core questions of WHAT, HOW, and FOR WHOM. Our interest here is to see how these questions are answered at present in the United States—that is,

* WHAT goods and services does the United States produce?
* HOW is that output produced?
* FOR WHOM is the output produced?

We focus on the big picture, without going into too much statistical detail. Along the way, we'll see how the U.S. economy stacks up against other nations.

What America Produces

In Chapter 10 we used the two-dimensional possibilities curve to describe WHAT output combinations can be produced. In reality, the mix of output includes so many different products that we could never fit them on a graph. We can, however, sketch what the U.S. mix of output looks like and how it has changed over the years.

How Much Output

The first challenge in describing the actual output of the economy is to somehow add up the millions of different products produced into a meaningful summary. The production-possibilities curve did this in *physical* terms, for only two products. We ended up with specific quantities of two goods. In principle, we could list all of the millions of products produced each year. But such a list would be longer than this textbook and a lot less useful. We need a summary measure of how much is produced.

The top panel of Table 12.1 illustrates the problem of obtaining a summary measure of output. Even if we produced only three products—oranges, disposable razors, and insurance policies—there is no obvious way of summarizing total output in *physical* terms. Should we count *units* of output? In that case, oranges would appear to be the most important good produced. Should we count the *weight* of different products? In that case, insurance policies wouldn't count at all. Should we tally their *sizes*? As you ponder these various physical measures of output, a summary statement seems impossible.

If we use monetary *value* instead of physical units to compute total output, we would have more success. In a market economy, every good and service commands a specific price. Hence the value of each product can be observed easily. ***By multiplying the physical output of each good by its price, we can determine the total value of each good produced.*** Notice in the bottom panel of Table 12.1 how easily these separate values can be added up. The resultant sum ($4.2 billion, in this case) is a measure of the *value of* total output.

gross domestic product
(GDP) The total value of final goods and services produced within a nation's borders in a given time period.

Gross Domestic Product   The summary measure of output most frequently used is called **gross domestic product (GDP)**. *GDP refers to the total value of all final goods and services produced in a country during a given time period: it is a summary measure of a nation's output.* GDP enables us to add oranges and razors and even insurance policies into a meaningful summary of economic activity (see Table 12.1).

TABLE 12.1
The Measurement of Output

It is impossible to add up all output when it is counted in *physical* terms. Accordingly, total output is measured in *monetary* terms, with each good or service valued at its market price. GDP refers to the total market value of all goods and services produced in a given time period. According to the numbers in this table, the total *value* of the oranges, razors, and insurance policies produced is $4.2 billion.

Output	Amount
Measuring output	
. . . **in physical terms**	
Oranges	6 billion
Disposable razors	3 billion
Insurance policies	7 million
Total	?
. . . **in monetary terms**	
6 billion oranges @ 20¢ each	$1.2 billion
3 billion razors @ 30¢ each	0.9 billion
7 million policies @ $300 each	2.1 billion
Total	$4.2 billion

Product	Physical Output		Unit Prices		Value of Output (billions)		
	Year 1	Year 2	Year 1	Year 2	Year 1 (@Year 1 prices)	Year 2 (@Year 2 prices)	Year 2 (@Year 1 prices)
Oranges	6 billion	6 billion	$0.20	$0.40	$1.2	$2.4	$1.2
Razors	3 billion	3 billion	0.30	0.60	0.9	1.8	0.9
Insurance	7 million	7 million	300.00	600.00	2.1	4.2	2.1
					$4.2	$8.4	$4.2

year 1 total = $4.2 billion

year 2 total = $8.4 billion

TABLE 12.2
Inflation Adjustments

If prices rise, so do the *values* of output. In this example, the nominal value of output doubles from Year 1 to Year 2, even though physical output remains unchanged. *Real* GDP corrects for such changing price levels. In this case *real* GDP in Year 2, measured in Year 1 prices, is unchanged at $4.2 billion.

Real GDP Although GDP is a convenient summary of total output produced in a year, it has some shortcomings. GDP is based on both physical output and prices. Accordingly, from one year to the next either rising prices or an increase in physical output could cause GDP to increase.

Notice in Table 12.2 what happens when all prices double. The measured value of total output also doubles—from $4.2 to $8.4 billion. That sounds like an impressive jump in output. In reality, however, no more goods are being produced; *physical quantities* are unchanged. So the apparent jump in GDP is an illusion caused by rising prices (inflation).

To provide a clearer picture of how much output we are producing, GDP numbers are routinely adjusted for inflation. These inflation adjustments delete the effects of rising prices by valuing output in *constant* prices. The end result of this effort is referred to as **real GDP,** an inflation-adjusted measure of total output.

real GDP The inflation-adjusted value of GDP: the value of output measured in constant prices.

In 2003, the U.S. economy produced roughly $11 *trillion* of output. That was a lot of oranges, razors, and insurance policies—not to mention the tens of thousands of other goods and services produced.

International Comparisons The $11 trillion of output that the United States produced in 2003 looks particularly impressive in a global context. The output of the entire world in 2003 was only $50 trillion. Hence the U.S. economy produces over 20 percent of the entire planet's output. With less than 5 percent of the world's population, that's a remarkable feat. It clearly establishes the United States as the world's economic giant.

Figure 12.1 provides some specific country comparisons for a recent year. The U.S. economy is two and a half times larger than Japan's, the world's third-largest. It is 12 times larger than Mexico's. In fact, the U.S. economy is so large that its output exceeds by a wide margin the *combined* production of *all* countries in Africa and South America.

Per Capita GDP Another way of putting these trillion-dollar figures into perspective is to relate them to individuals. This can be done by dividing a nation's total GDP by its population, a calculation that yields **per capita GDP.** Per capita GDP tells us how much output is potentially available to the average person. It doesn't tell us how much any specific person gets. *Per capita GDP is simply an indicator of how much output each person would get if all output were divided evenly among the population.*

per capita GDP Total GDP divided by total population: average GDP.

In 2003, per capita GDP in the United States was approximately $34,000—more than five times the world average. Individual country comparisons are

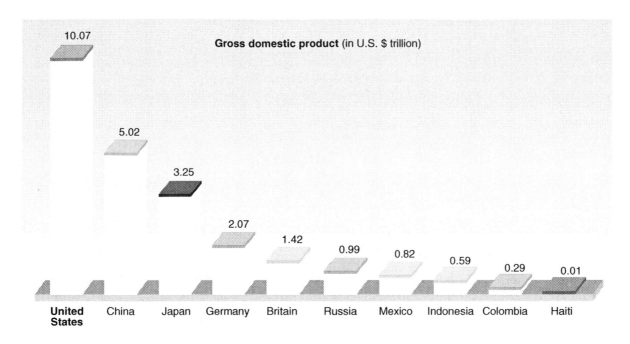

FIGURE 12.1 Real GDP (Output) of Specific Countries (2001)

The United States is by far the world's largest economy. America's annual output of goods and services is three times that of Japan's and equal to all of Western Europe. The output of Third World countries is only a tiny fraction of U.S. output.

Source: From *World Development Indicators, 2003* (Washington, DC: World Bank, 2003).

even more startling. In Ethiopia and Haiti, per capita incomes are less than $2,000—less than six dollars per day. *Homeless* people in the United States fare better than that—typically *much* better. Americans classified as poor have more food, more shelter, and more amenities than most people in the less developed nations even hope for. That is the reality depicted in the statistics of Table 12.3.

Historical Comparisons Still another way of digesting the dimensions of the American economy is to compare today's living standards with those of

TABLE 12.3

Per Capita Incomes around the World (2001)

The American standard of living is five times higher than the world average. People in the poorest nations of the world (e.g., Haiti, Ethiopia) barely survive on per capita incomes that are a tiny fraction of U.S. standards.

United States	$34,280
Japan	25,550
France	24,080
Spain	19,860
Greece	17,520
Mexico	8,240
World average	**7,370**
China	3,950
Jordan	3,880
Indonesia	2,830
India	2,820
Haiti	1,870
Ethiopia	800

Source: From *World Development Indicators, 2003.*

earlier times. People who the U.S. government currently classifies as poor not only enjoy a much higher living standard than the human masses in Third World nations, but they are also more comfortable than the *average* American family was in the 1950s. We now spend over a billion dollars a year on closet organizers alone, an expenditure people of other nations and earlier generations would find incomprehensible. Although many of us still complain that we don't have enough, we enjoy an array of goods and services that earlier generations only dreamed about.

What's even more amazing is that our abundance keeps growing. America's real GDP has increased by about 3 percent a year. That may not sound like much, but it adds up. With the U.S. population growing by only 1 percent a year, continued **economic growth** also implies more output per person. Like interest accumulating in the bank, economic growth keeps adding to our standard of living. If real GDP keeps growing 2 percentage points faster than our population, per capita incomes will double again in approximately 35 years.

economic growth An increase in output (real GDP); an expansion of production possibilities.

There is no certainty that the economy will continue to grow at that speed. From 1929 to 1939, real GDP didn't grow at all. As a consequence, U.S. living standards *fell* during the Great Depression. In other nations, the struggle between population growth and economic growth is a persistent source of anxiety. In the 1990s, output per capita actually *declined* in Haiti, Ethiopia, Kenya, Venezuela, Nigeria, and many other nations.

Social Welfare Although the United States has claim to being the world's largest economy, we must not confuse GDP with broader measures of social welfare. First of all, GDP measures only output produced for the market. It does not include home production or volunteer activities, even though these nonmarket activities affect our personal and community well-being. Neither do GDP statistics directly measure the noise, congestion, and pollution that often accompany increased output. Maybe we'd all be better off with a little less output and its related "bads." Finally, we have to recognize that GDP statistics *do* include the services of divorce lawyers, prison guards, and trash collectors. With more love, fewer crimes, and less pollution our social welfare might increase even if GDP declined.

Although GDP is an incomplete measure of social welfare, it is still important. The people in poor nations certainly appreciate the importance of more output and even Americans still strive for higher levels of material well-being. GDP statistics gauge how well we are doing in that regard.

However imperfect, the level of output (GDP) is undoubtedly the single best measure of a nation's economic well-being. Indeed, back in 1776 Adam Smith recognized that the wealth of nations was best measured by its output rather than by the amount of gold it possessed or the resources it owned. Today that standard of wealth is reflected in real GDP statistics.

The Mix of Output

In addition to the *level* of output, we also care about its *content*. As we observed in Chapter 10, there are many possible output combinations for any given level of GDP. In Chapter 10 we examined the different mixes of military and civilian output nations choose. More broadly, the content of output is described in terms of its major end uses. ***The major uses of total output include***

* ***Household consumption***
* ***Business investment***
* ***Government services***
* ***Exports***

Consumer Goods   Consumer goods account for two-thirds of America's total output. Consumer goods include everything from breakfast cereals to videos—anything and everything consumers buy.

Three types of consumer goods are often distinguished: *durable goods, nondurable goods,* and *services.* Consumer durables are expected to last at least three years. They tend to be big-ticket items like cars, appliances, and furniture. They are generally expensive and often purchased on credit. Because of this, consumers tend to postpone buying durables when they are worried about their incomes. Conversely, consumers tend to go on durables-spending sprees when times are good. This spending pattern makes durable goods output highly *cyclical,* that is, very sensitive to economic trends.

Nondurables and services are not as cyclical. Nondurables include clothes, food, gasoline, and other staples that consumers buy frequently. Services are the largest and fastest-growing component in consumption. At present, over half of all consumer output consists of medical care, entertainment, utilities, and other services.

Investment Goods   Investment goods are a completely different type of output. **Investment** goods include the plant, machinery, and equipment that are produced for use in the business sector. These investment goods are used

investment Expenditures on (production of) new plant and equipment (capital) in a given time period, plus changes in business inventories.

1. To replace worn-out equipment and factories, thus *maintaining* our production possibilities.
2. To increase and improve our stock of capital, thereby *expanding* our production possibilities.

We also count as investment goods those products that businesses hold as inventory for later sale to consumers.

The economic growth that has lifted our living standards so high was fueled by past investments. To attain even higher living standards, we must continue to devote some of our scarce resources to the production of new plant and equipment. This requires us to limit our immediate consumption (i.e., save) so scarce resources can be used for investment. Only 15 percent of America's GDP today consists of investment goods (see Figure 12.2).

Note that the term *investment* here refers to real output—plant and equipment produced for the business sector. This is not the way most

FIGURE 12.2
The Uses of GDP

Total GDP amounted to nearly $11 trillion in 2003. Over two-thirds of this output consisted of private consumer goods and services. The next-largest share (19 percent) of output consisted of public-sector goods and services. Investment absorbed 15 percent of GDP. Finally, because imports exceeded exports, we ended up consuming 4 percent more than we produced.

Source: U.S. Department of Commerce.

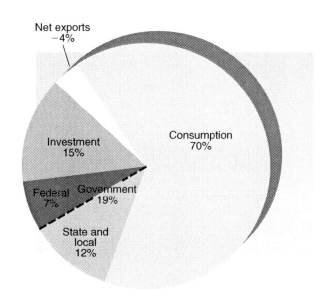

people use the term. People often speak, for example, of "investing" in the stock market. Purchases of corporate stock, however, do not create goods and services. Such *financial* investments merely transfer ownership of a corporation from one individual to another. Such *financial* investments may at times enable a corporation to purchase real plant and equipment. Tangible (economic) investment does not occur, however, until that plant and machinery are actually produced. Only tangible investment is counted in the mix of output.

Government Services The third type of output included in GDP is government services. Federal, state, and local governments purchase resources to police the streets, teach classes, write laws, and build highways. The resources used by the government sector for these purchases are unavailable for either consumption or investment. The production of government services currently absorbs nearly one-fifth of total output (Figure 12.2).

Notice the emphasis again on the production of real goods and services. The federal government *spends* well over $2 trillion a year. Much of that spending, however, is in the form of income transfers, not resource purchases. **Income transfers** are payments to individuals for which no direct service is provided. Social Security benefits, welfare checks, food stamps, and unemployment benefits are examples of income transfers. Such transfer payments account for half of all federal spending (see Figure 12.3). This spending is *not* part of our output of goods and services. *Only that part of federal spending used to acquire resources and produce services is counted in GDP.* In 2003, federal purchases (production) of goods and services accounted for only 6 percent of total output.

State and local governments use far more of our scarce resources than does the federal government. These are the governments that build roads; provide schools, police, and firefighters; administer hospitals; and provide social services. The output of all these state and local governments accounts for roughly 12 percent of total GDP. In doing so, they employ four times as many people (16 million) than does the federal government (4 million).

income transfers Payments to individuals for which no current goods or services are exchanged; e.g., Social Security, welfare, unemployment benefits.

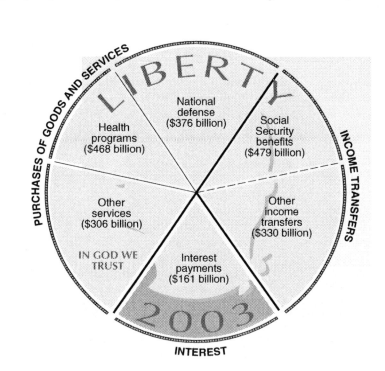

FIGURE 12.3
Federal Outlays, by Type
The federal government spent over $2.2 trillion in fiscal year 2003. Just over half of all this spending was for goods and services (including national defense, health programs, and all other services). Over $800 billion was spent on income transfers (Social Security benefits, government pensions, welfare, unemployment benefits, etc.). Interest payments on the national debt accounted for the rest of the budget.

Source: U.S. Office of Management and Budget.

exports Goods and services sold to foreign buyers.

imports Goods and services purchased from foreign sources.

Net Exports   Finally, we should note that some of the goods and services we produce each year are used abroad rather than at home. That is to say, we **export** some of our output to other countries, for whatever use they care to make of it. Thus GDP—the value of output *produced* within the United States—can be larger than the sum of our own consumption, investment, and government purchases if we export some of our output.

International trade is not a one-way street. While we export some of our own output, we also **import** goods and services from other countries. These imports may be used for consumption (Scotch whiskey, Japanese DVD players), investment (German ball bearings), or government (French radar screens). Whatever their use, imports represent goods and services that are used by Americans but are not produced in the United States.

The GDP accounts subtract imports from exports. The difference represents *net* exports. In 2003, the value of exports was less than the value of imports. This implies that we *used* more goods and services than we *produced* in that year. Hence, we have to subtract net imports from consumption, investment, and government services to figure out how much we actually *produced*. That is why net exports appear as a negative item in Figure 12.2.

Changing Industry Structure

As we noted earlier, many of the products we consume today did not exist ten or even two years ago. We have also observed how much the volume of output has grown over time. Throughout this process of economic growth, the mix of output has changed dramatically.

Decline in Farming   One of the most dramatic changes in the mix of output was the decline in the relative size of the farm sector. In 1900 farming was the most common occupation in the American economy. As Figure 12.4 illustrates, nearly four out of ten workers were employed in agriculture back then.

Today the mix of output is radically different. Between 1900 and 2000 over 25 *million* people left farms and sought jobs in the cities. As a result, less than 2 percent of the workforce is now employed in agriculture. And their number keeps shrinking a bit further every year as new technology makes it possible to grow *more* food with *fewer* workers.

Decline of Manufacturing Share   Most of the farmers displaced by technological advances in the early 1900s found jobs in the expanding manufacturing sector. The Industrial Revolution that flourished in the late 1800s led to a massive increase in manufacturing activity (e.g., steel, transportation systems, automobiles, airplanes). Between 1860 and 1920, the manufactured share of GDP doubled, reaching a peak at 27 percent. World War II also created a huge demand for ships, airplanes, trucks, and armaments, requiring an enlarged manufacturing sector. After World War II, the manufactured share of output declined, and now accounts for less than 20 percent of total output.

The *relative* decline in manufacturing does not mean that the manufacturing sector has actually shrunk. As in farming, technological advance has made it possible to increase manufacturing output tremendously, even though employment has grown only modestly. Just in the last 50 years, manufactured *output* has increased fourfold even though manufacturing *employment* has increased only 20 percent. As a result, the volume of manufacturing output has increased, even while the manufacturing *share* of GDP has declined.

Growth of Services   The *relative* decline in manufacturing is due primarily to the rapid expansion of the service sector. America has largely

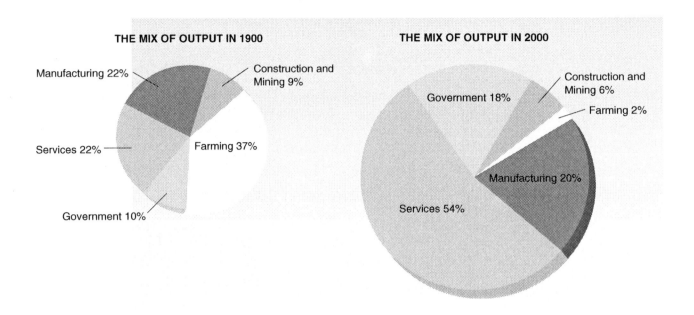

FIGURE 12.4 A Century of GDP Changes

In the 20th century the total output of the U.S. economy increased thirteenfold. As the economy has grown, the farm sector has shrunk and the manufactured *share* of total output has declined. Since 1930 the American economy has been predominantly a service economy, with output and job growth increasingly concentrated in retail trade, education, health care, entertainment, personal and business services, and government.

Source: U.S. Departments of Commerce and Labor.

become a service economy. A hundred years ago less than 25 percent of the labor force was employed in the service sector; today service industries (including government) generate over 70 percent of total output. Among the fastest-growing service industries are health care, computer science and software, financial services, retail trade, business services, and law. According to the U.S. Department of Labor, this trend will continue; 98 percent of net job growth between 2005 and 2015 will be in service industries.

Growth of Trade International trade also plays an increasingly important role in how goods are produced. Roughly one-eighth of the output Americans produce is exported. As noted earlier, an even larger share of output is imported (hence the negative "net exports" in Figure 12.2).

What is remarkable about these international transactions is how they have grown. The import ratio—imports divided by GDP—has increased from 5 percent in the 1920s to over 13 percent today. This increasing globalization of the U.S. economy is likely to continue. The slow but continuing removal of trade barriers (e.g., the North American free-trade zone) facilitates this globalization. Advances in communications and transportation technologies also make international trade and investment easier. You can click onto a British clothier's website just as easily as onto the site of a U.S. merchant. And consumers in other nations can easily purchase goods from American cybermerchants. Then FedEx or another overnight delivery service can move the goods across national borders. As a result, the volume of both imports and exports keeps growing rapidly. The growth of trade is also fueled by the increased consumption of *services* (e.g., travel, finance, movies, computer software) rather than goods. With trade in services, you don't even need overnight delivery services.

How America Produces

International trade has also affected HOW goods and services are produced. Hundreds of foreign-owned firms (e.g., Toyota, BMW, Shell, Air France) produce goods or services in the United States. Any output they produce within U.S. borders is counted in America's GDP. By contrast, U.S.-owned **factors of production** employed elsewhere (e.g., a Nike shoe factory in Malaysia) don't contribute directly to U.S. output. Foreign firms typically bring not only factors of production across national borders but often new technology as well.

factors of production Resource inputs used to produce goods and services, e.g., land, labor, capital, entrepreneurship.

Factors of Production

Even without foreign investments, the United States would have ample resources to produce goods and services. To begin with, the United States has the third-largest population in the world (behind China and India). The United States also has the world's fourth-largest land area (behind Russia, China, and by a hair, Canada) and profuse natural resources (e.g., oil, fertile soil, hydropower).

Abundant labor and natural resources give the United States a decided advantage. But superior resources alone don't explain America's economic dominance. After all, China has five times as many people as the United States and equally abundant natural resources. Yet China's annual output is less than one-half of America's output.

Capital Stock   In part, America's greater economic strength is explained by the abundance of capital. America has accumulated a massive stock of capital—over $30 *trillion* worth of machinery, factories, and buildings. As a result of all this prior investment, American production tends to be very **capital intensive.** The contrast with *labor-intensive* production in poorer countries is striking. A Chinese farmer mostly works with his or her hands and crude implements, whereas an American farmer works with computers, automated irrigation systems, and mechanized equipment. Russian business managers don't have the computer networks or telecommunications systems that make American business so efficient.

capital intensive Production processes that use a high ratio of capital to labor inputs.

Factor Quality   The greater **productivity**—output per worker—of American workers reflects not only the capital intensity of the production process but also the *quality* of both capital and labor. America invests each year not just in *more* plant and equipment but in *better* plant and equipment. Today's new computer is faster and more powerful than yesterday's. Today's laser surgery makes yesterday's surgical procedures look primitive. Even textbooks get better each year. Such improvements in the quality of capital expand production possibilities.

productivity Output per unit of input, e.g., output per labor hour.

Labor quality also improves with education and skill training. Indeed, one can invest in human capital, much like one invests in physical capital. **Human capital** refers to the productive capabilities of labor. In the Stone Age, one's productive capacity was largely determined by physical strength and endurance. In today's economy, human capital is largely a product of education, training, and experience. Hence a country can acquire more human capital even without more bodies.

human capital The knowledge and skills possessed by the work force.

Over time, the United States has invested heavily in human capital. In 1940, only one out of twenty young Americans graduated from college; today, over 30 percent of young people are college graduates. High school graduation rates have jumped from 38 percent to over 85 percent in the same time

America's enormous output is made possible by huge investments in physical and human capital. In poorer countries, how output is produced is constrained by low levels of education and the scarcity of plant and equipment.

Top: © Brian F. Peterson/Corbis; Bottom: © Vivian Moos/Corbis

period. In the poor countries of the Third World only one out of two youths ever *attends* high school, much less graduates (see Headline on the next page). As a consequence, over one billion people—one-sixth of the world's population—is unable to read or even write their own names.

America's tremendous output is thus explained not only by a wealth of resources but by their quality as well. ***The high productivity of the U.S. economy results from using highly educated workers in capital-intensive production processes.***

HEADLINE HUMAN CAPITAL

The Education Gap between Rich and Poor Nations

Virtually all Americans attend high school and roughly 85 percent graduate. In poor countries relatively few workers attend high school and even fewer graduate. Half of the workers in the world's poorest nations are illiterate.

Source: From *World Development Indicators, 2003* (Washington, DC: World Bank, 2003).

Enrollment in secondary schools (percent of school-age youth attending secondary schools)

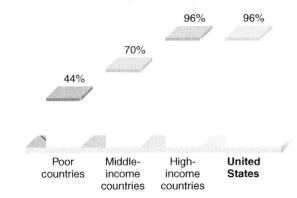

| Poor countries | Middle-income countries | High-income countries | **United States** |
| 44% | 70% | 96% | 96% |

NOTE: The high productivity of the American economy is explained in part by the quality of its labor resources. Workers in poorer, less developed countries get much less education or training.

Factor Mobility Our continuing ability to produce the goods and services that consumers demand also depends on our agility in *reallocating* resources from one industry to another. Every year, some industries expand and others contract. Thousands of new firms are created each year and almost as many others disappear. In the process, land, labor, capital, and entrepreneurship move from one industry to another in response to changing demands and technology. In 1975, Federal Express, Compaq Computer, Microsoft, America Online, Amgen, and Oracle didn't even exist. Today these companies collectively employ over 200,000 people. These workers came from other firms and industries that weren't growing as fast.

Business Organization

The factors of production released from some industries and acquired by others are organized into productive entities we call businesses. A business is an organization that uses factors of production to produce specific goods or services. Actual production activity takes place in the 20 million business firms that participate in the U.S. product markets.

Business Types Business firms come in all shapes and sizes. A basic distinction is made, however, among three different legal organizations:

* Corporations
* Partnerships
* Proprietorships

The primary distinction among these three business forms lies in their ownership characteristics. A single proprietorship is a firm owned by one individual. A partnership is owned by a small number of individuals. A corporation is typically owned by many—even hundreds of thousands of—individuals, each of whom owns shares (stock) of the corporation. An important characteristic of corporations is that their owners (stockholders) are not personally responsible (liable) for the debts or actions of the company. This limited liability makes it easier for corporations to pool the resources of thousands of individuals.

Corporate America   Because of their limited liability, corporations tend to be much larger than other businesses. Single proprietorships are typically quite small, because few individuals have vast sources of wealth or credit. The typical proprietorship has less than $10,000 in assets, whereas the average corporation has assets in excess of $4 million. As a result of their size, corporate America dominates market transactions, accounting for almost 90 percent of all business sales.

We can describe who's who in the business community, then, in two very different ways. In terms of numbers, the single proprietorship is the most common type of business firm in America. Proprietorships are particularly dominant in agriculture (the family farm), retail trade (the corner grocery store), and services (your dentist). In terms of size, however, the corporation is the dominant force in the U.S. economy (see Figure 12.5). The four largest nonfinancial corporations in the country (General Electric, ExxonMobil, Wal-Mart, Verizon) alone have more assets than *all* the 15 million proprietorships doing business in the United States. Even in agriculture, where corporate entities are still comparatively rare, the few agribusiness corporations are so large as to dominate many thousands of small farms.

Government Regulation
Although corporate America dominates the U.S. economy, it does not have the last word on WHAT, HOW, or FOR WHOM goods are produced. In our mixed economy, the government has a significant voice in all of these decisions. Even before America became an independent nation, royal charters bestowed the right to produce and trade specific goods. Even the European discovery of America was dependent on government financing and the establishment of exclusive rights to whatever treasures were found. Today over 50 federal agencies and thousands of state and local government entities

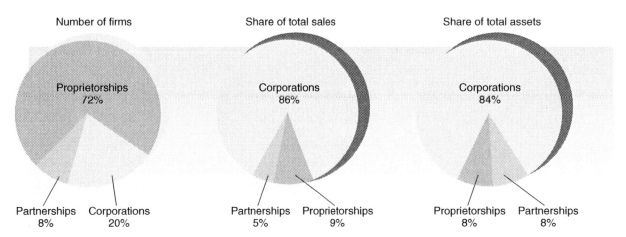

FIGURE 12.5   U.S. Business Firms: Numbers vs. Size

Proprietorships (individually owned companies) are the most common form of American business firm. Corporations are so large, however, that they account for most business sales and assets. Although only 20 percent of all firms are incorporated, corporations control 86 percent of all sales and 84 percent of all assets.

Source: U.S. Department of Commerce, *Statistical Abstract of the United States*, 2002.

regulate the production of goods. In the process, they profoundly affect HOW goods are produced.

Providing a Legal Framework One of the most basic functions of government is to establish and enforce the rules of the game. In some bygone era maybe a person's word was sufficient to guarantee delivery or payment. Businesses today, however, rely more on written contracts. The government gives legitimacy to contracts by establishing the rules for such pacts and by enforcing their provisions. In the absence of contractual rights, few companies would be willing to ship goods without prepayment (in cash). Without legally protected ownership rights, few individuals would buy or build factories. Even the incentive to write textbooks would disappear if government copyright laws didn't forbid unauthorized photocopying. By establishing ownership rights, contract rights, and other rules of the game, the government lays the foundation for market transactions.

Protecting Consumers Much government regulation is intended to protect the interests of consumers. One way to do this is to prevent individual business firms from becoming too powerful. In the extreme case, a single firm might have a **monopoly** on the production of a specific good. As the sole producer of that good, a monopolist could dictate the price, the quality, and the quantity of the product. In such a situation, consumers would likely end up with the short end of the stick—paying too much for too little.

To protect consumers from monopoly exploitation, the government tries to prevent individual firms from dominating specific markets. Antitrust laws prohibit mergers or acquisitions that would threaten competition. The U.S. Department of Justice and the Federal Trade Commission also regulate pricing practices, advertising claims, and other behavior that might put consumers at an unfair disadvantage in product markets. The "trustbusters" also forced Microsoft to change its licensing procedures in order to assure consumers more choice in computer operating and applications software. The Justice Department even sought to break up the company so as to create more competition in both markets. By changing HOW software systems are developed, the trustbusters hoped to encourage more innovation and lower prices.

Government also regulates the safety of many products. Consumers don't have enough expertise to assess the safety of various medicines, for example. If they rely on trial and error to determine drug safety, they might not get a second chance. To avoid this calamity, the government requires rigorous testing of new drugs, food additives, and other products.

Protecting Labor The government also regulates how our labor resources are used in the production process. As recently as 1920, children between the ages of 10 and 15 were employed in mines, factories, farms, and private homes. They picked cotton and cleaned shrimp in the South, cut sugar beets and pulled onions in the Northwest, processed coal in Appalachia, and pressed tobacco leaves in the Mid-Atlantic states. They often worked six days a week in abusive conditions, for a pittance in wages. Private employers got cheap labor, but society lost valuable resources when so much human capital remained uneducated and physically abused. First the state legislatures, then the U.S. Congress intervened to protect children from such abuse by limiting or forbidding the use of child labor and making school attendance mandatory. In poor nations, governments do much less to limit use of child labor. In Africa, for example, 40 percent of children under age 14 work to survive or to help support their families.

monopoly A firm that produces the entire market supply of a particular good or service.

Government regulations further change HOW goods are produced by setting standards for workplace safety and even minimum pay, fringe benefits, and overtime provisions. After decades of bloody confrontations, the government also established the right of workers to organize and set rules for union–management relations. Unemployment insurance, Social Security benefits, disability insurance, and guarantees for private pension benefits also had the effect of protecting labor from the vagaries of the marketplace. They have had a profound effect on how much people work, when they retire, and even on how long they live.

Protecting the Environment In earlier times, producers didn't have to concern themselves with the impact of their production activities on the environment. The steel mills around Pittsburgh blocked out the sun with clouds of sulfurous gases that spewed out of their furnaces. Timber companies laid waste to broad swaths of forestland, without regard to animal habitats or ecological balance. Paper mills used adjacent rivers as disposal sites, and ships at sea routinely dumped their waste overboard. Neither cars nor airplanes were equipped with controls for noise or air pollution.

In the absence of government intervention, such side effects would be common. Decisions on how to produce would be based on private costs alone, not on how the environment is affected. However, such **externalities**— spillover costs imposed on the broader community—affect our collective well-being. To reduce the external costs of production, the government limits air, water, and noise pollution and regulates environmental use.

externalities Costs (or benefits) of a market activity borne by a third party.

Striking a Balance

All of these government interventions are designed to change HOW goods and services are produced. Such interventions reflect the conviction that the market alone would not always select the best possible way of producing goods and services. The market's answer to the HOW question would be based on narrow, profit-and-loss calculations, not on broader measures of societal well-being. To redress this market failure, the government regulates production behavior.

As noted in Chapter 10, there is no guarantee that government regulation of HOW goods are produced always makes us better off. Excessive regulation may inhibit production, raise product prices, and limit consumer choices. In other words, *government* failure might replace *market* failure, leaving us no better off and possibly even worse off.

For Whom America Produces

However imperfect our answers to the WHAT and HOW questions might be, they cannot obscure how rich America is. As we have observed, the American economy produces a $11 trillion economic pie. The final question we have to address is how that pie will be sliced. Will everyone get an equal slice, or will some Americans be served gluttonous slices while others get only crumbs?

Were the slices of the pie carved by the market mechanism, the slices surely would not be equal. Markets reward individuals on the basis of their contribution to output. ***In a market economy, an individual's income depends on***

- ***The quantity and quality of resources owned.***
- ***The price that those resources command in the market.***

That's what concerned Karl Marx so much. As Marx saw it, the capitalists (owners of capital) had a decided advantage in this market-driven distribution. By owning the means of production, capitalists would continue to accumulate wealth, power, and income. Members of the proletariat would get only enough output to assure their survival. Differences in income within the capitalist class or within the working class were of no consequence in the face of these class divisions. All capitalists were rich, all workers poor.

Marx's predictions of how output would be distributed turned out to be wrong in two ways. First, labor's share of total output has risen greatly over time. Second, differences *within* the labor and capitalist classes have become more important than differences between the classes. Many workers are rich and a good many capitalists are poor. Moreover, the distinction between workers and capitalists has been blurred by profit-sharing plans, employee ownership, and widespread ownership of corporate stock. Accordingly, in today's economy it is more useful to examine how the economic pie is distributed across *individuals* rather than across labor and capitalist *classes*.

The Distribution of Income

Figure 12.6 illustrates how uneven the individual slices of the income pie are. Imagine dividing up the population into five subgroups of equal size, but sorted by income. Thus, the top fifth (or quintile) would include that 20 percent of all households with the most income. The bottom fifth would include the 20 percent of households with the least income. The rest of the population would be spread across the other three quintiles.

Figure 12.6 shows that the richest fifth of the population gets nearly *half* of the income pie. By contrast, the poorest fifth gets a tiny sliver. The dimensions of this inequality are spelled out in Table 12.4. Both the figure and the table underscore how unequally the FOR WHOM question is settled in the United States.

As shocking as U.S. income inequalities might appear, incomes are distributed even less equally in many other countries. The Headline on page 416 displays the share of total income received by the top decile (tenth) of households in various countries. In general, inequalities tend to be larger in poorer countries. As countries develop, the **personal distribution of income** tends to become more equal.

personal distribution of income The way total personal income is divided up among households or income classes.

FIGURE 12.6
Slices of the U.S. Income Pie

The richest fifth of U.S. households gets half of all the income—a huge slice of the income pie. By contrast, the poorest fifth gets only a sliver. Should the government do more to equalize the slices or let the market serve up the pie?

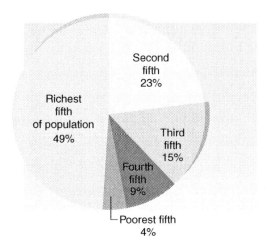

Income Group	2001 Income (dollars)	Average Income	Share of Total Income (percent)
Lowest fifth	0–$17,970	$10,136	3.5%
Fourth fifth	17,971–33,314	25,468	8.8
Third fifth	33,315–53,000	42,629	14.7
Second fifth	53,000–83,500	66,839	23.0
Highest fifth	above 83,500	145,470	50.0

Source: U.S. Department of Commerce, Bureau of the Census.

TABLE 12.4
Distribution of Personal Income, 2001

The size distribution of income indicates how total income is distributed among income classes. That fifth of our population with the lowest incomes received only 3.5 percent of total income. The highest income class (fifth) received nearly half of total income.

Income Mobility

Another important feature of any income distribution is how long people stay in any one position. Being poor isn't such a hardship if your poverty only lasts a week or even a month. Likewise, unequal slices of the economic pie aren't so unfair if the slices are redistributed frequently. In that case, everyone would have a chance to be rich or poor on occasion.

In reality, the slices of the pie are not distributed randomly every year. Some people do get large slices every year, and some other people always seem to end up with crumbs. Nevertheless, such *permanent* inequality is more the exception than the rule in the U.S. economy. One of the most distinctive features of the U.S. income distribution is how often people move up and down the income ladder. This kind of income *mobility* makes lifelong incomes much less unequal than annual incomes. In many nations, income inequalities are much more permanent.

In-Kind Income

When assessing the degree of inequality, we also have to recognize that *income* inequalities aren't a perfect gauge of how *output* is distributed. Income is the primary but not the only ticket to the GDP supermarket. Many goods and services are distributed directly as **in-kind income** rather than through market purchases. Many poor people, for example, live in public housing and pay little or no rent. As a consequence, they receive a larger share of total *output* than their money incomes imply. People with low incomes also receive food stamps, which allow them to purchase more food than their money incomes would allow. In this sense, food-stamp recipients are better off than the distribution of personal income (which omits food stamps) implies.

in-kind income Goods and services received directly, without payment in a market transaction.

Students who attend public schools and colleges also consume more goods and services than they directly pay for; public education is subsidized by all taxpayers. As a consequence, the distribution of money income understates the share of output received by students in public schools. All older Americans, regardless of income, also get subsidized health care from the Medicare program.

So long as some goods and services need not be purchased in the marketplace, *the distribution of money income is not synonymous with the distribution of goods and services.* Accordingly, the distribution of money receipts is not a complete answer to the question of FOR WHOM we produce. This measurement problem is particularly important when comparisons are made over time. For example, the federal government officially classifies people as "poor" if their money income is below a certain threshold. By this standard, we have made little progress in reducing the number of poor people in America during the last 20 years. In that time, however, we

Income Share of the Rich

Incomes are distributed much less equally in poor countries than in rich ones. In most developing countries the top tenth of all households receives 30–50 percent of all income. In the United States and other developed countries inequality is much less severe.

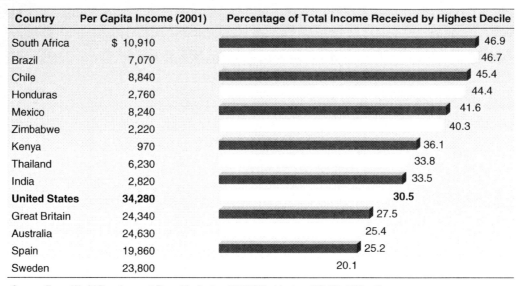

Country	Per Capita Income (2001)	Percentage of Total Income Received by Highest Decile
South Africa	$ 10,910	46.9
Brazil	7,070	46.7
Chile	8,840	45.4
Honduras	2,760	44.4
Mexico	8,240	41.6
Zimbabwe	2,220	40.3
Kenya	970	36.1
Thailand	6,230	33.8
India	2,820	33.5
United States	**34,280**	**30.5**
Great Britain	24,340	27.5
Australia	24,630	25.4
Spain	19,860	25.2
Sweden	23,800	20.1

Source: From *World Development Report Indicators,2003* (Washington, DC: World Bank)

Source: From *World Development Indicators, 2003* (Washington, DC: World Bank).

have provided a vastly increased amount of in-kind benefits to low-income people. Hence their living standards (*real* income) have risen much more than the *money* statistics indicate. In this case, money statistics exaggerate real inequalities.

The distinction between money incomes and real incomes also affects international comparisons. Many people in less developed countries rely more on home production than on market participation for essential goods and services. As a consequence, the measured distribution of money income overstates inequalities. This overstatement also affects comparisons between the United States and such countries as Sweden and Great Britain. In those countries, the governments provide more direct goods and services (e.g., housing, medical care) than the U.S. government does. Hence *real* income is more evenly distributed in those countries than money incomes imply.

Taxes and Transfers

In-kind benefits like food stamps. Medicaid, and public housing are examples of government intervention in the FOR WHOM question. Their goal is to increase the share of output received by people who receive little income from the market. Such in-kind benefits are part of the larger tax-transfer system.

progressive tax A tax system in which tax rates rise as incomes rise.

Taxes Taxes are also a critical mechanism for redistributing market incomes. A **progressive tax** does this by imposing higher tax *rates* on people

© AFP/Corbis

Income inequalities are more vivid in poor nations than in rich ones.

with larger incomes. Under such a system a rich person pays not only more taxes but also a larger *portion* of his or her income. Thus *a progressive tax makes after-tax incomes more equal than before-tax incomes.*

The federal income tax is designed to be progressive. Individuals with less than $7,000 of income paid no income tax in 2003 and might even have received a spendable tax credit from Uncle Sam. Middle-income households confronted an average tax rate of 20 percent, and rich households faced a federal income tax rate of 35 percent.

The rest of the American tax system is less progressive. Social Security payroll taxes and state and local sales taxes have the opposite effect on the FOR WHOM question. These are **regressive taxes** that impose higher tax rates on lower-income households. This may seem strange, but this reverse redistribution results from the way such taxes are levied. The amount of sales tax you pay, for example, depends on how much you spend. As a rule, poor people spend nearly all of their income, whereas rich people save a lot. As a consequence, poor people end up spending a greater *percentage* of their incomes on sales taxes. Thus sales and other regressive taxes tend to make the after-tax distribution of income less equal.

regressive tax A tax system in which tax rates fall as incomes rise.

When all taxes are added up the tax system appears to have little impact on the FOR WHOM question. The progressive nature of the federal income tax is just about offset by the regressive nature of other sales, payroll, and property taxes. As a result, *the tax system does not equalize incomes very much.*

Transfers Taxes are only half of the redistribution story. Equally important is who gets the income the government collects. The government completes the redistribution process by transferring income to consumers and providing services. The largest income-transfer program is Social Security, which pays over $500 billion a year to 50 million older or disabled persons. Although rich and poor alike get Social Security benefits, low-wage workers get more retirement benefits for every dollar of earnings. Hence the benefits of the Social Security program are distributed in a *progressive* fashion. Income transfers reserved exclusively for poor people—welfare benefits, food stamps, Medicaid, and the like—are even more progressive. As a result, *the income-transfer system gives lower-income households more output than the market itself would provide.* In the absence of transfer payments and taxes, the lowest income quintile would get only 1 percent of total income. The tax-transfer system raises their share to 4 percent. That's still not much of a slice, but it's more of the income pie than they got in the marketplace. To get a still larger slice, they need more market income or more government-led income redistribution.

SUMMARY

* The answers to the WHAT, HOW, and FOR WHOM questions are reflected in the dimensions of the economy. These answers are the product of market forces and government intervention.
* Gross domestic product (GDP) is the basic measure of how much an economy produces. Real GDP measures the inflation-adjusted value of output.
* The United States produces roughly $11 trillion of output, more than one-fifth of the world's total. American GDP per capita is five times the world average.
* The high level of U.S. per capita GDP reflects the high productivity of American workers. Abundant capital, education, technology, training, and management all contribute to high productivity.
* Over 70 percent of U.S. output consists of services. The service industries continue to grow faster than goods-producing industries.
* Most of America's output consists of consumer goods and services. Investment goods account for only 18 percent of total output.
* Proprietorships and partnerships outnumber corporations nearly five to one. Nevertheless, corporate America produces 90 percent of total output.
* Government intervenes in the economy to establish the rules of the (market) game and to correct the market's answers to the WHAT, HOW, and FOR WHOM questions. The risk of government failure spurs the search for the right mix of market reliance and government regulation.
* Incomes are distributed very unequally among households, with households in the highest income class (quintile) receiving 15 times more income than the average low-income (quintile) household.
* The tax system alone does little to equalize incomes. Tax-financed transfer payments like Social Security and welfare do redistribute a significant amount of income, however.

Terms to Remember

Define the following terms:

gross domestic product	exports	externality
real GDP	imports	personal distribution of income
per capita GDP	factors of production	in-kind income
economic growth	capital intensive	progressive tax
investment	productivity	regressive tax
income transfers	human capital	
	monopoly	

1. Americans already enjoy living standards that far exceed world averages. Do we have enough? Should we even try to produce more?
2. Why do we measure output in value terms rather than in physical terms? For that matter, why do we bother to measure output at all?
3. Why do people suggest that the United States needs to devote more output to investment goods? Why not produce just consumption goods?
4. The U.S. farm population has shrunk by over 25 million people since 1900. Where did they all go? Why did they move?
5. Rich people have over 15 times as much income as poor people. Is that fair? How should output be distributed?
6. If taxes were more progressive, would total output be affected?
7. Why might income inequalities diminish as an economy develops?
8. Why is per capita GDP so much higher in the United States than in Mexico?
9. Do we need more or less government intervention to decide WHAT, HOW, and FOR WHOM? Give specific examples.

1. Draw a production-possibilities curve with consumer goods on one axis and investment goods on the other axis.
    (a) Identify the opportunity cost of increased investment.
    (b) What will happen to future production possibilities if investment increases? Illustrate.
    (c) What will happen to future production possibilities if only consumer goods are produced?
2. Suppose the following data describe output in two different years:

Item	Year 1	Year 2
Apples	20,000 @25¢ each	30,000 @ 30¢ each
Computers	700 @ $800 each	650 @ $900 each
Video rentals	6,000 @ $1.50 each	7,000 @ $2.00 each

    (a) Compute GDP in each year.
    (b) By what percentage did GDP increase between Year 1 and Year 2?
    (c) Now compute *real* GDP in Year 2 by using the prices of Year 1.
    (d) How has real GDP changed from Year 1 to Year 2?
3. GDP per capita in the United States was approximately $38,000 in 2004. What will it be in the year 2014 if GDP per capita grows each year by
    (a) 0 percent
    (b) 2 percent
    (c) 4 percent
4. According to Figure 12.4
    (a) Has the *quantity* of manufactured output increased or decreased since 1900?
    (b) By how much (in percentage terms)?
    (c) Why has the manufacturing *share* of GDP fallen?
5. Assume that total output is determined by the formula:

$$\text{number of workers} \times \text{productivity} = \text{Total output}$$
$$(\text{output per work})$$

(a) If the number of workers increases by 1.0 percent a year and productivity doesn't improve, how fast will output grow?

(b) If productivity *and* the number of workers increase by 1 percent a
year, how fast will output grow?

6. According to Table 12.4,
   (a) What is the *average* income in the U.S.?
   (b) What percent of the income of people in the highest fifth would
   have to be taxed away to achieve that average?

7. According to the Headline on p. 48, what percent of their income
would the highest-decile households in Brazil have to give up to end
up with an *average* income?

8. Suppose that the following table describes the spending behavior of
individuals at various income levels:

Income	Total Spending	Sales Tax	Sales Tax Paid as Percentage of Income
$ 1,000	$ 1,000	————	————
2,000	1,800	————	————
3,000	2,400	————	————
5,000	3,500	————	————
10,000	6,000	————	————
100,000	40,000	————	————

Assuming that a sales tax of 10 percent is levied on all purchases,
calculate

(a) The amount of taxes paid at each income level

(b) The fraction of income paid in taxes at each income level

Is the sales tax progressive or regressive in relation to income?

Web Activities

1. Log on to www.economagic.com/popular.htm and find the statistics for
real gross domestic product.
   (a) Compare this period's real GDP to one year ago.
   (b) Has the economy experienced economic growth? Explain.

2. Log on to www.bea.doc.gov/bea/glance.htm and find the statistics on
balance of payments for goods and services for the last two years of
data available.
   (a) The balance of payments on the current account is often referred
   to by the media as the *trade deficit*. Which is larger, imports or
   exports of goods and services?
   (b) Does this imbalance in trade cause the value of GDP to increase
   or decrease?

Living Econ

Where Will I End Up?

Based on the important characteristics of the U.S. economy what can we say
about the future prospects of college students? Most of you will work in the
service sector, a part of the economy that includes over 70 percent of all current employment and nearly 100 percent of all new jobs.

Even though many service sector jobs are in government, chances are you
will produce consumption goods in the private sector. Most likely you'll work

for a corporation because they produce most of U.S. output. On average households earned about $42,000 in 2001, a figure that is likely to rise over time and, as a college graduate, your earnings will average more than sixty percent above those who complete only high school.

Of course it is misleading to talk about an *average* person. Even though non-service sector jobs are on the decline, the economy still needs manufacturers, farmers, and construction and mine workers. In addition, there are more than 20 million small proprietorships providing jobs to a number of individuals, even if these jobs are not their primary income source. And, average incomes hide the great discrepancy between the lowest 20% of households with incomes in 2001 below $18,000 and the top 20% of households with incomes over $83,500.

Money and Banks

Sophocles, the ancient Greek playwright, had very strong opinions about the role of money. As he saw it, "Of evils upon earth, the worst is money. It is money that sacks cities, and drives men forth from hearth and home; warps and seduces native intelligence, and breeds a habit of dishonesty."

In modern times, people may still be seduced by the lure of money and fashion their lives around its pursuit. Nevertheless, it is hard to imagine an economy functioning without money. Money affects not only morals and ideals but also the way an economy works.

The purpose of this chapter is to examine the role of money in the economy today. We begin with a very simple question:

* What is money?

As we shall discover, money isn't exactly what you think it is. Once we have established the characteristics of money, we go on to ask:

* Where does money come from?
* What role do banks play in the macro economy?

The Uses of Money

To appreciate the significance of money for a modern economy, imagine for a moment that there were no such thing as money. How would you get something for breakfast? If you wanted eggs for breakfast, you would have to tend your own chickens or go see Farmer Brown. But how would you pay Farmer Brown for his eggs? Without money, you would have to offer him goods or services that he could use. In other words, you would have to engage in primitive **barter**—the direct exchange of one good for another. You would get those eggs only if Farmer Brown happened to want the particular goods or services you had to offer and if the two of you could agree on the terms of the exchange.

The use of money greatly simplifies market transactions. It's a lot easier to exchange money for eggs at the supermarket than to go into the country and barter with farmers. Our ability to use money in market transactions, however, depends on the grocer's willingness to accept money as a *medium of exchange.* The grocer sells eggs for money only because he can use the same money to pay his help and buy the goods he himself desires. He, too, can exchange money for goods and services. Accordingly, money plays an essential role in facilitating the continuous series of exchanges that characterize a market economy.

Money has other desirable features. The grocer who accepts your money in exchange for a carton of eggs doesn't have to spend his income immediately. He can hold onto the money for a few days or months, without worrying about its spoiling. Hence money is also a useful *store of value,* that is, a mechanism for transforming current income into future purchases. Finally, common use of money serves as a *standard of value* for comparing the market worth of different goods. A dozen eggs is more valuable than a dozen onions if it costs more at the supermarket.

We may identify, then, several essential characteristics of what we call money. Specifically, ***anything that serves all of the following purposes can be thought of as money:***

- *Medium of exchange:* is accepted as payment for goods and services (and debts).
- *Store of value:* can be held for future purchases.
- *Standard of value:* serves as a yardstick for measuring the prices of goods and services.

The great virtue of money is that it facilitates the market exchanges that permit specialization in production. In fact, efficient division of labor requires a system whereby people can exchange the things they produce for the things they desire. Money makes this system of exchange possible.

Many Types of Money

Although markets cannot function without money, they can get along without *dollars.* U.S. dollars are just one example of money. In the early days of Colonial America, there were no U.S. dollars. A lot of business was conducted with Spanish and Portuguese gold coins. Later, people used Indian wampum, then tobacco, grain, fish, and furs as mediums of exchange. Throughout the colonies, gunpowder and bullets were frequently used for small change. These forms of money weren't as convenient as U.S. dollars, but they did the job. So long as they served as a medium of exchange, a store of value, and a standard of value, they were properly regarded as money.

The first paper money issued by the U.S. federal government consisted of $10 million worth of "greenbacks," printed in 1861 to finance the Civil War. The Confederate states also issued paper money to finance their side of the

barter The direct exchange of one good for another, without the use of money.

Goods Replace Rubles in Russia's Vast Web of Trade

Workers, paid in products, must make deals to survive; glasses, shoes, bras become new forms of currency

GUS-KHRUSTALNY, RUSSIA—Wrapped tightly against chilling winds, Valentina Novikova, a pensioner, stood expectantly at a lonely crossroads outside this old glass-and-crystal-making town, her champagne flutes tucked neatly into cardboard boxes, stacked on makeshift birch tables. . . .

The glass and crystal sold on the roadside here are the lifeblood of the local economy. Workers are paid in glass, receive their social benefits in glass and must sell the glass to stay alive. The glass has become a kind of substitute money.

The workers and their glass factory are part of a vast transactional web of barter, trading and debt—all using surrogates for the Russian ruble—that by some estimates now accounts for more than half of the Russian economy.

Virtually every sector, every factory and every worker in Russia has been touched by the flood of surrogate money.

What began a few years ago at a time of runaway inflation has persisted and become even more widespread as inflation has cooled yet industry remained moribund. From sheet metal to finished cars, from champagne glasses to shoes, goods are traded around Russia in lieu of money.

In Volgograd, workers at the Armina factory decided to go on strike this month, according to the newspaper *Izvestia*. The reason: Their monthly wage of about $50 is paid in brassieres. . . .

Movie theaters in the Siberian city of Altai started charging two eggs for admission because people had no cash to spare. But the theaters hit a problem in the winter, when hens lay fewer eggs and audiences began to dwindle. So now the movie houses are taking empty bottles as payment, turning them back in to the bottlers for cash.

—David Hoffman

Source: © 1997, the Washington Post. *Washington Post*, January 31, 1997, p. A15. Reprinted with permission.

NOTE: When people lose faith in a nation's currency, they must use something else as a medium of exchange. This greatly limits market activity.

Civil War. Confederate dollars became worthless, however, when the South lost and people no longer accepted Confederate currency in exchange for goods and services.

When communism collapsed in Eastern Europe, similar problems arose. In Poland, the zloty was shunned as a form of money in the early 1980s. Poles preferred to use cigarettes and vodka as mediums of exchange and stores of value. So much Polish currency (zlotys) was available that its value was suspect. The same problem undermined the value of the Russian ruble in the 1990s. Russian consumers preferred to hold and use American dollars rather than the rubles that few people would accept in payment for goods and services. Cigarettes, vodka, and even potatoes were a better form of money than Russian rubles. Notice in the accompanying Headline how movie tickets were sold in 1997 for eggs, not cash, and workers were paid in goods, not rubles.

The Money Supply

Cash vs. Money

In the U.S. economy today, such unusual forms of money are rarely used. Nevertheless, the concept of money includes more than the dollar bills and coins in your pocket or purse. Most people realize this when they offer to pay for goods with a check or debit card rather than cash. The money you have in a checking account can be used to buy goods and services or to pay debts, or it can be retained for future use. In these respects, your checking account balance is as much a part of your money as are the coins and dollars in your pocket or purse. In fact, if everyone accepted your checks (and if the checks could also operate vending machines and pay telephones), there would be no need to carry cash.

There is nothing unique about cash, then, insofar as the market is concerned. ***Checking accounts can and do perform the same market functions as cash.*** Accordingly, we must include checking account balances in our concept of **money**. The essence of money is not its taste, color, or feel but, rather, its ability to purchase goods and services.

money Anything generally accepted as a medium of exchange.

Transactions Accounts

In their competition for customers, banks have created all kinds of different checking accounts. Credit unions and other financial institutions have also created checking-account services. Although they have a variety of distinctive names, all checking accounts have a common feature: they permit depositors to spend their deposit balances easily, without making a special trip to the bank to withdraw funds. All you need is a checkbook, a debit card, an ATM card, or an Internet hookup.

transactions account A bank account that permits direct payment to a third party (e.g., with a check).

Because all such checking-account balances can be used directly in market transactions (without a trip to the bank), they are collectively referred to as *transactions accounts*. The distinguishing feature of all **transactions accounts** is that they permit direct payment to a third party, without requiring a trip to the bank to make a withdrawal. The payment itself may be in the form of a check, a debit-card transfer, or an automatic payment transfer. In all such cases, ***the balance in your transactions account substitutes for cash, and is, therefore, a form of money.***

Basic Money Supply

Because all transactions accounts can be spent as readily as cash, they are counted as part of our money supply. Adding transactions-account balances to the quantity of coins and currency held by the public gives us one measure of the amount of money available—that is, the basic **money supply**. The basic money supply is typically referred to by the abbreviation **M1**.

money supply (M1) Currency held by the public, plus balances in transactions accounts.

Figure 13.1 illustrates the actual composition of our money supply. The first component of MI is the cash people hold (currency in circulation

FIGURE 13.1

Composition of the Basic Money Supply (M1)

The money supply (M1) includes all cash held by the public plus balances people hold in transactions accounts (e.g., checking, NOW, ATS, and credit union share-draft accounts). Cash is only part of our money supply.

Source: Federal Reserve Board of Governors, September 2003.

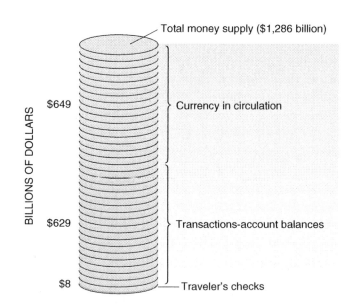

MEDIUMS OF EXCHANGE

Writing Checks Going Out of Style

U.S. consumers and businesses make 80 billion retail payments annually, nearly 50 billion by check and 30 billion by electronic instruments, such as credit cards, debit cards and the Automated Clearing House (ACH). Check writing in 2000 compared with 21 years ago:

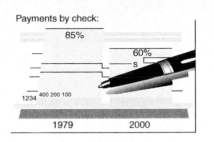

Payments by check:

85%

60%

1234 400 200 100

1979   2000

Source: *USA Today*, December 10, 2001, p. B1.

NOTE: Although people are writing fewer checks, checks are still the most common form of noncash payment. Checks are also used to pay most credit-card balances.

outside of commercial banks). Clearly, ***cash is only part of the money supply; most money consists of balances in transactions accounts.*** This really should not come as too much of a surprise. Most market transactions are still conducted in cash. But those cash transactions are typically small (e.g., for coffee, lunch, small items). They are vastly outspent by the 80 billion *non*-cash retail payments made each year. People prefer to use checks rather than cash for most large market transactions (see Headline). Checks are more convenient than cash, because they eliminate trips to the bank. Checks are also safer: lost or stolen cash is gone forever; checkbooks are easily replaced, at little or no cost.

Credit cards are another popular medium of exchange. People use credit cards for about one-third of all purchases. This use is not sufficient, however, to qualify credit cards as a form of money. Credit card balances must be paid by check or cash. Hence credit cards are simply a payment *service*, not a final form of payment (credit card companies charge fees and interest for this service). The cards themselves are not a store of value, in contrast to cash or bank account balances.

The last component of our basic money supply consists of traveler's checks issued by nonbank firms (e.g., American Express). These, too, can be used directly in market transactions, just like good old-fashioned cash.

Near Money

Transactions accounts are not the only substitute for cash. Even a conventional savings account can be used to finance market purchases. This use of a savings account may require a trip to the bank for a special withdrawal. But that is not too great a barrier to consumer spending. Many savings banks make that trip unnecessary by offering computerized withdrawals and transfers from their savings accounts, some even at supermarket service desks or cash machines. Others offer to pay your bills if you phone in instructions.

Not all savings accounts are so easily spendable. Certificates of deposit, for example, require a minimum balance to be kept in the bank for a specified number of months or years; early withdrawal results in a loss of interest. Funds held in certificates of deposit cannot be transferred automatically to a checking account (like passbook savings balances) or to a third party (like NOW-account balances). As a result, certificates of deposit are seldom used for everyday market purchases. Nevertheless, such accounts still function like "near money" in the sense that savers can go to the bank and withdraw cash if they really want to buy something.

Another popular way of holding money is to buy shares of money-market mutual funds. Deposits into money-market mutual funds are pooled and used to purchase interest-bearing securities (e.g., Treasury bills). The resultant interest payments are typically higher than those paid on regular checking accounts. Moreover, money-market funds can often be withdrawn *immediately,* just like those in transactions accounts. However, such accounts only allow a few checks to be written each month without paying a fee. Hence consumers don't use money-market funds as readily as other transactions accounts to finance everyday spending.

Additional measures of the money supply (M2, M3, etc.) have been constructed to account for the possibility of using money-market mutual funds and various other deposits to finance everyday spending. At the core of all such measures, however, are cash and transactions-account balances, the key elements of the basic money supply (M1). Accordingly, we will limit our discussion to just M1.

Aggregate Demand

Why do we care so much about the specifics of money? Does it really matter how people pay for their purchases?

Our concern about the specific nature of money stems from our broader interest in macro outcomes. As we have observed, total output, employment, and prices are all affected by changes in **aggregate demand.** How much money people have may be one of the determinants of their spending behavior. That's why it's important to know what "money" is and where it comes from.

aggregate demand The total quantity of output demanded at alternative price levels in a given time period, ceteris paribus.

Creation of Money

When people ponder where money comes from, they often have a simple answer: the government prints it. They may even have toured the Bureau of Engraving and Printing in Washington, D.C., and seen dollar bills running off the printing presses. Or maybe they visited the U.S. Mint in Denver or Philadelphia and saw coins being stamped.

There is something wrong with this explanation of the origin of money, however. As Figure 13.1 illustrates, ***most of what we call money is not cash but bank balances.*** Hence, the Bureau of Engraving and the two surviving U.S. mints may play only a minor role in creating money. The real power over the money supply must lie elsewhere.

Deposit Creation

To understand the origins of money, think about your own bank balance. How did you acquire a balance in your checking account? Did you deposit cash? Did you deposit a check? Or did you receive an automatic payroll transfer? If you typically make *non*cash deposits, your behavior is quite typical. Most deposits into transactions accounts are checks or computer transfers; hard cash is seldom used. When people get paid, for example, they typically deposit their paychecks at the bank. Some employers even arrange automatic payroll deposits, thereby eliminating the need to go to the bank at all. The employee never sees or deposits cash in these cases (see cartoon).

Less than half of our money supply consists of coins and currency. Most banking transactions entail check or computer deposits and payments.

Frank & Ernest reprinted by permission of Newspaper Enterprise Association. Inc.

If checks are used to make deposits, then the supply of checks provides an initial clue about where money comes from. Anyone can buy blank checks and sign them, of course. But banks won't cash checks without some assurance that there are funds in a bank to make the check good. Banks, in fact, hold checks for a few days to confirm the existence of sufficient account balances to cover the checks. Likewise, retailers won't accept checks unless they get some deposit confirmation or personal identification. The constraint on check writing, then, is not the supply of paper but the availability of transactions-account balances.

Like a good detective novel, the search for the origins of money seems to be going in a circle. It appears that transactions-account deposits come from transactions-account balances. This seeming riddle suggests that money creates money. But it offers no clue to us to how the money got there in the first place. Who created the first transactions-account balance? What was used as a deposit?

The solution to this mystery is totally unexpected: banks themselves create money. They don't print dollar bills. But they do make loans. The loans, in turn, become transactions-account balances and therefore part of the money supply. This is the answer to the riddle. Quite simply, ***in making a loan, a bank effectively creates money, because transactions-account balances are counted as part of the money supply.*** And you are free to spend that money, just as if you had earned it yourself.

To understand where money comes from, then, we must recognize two basic principles:

* Transactions-account balances are the largest part of the money supply.
* Banks create transactions-account balances by making loans.

In the following two sections we shall examine this process of creating money—**deposit creation**—more closely.

deposit creation The creation of transactions deposits by bank lending.

A Monopoly Bank

Suppose, to keep things simple, that there is only one bank in town, University Bank, and no one regulates bank behavior. Imagine also that you have been saving some of your income by putting loose change into a piggy bank. Now, after months of saving, you break the bank and discover that your thrift has yielded $100. You immediately deposit this money in a new checking account at University Bank.

Your initial deposit will have no immediate effect on the money supply (M1). The coins in your piggy bank were already counted as part of the money supply, because they represented cash held by the public. ***When you deposit cash or coins in a bank, you are changing the composition of the money supply, not its size.*** The public (you) now holds $100 less of coins but $100 more of transactions deposits. Accordingly, no money is lost or created by the demise of your piggy bank (the initial deposit).

What will University Bank do with your deposit? Will it just store the coins in its safe until you withdraw them (in person or by check)? That doesn't seem very likely. After all, banks are in business to earn a profit. And University Bank won't make much profit just storing your coins. To earn a profit on your deposit, University Bank will have to put your money to work. This means using your deposit as the basis for making a loan to someone else—someone who is willing to pay the bank interest for the use of money.

Typically, a bank does not have much difficulty finding someone who wants to borrow money. Many firms and individuals have expenditure desires that exceed their current money balances. These market participants are eager to borrow whatever funds banks are willing to lend. The question is, how much money can a bank lend? Can it lend your entire deposit? Or must University Bank keep some of your coins in reserve, in case you want to withdraw them? The answer may surprise you.

An Initial Loan   Suppose that University Bank decided to lend the entire $100 to Campus Radio. Campus Radio wants to buy a new antenna but doesn't have any money in its own checking account. To acquire the antenna, Campus Radio must take out a loan from University Bank.

When University Bank agrees to lend Campus Radio $100, it does so by crediting the account of Campus Radio. Instead of giving Campus Radio $100 cash, University Bank simply adds $100 to Campus Radio's checking-account balance. That is to say, the loan is made with a simple bookkeeping entry.

This simple bookkeeping entry is the key to creating money. At the very moment University Bank lends $100 to the Campus Radio account, it creates money. Keep in mind that transactions deposits are counted as part of the money supply. Once the $100 loan is credited to its account, Campus Radio can use this new money to purchase its desired antenna, without worrying that its check will bounce.

bank reserves Assets held by a bank to fulfill its deposit obligations.

Or can it? Once University Bank grants a loan to Campus Radio, both you and Campus Radio have $100 in your checking accounts to spend. But the bank is holding only $100 of **reserves** (your coins). In other words, the increased checking-account balance obtained by Campus Radio does not limit your ability to write checks. There has been a net *increase* in the value of transactions deposits, but no increase in bank reserves.

Using the Loan   What happens if Campus Radio actually spends the $100 on a new antenna? Won't this use up all the reserves held by the bank, and endanger your check-writing privileges? The answer is no.

Consider what happens when Atlas Antenna receives the check from Campus Radio. What will Atlas do with the check? Atlas could go to University Bank and exchange the check for $100 of cash (your coins). But Atlas probably doesn't have any immediate need for cash. Atlas may prefer to deposit the check in its own checking account at University Bank (still the only bank in town). In this way, Atlas not only avoids the necessity of going to the bank (it can deposit the check by mail), but also keeps its money in a safe place. Should Atlas later want to spend the money, it can simply write a check. In the meantime, the bank continues to hold its entire reserves (your coins) and both you and Atlas have $100 to spend.

Fractional Reserves   Notice what has happened here. The money supply has increased by $100 as a result of deposit creation (the loan to Campus Radio). Moreover, the bank has been able to support $200 of transaction deposits (your account and either the Campus Radio or Atlas account) with only $100 of reserves (your coins). In other words, *bank reserves are only a fraction of total transactions deposits.* In this case, University Bank's reserves (your $100 in coins) are only 50 percent of total deposits. Thus the bank's **reserve ratio** is 50 percent—that is,

reserve ratio The ratio of a bank's reserves to its total transactions deposits.

$$\bullet \ \text{Reserve ratio} = \frac{\text{bank reserves}}{\text{total deposits}}$$

The ability of University Bank to hold reserves that are only a fraction of total deposits results from two facts: (1) people use checks for most transactions, and (2) there is no other bank. Accordingly, reserves are rarely withdrawn from this monopoly bank. In fact, if people *never* withdrew their deposits in cash and *all* transactions accounts were held at University Bank, University Bank would not really need any reserves. Indeed, it could melt your coins and make a nice metal sculpture. So long as no one ever came to see or withdraw the coins, everybody would be blissfully ignorant. Merchants and consumers would just continue using checks, presuming that the bank could cover them when necessary. In this most unusual case, University Bank could continue to make as many loans as it wanted. Every loan made would increase the supply of money.

Reserve Requirements

If a bank could create money at will, if would have a lot of control over aggregate demand. In reality, no private bank has that much power. First of all, there are many banks available, not just a single monopoly bank. Hence *the power to create money resides in the banking system, not in any single bank.* Each of the thousands of banks in the system plays a relatively small role.

The second constraint on bank power is government regulation. The Federal Reserve System (the Fed) regulates bank lending. The Fed decides how many loans banks can make with their available reserves. Hence even an assumed monopoly bank could not make unlimited loans with your piggy bank's coins. *The Federal Reserve System requires banks to maintain some minimum reserve ratio.* The reserve requirement directly limits the ability of banks to grant new loans.

To see how Fed regulations limit bank lending (money creation), we have to do a little accounting. Suppose that the Federal Reserve had imposed a minimum reserve requirement of 75 percent on University Bank. That means the bank must hold reserves equal to at least 75 percent of total deposits.

A 75 percent reserve requirement would have prohibited University Bank from lending $100 to Campus Radio. That loan would have brought *total* deposits up to $200 (your $100 plus the $100 Campus Radio balance). But reserves (your coins) would still be only $100. Hence the ratio of reserves to deposits would have been 50 percent ($100 of reserves ÷ $200 of deposits). That would have violated the Fed's assumed 75 percent reserve requirement. A 75 percent reserve requirement means that University Bank must hold at all times **required reserves** equal to 75 percent of *total* deposits, including those created through loans.

required reserves The minimum amount of reserves a bank is required to hold by government regulation: equal to required reserve ratio times transactions deposits.

The bank's dilemma is evident in the following equation:

$$\bullet \ \text{Required reserves} = \text{required reserve ratio} \times \text{total deposits}$$

To support $200 of total deposits, University Bank would need to satisfy this equation:

$$\text{Required reserves} = 0.75 \times \$200 = \$150$$

But the bank has only $100 of reserves (your coins) and so would violate the reserve requirement if it increased total deposits to $200 by lending $100 to Campus Radio.

University Bank can still issue a loan to Campus Radio. But the loan must be less than $100 in order to keep the bank within the limits of the required reserve formula. Thus *a minimum reserve requirement directly limits deposit-creation possibilities*.

Excess Reserves

excess reserves Bank reserves in excess of required reserves.

Banks will sometimes hold reserves in excess of the minimum required by the Fed. Such reserves are called **excess reserves** and calculated as

- Excess reserves = total reserves − required reserves

Suppose again that University Bank's only deposit is the $100 in coins you deposited. Assume also a Fed reserve requirement of 75 percent. In this case, the initial ledger of the bank would look like this:

Assets		Liabilities	
Required reserves	$75	Your account balance	$100
Excess reserves	$25		
Total assets (your coins)	$100		

Notice two things in this T-account ledger. First, total assets equal total liabilities. This must always be the case, because someone must own every asset. Second, the bank has $25 of excess reserves. It is *required* to hold only $75; the remainder of its reserves ($25) are thus excess.

This bank is not fully using its lending capacity. **So long as a bank has excess reserves, it can make additional loans.** If it does, the nation's money supply will increase.

A Multibank World

In reality, there is more than one bank in town. Hence any loan University Bank makes may end up as a deposit in another bank rather than at its own. This complicates the arithmetic of deposit creation but doesn't change its basic character. Indeed, the existence of a multibank system makes the money-creation process even more powerful.

In a multibank world, *the key issue is not how much excess reserves any specific bank holds but how much excess reserves exist in the entire banking system.* If excess reserves exist anywhere in the system, then some banks still have unused lending authority.

The Money Multiplier

Excess reserves are the source of bank lending authority. If there are no excess reserves in the banking system, banks can't make any more loans.

Although an *absence* of excess reserves precludes further lending activity, the *amount* of excess reserves doesn't define the limit to further loans.

This surprising conclusion emerges from the way a multibank system works. Consider again what happens when someone borrows all of a bank's excess reserves. Suppose University Bank uses its $25 excess reserves to support a loan. If someone borrows that much money from University Bank, those excess reserves will be depleted. The money won't disappear, however. Once the borrower *spends* the money, someone else will *receive* $25. If that person deposits the $25 elsewhere, then another bank will acquire a new deposit.

If another bank gets a new deposit, the process of deposit creation will continue. The new deposit of $25 increases the second bank's *required* reserves as well as its *excess* reserves. We're talking about a $25 deposit. If the Federal Reserve minimum is 75 percent, then *required* reserves increase by $18.75. The remaining $6.25, therefore, represents *excess* reserves. This second bank can now make additional loans in the amount of $6.25.

Perhaps you are beginning to get a sense that the process of deposit creation will not come to an end quickly. On the contrary, it can continue indefinitely as loans get made and the loans are spent—over and over again. **Each loan made creates new excess reserves, which help fund the next loan.** This recurring sequence of loans and spending is very much like the income multiplier, which creates additional income every time income is spent. People often refer to deposit creation as the money-multiplier process, with the **money multiplier** expressed as the reciprocal of the required reserve ratio. That is

$$\text{Money multiplier} = \frac{1}{\text{required reserve ratio}}$$

money multiplier The number of deposit (loan) dollars that the banking system can create from $1 of excess reserves; equal to 1 ÷ required reserve ratio.

The money-multiplier process is illustrated in Figure 13.2. When a new deposit enters the banking system, it creates both excess and required reserves. The required reserves represent leakage from the flow of money, since they cannot be used to create new loans. Excess reserves, on the other hand, can be used for new loans. Once those loans are made, they typically become transactions deposits elsewhere in the banking system. Then some additional leakage into required reserves occurs, and further loans are made. The process continues until all excess reserves have leaked into required reserves. Once excess reserves have all disappeared, the total value of new loans will equal initial excess reserves multiplied by the money multiplier.

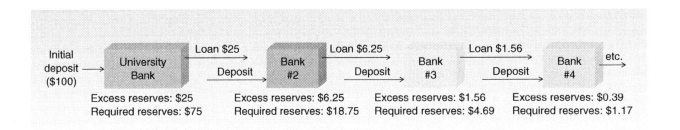

FIGURE 13.2 The Money-Multiplier Process

Each bank can use its excess reserves to make a loan. The loans will end up as deposits at other banks. These banks will then have some excess reserves and lending capacity. Bank #2 can lend 25 percent of the $25 deposit it receives.

Limits to Deposit Creation

The potential of the money multiplier to create loans is summarized by the equation

$$\bullet \quad \frac{\text{Excess reserves of}}{\text{banking system}} \times \frac{\text{money}}{\text{multiplier}} = \frac{\text{potential}}{\text{deposit creation}}$$

Notice how the money multiplier worked in our previous example. The value of the money multiplier was equal to 1.33, which is 1.0 divided by the required reserve ratio of 0.75. The banking system started out with the $25 of excess reserves created by your initial $100 deposit. According to the money multiplier, then, the deposit-creation potential of the banking system was

$$\frac{\text{Excess reserves}}{(\$25)} \times \frac{\text{money multiplier}}{(1.33)} = \frac{\text{potential deposit}}{\text{creation } (\$33.25)}$$

If all the banks fully utilize their excess reserves at each step of the money-multiplier process, the banking system could make loans in the amount of $33.25.

Excess Reserves as Lending Power

While you are reviewing the arithmetic of deposit creation, notice the critical role that excess reserves play in the process. A bank can make loans only if it has excess reserves. Without excess reserves, all of a bank's reserves are required, and no further liabilities (transactions deposits) can be created with new loans. On the other hand, a bank with excess reserves can make additional loans. In fact,

  * *Each bank may lend an amount equal to its excess reserves and no more.*

As such loans enter the circular flow and become deposits elsewhere, they create new excess reserves and further lending capacity. As a consequence,

  * *The entire banking system can increase the volume of loans by the amount of excess reserves multiplied by the money multiplier.*

By keeping track of excess reserves, then, we can gauge the lending capacity of any bank or, with the aid of the money multiplier, the entire banking system.

The Macro Role of Banks

The bookkeeping details of bank deposits and loans are complex and often frustrating. But they do demonstrate convincingly that **banks can create money.** Since virtually all market transactions involve the use of money, banks must have some influence on macro outcomes.

Financing Aggregate Demand

What we have demonstrated in this chapter is that banks perform two essential functions:

  * Banks transfer money from savers to spenders by lending funds (reserves) held on deposit.
  * The banking system creates additional money by making loans in excess of total reserves.

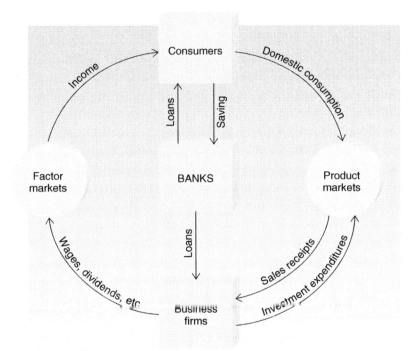

FIGURE 13.3
Banks in the Circular Flow

Banks help to transfer income from savers to spenders. They do this by using their deposits to make loans to business firms and consumers who desire to spend more money than they have. By lending money, banks help to maintain any desired rate of aggregate spending.

In performing these two functions, banks change not only the size of the money supply but aggregate demand as well. The loans banks offer to their customers will be used to purchase new cars, homes, business equipment, and other output. All of these purchases will add to aggregate demand. Hence ***increases in the money supply tend to increase aggregate demand.***

When banks curtail their lending activity, the opposite occurs. People can't get the loans or credit they need to finance desired consumption or investment. As a result, ***aggregate demand declines when the money supply shrinks.***

The central role of the banking system in the economy is emphasized in Figure 13.3. In this depiction of the circular flow, income flows from product markets through business firms to factor markets and returns to consumers in the form of disposable income. Consumers spend most of their income but also save (don't spend) some of it. This consumer saving could pose a problem for the economy if no one else were to step up and buy the goods and services consumers leave unsold.

The banking system is the key link between consumer savings and the demand originating in other sectors of the economy. To see how important that link is, imagine that *all* consumer saving was deposited in piggy banks rather than depository institutions (banks) and that no one used checks. Under these circumstances, banks could not transfer money from savers to spenders by holding deposits and making loans. The banks could not create the money needed to boost aggregate demand.

In reality, a substantial portion of consumer saving *is* deposited in banks. These and other bank deposits can be used as the bases of loans, thereby returning purchasing power to the circular flow. Moreover, because the banking system can make *multiple* loans from available reserves, banks don't have to receive all consumer saving in order to carry out their function. On the contrary, ***the banking system can create any desired level of money supply if allowed to expand or reduce loan activity at will.***

Constraints on Money Creation

If banks had unlimited power to create money (make loans), they could control aggregate demand. Their power isn't quite so vast, however. There are four major constraints on their lending activity.

Bank Deposits   The first constraint on the lending activity of banks is the willingness of people to keep deposits in the bank. If people preferred to hold cash rather than checkbooks, banks would not be able to acquire or maintain the reserves that are the foundation of bank lending activity.

Willing Borrowers   The second constraint on deposit creation is the willingness of consumers, businesses, and governments to borrow the money that banks make available. If no one wanted to borrow any money, deposit creation would never begin.

Willing Lenders   The banks themselves may not be willing to satisfy all credit demands. This was the case in the 1930s when the banks declined to use their excess reserves for loans they perceived to be too risky. In the recession of 1990–91 many banks again closed their loan windows.

Government Regulation   The last and most important constraint on deposit creation is the Federal Reserve System. In the absence of government regulation, individual banks would have tremendous power over the money supply and therewith all macroeconomic outcomes. The government limits this power by regulating bank lending practices.

POLICY PERSPECTIVES

Digital Money

The Internet has created a virtual mall that millions of people visit every day. In 2003 roughly $60 *billion* of goods and services were sold at that mall. Yet, experts say the sales potential of the Internet has barely been tapped. Only a tiny fraction of the consumers who browse through the Internet mall actually buy something. As a result, Internet sales remain a very small fraction of gross domestic product.

E-retailers say *money* is the problem. You can't pay cash at the Internet mall. And you can't hand over a check in cyberspace. So the most common forms of money used in bricks-and-mortar malls can't serve as a medium of exchange in electronic malls.

Credit Cards   Because cash and checks don't work in cyberspace, almost all Internet purchases are completed with credit cards. But dependence on credit cards limits the potential of e-commerce. To begin with, there is the question of security. Once you transmit your credit card number into cyberspace, you can't be 100 percent confident about its use. There are thousands of credit card thefts on the Internet. Hackers have even broken into databases that were supposed to provide security for credit card transactions.

Consumers also worry about privacy. Retail merchants compile databases on credit card purchasers. They even sell these data files to other merchants, unleashing a barrage of targeted advertising. Consumers don't want those marketing intrusions. And they don't want the world to know how often they visited a pornographic site or purchased sex toys in cyberspace.

E-Payments Dozens of Internet companies have tried to create alternative means of payment for cybershoppers. Some companies offer a quasi-banking service by storing purchasing power that consumers and e-retailers can access. To use this kind of e-cash, retailers have to install new software. Consumers must deposit e-cash with credit card advances. Digital "wallets" are a slight variation of digital cash. With wallets, however, the merchant actually receives a direct credit card charge rather than a form of Internet currency. Other companies simply act as umpires for specific purchases, holding final payment (via credit card) until the buyer is satisfied with the purchase.

Speed of Spending All of these digital means of payment are designed to make cyberspending faster and easier. When the credit card bills come due, however, consumers will still need real money (cash and checking-account balances) to pay for their purchases. Hence the amount of money available still counts; even in cyberspace. With easier and more secure payment mechanisms, however, virtual malls will allow consumers to spend money balances *faster*, thereby boosting aggregate demand.

SUMMARY

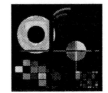

* In a market economy, money serves a critical function in facilitating exchanges and specialization, thus permitting increased output. "Money" in this context may refer to anything that serves as a medium of exchange, store of value, and standard of value.
* The most common measure of the money supply (M1) includes both cash and balances people hold in transactions accounts (e.g., checking, NOW, and ATS accounts).
* Banks have the power to create money simply by making loans. In making loans, banks create new transactions deposits, which become part of the money supply.
* The ability of banks to make loans—create money—depends on their reserves. Only if a bank has excess reserves—reserves greater than those required by federal regulation—can it make new loans.
* As loans are spent, they create deposits elsewhere, making it possible for other banks to make additional loans. The money multiplier (1 ÷ required reserve ratio) indicates the total value of deposits that can be created by the banking system from excess reserves.
* The role of banks in creating money includes the transfer of money from savers to spenders as well as deposit creation in excess of deposit balances. Taken together, these two functions give banks direct control over the amount of purchasing power available in the marketplace.
* The deposit-creation potential of the banking system is limited by government regulation. It is also limited by the willingness of market participants to hold deposits or borrow money. At times, banks themselves may be unwilling to use all their lending ability.

Define the following terms:

Terms to Remember

barter	aggregate demand	required reserves
money	deposit creation	excess reserves
transactions account	bank reserves	money multiplier
money supply (M1)	reserve ratio	

1. Do eggs satisfy the three conditions for money? Did barter make it easier or more difficult to go to the movies in Russia? (See Headline on page 425.)
2. If a friend asked you how much money you had to spend, what items would you include in your response?
3. Why aren't credit cards counted as money?
4. Does money have any intrinsic value? If not, why are people willing to accept money in exchange for goods and services?
5. Have you ever borrowed money to buy a car, pay tuition, or for any other purpose? In what form did you receive the money? How did your loan affect the money supply? Aggregate demand?
6. Does the fact that your bank keeps only a fraction of your account balance in reserve make you uncomfortable? Why don't people rush to the bank and retrieve their money? What would happen if they did?
7. If people never withdrew cash from banks, how much money could the banking system potentially create? Could this really happen? What might limit deposit creation in this case?
8. If all banks heeded Shakespeare's admonition "Neither a borrower nor a lender be," what would happen to the supply of money?

1. What percentage of your monthly spending do you pay with (*a*) cash, (*b*) check, (*c*) credit card, or (*d*) automatic transfers? How do you pay off the credit-card balance? How does your use of cash compare with the composition of the money supply (Figure 13.1)?
2. How large is the money multiplier when the required reserve ratio is 0.05? If the required reserve ratio increases to 0.0667, what happens to the money multiplier?
3. How large a loan can Bank #4 in Figure 13.2 make?
4. What volume of loans can the banking system in Figure 13.2 support? If the reserve requirement were 50 percent, what would the system's lending capacity be?
5. Suppose that an Irish Sweepstakes winner deposits $10 million in cash into her transactions account at the Bank of America. Assume a reserve requirement of 25 percent and no excess reserves in the banking system prior to this deposit. Show the changes on the Bank of America balance sheet when the $10 million is initially deposited.
6. In December 1994, a man in Ohio decided to deposit all of the *8 million* pennies he had been saving for nearly 65 years. (His deposit weighed over 48,000 pounds!) With a reserve requirement of 20 percent, how did his deposit change the lending capacity of
   (*a*) His bank?
   (*b*) The banking system?

1. Log on to www.federalreserve.gov/releases/h3/about.htm and access the latest release.
   (*a*) What is the latest level of required reserves?
   (*b*) Are banks keeping excess reserves?
2. Log on to http://research.stlouisfed.org/fred2 and click on "Monetary Aggregates." What is the average money multiplier for the last two weeks?

3. Log on to www.federalreserve.gov/releases/h3/about.htm and access the latest release.
   (a) Calculate excess reserves for the latest month reported.
   (b) Assuming a reserve requirement of 0.05, how much additional lending capacity exists in the banking system?
4. Log on to www.federalreserve.gov/releases/h6/about.htm.
   (a) How does the Fed define the terms M1, M2, and M3?
   (b) Click on the most recent statistical release. What are the most recent estimates for M1, M2, and M3?

How Do 1 Create Money?

When you hear the words "money creation," your first thought might be of counterfeiting. Certainly it occurs, but in this chapter you learned that the banking system creates money by lending—and it's perfectly legal. Banks take in the deposits of those who save and then lend the dollars to those who spend. The "magic" of money creation occurs because banks can lend out the portion of the deposits they do not hold as required reserves.

What role do you play in this process? Well, each time you deposit dollars into the banking system you allow a bank to lend more dollars. And each time you borrow dollars, to buy a car or pay your college tuition, you contribute to the demand for loans. If you and many others decide to take your money out of the banking system and keep it under a mattress, money creation will shrink. Or, if you and many others decide to stop borrowing money, the money creation process will also be reduced. So, without even thinking about the impact, you and I are likely to influence the amount of money creation and, ultimately, the size of the money supply.